Handbook of Adolescent Transition Education for Youth with Disabilities

Transition from secondary education to adulthood represents a period during which adolescents with disabilities face multiple responsibilities and changing roles that include establishing independence, attending postsecondary education or training, developing social networks, choosing a career, participating in their communities, and managing healthcare and financial affairs. Sponsored by the Division on Career Development and Transition (DCDT) of the Council for Exceptional Children, this handbook provides a comprehensive resource to the communities of educators, related service and agency personnel, families, caretakers, counselors, and other stakeholders who facilitate these complex transitions to adulthood for adolescents with disabilities.

Comprehensive — This comprehensive volume includes coverage of historical foundations, policy, transition programming and planning, development of student skills, and program structure. It also recommends transition supports for students with specific disabilities.

Organizing Taxonomy — The book is organized around a well recognized taxonomy for adolescent transition used by many states to design and reform their transition services.

Expertise — The volume editors are past-presidents of the Council for Exceptional Children's Division on Career Development and are leaders in transition research and practice. Contributors are well-recognized for their expertise in transition.

Chapter Structure — Each chapter includes a discussion of evidence-based research, recommended practices, suggestions for transition personnel and families, and additional resources.

This book is appropriate for researchers and graduate-level instructors in special education and vocational education, inservice administrators and policy makers, and transition service providers.

Michael L. Wehmeyer is Professor of Special Education; Director, Kansas University Center on Developmental Disabilities; and Senior Scientist, Beach Center on Disability, all at the University of Kansas. His research focus is on self-determination, technology use by people with cognitive disabilities, the intellectual disability construct, and access to the general education curriculum for students with severe disabilities. He is the past editor of the journal *Remedial and Special Education*, past president of the CEC Division on Career Development and Transition, and immediate past president of the American Association on Intellectual and Developmental Disabilities.

Kristine Wiest Webb is a Professor at the University of North Florida (UNF) and serves as Director of the Disability Resource Center. Prior to UNF, she served as Director of the Florida Network at the University of Florida. While pursuing her doctoral degree at the University of New Mexico, she directed the Intern Program. Kris taught for 17 years in New Mexico and Colorado. Her research includes transition to higher education, family involvement, and student-centered planning. She is a past president of the CEC Division on Career Development and Transition.

Handbook of Adolescent Transition Education for Youth with Disabilities

Edited by
Michael L. Wehmeyer
UNIVERSITY OF KANSAS

Kristine W. Webb
UNIVERSITY OF NORTH FLORIDA

Routledge
Taylor & Francis Group

NEW YORK AND LONDON

76773

First published 2012
by Routledge
711 Third Avenue, New York, NY 10017

Simultaneously published in the UK
by Routledge
2 Park Square, Milton Park, Abingdon, Oxon OX14 4RN

Routledge is an imprint of the Taylor & Francis Group, an informa business

© 2012 Taylor & Francis

Library of Congress Cataloging in Publication Data
Handbook of adolescent transition education for youth with disabilities /
edited by Michael L. Wehmeyer, Kristine W. Webb.
        p. cm.
    Includes bibliographical references and index.
    1. Teenagers with disabilities—Education—United States.   2. Teenagers
with disabilities—Vocational guidance—United States.   3. Teenagers with
disabilities—Services for—United States.   4. Students with disabilities—
Services for—United States.   I. Wehmeyer, Michael L.   II. Webb,
Kristine Wiest.
    LC4031.H358 2011
    371.90973–dc23

                                                                    2011026697

ISBN: 978–0–415–87278–2 (hbk)
ISBN: 978–0–415–87279–9 (pbk)
ISBN: 978–0–203–83732–0 (ebk)

Typeset in Bembo
by RefineCatch Limited, Bungay, Suffolk, UK

Printed and bound in the United States of America on acid-free paper
by Edwards Brothers, Inc.

Contents

Contents

Contents

Preface

Transition from secondary education to adulthood represents a period during which adolescents with disabilities face multiple responsibilities and changing roles that include establishing independence, attending postsecondary education or training, developing social networks, choosing a career, participating in their communities, and managing healthcare and financial affairs. The purpose of this handbook is to serve as a comprehensive resource to students, the communities of educators, related service and agency personnel, families, caretakers, counselors, and other stakeholders who facilitate these complex transitions to adulthood for adolescents with disabilities.

The editors have approached the process of assembling and editing this book with a number of key features in mind. First, our intent was to assemble a handbook that was comprehensive. Topics covered encompass historical foundations, policy, transition programming and planning, development of student skills, program structure, along with recommendations of transition supports for students with specific disabilities. Second, we recruited experts in the field of transition to ensure that information was grounded in theory and research. The co-editors (Wehmeyer and Webb) are past-presidents of the Council for Exceptional Children's Division on Career Development and Transition (DCDT), and this book was a collaborative effort between DCDT and the editors. All proceeds from the handbook will be donated to DCDT to support its mission "to promote national and international efforts to improve the quality of and access to, career/vocational and transition services, increase the participation of education in career development and transition goals and to influence policies affecting career development and transition services for persons with disabilities" (http://www.dcdt.org). Third, we have asked authors to ensure that the text is accessible to a wide array of potential readers, from academicians and undergraduate/graduate students to teachers, transition specialists, and vocational rehabilitation counselors, to parents and family members. Finally, if there is a single theme that runs throughout the text, it is that transition education should actively engage adolescents with disabilities in all aspects of the transition process, from planning to implementation and evaluation. Student involvement in transition planning and promoting self-determination and student-directed learning are critically important to success in the transition enterprise.

Foreword

Ginger Blalock

UNIVERSITY OF NEW MEXICO

By this point in history, after 35+ years of examining adolescent transition education, we are acutely familiar with most of the personal, social, career, community, and financial challenges of movement from secondary schooling to adult life faced by youth with disabilities. Although we know a great deal from these years of research, demonstration projects, and compliance monitoring, the field of secondary transition education (and education in general) is far from effectively, efficiently producing the young adult outcomes we all seek. We need continuing, research-driven professional development (in every broad sense of that word) to inform us, to raise the bar for the expectations that students, family members, and professionals hold, and to teach us all how to improve those outcomes. The field is fortunate that the *Handbook of Adolescent Transition Education for Youth with Disabilities* presents itself now, to offer very timely, validated strategies for advancing the post-school success of young adults. The issues and solutions discussed herein are based not only on results of scholarly studies judged empirically appropriate for publication and dissemination; these chapters additionally reflect significant investment in and commitment to student involvement in transition planning, student self-determination, and student voice, as readers will experience.

This handbook is practical and immediately useful for many reasons and for many individuals. This text features a comprehensive range of topics of shared concern and scholarly interest, beginning with student-focused planning and moving to student learning and then to program and system structures such as those found within secondary and postsecondary education and interagency connections. Also addressed are disability-specific transition issues and strategies, to ensure the applicability of this handbook to a wide range of readers.

The collection offers extremely contemporary thinking by a "star-studded" cast of transition experts whose names and topics are remarkable. These contributors have been organized and led by two noteworthy authors who've done their own ground-breaking work in their respective areas of concentration. Michael Wehmeyer is one of the most prolific and recognized authors of both policy and research publications regarding transition in general and provides inspiring national leadership regarding students with significant support needs as well as self-determination assessment and instruction. Through the 25 years I've witnessed Kristine Webb's work in New Mexico and Florida, she has provided significant influence at school, district, state, and national levels to enhance the capacity of youth with all types and levels of support needs to move into further learning after high school. These two worthy editors, both my friends and colleagues, elaborate on the contributions of their impressive team of experts in the introductory chapter. This chapter is important to read, as it provides unifying principles and perspectives to guide readers in digesting the body of works here, to maximize their utility.

The *Handbook* will be helpful to youth and young adults in transition, family members, practitioners, scholars, and policymakers—in other words, all engaged in secondary transition to adulthood. A unique contribution is the section focused on the issues and practices associated with specific disabilities, so that users can be fully equipped with state-of-the-art knowledge for enhancing ALL students' success. Themes of researach-based practices and interagency collaboration combine with student-focused decision-making to form foundational threads throughout the chapters. The *Handbook of Adolescent Transition Education for Youth with Disabilities* promises to provide assistance for years to come.

Ginger Blalock, Ph.D.
Emeritus Professor, Special Education
University of New Mexico

Section I

Introduction and Overview of Adolescent Transition Education

An Introduction to Adolescent Transition Education

Michael L. Wehmeyer

UNIVERSITY OF KANSAS

Kristine W. Webb

UNIVERSITY OF NORTH FLORIDA

Transition from secondary education to adulthood represents a period during which adolescents with disabilities face multiple responsibilities and changing roles that include establishing independence, attending postsecondary education or training, developing social networks, choosing a career, participating in their communities, and managing healthcare and financial affairs. The purpose of this handbook is to serve as a comprehensive resource to students, the communities of educators, related service and agency personnel, families, caretakers, counselors, and other stakeholders who facilitate these complex transitions to adulthood for adolescents with disabilities.

What is Transition?

The Individuals with Disabilities Education Act (IDEA), the federal law requiring all students with disabilities to receive a free, appropriate public education, has, since 1990, also required the educational programs of adolescents with disabilities receiving special education services to include a focus on services and instructional needs to enable the student to "transition" from secondary education to postsecondary education and adult life. The term "transition" refers, generally, to the "life changes, adjustments, and cumulative experiences that occur in the lives of young adults as they move from school environments to independent living and work environments" (Wehman, 2006, p. 4).

Therefore, the concept of transition implies movement and change. Change, as it applies to students who are preparing to leave high school, is associated with those new situations in which students will find themselves. These new situations come with certain demands and challenges that require an array of knowledge and skill sets to function successfully. The transition to the world after high school is complicated and needs informed and systematic attention.

Vertical and Horizontal Transitions

We experience many transitions throughout our lives. Some of these are normative and predictable (vertical), whereas others are individual-specific and occur at some specific point in time (horizontal) (Wehmeyer & Patton, in press). The life-span-related (i.e., vertical) transitions are associated with predictable life events, such as beginning school, leaving elementary school, and growing older. Coordinated planning for these transitions can minimize the anxiety that may arise, and make such transitions smoother, but in reality, little comprehensive planning occurs in the lives of most individuals. Horizontal transitions refer to movement from one situation or setting to another. One of the most important and frequently discussed horizontal transitions is the movement from separate settings to more inclusive ones. This is an example of a transition that is not age specific, as opportunities for such movement are available throughout the life span for persons with disabilities.

Transition Defined

Transition from school to postschool settings has been defined in different ways since its inception in the early 1980s. The Division on Career Development and Transition developed one of the most comprehensive definitions (Halpern, 1994). This definition underscores the realities associated with change. It points out that, as students leave school, they will have to assume a variety of adult roles in the community. It also stresses the proactive aspects of transition education and the importance of actively involving students in this process whenever possible. The definition, written by Halpern (1994), reads as follows:

> Transition refers to a change in status from behaving primarily as a student to assuming emergent adult roles in the community. These roles include employment, participating in postsecondary education, maintaining a home, becoming appropriately involved in the community, and experiencing satisfactory personal and social relationships. The process of enhancing transition involves the participation and coordination of school programs, adult agency services, and natural supports within the community. The foundations for transition should be laid during the elementary and middle school years, guided by the broad concept of career development. Transition planning should begin no later than age 14, and students should be encouraged, to the full extent of their capabilities, to assume a maximum amount of responsibility for such planning.
>
> (p. 117)

Rationale and Mandate

The transition movement in the education of children with disabilities has a long history, both in policy and practice, described in detail in Bassett and Kochhar-Bryant (Chapter 16) and Johnson (Chapter 2), and as such, we will not repeat the antecedents to the current focus on transition in the field. We do know that life outcomes have long been the core of services for individuals with disabilities. For example, as early as 1799, Jean-Marc-Gaspara Itard's goals for Victor, the "Wild Boy of Aveyron," were focused on the boy's social life, his sensibilities, range of ideas, use of speech and mental operations (Smith & Tyler, 2010). Several centuries later, transition for adolescents and young adults has become increasingly complex (Repetto & Webb, 1999).

Suffice it to say that by the mid-1980s, it was evident that students with disabilities were not achieving the types of transition-related outcomes desired by the relatively new Education for All Handicapped Children Act (now the Individuals with Disabilities Education Act). As the first generation of students with disabilities who received educational programming under this legislation began to graduate and leave school in the mid-1980s, a number of follow-up and follow-along studies were funded to track graduates and school leavers and to examine adult outcomes for these young people. Chadsey-Rusch, Rusch, and O'Reilly (1991) reviewed these studies, examining the research on employment, residential, and social/interpersonal relationship outcomes for youth with disabilities who made the transition from school to adulthood, and concluded:

> The outcomes experienced by youth with disabilities for employment, residential status, and social and interpersonal relationships are disappointing. Although rates vary from state to state, most youths with disabilities are either not employed or underemployed. Few youths live independently, many are not well integrated into their communities, and some appear to be lonely. Overall, youths with disabilities face a very uncertain future that holds little promise of improving as they age.
>
> (p. 28)

The National Longitudinal Transition Study of Special Education Students (NLTS), sponsored by the U.S. Department of Education, Office of Special Education Programs and running from 1985 to 1993, provided data regarding the adult outcomes of more than 8,000 youth with disabilities. This longitudinal study used a weighted sample which generalized to youth with disabilities across the nation (Blackorby & Wagner, 1996). The findings reinforced the need to focus more attention on transition-related outcomes and to identify practices that would better enable students with disabilities to become self-sufficient young people.

- The rate of competitive employment for youth with disabilities lagged significantly behind the employment rate of youth in the general population both 2 years after high school (46% to 59%) and 3 to 5 years out of school (57% to 69%).
- Gender, type of disability and ethnic background all impacted the probability that students would be competitively employed.
- Only 9% of competitively employed youth with disabilities two years out of school earned greater than $6.00 per hour, and that percentage grew to only 40% by 3–5 years.
- Only 14% of youth with disabilities who had been out of school for 2 years reported that they attended some type of postsecondary school compared with 53% of youth in the general population. At 3–5 years, 27% of youth reported having been involved in postsecondary education at some time after leaving secondary school, compared with 68% of peers in the general population.
- Thirty-three percent of youth in the general population were living independently less than 2 years after graduation, compared with 13% of youth with disabilities. By 3–5 years, 60% of non-disabled youth lived independently, compared with 37% of youth with disabilities.

Findings from the NLTS, along with results from numerous follow-up and follow-along studies, provided the impetus during the 1990 reauthorization of the Individuals with Disabilities Education Act to include requirements for documenting and providing transition services. The IDEA defines transition services within the Act as "a coordinated set of activities for a student with a disability that (1) is designed within an outcome-oriented process, that promotes movement from school to postschool activities, including postsecondary education, vocational training, integrated employment (including supported employment), continuing and adult education, adult services, independent living, or community participation; (2) is based on the individual student's needs, taking into account the student's preferences and interests" (IDEA, 2004, Sec 300.29). The law also requires that the educational program for any student age 16 or over who receives special education services include transition-related goals.

Along with school-based transition, the business community has impacted how we view transition services by projecting needs for the nation's workforce for 2000 and beyond. Efforts produced by the Department of Labor resulted in the Secretary's Commission on Achieving Necessary Skills (SCANS)(1991), a report that recommended skills that individuals will need for successful employment for the new millennium. The SCANS report offered ideas for parents, educators, and employers in the attainment of these skills.

The federal and state focus on transition services over the past twenty years has paid some dividends. A second National Longitudinal Transition Study, this one lasting 10 years, from 2000 to 2010, compared the outcomes of a nationally representative sample of over 10,000 youth with disabilities aged 13 to 16 years old with findings from the first NLTS. Newman, Wagner, Cameto, Knokey, and Shaver (2010) reported from this study that:

- Postsecondary enrollment rates were 19% higher in 2005 (46%) than in 1990 (26%) for youth with disabilities.
- Youth with disabilities were more likely to have been reported to be employed and/or attending postsecondary school at the time of the 2005 interview, as compared with the 1990 interview (86% vs. 65%, 21 percentage-point difference).
- Youth with disabilities were more likely to have a savings account in 2005 (56%) than in 1990 (44%).
- Reported rates of youth with disabilities participating in volunteer or community service activities were higher in 2005 (25%) than in 1990 (13%).

Unfortunately, the changes from 1990 to 2005 were not uniformly positive, as evidenced by:

- Youth with disabilities as a whole did not vary significantly between 1990 (62%) and 2005 (56%) in their reported employment status, job duration (15 months and 13 months, respectively), hours employed per week (38 hours and 35 hours), type of job, and average wages ($9.10 and $9.00, after adjusting 1990 wages for inflation).
- In 1990, youth with disabilities were more likely to report receiving paid vacation or sick leave, compared to 2005 (60 percent vs. 38 percent).
   It is clear that a concentrated focus on promoting the transition of youth from secondary education to postsecondary education and adulthood remains a critical component of the education of all youth with disabilities.

Key Elements of the Transition Planning/Services Process

The transition from school to life after high school is facilitated if the following elements (Wehmeyer & Patton, in press) have been implemented: comprehensive assessment of strengths, needs, preferences, and interests; development of a set of transition activities/services that is included in the IEP; implementation of the elements included in the IEP; and need for coordination (i.e., cooperation, collaboration, communication) among key school and adult service agency personnel. Although other factors, such as motivation or disposition of the student making the transition, also should be recognized as important, the basic elements are the *sine qua non* for successful transition (Wehmeyer & Patton, in press).

Transition Assessment and Planning

This first element primarily includes examining the student, who will be going through a transition, in terms of what he/she wants to do when school is over. Specific strategies for assessment are discussed subsequently in the text, so our treatment here is at the big picture level. Such assessment involves a look at the student's strengths as well as those areas that require attention now (i.e., instruction or experience) and those that will arise in the future. This assessment process requires a systematic and comprehensive way to obtain this information.

This phase should also involve closely looking at the receiving setting(s) into which the student will be going when high school is completed. In other words, the more the student, his/her family, and school-based transition personnel know about the receiving environment (i.e., what is demanded to be successful) and the existing strengths and challenges of the person who must deal with this subsequent setting, the better the chances for creating an effective transition to this new setting. How students perceive this process can be directly linked to their academic self-concepts, feelings of support, and aspirations (Eccles & Roeser, 2010; Osterman, 2000).

The results of a comprehensive assessment process should be discussed at an IEP meeting that is dedicated to the topic of transition and then ultimately written into the IEP for the student. As discussed in more detail subsequently, the student should be the one who leads the discussion of his/her transition preferences, interests, strengths, and needs, whenever possible.

This text includes chapters on IEP development (Wehman, this volume), assessment in transition (Neubert, this volume), planning strategies (Seabrooks-Blackmore & Williams, this volume), student involvement in transition planning (Martin, Test & Zhang, this volume), family involvement in transition planning (Wandry & Pleet, this volume), and self-determination (Wehmeyer, Field, & Thoma, this volume), all of which will provide information, resources, and strategies for stakeholders to more effectively engage in transition planning and assessment.

Acting on the Plans

Even high quality assessment and individualized planning become moot if the plan is not implemented effectively. Far too often, strategic plans are not put into effect. This important stage of the transition process suffers from two potential threats: (1) not being executed as planned and (2) some important aspects not being done because the assessment and/or the planning phase were performed inadequately.

There are a number of chapters in this volume written to assist stakeholders to use models, methods, and strategies to implement high quality transition instruction and supports. Test, Richter and Walker (this volume) overview life skills and community-based instructional strategies; Hanley-Maxwell and Izzo (this volume) provide information on employment skills instruction; Repetto and Andrews (this volume) address the career development process and vocational instruction. Chapters on the role of structured work experiences (Lindstrom, Doren, Flannery, & Benz, this volume), innovative employment models (Parent, this volume), job development and placement (Luecking & Buchanan, this volume), and assistive technology (Cavenaugh & Patterson, this volume) all provide strategies to enable educators to act on the plans developed. Chapters on social skills instruction and building social networks (Eisenman & Celestin, this volume) and self-determination (Wehmeyer et al., this volume) both address social issues and examine transition in the context of student and environment interactions.

School and Agency Coordination

The element of a successful transition is the coordination that can and should occur among key parties involved in the transition itself. Such coordination requires ongoing cooperation, collaboration, and at very least, communication. The movement of a student from school into any number of postschool settings such as a job or some type of further education setting is facilitated by coordination among various school and adult service providers. Interagency collaboration is addressed explicitly by Noonan and Morningstar (this volume), and collaboration and coordination are central features covered in chapters on family involvement (Wandry & Pleet, this volume), school completion (Kortering, this volume), cultural considerations (deFur & Trainor, this volume), and the transition to postsecondary education (Getzel & Webb, this volume).

These three elements (planning and assessment, action, school and agency collaboration) are also addressed by either age groupings (e.g., chapter on transition and middle school, Repetto, this volume) or by disability groups or categories, including a focus on the transition needs of students with autism (Smith-Myles & Steere, this volume), learning disabilities (Dunn & Curran, this volume), intellectual disability (Grigal, this volume), deaf and hard of hearing (Luckner, this volume), blind or visually impaired (Wolffe & Erin, this volume), emotional or behavioral disorders (Carter & Unruh, this volume), and mental health issues (Walker & Gowen, this volume).

Guiding Principles for Adolescent Transition

Certain principles are essential to guiding the transition process for students with disabilities. The guiding principles listed below represent a few of the many principles that should guide the transition process in schools and serve as a frame of reference for the implementation of transition planning and services.

- Transition efforts should start early.
- Planning must be comprehensive.
- Planning process must consider a student's preferences and interests.
- The transition planning process should be considered a capacity-building activity (i.e. consider a student's strengths).
- Student participation throughout the process is essential.
- Family involvement is desired, needed, and crucial.
- The transition planning process must be sensitive to diversity.
- Supports and services are useful and we all use them.
- Community-based activities provide extremely beneficial experiences.
- Interagency commitment and coordination is essential.
- Timing is crucial if certain linkages are to be made and a seamless transition to life after high school is to be achieved.
- Ranking of transition needs must occur for students who have an extensive set of challenges (Wehmeyer & Patton, in press).

A Framework for Addressing Transition

The federally funded National Secondary Transition Technical Assistance Center (NSTTAC, 2010) has established a framework, based upon seminal work conducted by Paula Kohler in creating a taxonomy for transition programming (Kohler, 1996). Kohler's taxonomy conceptualizes high quality transition programming as addressing five overarching areas: (1) Student-focused planning activities (IEP development, student involvement, planning strategies); (2) Student development activities (life skills instruction, career and vocational curricula, structured work experiences, assessment support services); (3) Family involvement (family training, family involvement, family empowerment); (4) Program structure (program philosophy, program policy, strategic planning, program evaluation, resource allocation, human resource development); and (5) Interagency collaboration (collaborative framework, collaborative service delivery). The NSTTAC framework has identified 33 evidence-based practices in secondary transition (Test et al., 2009b) linked to Kohler's primary areas, provided in Table 1.1. In addition, NSTTAC has identified 16 evidence-based predictors of post-school employment, education and independent living success, listed in Table 1.2 (Test et al., 2009b).

Table 1.1 Evidence-based practices in secondary transition

Kohler's taxonomy category	Evidence-based practices
Student-focused planning	• Involving students in the IEP process • Using the Self-Advocacy Strategy • Using the Self-Directed IEP
Student development	• Teaching: functional life skills • banking skills • restaurant purchasing skills • employment skills using CAI • grocery shopping skills • home maintenance • leisure skills • personal health skills • job-specific employment skills • purchasing using the "one more than" strategy • life skills using CAI • life skills using CBI • self-care skills • safety skills • self-determination skills • self-management for life skills • self-management for employment • self-advocacy skills • purchasing skills • functional reading skills • functional math skills • social skills • purchasing skills • completing a job application skills • job-related social communication skills • cooking and food preparation skills • employment skills using CBI
Family involvement	• Training parents about transition services
Program structure	• Providing community-based instruction • Extending services beyond secondary school • Using Check and Connect
Interagency coordination	• None

Source: Used by permission (public domain), National Secondary Transition Technical Assistance Center (2010).

Table 1.2 Evidence-based predictors of post-School Employment, Education and Independent Living Success

Predictors/outcomes	Education	Employment	Independent living
Career awareness	X	X	
Community experiences		X	
Exit exam equirements/ High school diploma status		X	
Inclusion in general education	X	X	X
Interagency collaboration	X	X	
Occupational courses	X	X	
Paid employment/work experience	X	X	X
Parental involvement		X	
Program of study		X	
Self-advocacy/self-determination	X	X	
Self-care/independent living	X	X	X
Social skills	X	X	
Student support	X	X	X
Transition program	X	X	
Vocational education	X	X	
Work study		X	

Source: Used by permission (public domain), National Secondary Transition Technical Assistance Center (2010).

Readers will find among the chapters in this text, a treatment of virtually every evidence-based practice or predictor listed in Table 1.1 or 1.2. It is our intent that in so doing, stakeholders in the transition process will be provided up-to-date information on the state of the field in adolescent transition.

References

Blackorby, J. & Wagner, M. (1996). Longitudinal postschool outcomes of youth with disabilities: Findings from the National Longitudinal Transition Study. *Exceptional Children, 62*, 399–414.

Chadsey-Rusch, J., Rusch, F., & O'Reilly, M. F. (1991). Transition from school to integrated communities. *Remedial and Special Education, 12*, 23–33.

Eccles, J. S., & Roeser, R. W. (2010). An ecological view of schools and development. In J. S. Meece & J. S. Eccles (Eds), *Handbook of research on schools, schooling, and human development* (pp.6–22). New York: Routledge.

Halpern, A. S. (1994). The transition of youth with disabilities to adult life: A position statement of the Division on Career Development and Transition. *Career Development for Exceptional Individuals, 17*(2), 115–124.

Individuals with Disabilities Education Improvement Act (IDEA) of 2004, PL 108–446, 20 U.S.C. ss 1,400 et seq.

Kohler, P. (1996). Taxonomy for transition programming. Champaign: University of Illinois.

National Secondary Transition Technical Assistance Center (2010). *Evidence-based practices and predictors in secondary transition: What we know and what we still need to know.* Charlotte, NC: NSTTAC.

Newman, L., Wagner, M., Cameto, R., Knokey, A.-M., & Shaver, D. (2010). *Comparisons across time of the outcomes of youth with disabilities up to 4 years after high school. A report of findings from the National Longitudinal Transition Study (NLTS) and the National Longitudinal Transition Study-2 (NLTS2)* (NCSER 2010-3008). Menlo Park, CA: SRI International.

Osterman, K. F. (2000). Students' need for belonging in the school community. *Review of Educational Research, 70*, 323–367.

Repetto, J. B. & Webb, K. W. (1999). Secondary special education. In deFur, S. & Patton, J. (Eds.), *The relationship of school-based services to the transition process.* Austin, TX: PRO-ED Inc.

Secretary's Commission on Achieving Necessary Skills (SCANS). (1991). *What work requires of schools: A SCANS report for America 2000.* Washington, DC: U.S. Department of Labor. (ERIC Document Reproduction Service No. ED 332 054.)

Smith, D. D. & Tyler, N. C. (2010). *Introduction to special education: Making a difference* (7th ed.). Upper Saddle River, NJ: Pearson Education, Inc.

Test, D. W., Fowler, C. H., Richter, S. M., Mazzotti, V., White, J., Walker, A. R., et al. (2009a). Evidence-based practices in secondary transition. *Career Development for Exceptional Individuals, 32*, 155–128.

Test, D. W., Mazzotti, V. L., Mustian, A. L., Fowler, C. H., Kortering, L. J., & Kohler, P. H. (2009b). Evidence-based secondary transition predictors for improving post-school outcomes for students with disabilities. *Career Development for Exceptional Individuals, 32*, 160–181.

Wehman, P. (2006). Transition: The bridge from youth to adulthood. In P. Wehman (Ed.), *Life beyond the classroom: Transition strategies for young people with disabilities* (4th ed.)(pp. 3–40). Baltimore: Paul H. Brookes.

Wehmeyer, M. L., & Patton, J. (in press). Transition to postsecondary education, employment and adult living. In D. Zager, M. L. Wehmeyer, & R. Simpson (Eds.), *Research-based principles and practices for educating students with autism.* New York: Taylor & Francis.

2

Policy and Adolescent Transition Education

David R. Johnson

UNIVERSITY OF MINNESOTA

For more than twenty-five years, federal legislation has played a major role in supporting the participation of youth with disabilities in secondary and postsecondary education programs, employment, and other aspects of community living. While an important policy framework has been advanced, and strides have been made in achieving the goals and intent of federal legislation, much more remains to be accomplished on behalf of youth and young adults with disabilities as they transition from school to adult life. Over the years, the federal government has assumed a key role in stimulating state and local efforts to improve transition services through a variety of policy, interagency, systems-change, model-demonstration, and research efforts (Johnson, Stodden, Emanuel, Luecking, & Mack, 2002). A major impetus for investing in these initiatives has been the recognition that many young adults with disabilities exit school unprepared for adult life.

Post-school follow-up and follow-along studies conducted over the past three decades provide substantial documentation concerning the difficulties these young adults with disabilities experience upon leaving school (Blackorby & Wagner, 1996; Halpern, 1985; Hasazi, Gordon, & Roe, 1985; Johnson, McGrew, Bloomberg, Bruininks, & Lin, 1997; Newman, Wagner, Cameto, & Knokey, 2009; Wagner, Newman, D'Amico, Jay, Butler-Nalin, Marder, & Cox 1991). These and other studies uniformly report high levels of unemployment and underemployment, economic instability, dependence, and social isolation, and low levels of participation in postsecondary education and training programs. Follow-up studies have played an important role in influencing and shaping public policies that have led to needed reforms and improvements in professional practices pertaining to the provision of transition and related services.

This chapter will examine transition policy from its historical roots to the present federal regulations of the Individuals with Disabilities Act (IDEA) Amendments of 2004. The chapter will also provide information on related federal legislation that is currently influencing school and post-school services for adolescents and adults with disabilities and discuss future directions in transition policy development.

Historical Background

As early as the late 1950s, cooperatively financed programs between special education and vocational rehabilitation were being established in several states. Much of the impetus for these cooperative programs stemmed from the availability of federal matching funds. The Vocational Rehabilitation Amendments of 1954 increased the federal reimbursement level to states from 50% to 60%, and was further raised to 75% in the Vocational Rehabilitation Amendments of 1965. This allowed states to match in-kind shares to receive a greater federal share. Consequently, third-party agreements were established with numerous local school districts, state correctional programs, state hospitals, and other state and local agencies. State funds from these programs, primarily in the form of in-kind contributions, were then matched to the higher federal level available for financing state vocational rehabilitation programs. The programs were commonly referred to as Cooperative School Vocational Rehabilitation Programs and employed individuals identified as vocational adjustment coordinators (VACs). These personnel were typically funded jointly by the state vocational rehabilitation agency and local school district special education programs. These collaborative programs flourished throughout the 1960s, and a significant number of school-age youth with disabilities were served. The programs declined in the 1970s due to changes in the federal vocational rehabilitation matching fund formula and the influences of other federal legislation.

In the Vocational Education Amendments of 1968, Congress took steps to provide students with disabilities access to vocational training programs. A 10% set-aside of vocational education funds earmarked for states was contained within this federal law. The Department of Health, Education, and Welfare (HEW)-commissioned evaluation of the 1968 Amendments found that 70% of all students with disabilities receiving vocational training were, however, enrolled in segregated classes (Olympus Research Corporation, 1974). Through 1975, the actual enrollment of students with disabilities in vocational education programs remained at less than 2% (Lee, 1975). The intent of the 1968 legislation clearly envisioned a broad range of vocational education opportunities that would be extended to students with disabilities, but state and local response was minimal.

The Vocational Rehabilitation Act of 1973 provided funds to states to assess "the rehabilitation potential" of individuals with disabilities of an employable age (beginning by age 16) in an effort to prepare for and engage in gainful employment. Section 504 of the Vocational Rehabilitation Act of 1973, linked with earlier civil rights legislation of the 1960s, prohibited discrimination on the basis of disability in any private or public program or agency receiving federal financial assistance. The Education for All Handicapped Children Act (EHA) of 1975 required that states provide all children with disabilities between ages 3 and 21 a free and appropriate public education, which included access to vocational education and career preparation. The law specifically identified industrial arts, consumer, and home-making programs as appropriate programs for students on individualized education programs (IEPs). EHA 1975 also required that parents, educators, and other specialists establish at least one career education objective in each IEP.

In the Vocational Education Amendments of 1976, Congress continued to strengthen the use of the 10% set-aside for students with disabilities and required that the programs be integrated and conducted in the least restrictive environment consistent with EHA 1975. As prescribed by law, plans for vocational education involvement of students with disabilities must be coordinated with their IEP team and goals included within the students' IEP. The individual rights of parents and students guaranteed under EHA 1975 were extended to students with disabilities served under the Vocational Education Amendments of 1976.

Thus, the Vocational Education Act, like EHA 1975, required for each person with a disability served: inclusion in non-discriminatory assessments; full parental involvement in developing the IEP; special education programming in the least restrictive environment; an IEP; and due process safeguards. Together, the Vocational Education Act of 1976, the Education for All Handicapped Children Act of 1975, and the Vocational Rehabilitation Act of 1973 and its Section 504 provisions formed the core of the legal mandates supporting the career development and vocational preparation of school-age children with disabilities from the mid-1970s through the early 1980s.

The first reference to transition services for students with disabilities was included in the Education for All Handicapped Children Act Amendments (EHA) of 1983. Section 626 of the 1983 Amendments, entitled "Secondary Education and Transitional Services for Handicapped Youth," authorized funding to support a series of discretionary grant programs intended to: (a) strengthen and coordinate education, training, and related services to assist youth with disabilities in the transition process from school to employment, independent adult living, and/or a postsecondary education; and (b) strengthen special education programs with the goal of eventual transition.

In 1986 the Education for All Handicapped Children Act was again amended. Language was added to Section 626 of the Amendments to the Act. This included: (a) an additional purpose "to stimulate the improvement of the vocational and life skills of students with handicaps to enable them to better prepare for transition to adult life and service" (Section 626(a)(3)); (b) expanded discretionary grant projects to include "conducting studies which provide information on ... why handicapped youths drop out of school, developing special education curriculum and instructional techniques that will improve handicapped students' acquisition of the skills necessary for transition to adult life and services, and specifically designed physical education and therapeutic recreation programs to increase the potential of handicapped youths for community participation" (Section 626(b)(8–10)); and (c) a new requirement that parents and students with disabilities be involved in the planning, development, and implementation of the aforementioned projects funded under the Act and "a description of the procedures that will be used for coordinating services among agencies for which handicapped youths are or will be eligible" (Section 626(d)(2)).

In 1990 Congress enacted the Individuals with Disabilities Act (IDEA). The title of the Act changed, from Education for All Handicapped Children Act to Individuals with Disabilities Act (IDEA), and several important statutory provisions intended to guide state and local actions in addressing the transition needs of youth with disabilities and families were included in the Act. IDEA 1990 mandated the inclusion of transition services in IEPs for students 16 years of age and older. The intent of the federal legislation was to promote "effective" transition programming by: (a) providing a definition of transition services; (b) listing the coordinated set of activities that constitute transition services and detailing the basis for determining which activities are appropriate for an individual student; (c) specifying the process by which a statement of needed transition services is to be included in the student's IEP; and (d) determining agency responsibilities and monitoring the provision of transition services (Johnson & Sharpe, 2000). The final regulations for IDEA 1990 were published in the fall of 1992. The most prescriptive aspects of the regulations pertained to four major transition service requirements and included: (1) parent notification; (2) student and agency participation in meetings; (3) content of the IEP; and (4) agency responsibility.

The re-authorization of IDEA in 1997 expanded the transition service requirements of the 1990 Act. In addition to transition services beginning at age 16, a statement of transition service needs was required at age 14. At age 14 and annually thereafter for updates, the IEP team looks at the child's courses of study (such as advanced placement courses or vocational education programs) and determines whether those courses are leading the student to where the student needs to be upon graduation. IDEA 1997 also required that students gain greater access to the general education curriculum and state and local assessment systems. IDEA was again re-authorized in 2004 with the intent of further strengthening and supporting students' transition from school to adult life. IDEA-2004 will be described in greater detail later in this chapter in relation to specific provisions contained within the law and federal regulations.

What has emerged based on these federal legislative developments in special education has been a coherent policy framework intended to guide state and local actions on behalf of young people with disabilities and their families as they prepare to leave public schools to enter adult life. The current challenge is to integrate and align the transition service requirements of IDEA 2004 with other major federal legislation, such as the No Child Left Behind Act of 2001, the Americans with Disabilities Act Amendments of 1998, the Workforce Investment Act of 1998, the Vocational Rehabilitation Act of 1973 and subsequent amendments, and other federal legislation. Each of these, and other federal laws, has helped to create a results–based policy framework intended to support young people in the transition from school to adult life.

Supporting Federal Legislation and Transition

While IDEA 2004 conveys the major transition services requirements for school-age youth with disabilities, additional federal legislation has also played a major role in supporting these students in achieving adult life outcomes. The policy intent and legislative goals of these acts reflect the expressed national commitment that youth and young adults with disabilities will be supported to develop skills and experience the opportunity to realize personal goals and choices about how to lead lives as productive, integrated, and empowered members of their communities and society. The following briefly summarizes these major legislative developments.

Rehabilitation Act of 1973 and Subsequent Amendments

The Rehabilitation Act of 1973 provided comprehensive services to all individuals with a disability, regardless of the severity of the disability, and outlawed discrimination against citizens with disabilities. Section 504 specifically prohibited discrimination against otherwise qualified persons with disabilities in any program or activity receiving federal funds. The Act also focused on youth and adults transitioning into employment settings and ensured the development and implementation of a comprehensive and coordinated program of vocational assistance for individuals with disabilities, thereby supporting independent living and maximizing employability and inclusion within communities.

Several amendments have been made to the Rehabilitation Act since 1973. The amendments of 1978 created the Independent Living Program and established independent living centers within states; the amendments of 1986 established supported employment as a viable vocational rehabilitation outcome and were introduced within states through federally supported technical assistance and demonstration programs; the amendments of 1992 brought forward the important concept of "consumer choice" relative to career options and defined competitive employment as the primary outcome for vocational rehabilitation programs; and the amendments of 1998 established linkages between state vocational rehabilitation programs and WIA programs and strengthened Section 508 of the Rehabilitation Act, which requires access to electronic and information technology provided by the federal government.

Americans with Disabilities Act of 1990 (ADA) and 2008 Amendments

ADA of 1990 guaranteed the civil rights of people with disabilities by prohibiting discrimination against anyone who has a mental or physical disability in the area of employment, public services, transportation, public accommodations, and telecommunications. The 2008 Amendments to ADA broadened the definition of "disability" and expanded the list of major "life activities" covered by the law, which includes, but is not limited to, caring for oneself, performing manual tasks, working, etc.

Technology-Related Assistance for Individuals with Disabilities Act of 1998 (Tech Act)

The 1998 Tech Act extended the programs formerly authorized under the Technology-Related Assistance for Individuals with Disabilities Act of 1988. The Tech Act assists states in developing comprehensive programs for technology-related assistance and promotes the availability of technology to individuals with disabilities and their families.

Workforce Investment Act of 1998 (WIA)

WIA created a comprehensive job-training system that consolidates a variety of federally funded programs into a streamlined process that allows individuals to easily access job-training employment services. WIA contained specific provisions that supported the participation of youth with disabilities. For example, WIA-funded programs offered services to individuals with disabilities that are fully integrated with services extended to other persons without disabilities. WIA also provided assurances that its system of one-stop centers included disability programs, such as state vocational rehabilitation agencies.

Ticket to Work and Work Incentives Improvement Act of 1999

The Ticket to Work Program made it possible for individuals with disabilities to join the workforce without fear of losing their Medicare or Medicaid coverage. The legislation created two new options for states. First, it created a new Medicaid buy-in demonstration to help people whose disability is not yet so severe that they cannot work. Second, it extended Medicare coverage for an additional four-and-a-half years for people in the disability insurance system who return to work.

No Child Left Behind Act of 2001 (NCLB)

NCLB redefined the federal goal in K–12 education as closing the achievement gap between typically performing students and economically disadvantaged, English-language learners, minority students, and students with disabilities. The legislation was based on four principles of the Bush administration's education reform plan: (a) to improve accountability for results; (b) expand flexibility and local control; (c) expand options for parents; and (d) emphasize proven teaching methods. Under NCLB, state assessments measure what children know and learn in reading and math (at a minimum) in grades 3–8. All students are tested annually. The assessment data are available in annual report cards on school performance and on annual statewide progress (annual yearly progress). The performance of students with disabilities is included and reported in these reports.

Carl D. Perkins Career and Technical Education Improvement Act of 2006

The Carl D. Perkins Vocational and Technical Education Act was first authorized by the federal government in 1994 and re-authorized in 1998. The Perkins Act, from its origin in 1984, has required states to ensure that special-population students have equal access to vocational education and that localities ensure the full participation of these students in programs that are approved using Perkins funds. States receiving federal vocational education money must fund, develop, and carry out activities and programs to eliminate gender bias, stereotyping, and discrimination in vocational education. The new law includes several major areas of revision: (a) using the term "career and technical education" instead of "vocational education," (b) maintaining the Tech-Prep Program as a separate federal funding stream within the legislation, (c) including new requirements for "programs of study" that link academic and technical content across secondary and postsecondary education, and (d) emphasizing the importance of developing rigorous academic standards and accountability measures for academic and technical skills.

Higher Education Opportunity Act of 2008

Congressional interest in strengthening colleges and universities and in providing financial assistance for students in postsecondary and higher education was originally included in the Higher Education Opportunity Act of 1965. The most recent re-authorization included several significant disability policy provisions, including: (a) a commission and model programs to increase access to instructional materials; (b) model programs for students with intellectual disabilities, including provisions for national technical assistance to support state and local programs; (c) access to federal financial aid for students with intellectual disabilities and veterans with disabilities; and (d) programs to train teachers and other personnel to teach students with disabilities.

IDEA Amendments of 2004: Key Provisions on Transition

President George W. Bush signed the Individuals with Disabilities Act (IDEA) Amendments into law on December 3, 2004. The provisions of the Act became effective on July 1, 2005, and the final regulations were first published on August 14, 2006. When examining the transition requirements of IDEA 2004, the simplest way to understand the statutory obligations is to separate the legal requirements into two distinct areas: (1) substantive obligations and (2) procedural obligations (Shorter, 2008). Substantive obligations are the statutory written law that governs the rights of those affected and the obligations of those who are subject to it. Statutory language conveys policy intent and goals, and defines the legal relationship between individuals affected or served by the law and administrative entities responsible for ensuring that the conditions of the law are met. Substantive law defines who will be served and under what conditions.

Procedural obligations (requirements), in contrast, are the legal rules that govern the process for determining the rights of those affected and the means by which the substantive obligations of law are carried out and administered. Another way of summarizing the difference between substantive and procedural law and obligations is: substantive law defines, creates, or confers substantive legal rights or legal status while procedural law deals with the technical aspects (practices and procedures) and prescribes the steps for enforcing those rights and duties. Presented and discussed in this chapter are the major provisions and requirements concerning transition services. Table 2.1 presents specific language contained within the law, with specific citations to and discussion of the IDEA 2004 federal regulations. The bold text indicates language changes added to the regulations from the IDEA 1997 federal regulations.

Purposes—Section 300.1

Congress added "further education" to IDEA's Purposes Section. This essentially represents a new outcome for special education programs. It acknowledges the importance of postsecondary

Table 2.1 Key transition provisions of IDEA 2004

300.1 Purposes. *The purposes of this title are –*

(a) To ensure that all individuals with disabilities have available to them a free appropriate public education that emphasizes special education and related services designed to meet their unique needs and prepare them **for further education**, employment, and independent living.

300.43 Transition Services (Definitions)

(a) The term "transition services" means a coordinated set of activities for a **child with a disability** that –

  (1) is designed to be **within a results**-oriented process, **that is focused on improving the academic and functional achievement of the child with a disability to facilitate the child's** movement from school to post-school activities, including postsecondary education, vocational education, integrated employment (including supported employment), continuing and adult education, adult services, independent living, or community participation;

  (2) is based on the individual child's needs, taking into account the **child's strengths**, preferences and interests; and includes instruction, related services, community experiences, the development of employment and other post-school adult living objectives, and, if appropriate, acquisition of daily-living skills and functional vocational evaluation.

300.102 Limitations – Exceptions to FAPE for certain ages

(a) **General**. The obligation to make FAPE available to all children with disabilities does not apply with respect to the following:

  (1) Children age 3, 4, 5, 18, 19, 20, or 21, in a State to the extent that its application to those children would be inconsistent with State law or practice, or the order of any court, respecting the provision of public education to children of those ages.

  (2) (i) Children age 18 through 21, in a State to the extent that State law does not require that special education or related services under Part B of the Act be provided to students with disabilities who, in the last educational placement prior to their incarceration in an adult correctional facility –

      (A) Were not actually identified as being a child with a disability under §300.8; and

      (B) Did not have an IEP under Part B of the Act.

    (ii) The exception in paragraph (a)(2)(i) of this section does not apply to children with disabilities, age 18 through 21, who –

      (A) Had been identified as a child with a disability under §300.8 and had received services in accordance with an IEP, but who left school prior to their incarceration; or

      (B) Did not have an IEP in their last educational setting, but who had actually been identified as a child with a disability under §300.8.

  (3) (i) Children with disabilities who have graduated from high school with a regular high school diploma.

    (ii) The exception in paragraph (a)(3)(i) of this section does not apply to children who have graduated from high school but have not been awarded a regular high school diploma.

    (iii) Graduation from high school with a regular high school diploma constitutes a change in placement, requiring written prior notice in accordance with §300.503.

    (iv) As used in paragraphs (a)(3)(i) through (a)(3)(iii) of this section, the term regular high school diploma does not include an alternative degree that is not fully aligned with the State's academic standards, such as a certificate or a general educational development credential (GED).

(b) **Documents relating to exceptions**. The State must assure that the information it has provided to the Secretary regarding the exceptions in paragraph (a) of this section, as required by §300.700 (for purposes of making grants to States under this part), is current and accurate. (Authority: 20 U.S.C. 1412(a)(1)(B)-(C))

300.321 Student Notification and Participation

(b) Transition services participants.

(Continued)

Table 2.1 (Continued).

(1)	In accordance with paragraph (a)(7) of this section, the public agency must invite a child with a disability to attend the child's IEP team meeting if a purpose of the meeting will be the consideration of the postsecondary goals for the child and the transition services needed to assist the child in reaching those goals under Sec. 300.320(b).
(2)	If the child does not attend the IEP team meeting, the public agency must take other steps to ensure that the child's preferences and interests are considered.

300.322 Parent Notification and Participation

(a) Public agency responsibility – general. Each public agency must take steps to ensure that one or both of the parents of a child with a disability are present at each IEP team meeting or are afforded the opportunity to participate, including –

   (2) For a child with a disability beginning not later than the first IEP to be in effect when the child turns 16, or younger if determined appropriate by the IEP team, the notice also must –

      (i) Indicate –

         (A) That a purpose of the meeting will be the consideration of the postsecondary goals and transition services for the child, in accordance with §300.320(b); and

         (B) That the agency will invite the student; and

      (ii) Identify any other agency that will be invited to send a representative.

300.321 Agency Notification and Participation

(b) Transition services participants.

   (3) To the extent appropriate, with the consent of the parents or a child who has reached the age of majority, in implementing the requirements of paragraph (b)(1) of this section, the public agency must invite a representative of any participating agency that is likely to be responsible for providing or paying for transition services.

300.305 Additional requirements for evaluations and re-evaluations

(e) **Evaluations before change in eligibility.**

   (1) **Except as provided in paragraph (e)(2)** of this section, a public agency must evaluate a child with a disability in accordance with §§300.303 through 300.311 before determining that the child is no longer a child with a disability.

   (2) **The evaluation described in paragraph (e)(1) of this section shall not be required before the termination of a child's eligibility under this part due to graduation from secondary school with a regular diploma, or due to exceeding the age eligibility for FAPE under State law.**

   (3) **For a child whose eligibility under this part terminates under circumstances described in paragraph (e)(2) of this section, a local education agency shall provide the child with a summary of the child's academic achievement and functional performance, which shall include recommendations on how to assist a child in meeting the child's postsecondary goals. (Authority: 20 U.S.C. 1414(c))**

300.320 Definition of individualized education program

(b) Transition services. **Beginning not later than the first IEP to be in effect when the child is 16, or younger if determined appropriate by the IEP team, and updated annually thereafter, the IEP must include –**

   (1) **appropriate measurable postsecondary goals based upon age appropriate transition assessments related to training, education, employment, and, where appropriate, independent living skills;**

   (2) **the transition services (including courses of study) needed to assist the child in reaching those goals.**

(c) Transfer of rights at the age of majority. Beginning **not later than** 1 year before the child reaches the age of majority under State law, a statement that the child has been informed of the child's rights under this title, if any, that will transfer to the child on reaching the age of majority under section 615(m),

(Continued)

300.324 Development of the IEP

(a) **Development of IEP**.
   (1) General. In developing each child's IEP, the IEP team must consider –
      (i) The strengths of the child;
      (ii) The concerns of the parents for enhancing the education of their child;
      (iii) The results of the initial or most recent evaluation of the child; and
      (iv) **The academic, developmental, and functional needs of the child.**

(c) **Failure to meet transition objectives.**
   (1) Participating agency failure. If a participating agency, other than the public agency, fails to provide the transition services described in the IEP in accordance with §300.320(b), the public agency must reconvene the IEP team to identify alternative strategies to meet the transition objectives for the child set out in the IEP.
   (2) Construction. Nothing in this part relieves any participating agency, including a State vocational rehabilitation agency, of the responsibility to provide or pay for any transition services that the agency would otherwise provide to children with disabilities who meet the eligibility criteria of that agency.

education, the value of which has increased significantly over the last decade. We recognize that, in order to be successful in achieving economic self-sufficiency and stable employment, a person must receive some form of postsecondary education. Today, increasing numbers of students with disabilities are enrolling and participating in two-year and four-year postsecondary education programs (Newman et al., 2009). The findings of the National Longitudinal Transition Study-2 indicated that 45% of youth with disabilities reported having continued on to postsecondary education within four years of leaving high school. This has increased dramatically, climbing from 2.6% in 1978, to 9.2% in 1994, to 19% in 1996 (Blackorby & Wagner, 1996; Gajar, 1992).

The addition of "further education" to IDEA 2004 underscores the importance that some form of postsecondary education and training plays in the post-school life-adjustment of young adults with disabilities. This added emphasis on postsecondary education will continue to increase in transition planning and decision-making discussions within states and local school districts nationwide in the coming years.

Definitions—Section 300.43(a)

Several changes were introduced in IDEA 2004 from IDEA 1997 regarding the definition of transition services. The definition of transition services was first introduced in the IDEA Amendments of 1990. The definition of transition services in IDEA 2004 now refers to a "child" instead of a "student." The law has always been child-focused, and the change in language makes the definition of transition services more consistent with language that appears elsewhere in the law. Several other changes that were made in IDEA 2004 are more substantial, however.

IDEA 2004 changed the language to say that transition services for a child with a disability must be "designed to be within a results-oriented process." Since 1990 the definition of transition services had made reference to "an outcome-oriented process." Again, this language was changed to be consistent with other sections of the law and regulations where the term "results" has been used in lieu of "outcomes." Additionally, however, "results" and "outcomes" have different meanings. While not defined within the statute, the term is likely used to imply additional accountability for IEP planning terms to determine whether an outcome has yielded or has the potential to yield positive results for the transition-age student.

IDEA 2004 now requires, within the definition of transition services, that the process be "focused on improving the academic and functional achievement of a child with a disability." The emphasis on academic achievement was strengthened in IDEA 1997, with its intent to achieve greater access to the general education curriculum and for students with disabilities to be included and counted in statewide assessment and accountability systems. The No Child Left Behind Act of 2001 required further consideration of students' academic development and achievement and specifically identified that this was to include students with disabilities. The new language in IDEA 2004 strengthens this alignment with the No Child Left Behind Act to emphasize the importance of academic achievement. Clearly, students' academic development and achievement have fast become the cornerstone of transition planning for transition-age youth with disabilities. The importance of this is also emphasized by the increased attention that IEP transition-planning teams are placing on students' access to postsecondary education and employment opportunities that are requiring increasingly higher levels of academic skills.

The term "functional achievement" is not specifically defined in IDEA 2004. In general terms, it implies skills other than academic skills that are identified as part of an overall transition planning process to facilitate transition. The U.S. Department of Education's response to comments regarding the term "functional achievement" when the final regulations for IDEA 2004 were published make an important point, that the development of functional skills pertains to any child with a disability and not just to those with significant cognitive disabilities (Federal Register, October 14, 2006, p. 46579). Functional skills are, however, typically defined as skills that can be used in everyday life situations across different environments, such as home, community-living, recreation, postsecondary education, employment, and the like.

IDEA 2004 did not make changes in the IEP requirement that transition planning be based on the individual child's needs. IDEA 1997 included language requiring that, when transition goals are established by IEP teams, full consideration be given to a child's preferences and interests. IDEA 2004 broadens this emphasis to include "taking into account the child's strengths," as well. This now requires that IEP teams, in addition to considering students' preferences and interests, should also review information concerning academic, functional, and other areas in which the child has performed well during the school experience. This is not intended to mean that consideration of a student's strengths or performance should outweigh the student's preferences and interests but suggests that such information is important in IEP team discussions when making decisions and setting goals.

IDEA 2004 also requires that the IEP team, at a minimum, consider each of the areas, including "instruction; related services; community experiences; development of employment and other post-school adult living objectives and, if appropriate, acquisition of daily-living skills; and, if appropriate, a functional vocational evaluation." In many cases, each of these areas, and possibly others, will be included in students' IEPs. There is no statutory limit on the types of services that may be provided to a child with a disability so long as the IEP team makes this determination. The acquisition of daily-living skills and functional vocational evaluation are important considerations that need to be discussed by the IEP team. Transition services may be provided by the education agency or, as outlined in Section 300.324(c)(2) of the regulations, by agencies outside the school. In either case, they must be written into the IEP and the responsible agency noted.

Exceptions to FAPE for Certain Ages

IDEA has always made it clear that there are some possible exceptions to the requirement of providing a free and appropriate public education (FAPE) for some students of transition age. For example, as illustrated in Table 2.1, FAPE does not apply with respect to children aged 3, 4, 5, 18, 19, 20, or 21, unless there is state law or practice to do so, or the order of a court requiring, for any reason, that these age groups be served. Parents must be aware of the state laws regarding the age at which the right to public education terminates.

IDEA 2004, like previous amendments of this Act, has extended special education services to children age 18–21 (with some state variations). Extended special education services, however, are not automatically provided but rather must be based on the IEP team's determination regarding the need for additional years of schooling. It is important for the IEP team to assess as early as possible the actual age at which termination of special education services will occur, either 18 or sometime up to or through age 21. This certainly has a significant bearing on the types of academic and functional skills the student will need to develop prior to graduation and the extent to which outside agency participation may be required to support the student in achieving post-school goals.

Section 300.102 notes that some students with disabilities who are incarcerated are not entitled to FAPE. Table 2.1 identifies conditions under which incarcerated youth may not be eligible for FAPE. According to these regulations, if prior to incarceration a student had been receiving special education services, but had dropped out of school or had been formally identified as a "child with a disability," that individual is still entitled to FAPE and to the transition services that it entails. In fact, transition planning may be particularly important for this group of students, given the high unemployment and recidivism rates among dropouts and incarcerated youth.

It is also important for parents and educators to know that, if a child graduates from high school with a regular high-school diploma, the child is no longer entitled to FAPE and special education, and the child's special education services end at that point. According to Section 300.102(a)(3)(ii–iii), the exception does not apply to students who have graduated but have not been awarded regular high-school diplomas or in situations where graduation from high school with a regular high-school diploma constitutes a change in placement, requiring prior written notice. Given this language, it is critical that the parents, student, and IEP team members carefully consider when a regular high-school diploma should be received. What has been problematic in situations when graduation has been challenged is that specific academic and functional goals included on the student's IEP have not, as yet, been fully met. In some cases, it may be advisable to delay formal receipt of the regular high-school diploma until all transition service requirements have been achieved or until students have been connected with adult services necessary to support their post-school education, employment, and independent living needs. Also noted in Table 2.1 is the requirement that states must have on file adequate documentation relating to any exemptions. This is identified in Section 300.102(b), Documents Relating to Exceptions.

Student Notification and Participation

The IDEA 2004 final regulations require that "a child with a disability, beginning not later than the first IEP to be in effect when the child turns 16, or younger, if determined appropriate by the IEP team, be invited to attend the IEP meeting if one of the purposes of the annual meeting will be the discussion of transition service needs." The requirement to involve students in the discussions of their future goals and plans reflects the values of self-determination and shared responsibility. Creating these opportunities, however, may pose challenges to parents and professionals to change procedures and develop strategies to ensure that students are given an active and meaningful role and voice in planning their future. Teachers and other professionals must play an important role in working with students on the knowledge and skills they will need to become active and effective decision-makers on their own behalf in IEP meetings. Several self-determination curricula have been developed and are readily available to support students in the development of the skills necessary to participate in their IEP meetings focused on transition outcomes (Field, Martin, Miller, Ward, & Wehmeyer, 1998; Martin & Marshall, 1995; Wehmeyer, Agran, & Hughes, 1998).

It is difficult to envision any situation where students with disabilities, irrespective of the level or significance of the disability, should not be invited to their IEP meetings with the expectation that they assume an active role in planning and decision-making. One exception may be the withdrawal of a child's participation by the parent if the child is below the age of majority and not in a legal decision-making capacity. In conditions under which a student would not attend his or her IEP meeting, the public agency must take other steps to make sure that the child's preferences and interests are considered. One example might be to collect information from the student prior to the meeting and request that informed family members, friends, and/or professionals present information at the meeting on behalf of the child. Whatever strategy is decided upon, it is important to make sure that someone at the meeting knows the student's preferences and interests, the student's ideas about his or her future post-school goals, and understands the student's expectations of needed transition services.

Parent Notification and Participation

The federal requirements are clear—parents must be notified when the purpose of the IEP meeting is to consider transition services. These specific provisions are noted in Table I, Section 300.322(a)(2). Ensuring that parents are informed in advance that transition goals will be discussed at the IEP meeting provides them the opportunity to prepare for the discussion. Encouraging parents to discuss future transition goals with their son or daughter prior to the meeting is also desirable. The first step, however, is providing appropriate notice to parents of the IEP meeting and its intent. In addition, by understanding what outside agencies are invited, parents can request that additional or alternative agencies be included. This also provides an opportunity for parents to request information about the services and policies of invited agencies. If parents are unable to attend, alternative strategies can be used to obtain their input regarding possible transition goals for their son or daughter. In these cases, strategies that have been used most often range from holding an individual meeting with parents outside the formal IEP meeting, conducting an informational conference over the phone, mailing a draft of the student's transition goals home for review and feedback by the parent, or inviting the parent to submit comments regarding the plan in writing (Johnson & Sharpe, 2000).

Agency Notification and Participation

The requirement to involve agencies responsible for providing or paying for services reflects the values of long-term, child-centered planning, service collaboration, and shared responsibility. It places responsibility on school personnel to become knowledgeable about the services and policies of community agencies that may be involved in a child's IEP when transition goals are discussed. Some possible agencies may include: vocational rehabilitation, employment and training, postsecondary education programs, health, mental health, developmental disabilities, social security, housing, and others relevant to the individual's needs and preferences.

One of the notable changes to IDEA 2004 was the incorporation of parent and adult child consent when an IEP team involves outside agency participation in the IEP meeting. This requirement is noted in Section 300.321(b)(3) and in Section 300.9 of the federal regulations. IDEA 2004 does not give school districts the authority to compel another agency to participate in planning the transition for a child with a disability (Shorter, 2008). The IDEA 2004 regulations removed the language from IDEA 1997 regulations that required a school district to ensure outside agency participation. Further, the IDEA 2004 regulations no longer include the requirement found in the IDEA 1997 regulations that, "if an agency invited to send a representative to a meeting does not do so, the public agency shall take other steps to obtain the participation of the other agency in the planning of any transition services" (Section 300.344(b)(3)(ii)). This means that if a participating agency that has been invited does not attend the meeting, the school district is no longer required to take other steps to obtain participation of another agency.

While achieving outside agency participation in IEP meetings is not required, this does not mean that steps cannot be taken to involve an outside agency even if agency representatives do not attend the meeting. Steps that may be taken, with the consent of the parents or a child who has reached the age of majority, include: forwarding a copy of the IEP to the agency for review, arranging for a subsequent meeting to discuss transition-specific issues with parents or the child, maintaining contact with the agency to promote involvement, and encouraging parents and the child to initiate contact and request information about services and policies and their involvement in future IEP meetings when transition goals are discussed.

Additional Requirements for Evaluations and Re-evaluations

Section 300.305(e)(3) of the IDEA 2004 regulations requires that all special education students who leave secondary education through graduation or by exceeding state eligibility are to be provided with a Summary of Performance (SOP) to use as they pursue their transition goals. The SOP is to be developed in lieu of an exit IEP and is intended to assist the student in transition from high school to postsecondary education, training, and/or employment. More specifically, the information contained in the SOP should provide information that is helpful under Section 504 of the Rehabilitation Act and the Americans with Disabilities Act when a student is attempting to establish eligibility for reasonable accommodations and supports in postsecondary education and other settings. Because of the implications of the SOP in establishing eligibility, as well as identifying accommodations and supports needed, the student should actively participate in the development of this document. Numerous resources are available that detail the steps necessary to develop the SOP (see Cortiella, 2007; Dukes, Shaw, & Madaus, 2007; Madaus, Bigaj, Chafouleas & Simonsen, 2006; Madaus & Shaw, 2007).

Definition of the Individualized Education Program

A major change occurred in IDEA 2004 that removed the requirement that IEP teams begin considering appropriate coursework at age 14. Section 300.320(b) shifts the transition planning to "not later than the first IEP to be in effect when the child is 16 ..." Many professionals and advocates have commented that age 16 is too late to start transition planning. Numerous comments were received regarding this age change, as the federal regulations were being reviewed and approved, following the enactment of IDEA's 2004 statutory language. The final regulations, however, in Section 300.320(b) included the phrase, "or younger, if determined appropriate by the IEP Team." Central to both the statutory language and final regulations is the understanding that IEP team decisions must always be individualized. Several states, however, have chosen to retain the IDEA-1997 younger age of 14 as the point at which the state requires transition services be considered by the IEP team.

IDEA 2004 required, as part of the IEP process for a child who is entitled to transition services, that appropriate, measurable postsecondary goals be developed. The notion that "appropriate" goals be developed means that such goals are based on the individual student's strengths, needs, interests, and preferences; and on age-appropriate transition assessments relating to training, education, employment, and, where appropriate, independent living skills. To be "measurable" means that there must be objective criteria that are observable and countable, which can determine if a student with a disability has achieved goals in their IEP. The term "postsecondary" means goals for the student to work toward while in high school in preparation for life after high school.

IDEA 2004 also required that the IEP team use appropriate transition assessments. The final regulations remained silent on what constitutes an appropriate transition assessment, and this decision is left up to individual states. IDEA 2004 is clear, however, that appropriate transition goals must include training, education, employment, and, where appropriate, independent living skills. Appropriate transition assessment information is critical in making such determinations. The Division on Career Development and Transition of the Council for Exceptional Children defines transition assessment as "an ongoing process of collecting data on the individual's needs, preferences, and interests as they relate to the demands of current and future working, educational, living, and personal and social environments" (Sitlington, Neubert, & Leconte, 1997). Transition assessments can be formal or informal, and the determination of what specific strategies states and local school district shall use has been left up to individual states (Kortering, Sitlington, & Braziel, 2004; Sitlington et al., 1997; Sitlington, Neubert, Begun, Lombard, & Leconte, 2007). Also noted in the federal regulations is the requirement that the transition services needed to assist the child in reaching these goals also include the student's courses of study.

The regulation provision that allows for the transfer of parental rights to students at the age of majority under state law is a further recognition of the importance of schools' responsibilities in assisting students to move from school to the adult world. In a state that transfers rights at the age of majority, beginning at least one year before a student reaches the age of majority, under state law, the student's IEP must include a statement that the student has been informed of his or her rights under Part B of the Act, if any, that will transfer to the student on reaching the age of majority. In addition, when the student reaches the age of majority, if rights are transferred, the school must provide any notice required by Part B regulations to both the student and the parents. Exceptions to this are rare. However, if, under state law, a state has a mechanism to determine that a student with a disability, who has reached the age of majority under state law that applies to all children and has not been determined incompetent under state law, does not have the ability to provide informed consent for his or her educational program, the state shall establish procedures for appointing the parent to represent the student's educational interests throughout the student's eligibility under Part B. If a parent is not available, another appropriate individual will be appointed.

This provision to transfer the rights at the age of majority was initiated in IDEA 1997 and was carried forward in the IDEA-2004 final regulations. The provision underscores the importance of empowering students with disabilities to become more knowledgeable and skilled in expressing their needs, preferences, and aspirations. This provision should also encourage educators and parents to ensure that appropriate opportunities and supports are available to students that promote self-determined behavior and attitudes well before the transition process and transfer of rights occur.

Development of the Individualized Education Program (Section 300.324)

Outside agencies that are identified by the IEP team as responsible for providing or paying for services to a child with a disability are not excused from those obligations as a result of IDEA-2004. The final regulations of IDEA-2004 parallel those of the IDEA 1997 regulations. As noted in Table I, if a participating agency, other than the public agency, fails to provide the transition services described in the IEP the public agency shall reconvene the IEP team to identify alternative strategies to meet the transition objectives for the student. Clearly, the ultimate responsibility for the provision of transition services under IDEA rests with the school district.

The IEP team may be able to identify alternative strategies without changing the student's IEP. In other instances, the IEP team may decide to revise the IEP, changing goals, short-term objectives, timelines, or statements about agency responsibility. For example, a student's IEP specifies that a community residential placement is needed within the next three months. If a community residence is not accessed by that time, the team would meet again to discuss the delay and to ascertain the status of access to the service. It may be that waiting lists indicate a six-month wait, but the likelihood of accessing services is high. In that case, the IEP team may decide to lengthen the timeline and meet in another three months to discuss progress. If the indication is that a community residence is likely not possible for this student, due to lack of availability, eligibility, or other reasons, the team may try to come up with other strategies to achieve the same goal. These strategies may include creative use of Social Security and other funds to purchase or rent housing, pooling resources of young adults with similar needs (both with and without disabilities), or obtaining other forms of support from parents and/or advocacy groups.

Section 300.324(c)(2) does not imply that the burden of services, programs, or financial responsibility falls solely on the educational agency when things do not turn out as planned. By giving parents and students an opportunity to re-engage with the planning team when things go wrong, the provision seeks to prevent students from falling through the cracks with no place to go for assistance and advocacy. The strength of this provision relies on the existence of state or local interagency agreements that delineate the financial and legal responsibilities of agencies involved in transition services. Without such agreements, the reconvention process may be ineffectual. Specific language within these interagency agreements to address the questions of "What services are available to meet individual student needs?" and "Who pays for these services?" is fundamental to ensuring that service needs are met for the student.

A Foundation for Future Transition Policy

Achieving more effective and coordinated transition services must begin with a coherent policy framework that incorporates greater consistency across public programs in philosophical values, goals, standards, and practices. Future policies that are intended to support students in making a successful transition from school to adult life can only be accomplished by: (a) developing consistent policy goals at all levels; (b) viewing the transition period as a shared responsibility among and between schools and community service agencies; (c) investing in research that leads to tested and valid practices, and engaging in continuous and sustained evaluation of programs to guide and inform the policy-making process; and (d) creating broad-based and comprehensive professional development opportunities.

Importance of Shared Beliefs, Values, and Guiding Principles

The first and perhaps the most essential step in achieving improved service planning and coordination and effectiveness in transition service programs is through renewed and explicit articulation of clearly stated and consistent values, beliefs, and principles to guide public policies. Currently, as noted throughout this chapter, no clearly articulated or widely accepted overarching public policy addresses the transition of youth with disabilities. Instead, transition services are engulfed by a myriad of federal and state laws and procedural requirements that typically must be patched together to meet the school and post-school needs of youth and young adults with disabilities. Given this complex array of public policies influencing the provision of transition services, guiding principles provide an important mechanism for adding a sense of coherence on what is "most" essential to achieve through federal and state policy development. More specifically, the principles are intended to: (a) guide and inform policy-makers as to what is of central importance in advancing policies and practices, (b) stimulate discussion about best practice in the provision of transition services, and (c) guide the actions and behaviors of professionals in everyday practice to ensure that students with disabilities achieve positive school and post-school results.

Over the years, several national organizations and professional associations, i.e., National Council on Disability, National Organization on Disability, Council for Exceptional Children, and others, have set forth various position statements that express the shared values, beliefs, and principles of these organizations and their members concerning youth with disabilities and their transition from school to adult life. Recently (October 2009), the Consortium for Citizens with Disabilities (CCD) published a list of essential transition principles for youth with disabilities. CCD is a coalition of more than a hundred national disability organizations and advocates for national public policy that ensures the inclusion of children and adults with disabilities in all aspects of community life. Collectively, CCD and its member organizations emphasize the following policy principles for transition:

- Federal and state policies should promote positive transition outcomes, including additional education opportunities, competitive employment, economic self-sufficiency, and community living.
- All transition-related statutory and policy changes should be driven by an underlying belief in high expectations for all youth, self-determination, and equality of opportunity (including nondiscrimination, individualization, inclusion, and integration).
- Transition planning and services must be based on self-determination and be individualized, person-centered, youth-driven, and based on the strengths and interests of the youth.
- Transition strategies should be evidence-based and include school-based preparatory experiences, career preparation and work-based learning experiences, youth development and leadership, connecting activities (such as services, activities, and supports that help youth gain access to chosen post-school options), and family involvement and supports.
- Businesses and employers need to be engaged as partners in the transition process.
- Agencies, programs, and organizations coordinating services and supports should align their missions, policies, procedures, data, and resources to serve all youth including those with disabilities, to provide a unified, flexible array of programs, services, accommodations, and supports. Definitions for transition and transition services should be embedded in relevant federal legislation and regulations.
- To achieve positive transition outcomes, federal and state policies should promote interagency coordination, agency responsibilities, and a set of incentives for Labor, Education, Vocational Rehabilitation, Medicaid, and other sources of public funds to maximize funding and develop cross-agency transition strategies.
- Schools and other relevant agencies should have adequate numbers of knowledgeable, responsive, accountable, and culturally competent staff to help youth achieve their goals.

Each of these guiding policy principles for transition is undeniably interdependent. Corresponding public policy, however, treats these principles in a piecemeal fashion within respective federal and state laws governing education, postsecondary education, employment, health care, community living, transportation, and the like, functioning as separate, independent programs and sets of services. Substantial and prolonged policy advocacy will be necessary for the integration of these guiding principles, as common elements of statutory law and procedural requirements, to achieve positive results for young people with disabilities and their families.

Importance of Shared Responsibility

As noted earlier in this chapter, federal legislation in special education and similarly in vocational rehabilitation, vocational education, health and human services, labor, and other service-delivery systems cannot compel another agency to participate in the development of transition plans or commit another agency to pay for services unless that agency agrees to do so. It is unlikely that Congress will dramatically change this situation on behalf of transition-age youth with disabilities, thus directing professionals and policy-makers to establish other mechanisms to improve the coordination and delivery of services.

Efforts to achieve greater coordination of services to address the lifelong needs of individuals with disabilities have been a long-standing preoccupation of public policy in education and human services. The policy intent to increase interagency collaboration has already been established at the federal level through written joint policy statements between the Offices of Special Education Programs, Vocational Rehabilitation, Vocational Education, Labor, Health and Human Services, Social Security, and other federal agencies. In addition, since the mid-1970s, this emphasis on the need for improved coordination of services has been urged upon states in the form of federal legislative mandates to establish interagency agreements at both the state and local levels.

Because of conflicting policy goals, eligibility criteria, funding patterns, and other factors that differ across agencies and states, however, many of these interagency agreements carry little force or are difficult to implement with the flexibility needed to provide appropriate services for youth and young adults with disabilities. Title I of the Rehabilitation Act, for example, requires the development of state interagency agreements between special education and vocational rehabilitation, focused on the transition of youth with disabilities. A recent national study on state vocational rehabilitation agency policies and practices concerning transition-age youth with disabilities found that while 90% of states have interagency agreements between state vocational rehabilitation and education agencies, far fewer agreements are in place at the local level (Norman, Johnson, Timmons, Cobb, & Albright, 2007). State vocational rehabilitation officials, however, report that local interagency agreements are critical in establishing the level of service coordination needed to support students during the period of transition from school to adult life.

In reviewing state vocational rehabilitation interagency agreements, Norman et al. (2007) found that, while these state-level agreements were important, agency officials deemed them not specific enough concerning the roles and responsibilities that special education and vocational rehabilitation agencies should assume in addressing the transition needs of youth with disabilities. Given the importance of determining the type and level of transition services and supports provided to youth with disabilities at the local level, increased attention to the development of local interagency agreements should be emphasized in future federal policy discussions at the federal and state levels. Several policy-related implications should be considered: (a) identifying, and stating in state vocational rehabilitation plans, specific sets of activities and actions in which local interagency teams should engage; (b) including in the job responsibilities of vocational rehabilitation counselors' participation on local interagency teams; (c) clarifying agency responsibilities for providing and paying for specific types of services; and (d) undertaking evaluations of the effectiveness of local interagency processes in achieving employment and related adult-life outcomes for transition-age youth and youth with disabilities.

Importance of Investing in Research and Evaluation

At all levels of the service delivery system, there is a critical need to engage in comprehensive research on effective interventions and strategies and systematic evaluations of policies, programs, and services. For the past three decades, the U.S. Department of Education's Office of Special Education Programs and, more recently, the Institute of Education Sciences have sponsored transition research and related initiatives that have resulted in a knowledge base of promising interventions, approaches, and strategies for the delivery of transition services for students with disabilities. Advances and innovations in functional skill development, vocational training, job acquisition, access to postsecondary education, transition planning, student and parent involvement in school and post-school decision-making, development of adult living skills, and self-determination and self-advocacy are all valued examples of previous and current efforts (Johnson et al., 2002). These and other varied approaches supported through the discretionary grant programs of other federal and state agencies have served as a foundation upon which transition services are provided to youth with disabilities and their families. Federal policies must continue to maintain and expand research on these and other interventions and strategies that will go a long way toward ensuring that youth with disabilities achieve the positive school and post-school results essential for successful transition.

Schools and community service agencies also need evaluation data to provide decision-makers with reliable information to modify programs and improve transition services. Follow-up and follow-along studies have been the primary evaluation strategy to assess the post-school status of youth and young adults with disabilities. Many states are now in the process of developing and conducting post-school follow-up data systems on former special education students. IDEA 2004 specifically required states to gather information on a minimum set of post-school outcomes focused on employment and access to postsecondary education. This requirement has helped to establish a minimum baseline of knowledge regarding the post-school experiences of these young people.

A particular need persists, however, to go beyond present approaches. We need improved information on: (a) the longitudinal nature of post-school adjustment that examines the community status of older-age cohorts, now in their 30s, who may have remained in the care of their families, without access to independent living, employment services, and other opportunities; (b) post-school evaluations on students with disabilities who fail to complete their public education programs and are trying to "make it" in our communities; (c) studies that document not only access to postsecondary education but also the rates of successful completion and entry into gainful employment; and (d) studies on the financial and emotional impact of the critical transition years on families. Findings in such studies could provide a sound, empirical foundation for improving secondary education programs, developing critical transition service programs for students leaving school, structuring more complex research and evaluation efforts, and establishing more effective educational and community services.

At least two additional evaluation considerations have been neglected and require policy advocacy. First, there is a general lack of information on the benefits and costs of special education and other community services as they prepare students for the transition to adulthood. Given the current economic climate of our country, policy-makers and agency administrators must base decisions regarding current and future program investments on both the costs and benefits or outcomes that such services can achieve. Advances have been made in benefit–cost methodology that allow for the evaluation of important quality-of-life dimensions in statistical analyses and that make the methodology feasible within the constraints that exist in school systems and community service agencies.

Second, while interagency collaboration has, for more than forty years, been touted as the primary means through which many students with disabilities can only experience success in their post-school, adult-life experiences, discussions in published literature during this time have repeatedly revealed numerous barriers and challenges to achieving improved service coordination (Benz, Johnson, Mikkelsen, & Lindstrom, 1995; Furney, Hasazi, & DeStefano,

1997; Hasazi, Furney, & DeStefano, 1999; Johnson et al., 2002; Luecking & Crane, 2002; Stodden, 1998). Despite the importance of interagency collaboration in achieving positive school and post-school results for youth with disabilities, the approaches, processes, and outcomes of collaboration have not been subjected to systematic evaluations or rigorous research. In the absence of such evaluations or research, we are left with few models that clearly delineate the critical process steps needed by key administrative personnel to carry out inter-agency planning and service coordination effectively. Limitations or failures in achieving improved levels of interagency coordination result not only from inadequate understanding of the functioning of other agencies (goals, regulations, eligibility criteria, funding, etc.), but also from limited understanding of the process skills necessary to manage successfully a comprehen-sive planning process composed of parents and multiple agency members. There are arenas, however, where collaborative processes have been successfully investigated in the public and private sectors (Bennis, Benne, Chin, & Corey, 1976; Bryson, 2004; Delbecq, Van de Ven, & Gustafson, 1975). Without systematic efforts to investigate the usefulness of these effective management tools, interagency collaboration will remain an illusory goal. If Congress and state legislatures continue to embed language with increasing requirements for cross-agency collab-oration, commitments and investments must be made to research the efficacy of collaboration in achieving positive results.

Importance of Comprehensive Professional Development

Nowhere is the need for professional development more pronounced than in efforts to ensure that education and community service professionals have the knowledge, skills, and tools necessary to support students during the critical transition period. Currently, few institutions of higher education offer formal pre-service training programs that provide a specialized emphasis on secondary education and transition services. The challenging nature of state licensing and certification standards and requirements have presented limited opportunities to embed sufficient content into pre-service training programs to prepare future teachers and other professionals to address the transition needs of youth with disabilities. Consequently, many new professionals enter the field without the specific knowledge and skills needed to support transition. Further, most university-based training programs provide instruction along disciplinary lines; however, transition, by its very premise, is multi-disciplinary in its practice. Today there is increased attention to the transition not only of youth with disabilities but of all students. The rapidly emerging interest in ensuring that a greater number of students exiting high school access postsecondary education has fueled this discussion. College readiness programs, individual graduation plans focused on all students, and other developments have all focused on a need to better prepare and support all students in the transition from school to postsecondary education, employment, and other aspects of community living. Future policy development must acknowledge these emerging trends and developments and examine current licensing and certification practices and the investments that must be made in university and college training programs to prepare future professionals.

Beyond pre-service training, high-quality continuing professional development is needed to ensure that current educators and other professionals are up-to-date and fully able to support students in the transition from school to adulthood. Here, too, there are many challenges in making available continuing education programs for professionals. Limited state and local school district and community service agency budgets have made it difficult to make available in-service training related to transition services. Cost-effective training models and approaches using on-line instruction, webinars, podcasts, and other strategies offer promising opportunities to support professionals in the development of skills needed to support students during their transition (Kim & Morningstar, 2007; Morningstar & Clark, 2003; Morningstar, Kim, & Clark, 2008).

Conclusion

Achieving improvements in transition services nationally must begin with a coherent policy framework that incorporates greater consistency across public programs in philosophical values, goals, standards, and practices to guide the ongoing management of education and community services to youth and young adults with disabilities. Federal and state legislation has served as the primary impetus for addressing the critical transition period and will continue to do so into the future. How we move forward, with what sense of priority concerning the needs that must be met for individuals and their families, is the critical question. As E. F. Schumacher (1973) argued many years ago, our policies are mirrored in their implementation. Reforming current operating practices is essential to the economic, personal, and social integration of youth and adults with disabilities.

References

Bennis, W. G., Benne, K. D., Chin, R., & Corey, K. E. (1976). *The planning of change.* New York: Holt, Rinehart, & Winston.

Benz, M., Johnson, D. K., Mikkelsen, K. S., & Lindstrom, L. E. (1995). Improving collaboration between schools and vocational rehabilitation: Stakeholder identified barriers and strategies. *Career Development for Exceptional Individuals, 18*(2), 133–144.

Blackorby, J., & Wagner, M. (1996). Longitudinal postschool outcomes of youth with disabilities: Findings from the National Longitudinal Transition Study. *Exceptional Children, 62*(5), 399–414.

Bryson, J. M. (2004). *Strategic planning for public and nonprofit organizations: A guide to strengthening and sustaining organizational achievement.* 3rd edition. San Francisco: Jossey-Bass.

Cortiella, C. (2007). Summary of performance: A new tool for successful transition. *Exceptional Parent, 37*(11), 97.

Delbecq, A. L., Van de Ven, A., & Gustafson, D. (1975). *Group techniques for program planning: A guide to Nominal Group and Delphi.* Chicago: Scott, Foresman.

Dukes, L., Shaw, S., & Madaus, J. (2007). How to complete a summary of performance for students exiting to postsecondary education. *Assessment for Effective Intervention, 32*(3), 143–159.

Federal Register, October 14, 2006, p. 46579. Washington, DC: U.S. Government Printing Office.

Field, S., Martin, J. E., Miller, R., Ward, M., & Wehmeyer, M. (1998). *A practical guide for teaching self-determination in the schools.* Reston, VA: The Council for Exceptional Children. (ERIC Document Reproduction Service No. ED 442207.)

Furney, K. S., Hasazi, S. B., & DeStefano, L. (1997). Transition policies, practices, and promises: Lessons from three states. *Exceptional Children, 63*(3), 343–355.

Gajar, A. (1992). University-based models for students with learning disabilities: The Pennsylvania State University Model. In F. R. Rusch, L. DeStefano, J. G. Chadsey-Rusch, L. A. Phelps, & E. Szymanski (Eds.), *Transition from school to adult life: Models, linkages, and policy.* Sycamore, IL: Sycamore Publishing Company.

Halpern, A. S. (1985). Transition: A look at the foundations. *Exceptional Children, 51*(6), 479–486.

Hasazi, S. B., Furney, K. S., & DeStefano, L. (1999). Implementing the IDEA transition mandates. *Exceptional Children, 65*(4), 555–566.

Hasazi, S. B., Gordon, L. R., & Roe, C. A. (1985). Factors associated with the employment status of handicapped youth exiting high school from 1979 to 1983. *Exceptional Children, 51*(6), 455–469.

Johnson, D. R., McGrew, K., Bloomberg, L., Bruininks, R. H., & Lin, H. C. (1997). *Policy research brief: A national perspective on the postschool outcomes and community adjustment of individuals with severe disabilities.* Minneapolis, MN: University of Minnesota, Institute on Community Integration.

Johnson, D. R., & Sharpe, M. N. (2000). Results of a national survey on the implementation transition service requirements of IDEA of 1990. *Journal of Special Education Leadership, 13*(2), 15–26.

Johnson, D. R., Stodden, R. A., Emanuel, E. J., Luecking, R., & Mack, M. (2002). Current challenges facing secondary education and transition services for youth with disabilities: What research tells us. *Exceptional Children, 68*(4), 519–531.

Kim, K. H., & Morningstar, M. E. (2007). Online inservice training: Enhancing secondary special education teachers' knowledge and competencies in working with culturally and linguistically diverse families. *Career Development for Exceptional Individuals, 30*(2), 116–128.

Kortering, L., Sitlington, P., & Braziel, P. (2004). The use of vocational assessment and planning as a strategic intervention to help keep youths with emotional or behavioral disorders in school. In D. Cheney (Ed.), *Transition of Students with Emotional or Behavioral Disorders: Current approaches for positive outcomes.* Arlington, VA: Council for Children with Behavioral Disorders and Division on Career Development.

Lee, A. M. (1975). *Learning a living across the nation: Project baseline.* Flagstaff, AZ: Northern Arizona University.

Luecking, R., & Crane, K. (2002). Addressing the transition needs of youth with disabilities through the WIA system. *National Center on Secondary Education and Transition Issue Brief, 1*(6). Minneapolis, MN: University of Minnesota.

Madaus, J., Bigaj, S., Chafouleas S., & Simonsen, B. (2006). What key information can be included in a comprehensive summary of performance? *Career Development for Exceptional Individuals, 29*(1), 90–99.

Madaus, J. W., & Shaw, S. F. (2007). Transition assessment: Introduction to the special series. *Assessment for Effective Intervention, 32*, 130–132.

Martin, J. E., & Marshall, L. H. (1995). ChoiceMaker: A comprehensive self-determination program. *Intervention in School and Clinic, 30*(3), 147–156. (ERIC Document Reproduction Service No. EJ 497548.)

Morningstar, M. E., & Clark, G. M. (2003). The status of personnel preparation for transition education and services: what is the critical content? How can it be offered? *Career Development for Exceptional Individuals, 26*(2), 227–238.

Morningstar, M. E., Kim, K., & Clark, G. M. (2008). Evaluating a transition personnel preparation program: Identifying transition competencies of practitioners. *Teacher Education and Special Education, 31*(1), 47–58.

Newman, L., Wagner, M., Cameto, R., & Knokey, A.-M. (2009). *The post-high school outcomes of youth with disabilities up to 4 years after high school: A report of findings from the National Longitudinal Transition Study-2 (NLTS2) (NCSER 2009-2017).* Menlo Park CA: SRI International. Available at www.nlts2. org.reports/2009_04/nlts2_report_2009_04_complete.pdf

Norman, M., Johnson, D. R., Timmons, J., Cobb, B., & Albright, L. (2007). *An assessment of transition policies and practices in state vocational rehabilitation agencies: Final draft report to the Rehabilitation Services Administration.* Kill Devil Hills, NC: The Study Group Inc.

Olympus Research Corporation. (1974). An *assessment of vocational education programs for the handicapped under Part B of the 1968 Amendments to the Vocational Education Act.* Salt Lake City, UT: Olympus Research Corporation.

Schumacher, E. F. (1973). *Small is beautiful: Economics as if people mattered.* New York: Harper & Row.

Shorter, T. N. (2008). *From school to post-school activities: Understanding the IDEA's transition requirements.* Horsham, PA: LRP Publications.

Sitlington, P. L., Neubert, D. A., Begun, W. H., Lombard, R. C., & Leconte, P. J. (2007). *Assess for success: A practitioner's handbook on transition assessment* (2nd ed.). Thousand Oaks, CA: Corwin Press.

Sitlington, P. L., Neubert, D. A., & Leconte, P. J. (1997). Transition assessment: The position of the Division on Career Development and Transition. *Career Development for Exceptional Individuals, 20*(1), 69–79.

Stodden, R. A. (1998). School-to-work transition: Overview of disability legislation. In F. Rusch & J. Chadsey (Eds.), *Beyond high school: Transition from school to work.* Belmont, CA: Wadsworth.

Wagner, M., Newman, L., D'Amico, R., Jay, E. D., Butler-Nalin, P., Marder, C., et al. (1991). *Youth with disabilities: How are they doing? The first comprehensive report from the national longitudinal transition study of special education students.* SRI International (Contract 300-87-0054). Washington, DC: U.S. Department of Education, Office of Special Education Programs.

Wehmeyer, M. L., Agran, M., & Hughes, C. (1998). *Teaching self-determination to students with disabilities: Basic skills for successful transition.* Baltimore: Paul H. Brookes Publishing Company. (ERIC Document Reproduction Service No. ED 419361.)

Section II

Adolescent Transition
Education Planning

3

IEP Development in Adolescent Transition Education

Paul Wehman and Pamela S. Targett

VIRGINIA COMMONWEALTH UNIVERSITY

The transition of young people with disabilities is continuing to receive significant attention (Rusch, Hughes, Agran, Martin, & Johnson, 2009; Test, Mazzotti, Mustian, Fowler, Kortering, & Kohler, 2009; and Wehman, 2010). Transition is the normal culmination of years of schooling, growth, and development. For adolescents with disabilities there is an especially strong need for a blueprint for the future. This blueprint can be formatted on a transition IEP and should reflect a balance of work, community and social skills, travel, financial literacy, and self-determination.

A. Turnbull and R. Turnbull (2009) talked about young people with disabilities as having "whole lives." Whenever a student with a disability and/or family member is asked what this means, the answers often sound something like this: "Having a whole life means being part of a community, working, living independently, having friends and fun with those who have similar interests, safely getting to and from places on time, and using earnings to buy things and do what one wants to do." The transition IEP is the mechanism to bring this to fruition. For many people, this does not sound unreasonable. As a matter of fact, it sounds quite typical of what most have come to expect during a lifetime.

Unfortunately, though, these expectations are more difficult to attain for many students with disabilities and particularly students with more intensive support needs (Wehman, 2006). Frequently, these students may be relegated to living an incomplete life, one that is missing the basic aspects that most of us have come to expect. And although what is left out varies from person to person, quite often it will include opportunities to work for real pay, go to college, and live in the community. This, in turn, infringes on the most basic of human rights—the opportunity to pursue happiness.

Many students with disabilities exit school unemployed and never go to work in the community (Wehman, 2006; Wehman, Inge, Revell, & Brooke, 2007). Instead they find themselves living and working in long-term segregated settings (Gill, 2005). In the workshop a person may be performing various types of rote tasks like putting together ink pens or stuffing envelopes to fulfill a contract with business or the government.

Young people with more intensive support needs are often channeled into day activity centers (Wehman, 2006; Wehman et al., 2007; Braddock, Hemp, & Rizzolo, 2008). In these settings individuals may be observed trying to put together a puzzle intended for a kindergarten-age student or using a blue crayon to scribble in a coloring book. Or perhaps, a person may be seen spinning a bottle cap around on a table, time after time again, or sitting in a chair located in a distant corner of the room rocking back and forth, off beat, to loud music that staff chose to play for the day.

In either setting, a workshop or day activity center, personal choices are highly limited (Gill, 2005). Paid staff often make decisions for those in attendance. Staff may tell a person what to do, when to do it, and where to do it. Even the most basic decisions are denied. For instance, the person will have lunch served at a set time, sit in a particular spot, and eat whatever the cook decided to serve that day.

In part this stems from society's inability to believe in the abilities of people with disabilities and a self-righteous desire to protect them. No matter what the reasons, the outcome remains the same—many people with disabilities go on to experience lives that are far removed from being "whole lives." For some people, this may go on for a long time and for others it may last a lifetime.

In addition to a lack of opportunity to work, the main outlets for recreation and socialization for many students with disabilities may involve participating in activities with immediate family. This, of course, is only required when others are not being paid to "have fun" with them. Furthermore, many youth with disabilities continue to reside at home with their aging parents after exiting from school. This goes on until one day a parent is no longer able to care for an adult son or daughter. Then what?

Fortunately, it does not have to be this way. Youth with disabilities do not have to be destined to live incomplete lives but can and should live whole lives. Of utmost importance to pursuing this endeavor is a commitment from family, special educators, and other partners in transition, to stay abreast of and follow best practices in transition for youth with disabilities, and specifically to design and implement a transition plan that provides a roadmap to the future (Wehman, 2006; Wehman & Wittig, 2009). Such a plan is carefully crafted for one student at a time (Wehman & Wittig, 2009). That is the focus of this chapter.

It is, of course, critical to understand the legal context for transition, and readers are referred to Chapter 4 in this Volume for a comprehensive review of policy and legislation pertaining to transition. In this chapter, we review some of the organizations where professionals may serve on a student's transition team. This is followed by a description of some ways to individualize the student's transition IEP including person-centered planning and approaches to assessment. Then the chapter concludes by taking a look at the transition IEP meeting. Logistics, ways to enhance student involvement, challenges that may be encountered at this time, and goal writing are covered. In addition, a sample transition IEP is provided.

The Team

Transition planning should begin early enough to ensure that when a student exits school, he or she has developed some important skills to function as an adult. Many leaders in the field advocate for starting the plan early, around age 14 (Wehman, 2006). According to IDEA 2004, the first transition IEP should be in effect no later than age 16. At this time the student, to the greatest extent possible, and his or her team develop a transition IEP.

In addition to the student, transition IEP team members typically include family, school personnel, and representatives from outside agencies. Educators will want to establish relationships with adult service systems such as vocational rehabilitation, state mental health and developmental disabilities, one-stop career centers, and employment service organizations. Then, as indicated, representatives should be recruited to serve on a student's team (Wehman, 2006; Wehman & Wittig, 2009). A description of some of the agencies where future collaborators may be found is offered below.

State Vocational Rehabilitation

The Vocational Rehabilitation program is mandated through the Rehabilitation Act Amendments of 1998 (PL 105–220). Each state has its own operational structure. However, federal government regulations provide considerable resources and direction to help ensure that a common set of practices and procedures is followed to provide and pay for various services. The state's organization may be referred to as an Office of Vocational Rehabilitation or State Department of Vocational Rehabilitation services where vocational rehabilitation counselors offer a wide range of cost and no-cost services. Some services are offered in house, such as career guidance and counseling, assessment, and job placement services. Other services, such as supported employment, may be referred out to a community service provider.

To be eligible for the state's vocational rehabilitation services a student needs assistance to prepare for, secure, retain, or regain employment. Students who receive supplementary security income (SSI) are automatically presumed to be eligible for services. Some states also specify that students eligible for long-term supports from the mental health and developmental disabilities agencies who are pursuing supported employment are eligible for services. Furthermore, vocational rehabilitation may be able to augment or pay for job coaches or supported employment services.

Because of finite resources, the state's vocational rehabilitation program may operate under a selection order, serving those first with significant disabilities who are the hardest to serve. This offers an excellent opportunity for youth with more severe disabilities to tap into needed support services.

Youth should be referred early on, in their secondary school years. Federal regulations favor active participation of vocational rehabilitation in transition planning and interagency cooperation so services are delivered as efficiently as possible. This is an extremely important resource that students need to access. Rights must be understood and able to be resolved that relate to accessing appropriate services, roles, and funding.

State Mental Health and Developmental Disabilities Agencies

Each state has agencies that deliver mental health and services to individuals with intellectual and developmental disabilities. They are managed by state administration, community service boards, or distinct state regions. Eligibility guidelines differ from state to state. Not all youth are eligible for services. In addition, availability of funding depends on public funds and waiting lists are not unusual.

Fortunately, some states have made transitioning youth a priority for funding. Usually, these entities offer a range of services and are typically well known by school districts. For example, youth with emotional or mental health disabilities may receive case management, clinical services, counseling, and medication management. Services for youth with intellectual and development disabilities may include case management, housing, and employment services. Sometimes the organization provides direct services like job coaching or supported employment. Once again, stakeholders need to know what options are available to youth through a particular agency and what rights a young person is entitled to in order to resolve any difficulties.

One-Stop Career Centers

The Workforce Investment Act (WIA) of 1998 (PL 105–220) marked a major reform in the nation's job-training system. It consolidated more than 60 federal training programs into three

Table 3.1 One-Stop Career Centers

One-Stop Career Centers
Service: Core
Description: Core services provide basic job-search assistance and usually include assistance with accessing job postings by community employers, resources to search for and apply for work (telephones, fax machines, computers, internet services), and screening to identify the need for more intense employment services
Available to: anyone who wants basic job-search assistance
Service: Intensive
Description: Intensive services may include career guidance and counseling, vocational assessment, and case management, and short-term services such as resume development and professional conduct training
Available to: certain categories of jobseekers such as those with low income or who have been laid off
Service: Training
Description: Training services may include training and education related to good worker traits and skills, on-the-job training, adult education, and literacy activities, occupational skills training, etc.
Available to: only those who meet eligibility requirements

block grants to states: adult employment and training, disadvantaged youth employment and training, and adult education and family literacy. The act was passed to overcome many weaknesses in the current system by consolidating, coordinating, and improving employment, training, literacy, and vocational rehabilitation programs. The cornerstone of this legislation is a national system of One-Stop Career Centers, which serve as key employment resources to communities.

One-Stop Career Centers are a place in the community where anyone can go to obtain employment-related resources and multiple services, all located under the same roof. The One-Stop Career Centers are under federal mandate to offer three levels of services, described in Table 3.1.

Notably, core services are available to anyone age 18 or older, with no maximum age. The goal is to provide youth with career and job search assistance without them having to wait for eligibility determination or referrals.

Those involved with assisting students with transitioning to work will want to know about the various services and how these can be of benefit to students with disabilities. For example, information about the local labor market and hiring trends can be accessed along with youth employment programs or generic career development and training services. In addition, vocational rehabilitation and employment services are located there.

Some One-Stop Career Centers have a staff member on board who specializes in assisting persons with disabilities with a customized employment process. This specialist makes direct contact with businesses in an effort to locate potential work options and negotiate a viable opportunity for the jobseeker (Wehman et al., 2007). However, some Career One-Stops may seem unfamiliar with serving students with more significant support needs. Therefore, education and training may be required. In addition, some students may need assistance with advocating for their right to access One-Stop services.

Employment Service Providers

Employment service providers play an important role in assisting students with transitioning from school to work and are likely available in larger communities and cities. Providers may be more difficult to find in smaller communities and rural areas.

Generally, employment service providers are contracted by state vocational rehabilitation services and other agencies, including schools, to provide vocational support. Many perform community-based and functional vocational assessments, as well as other support services, to help a student gain and maintain work. Services range from help with pre-employment activities like locating work options, applying and interviewing for jobs to much more intensive services such as supported employment that offers one-on-one assistance with locating or creating a job, on-the-job training and support, and long-term follow-along (Wehman, 2006).

Resource Mapping

One way to gather information about services is through community resource or asset mapping. The process involves identifying and cataloging resources that are available within a designated region to fulfill a specific purpose. The process focuses on what is available rather than what is needed. Because of this, it may not be particularly useful in areas where resources are limited. Information collected includes: organization and/or person to contact, address, telephone and email address, best time to reach, alternative contact if applicable, overview of services offered (free of charge versus cost), eligibility requirements including areas served, recommendations on when to reach to avoid waiting for services, willingness to attend student planning meetings, and how to schedule appointments.

Roles

Professionals recruited from various organizations play important roles as members of a student's transition IEP team by providing services and a wealth of knowledge. Although it is crucial to have team support, it is not necessary to have representation from every agency. It is possible that some members may serve multiple roles. For instance, a vocational rehabilitation counselor may be able to discuss social security benefits, or parents will likely have expertise in how to interpret their child's nonverbal communications. Some examples of the roles of team members are offered in Table 3.2.

Notably, Certo et al. (2008) have called for seamless transition and federal entitlement to long-term support behind the three public systems responsible for employment and adult living outcome: the school, vocational rehabilitation, and developmental disabilities. If laws are amended under this change, among other things the school would be able to subcontract with adult agencies to help produce positive employment and adult-living outcomes. To support this recommendation, Certo et al. (2008) described and provided outcome data for the Transition Services Integration Model (TSIM). This approach includes integrating staff from different agencies and funding sources to offer services in the community. Public schools were able to subcontract with agencies to provide community-based services to students. Data revealed post-school outcomes were better than the national average for students with intellectual disabilities.

For a team to develop a transition IEP, they will need information about the student (Wehman, 2006; Wehman & Wittig, 2007). They will need to understand the student's vision for the future and his or her current levels of performance across the various adult life domains. Some possible ways to gather this important information are reviewed in the next section.

Individualized Transition Planning

The transition from adolescence to adulthood is an increased time of decision making and goal setting for living a whole life, including decisions involving independent living and

Table 3.2 Examples of team member roles

Examples of team member roles

State vocational rehabilitation counselor
Describes services (cost and no cost) and eligibility requirements
Assists with completing application
Provides career guidance and counseling
Provides information on Social Security, including use of work incentives
Recommends and coordinates services with community employment providers
Provides information on local labor market
Shares employer network information
Shares information on other resources
Provides information on transportation
Discusses disability disclosure options
Provides funding or blends funds
Helps solves problems related to accessing services, funding etc.
Helps determine postsecondary education, training, and employment-related goals
Helps determine activities required to reach goals

State mental health and developmental disability service case manager
Describes services and eligibility requirements
Assists with completing application process for various services
Provides case management
Coordinates service delivery
Provides funds or blends funds
Helps problem solve
Helps determine postsecondary goals across life domains
Helps determine activities required to reach goals

One-stop career centers
Describes services
Creatively problem solves to ensure services are provided to all, including youth with significant support needs

Employment services provider
Provides functional vocational assessment including situational assessments
Writes vocational reports
Recommends workplace supports
Recommends ideas for job creation
Customizes employment services offering intense (supported employment) and less intense services
Helps determine employment-related goals
Helps determine activities required to reach goals

employment. This means acquiring some of the new knowledge and skills as well as accessing any needed supports to live as independently as possible in the community (Wehman, 2006; Wehman & Wittig, 2009). For example, this may require learning to take more care of one's basic needs (hygiene, eating, toileting, etc.), keeping house, getting around safely and accessing community resources (shopping, recreation, etc.), handling finances (making purchases, maintaining bank accounts, understanding social security benefits, etc.) and estate planning.

This period also means going to work in the community (Luecking, 2009; Wehman et al., 2007). Some students may choose a career path that requires a college degree or specialized training prior to pursuing that particular vocation. Other students may go straight to work in the community. Some of these students may be continuing on in a job that he or she secured while still in school and perhaps be looking at a move from a part- to full-time status. If best practices in transition have not been followed, some will find themselves looking for work for the first time. Some will need to access some type of vocational support services like job placement assistance or supported employment to assist them with gaining and maintaining work.

No matter what the scenario, one of the most important things to do is to teach and support youth with disabilities to develop the skills and knowledge to move into adulthood (Bouck, 2009; Wehman & Kregel, in press). This also means embracing the fact that some students, especially students with more intensive support needs, will require varying levels of assistance along the way.

This is why transition planning is so important. When done in a timely and meaningful way, transition planning assists students in learning more about themselves. In turn this allows the student and family to envision a more positive future, knowing they can access instruction, services, and needed supports to help move closer toward the desired outcome (Sitlington, Neubert, Begun, Lombard, & Leconte, 2007).

On the other hand, when performed in a thoughtless manner, students may have limited or no direction for their future. For some, this will lead to an increased dependency on others for many of life's most basic necessities, or lowered self-esteem resulting from feelings of hopelessness and no sense of purpose. Others may exhibit negative or destructive behaviors, such as drug use and/or dropping out of school. No matter what the scenario, the outcome will be the same: an incomplete or ineffective education that results in a student who is at best ill equipped to lead a productive adult life.

Person-Centered Planning

Person-centered planning helps a student and family members think about and develop a positive vision for the future. Usually, a group of people is invited to come together to be part of a student's person-centered planning process. The group often includes family, friends, and select members of the student's support network. Sometimes, members of the student's transition IEP team are present.

As a matter of fact, sometimes a team chooses to use person-centered planning like a Plan for Achieving Tomorrows with Hope (PATH) to guide the development of a student's transition IEP. For example, during a PATH, those present envision the student's "positive, possible future." Then, with this vision in mind, the group works backwards to examine what would need to happen in order to help the student get there, including timeframes. Personal interests, preferences, abilities, support needs, and potential supports are also usually identified along the way. Those present may choose to enlist themselves to help with certain activities. At the close of the meeting, a date for the next one is established. The plan is then used to guide future actions and choices (Mount, 2000).

Person-centered planning has been extensively researched across disabilities and perspectives, including ways to individualize and maximize the effectiveness of a student's transition plan (deFur, 2003; Hosp, Griller-Clark, & Rutherford, 2001; Martin, Greene, & Borland, 2004; Martin, Marshall, & Sale, 2004; Martin et al., 2006; Myers & Eisenman, 2005; Nelson, 2005; Powers et al., 2005). For example, when developing the transition IEP, the student with support can share the plan with the team. In turn, this information should stimulate student-focused discussions around his or her vision for the future. The team members can reflect on this, along with the results from transition assessments, to formulate student-centered goals and objectives.

Perhaps assessments results reveal a number of adult life skills that a student needs to acquire. Referring back to the person-centered plan may help the team prioritize what should happen first, second, and so on.

Transition Assessment

Before developing the student's transition IEP, an evaluation of his or her current level of performance across the various adult-life domains like employment and community living takes place. A variety of data gathering devices can be used to obtain this type of information, which is vital to establishing a suitable direction for the student's future education as well as designing educational and training experiences. Some examples of the types of instruments used are formal inventories, questionnaires, surveys, interviews, and observations (Sitlington et al., 2007; Wehman & Wittig, 2009).

Approaches

There are a variety of formal and informal approaches to assessment. The techniques that are most likely to render the most useful information are the ones that should be used. Standardized or formal assessment instruments have documented an acceptable level of validity and reliability. There are many examples of standardized or formal assessments (Sitlington et al., 2007; Wehman & Wittig, 2007). Some of the most widely used include achievement tests, aptitude tests, intelligence tests, adaptive behavioral scales, and interest inventories. Only a few published standardized assessment instruments are specifically related to transition.

An informal approach is often the preferred method for gathering information about a student's current levels of performance. Examples of informal assessment tools include: interviews, surveys, observations of a student in natural environments, and adaptive behavioral or functional skill inventories (Wehman & Wittig, 2007; Sitlington et al., 2007). Sometimes a variety of informal assessments, usually designed by teachers, have to take place before any useful information is found.

Some of the most useful information can be obtained by talking to people who know the student best and spending time to get to know the student (Wehman, 2006). For instance, parents and others who know the student best will have a wealth of information to share. Information on their views may be obtained through written surveys, checklists, or face-to-face interviews that have been specifically designed to further assess a student's current levels of competency as related to assuming adult roles and responsibilities in the future. Information is also gathered about the student's interests, likes, and dislikes.

Students may also be interviewed. Some students will be able to express their thoughts. Others will need some type or level of support to communicate personal preferences, likes, and dislikes. For instance, information may have to come primarily from those who know the student along with first-hand observations. Some examples of questions to help survey a student's or family member's perspectives are offered in Table 3.3.

No functional assessment would be complete without observing the student in community-based settings. Observation of the student's abilities in natural environments is essential. This is true not only when the student has difficulty communicating but also when experience is limited. When it comes to assuming many of the roles and responsibilities associated with adulthood such as work, managing a household and finances, mobility in the community, etc., many students will likely have limited knowledge, skills, and abilities in many areas.

Two types of assessment that allow the student to perform in natural environments while the evaluator observes and collects data are ecological evaluations and situational assessments. Table 3.4 provides a brief description.

One of the main advantages of either approach is that the student is more likely to give an authentic response. This, in turn, helps ensure that the data collected are representative of the student's current skills and abilities. For students with more significant disabilities, a functional or practical approach to assessment is usually required.

Table 3.3 Basic questions to ask

Basic questions to ask*
What does X like to do or show an interest in?
What does X do on a typical day/weekend?
What would X like to do after leaving school?
Where will X live and with whom?
What responsibilities does X have in the home?
What skills do you think X needs to develop to be more independent at home?
What supports will X need to live as independently as possible?
Where will X work?
What types of jobs and careers have been explored?
What characteristics make up a dream job (indoor/outdoor; work with people, data, or things; pay; distance from home; level of supervision)?
What types of supports will X need to be successful (transportation, housing, personal care, job coaching, etc.)
What, if anything, might interfere with success at work or living in the community?

Note: * Questions are written for a third party, e.g., parents, and need be rephrased to address a student.

Table 3.4 Assessments occurring in natural environments

Assessments occurring in natural environments
Ecological evaluation – performed across natural environments (school, home, places where student has fun, shops, etc.). Includes perceptions of others and observations over time as the student is engaged in normal routines. The process usually entails a review of current records from classroom teachers, therapists, psychologists, etc., and talking to the family and student. Similarities and discrepancies in findings are noted for future verification. Next, considerable time is spent observing student in a variety of settings (e.g., classroom, cafeteria, during free time, at home, at work-training site). To ensure consistency in data collection, oftentimes observational checklistsare used to collect data. Information is also collected from the student (to the degree possible) and those who best know the student's strengths, interests, and support needs.
Situational assessment – performed in particular location, often a vocational setting. When conducting the assessment, the evaluator observes in the same location for a period of time rather than across domains. Students are assessed on abilities, interests, and support needs while performing tasks in employment settings. Data are collected on skill acquisition and response-to-teaching strategies using a task analysis and productivity, including time on- and off-task behavior. Information on likes and dislikes, social skills, and self-determination is collected. In addition, goals and objectives related to achieving priorities can be suggested. Guidelines under the Fair Standards Labor Act are followed. These assessments may be conducted as part of a community-based vocational education program, taking place at various businesses.

Data Analysis

Teachers or others charged with assessment must have adequate tools and knowledge to analyze and interpret common assessment data. The type of analysis necessary is usually determined when the evaluation is designed. While the topic of data analysis is also beyond the scope of this chapter, a few guidelines are offered.

First, it is important to note that the analysis and interpretation of the data will only be as reliable as the data themselves. Therefore, any incorrect or insufficient data should be thrown out. Second, treat data confidentially. Be sure this has been communicated to the student and family in advance. Also, reiterate the need for confidentiality with team members. Finally, try to keep the data analysis simple. Use the simplest statistics possible and only what is needed to draw a conclusion. With a summary of the results from the various transition assessments available, it will be time to convene the student's team and develop his or her transition IEP.

Transition IEP Meeting

Team members should come together with the understanding that, regardless of the student's disability, transition is a time to build skills and find support options. Do not rule out any possibilities for employment and independent living (Wehman & Wittig, 2009). Upon reviewing the results from the transition assessment, the team may find that a student has either few or extensive needs to address. One student may need to enhance social skills and begin making preparations to eventually enter college. Another may need to learn many of the skills associated with independent living as well as access assistance to gain and maintain employment in the community, such as supported employment.

No matter what the student's situation, it is important to make sure that the time the team spends together is time well spent. This section reviews tips on meeting logistics, offers insight on ways to promote student involvement, concludes with some of the challenges the team may face, and outlines guidelines for developing student goals.

Logistics

The team leader should be sure the meeting takes place at a time when the student, family members, and the core members of the team can be present. Some states have specific guidelines on attendance and what to do if a parent or other party cannot attend. Some tips to keep in mind when planning a student's transition IEP meeting are offered in Table 3.5.

In addition to coordinating the meeting, a person must be designated to take on lead responsibilities. Some of the key functions that the team leader or another designee may assume are provided in Table 3.6.

It is important to note that these may be some of the things a student can do or at least help with. Eventually, over time and with training and/or support, some students will lead the meeting. Cameto (2005) provides National Longitudinal Study 2 data on students' post-high school goals as well as who the active participants are in most efforts at transition planning.

Table 3.5 Meeting planning tips

Meeting planning tips
Find out if attendees prefer morning meetings.
Tuesdays and Thursdays are popular meeting days for professionals.
Avoid Friday meetings if possible.
Avoid meetings on holidays and the night before holidays.
Be sensitive to attendee travel requirements.
Notify attendees early enough so they have time to plan to attend.
Invite people early and continue reminding them even if they have confirmed attendance.
Tell parents the purpose, time, and location of the meeting and who will attend.
Encourage the parents to invite people who have knowledge of or special expertise about the child.
Create an agenda and stick to it (e.g., start and end on time).
Keep the agenda focused and do not overwhelm attendees (e.g., be sure to schedule breaks).
Support the student in getting involved in setting up the meeting (e.g., phone calls and sending emails to extend invitations and reminders about the event, etc.).
Be sure the meeting room has comfortable seating, lighting, noise levels, and temperature.

Table 3.6 Possible responsibilities for meeting facilitator

Possible responsibilities for meeting facilitator
Gathers all pertinent information about the student prior to the meeting
Makes sure releases are signed
Sends information needing advance review to team members
Coordinates meeting with individuals and agency members who need to be present
Calls meeting to order on time
Discusses ground rules
States mission and values
Emphasizes that student and family members provide input and make final decisions
Supports student in participating/leading the meeting to greatest extent possible
Summarizes key information about student, including personal vision and assessment results
Initiates discussion about outcomes and possible supports
Fosters open and honest communication (remember that everyone needs to be heard)
Encourages team members to voice opinions, including any concerns about potential outcomes or support services
Ensures team members know responsibilities and timeframe for action
Adjourns meeting on time
Supports student in sending follow-up communications and thanks attendees

Cameto indicated that while 58% of students provide some input to their transition planning, only 12% take a leadership role.

Student Involvement

The student must be invited to his or her transition IEP meeting and should participate to the greatest extent possible (Thoma & Wehman, 2010). Having students take ownership and a leading role in the planning process further supports the large body of research related to self-determination and self-advocacy (Wehmeyer, Palmer, Agran, Mithaug, & Martin, 2000). There are a number of curricula described in Chapter 6 of this Volume that can be used to assist students with developing skills associated with self-determination and advocacy. These skills can be shaped and advanced further during various activities associated with plan development.

In conclusion, with regard to planning, we would note that some principles that are directly aligned with work include the following: the best place to learn about work is in an actual workplace (students do not have to "get ready" to work); students should be employed prior to exiting school; and students will need varying levels of support to gain and maintain employment (e.g., supported employment) and live in the community (Wehman, 2006). It may be useful to send a list of these and other guiding principles to team members in advance along with the meeting agenda or, at the very least, to briefly review them when the team convenes.

Challenges

Transition planning is not always easy and straightforward. Sometimes challenges are encountered along the way since there is no such thing as a service menu for students with disabilities.

Obviously, accessing readily available services through existing community resources will be much easier than having to create new options. However, given the vast difference among students with disabilities and the lack of available or quality services within some communities, resource development may sometimes be necessary. For example, consider Alice, a young woman with a severe intellectual disability. In order to gain and maintain employment in her community, she will require intense advocacy support services like those offered in a supported-employment approach. Supported employment provides one-on-one assistance to help a person gain employment and then, once hired, offers on- and off-the-job supports to help the person maintain work. The only supported employment provider in town is a workshop that offers a group placement approach, called an enclave. In addition, the waiting list for services is long. Many of the individuals who are referred there for employment services end up working in the workshop for many years. What does this mean for Alice and her parents? Do they have to settle for the "only game in town"? Is the vision of a real job for real pay in Alice's future really just a dream?

The answer is no, at least not when best practices in transition are followed. Instead, creative problem solving can be used to develop and implement services specifically designed to meet Alice's preferences and needs, rather than forcing her to fit into an antiquated, one-size-fits-all service option that just happens to be readily available.

On the other hand, some students will be able to have their needs and preferences met through existing service options. For example, consider Marion, a student with a physical disability who wants to attend college. He is ready to start thinking about where he will apply. As part of the process, Marion will require some support with determining what types of accommodations he will need and requesting those from the school's disability services office. A vocational rehabilitation counselor will help him.

The take-away point is teams must understand that each student must be served—one person at a time. Some other challenges that may be faced are highlighted in Table 3.7.

Goals

A student's transition IEP should include a number of things including goals and a description of the transition services the student needs to reach them. Down the road, when it is time to update the transition IEP, teams should be able to measure a student's progress by reviewing his or her current levels of performance in relation to the intended outcomes—the goals. Then, as indicated, additional assessment and/or person-centered planning may take place to modify or develop new student goals.

Table 3.7 Challenges associated with transition

Some of the challenges associated with transition

Different degrees of expectations for students with disabilities and varying levels of staff competency lead to an uneven provision of services to assist individuals with planning and preparing for life after school.

Upon leaving school, an individual no longer has legal right to services (vocational services, transportation, life skills training, counseling, etc.).

The individual may need ongoing support to expand opportunities and potential to lead a whole life.

Locating, obtaining, and financing services may be difficult, requiring navigation of a complicated adult-service-delivery system.

Services needed may not exist or funding may not be present and, rather than putting the student's needs first and finding another way, the student is expected to accept what is available.

Community employment services may not be tailored to serving one person at a time or may serve individuals with only specific types of disabilities.

Effective planning requires a review of issues surrounding disability benefits provided by Social Security Administration, which means involvement with one or more complex and confusing program.

When formulating goals, the team should keep the following points in mind. As previously mentioned, the team should have high expectations for the student regardless of the severity of his or her disability. Transition planning should start early, by age 14 or sooner, as needed. This is critical to help some students reach their goals, including those that other people may have deemed impossible.

It is also important to remember that whenever a student has difficulty or cannot learn something, supports should be considered. Supports help promote independence and might include adaptations or modifications to how an activity is completed.

Furthermore, students should not have artificial limitations imposed on them. For example, a goal that states a student needs to first learn how to perform tasks in the school cafeteria before a community-based work experience or real employment is not acceptable. The student should not have to jump through these hoops. On the other hand, this may be the scenario because of ease of implementation. It is a lot easier to work with students in the classroom or on campus than in real work settings. But this is not the best practice and simply exacerbates the problem of unemployment among students with disabilities.

Once again, it is important to remember that post-school goals should be driven by student and family choice rather than available resources and funding. Teams should anticipate this need and be prepared to use creative problem solving to ensure a student's education is relevant and that individual needs are being met.

As indicated throughout this chapter, transition goals are developed with the student's post-school life in mind. Assessment results should indicate a student's current level of performance in various adult-life domains. The discrepancy between where the student is now and where the student needs to be in adulthood can be broken down to form annual goals. Then each goal is broken down into specific objectives that, when combined, will achieve the targeted outcome. The process is completed across all domains relevant to a student's desired future and current situation. Table 3.8 provides an excerpt from a plan.

What comes next is an integral part of the process. It is important to make sure the student, family, and others are aware of what results are expected. Along the way data will be collected, analyzed, and interpreted. Based on an analysis of the information collected, changes in the program may be necessary. Adjustments must be made.

Finally, unacceptable results, such as a student's lack of progress towards reaching goals, should be examined. Reasons may include improper IEP content, ineffective teaching strategies, or lack of motivation of participants (student or teacher). Every part of the program should be examined and, as indicated, changes should be made.

Transition IEP

We conclude with a sample of a student's IEP for transition. Teachers may want to use the format provided here for future IEP planning and development. The reader may note that the template crosses over all major life domains. Numerous other examples can be found in *Transition IEPs: A Curriculum Guide for Teachers and Transition Practitioners* (Wehman & Wittig, 2009).

Summary

Although post-school outcomes are improving for youth with disabilities, much remains to be done (Wehman, 2006). Transition planning should begin early enough to make sure that when a student exits school, he or she has developed some important skills to function as a responsible adult in society. The plan should include measurable goals that are based on assessments related

Table 3.8 Excerpts of post-school vision, goals, and objectives across adult life domains

---

Excerpts of post-school vision, goals, and objectives across adult life domains

---

Post-School Vision: Sherry will work full-time in a job in the community that interests her.
Domain: Employment.
Ask: Where does the student want to be? Where and/or what type of work might the student pursue? (Keep in mind that work is often expressed in terms other than a vocational goal and sometimes jobs are created for individuals with significant support needs.) Does the student plan to pursue postsecondary education or technical skills training for employment and, if so, what might this be and where will it take place? Where will the student live?
Source: This may come from a person-centered life planning meeting and/or a transition assessment that focuses on work, e.g., interviewing family, vocational situational assessments. Note: the student's vision statement should be in alignment with whatever is generally expected from youth; this means competitive work, a decent paying job in the community, etc. (Sheltered employment, enclaves, and mobile work crew should not be considered as options.) It means living in one's own home, renting a room or apartment in the community. (Living options like group homes or adult homes should not be considered as options.) Obviously, some students will need intensive support at work, at home, or in the community to achieve this natural adult lifestyle (e.g., supported employment, supported living, and case management services).
Present level of performance: Sherry is 14 years old and has limited knowledge about work. When asked, she will tell you her mother works with the "sick" (at a hospital) and her dad works for the president (at the state department of transportation). Her parents indicated that Sherry takes care of all of her personal needs at home except for washing her hair. She uses some small appliances when assisting her mother with meal preparation and she vacuums the house. She also assists her father with some aspects of lawn care and gardening. Sometimes she sits down in mid-task and refuses to get up. Her parents ignore her behavior (unless it is raining or cold outside) and eventually (after about 15 minutes) she usually gets up and moves on to some other preferred activity (watching television, playing video games, etc.). A survey with her teacher revealed that last year she had toured local businesses including the bakery, airport, and hospital. She looked happy during the tours, smiling much of the time. However, during the bakery tour there was a loud noise and she attempted to flee the immediate setting. Due to this, she was paired with the teacher or teacher's aide on all future trips. The behavior was not observed again.
Ask: What is the student doing now? What is his or her current level of performance across adult life domains? This information comes from person-centered planning or transition assessment data from interviews, surveys, observations, etc.
Sample Annual Goal: Using cue cards, Sherry will express her likes and dislikes by May for at least 12 different types of job tasks across three different types of employment settings.
Ask: What skills and/or knowledge would enhance the student's ability to work in the community in a real job for real pay? What skills and/or knowledge would enhance the student's ability to live as independently as possible? Does it describe the behavior the student will be doing when the goal is met? Does it state what will be observed? Does it state what the student will do and to what level or degree? Does the goal make sense to other members of the team? Does it avoid jargon?
Sample Objective: For each new job task tried, on at least five different occasions, Sherry will use cue cards to indicate if she likes or dislikes it.
Ask the following questions: Does it state what the student will need to do to reach the goal? Does it describe the behavior the student will be exhibiting when the short-term objective or benchmark is achieved?
Steps needed to accomplish goals: (1) obtain permissions (teacher); (2) set up situational assessment sites (transition specialist); (3) conduct one assessment per month (community service provider); (4) review findings with Sherry and parents to help determine work preferences and ideas for job creations (vocational rehabilitation counselor); (5) apply for vocational rehabilitation services, requesting supported employment (parent); (6) interview and choose a supported employment provider (parent).
Ask: What major activities need to happen? Who is the primary person responsible for overseeing that the activity takes place? (This should indicate who is responsible for making sure the activity takes place. Who actually carries out the activity may or may not be the person listed.)

Table 3.9 Transition individualized education program

Student's name		
Last: Manfred	**First: Leah**	**M.I.**
Birthdate: 1/17/1988	**School: Great Plains High School**	
Student's I.D. #: 102	**IEP conference date: 8/21/09**	

Participants	
Name	**Position**
Leah Manfred	student
Mary and Sam Manfred	parents
Kendra Watson	IEP case manager
Tina Wendt	job coach
Roy Simms	VR counselor
Kent Bandon	transition coordinator
Jarrod Exeter	horticulture teacher
Ivy Robinson	CSB case manager
Jed Johnson	Great Plains Community College, DSS office
Katrina Roberts	Dept. of Parks and Recreation
David Hart	Center for Independent Living

Student profile
(Note: Include recent transition assessments and student's post-school vision.)

Leah is a 19-year-old senior who attends a large comprehensive high school. She is very outgoing and popular. She can read and write at about the second-grade level. She has very supportive parents and is involved in many family and church activities.

Leah has various jobs at school, including serving as a messenger for the guidance office. She has also worked at school-supported community-based job sites with other students. Those jobs included stocking shelves at a local department store, scanning and counting items for inventory, and serving as hostess in the snack bar. Over the summer she obtained a part-time job at a major home improvement store working two half-days a week, and she attends the horticulture program part of the day at the school's technical center. Leah enjoys working with plants and has recently transferred into the garden shop at her current job.

I. Career and economic self-sufficiency outcomes

1. Employment goal: (may include integrated employment and supported employment):
Leah will work full-time with support in a home improvement store garden center by July 2008.

Level of present performance:	Leah received VR services for assessment in a home improvement store for one month during the spring and was employed with wages for two 4-hour shifts with a job coach. She has developed several skills in this site including inventory and pricing. She has told everyone how much she enjoys her work.
Steps needed to accomplish goal:	(1) obtain continued job coach support beyond assessment; (2) decrease level of support on the job; (3) coordinate transportation between job and school.
Date of completion:	May 2008
Person(s) responsible for implementation:	Leah, transition coordinator, parents

2. Vocational/technical training goal (may include apprenticeship, workforce training):
Leah will develop skills in the area of horticulture by June, 2008.

Level of present performance:	Leah has an interest in working with plants and attends a basic horticulture program five days a week. She experiences some difficulty with the assignments and has boarded the wrong bus to the tech center a couple of times. She enjoys working in her family's garden and is able to seed, weed, and harvest vegetables with no support at home.
Steps needed to accomplish goal:	(1) Provide Leah with a visual cue for the correct bus and identify a peer she can ask if she needs assistance; (2) Meet with the horticulture teacher to modify assignments for Leah; (3) Explore career options using horticulture skill sets with Leah and VR counselor during the 2007–08 academic year.
Date of completion:	May 2008
Person(s) responsible for implementation:	Leah, IEP case manager, horticulture teacher

II. Postsecondary education and training outcomes

3. Higher education goal:
Leah will improve skills in the field of horticulture to improve job opportunities by June, 2010.

Level of present performance:	Leah will graduate with a 2-year certificate in horticulture in June 2010. She has developed good skills at home in this area. She wants to go to a local community college to improve her skills.
Steps needed to accomplish goal:	(1) Visit Great Plains Community College horticulture program with Transition Coordinator by September, 2007; (2) Apply for assistance for this postsecondary program at the local community college with VR counselor by October 2007; (3) Attend 1 class twice per week for audit purposes during spring 2008; (4) Attend program by August 2008.
Date of completion:	Ongoing
Person(s) responsible for implementation:	Leah, VR counselor, parents, Disability Support Services counselor, GPCC

4. Continuing and adult education, career/technical education goal (may include public or private technical school): N/A at this time

Level of present performance:	
Steps needed to accomplish goal:	
Date of completion:	
Person(s) responsible for implementation:	

III. Community integration and functional participation outcomes

5. Residential goal: Leah will cook two meals per week at home independently by April 2008.

Level of present performance:	Leah depends on others to prepare her meals. She recently has learned to cook basic recipes using a microwave oven. Her mother assists with the development of a weekly menu, and Leah cooks, with support, on Tuesday evenings. Her greatest challenge is managing her time during meal preparation.

Steps needed to accomplish goal:	Leah will (1) prepare two meals per week using visual cue cards; and (2) use a visual timer and watch alarm to begin and end meal preparation at the designated times.
Date of completion:	April 2008
Person(s) responsible for implementation:	Leah, parents

6. Transportation/mobility goal: Leah will travel to and from work independently by June 2008.

Level of present performance:	Leah gets to and from work by school bus and by her parents transporting her. She recently took part in a transportation practice day sponsored by the local Center for Independent Living.
Steps needed to accomplish goal:	Leah will (1) apply for specialized public transportation; (2) learn to use specialized public transportation by (a) learning how to call the service and (b) learning to purchase tickets.
Date of completion:	March 2008
Person(s) responsible for Implementation:	CSB case manager, Leah, parents

7. Financial/income needs goal: Leah will independently deposit paycheck into her bank account.

Level of present performance:	Leah's bank account was opened for her by her parents, who handle all of her finances. She has decided to learn this task so that she can "have a lot of money."
Steps needed to accomplish goal:	Leah will (1) learn to sign checks and complete deposit slips; (2) practice making deposits at the bank.
Date of completion:	June 2008
Person(s) responsible for implementation:	Leah, IEP case manager, parents

8. Self-determination goal: Leah will identify needs for assistance at the work-site by January 2008.

Level of present performance:	Leah is articulate about her needs but waits for the last possible moment to ask for assistance, which leads to unfinished tasks. She has observed classmates and co-workers speaking up for themselves and is motivated to do this.
Steps needed to accomplish goal:	Leah will (1) identify appropriate means and situations for advocacy at the work place; (2) role-play situations; and (3) attend a class sponsored by the Center for Independent Living.
Date of completion:	November 2007
Person(s) responsible for implementation:	Leah, Center for Independent Living, job coach

9. Social competence goal: Leah will maintain friendships after graduation

Level of present performance:	Leah has made several close friends in high school. She has seen several classmates leave school and has lost touch with them, which is "making her sad." Leah has asked for assistance in this area.
Steps needed to accomplish goal:	Leah will (1) keep an address book of friends; (2) identify monthly dates for suitable activities to engage in with friends; (3) arrange transportation to activities by December 2007.

Date of completion:	Ongoing
Person(s) responsible for implementation:	Leah, IEP case manager, parents

10. Health/safety goal:

Leah will identify unsafe situations at the work-site and report them to her manager or parents (via cell phone).

Level of present performance:	Leah is friendly and assists customers as a part of her job at the home improvement store. She occasionally helps customers take items to their vehicles. She has good self-awareness of safety issues but rarely reports issues until after the fact. A recent scare in which a customer tried to lure her into a truck prompted Leah, her school, and other transition team members to make this a priority.
Steps needed to accomplish goal:	(1) Leah will carry her cell phone attached to her work apron at all times. (2) Leah will, with support, call the front desk to announce her departure from the store and (3) go to the front desk to announce her arrival back. (4) Leah will role play calling in for an emergency at home, work, and at school.
Date of completion:	January 2008
Person(s) responsible for implementation:	Leah, job coach, VR counselor
Student's career preference:	Full-time competitive employment, preferably working with plants.
Student's major transition needs:	1. Personal safety 2. Continued education in horticulture field 3. Transportation 4. 5.

Summary of performance	
Student's name: Leah Manfred	**Student I.D. #102**
Disability: Intellectual disability	
Student's address: **4219 Omaha Blvd.,Great Plains, ND**	**Phone number:** **555–1212**
School Address: 200 School Way, GP, ND	**Phone number:** **555–1212**
Post-secondary goals	

Employment: Leah will work full time with supports after high school.

Education/Training: Leah will earn program certification in horticulture within three years after graduation.

Independent living/community participation: Leah will maintain her ties with friends and church members after graduation. She will increase her independence with transportation by June 2010.

Current academic achievement (include courses of study)
Leah will earn a transition diploma this June.

Current functional performance
Leah follows routines well and enjoys learning new tasks at work. She is also learning basic household tasks such as cooking and doing her own laundry.

Recommendations for achieving postsecondary goals
1. Maintain support system with VR counselor and CSB case manager by meeting with them at least once a month. 2. Maintain employment. Attached is a resource directory of community and adult service agencies. To obtain a copy of transcripts, contact the school guidance office. To obtain copies of Special Education documentation, contact the Office of Special Education, School Board Office.

Additional notes

Source: Based on Barrett, Wehman, & Wittig, 2009.

to training, education, employment and, where appropriate, independent living skills. It should also include a description of the transition services the student needs to reach the goals.

A number of people serve on the student's transition team. Educators need to have first-hand knowledge of these services and to work closely with them.

Person-centered planning can enrich the transition IEP. This process provides a way to identify and clarify a student's preferences, strengths, and support needs. It can also help prioritize areas to address first. There are formal and informal approaches to assessment. The techniques that render the most useful information to the planners are the ones that should be used. Sometimes a variety of assessments will be needed before useful information is found. For students with the most significant disabilities, a functional approach to assessment is required.

Educators should be familiar with some tips to help plan and implement the transition IEP meeting, including ways to involve the student. Transition planning is not always easy or straightforward and teams should expect to encounter some challenges. A student's plan should include goals, objectives, and a description of the transition services needed to reach specific goals goals. If a student is not showing progress, the plan may need to be redesigned.

References

Barrett, V. Z, Wehman, P. & Wittig, K. M. (2009). Transition IEPs for youth with intellectual disabilities. In P. Wehman & K. M. Wittig (Eds.). *Transition IEPs: A curriculum guide for teachers and transition practitioners* (3rd ed., pp. 148–154). Austin, TX: PRO-ED Publishing.

Bouck, E. C. (2009). Functional curriculum models for secondary students with mild mental impairment. *Education and Training in Developmental Disabilities, 44*(4), 435–443.

Braddock, D., Hemp, R., & Rizzolo, M. C. (2008). *The state of the states in developmental disabilities: 2008.* Boulder, CO: University of Colorado, Department of Psychiatry and Coleman Institute for Cognitive Disabilities.

Cameto, R. (2005). The transition planning process. *National Longitudinal Transition Study 2, 4* (1). National Center on Secondary Education and Transition, Minneapolis: University of Minnesota.

Certo, N. J., Luecking, R. G., Courey, S., Brown, L., Murphy, S., & Mautz, D. (2008). Plugging the policy gap at the point for transition for individuals with severe intellectual disabilities: An argument for seamless transition and federal entitlement to long term support. *Research and Practice for Persons with Severe Disabilities, 33*(3), 85–95.

deFur, S. H. (2003). IEP transition planning-from compliance to quality. *Exceptionality*, 11(2), 115–128.

Gill, M. (2005). The myth of transition: Contractualizing disability in the sheltered workshop. *Disability and Society, 20*(6), pp. 613–623.

Hosp, M. K., Griller-Clark, H., & Rutherford, R. B. (2001). Incarcerated youth with disabilities: Their knowledge of transition plans. *Journal of Correctional Education, 52*(3), 126–130.

Individuals with Disabilities Education Act (IDEA), 20 U.S.C. Sec. 1401 (34).

Luecking, R. G. (2009). *The way to work: How to facilitate work experiences for youth in transition.* Baltimore: Paul Brookes Publishing Co.

Martin, J. E., Greene, B. A., & Borland, B. J. (2004). Secondary students' involvement in their IEP meetings: Administrators' perceptions. *Career Development for Exceptional Individuals, 27*(2), 177–188.

Martin, J. E., Marshall, L. H., & Sale, P. (2004). A 3-year study of middle, junior, and high school IEP meetings. *Exceptional Children, 70* (3), 285–298.

Martin, J. E., Van Dycke, J. L., Christensen, W. R., Greene, B. A., Gardner, J. E., & Lovett, D. L. (2006). Increasing student participation in IEP meetings: Establishing the self-directed IEP as an evidence-based practice. *Exceptional Children, 72*(3), 299–316.

Mount, B. (2000) *Person-centered planning. Finding directions for change using personal futures planning.* Amenia, NY: Capacity Works.

Myers, A., & Eisenman, L. (2005). Student-led IEPs: Take the first step. *TEACHING Exceptional Children, 37*(4), 52–58.

Nelson, B. (2005). Creating positive outcomes for deafblind youth and young adults: A personal futures planning transition model. *REview, 36*(4), 173–180.

Powers, K. M., Gil-Kashiwabara, E., Geenen, S. J., Powers, L. E., Balandran, J., & Palmer, C. (2005). Mandates and effective transition planning practices reflected in IEPs, *Career Development for Exceptional Individuals, 28*, 47–59.

Rusch, F. R., Hughes, C., Agran, M., Martin, J. E. & Johnson, J. R. (2009). Toward self-directed learning, post-high school placement, and coordinated support: Constructing new transition bridges to adult life. *Career Development for Exceptional Individuals, 32*, 1–7.

Sitlington, P. L., Neubert, D. A., Begun, W. H., Lombard, R. C., & Leconte, P. J. (2007). *Assess for success: Handbook on transition assessment.* Reston, VA: Council for Exceptional Children, Division of Career Development and Transition.

Test, D. W., Mazzotti, V. L., Mustian, A. L., Fowler, C. H., Kortering, L., & Kohler, P. (2009). Evidence-based secondary transition predictors for improving postschool outcomes for students with disabilities. *Career Development for Exceptional Individuals, 32*(3) 160–118.

Thoma, C., & Wehman, P. (2010). *Student directed IEPs.* Baltimore: Paul Brookes Publishing Co.

Turnbull, A., & Turnbull, R. (2009). *Whole lives: A curriculum for young people in transition from school to adulthood.* Lawrence, KS, University of Kansas, Beach Center on Disability.

Wehman, P. (2006). *Life beyond the classroom: Transition strategies for young people with disabilities* (4th ed.). Baltimore: Paul Brookes Publishing Co.

Wehman, P. (2010) *Essentials of transition planning.* Baltimore: Paul H. Brookes.

Wehman, P., Inge, K. J., Revell, W. G., & Brooke, V. A. (2007). *Real work for real pay: Inclusive employment for people with disabilities.* Baltimore: Paul Brookes Publishing Co.

Wehman, P., & Kregel, J. (in press). *Functional curriculum for elementary, middle, secondary age students with special needs* (3rd ed). Austin, TX: PRO-ED Publishing.

Wehman P., & Wittig, K. M. (2009). *Transition IEPs: A curriculum guide for teachers and transition practitioners* (3rd ed., p. 8). Austin, TX: PRO-ED.

Wehmeyer, M. L., Palmer, S. B., Agran, M., Mithaug, D. E., & Martin, J. E., (2000). Promoting causal agency: The self determined learning model of instruction. *Exceptional Children 6*(4), 439–453.

4

Student Involvement in the Transition Process

James Martin

UNIVERSITY OF OKLAHOMA

Dan Dalun Zhang

TEXAS A & M UNIVERSITY

David W. Test

UNIVERSITY OF NORTH CAROLINA AT CHARLOTTE

Active student participation in the transition education process represents a foundational secondary special education practice (Kohler & Field, 2003; Rusch, Hughes, Agran, Martin, & Johnson, 2009). Federal legislation and research on transition education practices have provided strong support for students with disabilities to be involved in transition education practices. Federal special education law requires that students of transition age be invited to participate in their transition IEP planning meetings, and the implied assumption is that students actively participate in the transition discussions to help ensure that IEPs are written based upon the students' needs, while considering the students' strengths, preferences, and interests (Flexer & Baer, 2008). The federal government mandates that state and local education agencies comply with these legal requirements, and enforces compliance with monitoring activities that include site visits and review of documents. Clearly, federal mandates serve as a strong support for students to participate in and contribute to the development of the transition IEP.

Over the past two decades, effective models and strategies have been developed and researched that teach students the skills to become active participants in transition planning, and opportunities have been increased at schools so that students can use and master the learned skills. Researchers and practitioners have identified transition education best practices. Kohler's pioneering work created the Taxonomy for Transition Programming (Kohler, 1993; 1996). Two of the five categories in the Transition Taxonomy encourage student involvement in the transition education process. The Student-Focused Planning Taxonomy domain, for instance, considers student involvement in the transition planning process essential to developing a meaningful plan. The Student Development Taxonomy domain includes student-directed goal setting, decision-making, and self-advocacy, which encourage even more student involvement in the transition education process (Kohler & Field, 2003).

A more recent review of the transition literature resulted in a core of 12 best practices, one of which is student-focused planning that involves active student participation in the transition education process (Greene, 2009). Landmark, Ju, and Zhang (2010) identified self-determination instruction, including active student involvement in transition education activities, as one of eight effective transition practices. Cobb and Alwell (2009) in an analysis of transition research found that Student-Focused Planning and Student Development interventions had the greatest number of research studies supporting their use, and recommended their use in transition education. Test, et al. (2009) mapped evidence-based practices by Kohler's (1996) Taxonomy for Transition Programming. Thirty-two evidence-based practices were identified, which included two Student-Focused Planning instructional practices that increased student involvement in their IEP meetings.

Researchers and practitioners have developed strategies to promote student involvement in the transition process. Zhang and Stecker (2001), for instance, suggested three opportunities for students to become involved: (a) before the meeting, educators need to arrange opportunities for students to talk to teachers and family to discuss school and postschool interests, needs, and wants, and educators need to teach students what to do at their IEP meeting; (b) during the meeting, students need to actively participate in discussions, and teachers need to facilitate student involvement; and (c) after the meeting, educators need to facilitate student discussions with school personnel about attaining transition goals and related activities.

Konrad and Test (2004) suggested that the IEP process be divided into four stages, so that student involvement can become more focused: (a) planning, (b) drafting the plan, (c) meeting to revise the plan, and (d) implementing the plan. Research has documented that students with disabilities can be actively involved in each of these stages. For example, Cross, Cooke, Wood and Test (1999); Keyes and Owens-Johnson (2003); Powers, et al. (2001); and Woods, Sylvester, and Martin (2010) conducted studies that resulted in students being able to actively identify and discuss their strengths and needs as part of IEP planning. Konrad and Test (2004), Konrad, Trela, and Test (2006), and Konrad and Test (2007) successfully taught students to write drafts of IEPs, including choosing and writing goals and objectives. Test, et al. (2004) found 16 studies in which students with disabilities were taught to be involved in their IEP meeting. Finally, Agran, Blanchard, & Wehmeyer (2000) and German, Martin, Marshall, & Sale (2000) provided evidence that students could be taught strategies to implement their IEP plan and attain their IEP goals.

This chapter will first discuss student involvement in the transition assessment process as a means for students to identify postschool and annual transition goals. Second, student involvement in the transition IEP meeting will be explored as a means to ensure that students have the opportunity to discuss their IEP and offer input. Third, and last, this chapter will examine the emerging practice of student involvement in attaining their annual transition goals at school and in the community as a means to teach students critical goal attainment skills, and that the transition goals become meaningful targets that students work to attain.

Student Involvement in Transition Assessment

Federal special education law requires that transition goals be based upon information obtained through transition assessments (Miller, Lombard, & Corbey 2007). To meet the intent of the law and inform students so they can meaningfully participate at IEP transition meetings, the transition assessment process must meaningfully include and involve students (Field & Hoffman, 2007). For students to become involved in the transition assessment process in a participatory manner, educators need to provide students opportunities to (a) complete student versions of transition assessments, (b) understand information gleaned from the student, parent, and educator transition assessment versions, and (c) formulate postsecondary and annual transition goals using transition assessment results. Transition assessments provide information that students can use to answer critical questions to build postsecondary and annual transition goals.

Thus, student involvement in the transition assessment process should begin with students learning the six questions that transition assessments will attempt to answer.

Key Transition Assessment Questions that Students Need to Answer

The transition assessment process begins with students knowing these questions and perhaps developing tentative answers.

Postsecondary Goal Questions

- Where do I want to live after high school?
- Where do I want to work after high school?
- Where do I want to learn after high school?

Annual Transition Goal Questions

- What do I need to learn this year to live where I want after graduation from high school?
- What do I need to learn this year to obtain the career I want after graduation from high school?
- What do I need to learn this year to have the education I want after graduation from high school?

Transition assessments, structured interviews, experiences, and input from family members and educators will enable students with disabilities to answer the above questions, and from these answers, postsecondary and annual transition goals can be built (Martin & McConnell, 2011).

Complete Student Versions of Transition Assessments

To build employment, independent living, and further education postsecondary and annual transition goals, three types of assessments need to be completed: (a) career interests and skills, (b) independent living, and (c) self-determination assessments. Several free or low cost transition assessments that have student assessment versions are available online at http://www.zarrowcenter.ou.edu. Educator selection of assessments depends upon student abilities, and the opportunities students have to meaningfully participate in the assessment process. No one assessment is appropriate for all students nor does it assess all the areas that students, educators, and families need to consider to develop the IEP transition section.

Career Interests and Exploration

Loren is a high school freshman who has a learning disability. Her special education teacher arranged for Loren to complete the Career Clusters interest survey (Career Clusters, 2011), which produced a ranked list of preferred career clusters. She wanted Loren to use this assessment because Loren will most likely attend the local Career Technology Center part-time during her last two years of high school, and the results from the Career Clusters Assessment match the Career Technology's degree programs. After completing the assessment, Loren scored it and discovered her top career clusters were health science, hospitality and tourism, and human service. Over the next two weeks, Loren watched a series of videos at the Career One Stop website (http://acinet.org/acinet/videos.asp?id=27,&nodeid=27%00) that described various jobs by cluster, hiring opportunities, and qualifications across her top three job clusters.

After thinking about the information and gathering information that described the requirements for different Career Tech Center programs, Loren talked it over with her family and special education teacher. Loren decided to pursue a career in health care and searched for a vocational school to enable her to become a phlebotomist and obtain employment at the local hospital. Through the use of transition assessments, she developed her postsecondary employment and further education goals.

Independent Living Assessment

Loren plans to live at home with her Mom after graduation from high school for a few years until she obtains a job and saves some money. Then, she would like to move into her own apartment. To determine if Loren's level of attainment across crucial independent living skills needs instructional attention, the special education teacher asked Loren and her mother to complete the Life Skills Inventory (Washington State Department of Social and Health Services, 2000). This inventory built a level of attainment profile across 15 independent living domains, including money management, food management, housekeeping, and emergency and safety skills. It rated her attainment across each domain at the basic, intermediate, advanced, or exceptional levels. After completing the assessment and comparing the results with her Mom's, Loren was higher in a few areas (money management, pregnancy prevention, and transportation), but on the other domains their scores matched. Loren, with input from her Mom and teacher, decided that an annual transition goal would be developed to improve her emergency and safety skills, because her level of attainment in this domain was at the basic level.

Self-Determination Assessment

Loren's teacher asked her to complete the student version of the AIR Self-Determination Assessment (Wolman, Campeau, DuBois, Mithaug, & Stolarski, 1994). Loren's teacher scored the assessment and told Loren that she had obtained an overall self-determination score of 72%, which meant that she had developed many of the skills and had many opportunities to learn and practice them, but she still had more to learn. Loren's teacher explained that the opportunities at school to practice the self-determination skills needed to be increased, especially expecting Loren to set and attain her transition goals. Likewise, she had to learn more about setting and making her goals happen. Because of this assessment, Loren asked that setting and attaining her transition goals become an annual further education IEP goal.

Lesson Package that Uses Student Self-Assessment to Build IEP Sections

To encourage student involvement in the transition planning process, the Student-Directed Transition Planning (SDTP) lessons (Sylvester, Woods, & Martin, 2009) provide students a means to complete transition assessments in a guided process and link the results to the other transition planning components. To increase students' participation in transition discussions at their IEP meeting, Sylvester et al. (2009) created the eight-lesson SDTP sequence to enable students to become self-aware for developing postschool employment, independent living, and further education goals, to write a course of study to prepare them for attaining the goals, to connect with needed adult services, and to develop a script for students to use and discuss transition information at their IEP meeting. Educators may freely download the scripted lesson manual and lessons, and present them to students via PowerPoint files, associated exercises, and knowledge tests (http://www.zarrowcenter.ou.edu). Through the lessons, students obtain information from family members and educators, then add their own thoughts. After consideration, students write their opinions on topics such as their career strengths.

Woods et al. (2010) found that the lessons significantly increased students' transition knowledge and self-efficacy. At the end of the lessons, the students believed that:

- At the next IEP meeting, I know I can talk about my disability.
- I know the employment, further education, and adult living goals that I will talk about at my next IEP meeting.
- I know I can tell my IEP team about the job I want after graduation.
- I know I can tell my IEP team about the plan of study that will help me reach my transition goals.
- I know I can tell my IEP team about the adult supports and services I might need after graduation.

The SDTP lesson package specifically teaches students the content needed to become actively involved in the transition discussions at their IEP meeting. As a part of the lessons, students complete several transition assessments and use the information, along with input from family and educators, to help build postsecondary transition goals. As students complete the lessons, they build a script of what they want to say about transition issues at their IEP meeting.

Student Involvement in the Transition IEP Meeting

Martin, Marshall, and Maxson (1993) indicated that the IEP process provides repeated opportunities for students to make decisions and to self-advocate by learning to develop, participate, and manage their IEP. Test et al. (2004) suggested that the IEP meeting provides the opportunity for teaching and practicing a variety of important self-determination and self-advocacy skills, including (a) describing a disability, strengths, needs, and present level of performance; (b) evaluating progress and alternative goals; (c) preparing for a formal presentation and self-advocating in a formal meeting; (d) communicating interests and preferences; (e) taking responsibility for improvements; (f) participating in discussions about post-school goals and plans; and (g) determining and requesting accommodations.

Martin and Marshall (1995) indicated that students need opportunities to learn the leadership skills to manage and actively participate in their IEP meeting, and to tell their IEP team their "interests, skills, limits, and goals" (p. 152). Since IEP meetings must occur annually, they allow students to become involved at an early age and their involvement can increase and continue over multiple years. As such, it is more likely that students would master these skills, as well as increase the chances of skill generalization and maintenance once they leave high school. Martin et al. (1993) suggested that students in elementary school observe and minimally participate in their IEP meetings. By middle school, students will actively participate in their IEP meetings, and during the high school years, students will manage their IEP meeting and process. This all will be done, of course, with educator preparation and coaching. "If educators and families are serious about involving students in their IEP process, then students must be taught their role. This means that even in fully included schools, students who have an IEP must receive instruction about the IEP process and their role in it" (Martin, Marshall, and DePry, 2008, p. 358). However, educator-directed IEP meetings dominate secondary special education practice.

Lack of Student Involvement in Educator-Directed IEP Meetings

In spite of strides being made in teaching students skills and providing opportunities for them to participate in the IEP process, special education has a long history of not actively involving students in their IEP meetings. For example, Lovitt and Cushing (1994) and Thoma, Rogan, & Baker (2001) indicated that students were unfamiliar with the IEP process. These data were supported by Mason, Field, & Sawilowsky (2004) who surveyed teachers, administrators, and related services personnel and found that only 46% of students attended IEP meetings, and that students who attended were "not that involved" (p. 445).

Powers, Turner, Matuszewski, Wilson, & Loesch (1999) interviewed students after they participated in educator-directed meetings. Their students reported the meetings to be boring, that they did not understand much of what was said, and they felt ignored by the adults at the meeting. Over a three-year period, Martin, Marshall, and Sale (2004) examined the perceptions of over 1,600 IEP team members. The student team members reported dismal findings. They indicated that they knew the reason for the IEP meetings, knew what to do at the meetings, talked at the meetings, and felt good about the meetings less than any other team member.

Martin, Greene, and Borland (2004) found in a statewide survey of special education leaders that most believed their students with mild to moderate disabilities almost always were invited to attend IEP meetings, but only a few of their special educators had received any in-service training on facilitating student involvement. Not surprisingly, these administrators reported that students were only somewhat involved in the IEP meetings. Interestingly, the administrators furthest away from the meetings reported higher rates of student involvement than those who regularly attended IEP meetings. Martin, Van Dycke, Greene, et al. (2006) directly observed 109 middle and high school IEP meetings. The observations found that students spoke only 3% of the time, as opposed to 51% for special education teachers. At the observed transition IEP meetings, only a few of the students stated the purpose of the meeting, introduced everyone, or reviewed progress made on their past goals. Almost 50% of the students did discuss their interests, 27.1% discussed goals, and 20% discussed strengths and weaknesses.

Martin, Van Dycke, Greene, et al. (2006) observed 109 secondary IEP meetings and at the conclusion of each meeting team members completed a survey. On a "not at all" to "a lot" survey scale, the IEP team members gave the transition participation questions the lowest scores of the survey, which suggests only minimal team transition planning discussions. The discussions that did happen focused on the jobs students might do after high school, educational opportunities after high school, and further supports. The teams gave a "somewhat" rating to the item that asked if the IEPs reflected the students' post-school visions, and another "somewhat" rating to the item that asked if the team members thought students could attain the identified postschool goals.

A recent study examined IEP documents of secondary students with disabilities for transition compliance and found that 93% of the students were invited to participate in their IEP meeting (Landmark & Zhang, 2010). However, simply being invited to the meeting, although it meets IDEA compliance requirements, is the lowest level of involvement. For the student, simply being invited to the meeting or being present at the meeting does not necessarily mean active student participation. For educators, simply providing the opportunity for students to attend the meeting, without teaching students what to do at the IEP meeting and offering them the opportunity to learn transition knowledge about themselves, misses the intent of IDEA 2004 (Woods et al., 2010).

Recent data from the National Longitudinal Transition Study 2 indicated that 73.4% of all students receiving special education had attended an IEP meeting in the past two years (National Longitudinal Transition Study 2, 2009). Percentages ranged from a low of 68.5% for students identified with autism to a high of 86.7% for students with traumatic brain injury. But, attendance at IEP meetings, as established through the already discussed survey and direct observation studies, does not assume participation.

Lack of Student Involvement in Transition Planning Discussions

Martin, Van Dycke, Christensen et al. (2006) observed 129 transition IEP meetings and found that 25% of the meeting time was used discussing transition issues. Adult IEP team members dominated the transition discussions by talking 90% of the time, with students only talking 10% of the time. Special education teachers clearly dominated the transition discussions by talking 50% of the time. Family members and administrators both talked about 10% of time. Although students were present at these transition discussions, clearly adults talked to adults about students' transition plans, and students had minimal input into their transition plan.

Summary

Despite the history of continued lack of active student involvement in the IEP meeting, research has indicated a widespread interest in increasing the level of student involvement in the IEP meeting. Both Agran, Snow, and Swaner (1999) and Mason et al. (2004) found that teachers and administrators were interested in learning how to prepare students to be actively involved in their IEP process. Grigal, Neubert, Moon, & Graham (2003) indicated that parents and teachers felt that students should be prepared to participate in their IEP meetings.

Strategies for Involving Students in IEP Meetings

While research indicates that historically students have not been actively involved in their IEP meetings, a growing body of research indicates that students can learn to become active participants in their IEP meetings. Test et al.'s (2004) review of the literature found that 16 studies demonstrated successful strategies designed to increase student involvement in IEP meetings. Their findings indicated that students with a variety of disabilities could learn to become active participants in their IEP meeting using either published student-directed or person-centered planning strategies. When published curricula were used, a combination of direct skill instruction and role-playing was the most commonly used instruction technique. Each of the lesson packages require the students be taught skills prior to their IEP meetings, and that educators provide opportunities for students to use the learned skills during the meetings.

Using Published Curricula to Teach Student Involvement in IEP Meetings

Test et al. (2009) conducted a literature review to identify evidence-based practices in secondary transition. Only studies that met the quality indicators for group experimental research (Gersten et al., 2005) or single subject research (Horner et al., 2005) were included in the summary. Based on that review, two published curricula for teaching students to become active participants in their IEP meetings met the criteria to become an evidence-based best practice. The two lesson packages were the *Self-Advocacy Strategy* (Van Reusen, Bos, Schumaker, & Deshler, 1994) and the *Self-Directed IEP* (Martin, Marshall, Maxson, & Jerman, 1996). A recent study by Wehmeyer, Palmer, Lee, Williams-Diehm, and Shogren (2011) provides causal evidence of the efficacy of the *Whose Future is it Anyway?* process.

The *Self-Advocacy Strategy* teaches students to participate in an education or transition-planning meeting. The steps of the strategy are called IPLAN (Van Reusen & Bos, 1994):

1   Inventory your strengths, areas to improve or learn, goals, and choices for learning or accommodations. Students complete an inventory sheet that identifies strengths, areas to improve or learn, goals, and choices for learning or accommodations that they can use at their meetings.

2   *Provide your inventory information.* Students use their inventory sheet during IEP meeting discussions.
3   *Listen and respond.* Students learn proper times to listen (e.g., when someone is making a statement, when someone is asking a question) and respond (e.g., when someone asks a question, when you have information to add).
4   *Ask questions.* Students learn how to ask questions when they do not understand what people are saying.
5   *Name your goals.* Students learn to name goals they would like included in their IEP.

The *Self-Advocacy Strategy* has been used to teach males and females aged 12–17 with mild to moderate disabilities to participate in their IEP meeting. The *Self-Advocacy Strategy* has been taught using both teacher-led instruction and technology using hypermedia and CD-ROM. For example, Test and Neale (2004) effectively taught the *Self-Advocacy Strategy* to four middle school students with disabilities in ten 20–45 minute tutoring sessions over two weeks.

The *Self-Directed IEP* teaches students 11 steps to follow to be able to lead their own IEP meeting in six to ten 45-minute sessions. The *Self-Directed IEP* includes assessments, videotape, and a student workbook. The 11 steps are:

- *Step 1: Begin meeting by stating the purpose*, which involves students learning how to explicitly state the purpose of the meeting (e.g., review goals).
- *Step 2: Introduce everyone*, which involves students learning who is required to be at an IEP meeting and who else they would like to invite, as well as practicing introducing these individuals.
- *Step 3: Review past goals and performance*, which involves students stating their goals and learning which actions can be taken to help meet their goals.
- *Step 4: Ask for others' feedback*, which involves students learning what feedback is and the different ways they can receive feedback on their goals.
- *Step 5: State your school and transition goals*, which involves students identifying their interests, skills, and needs and the goals they would like to achieve in school.
- *Step 6: Ask questions if you don't understand*, which involves students learning how to ask questions for clarification.
- *Step 7: Deal with differences in opinion*, which involves students learning the LUCK strategy (Listening to the other person's opinion, Using a respectful tone of voice, Compromising or Changing your opinion if necessary, and Knowing and stating the reasons for your opinion.)
- *Step 8: State the support you will need to reach your goal*, which involves students learning about supports that will help achieve their goals.
- *Step 9: Summarize your current goals*, which involves students restating their goals, actions they will take to meet those goals, and how they would receive feedback in meeting those goals.
- *Step 10: Close meeting by thanking everyone*, which involves students learning how to end the meeting by using closing statements and thanking everyone for attending.
- *Step 11: Work on IEP goals all year*, which involves students being reminded to work on their goals all year by taking actions and receiving feedback and support to accomplish these goals.

The *Self-Directed IEP* has been used to teach males and females, aged 12–21, identified as having mild to moderate disabilities, to participate in their IEP meeting. The *Self-Directed IEP* has primarily been taught following the procedures outlined in the teacher's workbook combined with a model-lead-test prompting procedure (Allen, Smith, Test, Flowers, & Wood, 2001; Arndt, Konrad, & Test, 2006).

Whose Future is it Anyway? (WFA), the third published curriculum, is now in its second edition (Wehmeyer, Lawrence, Garner, Soukup, & Palmer, 2004), and has some research supporting its use. WFA was developed primarily for secondary transition-aged students with disabilities. It is taught in 36 sessions with materials that are written for students. In addition, there is a Coach's Guide to help teachers provide any needed support to students. The five sections of the WFA include:

1. Getting to Know You: introduces students to the concept of transition and transition planning, four transition outcome areas (i.e., employment, community living, postsecondary education, recreation and leisure), and disability awareness. During this section students identify their unique learning and support needs related to their disability.
2. Making Decisions: introduces students to DO IT!, a decision-making process that is then applied to the four transition outcome areas. Students learn to use DO IT! to make a decision about a possible living arrangement and then apply the decision-making strategy to each of the other three outcome areas.
3. How to Get What You Need, Sec. 101: teaches students to identify potential community supports for each transition outcome area.
4. Goals, Objectives, and the Future: teaches students to write goals and objectives, as well as strategies they can use to track progress on their goals and objectives.
5. Communicatin': teaches students about effective small-group communication strategies, types of communication (e.g., verbal, nonverbal), how to be assertive, not aggressive, how to negotiate and compromise, and how to use persuasion.

The WFA has been used with high school and middle school students with intellectual disability and learning disabilities. WFA has been primarily taught using printed workbooks, but recently was taught using a computer-based reading support program called *Rocket Reader* (Lee et al., 2011). Wehmeyer and Lawrence (1995) conducted an initial evaluation of the WFA, determining its efficacy in promoting transition knowledge and self-efficacy for transition planning. Wehmeyer et al. (2011) conducted a randomized-trial placebo control group evaluation of the effects of the WFA with more than 400 high school students, determining that instruction using the WFA process resulted in significant, positive differences in self-determination when compared with a placebo-control group, and that students who received instruction with the WFA process gained transition knowledge and skills.

Strategies for Teaching Students to Draft their IEP

So far the strategies described have focused on teaching students to actively participate in their IEP meeting. This section describes two strategies that can be used not only to teach students to write parts of their IEP, but also to infuse teaching self-determination skills into academic writing instruction. The two strategies include using an IEP template (Konrad & Test, 2004) and the GO 4 IT ... NOW! Strategy (Konrad, Trela, & Test, 2006).

The IEP Template is a "fill-in-the-blank" IEP that students use to write a draft of a first-person IEP in complete sentences (Konrad & Test, 2004). The Template helps students understand IEP content and format. Teachers can prepare students to use the Template by (a) using online interest and career inventories and working with their school guidance counselors to help students develop vision statements about their post-school goals, (b) working with students to identify strengths and academic, functional, social, and behavioral needs, (c) teaching students how to turn a need into a goal, and (d) using modeling and guided and independent practice to teach students to complete the Template. While teaching students to complete the

Template, teachers can also teach writing and communication skills. For example, they can teach capitalization, punctuation, and parts of a sentence (subject, verb) using sentences from student Templates. Students can then learn to use transition words and phrases to combine sentences into paragraphs. Next, teachers can also teach letter-writing skills by having students write letters to invite IEP team members to their meetings. Finally, students can be encouraged to participate in their IEP meetings by bringing their completed Templates and/or paragraphs to the meetings or developing presentations from their Templates.

GO 4 IT . . . NOW! is a learning strategy designed to teach students how to write paragraphs about their IEP goals (Konrad & Test, 2007), and it has been used effectively with a variety of students (Konrad et al., 2006). Students are taught: (a) that one paragraph is about one goal and that goal is the topic of the paragraphs, (b) objectives are the supporting details, and (c) to restate the goal and indicate how long it will take to complete as a concluding sentence. The GO 4 IT . . . NOW! mnemonic is:

G – **G**oals
O – **O**bjectives
4 – **4** objectives
IT – **I**dentify **T**imeline
N – Did I **NAME** my topic?
O – Did I **ORDER** my steps?
W – Did I **WRAP** it up and restate my topic?

Teachers can use GO 4 IT . . . NOW! by (a) helping students identify their academic, functional, social, and behavioral needs and then explicitly teaching students to turn a need into a goal using an "I will" statement; and (b) providing explicit instruction on how to write a goal paragraph, using modeling and guided and independent practice and "transition words" to teach students to put objectives into a logical order. Once students are able to write effective paragraphs, students can be taught to combine their paragraphs to create longer essays. Finally, students can be encouraged to share their paragraphs and essays at their IEP meeting or send them with the IEP invitation letters to prepare team members for the meeting.

Teach Students to Develop and Use their Summary of Performance with the SDTP Lessons

IDEA 2004 requires that, for a child whose eligibility under special education terminates due to graduation with a regular diploma or due to exceeding the age of eligibility, the local education agency ". . . shall provide the child with a summary of the child's academic achievement and functional performance, which shall include recommendations on how to assist the child in meeting the child's postsecondary goals" (Kochhar-Bryant & Izzo, 2006, p 71). The purpose of the Summary of Performance (SOP) is to assist the student in the transition from high school to further education, employment, and independent living. While IDEA does not provide much detail on the content of the SOP, the field has developed a number of forms and practices to make the SOP more comprehensive and useful. Moreover, lessons have been developed to teach students to self-direct the writing of their SOP, and to use the SOP to provide essential transition information that students can use to help with transition discussions during the IEP meeting, and for student-presentation of the SOP at the exit IEP meeting (Martin, Van Dycke, D'Ottavio, & Nickerson, 2007).

The Student-Directed Transition Planning lesson package (Sylvester et al., 2009), which was described earlier in the student involvement in transition assessment section, teaches students to systematically construct their own SOP. Students bring the completed SOP to their IEP meeting and use it as a script to provide essential transition information. To date, one published study validates SDTP's effectiveness to increase students' knowledge of transition (Woods et al., 2010).

The Me! Self-Awareness and Self-Advocacy lesson package (Cantley, Little, & Martin, 2010) uses the IEP and other resources to teach students to understand their disability and advocate for themselves using the information contained in their IEP. Knowledge quizzes provide feedback on student acquisition of crucial knowledge. Projects include the Me! portfolio in which students compile their own special education history, along with detailed information about their disability, skills, and limits. Students take this additional information into their IEP meeting, and use it to participate in meaningful conversations. This lesson package is freely available by downloading it from the OU Zarrow Center web page (http://www.zarrow-center.ou.edu/content/education/centers-and-partnerships/zarrow/trasition-education-materials/).

Using Person-Centered Planning Strategies to Increase Student Participation in IEP Meetings

Test et al. (2004) identified a number of studies that used person-centered planning strategies to increase student involvement in the IEP meeting, including *Whole-Life Planning* (Timmons & Whitney-Thomas, 1998), *Personal Futures Planning* (Miner & Bates, 1997a), and *McGill Action Planning System* (Vandercook, York, & Forest, 1989). Person-centered planning maintains an explicit emphasis on empowerment of and primary direction from the individual for whom the planning is being conducted (Timmons & Whitney-Thomas, 1998), and therefore is an excellent tool for gathering information on a student's future vision and putting the student as the central focus of the transition planning process. Person-centered planning is particularly applicable to the transition process because of its ability to mobilize and empower families, community members, and students as full participants in the collaboration process (Michaels & Ferrara, 2005). Based on research with 10 students, Timmons and Whitney-Thomas (1998) found that student participation in transition planning is greatly enhanced if the person-centered planning approach is taken and student personal conversation style is taken into consideration. Person-centered planning can be used to develop the student's personal profile. School teams are encouraged to offer opportunities for the student and family to use their dreams for their student's future to help with transition planning (Michaels & Ferrara, 2005).

Person-centered planning strategies are typically a facilitated process designed to plan and develop supports to meet the specific desires of the focal person. Students need little to no prior instruction and the facilitation takes place during the actual meetings. While PCP strategies vary, they typically involve similar steps. The student and family members identify a group of people who have an interest in developing goals and future supports, then the group meets at a convenient location, such as the student's home or a restaurant. During the meeting, a facilitator guides the group through a series of questions designed to solicit information that can then be used to develop a plan that includes goals, action steps, and responsible persons for helping to achieve the student's goals. For example, the *McGill Action Planning System* (Vandercook et al., 1989) asks the following questions:

1 What is the individual's history?
2 What is your dream for the future?
3 What is your nightmare?
4 Who is the individual?
5 What are the individual's strengths, gifts, and abilities?
6 What are the individual's needs?

7   What would the individual's ideal day at school look like?

8   What must be done to make it happen?

Miner and Bates (1997b) suggested four steps for developing a personal profile:

- Draw a "circle of support map," with the student being in the center, close friends and family members immediately outside the student, and other support personnel in the outer circle.
- Draw a "community presence" map, consisting of a list of community settings that the student uses or can use.
- Make a list of things that work or do not work for the student.
- List the student's gifts and capacities.

Person-centered planning strategies have been used primarily with students with moderate to severe intellectual disabilities. Person-centered planning meetings can be conducted either in school settings or in community settings with the final plan shared at the student's IEP meeting. At times, these meetings are used to develop students' IEPs.

Summary

Research has clearly demonstrated that students with a variety of ability levels and ages can be taught to actively participate in writing a draft IEP and meeting to write the final draft. Strategies include three research-based curricula: *The Self-Advocacy Strategy, The Self-Directed IEP*, and *Who's Future is it Anyway?*, along with person-centered planning strategies. Finally, the IEP Template and GO 4 IT ... NOW! can be used to teach students to write their IEPs, as well as include self-determination skills when teaching academic writing skills. Next, student involvement in achieving their goals will be discussed.

Student Involvement in Attaining their Annual Transition Goals

Good transition planning does not necessarily lead to appropriate actions if adequate follow-up actions are not taken. Too often the transition IEP becomes stored in students' files, while instructional activities or transition services laid out in the plan are not implemented. To ensure adequate implementation, we believe that students need to be actively involved in attaining their transition goals. The last section of this chapter will explore methods to involve students in attaining their transition IEP goals.

Self-Determination and Goal Attainment

Self-determination refers to skills that enable students to engage in goal-directed behavior (Field et al., 1998), and self-determined individuals will choose their goals and "doggedly pursue them" (Martin & Marshall, 1995, p. 147).

Take Action Goal Attainment Process

The ChoiceMaker Curriculum has three main sections that teach students to become more self-determined: (a) choosing transition goals, (b) expressing transition goals by being an active IEP meeting participant, and (c) taking action to attain transition goals. The Take Action lesson package (Marshall et al., 1999) teaches students to attain transition goals by building a plan that

- Breaks an annual transition goal into smaller, doable short-term goals that can be accomplished in a week.
- Sets a standard to know when a short-term goal has been attained.
- Describes feedback on performance toward attaining the goal.
- Identifies motivation factors associated with attaining the goal.
- Identifies strategies that will be used to attain the goal.
- Lists needed supports to attain the goal.
- Schedules when work on short-term goals will be done (Martin & Marshall, 1995).

After the plan has been implemented, students evaluate performance and make any adjustments in the plan if the short-term goal has not been accomplished. The following studies have demonstrated the usefulness of the Take Action process to enable students to attain their IEP goals.

German et al. (2000) demonstrated the usefulness of the Take Action lesson package to teach six high school students with intellectual disability to attain IEP goals using the plan, act, evaluate, and adjust process. Using the modified Take Action Process, the students built daily plans that answered three questions: (a) What will I do? (b) What help will I need? and (c) When will I do it? Students then implemented the plan, evaluated their performance, and made adjustments to be included in the next day's plan. Instruction in the Take Action goal attainment strategy produced an increase in the number of daily goals attained, and this level of goal attainment was maintained after withdrawal of teacher instruction. This brief instructional intervention provided students with 360 minutes of instruction and four to six days of guided practice. Teacher observations noted that daily evaluation and plan adjustments taught students how to make changes in their plans so their goals could be attained.

Martin, Marshall, and El-Kazimi (2011) taught the Take Action goal attainment process to 101 middle school students in general education English classes. Overall, the results found statistically significant improvement in the number of long-term goals the students set and met and in self-determination assessment results. The mean growth percentage found the largest gain among the students with disabilities in the general education English classes. Student positive comments indicated that the Take Action process enabled them to be more organized and focused on tasks. Martin, Martin, and Osmani (2011) used the Take Action process to teach nine high school juniors with learning disabilities to attain their annual transition goals. Students first learned the Take Action goal attainment process, then the students applied the Take Action plan, act, evaluate, and adjust process to attain self-selected annual transition goals.

Self-Determined Learning Model of Instruction (SDLMI)

The SDLMI (Mithaug, Wehmeyer, Agran, Martin, & Palmer, 1998; Wehmeyer, Palmer, Agran, Mithaug, & Martin, 2000) provides a series of questions to enable teachers to teach students to self-select and attain goals. The SDLMI consists of three phases: (a) learn to set a goal; (b) develop and implement a self-directed action plan to achieve the goal and (c) design and implement a self-monitoring plan and use the plan to evaluate progress toward the goal, and make necessary adjustments based on the evaluation. Instruction in each phase is presented by posting a series of four challenging questions to the student, who is required to answer the questions and solve the problem. Unique features of this model include teacher objectives that are linked to student questions, a list of educational supports that teachers can use to enable students to self-direct learning, and the three phases are progressively connected so that the student learns a sequence of skills that are essential for goal setting and attainment. The overall theme and goal of the model are for the student to become the primary causal agent for choices, decisions, and actions.

Agran et al. (2000) used the SDLMI at job sites with 19 secondary aged youth who had multiple disabilities, including intellectual disability. Each student, with teacher support and the students' IEPs, selected a target behavior, including social skills, community living skills, and employment related skills. The students learned the SDLMI process that involved developing a plan, evaluating the plan, and revising the plan as needed to attain their goals. Students determined their goal by answering four questions: (a) What do I want to learn? (b) What do I know about it now? (c) What must change for me to learn what I don't know? and (d) What can I do to make this happen?

To begin to attain their goals, students moved into Phase 2 of the SDLMI and answered another four questions: (a) What can I do to learn what I don't know? (b) What could keep me from taking action? (c) What can I do to remove these barriers, and (d) When will I take action? The answers produced the action plans. After the action plan had been implemented, students answered Phase 3 SDLMI questions: (a) What actions have I taken? (b) What barriers have I removed? (c) What has changed about what I don't know? and (d) Do I know what I want to know? Goal attainment scaling indicated that over two-thirds of the students exceeded the expectation of their teachers, and that 89% of the students achieved their goals at or above the levels initially expected by their teachers.

McGlashing-Johnson, Agran, Sitlington, Cavin, and Wehmeyer (2003) used the SDLMI with four high school students with mental retardation who had extensive to pervasive support needs to self-select work-place goals at their community-based work experience site. The students set their own goals, developed an action plan, and evaluated their progress. The active problem solving enabled students to improve their work performance.

Conclusions

This chapter began with the premise that active student participation in the transition education process represents best practice. Federal special education rules and regulations and numerous researchers strongly support meaningful student involvement in the transition planning process through three primary means. First, students need to become involved in the transition assessment process to have input, and then learn the results to develop postsecondary and annual transition goals. Second, students need to learn how to become active members of the IEP team and learn transition-relevant information about themselves to participate in planning discussions. Educators need to teach students IEP involvement skills, and provide opportunities for students to learn transition knowledge about themselves, and then provide students opportunities to actively participate in their IEP meetings. Third, students need to learn goal attainment skills to be able to actively work on achieving their postsecondary and annual transition goals. Educators need to teach students these skills and then provide opportunities for students to practice their skills in attaining their transition and other educational goals. Together, educators and family members need to provide opportunities and teach needed skills so that the transition education process prepares students for further education, employment, and independent living.

References

Agran, M., Blanchard, C., & Wehmeyer, M. L. (2000). Promoting transition goals and self-determination through student self-directed learning: The self-determined learning model of instruction. *Education and Training in Mental Retardation and Developmental Disabilities, 35*, 351–364.

Agran, M., Snow, K., & Swaner, J. (1999). Teacher perceptions of self-determination: Benefits, characteristics, strategies. *Education and Training in Mental Retardation and Developmental Disabilities, 34*, 293–301.

Allen, S. K., Smith, A. C., Test, D. W., Flowers, C., & Wood, W. M. (2001). The effects of *Self-Directed IEP* on student participation in IEP meetings. *Career Development for Exceptional Individuals, 24*, 107–120.

Arndt, S. A., Konrad, M., & Test, D. W. (2006). Effects of the *Self-Directed IEP* on student participation in planning meetings. *Remedial and Special Education, 27,* 194–207.

Cantley, P., Little, K., & Martin, J. (2010). *Me! Lessons for teaching self-awareness & self-advocacy.* Norman, OK: University of Oklahoma, Zarrow Center for Learning Enrichment. Retrieved from: http://www.ou.edu/content/education/centers-and-partnerships/zarrow/trasition-education-materials/me-lessons-for-teaching-self-awareness-and-self-advocacy.html

Career Clusters (2011). *Career Clusters Interest Survey.* Retrieved from http://careerclusters.org/ccinterest-survey.php

Career One Stop. (2011). *Explore Career Videos.* Retrieved from: http://acinet.org/acinet/videos.asp?id=27,&nodeid=27%00

Cobb, R. B., & Alwell, M. (2009). Transition planning/coordinating interventions for youth with disabilities: A systematic review. *Career Development for Exceptional Individuals, 32,* 70–81.

Cross, T., Cooke, N. L., Wood, W. M., & Test, D. W. (1999). Comparison of the effects of *MAPS* and *ChoiceMaker* on student self-determination skills. *Education and Training in Mental Retardation and Developmental Disabilities, 34,* 499–510.

Field, S., & Hoffman, A. (2007). Self-determination in secondary transition assessment. *Assessment for Effective Intervention, 32,* 181–190.

Field, S., Martin, J., Miller, R., Ward, M., & Wehmeyer, M. (1998). *A practical guide for teaching self-determination.* Reston, VA: The Council for Exceptional Children.

Flexer, R. W., & Baer, R. M. (2008). Transition legislation and models. In R. W. Flexer, R. M. Baer, P. Luft, & T. J. Simmons (Eds.), *Transition planning for secondary students with disabilities* (3rd ed.). Upper Saddle River, NJ: Pearson.

German, S. L., Martin, J. E., Marshall, L. H., & Sale, R. P. (2000). Promoting self-determination: Using *Take Action* to teach goal attainment. *Career Development for Exceptional Individuals, 23,* 27–38.

Gersten, R., Fuchs, L. S., Compton, D., Coyne, M., Greenwood, C., & Innocenti, M. S. (2005). Quality indicators for group experimental and quasi-experimental research in special education. *Exceptional Children, 71,* 149–164.

Greene, G. (2009). Best practices in transition. In C. A. Kochhar-Bryant & G. Greene (Eds.), *Pathways to successful transition for youth with disabilities* (pp.196–235). Upper Saddle River, NJ: Pearson.

Grigal, M., Neubert, D. A., Moon, M. S., & Graham, S. (2003). Self-determination for students with disabilities: Views of parents and teachers. *Exceptional Children, 70,* 97–112.

Horner, R. H., Carr, E. G., Halle, J., McGee, G., Odom, S., & Wolery, M. (2005). The use of single-subject research to identify evidence-based practice in special education. *Exceptional Children, 71,* 165–179.

Individuals with Disabilities Education Improvement Act of 2004, PL 108-446, 20 U.S.C. §§ 1400 et seq. (2004).

Keyes, M. W., & Owens-Johnson, L. (2003). Developing person-centered IEPs. *Intervention in School and Clinic, 38,* 145–152.

Kochhar-Bryant, C. A., & Izzo, M. V. (2006). Access to post-high school services: Transition assessment and the summary of performance. *Career Development for Exceptional Individuals, 29,* 70–89.

Kohler, P. D. (1993). Best practices in transition: Substantiated or implied? *Career Development for Exceptional Individuals, 16*(2), 107–121.

Kohler, P. (1996). *A taxonomy for transition programming: Linking research and practice.* Champaign, IL: Transition Research Institute, University of Illinois.

Kohler, P. D., & Field, S. (2003). Transition-focused education: Foundation for the future. *The Journal of Special Education, 37,* 174–183.

Konrad, M., & Test, D. W. (2004). Teaching middle-school students with disabilities to use an IEP template. *Career Development for Exceptional Individuals, 27,* 101–124.

Konrad, M., & Test, D. W. (2007). Effects of GO 4 IT … NOW! strategy instruction on the written IEP goal articulation and paragraph-writing skills of middle school students with disabilities. *Remedial and Special Education, 28,* 277–291.

Konrad, M., Trela, K., & Test, D. W. (2006). Using IEP goals and objectives to teach paragraph writing to high school students with physical and cognitive disabilities. *Education and Training in Developmental Disabilities, 41,* 111–124.

Landmark, L. J., Ju, S., & Zhang, D. (2010). Substantiated best practices in transition: Fifteen plus years later. *Career Development for Exceptional Individuals, 33,* 165–176.

Landmark, L. J., & Zhang, D. (2010). Compliance and best practices in transition planning: Effects of disability and ethnicity. Manuscript submitted for publication.

Lee, Y., Wehmeyer, M. L., Palmer, S. B., Williams-Diehm, K., Davies, D. K., & Stock, S. E. (2011). The effect of student-directed transition planning with a computer-based reading support program on the self-determination of students with disabilities. *Journal of Special Education, 45*(2), 104–117.

Lovitt, T. C., & Cushing, S. S. (1994). High school students rate their IEPs: Low opinions and lack of ownership. *Intervention in School and Clinic, 30*, 34–37.

Marshall, L. H., Martin, J. E., Maxson, L. M., Miller, T. L., McGill, T., Hughes, W. M., et al. (1999). *Take action: Making goals happen.* Longmont, CO: Sopris West, Inc.

Martin, J. D., Martin, J. E., & Osmani, K. (2011). *Teaching high school students to attain their annual transition goals.* Manuscript in preparation.

Martin, J. E., Greene, B. A., & Borland, B. J. (2004). Secondary students' involvement in their IEP meetings: Administrators' perceptions. *Career Development for Exceptional Individuals, 27*, 177–188.

Martin, J. E., & Marshall, L. H. (1995). *ChoiceMaker:* A comprehensive self-determination transition program. *Intervention in School and Clinic, 30*(3), 147–156.

Martin, J. E., Marshall, L. H., & El-Kazimi, N. (2011). *Teaching goal attainment in an inclusive middle school general education setting.* Manuscript submitted for publication.

Martin, J. E., Marshall, L. H., & DePry, R. L. (2008). Participatory decision-making: Innovative practices that increase student self-determination. In R.W. Flexer, T. J. Simmons, P. Luft, & R. M. Baer (Eds.), *Transition planning for secondary students with disabilities* (3rd ed., pp. 340–366). Columbus: Merrill Prentice Hall.

Martin, J. E., Marshall, L. H., & Maxson, L. (1993). Transition policy: Infusing student self-determination and self-advocacy into transition programs. *Career Development for Exceptional Individuals, 16*, 53–61.

Martin, J. E., Marshall, L. H., Maxson, L., & Jerman, P. (1996). *The self-directed IEP.* Longmont, CO: Sopris West.

Martin, J. E., Marshall, L., & Sale, P. (2004). A 3-year study of middle, junior high, and high school IEP meetings. *Exceptional Children, 70*, 285–297.

Martin, J. E., & McConnell. A. (2011). *A three-part transition assessment process: Enabling students to build their own postsecondary and annual transition goals.* Manuscript in preparation.

Martin, J. E., Van Dycke, J. L., Christensen, W. R., Greene, B. A., Gardner, J. E., & Lovett, D. L. (2006). Increasing student participation in IEP meetings: Establishing the *Self-Directed IEP* as an evidenced-based practice. *Exceptional Children, 72*, 299–316.

Martin, J. E., Van Dycke, J., D'Ottavio, M., & Nickerson, K. (2007). The student-directed summary of performance: Increasing student and family involvement in the transition planning process. *Career Development for Exceptional Individuals, 30*, 13–26

Martin, J. E., Van Dycke, J. L., Greene, B. A., Gardner, J. E., Christensen, W. R., Woods, L. L., et al. (2006). Direct observation of teacher-directed secondary IEP meetings: Establishing the need for self-determination and student participation instruction. *Exceptional Children, 72*, 187–200.

Mason, C., Field, S., & Sawilowsky, S. (2004). Implementation of self-determination activities and student participation in IEPs. *Exceptional Children, 70*, 441–451.

McGlashing-Johnson, J., Agran, M., Sitlington, P., Cavin, M., & Wehmeyer, M. (2003). Enhancing the job performance of youth with moderate to severe cognitive disabilities using the self-determined learning model of instruction. *Research and Practice for Persons with Severe Disabilities, 28*, 194–204.

Michaels, C. A., & Ferrara, D. L. (2005). Promoting post-school success for all: The role of collaboration in person-centered transition planning. *Journal of Educational and Psychological Consultation, 16*, 287–313.

Miller, R. J., Lombard, R. C., & Corbey, S. A. (2007). *Transition assessment: Planning transition and IEP development for youth with mild to moderate disabilities.* Boston: Pearson.

Miner, C. A., & Bates, P. E. (1997a). The effect of person centered planning activities on the IEP/ transition planning process. *Education and Training in Mental Retardation and Developmental Disabilities, 32*, 105–112.

Miner, C. A., & Bates, P. E. (1997b). Person-centered transition planning. *Teaching Exceptional Children, 30(1)*, 66–69.

Mithaug, D., Wehmeyer, M. L., Agran, M., Martin, J., & Palmer, S. (1998). The self-determined learning model of instruction: Engaging students to solve their learning problems. In M. L. Wehmeyer & D. J. Sands (Eds.), *Making it happen: Students involvement in educational planning, decision-making and instruction* (pp. 299-328). Baltimore: Brookes.

National Longitudinal Transition Study 2. (2009). *NLTS2 data tables.* Retrieved from http://www.nlts2.org

Powers, L., Turner, A., Matuszewski, J., Wilson, R., & Loesch, C. (1999). A qualitative analysis of student involvement in transition planning. *The Journal for Vocational Special Needs Education, 21*(3), 18–26.

Powers, L. E., Turner, A., Westwood, D., Matuszewski, J., Wilson, R., & Phillips, A. (2001). *TAKE CHARGE for the Future*: A controlled field-test of a model to promote student involvement in transition planning. *Career Development for Exceptional Individuals, 24*, 89–104.

Rusch, F. R., Hughes, C., Agran, M., Martin, J. E., & Johnson, J. R. (2009). Toward self-directed learning, post-high school placement, and coordinated support: Constructing new transition bridges to adult life. *Career Development for Exceptional Individuals, 32*, 53–59.

Sylvester, L., Woods, L. L., & Martin, J. E. (2009). *Student-directed transition planning*. Norman, OK: University of Oklahoma, Zarrow Center. Retrieved from http://www.ou.edu/content/education/centers-and-partnerships/zarrow/trasition-education-materials/student-directed-transition-planning.html

Test, D. W., Fowler, C. H., Richter, S. M., White, J., Mazzotti, V., Walker, A. R., et al. (2009). Evidence-based practices in secondary transition. *Career Development for Exceptional Individuals, 32*, 115–128.

Test, D. W., & Neale, M. (2004). Using the *Self-Advocacy Strategy* to increase middle graders' IEP participation. *Journal of Behavioral Education, 13*, 135–145.

Test, D. W., Mason, C., Hughes, C., Konrad, M., Neale, M., & Wood, W. (2004). Student involvement in individualized education program meetings. *Exceptional Children, 70*, 391–412.

Thoma, C. A., Rogan, P., & Baker, S. R. (2001). Student involvement in transition planning: Unheard voices. *Education and Training in Mental Retardation and Developmental Disabilities, 36*, 16–29.

Timmons, J. S., & Whitney-Thomas, J. (1998). The most important member: Facilitating the focus person's participation in person centered planning. *Research to Practice, 4*(1), 3–6.

Vandercook, T., York, J., & Forest, M. (1989). The *McGill Action Planning System* (MAPS): A strategy for building the vision. *Journal of the Association of Persons with Severe Handicaps, 14*, 205–215.

Van Reusen, A. K., & Bos, C. S. (1994). Facilitating student participation in the individualized education programs through motivation strategy instruction. *Exceptional Children, 60*, 466–475.

Van Reusen, A. K., Bos, C. S., Schumaker, J. B., & Deshler, D. D. (1994). *The self-advocacy strategy for education and transition planning*. Lawrence, KS: Edge Enterprises.

Washington State Department of Social and Health Services (2000). *Life Skills Inventory*. Retrieved from http://www.dshs.wa.gov/pdf/ms/forms/10_267.pdf

Wehmeyer, M. L., & Lawrence, M. (1995). Whose future is it anyway? Promoting student involvement in transition planning with a student-directed process. *Career Development for Exceptional Individuals, 18*, 69–83.

Wehmeyer, M., Lawrence, M., Garner, N., Soukup, J. & Palmer, S. (2004). *Whose Future is it Anyway? A Student-Directed Transition Planning Process* (2nd ed.). Lawrence, KS: Beach Center on Disability.

Wehmeyer, M. L., Palmer, S. B., Agran, M., Mithaug, D. E., & Martin, J. E. (2000). Promoting causal agency: The self-determined learning model of instruction. *Exceptional Children, 66*, 439–453.

Wehmeyer, M. L., Palmer, S. B., Lee, Y., Williams-Diehm, K., & Shogren, K. A. (2011). A randomized-trial evaluation of the effect of *Whose Future is it Anyway?* on self-determination. *Career Development for Exceptional Individuals, 34*(1), 45–56.

Wolman, J. M., Campeau, P. L., DuBois, P. A., Mithaug, D. E., & Stolarski, V. S. (1994). *AIR Self-Determination Scale and User Guide*. Retrieved from http://www.ou.edu/content/education/centers-and-partnerships/zarrow/self-determination-assessment-tools/air-self-determination-assessment.html

Woods, L. L., Sylvester, L., & Martin, J. E. (2010). *Student-Directed Transition Planning*: Increasing student knowledge and self-efficacy in the transition planning process. *Career Development for Exceptional Individuals, 33*, 106–114.

Zhang, D., & Stecker, P. (2001). Student involvement in transition planning: Are we there yet? *Education and Training in Mental Retardation and Developmental Disabilities, 36*, 293–303.

5

Transition Assessment for Adolescents

Debra A. Neubert

UNIVERSITY OF MARYLAND

Introduction

During the adolescent years, assessment occurs for different purposes and students spend considerable time preparing for and taking various assessments. In classrooms, teachers use assessments to determine the concepts and skills students have mastered, to determine grades for a course, and to make recommendations for future courses concerning remedial or advanced placements (Dorn, 2010). Guidance counselors administer interest inventories to assess adolescents' interests and preferences. Students take annual state-mandated assessments to measure their mastery of content standards and school systems use the results to determine if schools are making adequate yearly progress (Payne-Tsoupros, 2010). A small percentage of students participate in alternate state assessments if their disability precludes them from taking the state assessments with accommodations (Hodgson, Lazarus, & Thurlow, 2010). In some states, students take exit exams to determine the type of diploma they will receive as they exit the public school system (Johnson, Stout, & Thurlow, 2009). Other assessment activities during the secondary years vary by a student's postsecondary goal and may include admission exams such as the Scholastic Aptitude Test (SAT) or the Armed Services Vocational Aptitude Battery (ASVAB).

While assessments vary, the results should be used to inform adolescents and their families as they plan secondary courses and work towards postsecondary goals for learning, living and working in the community. However, many adolescents have difficulty setting postsecondary goals and accessing secondary courses that will lead to optimal college and employment opportunities (Dougherty, 2010). Therefore, policy makers continue to focus on initiatives and mandates that require state and local school systems to assess students not only for academic content but also their readiness for life after school. For example, assessments and standards for college and career readiness are targeted in recent educational reform (Achieve, 2005; ACT, 2010; Dougherty, Mellor, & Smith, 2006). For adolescents with disabilities, policy makers have targeted age-appropriate transition assessment to plan a student's secondary course of study and post-school goals under the Individuals with Disabilities Education Improvement Act of 2004 (IDEA 2004). In fact, one of the purposes of IDEA 2004 is to ensure that all students with disabilities have a free, appropriate public education that includes services that will assist them in preparation for further education, employment and independent living. Despite such mandates, youth with disabilities continue to experience poor employment and college outcomes (National Disability Rights Network, 2011; Newman, Wagner, Cameto, & Knokey, 2009).

In this chapter, the purposes, models, and methods of transition assessment (TA) are described for adolescents. Models and methods can provide educators, counselors, school psychologists, and related personnel with a structure to work collaboratively with students and families in collecting, compiling, and sharing assessment results that inform the transition planning process. While TA is now an integral part of the IEP process under IDEA 2004, educators and related personnel are not always clear on what TA should encompass, who is responsible, and how to share the information effectively. While the term age-appropriate TA specifically applies to adolescents with disabilities eligible for services under IDEA 2004, the process can be used for all students and can certainly be viewed within the college and career readiness movement in education.

History, Definitions, and Legislation

While the need for planning transition services for adolescents with disabilities has been addressed in special education legislation since 1990, the term and the focus on TA are more recent. IDEA 2004 included language that "age-appropriate TA" form the basis for determining adolescents with disabilities to identify post-school goals to plan for secondary course of study through the Individualized Education Program (IEP) process, beginning at age 14 or 16 and updated annually. TA builds on the earlier concepts of vocational evaluation, vocational assessment, and career assessment (Leconte, 1994; 2006; Sitlington, Neubert, & Clark, 2010). A brief history of these concepts is provided first so that TA can be put into context when choosing models and methods to guide the process for adolescents in schools today.

Vocational Evaluation

The term vocational evaluation was originally used in the field of vocational rehabilitation (VR) and refers to an assessment process that helps counselors determine an individual's eligibility for VR along with the services and supports needed to reach a specific employment goal. Vocational evaluation methods in the 20th century came from psychology, the military, industrial engineering and production management, and medicine (Leconte, 1994). Theses methods included: (a) psychometric instruments to determine an individual's interests, aptitudes, cognitive abilities, personality traits, and career maturity; (b) commercial or information work samples to assess an individual's interests, aptitudes, and abilities in relation to tasks associated with certain jobs or tasks; (c) situational assessments or job tryouts to observe an individual's ability to perform tasks in a specific work or simulated environments. Initially, vocational evaluation was conducted in a rehabilitation center, at a sheltered workshop, or by counselors in VR offices. A vocational evaluator would administer assessments and write a report with recommendations related to the individual's ability and potential to work or live independently.

Today, these assessment methods continue to be used in VR to identify an individual's unique strengths, resources, priorities, employment patterns, abilities, interests, social skills, work habits and level of self-determination or consumer empowerment (Donoso, Hernandez, & Horin, 2010; Peer & Tenhula, 2010). Since state VR agencies have targeted adolescents with disabilities as a priority for assessments to determine their eligibility for VR services and to identify specific time-limited services and supports needed to reach an employment outcome (National Council on Disability, 2008), some may participate in the VR assessment process before they exit the school system. In this case, these assessment results can supplement the school's TA process. On the other hand, school personnel can share their TA results with VR personnel to use in determining if the student is eligible for VR services, to assign a priority for services, or to identify additional assessments that may be helpful in determining an employment outcome (Rehabilitation Act Amendments of 1998). Therefore, adolescents with disabilities, their families, and secondary educators need to be aware of these possible links and collaborate with VR personnel in planning future services and in sharing the results of assessments (Neubert & Moon, 2000; Lamb, 2007).

Vocational Evaluation/Assessment

Vocational evaluation was also used in some public school systems to help students determine career goals and explore secondary vocational programs by the 1970s. Vocational evaluation was first evident in public schools in separate work experience programs and in vocational evaluation units associated with CTE programs (Cobb & Neubert, 1998; Leconte, 1994). Similar to VR, commercial and informal work samples, psychometric tests, and situational assessments were used to assess a student's interests and skills and/or to recommend programs in a specific CTE area or for employment (Adami & Neubert, 1991).

As special education interest in vocational assessment grew, a curriculum-based vocational assessment (CBVA) model was also developed to assess and support students in CTE programs (Albright & Cobb, 1988). CBVA models focused on the curriculum, exploration of careers, and situational assessment in school environments. Until 1990, school systems often provided vocational evaluation or assessment services to students with funding and personnel from special set-aside monies in CTE legislation (Cobb & Neubert, 1998). Once this set-aside money was no longer available, many schools systems no longer funded vocational evaluation or assessment programs or personnel.

Special Education—Vocational, Career, and Transition Assessment

As interest in providing vocational assessment expanded in the school system, other terms and models evolved. With the focus on career education in the 1970s and early 1980s, preparing all students for careers and work became a focal point for school systems. The idea of career education and transition planning resurfaced with the School to Work Opportunities ACT of 1994 for all students in education. Concepts from this Act, such as school-based learning, work-based learning, and connecting activities remain integrated into school systems today, especially in Career and Technology Education (CTE) programs.

In special education, the term "career assessment" emerged with the career education movement and was associated with assessing students with disabilities to prepare for life roles such as independent living, social/personal, and vocational skills (Sitlington et al., 2010). Career assessment was defined "a developmental process beginning at the elementary-school level and continuing through adulthood" in a position paper for the Division on Career Development (Sitlington, Brolin, Clark, & Vacanti, 1985, p. 3). The idea of preparing students with disabilities for multiple life roles to work, live, and learn in the community remains evident in the IDEA 2004 definition of transition services.

As students with more significant disabilities participated in neighborhood schools and supported employment in the community during the 1980s and 1990s, the traditional methods of vocational evaluation or assessment (i.e., work samples, standardized tests) were replaced with a greater focus on situational assessments in the community (Inge & Moon, 2006). Person-centered planning, ecological assessments, and community-based instruction yielded more useful assessment data to assist students and families planning transition services and postsecondary goals. These methods remain important components of TA today (Sax & Thoma, 2002). The need for ongoing assessment in the community is especially critical for young adults who remain in the school system until age 21 and need to plan for supports and services to work, live, and go to college (Neubert, Moon, & Grigal, 2004; Walker, Updhold, Richter, & Test, 2010).

Just as career assessment was proposed to address the information needs of career education, TA addresses the information needs of transition services. In 1990 the IDEA required special educators to include a statement of services with a coordinated set of activities as part of the IEP process for students with disabilities by age 16. Post-school outcomes for students were to be based on the students' needs and interests. Unlike the vocational evaluation or assessment programs funded through CTE legislation, special educators were responsible for assessing students and transition services through the IEP process. The Council for Exceptional Children (CEC, 2009) has included skills and competencies related to career education, vocational assessment, interagency collaboration, and transition services in its Professional Standards for special educators over the past two decades.

By 1997, the (renamed) Division on Career Development and Transition (DCDT) endorsed a position paper that defined TA as an ongoing process of collecting data that focused on a student's needs, preferences, and interests as they related to working, educational, living, and personal and social environments. In addition "assessment data serve as the common thread in the transition process and form the basis for defining goals and services to be included in the Individualized Education Program (IEP)" (Sitlington, Neubert, & Leconte, 1997, pp. 70–71). This definition was expanded by Sitlington, Neubert, Begun, Lombard, & Leconte, (2007, pp. 2–3) to the following:

> an ongoing process of collecting information on the student's strengths, needs, preferences, and interests as they relate to the demands of current and future living, learning, and working environments. This process should begin in middle school and continue until the student graduates or exits high school. Information from this process should be used to drive the IEP and transition planning process and to develop the Summary of Performance document detailing the student's academic and functional performance and post-secondary goals.

This definition addresses the requirements for TA in IDEA 2004 and provides the foundation for the TA model—*Making the Match* (Sitlington et al., 2007). This model incorporates a conceptual framework of assessing students (the individual domain), assessing environments (the ecological domain), and making the match between students and their ecologies (the congruence domain) (Leconte, 2006). The section on TA methods in this chapter is adapted from this model.

IDEA 2004

IDEA 2004 provides the IEP team with the strongest language to conduct TA and to use the results/data when planning transition services and postsecondary outcomes for students with disabilities. While many states begin the transition process at age 14, IDEA 2004 mandates a student's IEP must be updated annually after age 16 and include:

- Measurable postsecondary goals that are based on age-appropriate transition assessment related to training, education, employment, and independent living skills;
- Transition services including courses of study needed for students to reach the goals.

Transition services must also include: (a) coordinated activities that focus on a results-oriented process, (b) the academic and functional achievement of the student to move from school to post-school activities, and (c) be based on the student's needs, strengths, preferences, and interests (IDEA, 2004). This definition of transition services also reinforces the need for students to develop self-determination skills and to have a voice in identifying their post-school goals. Carter, Trainor, Sun, & Owens (2009) further note the that TA should allow a student to explore and to focus on strengths rather than deficits.

IDEA 2004 also implies the need for ongoing assessment in the Summary of Performance (SOP). Students with disabilities must exit the school system with an SOP as they graduate or exit due to exceeding the eligible age limit of the state. Leconte (2006) posits that the SOP provides an updated and improved way to transfer TA information to postsecondary providers. The SOP must include a summary of the student's academic and functional performance along with recommendations on how to assist him or her in meeting postsecondary goals (IDEA, 2004). While state education agencies determine the format and name of the SOP, guidelines emphasize the need to use and update TA data (Kochhar-Bryant & Izzo, 2006; Sitlington et al., 2010). The intent is for students and families, VR counselors, adult agency personnel, and college disability providers to use the SOP in planning services, accommodations, and supports once the student exits the school system (Izzo & Kochhar-Bryant, 2006; Shaw, 2006).

Conceptualizing Age-Appropriate Transition

There is little federal guidance in terms of what constitutes "age-appropriate TA" for adolescents with disabilities. IDEA 2004 does not include a specific definition for this term but does state that a student's measurable postsecondary goals and course of study needed to reach the goals be based on age-appropriate TA. A review of the Final Regulations for IDEA 2004 indicates a number of comments requesting clarification on this term such as: when TA should begin so that transition services could be addressed by a student's 16th birthday, what methods to include under TA, and how methods might differ for students by age and type of disability (U.S. Department of Education, OSEP, 2006). While no further clarifications were included in the Final Regulations, OSEP did explain its reasoning. To address when TA should begin, it was noted that Section 614 required transition services be included in a student's IEP no later than age 16 and that "the Act does not require transition planning or TA, as recommended by some commenters" (U.S. Department of Education, p. 46667). In terms of the types of methods used in TA, OSEP said there was no need to clarify "… because the specific transition assessments used to determine appropriate measurable post-secondary goals will depend of the individual needs of the child, and are, therefore, best left to States and districts to determine on an individual basis."

However, there is little clarification at the state level regarding the "hows and whys" of TA. In a survey of state education agencies, Morningstar and Liss (2008) found only five (of 36 respondents) had developed policy or guidance for educators. Although there is agreement in the field that TA must be an ongoing process, Morningstar and Liss found that 13 states had identified a specific timeframe for conducting TAs. This varied from annually, to students in middle school, to part of the triennial process. The authors concluded, "It is unclear how well secondary special education teachers understand the significance of a systematic TA process (p. 53)." Similar results have been documented when special educators are surveyed about their knowledge of or use of TAs (e.g., Thoma, Held, & Sadler, 2002; Zhang, Ivester, Chen, & Katsiyannis, & Zhang, 2005).

These findings are unfortunate as vocational, career, or TA have long been identified as a necessary competency area in preparing secondary special educators and transition specialists (e.g., Anderson et al., 2004; Morningstar, Kim, & Clark, 2008). In addition, vocational or TA have also been recognized as a domain, best practice, or component of secondary transition programs (Benitez, Morningstar, & Frey, 2009; Kohler & Field, 2003; Landmark, Ju, & Zhang, 2010). Finally, when students with disabilities are taught to identify their needs, strengths, preferences, and interests and set goals through self-determination instruction, they are able to participate actively in their IEP meetings and to use assessment results in developing the SOP (Wehmeyer, 2002; Woods Sylverster, & Martin, 2010).

Indicator 13

IDEA 2004 requires each state to develop and implement a state performance plan that involves collecting data annually on 20 indicators. Indictor 13 requires that states report the percentage of youth ages 16 and above with an IEP that includes appropriate measurable postsecondary goals updated annually and based upon an age-appropriate TA and transition services, including courses of study, that will reasonably enable the student to meet those postsecondary goals, and annual IEP goals related to the student's transition services needs (20 U.S.C. 1416(a)(3)(B)).

To assist states with collecting this information, the National Secondary Technical Assistance Transition Center (NSTTAC, 2007) developed the *Indicator 13 Checklist, Instructions for Completing NSTTAC Indicator Checklist*, and a fact sheet on age-appropriate TA. The checklist requires a review of students' IEPs and includes the following questions: "Is there evidence that the measurable post-secondary goal(s) were based on age-appropriate transition? Is the use of TA(s) for the post-secondary goals(s) mentioned in the IEP or evident in the student's file?" In addition, NSTTAC's fact sheet on age-appropriate TA provides guidance and instructions concerning what type of assessment information all students should have in their files (e.g., current psychological data, state-mandated assessment scores, grades and progress notes, and career interests inventory or adaptive behavior scale. Guidelines are also provided for information that should be included in students' files if their goal is related to postsecondary education or independent living.

In summary, while TA for adolescents with disabilities has evolved from a variety of disciplines, it is now the responsibility of the special educator and the IEP team under IDEA 2004. Under this law, TA must be age-appropriate and students' post-school outcomes and course of study are to be based on the data gathered through this assessment process. NSTTAC provides guidance on how age-appropriate TA must be documented in the IEP and/or student file. While the TA models and methods described in the next section center on adolescents with disabilities, the concepts and practices can be applied to all adolescents engaged in the transition planning process.

TA Models

Given there is little federal or state guidance on age-appropriate TA, it is important that educators, students, and families have access to the available resources. There are a number of position papers, manuals, and textbooks that can assist school personnel to: (a) identify models or frameworks to organize the age-appropriate TA process, (b) identify and select methods for conducting assessments, and (c) summarize and use the data from TA in meaningful ways.

Models have been published in books specifically on TA (e.g., Miller, Lombard, & Corbey, 2007; Sax & Thoma, 2002; Sitlington et al., 2007) and in chapters of transition textbooks (e.g., Flexer, Baer, Luft, & Simmons, 2008; Kochhar-Bryant & Greene 2009; Sitlington et al., 2010). Models and manuals on the Internet can also provide information on TA and many are available for a free download. The *Age-Appropriate TA Toolkit* (definition, models, and methods) is available at the NSTTAC website (Walker, Kortering, Fowler, & Rowe, 2010) along with an annotated bibliography to help educators identify TA sources (Rowe, 2009). Two additional manuals that provide strategies for TA along with career planning include: *Career Planning Starts with Assessments* (Timmons, Podmostko, Bremer, Lavin, & Wills, 2005) and *Career Investigations for Transitioning Youth* (Mattis, Taymans, & Anderson, 2010). There are also several state department of education websites that depict TA models or recommend methods. For example, the Iowa Model for Age-Appropriate Transition Assessment (n.d.) provides a model planning process for teachers and methods to conduct assessment. The Virginia Department of Education has an *Assessment Transition Packet* at http://www.vcu.edu/ttac/transition/assessment.shtm. Finally, it is also important to consider the types of career development activities that are offered to all students within a school system and integrate these into the TA process (Carter, Trainor, Cakiroglu, Sweeden, & Owens, 2010; Fives, 2008; Mattis et al., 2010; Sitlington et al., 2007). Without a model or framework, TA may become a compliance issue for the IEP team (e.g., a checkbox that indicates the student has taken an interest inventory or participated in an interview) rather than a process that allows students the opportunity to prepare for realistic postsecondary goals. The common threads among age-appropriate TA models are to:

- Assess adolescents' needs, strengths, interests, and preferences over time;
- Plan for additional assessments for the student and ensure that information on current and potential environments also be collected;
- Use multiple methods to collect and triangulate assessment data;
- Summarize and profile the results for students, families, and other stakeholders;
- Use the results to guide the IEP planning process for transition services;
- Build collaboration among school, adult service, college, and community personnel to use the results of the TA process.

Transition Assessment Methods

While models vary, the methods used within these TA frameworks overlap. When selecting methods, the student's age/grade, postsecondary goals, career maturity, exposure to secondary programs and courses, and the community must be taken into account. To comply with age-appropriate requirement, TA methods should obviously vary for middle school students (e.g., Neubert, 2003; Repetto, Webb, Neubert, & Curran, 2006), for high school students (Sitlington & Clark, 2007), and for students ready to exit the school system (Dukes, Shaw, & Madaus, 2007; Roessler, Hennessey, Hogan, & Savickas, 2009). One approach to individualizing and selecting methods for TA is to develop a plan for each student or to answer a series of questions that guide the IEP process. Examples include *Sample Questions To Ask During TA* (Sitlington et al., 2007), a *Transition Checklist* (Thoma, Bartholomew, & Scott, 2009), and questions to answer for the IEP process from the Iowa Model for Transition Assessment (n.d).

Selecting age-appropriate methods for TA can be a daunting task and only a brief description of selected methods follows. For addition descriptions of methods along with the publishers of standardized instruments and informal assessments (checklists, questionnaires, or environmental analysis forms) readers are referred to: Clark, 2007; Clark & Patton, 2006; Clark, Patton, & Moulton, 2000; Miller et al., 2007; Sax & Thoma, 2002; Sitlington, Clark, & Patton, 2008; Sitlington et al., 2007; Sitlington et al., 2010; Synatschk, Clark, & Patton, 2008; Timmons et al., 2005; Walker, Kortering, Fowler, & Rowe, 2010). In the following section, methods for assessing students and environments are briefly described using *Making the Match* (Leconte, 2006; Sitlington et al., 2007).

Assessing Students—the Individual Domain

Methods for assessing students generally include: background reviews, interviews, standardized and informal assessments, behavior observation, performance or work samples, situational assessments, and person-centered planning. A variety of methods must be used to assess a student and to triangulate the findings about the student.

Background Reviews

One of the first sources of information for TA should be obtained from a review of the student's records. Gathering relevant background information is a skill that all beginning special educators should have according to the Council for Exceptional Children common core standards (2009). Depending on the student's age, postsecondary goals, and characteristics, this review can include:

- Observations from previous teachers, support staff, and agency staff;
- Transition-related goals, academic progress, and functional skills from the IEP;
- Results of formal assessments (e.g., achievement, IQ, adaptive behavior);
- GPA, attendance patterns, discipline referrals, courses taken;
- Results of state assessments and accommodations recommended/used;
- Accommodations, supports, technology used in content classes or the community;
- Medical information (e.g., allergies, medications, endurance);
- Results of interest inventories, career exploration activities;
- Functional behavior assessments, behavior intervention plans;
- Assistive technology evaluations/assessments;
- Assessments relevant to postsecondary goals (e.g., ACT; ASVAB; SAT).

A background review provides practitioners with a good idea of what is known about the student and what additional TA questions need to be asked to ensure the student progresses toward measurable postsecondary outcomes. For example, a 14-year-old student transferring to middle school with incomplete records may need psychological assessment to update academic and functional skills and an interview to ascertain future interests and goals. For a 12th grade student with a goal of postsecondary education, a GPA of 3.2, and the results of a college entrance exam, it is most important to analyze a variety of postsecondary education environments to determine the match between the student and the requirements and supports of the institution. An interview with the family would be helpful in determining expectations for the student to go to college (e.g., financial, distance from home, type of institution). Finally, recommendations for accommodations and support should be recorded on the SOP.

School personnel should choose a format(s) to summarize or profile the key results of the background review to serve as the foundation for summarizing TA results (Izzo & Kochhar-Bryant, 2006; Neubert & Moon, 2000). A transition profile or SOP also provides a vehicle for sharing assessment data with school and community personnel. To meet the requirements for Indicator 13, the results of assessments need to be summarized on a student's IEP, profile, or school file.

Interviews

The next source of information should be from the student and the family if possible. Families play a major role in shaping adolescents' career aspirations and goals for the future (Lindstrom, Doren, Metheny, Johnson, & Zane, 2007; Wandry & Pleet, 2004) and there are many formats and questions to guide the interview process. The results of the background review can be valuable in framing additional questions to ask the student or family or to request missing information.

An interview with a student should include questions related to expressed interests and preferences along with his or her knowledge of courses of study for the secondary years

(Neubert, 2003). Interviewing the student should provide the IEP team with the best source of information about a student's dreams, wishes, and post-school goals for living, learning, and working in the community. Interviewing the family should facilitate an understanding of the cultural and economic expectations a student might face after school for living and working independently and if the goals of the student and family are similar. Interviews with a student's teachers, counselor, support staff, or employer can also provide information on how the adolescent functions in school or the community. This information should be added to the student's file, transition profile, or SOP. NSTTAC (2007) recommends that informal interviews with the student and an interest inventory or questionnaire to determine student interests and preferences meet the basic requirements of age-appropriate TA in terms of Indicator 13.

Standardized and Informal Assessments

Most students with disabilities will have information on academic and functional skills in their IEPs and/or a psychological report in their files. While this information should be obtained in a background review, several states reported they would try to link TA to a student's triennial evaluation (Morningstar & Liss, 2008). The IEP team should work with the school psychologists and counselors in updating assessments and in identifying vocational interests and aptitudes over time (Fives, 2008). Such collaborative efforts can free special educators to focus on other methods of TA and to summarize the results of the process.

There are standardized instruments and informal assessments (checklists, questionnaires, rating scales) specifically developed for TA and planning transition services. These should be selected after a review of available resources and with a student's age, goals, and academic abilities in mind. In general, categories of assessments used in TA include the following: interest inventories, self-determination assessments, aptitude tests, career maturity assessments, transition planning inventories, adaptive behavior and independent living skill assessments, social skills or behavior rating scales, work behaviors, and personality or preference inventories.

Morningstar & Liss (2008) found that half of the 36 state education agencies responding to a survey indicated that specific instruments for TA would be recommended to educators. These included the Enderle Severson Transition Rating Scale, social skills rating forms, the Life Centered Career Education competency based assessments, self-determination assessments, the SAT, the Next Step Curriculum student portfolio, learning styles, and job analyses.

Curriculum-Based Assessment

Curriculum-based assessment (CBA) is an approach rather than a specific method. CBA is often teacher developed and is based on the curriculum the student encounters in various classes. Examples of curriculum-based assessment techniques include criterion-referenced testing, domain-referenced testing, curriculum-based measurement, and portfolio assessment. CBA can be valuable in tracking a student's progress in academic content areas as well as in CTE courses. This information can be valuable for determining accommodations and supports needed in postsecondary education or the workplace.

Behavior Observation

Behavior observation approaches are often used in gathering assessment data as a student participates in specific courses (their course of study), job tryouts or situational assessments, community-based instruction, or performance/work samples. Observing and recording a student's behavior over time in a variety of settings provides valuable information on interests, preferences, strengths, and needs at school, home, and the community. Observing a student's behavior also allows someone to document the student's use of or need for accommodations, technology, and support from one class (or environment) to the next. There are a number of strategies that can be used to observe and record behavior such as narrative reports, time sampling, trials to performance criterion, and time motion studies (Sitlington et al., 2007).

Performance / Work Samples

Work samples are often used as part of the assessment process in VR settings (Power, 2006). Work samples or work sample systems can be standardized and normed, often according to a group of workers who perform similar tasks in employment settings. Work samples generally have a set of directions, tasks, materials, and key behaviors to observe.

While some school systems may use formal or commercial work samples, it is more common to find a teacher-made performance or work sample that involves the tasks, materials, and tools that are similar to those used in the actual living, learning, or working setting. The demands of the environment (e.g., work tasks, independent living tasks, and community functioning skills) can be varied while recording behaviors such as interest, preference, skill level, organization of materials and tasks, and social interactions occurs. To determine the tasks to be included in the sample, it is important to conduct an analysis of the actual living, learning, or work setting that will be the focus of the sample. The key to administering work samples is to observe and document information concerning the student's level of interest, attention to tasks, and requests for assistance or clarification in addition to actual performance of the tasks.

Situational Assessment

Situational assessments are often used in school and rehabilitation settings to observe behaviors, skills, and interests in a specific environment. For example, a situational assessment could be arranged for a student to sell snacks or supplies in the school store. Situational assessments are often conducted in the community to determine interests, preferences, needs, and strengths at various employment sites or as part of community-based instruction.

To record behaviors, school personnel may use informal checklists or develop skill lists relevant to the site. There are also standardized instruments for situational assessments, more commonly used in rehabilitation settings. In a review of instruments that targeted vocational functioning, Peer and Tunhula (2010) found that common domains in situational assessment included social skills, work quality, work habits, personal presentation, and confidence/initiative. The key is to determine work preferences by documenting observations about the student at various sites and/or to ask the student about interests or preferences for each site (Cobigo, Morin, & Lachapelle, 2007).

Situational assessment can also relate to independent living environments. For example, how does the student navigate a transportation system after training has been provided? (Moon, Luedtke, & Halloran-Tornquist, 2010). Does the student enjoy spending a night in dormitory on a college campus with a sibling or a friend? Is the student able to use a cell phone if he or she is separated from a group or individual who is leading a community outing?

The advantage of situational assessment is that students can experience environments outside of the school and the home. In both performance samples and situational assessments, it is critical to systematically observe and record student behavior and skills. The data collected can then be used in planning and placement decisions concerning further situational assessment sites, types of programs or courses to consider for placement, and accommodations needed in specific situations. Situational assessments provide data to discuss at the student's IEP meeting or to add to the student's profile or SOP, such as observed preferences and interests, strengths and skills performed, interpersonal and social skills, and needs in school, work, and community sites.

Person-Centered Planning (PCP)

Individual choice is a primary policy theme reflected in IDEA 2004 and VR legislation. PCP approaches (e.g., PATH, MAPS, person futures planning) allow for ongoing planning that centers on the ideas and contributions of students, their families, and others who provide support to the student in classes, at home, and in the community. PCP provides an opportunity for the student and family to explore ideas for living, working, and learning in a group situation with ideas and support from a variety of people.

Using a PCP approach as part of the TA process allows for students and families to actively participate in the planning for the future and to identify cultural, economic, and community variables that may impact transition planning (Croke & Thompson, 2011; Trainor, 2007). The PACER center, the Minnesota Parent and Training Center (http://www.pacer.org/tatra/resources/personal.asp), identifies resources and guidelines for using PCP.

Assessing Environments—the Environmental Domain

To help students identify postsecondary goals as part of the IEP planning process, educators must also consider the requirements of current environments (secondary courses and activities) and future environments as they transition from school to adult life. This includes opportunities for postsecondary education, employment, adult services, and living in a community. An analysis of current and future environments will depend on an individual's postsecondary goals. While this type of assessment is probably less familiar to personnel in school systems, it is commonly used in rehabilitation, adult services, and in secondary community-based programs. While some environmental analyses will be specific to a student or small group of students based on their postsecondary goals (e.g., attend a small postsecondary institution near relatives in the Midwest), other environmental analyses, such as a Community Analysis, will be applicable to many students once it has been completed. Examples of informal assessments for collecting information about job sites, the community, secondary and postsecondary education programs, and adult services can be found in Clark, 2007; Miller et al., 2007; Sitlington et al., 2008; Sitlington et al., 2007; Sitlington et al., 2010; Synatschk et al., 2008. These forms should be easy for school personnel to modify depending on the needs of a student or a specific community. When possible, students and their families should participate in collecting these data when taking a tour of an adult agency or at a college.

Analysis of Secondary Courses

Analysis of secondary courses involves analyzing current environments or courses of study that are an important part of TA. This can include collecting information on CTE programs, college readiness courses, work-based learning opportunities, elective classes, community-based instruction, programs for students ages 18–21 in the community, diploma options, and extracurricular activities (Sitlington et al., 2010). Collecting and compiling information on programs, courses, and opportunities within specific school systems is one of the easiest environments for educators to analyze. Much of the information is available on the Internet via the school system or can be obtained from guidance counselors, school psychologists, CTE teachers, coaches, and other related school personnel. A school analysis can include the following:

- Programs and courses (dual enrollment, advanced placement courses (AP), international baccalaureate courses (IB)) for students interested in college, guidance department activities to assist students explore and apply to college;
- Programs and courses for employment preparation such as internships, work experience, career development courses, volunteer experiences, CTE programs that have a work-based component;
- Electives (and sequence of courses) for students interested in art, drama, music, photography, foreign languages, technology, ROTC; opportunities for after school or summer exploratory programs in the school system;
- Transition specialists in the school system to assist students with disabilities in plan-specific transition services; transition fairs; supports or programs on college or community campuses for students ages 18–21;
- Clubs, teams, and extracurricular at school.

Collecting and sharing information on opportunities with the school system is a great chance for students to engage in career exploration activities, such as visiting CTE courses, selecting content and elective courses that match their interests, and participating in activities outside the classroom (Neubert, 2003). While this process may be easy for some students and their families, for others it needs be highly structured to ensure all are familiar with the structure of the school system, graduation requirements, and courses of study to prepare for postsecondary goals.

Analysis of Work Environments

Task and job analysis techniques are methods to assess current and future environments related to a student's goal for employment (e.g., situational assessments, work sample, jobs in the community). A job analysis involves analyzing the demands of a work environment by conducting a task analysis of the job duties or obtaining a list of the essential functions of the job. It also includes obtaining information on where the work is done and under what conditions (e.g., amount of supervision, production requirements, culture of the workplace, and transportation near the worksite). This information should be collected from interviewing the employer, observing the worksite, and/or obtaining a description of the essential functions of the job from the employer or human resource personnel.

For a student who is interested in working during school or after leaving the school system, it is important to consider the demands of different workplaces in relation to an individual's interests and preferences along with strengths (reading and math ability, dexterity, endurance) and needs (accommodations, support personnel). Once the information is collected, it should be compared with information collected on the student to determine if there is a match between the individual and the work environment. This also provides a way to determine if there is a need for a student to have accommodations, support, job carving, or assistive technology devices to do the required job tasks and to manage social interactions in the workplace.

Assessing Communities

The *Community Assessment Form* was designed for teachers, students, and families to identify the following:

- Community resources (recreation and religious programs);
- Adult services (VR, Developmental Disabilities agencies, social security office, independent living options);

- Employment resources such as One-Stop Centers;
- Postsecondary education (universities, career colleges, adult education programs);
- Transportation options (Neubert & Moon, 2006; Sitlington et al., 2010).

While time-consuming initially, once the Community Assessment is completed it requires only periodic updating. In addition, much of the information can be found on the internet before venturing into the community to complete the form. A Community Assessment works well for teachers working with students with disabilities who remain in school until age 21 or who require adult services from a number of service systems, such as VR, social services, and mental health services. It can be duplicated for teachers across a school system and also shared with students and families at IEP meetings when planning transition services.

For some students and families with intellectual disabilities, it may be important to analyze a number of adult agencies in more detail before selecting a provider for ongoing services (Moon, Simonson, & Neubert, 2011). McDonough & Revell (2010) suggest exploring a range of employment support options for individuals with autism through VR, community rehabilitation programs, developmental disabilities agencies, one-stop career centers, and work incentive projects. Neubert (2010) developed a form to use in collecting information from specific community rehabilitation programs or adult service providers.

Analyzing Postsecondary Education Options

While many adolescents with and without disabilities express a desire to go to college after high school, the number who enroll and complete a credential is less than optimal (Radford, Berkner, Wheeless, & Shepherd, 2010). Exploring a variety of postsecondary options such as community colleges, career schools that offer degrees or certificates, universities and colleges, on-the-job training programs, adult education programs, and training through the military is an important part of TA. A thorough analysis of postsecondary education options should provide a student with realistic information about the program or institution so he or she can determine what is the best match based on their needs, strengths, interests, and preferences. Students and families should be encouraged to collect this information when possible and information compiled by school personnel can be used for many students.

Key information to collect in analyzing postsecondary education environments includes: (a) college entrance exams and other admission requirements; (b) financial considerations; (c) majors and programs available; (d) size of the institution/program; (e) distance from family and other supports; (f) options for residential living; and (g) support services available including tutoring services, study skills assistance, writing center assistance, disability services, career and counseling services; (h) options for students with intellectual and other disabilities. Sitlington et al. (2008) provide forms for analyzing and preparing for postsecondary education. Additional resources for students with intellectual disabilities include Getzel and Wehman (2005) and Grigal and Hart (2010).

The Critical Piece: Using TA Data to Make a Match

There are a number of reoccurring concerns related to using transition assessment data. One centers on how the results of the TA process are used in the IEP process and the data are linked to planning postsecondary goals (Carter et al., 2009; Leconte, 2006; Mazzotti et al., 2009). Even with the recent focus on age-appropriate TA in IDEA 2004, Morningstar and Liss (2008) found only one state department of education that required teachers to update secondary students' IEPs with data collected through the transition assessment process. Another concern is how to ensure that students understand why they are participating in age-appropriate TA and how this process ties into planning transition services at IEP meetings (Kortering & Braziel, 2008). A continuing issue relates to summarizing relevant data in the SOP or profile as a student exits the school system; is this information used in the next environment to inform employers, college personnel, or adult providers about the student's interests, preferences, strengths, and needs?

During the high school years, TA should be structured to assist students and their families to understand the demands of different postsecondary environments and then determine if there is a match between the individual and the potential environment. Sitlington et al. (2007) suggest that making this match requires consideration of three options. In the event that there is a good match between the student and the target environment, the IEP team should work with the student to gain entrance into a specific secondary course, plan a course of study, or apply to the future environment (e.g., employment agency, college, technical training institution or adult service agency). This information is then included in the student's IEP and the SOP. If the match is for a secondary course of study, the student's progress is monitored and reviewed at least yearly at the IEP meeting. Changes to the course of study or postsecondary goals can be made in the event that a student changes his or her mind about postsecondary options. Thoma et al. (2009) provide guidance and forms for incorporating universal design into this part of the transition process.

The second option involves the need to look at the student and the requirements of the target environment and determine if there are supports, accommodations, services or technology that can help bridge the gap. This can also include additional courses, related services, assistive technology, technology, universal design for learning, job coaches, educational coaches, job carving and other supports through schools and adult agencies. For example, Wehmeyer et al. (2006) found that technology and universal design can enhance employment outcomes. Identifying and planning appropriate supports and services enhance college participation for students with intellectual disabilities (Grigal & Hart, 2010).

In the event that the student, family, and IEP team determine there is not a good match even with additional technology, supports or accommodations, the TA process continues. Option 3 involves collecting more information on the student and analyzing different environments before reconvening the student, family, and IEP team to use the making-the-match process again. If students with disabilities and their families are taught the process of matching an individual's profile (needs, strengths, interests, and preferences) to a variety of possible environments during the secondary years, they will likely have learned a life-long skill.

Summary

Assessment has long been identified as an important practice in special education, CTE, and vocational rehabilitation services. Despite the many kinds of assessments in which adolescents may participate during the secondary school years, an ongoing problem in the field is to synthesize the results of various assessments and to use the data for planning secondary courses and experiences that will lead to optimal postsecondary outcomes. Providing appropriate supports for all students through universal design for learning, technology, career development activities, and related school services is needed to ensure students are career and college ready for opportunities in the 21st century.

For students with disabilities, the recent focus on using age-appropriate TA in IDEA 2004 to determine a student's postsecondary goals and a course of study provides an additional avenue to enhance post-school outcomes. The TA ideas, models and methods described in this chapter should assist students, their families, and school systems in planning a course of study to reach measurable post-school goals, monitoring a student's progress toward those goals, and ensuring that accommodations and supports, universal design, technology, career development, and related services are provided to enhance success in school and in the future. Continuing challenges in the field are to make sure students, educators, and families are aware of and use available resources to enhance the transition assessment process and for researchers to document evidence-based practices and to demonstrate how the TA process contributes to more successful measurable postsecondary outcomes for adolescents with disabilities

References

Achieve, Inc. (2005). *Rising to the challenge: Are high school graduates prepared for college and work? A study of recent high school graduates, college instructors, and employers.* Washington, DC: Author.

ACT (2010). *The condition of college and career readiness.* Retrieved from http://www.act.org/research/policymakers/cccr10/index.html?utm_source=researchlink&utm_medium=web&utm_campaign=cccr10

Adami, H., & Neubert, D. A. (1991). A follow-up of vocational assessment recommendations and placement in secondary vocational education programs for students with disabilities. *Vocational Evaluation and Work Adjustment Bulletin, 24*(3), 101–107.

Albright, L., & Cobb, R. B. (1988). Curriculum-based vocational assessment: A concept whose time has come. *The Journal of Vocational Special Needs Education, 10,* 13–16.

Anderson, D., Kleinhammer-Tramill, P. J., Morningstar, M. E., Lehmann, J., Bassett, D. S., Kohler, P., et al. (2004). What's happening in personnel preparation in transition? A national survey. *Career Development for Exceptional Individuals, 26,* 145–160.

Benitez, D. T., Morningstar, M. E., & Frey, B. B. (2009). A multistate survey of special education teachers' perceptions of their transition competencies. *Career Development for Exceptional Individuals, 32,* 6–16.

Carter, E. W., Trainor, A. A., Cakiroglu, O., Sweeden, B., & Owens, L. A. (2010). Availability of and access to career development activities for transition-age youth. *Career Development for Exceptional Individuals, 33,* 13–24.

Carter, E. W., Trainor, A. A., Sun, Y., & Owens, L. (2009). Assessing the transition related strengths and needs of adolescents with high-incidence disabilities. *Exceptional Children, 76,* 74–94.

Clark, G. M. (2007). *Assessment for transitions planning* (2nd ed.). Austin, TX: PRO-ED.

Clark, G. M. & Patton, J. R. (2006). *TPI-Transition planning inventory (Updated Version): Administration and resource guide.* Austin, TX: PRO-ED.

Clark, G. M., Patton, J. R., & Moulton, L. R. (2000). *Informal assessments for transition planning.* Austin, TX: PRO-ED.

Cobb, R. B., & Neubert, D. A. (1998). Vocational education: Emerging vocationalism. In F. Rusch & J. Chadsey (Eds.), *Beyond high school: Transition from school to work* (pp. 101–126). Boston, MA: Chadsworth Publishing Co.

Cobigo, V., Morin, D., & Lachapelle, Y. (2007). Assessing work task preferences among persons with intellectual disabilities: An integrative review of literature. *Education and Training in Developmental Disabilities, 42,* 286–300.

Council for Exceptional Children (CEC). (2009). *What every special educator must know: The international standards for the preparation and certification of special educators* (6th ed.). Arlington, VA: Author.

Croke, E. E., & Thompson, A. B. (2011). Person centered planning in a transition program for Bronx youth. *Children and Youth Sciences Review.* doi:10.1016/jchildyouth.2010.11.25

Donoso, O. A., Hernandez, B., & Horin, E. V. (2010). Use of psychological tests within vocational rehabilitation. *Journal of Vocational Rehabilitation, 32,* 191–200. DOI: 10:3233/JVR-2010-0509

Dorn, S. (2010). The political dilemmas of formative assessment. *Exceptional Children, 76,* 325–337.

Dougherty, C. (2010) *Using the right data to determine if high school interventions are working to prepare students for college and careers.* Washington, DC: National High School Center at American Institutes for Research. Retrieved from http://www.betterhighschools.org/

Dougherty, C., Mellor, L., & Smith, N. (2006*). Identifying appropriate college readiness standards for all students.* Austin, TX: National Center for Education Excellence.

Dukes, L. L., Shaw, S. F., & Madaus, J. W. (2007). How to complete a summary of performance for students exiting to post-secondary education. *Assessment for Effective Intervention, 32*(3), 143–159.

Fives, C. J. (2008). Vocational assessment of secondary students with disabilities and the school psychologist. *Psychology in the Schools, 46,* 508–544.

Flexer, R. W., Baer, R. M., Luft, P., & Simmons, T. J. (2008). Transition planning for secondary students with disabilities (3rd ed.).

Getzel, E. E., & Wehman, P. (2005). *Going to college: Expanding opportunities for people with disabilities.* Baltimore, MD: Brookes Publishing.

Grigal, M., & Hart, D. (2010). *Think college!* Baltimore, MD: Brookes Publishing.

Hodgson, J. R., Lazarus, S. S., & Thurlow, M. L. (2010). *Characteristics of states' alternate assessments based on modified academic achievement standards in 2009-2010* (Synthesis Report 80). Minneapolis, MN: National Center on Educational Outcomes. Retrieved from http://www.cehd.umn.edu/NCEO/

Individuals with Disabilities Education Improvement Act of 2004 (IDEA), 20 U.S.C. § 1400 et seq. (2004).

Inge, K. J., & Moon, M. S. (2006). Vocational preparation and transition. In M.E. Snell, & F. Brown (Eds.). Instruction of students with severe disabilities (6th ed.). 569–609.

Iowa Model for Age-Appropriate Transition Assessment (n.d). Retrieved from http://transitionassessment.northcentralrrc.org/IowaModel.aspx

Izzo, M. V., & Kochhar-Bryant, C. A. (2006). Implementing the SOP for effective transition: Two case studies. *Career Development for Exceptional Individuals, 29,* 100–107.

Johnson, D. R., Stout, K. E., & Thurlow, M. L. (2009). Diploma options and perceived consequences for students with disabilities. *Exceptionality, 17*(3), 119–134.

Kochhar-Bryant, C. A., & Greene, G. (2009). *Pathways to successful transition for youth with disabilities: A developmental process* (2nd ed.). Upper Saddle River, NJ: Pearson.

Kochhar-Bryant, C. A., & Izzo, M. V. (2006). Access to post-high school services: Transition assessment and summary of performance. *Career Development for Exceptional Individuals, 29,* 70–89.

Kohler, P. D., & Field, S. (2003). Transition-focused education: Foundation for the future. *Journal of Special Education, 37,* 174–184.

Kortering, L., & Braziel, P. M. (2008). The use of vocational assessments: What do students have to say. *The Journal for At-Risk Issues,* 14 (2), 27–35.

Lamb, P. (2007). Implications of the summary of performance for vocational rehabilitation counselors. *Career Development for Exceptional Individuals, 30,* 3–12.

Landmark, L. J., Ju, S. J., & Zhang, D. (2010). Substantiated best practices in transition: Fifteen plus years later. *Career Development for Exceptional Individuals, 33,* 165–176. doi: 10.1177/0885728810376410.

Leconte, P. J. (2006). The evolution of career, vocational, and transition assessment: Implications for the summary of performance. *Career Development for Exceptional Individuals, 29,* 114–124.

Leconte, P. J. (1994). Vocational appraisal services: Evolution from multidisciplinary origins and applications to interdisciplinary practices. *Vocational Evaluation and Work Adjustment Bulletin, 27,* 119–127.

Lindstrom, L., Doren, B., Metheny, J., Johnson, P., & Zane, C. (2007). Transition to employment: Role of the family in career development. *Exceptional Children, 73,* 348–366.

Mattis, J., Taymans, J., & Anderson, L. (2010). *Career investigations for transitioning youth (CITY).* Washington DC: George Washington University, http://gsehd.gwu.edu/tse-city

Mazzotti, V. L., Rowe, D. A., Kelley, K. R., Test, D. W., Kohler, P. D., & Kortering, L. J. (2009). Linking transition assessment and post-secondary goals. *Teaching Exceptional Children, 42,* 44–51.

McDonough, J. T., & Revell, G. (2010). Accessing employment supports in the adult system for transitioning youth with autism spectrum disorders. *Journal of Vocational Rehabilitation, 32,* 89–100.

Miller, R. J., Lombard, R. C., & Corbey, S. A. (2007). *Transition assessment: Planning transition assessment and IEP development for youth with mild and moderate disabilities.* Boston, MA: Pearson.

Moon, M. S., Luedtke, E. M., & Halloran-Tornquist, E. (2010). *Getting around town: Teaching community mobility skills to students with disabilities.* Arlington, VA: Council for Exceptional Children.

Moon, M. S., Simonson, M., & Neubert, D. A. (2011). Perceptions of supported employment providers: What students with developmental disabilities, families, and educators need to know for transition planning. *Education and Training in Autism and Developmental Disabilities,*

Morningstar, M. E., & Liss, J. M. (2008). A preliminary investigation of how states are responding to the transition assessment requirements under IDEIA 2004. *Career Development for Exceptional Children, 31,* 48–55.

Morningstar, M. E., Kim, K., & Clark, G. M. (2008). Evaluating a transition personnel preparation program: Identifying transition competencies of practitioners. *Teacher Education and Special Education, 31,* 47–58.

National Council on Disability (2008). *The Rehabilitation Act: Outcomes for transitioning youth.* Washington, DC: Author.

National Disability Rights Network (2011.). *Segregated and exploited: The failure of the disability system to provide quality work.* Retrieved from http://www.napas.org/

National Secondary Transition Technical Assistance Center (NSTTAC) (2007). *Indicator 13 Training Materials*. Charlotte, NC: Author. Retrieved from http://www.nsttac.org/tm_materials/y5ageappro-priatenessassessment.aspx

Neubert, D. A. (2003). The role of assessment in the transition to adult life process for individuals with disabilities. *Exceptionality, 11*, 63–71.

Neubert, D. A. (2010). *Community rehabilitation program (adult service provider) analysis*. College Park, MD: University of Maryland. http://www.education.umd.edu/oco/

Neubert, D. A., & Moon, M. S. (2000). How a transition profile helps students prepare for life in the community. *Teaching Exceptional Children, 32*(2), 20–25.

Neubert, D. A., & Moon, M. S. (2006). *Community assessment*. College Park, MD: University of Maryland. http://www.education.umd.edu/oco/

Neubert, D. A., Moon, M. S., & Grigal, M. (2004). Activities of students with significant disabilities receiving services in post-secondary settings. *Education and Training in Developmental Disabilities, 39*(1), 16–25.

Newman, L., Wagner, M., Cameto, R., & Knokey, A. M. (2009). *The post-high school outcomes of youth with disabilities up to 4 years after high school. A report of findings from the National Longitudinal Transition Study-2 (NLTS2)* (NCSER 2009-3017). Retrieved from http://www.nlts2.org/reports/2009_04/nlts2_report_2009_04_complete.pdf

Payne-Tsoupros, K. (2010). No child left behind. Disincentives to focus instruction on students above the passing threshold. *Journal of Law & Education, 39*, 471–501.

Peer, J. A., & Tenhula, W. (2010). Assessment of vocational functioning in serious mental illness: A review of situational assessment and performance-based measures. *Journal of Vocational Rehabilitation, 32*, 175–189.

Power, P. W. (2006). *A guide to vocational assessment* (4th ed.). Austin, TX: PRO-ED.

Radford, A. W., Berkner, L., Wheeless, S. C., & Shepherd, B. (2010). *Persistence and attainment of 2003–04 beginning post-secondary students: After 6 years (NCES 2011-151)*. Washington, DC: National Center for Education Statistics. from http://nces.ed.gov/pubsearch

Rehabilitation Act Amendments of 1998, Title IV of PL 105–220 (Workforce Investment Act of 1998).

Repetto, J. B., Webb, K. W., Neubert, D. A., & Curran, C. (2006). *The middle school experience: Successful teaching and transition planning for diverse learners*. Austin, TX: PRO-ED.

Roessler, R. T., Hennessey, M. L. Hogan, E. M., & Savickas, S. (2009). Career assessment and planning strategies for post-secondary students with disabilities. *Journal of Post-secondary Education and Disability, 21*, 126–137.

Rowe, D. A. (2009). *Transition assessment annotated bibliography*. Retrieved National Secondary Transition Technical Center website: http://www.nsttac.org/

Sax, C. L., & Thoma, C. (2002). *Transition assessment: Wise practices for quality lives*. Baltimore, MD: Paul H. Brookes.

Shaw, S. (2006). Legal and policy perspectives on transition assessment and documentation. *Career Development for Exceptional Individuals, 29*, 108–113.

Sitlington, P. L., Brolin, D. E., Clark, G. M., & Vacanti, J. M. (1985). Career/vocational assessment in the public school setting: The position of the Division on Career Development. *Career Development for Exceptional Individuals, 8*, 3–6.

Sitlington, P. L., & Clark, G. M. (2007). The transition assessment process and IDEIA 2004. *Assessment for Effective Intervention, 32*, 133–142.

Sitlington, P. L., Clark, G. M., & Patton, J. R. (2008). *Informal assessments for transition: Post-secondary education and training*. Austin, TX: PRO-ED.

Sitlington, P. L., Neubert, D. A., Begun, W. H., Lombard, R. C., & Leconte, P. J. (2007). *Assess for success: A practitioner's handbook on transition assessment* (2nd ed.). Thousand Oaks, CA: Corwin Press.

Sitlington, P. L., Neubert, D. A., & Clark, G. (2010). *Transition education and services for adolescents with disabilities* (5th ed.). Boston, MA: Pearson: Allyn & Bacon.

Sitlington, P. L., Neubert, D. A., & Leconte, P. J. (1997). Transition assessment: The position of the Division on Career Development and Transition. *Career Development for Exceptional Individuals, 20*, 69–79.

Synatschk, K. O., Clark, G. M., & Patton, J. R. (2008). *Informal assessments for transition: Independent living and community participation*. Austin, TX: PRO-ED.

Thoma, C. A., Bartholomew, C. C. & Scott, L. A. (2009). *Universal design for transition: A roadmap for planning and instruction.* Baltimore, MD: Paul H. Brookes Publishing.

Thoma, C. A., Held, M. F., & Saddler, S. (2002). Transition assessment practices in Nevada and Arizona: Are they tied to best practices? *Focus on Autism and Other Developmental Disabilities, 17*, 242–250.

Timmons, J., Podmostko, M., Bremer, C., Lavin, D., & Wills, J. (2005). *Career planning begins with assessment: A guide for professionals serving youth with educational & career development challenges* (rev. ed.). Washington, D.C.: National Collaborative on Workforce and Disability for Youth. Available at www.ncwdyouth.info/

Trainor, A., (2007). Person-centered planning in two culturally distinct communities: Responding to divergent needs and preferences. *Career Development for Exceptional Individuals, 30*, 92–103.

U.S. Department of Education (2006). Assistance to states for the education of children with disabilities and preschool grants for children with disabilities: Final rule. *Federal Register, 71*(156), 46539–46845.

Walker, A. R., Kortering, L. J., Fowler, C. H., & Rowe. D. (2010). *Age-appropriate transition assessment guide* (2nd ed.). Retrieved National Secondary Transition Technical Center (NSTTAC) website: http://www.nsttac.org/

Walker, A. R., Uphold, N. M., Richter, S., & Test, D. W. (2010). Review of literature on community-based instruction across the grades. *Education and Training in Autism and Developmental Disabilities, 45*, 242–267.

Wandry, D., & Pleet, A. (2004). *The role of families in secondary transition: A practitioner's facilitation guide.* Arlington, VA: Council for Exceptional Children.

Wehmeyer, M. (2002). Transition assessment: Critical components for transition planning. In C.L. Sax & C. Thoma, *Transition assessment: Wise practices for quality lives* (pp. 25–28). Baltimore, MD: Paul H. Brookes.

Wehmeyer, M. L., Palmer, S. B., Smith, S. J., Parent, W., Davies, D. K., & Stock, S. (2006). Technology use by people with intellectual developmental disabilities: A single subject design meta-analysis. *Journal of Vocational Rehabilitation, 24*, 81–86.

Woods, L. L., Sylverster, L., & Martin, J. E. (2010). Student-directed transition planning: Increasing student knowledge and self-efficacy in the transition planning process. *Career Development for Exceptional Individuals, 33*, 106–114.

Zhang, D., Sylverster, J. G., Chen, L., & Katsiyannis, A. (2005). Perspectives on transition practices. *Career Development for Exceptional Individuals, 28*, 15–25.

6

Transition Planning Strategies

Janice Seabrooks-Blackmore

UNIVERSITY OF NORTH FLORIDA

Gwendolyn Williams

WEST TEXAS A&M UNIVERSITY

In this chapter, many of the types of strategies available for use in supporting best practices in transition are presented. The strategies identified are considered informal, with most being available at a very low cost, while others can be obtained at no cost. In most cases, all transition-planning strategies can be categorized as person-centered and self-determined. Therefore, this chapter will describe the broader category of person-centered planning and then more specifically address those that have a high emphasis on student-led strategies which focus on the development of self-determination.

Evidence of a "results-oriented process" (IDEA 2004) is reflected by the involvement of students with disabilities in transition programs that incorporate instructional and planning materials and procedures which help them and/or their parents successfully participate in the mandated planning process. Although person-centered strategies are often considered time-consuming and reserved for those students who have more complex needs, understanding the underlying spirit and use of person-centered strategies is aligned with the directive of IDEA 2004. The application of these approaches can lead to building quality transition plans for each student with disabilities in special education.

Person-Centered Approaches

A person-centered approach involves a systematic process that focuses on an understanding of the needs of the person with disabilities and not the system that serves them. Person-centered approaches help generate an action plan whose primary focus is to empower people with disabilities, a team of professionals, and interested others to ultimately build capacity for individuals with disabilities to have greater inclusion as valued members of society (Pearpoint, O'Brien, & Forest, 1998; O'Brien & O'Brien, 2000). For students with disabilities, these approaches strengthen opportunities for the development of post-school roles to be well defined and activated during high school.

Each person-centered planning approach begins with a team-assessment process that uses a set of maps which helps build a profile of an individual. The maps vary based on the goals, wants, and needs of the individual (Wehman, 2001). Three basic features for each approach are: (1) examination of everyday events and activities in which the individual participates; (2) exploration of family and connections within the community; and (3) planning with the individual who is disabled and a group of people who know the person well and are committed to helping him/her achieve identified personal goals (Falvey, Forest, Pearpoint & Rosenberg, 1994). Additionally, each approach is led by a facilitator who uses group graphics (e.g., color, photographs, symbols, words, texture) to capture the team's thoughts on flip-chart paper (Mount & Zwernik, 1990; Pearpoint et al., 1998; Westgate & Blessing, 2005). This process is user-friendly for everyone involved in the problem-solving process. The heavy reliance on visual representation of text helps eliminate the burden of reading professional or perhaps complex language.

Although many person-centered approaches have been developed primarily for people with developmental disabilities as the target audience (Test, Mason, Hughes, Konrad, Neale, & Wood, 2004), only those that are most often cited and recently used in school and community settings will be discussed here. Those approaches include: Personal Futures Planning (PFP), Making Action Plans (MAPS), Planning Alternative Tomorrows with Hope (PATH), Group Action Planning (GAP), Choosing Options and Accommodations for Children (COACH), and Essential Lifestyles Planning.

Personal Futures Planning (PFP)

PFP is a creative process designed to help a group develop a blueprint of meaningful opportunities for post-school living. A team may use this process when a student's participation options in high school seem limited due to various factors (e.g., health, cognitive ability, family resources, behavior). Using this process can enhance the team's ability to identify appropriate resources and opportunities in school and community environments that generate a results-oriented process aligned with current mandates.

The facilitator is a person who is committed to an ongoing problem-solving process. This person plays a critical role in assuring that the plan and the process are implemented and embraces the challenge of people working together to build a better future for the youth with a disability during and after high school (Mount & Zwernik, 1990).

Five basic components are included that provide impetus for the greatest quality change in a person's life. They include:

1. People begin with a clear appreciation of the gifts and capacities of the focus person.
2. Committed people develop a common understanding of a specific positive future—a common dream.
3. Committed people agree to meet regularly to brainstorm and make commitments to act. These people are often those who spend a lot of time with the person or have known the person for a long time.
4. The group includes at least one person—a family member, advocate, community member, staff person, or the person who is the focus of the planning—who is a champion of the dream. This person makes extraordinary efforts to bring the dream into reality.
5. At least one agency or community organization is committed to supporting the implementation of the plan (Mount & Zwernik, 1990, p. 11).

The facilitator helps the group collect information through the use of frameworks, often called maps. The most common frameworks explore the following areas: relationships, places, background, preferences, dreams, and hopes and fears.

Making Action Plans (MAPS)

This form of person-centered planning was initially developed to focus on the integration and inclusion of elementary children with disabilities in general education. However, it has become a familiar tool that is used when addressing transition issues for students with disabilities whose planning requires alternative perspectives for enhancing post-school options.

Similar to PFP, MAPS primarily brings family members, friends of the family, regular and special educators, the student and the student's friends together to look at what the student with disabilities can do instead of working from the perspective of what he/she cannot do (Kansas State Board of Education, 1990).

There are seven driving questions in this process:

- What is the child's history?
- What is your dream for the child?
- What is your nightmare?
- Who is the student?
- What are student's gifts?
- What are the student's needs?
- What would an ideal day at school be like for the student? (Kansas Board of Education, 1990; Vandercook, York, & Forest, 1989).

One should be mindful that MAPS is also an ongoing problem-solving process. Although the driving questions seem clear and easy to address, each may take a committed amount of time to explore the depths of what each entails to portray the best picture of what is occurring and what needs to happen in a student's life for successful transition planning.

The group of professionals, family, and interested others work with a facilitator to ensure that the loudest voice in this action planning process is that of the student with a disability. The beauty of this process is that if the student has difficulty expressing himself/herself, a family member or someone close to the student is acknowledged as the spokesperson for the student, and the process can continue.

Planning Alternative Tomorrows with Hope (PATH)

PATH addresses both long- and short-term planning. Through an eight-step process, a dream is defined, and then a positive goal is set for the next six months to a year. Once the dream and goals are agreed upon, action plans are developed and people are asked to volunteer their support. In this process a graphic depiction of a person's dream is displayed and referred to as the path, with the North Star being the dream. The focus of the planning process is to think backwards from the dream to committing to the first step in helping accomplish the dream (Pearpoint, et al., 1998). The focus person is known as the pathfinder. A brief description of the steps follows:

- Touching the dream—a graphic depiction of the pathfinder's dream (the North Star)
- Sensing the goal—focuses on what needs to happen within the next year in reaching the dream
- Grounding in the now—currently taking a look at where the pathfinder is now in relation to the dream
- Identifying people to enroll—focuses on identifying those who are willing to share a commitment to accomplish the steps toward the dream
- Recognizing ways to build strength—focuses on helping the pathfinder acknowledge current strengths and ways to become stronger
- Charting action for the next few months—focuses on prioritizing actions that need to take place in the next three months toward the dream

- Planning the next month's work—focuses on specifying who will do what, when
- Committing to the first step—focuses on identifying the biggest hurdle of what needs to happen first to make movement toward the dream.

Group Action Planning (GAP)

GAP provides the opportunity for persons with difficult behaviors to be supported by a unified, reliable alliance that includes the focus person, family members, friends, and professionals. GAP helps individuals and their families envision the best possible outcomes for the focus person and helps bring their vision to fruition. GAP's members commit to accomplishing, monitoring, and adjusting those goals that provide continuous, ongoing support to focus individuals and their families.

The GAP process involves: (1) inviting people from the individual's natural network who can be helpful to participate in the planning process; (2) choosing a facilitator who connects well with others, makes people feel valued, sets a positive tone, helps keep comments relevant, and is willing to assign tasks; (3) involving the focus person and family as much as possible; (4) emphasizing information based on personal knowledge (vs. professional "knowledge"); (5) fostering dynamic dreams for the future, directed and controlled by the focus person and family; (6) brainstorming solutions to problems that encourage everyone's input and that are fueled by high expectations, and (7) continuously celebrating progress made by the team. The purpose of the GAP process is to support the individual with a disability to create a vision of how he or she wants to live life and then to make a long-term commitment to the individual to transform that vision into reality (Turnbull, et al., 1996).

Choosing Options and Accommodations for Children (COACH)

Although a family versus student-centered approach, COACH is included here because it embraces the same problem-solving process as the other approaches included in this chapter except that the family is the focal point. COACH was designed to include the family's values and dreams in the individualized educational program planning for students with moderate to severe disabilities (Giangreco, Cloninger, & Iverson, 1993). It has three major parts: (1) family prioritization interview; (2) defining the educational program components; (3) and addressing the educational program components in inclusive settings. In this process, the family's values are of utmost importance. This may prove to be a particularly useful transition-planning strategy for culturally and linguistically diverse families who have children with disabilities.

Essential Lifestyles Planning

Essential Lifestyles Planning is a different and unique process among the person-centered approaches. It aims to build agreements among a variety of service providers to address important issues for each focus person. The intent is to address power struggles that can lead to mistrust and unhappiness with little resolve for the individual in which everyone claims commitment. O'Brien and O'Brien (2000) emphasized that this process:

> . . . has generated an array of tools for discovering what matters to people, building a very finely grained understanding of the rituals and routines that allow people to express their uniqueness, reviewing the quality of plans, incorporating the perspective of skilled

service providers, dealing with conflicts, supporting necessary organizational changes, and bridging to other person-centered approaches as a person's dreams grow bigger and stronger and a person's relationships with potential allies grow wider and deeper (pp. 23–24).

Because some youth may require a combination of unique strategies to effectively compose a "results-oriented" transition plan from high to post-school settings, the Essential Lifestyles Planning process is a planning strategy that can be used to coordinate all the efforts into a compilation of activities.

Self-Determination Approaches

A self-determined person is better equipped to control his or her own destiny. The concept of self-determination includes both attitudes and abilities that lead to goal-setting as well as the initiative needed to reach these goals (Ward, 1994). Activities that lead to student self-determination include increasing self-awareness; improving decision-making, goal-setting, and goal-attainment skills (Wehmeyer, Argan, & Hughes, 1998); enhancing communication and relationship skills (Field, Hoffman, & Spezia, 1998); and developing the ability to celebrate success and learn from reflecting on experiences. Self-determination instructional programs help students learn how to participate more actively in educational decision-making by (a) helping students become familiar with the educational planning process, (b) assisting students to identify information they would like to share at educational planning meetings, and (c) supporting students to develop skills to effectively communicate their needs and wants.

Examples of activities used in self-determination instructional programs include (a) reflecting on daydreams to help students decide what is important to them; (b) teaching students how to set goals that are important to them and then, with the support of peers, family members, and teachers, taking steps to achieve those goals. Contextual supports and opportunities for students, such as coaching for problem-solving and offering opportunities for choice, are critical elements that lead to social competence, autonomy, and relatedness and, as a result, increase self-determination.

Self-determination is a lifelong process (further information about self-determination strategies can be found in Chapter 13 of this handbook). Both school and home can provide rich opportunities for developing the skills, attitudes, and support for self-determination. It is critical that students begin developing these skills by the time they start participating in their transition-planning process. Self-advocacy and self-determination skill instruction should begin before students reach the mandated age of 16 as required by the Individuals with Disabilities Education Improvement Act (IDEA) 2004. Ideally, students should prepare to participate in their transition-planning process by completing a self-determination skill curriculum before reaching secondary school. The primary skills taught by self-determination curricula include:

1   Student self-awareness—This includes their strengths, needs, interests, and preferences. Students should have an understanding of their disability, learning styles, and accommodations as well as their legal rights and responsibilities. This self-awareness must lead to increased positive self-esteem and confidence.
2   Problem-solving and decision-making—Students should be able to define the problem, gather information and resources, identify pros and cons, make informed decisions, and communicate preferences.

3   Goal-setting—Students should learn the skills to identify their vision and long-range goals, identify all possible resources, develop an action plan to reach these goals, and evaluate the outcomes. Goal-setting also includes the ability to take informed risks and to take responsibility for the consequences of student actions.

4   Communication skills—These skills include body image and posture, clearly expressing ideas and feelings, listening to what others have to say, asking questions, planning and organizing thoughts, and accepting comments and criticism. In addition, most self-determination curricula provide opportunities and support for students to use their new skills. Typically, these opportunities have focused on student-directed individualized education programs (IEPs) in which the student takes primary responsibility for developing the IEP goals and actually directing the IEP meetings. Several of the curricula offer strategies for increasing student involvement in making decisions regarding their employment, future living options, social relationships, and community participation. The following planning strategies may be used to foster self-determination.

Self-advocacy Planning Strategy for Education and Transition Planning

The Self-Advocacy Strategy for Education and Transition Planning (Van Reusen, Bos, Schumaker, & Deshler, 1994) is a motivational strategy that students use to prepare for and participate in their Transition IEP meeting. This strategy teaches students how to get organized prior to the meeting and how to communicate during the meeting. Students use the acronym "I-PLAN" to remember the five steps in the planning strategy. This planning strategy is part of the Strategic Instruction Model from the University of Kansas. It is most appropriate for students with disabilities who take part in the general education curriculum with accommodations. It may also be used by students in more segregated settings who function at independent levels. The Self-Advocacy Strategy for Education and Transition Planning may be used with students of all ages.

The purpose of the strategy is fivefold. First, as a motivation strategy, it is designed to enable students to systematically gain a sense of control and influence over their own learning and development. Second, the strategy focuses students' attention on their learning and transition-skill strengths and provides them with a systematic process for identifying or determining specific skills they want to learn or improve. Third, mastery of the strategy enables students to take an active role in making decisions related to their learning and development experiences. Fourth, the strategy provides students with a way of getting organized before any type of conference or meeting. Finally, the steps of the strategy remind students about behaviors and techniques needed for effectively communicating and advocating their education and transition goals.

The acronym "IPLAN" is used to help students remember the five steps of the strategy, which are described below. "IPLAN" represents:

I—Inventory your strengths, weaknesses needed to improve goals, interests, and choices for learning. This step will prepare students for their upcoming IEP conference.

P—Provide your inventory information, involves indentifying appropriate time for individuals to share information during the conference, speaking clearly and completely and referring to the inventory as needed.

L—Listen and respond, addresses being an active listener and responding to statements made by others in a positive manner.

A—Ask questions, focuses on asking appropriate questions to gather needed information.

N—Name your goals, focuses communicating goals and ideas on actions to be taken.

Next Student Transition and Educational Planning (S.T.E.P) Curriculum

The Next S.T.E.P. Curriculum and instructional program is designed to be presented to students, with or without disabilities, in a classroom setting. The curriculum includes 19 lessons and requires a minimum of three months to complete, but preferably continues for at least one year. It is recommended that instruction occur two times per week. The scope and sequence of the instructional program involves the following main units: (1) overview of transition planning, (2) self-evaluation, (3) goal development, (4) goal implementation, and (5) student direction of his/her transition-planning meeting. Lesson formats vary from large-group instruction to one-on-one instruction, depending on the nature of the tasks being addressed. As one outcome of the program, each student creates and begins implementation of a unique transition plan addressing four areas: (a) education and training, (b) jobs, (c) personal life, and (d) living on your own. Each student, to the extent of his/her capabilities, also directs the transition-planning IEP meeting (Halpern, Herr, Doren, & Wolf, 2000).

Opportunities in Postsecondary Education Through Networking (OPEN)

The Opportunities in Postsecondary Education through Networking (OPEN) Model is designed to assist students, parents, and school personnel in decision-making, planning, and preparation processes that result in college enrollment for students with disabilities. The OPEN model's first step is *Deciding* or making the decision to attend a college. The next step in the OPEN Model is *Planning* and is subdivided into three domains: academic planning, career planning and personal–social planning. The *Preparing* process is the third step in the OPEN model. Students explore, practice, and master strategies needed for participation in a postsecondary education setting. *Exploring* is the fourth step of the model, which assists students in exploring college options. During this step, students investigate and evaluate their final college choices with support from their IEP team members who have created an Individualized Transition Plan. Following that step, students select the final college that aligns with their interests, abilities, and needs. Once students select their college of best fit, the next step in the OPEN Model is to assist students in completing the admissions process to the college of their choice (Webb, 2000).

The Model for Self-Determination

The Model for Self-Determination focuses on and delineates variables related to self-determination that are within the individual's control and are potential targets for instructional intervention. The model contains five components: (1) know yourself, (2) value yourself, (3) plan, (4) act, and (5) experience outcomes and learn. Each of these components is further divided into sub-components. Students develop an awareness of strengths, interests, and needs, as well as rights and responsibilities.

The curriculum also covers assertive communication, conflict resolution, and problem solving. The package includes an instructor's guide, student activity book, and pre/post assessments. The Model for Self-Determination may be used with middle and secondary students. It has been used with students with disabilities participating in the general education curriculum with accommodations as well as with students who function on a more independent level (Field, et al., 1998).

Whose Future Is It Anyway?

Whose Future Is It Anyway? (Wehmeyer & Kelchner, 1995) is designed for persons with mild cognitive and developmental disabilities. This curriculum consists of 36 lessons that address

(a) having self-awareness, (b) making decisions, (c) obtaining supports and transition services, (d) writing and evaluating transition objectives, and (e) learning leadership skills. Each section in the curriculum includes an action-plan goal, introductory material, sample problems or examples from the lives of people with disabilities, and exercises to practice.

Self-determined Learning Model of Instruction

The Self-Determined Learning Model of Instruction (Wehmeyer, Palmer, Agran, Mithaug, & Martin, 2000) focuses on empowering students to self-regulate decision-making strategies that position them to become causal agents in their own lives. Its intent is to improve self-directed outcomes of students as they set their transition goals, act on them, and through evaluation, make needed adjustments. At the core of each of this three-phase instructional process is a set of four student questions. In each phase, the student's voice takes the lead for choices, decisions, and actions, even when some actions need teacher-direction. This is a model that can be used in a variety of content areas based on a universal problem-solving approach.

ChoiceMaker Self-Determination Transition Curriculum

The ChoiceMaker Self-Determination Transition Curriculum (Martin & Huber Marshall, 1995) is designed to teach secondary students the self-determination skills needed to be successful in adult life. It consists of three strands: (a) choosing goals, (b) expressing goals and (c) taking action. Each strand addresses three transition areas: (a) education, (b) employment, and (c) personal objectives. The instructional sets contain lessons and videos to teach students to identify their interests, skills, and limits. Students are taught to use this information to set and accomplish goals in different areas across six transition domains: (a) high school, (b) employment, (c) post high school, (d) personal, (e) housing and daily living, and (f) community participation. More information on the ChoiceMaker curriculum is provided in Chapter 4.

Self-Directed IEP

The purpose of the Self-Directed IEP (Martin, Marshall, Maxson, & Jerman, 1996) is to help students learn how to assume a leadership role in their educational program. It teaches students to become active participants in their IEP meetings and to lead their IEP meeting, with coaching being provided as needed by the teacher who taught the lessons. The *Self-Directed IEP* contains 11 sequential lessons that typically take six to ten 45-minute sessions to teach. Lessons may be taught in a resource room, study-skills class, or other settings. To teach students who are fully included in general education classes, teachers may choose to meet students during study skills or a similar class. Some teachers find that removing the students from school for an IEP Leadership retreat day is an effective method to provide students opportunities to learn the IEP-meeting participation skills.

The *Self-Directed IEP* contains four instructional tools:

- *Self-Directed IEP in Action* video (seven minutes). This video depicts students with different disabilities using the self-directed IEP lessons in their classes and talking about their experiences. This video is used to introduce the self-directed IEP to students, parents, teachers, and administrators.
- *Self-Directed IEP* video (17 minutes). This video shows a student describing to a younger, reluctant friend how he led his IEP meeting. Through flashbacks, the student models each of the 11 steps of the *Self-Directed IEP*.

- Teacher's Manual. This manual provides background information, detailed lesson plans and a teacher answer key to the quizzes and activities. Detailed lessons include a variety of activities to teach each step, including a mnemonic learning strategy, vocabulary-building exercises, role-playing, discussion, and brief reading and writing activities. The lessons are all presented in a model-lead-test approach.
- Student Workbook. This consumable workbook provides students an opportunity to apply each step of the *Self-Directed IEP* to their own meeting. Students complete a script, which summarizes all the steps, to take with them to their own IEP meetings.

The *Self-Directed IEP* Steps include:

1   Begin the meeting by stating the purpose.
2   Introduce everyone.
3   Review past goals and performance.
4   Ask for others' feedback.
5   State your school and transition goals.
6   Ask questions if you don't understand.
7   Deal with differences in opinion.
8   State what support you'll need.
9   Summarize your goals.
10 Close meeting by thanking everyone.
11 Work on IEP goals all year.

Dare to Dream Revised

Dare to Dream Revised (Webb, et al., 1999) is designed for secondary students with mild-to-moderate disabilities. The guide stresses student involvement in transition planning. It is an excellent pre-planning tool for students to identify their strengths, preferences, and needs in the areas of post-school adult living, employment, social, and community areas. Students complete exercises that promote their involvement in transition planning and help them start thinking about decisions for the future. Consideration is given to: (a) the student's dreams for the future, (b) supports for the student, (c) the individualized transition plan and who might be involved, (d) where the student might live in the future, (e) skills and education needed for employment, free time, helping others in the community, (f) transportation within the community, (g) desired post-school outcomes, (h) learning styles, (i) requirements for graduation, and (j) making one's dreams come true. Types of housing options are identified, including geographic choices, types of housing and alternative living arrangements.

Questions are provided to help the student clarify what type of work would be appealing, and the level/type of training required for various job categories is specified. Skills for independent living, work, leisure, and community participation are also identified.

Dare to Dream for Adults

Dare to Dream for Adults (Webb & Peller, 2004) assists adults with disabilities in identifying interests, accomplishments, and needs; setting goals; and obtaining the necessary supports and resources to reach their dreams. It is an ideal resource for secondary students with disabilities who have previously used *Dare to Dream Revised*, and are ready to move to another level of transition planning. A free download of this publication in English is available at http://www.

fldoe.org/ese/pdf/dream_adults.pdf and in Spanish at http://www.fldoe.org/ese/pdf/dream_span.pdf

TAKE CHARGE for the Future

TAKE CHARGE for the Future is a student-directed, collaborative model that includes (a) coaching adolescents in the application of self-determination skills to achieve personal goals, (b) mentorship experiences for adolescents, and (c) information and support to assist parents to promote the achievement and positive self-attributions of their sons and daughters (Powers, et al., 1996). The model is designed to be collaboratively implemented by schools and community organizations, independent living centers, and family support programs. TAKE CHARGE for the Future's centerpiece is adolescent-directed participation in personally relevant activities in school, community, and home settings. Students learn through coaching strategies that they are responsible for promoting their own independence, self-confidence, and personal goals.

Summary

Research and best practice suggest that students with disabilities participate in the development of their own transition plans. The transition-planning strategies presented in this chapter portray several processes that can be used to assist students with disabilities to develop skills for making decisions about their future. These processes are not done *for* the student, but *with* the student. Students attend all meetings related to transition and the development of their IEPs. They work, on an ongoing basis, during their school programs to learn to advocate for their vision of the future. Self-advocacy and self-determination skills are essential for full participation in the transition-planning process.

The transition-planning strategies that are presented in this chapter represent only a small number of the strategies available to support student participation in the development of their transition plans. These strategies are not new; many have existed since the early 1990s. They are, for the most part, informal, non-expensive, person-centered and self-determined. Many transition-planning strategies consist of the following components: (a) student-focused planning, (b) family involvement, (c) interagency collaboration, and (d) a commitment from the team to support the focus student to prepare for post-school options across a variety of settings. The strategies presented are designed to be person-centered and student-led, and to focus on the development of self-determination.

References

Falvey, M. A., Forest, M., Pearpoint, J., & Rosenberg, R. (1994). *All my life's a circle. Using the tools: Circles, MAP's and PATH.* Toronto, Canada: Inclusion Press.

Field, S., Hoffman, A., Spezia, S. (1998). *Self-determination strategies for adolescents in transition.* Austin, TX: PRO-ED.

Giangreco, M., Cloninger, C., & Iverson, V. (1993). *Choosing options and accommodations for children: A guide to planning inclusive education.* Baltimore: Paul H. Brookes.

Halpern, A., Herr, C., Doren, B., & Wolf, N. (2000). *NEXT S.T.E.P.: Student transition and educational planning.* Austin, TX: PRO-ED.

Individuals with Disabilities Education Improvement Act (IDEA) (2004), 20 U.S.C. § 1400 et seq. (2004).

Kansas State Board of Education. (1990). *MAPS: A plan for including all children in schools.* (1990). Topeka, Kansas: Author.

Martin, J. E., & Huber Marshall, L. H. (1995). ChoiceMaker: A comprehensive self-determination transition program. *Intervention School and Clinic, 30*, 147–156.

Martin, J. E., Marshall, L. H., Maxson, L. M., & Jerman, P. L. (1996). *The self-directed IEP*. Longmont, CO: Sopris West.

Mount, B., & Zwernik, K. (1990). *Making futures happen: A manual for facilitators of Personal Futures Planning*. St. Paul, MN: Minnesota Governor's Planning Council on Developmental Disabilities.

O'Brien, C., & O'Brien, J. (2000). *The origins of person-centered planning: A community of practice perspective*. Retrieved November 10, 2009, from http://thechp.syr.edu/PCP_History.pdf

Pearpoint, J., O'Brien, J., & Forest, M. (1998). *PATH: A workbook for planning possible futures* (2nd ed.). Toronto, Canada: Inclusion Press.

Powers, L. E., Sowers, J., Turner, A., Nesbitt, M., Knowles, E., & Ellison, R. (1996). Take charge: A model for promoting self-determination among adolescents with challenges. In L. E. Powers, G. H. S. Singer, & J. Sowers (Eds.), *On the road to autonomy: Promoting self-competence for children and adolescents with disabilities* (291–322). Baltimore: Paul H. Brookes.

Test, D., Mason, C., Hughes, C., Konrad, M., Neale, M., & Wood, W. (2004). Student involvement in individualized education program meetings. *Exceptional Children, 70*, 391–412.

Turnbull, A. P., Blue-Banning, M. J., Anderson, E. L., Turnbull, H. R., Seaton, K. A., & Dinas, P. A. (1996). Enhancing self-determination through Group Action Planning: A holistic emphasis. In D. J. Sands & M. L. Wehmeyer (Eds.), *Self-determination across the life span: Independence and choice for people with disabilities* (pp. 237–256). Baltimore, MD: Paul H. Brookes.

Vandercook, T., York, J., Forest, M. (1989). The McGill action planning systems (MAPS). A strategy for building the vision. *Journal of the Association for persons with Severe Handicaps, 14*(3), 205–215.

Van Reusen, A. K., Bos, C. S., Schumaker, J. B., & Deshler, D. D. (1994) *Self-advocacy strategy for education and transition planning*. Lawrence, KS: Edge Enterprises.

Ward, M., (1994). Self-determination: A means to an end. *Impact, 6*, 8.

Webb, K. W. (2000). *Transition to postsecondary education*. Austin, TX: PRO-ED.

Webb, K. W., & Peller, J. (2004). *Dare to dream for adults*. Tallahassee, FL: Bureau of Instructional Support and Community Services, Florida Department of Education.

Webb, K., Repetto, J., Beutel, A., Perkins, D., Bailey, M., & Schwartz, S. (1999). *Dare to dream revised – A guide to planning your future*. Tallahassee, FL: Bureau of Instructional Support and Community Services, Florida Department of Education.

Wehman, P. (2001). *Life beyond the classroom: Transition strategies for young people with disabilities* (3rd ed.). Baltimore, MD: Paul Brookes.

Wehmeyer, M., Argan, M., & Hughes, C. (1998). *Teaching self-determination to students with disabilities: Basic skills for successful transition*. Baltimore, MD: Paul H. Brookes.

Wehmeyer, M., & Kelchner, K. (1995). *Whose future is it anyway? A student-directed transition planning process*. Arlington, TX: The Arc.

Wehmeyer, M., Palmer, S. Argan, M, Mithaug, D., & Martin, J. (2000). Promoting causal agency: The self-determined learning instruction model. *Exceptional Children, 66* (4), 439–453.

Westgate, R., & Blessing, C. (2005). The power of person-centered planning. *TEACHING Exceptional Children Plus, 2*(2) Article 2. Retrieved December 8, 2009 from http://escholarship.bc.edu/education/tecplus/vol2/iss2/art2/

7

Family Involvement in Transition Planning

Donna L. Wandry

WEST CHESTER UNIVERSITY OF PENNSYLVANIA

Amy M. Pleet

UNIVERSITY OF DELAWARE

As will be established throughout this book, the art of transition planning for adolescents with disabilities is a complex undertaking if it is done thoroughly and appropriately. The participants in effective transition assessment, planning, and implementation span multiple disciplines and systemic structures. However, the primary focus, as across the entire service spectrum for individuals with disabilities, must rest upon serving the individual needs of the primary consumers: the youth and peripherally, the family.

This chapter will assist parents, other family members, and practitioners in maximizing their partnerships within the transition process. These partnerships must, first and foremost, be viewed as dynamic, egalitarian, and reciprocal. A necessary foundation is stakeholder acceptance of the value of family partnerships.

Importance of Family Partnerships

The importance of family involvement in any student's school life has been well documented. Students whose parents are involved in homework and school activities have increased academic, social, and behavioral performance (Henderson, Mapp, Johnson, & Davies, 2007; Johnstone, 2004; Snodgrass, 1991). The quality of the partnership is engendered in its ability to bring a community of adults together to work toward the common goal of student success. However, within that community, the effectiveness of the partnership is maximized only when the parents are perceived as important resources (Lazar & Slostad, 1999) and members of an equal partnership who can express their needs and have their contributions treated as intrinsically important (O'Connor, 2008; Pollack-Prezant & Marshak, 2006). In recognition of the value of this partnership, there is an active movement to build family engagement relationships (Henderson et al., 2007) as systems of support that view parents as participants, focus on empowerment and information, and create a partnership that includes parents and family members as collaborators and not as clients (Bloch, 2008).

Among families of adolescents with disabilities, the benefits of family involvement also are documented through research. Healthy family relationships, especially high levels of involvement with schools, result in greater growth of students with disabilities (Bennett, 2007). Special education teacher candidates perceive parent involvement as being the most critical aspect of transition planning (Wandry, Webb, Williams, Bassett, Asselin, & Hutchinson, 2008). Since family members are the continuous advocates, informants, and supporters for students with disabilities (Brolin & Loyd, 2004; Park, 2008), their role cannot ethically be subordinated or diminished.

Benefits of Family Partnership within the Transition Process

For youth with disabilities, transition is an ongoing process of planning, implementing, evaluating, and balancing details to achieve an integrated quality of life for the entire family (Ankeny, Wilkins, & Spain, 2009). Family participation and student self-determination have been linked in research on transition planning with increased graduation rates, employment, and achievement of positive post-school outcomes (Mason, McGahee, Kovac, Johnson, & Stilerman, 2002; Wehmeyer & Palmer, 2003). Families often have a greater impact on the career development process than their young adults' peers (Lindstrom, Doren, Metheny, Johnson, & Zane, 2007). In a meta-analysis of research in ongoing transition practices and their link to Kohler Taxonomy components, the influence of families on career choices and job acquisition is one of the primary emergent themes across multiple disability groups and studies (Cobb & Alwell, 2009). Best practices, therefore, show that students and parents should be actively involved in planning for post-school transitions (Rusch & Loomis, 2005; Park, 2008).

Unfortunately, information about student outcomes has caused advocates, families, and educators to question the efficacy of their transition programming experiences (Goupil, Tassé, Garcin, & Doré, 2002; Kohler & Field, 2003). Student and family participation remains one of the highest national challenges facing transition services (Johnson, Stodden, Emanuel, Luecking & Mack, 2002). The period of transition into adulthood is pivotal in the lives of parents of children with disabilities (Rapanaro, Bartu, & Lee, 2008). It also presents one of the highest stressors in families as they face variables of social-sexual adjustment, vocational options, guardianship, financial security, residential choices, etc. (Ankeny et al., 2009).

Effective transition programs, simply stated, have high degrees of productive parent and student participation (Kohler & Field, 2003; Zhang, Ivester, Chen, & Katsiyannis, 2005). Family members remain a primary source of economic and psychological support during the transition period (Glidden & Jobe, 2007). They also help their young adults negotiate this life change by aiding in resource exploration, goal-setting, and instruction/reinforcement of independent living skills (Sitlington, Clark, & Kolstoc, 2000).

Characteristics of Effective Family Partnership Practices

Given the potential impact of family participation, school practitioners need to consider the essential ingredients of strong family engagement. Mutual trust and respect are the foundation of collaborative partnerships (deFur, 2009). Understanding this dynamic, and actively pursuing it, will establish a solid basis upon which all other aspects of the partnership will rest.

Parent-identified factors that improve their participation are based on the development of personal, rather than bureaucratic, "system-culture" relationships (deFur, Todd-Allen, & Getzel, 2001; Kohler & Field, 2003). Partnerships should be promoted as the cumulative product of interdependent, equitable, and trusting relationships among all stakeholders (O'Connor, 2008). Parents desire these relationships to be based on respect, collaboration, communication, shared decision-making, and information-sharing (Marshak & Prezant, 2007; Mundschenk & Foley, 1994; Patterson, Webb, & Krudwig, 2009; Pollack & Marshak, 2006).

Trust is a key factor when examining the collaboration of parents of children with disabilities and school personnel and may be a key ingredient in positive student achievement (Smith, Hoy, & Sweetland 2001); however, some parents may have difficulty in recognizing their levels of trust. Other variables that may affect its formation are evidence of child-based orientations, communication, shared knowledge about student characteristics, and school climate regarding collaborating with families (Angell, Stoner, & Shelden, 2009).

Parents in broken trust relationships with schools have difficulty accepting suggestions from those personnel; they may lack the confidence to fully accept the professionals' demonstration of good-faith efforts (Lake & Billingsley, 2000). One must consider the enormous implication for post-school planning when that trust is broken. As decisions critical to the transition process—assessment, goal-setting, courses of study, needed post-school supports—are brought to the discussion, a broken trust can stall these decisions and indeed the overall productivity of the transition process. Harry (2008) summarized the shift in professional regard for the value of partnership with families, stating that "professionals gradually have come to understand that caregivers' reactions to disabilities represent resilience and adaptation rather than pathology, and that providing adequate external supports can make a tremendous difference in outcomes for family members with disabilities" (p. 373). Practitioners must identify their own willingness to trust that parents and families can play essential roles, with inherent accountabilities, in the transition process.

Identifying Family Roles

The purpose of this chapter is to examine ways to build family engagement at both the student-based and systems-based levels to permeate transition assessment, planning, and implementation activities. Several frameworks for conceptualizing family (particularly parent) engagement have been proposed. Ryan (2003) and Thomas and Vaughan (2004) discussed three roles for parents: parents as consumers (choosing a good education for their child), parents as partners (working with educational and other professionals), and parents as responsible (focusing on their emotional, social, and intellectual investment in their child). Through her research at the National Network of Partnership Schools, Epstein established a framework based on types of family involvement: parenting, communicating, volunteering, learning at home, decision-making, and collaborating with the community (Epstein, Sanders, Simon, Salinas, Jansorn, & Van Voorhis, 2002). In a study by Heslop and Abbott (2007), parents identified major process issues that are essential to these home–school partnerships: being proactive, having sufficient information, being well connected with other parents or with key professionals, and engaging in good forward planning. Similarly, The Appleseed Group recommended three overarching actions for parents in their partnerships with schools: becoming fully informed, supporting their youth to get the most out of their education, and advocating for school improvement (Coleman, Starzynksi, Winnick, Palmer & Furr, 2007). Henderson et al. (2007) developed a five-part framework to assess the quality of family school partnership: building relationships, linking to learning, addressing differences, supporting advocacy, and sharing power. Specific to the field of transition, Kohler (1998) suggested three levels of family involvement in school transitions services: participation, empowerment, and training. Wandry and Pleet (2003, 2009) contributed critical roles parents can play throughout the transition process at both the "my child" and systemic levels: parents as collaborators; evaluators and decision-makers; peer mentors; instructors in their adolescents' emergent independence; and systems change agents. Common themes emerge when these models are examined, and serve as the foundation for seven strategies recommended, as well as accompanying self-evaluative indicators, throughout the remainder of this chapter.

Seven Strategies for Engaging Families During Transition

Strategy 1: Establish Two-way Communication

Schools that recognize the important contributions families make will establish regular procedures for a two-way flow of information. They will seek family perspectives on their needs, concerns, hopes, and dreams. They will clearly invite parent-initiated discussions at IEP meetings as well as during other school-sponsored events. They will maintain open lines of communication, welcoming family questions, requests, and feedback (Trainor, 2005). This is critical for families during the transition years. School personnel who take the time to truly listen when families share their stories will build trusting relationships and a foundation for the collaborative work they must do together in supporting a smooth transition for each youth with disabilities into adulthood (Hess, Molina, Kozleski, 2006).

The lines of communication must be reciprocal, not only seeking information but offering it freely as well. Families need information about many aspects of the transition process from assessment and planning through implementation and community linkages. Each school must consider the most effective way to deliver that information. Will parents read a newsletter or packets of information? Will they come to a parent night? Will they turn out at an event held in a community center rather than the school itself? How many would access information on

Table 7.1 Strategy 1: establish two-way communication

Establish two-way communication

- ☐ I actively and systematically seek family perspective during transition and futures planning.
- ☐ I encourage open discourse during IEP meetings.
- ☐ I continually seek appropriate methods for gathering and disseminating critical information to family members.
- ☐ I make family members aware of other, non-school sources of pertinent transition-related information.
- ☐ I am instrumental in creating information networks among and in behalf of families.

Table 7.2 Dilemma #1 establish two-way communication

Dilemma #1 establish two-way communication

On parent night Ms. Ryanowski approached the school building, holding her breath. She was there only because she had promised Charlie that she would come just this once. She knew that high school was important to him after all he'd done to get past his reading problems. If all went well, he would be the first in the family to graduate. She would do almost anything for her son, but she had vowed years before that she would never enter a high school again. Well, here she was.

She looked up as a man in a suit handed her a paper with columns of numbers and directed her into the auditorium where someone behind a podium – probably the principal—was making a speech. He was saying something about budget deficits (whatever that meant) that would affect programs such as vocational training. Charlie had told her that they would be talking about a work-study program, but maybe he was wrong. She had hoped to be able to ask questions about that program and maybe share some hopes for programs that would help her Charlie. Whoever said, "They won't care how much you know until they know how much you care?" Well, did anybody here care about her and her boy and his goals for his future? Already, she regretted that she had come.

What are the issues for school improvement and family engagement? What would you do?

the internet or benefit from a DVD? Practitioners may want to consult with some families to determine the optimum channels of communication that would reach the most families. In many local education agencies, parents are hired to manage a parent information and training center. These parents are provided information about services, programs, and community resource options. They are responsible for developing multiple venues for delivering information to parents. In other locations, schools establish informal networks of parents who can share information with each other—especially during the transition years.

Strategy 2: Develop Cultural Acceptance

One of the challenges to building collaborative relationships with families is practitioner awareness and acceptance of family cultural values and mores. Often families served by a school represent a wide range of differences in race, social class, and culture. If school personnel come from differing backgrounds, these disparities can lead to misunderstandings about any family behaviors that vary from their own. Consider the negative judgments expressed in these statements: "Parents from that neighborhood don't attend IEP meetings. They don't care about their children's success." "These families don't value education the way we do." "Her mother is overprotective. She won't let Shaquita participate in job shadowing at the stadium." Henderson et al. (2007) suggested that the school team start planning for parent engagement with this premise: "All families, no matter what their income, race, education, language, or culture, want their children to do well in school—and can make an important contribution to their children's learning" (p. 115). Within this context, team members are more likely to have high expectations for family partnerships.

Table 7.3 Strategy 2: develop cultural acceptance

Develop cultural acceptance
☐ I am knowledgeable about the demographics of the students I serve.
☐ I distribute culturally appropriate and sensitive materials to all families with whom I work.
☐ I welcome culturally and linguistically diverse families to participate in their youth's transition planning as well as at the systems level.
☐ I endeavor to build my cultural awareness at the subtle level and use cultural reciprocity to resolve cultural differences during transition planning and implementation.
☐ I operate within culturally sensitive parameters when facilitating self-determination practices in my students.

Table 7.4 Dilemma #2 develop cultural acceptance

Develop cultural acceptance
Rachel Freeman was the sixth child of eight in her family. Like others who attended her synagogue, she would only eat kosher food and could not attend events from sundown on Friday until sundown on the Sabbath. The sophomore class was hosting their ring dance next Friday night and serving pizza. Mr. Roberts, the transition coordinator, decided that since parents would be dropping their children off for the dance, he would hold a parents' meeting, beginning at the same time as the ring dance (and also serving pizza). He thought that he could distribute information about summer community employment opportunities for juniors and give parents an opportunity to talk about their concerns in the transition process.
What are the issues for school improvement and family engagement? What would you do?

Educators need to be fully informed about the populations their schools serve and aware of the cultural context in the school. What ethnic, religious, socio-economic and racial groups are represented and in what proportion of the school population? What beliefs and customs, practiced by those groups, may differ from the traditional beliefs and customs held by the majority? There is a danger, however, that this information could lead to stereotyping groups of families if these data are used in isolation, leading to reinforced prejudices about families that hold differing cultural perspectives and values. Developing cultural awareness and employing it discerningly with each family, however, can have a positive benefit when value-laden topics such as post-school options, self-determination, and desired outcomes are discussed.

The levels of cultural awareness developed by Kalyanpur and Harry (1997, 1999) provide a useful framework for understanding cultural differences. A professional operating at the *overt* level of awareness attends to observable external differences such as language, accent, or style of dress. Stereotyping families at this stage is common. Those who operate at the *covert* level begin to look past the surface appearance to gain additional information about a family's orientation, including religious affiliation, cultural attitudes toward authority, and social networks. Professionals need information about generalized cultural perspectives and traditions for categories of families served by their schools, but they will need to move to a deeper level of awareness if they are committed to powerful partnerships with families. Operating at the *subtle* level of awareness, they explore individual families' beliefs and values, recognizing that acculturation levels of families vary greatly. They would investigate each family's attitudes about important transition issues such as independence vs. family interdependence, youth respecting authority vs. asserting themselves, adults' deference to school authority vs. agreement, and individual rights vs. importance of the collective (Harry, 2008; Kozleski et al., 2008; Zhang, 2005).

Kalyanpur and Harry (1997, 1999) describe four steps to the process of cultural reciprocity: (1) reflect on your own values and reactions and those of the school; (2) investigate the values of the family; (3) iterate the differences between the two value systems; and (4) work collaboratively with the family to come to a resolution that respects the values of all. For example, many school-transition programs provide opportunities for students to gain skills in advocating for their rights. Suppose one student's family recently immigrated from a culture that taught young people to silently respect their elders, deferring to their wishes. A professional who can respectfully articulate the two divergent viewpoints and can facilitate a discussion is more likely to build a stronger relationship with the family in the process of resolving a potential conflict that might influence the "student voice" as part of transition planning.

The stance of cultural reciprocity has significant application to the practice of developing self-advocacy and self-determination skills in youth from non-Anglo cultures. Researchers (Zhang, 2005; Zhang, Wehmeyer, & Chen, 2005) discuss the impact of diverse cultural values on families' support of school-endorsed self-advocacy values. When the values of the educational system and those of the family are in conflict, professionals will want to use the steps of cultural reciprocity to articulate the differences and discuss compromises that will lead to individual agreements made with those families.

Strategy 3: Engage in Shared Decision-Making

The shared responsibility for transition planning and implementation activities, based on student needs, has already been well established. Having specific strategies for effectively engaging parents in decision-making is essential to maintaining the health of that shared responsibility. Throughout the relationship, practitioners should take a welcoming stance, send positive messages about students' needs, challenge stereotypical assumptions about parents, and collaborate sincerely with them, working together while keeping student and parent goals at the

Table 7.5 Strategy 3: engage in shared decision-making

Engage in shared decision-making

☐ I make direct efforts to seek and incorporate information from families for transition-related decisions.

☐ I create an environment that supports open discourse and active power-sharing with families about transition planning.

☐ I strive to function as a collaborator, empowering parents to move from the periphery of transition decision-making to full partnership in the process.

☐ I model effective problem-solving free from pre-conceived biases about my students' or their families' abilities to participate with complete equity.

☐ There is an atmosphere of active power-sharing in decisions about my students' future employment, educational, residential, and community access options.

Table 7.6 Dilemma #3 engage in shared decision-making

Dilemma #3 engage in shared decision-making

Rhianna's parents had never attended any school event, including IEP meetings. Preparing for her spring IEP meeting, the transition coordinator was concerned about all the decisions that would be made in preparation for her approaching senior year. Was she going to take college preparation courses or register for a half-day, work-study program? Would she be able to explain her learning disability and advocate for accommodations in either program? Although she had taken home information about the SAT, Rhianna said her mother had not taken her on testing day. What were her plans for this summer? Rhianna had taken information about the summer Single Step program at the community college. Would her parents allow her to attend or would she gain valuable work experience? What did they want for Rhianna's future and what did they consider a priority? It was easy to dismiss her family as not interested or unsupportive, but maybe there were other factors to be considered. Perhaps it was just up to the school to go ahead with the decisions and inform Rhianna's parents of the direction to take that would be in her best interest.

What are the issues for school improvement and family engagement? What would you do?

---

center of the partnership (Michaels & Ferrara, 2005; Patterson et al., 2009). This will assist in fostering an open environment that values divergent perspectives and priorities, which must exist if shared decision-making is to occur.

The parameters of an appropriate education for children and young adults with disabilities grant parents the opportunity for shared decision-making (Lake & Billingsley, 2000), validating that all participants have valuable information to contribute (Patterson et al., 2009). Van Haren and Fiedler (2008) discuss strategies for empowering families to emerge as full partners in ways that will: (1) enhance families' sense of self-efficacy, (2) model effective problem solving for families, and (3) increase family coping skills. The healthy partnership needs to move together in the direction of the outcome, adjusting the system as it shifts from a disability-focused, deficit-driven model to a service–delivery approach that is based on abilities, options, and self-determination (Kohler & Field, 2003).

Phelps (1999) suggested that school–parent partnerships should rest on a model of true partnership akin to an organizational form: one requiring consultation, involvement, and reciprocity. It should not replicate a limited partnership organizational form, which results when one partner supplies the investment (in this case, the parent providing the "capital"—the student) while the other controls the daily running of the business (in this case, the school professional controlling the educational enterprise). Perceived diminished partnership relationships may be attributed to the concept of "professional gate-keeping," where limited communication relegates parents to the periphery of the decision-making process (O'Connor, 2008). This inability to recognize diverse perspectives severely impedes the quality of the transition process (Cooney, 2002).

Therefore, models of effective interaction have and should continue to move away from the practice of treating parents like clients to recognizing them as partners who collaborate with professionals on decisions relating to their child's education, with a foundation built from power-sharing (O'Connor, 2008). This shared power stance is critical to the act of managing disputes between home and school. Transition planning and implementation requires new, unfamiliar discussions among students, their families, and their teachers regarding post-school employment, educational, residential, and community access options, course-of-study decisions, and possible movement to community agency supports. Entering successfully into that new discussion and decision-making context requires a sense of equitable, mutually recognized empowerment.

Strategy 4: Resolve Disputes

Conflict is part of the human condition and is inevitable. The conflict, however, is not always the problem; the way it is handled and the outcomes may be the problem. Barriers that directly affect productive communication exist at all levels. Time, feelings of inadequacy, misunderstandings, language and cultural differences, intimidation, lack of feeling welcome may contribute to dwindling levels of communication and collaboration at the secondary level (DeMoss, Vaughan, & Langenbach, 1996)

Table 7.7 Strategy 4: resolve disputes

Resolve disputes

☐ I am open to the fact that family members may have information I do not possess.
☐ I embrace divergent family opinions without perceiving them as rigid or uninformed.
☐ I work with families to clearly articulate mutual vision as a context for our partnership before discussing our differences.
☐ I recognize that families may have different outcomes in mind than I for their young adult and am willing to listen and respect those desires.
☐ I trust that both my student's family and I have positive goals and wishes for that student.

Table 7.8 Dilemma #4 resolve disputes

Dilemma #4 resolve disputes

Mr. Tanner closed the door and asked everyone to take a seat. "Now, before Mrs. Whiley and her advocate come in, have we reached consensus about what we can provide for William?" The psychologist referred to her notes and provided information about William's ability and continued reading deficiencies.

Mr. Tanner thanked her and reminded everyone that they would propose that William pursue the half-day, work-study for the coming year. "William just doesn't have the reading skills to make it in most of our courses, right? He just gets frustrated and becomes a behavior problem."

"But if William is so low in reading," the transition coordinator asked, "why aren't we giving him reading intervention support so that he can improve or at least learn how to get meaning from grade level texts? He is clearly bright enough to go on to college."

Mr. Tanner frowned. "Please don't bring that up when Mrs. Whiley is here. You know that our reading specialist has been cut from the budget for next year. Telling her will just open a can of worms about the options available to him."

What are the issues for school improvement and family engagement? What would you do?

In a study by Rueda, Monzo, Shapiro, Gomez, & Blacher (2005), parent respondents believed that educators devalued parent knowledge of their children while promulgating their belief that their professional expertise made those educators correct. In a study by Lake and Billingsley (2000), school professionals reported their impression that parents can be too "single-minded," whereas parents might view that as determination. The traditional answer to the question: "Who makes the decisions and is in control?" is the professionals, who are perceived as the experts (Michaels & Ferrara, 2005).

When one considers the effect this can have on transition planning and programming, it is easy to project that the disputes will hinder movement toward outcomes. In fact, the point of dispute may rest within deciding what those outcomes might be, what course of study decisions are made to support those outcomes, what people at both home and school want at the IEP planning table or any other point of the process at which, minimally, agreement, and maximally, mutual support, are critical.

The essential truth is that power bases and tactical maneuvers are used by both parents and schools in attempts to resolve conflicts (Lake & Billingsley, 2000). The challenge, then, is to recognize power bases but make them productive and mutually beneficial. This means shared parity and accountability. As long as service providers view themselves (or are perceived) as housing all the solutions, and families are perceived as lacking essential expertise or expecting unreasonable services, family and practitioner collaboration will be blocked. Practitioners must recognize that families may make different choices than what they might traditionally recommend, and families need to recognize that practitioners may offer suggestions that the family members and student have not considered (deFur, 2009). Each end of the partnership must trust that they should be able to question the process without being labeled "difficult."

Strategy 5: Foster Youth Ownership

As is explained elsewhere in this book, when youths transition from the entitlement system mandated by the Individuals with Disabilities Education Improvement Acts of 2004 (P.L. 108–466) to the eligibility adult-service system, they will only have the protections and services specified by the Americans with Disabilities Act and the Rehabilitation Act if they self-disclose and advocate for themselves. A substantial body of research indicates that students who have developed self-advocacy skills exhibit a sense of competence, autonomy, and positive personal relationships (Eisenman, Chamberlin, & McGahee-Kovac, 2005; Fiedler & Danneker, 2007). During the middle and high school years, schools have the responsibility of equipping students with these skills by giving them opportunities to make choices, to learn about their disabilities and their legal rights, and to participate in their IEP meetings (Fiedler & Danneker, 2007; Konrad, 2008). By engaging families in a united collaborative approach, they will provide adolescents a wrap-around support system that is more likely to lead to successful self-determined behavior (Lee, Palmer, Turnbull, & Wehmeyer 2006). Once professionals and families have agreed on the aspects of self-determination that align with the family's cultural values, they can establish a multi-dimensional approach to fostering the youth's self-determination and adult behaviors.

Uphold, Walker, & Test (2007) proposed a self-advocacy conceptual framework that builds youths' (1) knowledge of self, (2) knowledge of rights, (3) communication, and (4) leadership. As adolescents are learning about their own disability and its implications for their future planning, teachers can reinforce acquisition of skills related to advocating for accommodations. Families can help them determine how their disability will impact their home life and future plans. When teachers mentor students to develop a personal organizational system for their homework responsibilities, families can support their children to manage a personal budget and make their own medical appointments. While transition coordinators arrange job shadowing

Table 7.9 Strategy 5: Foster youth ownership

Foster youth ownership

☐ I am familiar with legal rights and responsibilities my students have regarding self-disclosure.
☐ I am aware of family-specific cultural influences on the development of student self-determination skills.
☐ I work with my students' families to collaborate in teaching skills for independence in home and school environments.
☐ I work with families and youth to discover ways to reinforce student ownership of the IEP/transition planning process.
☐ I work to provide information and supports to youth and families that will increase ownership of the transition process.

Table 7.10 Dilemma #5 foster youth development

Dilemma #5 foster youth development

Northern High School launched a new initiative this year to support students practicing self-advocacy during their IEP meetings. They planned to provide opportunities for students to learn about their disabilities and the rights they will have in higher education and employment. Most of their energy would focus on coaching students to write their own IEP goals. Recognizing that families are critical allies in this endeavor, they invited families to an evening gathering, providing refreshments and babysitting.

Mrs. Allison was pleased to learn that her daughter, Monica, would be supported in interviewing teachers about her own strengths and needs as a student and would work with teachers to understand her test scores. She and her husband had already begun at home with helping her set goals for budgeting her paycheck. "I know that Monica will need to set goals for herself in two years when she goes away to college," Mrs. Allison said. "Can you also work with her on making choices in dating?"

Mrs. Tran, on the other hand, was quiet. In the Vietnamese tradition, Ming's future would be decided by family elders. It would be considered rude for her to put her personal preferences ahead of the collective good. Were these teachers really going to violate her family traditions by insisting that Ming voice her own opinions?

What are the issues for school improvement and family engagement? What would you do?

---

experiences, families can discuss types of jobs available in their community. At a time when transition coordinators are discussing how to decide if and when to disclose a disability, families can coach their children in appropriate ways to explain it and practice within the family. If school professionals are preparing the student to lead their IEP meeting, families reinforce these emerging leadership skills before, during, and after the meeting. As guidance counselors are describing the process of applying for financial aid for college, families can take the student to the college disability services office or an adult service-provider open house. To establish this kind of collaborative, unified support for the young adult, professionals will need to investigate what information and understandings parents will need, and take steps to provide such support.

The Self-Determination Instructional Partnership (Ward, 2009) is another framework families can use to support their adolescents as they gain skills they need to become self-advocates. First, students with parents' and educators' support identify skill priorities; second, they determine the best methodology to become proficient in those skills; and third, they assume ownership for self-regulation and evaluation. Students will emerge as self-determined leaders in their own lives with combined support from home and school.

Strategy 6: Include Families in School/Agency Improvement Efforts

During transition, families rely on educators and other professionals to provide information about future options for their young adults (Ankeny et al., 2009; Wagner, Newman, Cameto, Levine, & Marder, 2007). Despite this reliance, families experience higher satisfaction with services if they have even limited involvement in aspects of service delivery (Ankeny et al., 2009). In a study by Lindstrom et al. (2007), parents were grateful for ongoing work by school transition personnel but rarely described any opportunities for working in partnership with those personnel in providing career-related activities. What is needed, then, is a tangible set of activities in which parents and families might become involved to impact service provision on a larger scale.

It can be argued that the most efficient way to effect systems change is to work from within. Sadly, family representation on policy-making and advocacy groups often is lacking. However, school professionals may limit family involvement to raising money instead of making decisions (DeMoss et al., 1996). It must be noted that parents may serve on school boards, site-planning

Table 7.11 Strategy 6: include families in school/agency improvement efforts

Include families in school/agency improvement efforts

- ☐ I envision families as participants in the school-improvement process beyond traditional support roles.
- ☐ I recommend my students' parents for roles on local school councils, advisory teams, and transition councils.
- ☐ I provide information or resources for parents so they feel more secure as they become involved in school-improvement efforts.
- ☐ I work to make sure my students' parents feel they can have input on all aspects of transition assessment, planning, and implementation processes and procedures.
- ☐ I urge family members to help me understand the level of involvement with which they feel comfortable.

Table 7.12 Dilemma #6 include families in school/agency improvement efforts

Dilemma #6 include families in school/ agency improvement efforts

Mr. Stanley, principal of Central High School, called Mrs. Joyner, the Special Education chair, into his office. He reminded her of three concerns: "As you know, we didn't fare well in our last audit. Our school was cited for not making Adequate Yearly Progress for the second year in a row – students receiving special education services had actually declined. During the last audit our IEPs did not meet Indicator 13 compliance expectations. And our drop-out rate for students with special education services is not improving. So, Mrs. Joyner, what is your plan?"

Mrs. Joyner was aware of the problems. She told him that her students were struggling with the newly implemented inclusion model, and teachers didn't know how to support them. Students who had previously taken their academic courses in self-contained special education classes did not know how to advocate for themselves and didn't know what learning strategies worked for them. She hoped that the newly hired transition coordinator would be able to help with her on these issues and the two IDEA indicators. She promised to investigate resources, such as local consultants and specialists from the local university, who might be available with school improvement funding. She wondered if there was any way to engage families to support their efforts toward program improvement. No – wait – that was maybe not a good idea to involve parents who might just be looking for a bone to pick. They should just focus on their own child's daily schoolwork.

What are the issues for school improvement and family engagement? What would you do?

committees and parent organization boards that have a say in school policy (DeMoss et al., 1996). The Individuals with Disabilities Education Improvement Acts of 2004 is clear in its directives, for example, that (a) the majority of members on state advisory panels must be individuals with disabilities or their families, (b) parents are to be integral members of state and local performance plans, and (c) parents are to provide direct input into compliance-monitoring activities. A parallel family empowerment structure also exists within the Rehabilitation Act, which has continually strengthened the voice of the consumer and his/her family through mandated representation on State Rehabilitation Councils.

Parents should be encouraged to join advocacy groups and networks (Ankeny et al., 2009). Schools should engage parents in school councils, advisory teams, and other well-publicized committees that provide venues for formal parent input (DeMoss, Vaughan, & Langenbach, 1996). Often, parents may be reticent to participate at this level because they lack relevant information so they can fully participate. In a study by Park (2008), teachers identified informing parents about the transition process as one of the most challenging yet crucial tasks in supporting families during the transition period. However, one of the largest variables affecting parental participation in transition planning is simply a lack of information about services and support (Heron & Harris, 2001).

Strategy 7: Build Capacity for Expansion of Family Engagement

Schools that are committed to establishing strong partnerships with families will need to systematically plan to build their own capacity. Professional literature is replete with recommendations, such as the Coalition on Community and Family Engagement's six keys to community and family engagement (Berg, Melaville, & Blank, 2006). Their framework, co-produced with the National Association of Secondary School Principals and National Association of Elementary School Principals, is based on interviews and focus groups with 46 school principals from across the United States, and recommends the following tactics: (1) know where you're going, (2) share leadership, (3) reach out, (4) don't ignore the elephant in the room, (5) tell your school's story, and (6) stay on course. In their view, school leaders committed to building capacity for expanded family engagement will develop a vision and plan for partnerships with families, encourage families' contributions and leadership, meet families where they are, have welcoming and honest conversations about the diversity of families, become visible in the community in ways that are recognized and appreciated by families, and continually assess progress.

Schools will need to determine their current strengths in parent engagement and anticipate professional development needs of their teachers, counselors, transition coordinators, and other

---

Table 7.13 Strategy 7: build capacity for expansion of family engagement

Build capacity for expansion of family engagement

- ☐ I actively seek to contribute to a positive vision of family engagement in my school.
- ☐ I seek ways to become useful in environments and activities outside of school that are of high value to my students' parents.
- ☐ I assess and address my own need for information on family diversity, collaborative problem-solving methods, and the like so that I might become a more informed support.
- ☐ I support parents and other family members as they mentor others.
- ☐ I work with my administrators to investigate new ways for my school to engage families more fully in transition programming at the "my child" and the systems levels.

Table 7.14 Dilemma #7 build capacity for expansion of family engagement

---

Dilemma #7 build capacity for expansion of family engagement

"You'd better keep in touch to let me know how your children are doing! I'm going to miss you all," Ms. Chen finished with a smile and sat down.

Mrs. Green stood up, "Before we talk about the graduation party, who has a challenge for us to work on tonight? Come on now, this is our last official meeting with Ms. Chen although I know some of us will still be here on the first Monday of every month."

Ms. Chen looked around the room, counting over 35 parents and other family members. She thought about how far they had come in four years. In her first three years at Eastside High, only six parents had attended IEP meetings, but she hadn't been satisfied with her colleagues' explanation that these parents had other priorities. When she was told that she would be case manager for the incoming ninth grade class, she decided to do something to get parents involved. Searching the internet for ideas, she discovered evidence-based national models and strategies. The findings from those studies increased her resolve, but there was no available support in her school for reaching out to families. She started buying her bread at Mrs. Green's bakery and saw motherly pride in Simon's gift with cake decorating. She met Mrs. Fisher and Mr. Rothenburg the first Saturday that she rode the ice cream truck through the neighborhood. Mr. Rothenburg had arranged for them to meet here in the church hall every month. Mrs. Fisher had told her about Friday nights at Ricardo's Pizza, where she had been introduced to several more. Ms. Chen couldn't remember whose idea it was to begin meeting on Mondays, but the tradition had continued throughout the four years – and it had grown to include aunts, uncles, and grandparents. Sometimes they had requested guest speakers, but they always took time to problem solve on a challenge one or more of them was facing with their kids. She knew that the summer employment program would not have expanded if these parents had not organized and descended on the school board and the state legislature. Since Ms. Dieker from the community college Disability Services Office and Mr. Minowski from the Division of Vocational Rehabilitation had come to some of these meetings, she knew they would support their children in keeping those connections. Who would have thought that these fine men and women would have become her friends or that they would have surprised her with a bridal shower? She had come to know their teenagers so well through their families' eyes. Together they had handled many problems early before they erupted into major problems at school. Yes, she would miss them. Too bad her colleagues hadn't reached out to parents. They didn't know what they were missing.

What are the issues for school improvement and family engagement? What would you do?

---

related personnel (Harry, 2008). These needs may include knowledge of the potential power of family engagement, awareness of family diversity within their school community, issues related to self-determination and disability disclosure. Professionals may also need to develop enhanced skills in listening, collaboration, cultural reciprocity, problem solving, dispute resolution, and mentoring. Finally, they will need facility in reflective self-evaluation related to their own effectiveness in working with families during the transition years.

Another emerging venue for building capacity rests with the families themselves. As families discover the satisfaction of becoming partners with the school, many will be willing to take the next step of becoming a spokesperson for families—whether on advisory boards or panels, speaking to policy-making leadership groups or in mentoring other families (Morningstar, 2009; Ripley, 2009). Schools would be well served to nurture these family members and create systems for building the capacity of parents to take on this broader context for their advocacy (Trainor, 2005). As students progress through the transition process, leaving school buildings for adult community settings, their families who have become more informed, engaged partners will then shift their focus from school to adult services. Those parents who have become valuable partners in systemic reform at the school level may only serve in that capacity for a few short years, and educators will need to continually use strategic methods to solicit perspectives from families of youth entering the transition process about their support needs and willingness to enter expanded levels of involvement.

Evaluating Engagement Practices

Inherent in this capacity building as in all other improvement efforts is a strategic way of evaluating the effectiveness of practices (Henderson et al., 2007; Trainor, 2005). Are there systematic ways to collect and analyze data to inform evaluation of family engagement practices? Which methods are the best in communicating with families—both for gathering their perspectives

Table 7.15 Resources

HEATH Resource Center. Washington, DC: www.heath.gwu.edu
HEATH Resource Center Clearinghouse has information for students with disabilities and their families on educational disability support services, policies, procedures, adaptations, accessing college or university campuses, career-technical schools, and other postsecondary training entities.

National Coalition for Parent Involvement in Education. Washington, DC: www.ncpie.org
NCPIE's mission is to advocate the involvement of parents and families in their children's education, and to foster relationships between home, school, and community to enhance the education of all young people. They serve as a visible representative for strong parent and family involvement initiatives at the national level, conduct activities that involve efforts to increase family involvement, and provide resources and legislative information that promote parent and family involvement.

National Collaborative on Workforce and Disability for Youth (2005). *The 411 on disability disclosure workbook.* Washington, DC: Institute for Educational Leadership.
Parents and practitioners can guide youth through the process of considering benefits and disadvantages of disclosure.

National Dissemination Center for Children with Disabilities. Washington, DC: www.nichcy.org
NICHCY provides family-friendly information about disabilities in children and youth; programs and services for infants, children, and youth with disabilities, and research-based information on effective practices for children with disabilities.

National Network of Partnership Schools, Johns Hopkins University, Baltimore, MD: nnps@csos.jhu.edu
Established at Johns Hopkins University in 1996, NNPS invites schools, districts, states, and organizations to join together and use research-based approaches to organize and sustain excellent programs of family and community involvement that will increase student success in school.

PACER Center. Minneapolis, MN: www.pacer.org
PACER provides coordination, training, and technical assistance to and through federally funded parent centers, as well as several publication and projects dedicated to parent–professional partnerships.

Parent Educational Advocacy Training Center. Falls Church, VA: www.peatc.org
PEATC offers, among many other family-centered supports, a transition series for training parent and professional teams in building transition partnerships, called NEXT STEPS.

Technical Assistance Alliance for Parent Centers. Minneapolis, MN: www.taalliance.org
The Technical Assistance ALLIANCE for Parent Centers is a partnership of one national and six regional parent technical assistance centers that coordinate support to over 100 Parent Training and Information Centers and Community Parent Resource Centers nationally, all of them focused on assisting parents of children, youth, and young adults with disabilities. The Alliance provides media resources, conferences, and training designed to build effective home-school partnerships.

Zarrow Center for Learning Enrichment. Norman, OK: www.ou.edu/zarrow
The Zarrow Center for Learning Enrichment, housed at the University of Oklahoma, facilitates successful secondary and postsecondary educational, vocational and personal outcomes for students and adults with disabilities through self-determination oriented evaluation, research, development, transition education instruction, and dissemination of best educational and support practices.

---

and for delivering information? Is the school making progress with cultural acceptance? Are families engaged in decision making and are disputes being resolved in ways in which all can win? Are families included as full partners in strategies to develop their adolescents' leadership and ownership skills? Are family engagement activities attracting increasing numbers of families and are there parallel increases in student outcome data? Finally, are family voices integral to efforts to build capacity of professionals to work with families and are diverse families emerging as leaders?

Table 7.15 provides information on resources teachers can use. By employing the strategies suggested in this chapter, and formatively evaluating those efforts through systematic self-examination using the Engagement Indicators for Practitioners and the related Dilemmas for Discussion scenarios, the reader should find that positive professional growth has occurred. When formative measures are successful, responses to the questions stated above should begin to reveal a new trend for transition-related parent engagement practices in the reader's respective settings.

References

Angell, M. E., Stoner, J. B., & Shelden, D. L. (2009). Trust in education professionals: Perspectives of mothers of children with disabilities. *Remedial and Special Education, 30*(3), 160–176.

Ankeny, E. M., Wilkins, J., & Spain, J. (2009). Mothers' experiences of transition planning for their children with disabilities. *Teaching Exceptional Children, 41*(6), 26–36.

Bennett, K. S. (2007). The role of family in the development of social skills in children with physical disabilities. *International Journal of Disability, Development and Education, 54*(4), 381–397.

Berg, A. C., Melaville, A., & Blank, M. J. (2006). *Community & Family Engagement: Principals Share What Works.* Retrieved November 17, 2009 from http://www.communityschools.org/assets/1/AssetManager/CommunityAndFamilyEngagement.pdf

Bloch, J. S. (2008). The home/school collaborative model. *Children and Schools, 30*(3), 189–191.

Brolin, D. D., & Loyd, R. J. (2004). Career development and transition services: A functional life skills approach (4th ed.). Upper Saddle River, NJ: Pearson.

Cobb, R. B., & Alwell, M. (2009). Transition planning/coordinating interventions for youth with disabilities: A systematic review. *Career Development for Exceptional Individuals, 32*(2), 70–81.

Coleman, A. L., Starzynski, A. L., Winnick, S. Y., Palmer, S. R., & Furr, J.E. (2007) It Takes A Parent: Transforming Education in the Wake of the No Child Left Behind Act. Appleseed downloaded from http://www.educationcounsel.com/resources/files/It Takes a Parent.pdf

Cooney, B. F. (2002). Exploring perspectives on transition of youth with disabilities: Voices of young adults, parents, and professionals. *Mental Retardation, 40*(6), 425–436.

deFur, S. H. (2009). Parents as collaborators: Building partnerships with school and community-based providers. In Wandry, D., & Pleet, A. (Eds.), *Engaging and empowering families in secondary transition* (pp. 33–50). Arlington, VA: Council for Exceptional Children.

deFur, S. H., Todd-Allen, M., & Getzel, E. E. (2001) Parent participation in the transition planning process. *Career Development for Exceptional Individuals, 24,* 19–36.

DeMoss, S. E., Vaughan, C., & Langenbach, M. (1996). Parental perceptions of long-term involvement with their children's schooling. *National Association of Secondary School Principals, 80*(92), 92–101.

Eisenman, L., Chamberlin, M., & McGahee-Kovac, M. (2005). A teacher inquiry group on student-led IEPs: Starting small to make a difference. *Teacher Education and Special Education, 28*(3–4), 195–206.

Epstein, J. L., Sanders, M. G., Simon, B. S., Salinas, K. C., Jansorn, N. R., & Van Voorhis, F. L. (2002). *School, family, and community partnerships: Your handbook for action,* 2nd ed. Thousand Oaks, CA: Corwin Press.

Fiedler, C. R., & Danneker, J. E. (2007, April). Self-advocacy instruction: Bridging the research-to-practice gap. *Focus on Exceptional Children, 39*(8), 1–20.

Glidden, L. M., & Jobe, B. M. (2007). Measuring parental daily rewards and worries in the transition to adulthood. *American Journal of Mental Retardation, 112*(4), 275–288.

Goupil, G., Tassé, M. J., Garcin, N., & Doré, C. (2002). Parent and teacher perceptions of individualized transition planning. *British Journal of Special Education, 29*(3), 127–135.

Harry, B. (2008, Spring). Collaboration with culturally and linguistically diverse families: Ideal versus reality. *Exceptional Children, 74*(3), 372–388.

Henderson, A. T., Mapp, K. L., Johnson, V. R. & Davies, D. (2007). *Beyond the bake sale: The essential guide to family-school partnerships*. New York: The New Press.

Heron, T. E., & Harris, K. C. (2001). *The educational consultant: Helping professionals, parents, and students in inclusive classrooms* (4th ed.). Austin, TX: PRO-ED.

Heslop, P., & Abbott, D. (2007). School's out: Pathways for young people with intellectual disabilities from out-of-area residential schools or colleges. *Journal of Intellectual Disability Research, 51*(7), 489–496.

Hess, R. S., Molina, A. M., & Kozleski, E. G. (2006). Until somebody hears me: parent voice and advocacy in special education decision making. *British Journal of Special Education, 33*(3), 148–157.

Johnson, D. R., Stodden, R. A., Emanuel, E. J., Luecking, R., & Mack, M. (2002). Current challenges facing secondary education and transition: What research tells us. *Exceptional Children, 68*, 519–531.

Johnstone, D. (2004). Effective partnerships with parents. *Education Journal, 73*, 7.

Kalyanpur, M., & Harry, B. (1997) A posture of reciprocity: A practical approach to collaboration between professionals and parents of culturally diverse backgrounds. *Journal of Child & Family Studies, 6*(4), 487–509.

Kalyanpur, M., & Harry, B. (1999) *Culture in special education: Building reciprocal family-professional relationships*. Baltimore: Paul H. Brookes.

Kohler, P. D. (1998). Implementing a transition perspective of education: A comprehensive approach to planning and delivering secondary education and transition services. In F. R. Rusch & J. Chadsey (Eds.), *High school and beyond: Transition from school to work* (pp. 179–205). Belmont, CA: Wadsworth Publishing.

Kohler, P. D., & Field, S. (2003). Transition-focused education: Foundation for the future. *Journal of Special Education, 37*(3), 174–183.

Konrad, M. (2008). Involve students in the IEP process. *Intervention in the School & Clinic, 43*(4), 236–239.

Kozleski, E. B., Engelbrecht, P., Hess, R., Swart, E., Eloff, Oswald, M. et al. (2008) Where differences matter: A cross-cultural analysis of family voices in special education. *Journal of Special Education, 42*(1), 26–35.

Lake, J.F., & Billingsley, B. S. (2000). An analysis of factors that contribute to parent-school conflict in special education. *Remedial and Special Education, 21*(4), 240–252.

Lazar, A., & Solstad, F. (1999). How to overcome obstacles to parent-teacher partnerships. *Clearing House, (72)*4, 206–210.

Lee, S., Palmer, S. B., Turnbull, A. & Wehmeyer, M. (2006) A model for parent-teacher collaboration to promote self-determination in young children with disabilities. *Teaching Exceptional Children, 38* (3), 36–41.

Lindstrom, L., Doren, B., Metheny, J., Johnson, P., & Zane, C. (2007). Transition to employment: Role of the family in career development. *Exceptional Children, 73*(3), 348–366.

Marshak, L. E., & Prezant, F. P. (2007). *Married with special needs children: A couples' guide to keeping connected*. Bethesda, MD: Woodbine House.

Mason, C. Y., McGahee-Kovac, M., Johnson, L., & Stilerman, S. (2002). Implementing student-led IEPs: Student participation and student and teacher reaction. *Career Development for Exceptional Individuals, 25*, 171–192.

Michaels, C. A., & Ferrara, D. L. (2005). Promoting post-school success for all: The role of collaboration in person-centered transition planning. *Journal of Educational and Psychological Consultation, 16*(4), 287–313.

Morningstar, M. (2009) Parents as systems change agents. In Wandry, D. L. & Pleet, A. M. (Eds.) *Engaging and Empowering Families in Secondary Transition: A Practitioner's Guide* (pp. 119–139). Alexandria, VA: Council for Exceptional Children.

Mundschenk, N. A., & Foley, R. M. (1994). Collaborative relationships between school and home: Implications for service delivery. *Preventing School Failure, 39*(1), 16–21.

O'Connor, U. (2008). Meeting in the middle? A study of parent–professional partnerships. *European Journal of Special Needs Education, 23*(3), 253–268.

Park, Y. (2008). Transition services for high school students with disabilities: Perspectives of special education teachers. *Exceptionality Education Canada, 18*(3), 95–111.

Patterson, K. B., Webb, K. W., & Krudwig, K. M. (2009). Family as faculty parents: Influence on teachers' beliefs about family partnerships. *Preventing School Failure, 54*(1), 41–50.

Phelps, P. H. (1999). Secondary teachers' perspectives on partnerships. *Contemporary Education, 70*(3), 29–32.

Pollack-Prezant, F., & Marshak, L. (2006). Helpful actions seen through the eyes of parents of children with disabilities. *Disability and Society, 21*(1), 31–45.

Rapanaro, C., Bartu, A., & Lee, A. H. (2008). Perceived benefits and negative impact of challenges encountered in caring for young adults with intellectual disabilities in the transition to adulthood. *Journal of Applied Research in Intellectual Disabilities, 21*(1), 34–47.

Ripley, S. (2009) Parents as peer mentors. In Wandry, D. L. & Pleet, A. M. (Eds.), *Engaging and Empowering Families in Secondary Transition: A Practitioner's Guide* (pp. 101–117). Alexandria, VA: Council for Exceptional Children.

Rueda, R., Monzo, L., Shapiro, J., Gomez, J., & Blacher, J. (2005). Cultural models and practices regarding transition: A view from Latina mothers of young adults with developmental disabilities. *Exceptional Children, 71*, 401–414.

Rusch, F. R., & Loomis, F.D. (2005). The unfulfilled promise of special education: The transition from education to work for young adults with disabilities. *Exceptional Parent, 35*(9), 72–74.

Ryan, J. (2003). Reading diverse schools: Headteachers and inclusion. *Improving Schools, 6*, 43–62.

Sitlington, P. L., Clark, G. M., & Kolstoe, O. P. (2000). *Transition education and services for adolescents with disabilities.* Boston, MA: Allyn & Bacon.

Smith, P. A., Hoy, W. K., & Sweetland, S. R. (2001). Organizational health of high schools and dimensions of faculty trust. *Journal of School Leadership, 12*, 135–150.

Snodgrass, D. M. (1991). The parent connection. *Adolescence, 26*(101), 83–87.

Thomas, G., & Vaughan, M. (2004). Inclusive education: Readings and reflections. Maidenhead, Berkshire, UK: (McGraw-Hill) Open University Press.

Trainor, A. (2005). Self-determination perceptions and behaviors of diverse students with LD during the transition planning process. *Journal of Learning Disabilities, 38*(3), 233–249.

Uphold, N. M., Walker, A. R., & Test, D. W. (2007). Resources for involving students in their IEP process. *TEACHING Exceptional Children Plus*, 3(4) Article 1. Retrieved November 17, 2009 from http://escholarship.bc.edu/education/tecplus/vol3/iss4/art1

Van Haren, B., & Fiedler, C. (2008, March). Support and empower families of children with disabilities. *Intervention in School and Clinic, 43*(4), 231–135.

Wagner, M., Newman, L., Cameto, R., Levine, P., & Marder, C. (2007). *Perceptions and expectations of youth with disabilities. A special topics report of findings from the National Longitudinal Transition Study-2 (NLTS-2).* Menlo Park, CA: SRI International.

Wandry, D., & Pleet, A. (Eds.) (2003) *A practitioner's guide to involving families in secondary transition.* Arlington, VA: Council for Exceptional Children.

Wandry, D., & Pleet, A. (Eds.) (2009) *Engaging and empowering families in secondary transition.* Arlington, VA: Council for Exceptional Children.

Wandry, D. L., Webb, K. W., Williams, J. M., Bassett, D. S., Asselin, S. B. & Hutchinson, S. R. (2008). Teacher candidates' perceptions of barriers to effective transition programming. *Career Development for Exceptional Individuals, 31*(1), 14–25.

Ward, M. (2009) Parents as partners in their youths' emergent independence. In Wandry, D. L. & Pleet, A. M. (Eds.), *Engaging and empowering families in secondary transition: A practitioner's guide* (pp. 53–79). Alexandria, VA: Council for Exceptional Children.

Wehmeyer, M., & Palmer, S. B. (2003). Adult outcomes for students with cognitive disabilities three years after high school: The impact of self-determination. *Education and Training in Developmental Disabilities, 38*, 131–144.

Zhang, D. (2005). Parent practices in facilitating self-determination skills: The influences of culture, socio-economic status, and children's special education status. *Research and Practice for Persons with Severe Disabilities, 30*(3), 154–162.

Zhang, D., Ivester, J. G., Chen, L., & Katsiyannis, A. (2005). Perspectives on transition practices. *Career Development for Exceptional Individuals, 28*(1), 15–25.

Zhang, D., Wehmeyer, M, & Chen, L. (2005). Parent and teacher engagement in fostering the self-determination of students with disabilities. *Remedial and Special Education*, 26(1), 55–64.

Section III

Student Development in Adolescent Transition Education

8

Life Skills and Community-Based Instruction

David W. Test

UNIVERSITY OF NORTH CAROLINA AT CHARLOTTE

Sharon Richter

APPALACHIAN STATE UNIVERSITY

Allison R. Walker

UNIVERSITY OF NORTH CAROLINA–WILMINGTON

Introduction

While early transition education movements (1960–1980) focused on cooperative work study programs and career education (Halpern, 1992), and Will's (1984) "bridges model" of transition had employment as the primary outcome of the secondary transition process, Halpern's (1985) transition model maintained the employment focus while expanding the model to include a broader focus called "community adjustment." According to Halpern (1985), community adjustment rested on three pillars called residential environment, employment, and social and interpersonal networks. Since then, the field of secondary transition has continued to recognize that there is more to life than just work.

This reality is recognized in the Individuals with Disabilities Education Improvement Act (IDEA) of 2004 which states that one of the purposes of IDEA is "To ensure that all children with disabilities have available to them a free appropriate public education that emphasizes special education and related services designed to meet their unique needs and prepare them for further education, employment, and independent living" [§300.1(a)]. As a result of independent living skills, or life skills, being viewed as a primary outcome for students with disabilities, it is important that students receive instruction on these skills throughout their school years (Walker, Uphold, Richter, & Test, 2010).

Independent living skills have been referred to using many different terms including "adaptability skills" (Mithaug, Martin, & Agran, 1987) and "life skills" (Cronin, 1996). More recently, Smith (2004) called them "functional skills" and Storms, O'Leary, & Williams (2000) used the phrase "daily living skills."

Throughout this chapter we will use the term life skills and define it as "those skills or tasks that contribute to the successful independent functioning of an individual in adulthood" (Cronin, 1996, p. 54). In addition, we will advocate for using a life skills instruction approach supported by the Division on Career Development and Transition of the Council for Exceptional Children (DCDT; Clark, Field, Patton, Brolin, & Sitlington, 1994). In the DCDT position paper, life skills instruction was described as providing instruction in the areas of "personal responsibility, social competence, interpersonal relationships, health (physical and mental), home living, employability, occupational awareness, job skills, recreation and leisure skills, consumer skills, and community participation" (Clark et al., 1994, p. 126). This chapter will focus on teaching non-employment-related life skills.

Importance of Life Skills

Although IDEA (2004) emphasized the importance of preparing students with disabilities for independent living, recent data from the National Longitudinal Transition Study–2 (NLTS2; Newman, Wagner, Cameto, & Knokey, 2009) indicated that within the first few years after leaving high school only 25% of students with disabilities lived independently (on their own or with spouse, partner, or roommate) and 6% lived semi-independently (in college dorm or military). Other findings related to life skills indicated that 46% of students with disabilities had a checking account (compared to 68% of the general population) and 28% had a credit card in their name (compared to 50% in the general population). Finally, 69% had either a driver's license or learner's permit and 67% had voted.

One strategy that may help improve post-school outcomes for independent living is for practitioners to incorporate evidence-based practices and predictors of post-school success into their instruction. Findings from the recent reviews of experimental and correlational literature conducted by the National Secondary Transition Technical Assistance Center (Test, Fowler et al. 2009; Test, Mazzotti, et al., 2009) can provide a starting point for designing instruction to teach life skills. First, Test, Fowler et al. (2009) identified 32 secondary transition evidence-based practices based on their review of experimental research using both group and single-subject designs. Of these 32 practices, 20 would be considered life skills (see Table 8.1

Table 8.1 NSTTAC evidence-based practices related to life skills

NSTTAC evidence-based practices related to life skills
Teaching functional life skills
Teaching banking skills
Teaching cooking and food preparation skills
Teaching grocery shopping skills
Teaching home maintenance skills
Teaching leisure skills
Teaching personal health skills
Teaching purchasing skills
Teaching purchasing using the "one-more-than" strategy
Teaching restaurant purchasing skills
Teaching safety skills
Teaching self-care skills
Teaching life skills using community-based instruction
Teaching life skills using computer-assisted instruction
Teaching self-management for life skills
Teaching self-determination skills
Teaching self-advocacy skills
Teaching functional reading skills
Teaching functional math skills
Social-skills training

for a list of evidence-based practices related to life skills). Further information about each practice can be found at http://www.nsttac.org/content/evidence-based-practices and lesson plans for each of these skills can be found at http://www.nsttac.org/content/lesson-plan-starters. Each lesson plan starter includes an objective, setting/materials, content taught, teaching procedures, and evaluation information. See Table 8.2 for an example lesson plan starter for teaching students to use the "one-more-than" technique to purchase items at a store.

Second, Test, Mazzotti et al. (2009) reviewed the secondary transition correlational literature to identify in-school predictors that related to improved post-school outcomes for

Table 8.2 Research to practice lesson plan starter for purchasing items using the "one-more-than" technique

"One-more-than" technique

Objective: To teach purchasing skills by using the "one-more-than" technique with the "cents pile modification" with one-, five-, and ten-dollar bills.

Setting and materials

Setting: Instruction is conducted in the school library four times each week. Skill generalization is measured in the community at stores and restaurants near the school.

Materials: Each student was given 5 one-dollar bills, 1 five-dollar bill, and 1 ten-dollar bill during all instructional sessions.

Content taught

The "one-more-than" technique with the "cents pile modification" is a strategy to increase students' abilities to use money for purchases. By using this functional strategy, learners can successfully purchase items by using currency without mastering skills related to coin usage and coin value, which can be barriers to successful purchasing in the community.

The following description of this strategy has been developed based on information in the article.

1 The purchaser listens for the price of an item (e.g., "Three dollars and forty-eight cents").

2 The purchaser counts one dollar for the "cents pile" (i.e., 48 cents) and puts it aside.

3 The purchaser then places the number of dollar bills identified in the price (i.e., 3) and places these on the "cents pile" dollar.

4 The purchaser then pays for the item using all of the bills in the pile.

Teaching procedures

1 Tell students that you will teach them a method they can use to go to the store and buy things themselves.

2 Orally describe and model to introduce the concept of "one-more-than" with "cents-pile modifications." For example, say: "If the salesperson says 'two dollars and fifteen cents,' you put one dollar to the side for the 'cents pile,' and then count out two dollars."

3 Tell students they are going to role-play purchasing items using the method.

4 Separate training items into 4 price groups, 0–$4.99, $5.00–$9.99, $10.00–$14.99, and $15.00–$20.00.

5 For the first price group, 0–$4.99, students will use the "cents-pile modification" to count out one more dollar than the amount requested.

6 Name a price between 0 and $4.99. in one of the following ways:
   (a) With the terms "dollars" and "cents" included (e.g., "That will be four dollars and twenty cents").
   (b) Without dollars and cents (e.g. "That will be four twenty").

7 Model "paying" the first training amount, by counting one dollar to the side for the "cents pile" and then count out the number of dollars requested.

8 Have students practice "paying" the first training amount.

9 For each correct response, provide descriptive verbal praise on a continuous reinforcement (CRF) schedule by pointing out that the student had just given enough dollars to pay for items, such as "Good job. You just gave me enough dollars."

10 For each incorrect response, verbally describe and model the correct response and then have the student try again. If student then responds appropriately, provide praise. If the student responds incorrectly, move to the next item by saying, "Let's try another one."

11 Provide students with three additional training amounts from the same price group using one of the ways to state the price identified in item #6 above.

12 Use the same procedure for all price groups (0–$4.99, $5.00–$9.99, $10.00–$14.99, $15.00–$20.00) with additional instruction related to counting on from five- and ten-dollar bills.

13 Show the students the bill(s), model "counting-on" from the bill(s), and then model the example item for that price group (e.g., for seven dollars, start with a five dollar bill and count on. As you place a five dollar bill on the table, say, "Five." As you place each dollar bill on the five dollar bill, say "Six" as you place the first bill and "Seven" as you place the next bill on the money stack.

14 Ask students to repeat the modeled item.

15 During training sessions, use 12 amounts that were not used in previous training sessions.

16 When students achieve 12 correct responses out of 12 opportunities, present "mixed practice" to students by randomly distributing three amounts from each of the four price groups across the 12 training items.

Evaluation

Collect student performance data on the percent correct on 12-item daily probes. Probes should include prices from the three price ranges (0–$4.99, $5.00–$9.99, $10.00–$14.99, $15.00–$20.00) and be stated to students in one of the following ways:

1. With the terms "dollars" and "cents" included (e.g., "That will be five dollars and twenty cents").
2. Without dollars and cents (e.g. "That will be five twenty").

Lesson plan based on:

Denny, P., & Test, D. (1995).Using the "one-more-than" technique to teach money counting to individuals with moderate mental retardation: A systematic replication. *Education & Treatment of Children, 18,* 422–32.

---

students with disabilities in the areas of employment, education, and independent living. Based on their review, 16 evidence-based predictors were identified. The four predictors for post-school success in independent living were (a) being included in general education classes (Heal, Khoju, & Rusch, 1997), (b) having a paid work experience (Bullis, Davis, Bull, & Johnson, 1995), (c) having self-care/independent living skills (Heal & Rusch, 1994), and (d) having family and friend support (Heal, Khoju, et al., 1999.)

In conclusion, while life skills and life skills instruction are viewed as important by the field of secondary transition, NLTS2 data reveal that post-school outcomes in this area can still be improved. As a result, the remainder of this chapter will focus on helping practitioners interested in teaching life skills to students with disabilities to understand what to teach and how to teach these critical skills.

What Life Skills Should Practitioners Teach?

Once practitioners have a clear understanding of the definition of life skills, they may consult different types of curricula to help drive their delivery of instruction. According to Polloway, Patton, & Serna (2008), practitioners usually refer to three types of curricula (i.e., explicit curriculum, hidden curriculum, and absent curriculum); however, the most commonly used type of curriculum for practitioners teaching life skills is called the absent curriculum. Polloway et al. (2008) refer to this curriculum as instruction that is not part of the formal curriculum driven by state standards. In other words, absent curriculum typically includes content (e.g., life skill instruction) chosen by the teacher, that may not be a common theme in a formal explicit curriculum. Therefore, practitioners are confronted with the task of not only identifying the type of curriculum to use in their teaching but also to specifically identify what life skills to teach. Consequently, it is imperative that practitioners refer to each student's individualized education plan (IEP) as the first step in identifying which skills to teach. According to Heward (2009), each IEP should include seven components. Of these seven components, students must have:

A statement of measurable annual goals, including academic and functional goals, designed to—(a) meet the child's needs that result from the child's disability to enable the child to be involved in and make progress in the general education curriculum; and (b) meet each of the child's other educational needs that result from the child's disability. (p. 63)

Once practitioners locate and identify each student's functional goals, they still may be confronted with the following question: What functional skill(s) do I teach? The first step in answering this question would be to determine what skills the student already has in his/her repertoire. In order to do this, practitioners should refer to the student's present level of academic and functional performance documented in the IEP. This information would serve as a baseline of data indicating the current skills in the student's repertoire. For example, a student's present level of functional performance may include the following statement: "John can dress himself with 95% accuracy." However, according to Gibb and Dyches (2007), one of the elements of the present level of academic achievement and functional performance statement in the IEP is to write the statement with enough detail that will provide practitioners with information needed to write complementary annual goals. Therefore, when reading the statement "John can dress himself with 95% accuracy", it would be difficult to know what skills John already has in his repertoire. Consequently, it would be beneficial if John's teacher conducted additional assessments to provide detailed information about his current strengths and needs and most importantly address the essential question: What functional(s) skills do I teach?

Life-skills Assessment

The concept of assessment has many different interpretations in education; however, when referring to assessing life skills, researchers often refer to the broader term of transition assessment. According to Sitlington, Neubert, & Leconte (1997), the Division on Career Development and Transition (DCDT) defines transition assessment as:

The ongoing process of collecting data on the individual's needs, preferences, and interests, as they relate to the demands of current and future working, educational, living, and personal and social environments. Assessment data serve as the common thread in the transition process and form the basis for defining goals and services to be included in the Individualized Education Program (IEP). (pp. 70–71)

When identifying a student skill level in the work, educational, living, and personal and social environment, different types of assessments ranging from informal to formal assessments are available for measuring a student's interests, preferences, and needs. According to Thoma, Held, & Saddler (2002), formal assessments are standardized instruments that have been widely tested using validity and reliability measures to gather information on student performance. In contrast, informal assessments are not standardized and are typically developed by practitioners to be administered in various settings to collect a wide array of information. Additionally, informal assessments are used most often to collect information about a student's functional skills and interests because of the ability to individualize these assessments. Examples of informal assessments include surveys, interviews, direct observations, and task analysis.

According to the previous example, it was stated that *John can dress himself with 95% accuracy.* However, the information provided is unclear and makes it difficult to determine what skills the practitioner should teach. Therefore, one method that can be used to answer the question, *What skills do I teach?*, would be to conduct a task analysis. A task analysis is a systematic procedure using a series of steps to teach a specific behavior. For example, John's teacher may write a task analysis that includes all of the steps for getting dressed in the morning, which would include putting on underwear, a shirt, socks, pants, belt, and shoes. Next, John's teacher could ask John's parents to use this task analysis across several days to check off which skills he is able to perform without assistance. Last, John's teacher can use the data from the task analysis to determine what skills to teach. In other words, if John was able to complete all of the steps to put on his shoes without assistance but was not able to complete the steps in tying his shoes, this would be helpful data for John's teacher. These data will allow John's teacher to prepare and deliver the appropriate instruction so that his needs are met and he is able to perform a functional life skill successfully.

Once the assessments have been administered and skills have been identified, practitioners may organize their instruction by categorizing these life skills into the main three post-secondary goal areas (i.e., postsecondary education, independent living, and employment) indicated in IDEA (2004). This categorization will also allow practitioners to determine whether the intended life skills are age-appropriate and socially important. In other words, practitioners need to make sure that the intended skills are chronologically age-appropriate, meaning that a student's same-age peer would typically learn the same skill. For example, it would be chronologically age-appropriate for a 16-year-old student to learn the meaning of road signs when studying for the driver's test; however, it would not be chronologically age-appropriate for a 10-year-old to learn the same skill. Therefore, practitioners need to ensure that the life skills they are teaching are chronologically age-appropriate rather than developmentally age-appropriate. Table 8.3 provides examples of age-appropriate life skills across the elementary, middle, and high school grade level. In addition, it is essential that the social importance of each skill is examined to make sure a student will actually benefit from learning the intended skill. For example, it may be beneficial for a student to learn how to read a course schedule if he/she is taking classes at the local community college; however, it may not be beneficial for that student to learn to drive if he/she has a severe visual impairment.

Self-determination and Life Skills

For over a decade, researchers and practitioners have emphasized the importance of teaching self-determination skills to students with disabilities (Algozzine, Browder, Karvonen, Test, & Wood, 2001; Field, Martin, Miller, Ward, & Wehmeyer, 1998). These self-determination skills include choice making, decision making, problem solving, goal setting, self-awareness, self-

Table 8.3 Age-appropriate life skills across elementary, middle, and high school

Examples of life skills	Grade level
Brushing and combing hair Eating meals Washing hands and face Using caution with strangers	Elementary
Preparing simple meals Using skin care products Crossing the street independently Washing hair	Middle
Taking medicine Avoiding alcohol and other drugs Budgeting checking or savings account Driving a car	High

advocacy, and self-regulation. In addition, researchers have also provided evidence to support the benefits of teaching these skills to students prior to transitioning into adult life (Wehmeyer & Palmer, 2003). Therefore, practitioners sometimes need to find creative ways of infusing these self-determination skills into their life-skills curriculum. For example, if a student is learning how to enroll in a college course at the local community college, learning how to request his/her accommodations (i.e., self-advocacy) would be an appropriate self-determined behavior that could be taught simultaneously. Table 8.4 provides examples of ways in which self-determination can be infused within specific life skills, and readers can learn more about self-determination from Chapter 13 in this Volume.

Why is Life-skills Instruction Different?

Life skills, as the term implies, are essential to life for all people, including individuals with intellectual disability. Life skills include those skills that, if individuals cannot do for themselves, another person will have to do for them. Unlike knowledge of history and literature (i.e., skills that are important to success in certain settings such as a World Civilization classroom or a book discussion group, respectively), life skills are unique. These skills are important to everyday functioning in *all* of the settings of life, including the home in which we reside, the school we attend, and the community where we live. When we (a) participate in groups related to our interests such as gardening and record collecting, (b) shop for new jeans, (c) eat out with family and friends, (d) see health care professionals, (e) buy stamps, (f) take a hike on a trail, (g) buy groceries, (h) volunteer in a soup kitchen, (i) take a bus, (j) see a band, (k) meet new people, (l) exercise, and (m) work, we are using life skills. Given that all individuals seek independence, self-respect, feelings of accomplishment, and the prerequisite skills to "sit in the driver's seat" of their life, life skills are critical to quality of life for all individuals and, therefore, a fundamental component of instructional content.

Each day, special educators teach life skills via traditional classroom instruction (i.e., ways that are similar to teaching any other skill such as how to read [e.g., constant time delay], how to write your name [e.g., modeling], and how to add using a calculator [e.g., least-to-most prompting]); however, as teachers, we also employ instructional strategies that are specially designed to teach skills for life to students with disabilities. In order to facilitate acquisition of life skills that are critical to community participation, special educators must design instruction for students with disabilities that consider the settings in which they are typically used, including *community-referenced instruction* and *community-based instruction*.

Community-referenced instruction is instruction that is designed to support students' use of skills in their current and subsequent community settings. Community-referenced instruction refers

Table 8.4 Self-determination and life skills infusion

Examples of life skills	Self-determination component	Infusion
Eating meals	Choice making	Student can choose which meal he/she would like to eat for lunch.
Budgeting checking or savings account	Goal setting	Student can set a goal of having $100 in his/her savings account and list the steps that will be followed to reach that goal.
Using caution with strangers	Problem solving	Student can write an action plan in case of an emergency if he/she was approached by a stranger.

to teaching instructional content that is essential to students' success in community settings. Examples of community-referenced instruction include skills such as teaching students to (a) make purchases, (b) use public transportation, (c) make a deposit at the bank, (d) read community signs, (e) have fun, (f) act safely and appropriately, (g) order lunch, and (h) cross the street.

Community-based instruction is instruction that is community-referenced and takes place in the community, where the skill is typically performed. For example, teaching students to purchase toothpaste could be taught at either a drug store or a grocery store.

Although the content of community-referenced instruction is based on the expectations and consequences that occur naturally in community settings, this type of instruction may also be implemented in simulated settings such as the classroom.

Simulated instruction is instruction that is community-referenced (i.e., based on the expectations of the community) which takes place in a non-community setting, usually a classroom. To design simulated instruction to support student's acquisition of community skills, teachers attempt to mimic the materials, procedures, and expectations of the community setting in which students will actually use the skills. For example, paying for items is a skill needed in the community; therefore, it is a type of community-referenced instruction.

What Does the Research Say about Simulated Instruction?

Research indicates that students with disabilities can acquire a number of skills via simulated instruction. In simulated settings, students have learned social skills needed for employment through scripted lessons (Montague, 1988). Additionally, video-based simulated instruction provided students with an opportunity to watch a video depicting a targeted skill performed in a natural setting, such as how to buy a soda from a vending machine. Through video-based instruction, students with disabilities have improved their ability to order meals at fast food restaurants (Mechling & Cronin, 2006), use debit cards at bank machines (Alberto, Cihak, & Gama, 2005), and read words found in grocery stores (Mechling, Gast, & Langone, 2002). Given that research indicates that simulated instruction is an effective instructional strategy, practitioners should consider its use while keeping in mind some advantages and disadvantages associated with simulated instruction.

What are the Advantages of Simulated Instruction?

Simulated instruction can be done in most school settings and at most times of the day. Consequently, teachers can design instruction that targets areas of student need frequently throughout the school day via massed trials or distributed trials, which will likely not be reasonable in a community setting. For example, through data collection, a teacher may identify that a student is independently completing all skills associated with eating in a restaurant, excluding leaving a tip. To target this skill in a simulated setting, a teacher could provide opportunities for a student to leave a tip several times each day; however, in the community setting at a local restaurant, only one such opportunity is likely: when the bill is paid.

Table 8.5 Introducing Ms. Shepherd

Ms. Shepherd is a high-school special education teacher of students with intellectual disability. She is a third-year teacher who decides that she will teach the skill, paying for items, via *simulated instruction* in her classroom. She plans that each day, she and her paraprofessional will role-play as cashiers and the students will use money to practice paying for items.

Additionally, simulated instruction can be implemented using many strategies that are familiar to teachers such as whole group, small group, and individualized instruction.

What are the Disadvantages of Simulated Instruction?

Simulated instruction is designed to imitate the setting in which students will use skills, but developing experiences that actually expose students to the characteristics of the community setting can pose challenges. First, when using simulated instruction, teachers must create materials that are realistic but also reasonable to create in terms of cost, time, and skill. For example, researchers developed materials designed to replicate the experience of using an ATM so students could learn this skill via simulated instruction. First, Shafer, Inge, & Hill (1986) used plywood to create a replica of an ATM. Next, Davies, Stock, & Wehmeyer (2003) utilized a computer-based application. Creation of authentic instructional materials such as these may be prohibitive in terms of cost and time. Second, situations occur in the natural setting that are unpredictable and are, therefore, difficult to embed in simulated instruction. For example, when teaching students to use an ATM in the community, teachable moments are likely such as the presence of other ATM users or encountering a machine that is out of money. Other examples of unpredictable teachable moments include fire drills, power outages, and a sidewalk being closed for construction. The unpredictability that is common in natural settings provides opportunities for students to develop independence in responding to the authentic challenges of community settings and can be quite difficult for teachers to approximate.

Community-based instruction is also instruction that is community-referenced. However, unlike simulated instruction, community-based refers to the *setting* in which instruction takes place. Community-based instruction (CBI) provides instruction in one specific setting: the community. Potential instructional sites are endless: CBI can take place anywhere in the community around you.

What Does the Research Say about CBI?

Research indicates that students with disabilities have acquired a number of skills via CBI. First, Ferguson & McDonnell (1991) successfully taught grocery skills to teenagers with significant cognitive disabilities via instruction in three grocery stores. Second, Berg, Wacker, Ebbers, Wiggins, Fowler, et al. (1995) indicated that all participants gained skills such as ordering a meal and purchasing items at a sandwich counter at a shopping mall, a fast food restaurant, a cookie

Table 8.6

Although Ms. Shepherd was planning to teach her high school students to pay for items via simulated instruction, she became overwhelmed by trying to closely represent the expectations of the community. She didn't have a cash register, an electronic device to display the prices, or a counter similar to that in a store. Further, she didn't think she could represent all of the social interactions with cashiers such as greetings (e.g., Hello, sir," "Did you find everything you were looking for today?," "Having a good day?," "Do you think this rain will ever stop?") and requests for money (e.g., "Nine eighty-seven, please," "Nine dollars and eighty-seven cents," "That'll be nine eighty-seven," "Nine eighty-seven is your total"), let alone that a real store has noisy announcements and other people (usually strangers) who are in line in front of you and behind. She was overwhelmed by the responsibility to her students. If she did not closely simulate the community setting to teach purchasing skills in her classroom, her students would no be able to actually make purchases where it really matters—in the community setting. Ms. Shepherd had a brilliant idea. She decided that she would teach her students purchasing skills via *community-based instruction*.

Table 8.7

Ms. Shepherd started planning with her paraprofessionals to teach purchasing skills in the community. She would choose some stores that are close to her school and take her students to each a few times each week. She planned out the logistics of providing CBI to her students (e.g., parent permission forms, transportation, money, adapting teaching strategies for community use). Given all of the other learning objectives and school activities that she and her students were involved in, they only had time to go to a store in the community each Friday. She would be able to teach her students purchasing skills in the setting where they would be used and she was excited for their shopping plans.

---

store at a shopping mall, and a deli counter at a grocery store. Finally, Souza and Kennedy (2003) indicated training on a bus and in a cafeteria can be effective in improving social interactions in community settings.

What are the Advantages of CBI?

In natural settings, students are exposed to an array of materials and experiences that are naturally present in community settings, eliminating the need for special materials designed by a teacher. Additionally, by training in the community, teachers are facilitating students' application of skills in the settings in which they are used; therefore, teachers minimize the need for additional training aimed to foster generalization since these considerations are inherent to instruction provided in community settings.

What are the Disadvantages of CBI?

CBI is effective in improving and maintaining functional skills needed for postsecondary life among students with disabilities; however, planning and implementing CBI poses challenges not present in instruction provided in school settings (Wissick, Gardner, & Langone, 1999). Designing CBI must include plans to (a) transport students to instructional sites (e.g., walking, using a school bus or city bus), (b) gain needed permissions to regularly leave the school campus (e.g., principal permission, parent permission), (c) pay for transportation and community services (e.g., to practice purchasing skills in the community through shopping at a grocery store, students will need money), and (d) reflect coordination of schedules between the school and the community site (e.g., scheduling around lunch periods, gym class, occupational therapy).

In addition to logistics associated with planning CBI, teachers must also consider the CBI setting to design instruction that is appropriate for the CBI setting. First, specially designed instruction is planned with respect to the natural ratios of society. Second, teachers must use inconspicuous strategies and materials.

Natural Ratios

Teachers must not infringe upon the *natural ratios* of persons with disabilities to persons without disabilities typically present in the community. For example, planning a holiday shopping trip for 30 high schoolers would certainly violate the guiding principle of natural ratios. It is obvious that this group would violate natural ratios if shopping as one large (very large!) group; however, even 15 student pairs, each working with one school employee, would breach this rule. This rule is not employed because large groups of individuals with disabilities are unwelcome; rather, it is upheld to facilitate meaningful instruction. Overwhelming, a CBI setting with individuals with disabilities results in an instructional setting that is flawed. The expectations and challenges typically associated with the setting are not present. Additionally, it would be extremely difficult to actually provide instruction to such a large group. Finally, using the previous example, it is unreasonable to imply that going shopping ever occurs with 30 people you know.

Inconspicuous Strategies and Materials

Teachers must provide instruction in a manner that teaches with regard to the expectations and challenges naturally present in the community. For example, individuals usually wait in line among strangers to purchase items at a drug store. Therefore, rather than teaching purchasing at a cash register with six students in the same line, students should make transactions in different cash register aisles mixed in with shoppers unknown to them. Next, it is important that instruction does not diminish the perceived competence of the student being trained nor attract the attention of the general public. For example, students improved on-task behavior by using audio prompting in a restaurant (Davis, Brady, Williams, & Burta, 1992), rather than using a large schedule displayed on the wall. Next, instruction should provide strategies that improve the independence of the student. For example, teachers should consider self-prompting and self-monitoring strategies. Students increased shopping skills by using grocery lists with photographs of anticipated purchases in the grocery store (Morse & Schuster, 2000). Finally, instruction should include items that will be available to students in postsecondary life. For example, if a student uses an assistive technology device that is owned by the school district, and will not have access to this device after graduation, teachers should fade the use of such devices and teach strategies to compensate for the absence of the device.

Recommendation: Pair Simulated Instruction with CBI

Although challenges exist in designing and implementing both simulated instruction and CBI, skills for community participation are essential for students with disabilities. Here is the solution: Instruction that integrates both natural and simulated settings is effective in teaching life skills for community participation to students with disabilities (Alberto et al., 2005). Further, recent research indicates that *CBI paired with simulated instruction* is more effective than either simulated instruction alone or CBI alone (Cihak, Alberto, Kessler, & Taber, 2004). The general rule is this: Teachers of students with disabilities who cannot provide all instruction in the community should provide concurrent instruction in both settings to support skill acquisition (Nietupski, Hamre-Nietupski, Clancy, & Veerhusen, 1986).

What Does the Research Say about Simulated Instruction Paired with CBI?

Several community skills have been taught using a combination of simulated and community-based instruction including safe street crossing (i.e., simulated instruction including photos of

Table 8.8

After four Fridays of CBI focused on purchasing skills, Ms. Shepherd had to face a difficult reality. Despite teaching skills in the community setting, none of her students had shown any consistent improvement in purchasing skills in comparison to the first week of instruction. She was mostly concerned that one day each week was insufficient for her students to learn the skills in a reasonable time frame. The old familiar feeling of "overwhelmed" again set in. What should Ms. Shepherd do? Her students are high-school age, so they would graduate from public school soon. Given that purchasing skills, like all life skills, are used frequently, if not daily in adult life, the students simply had to learn these skills efficiently and to the extent that they would be able to use them where it counted—in a store or other community setting.

Table 8.9

The brilliant Ms. Shepherd again changed her plans: She would teach purchasing skills via a combination of simulated instruction and CBI. With simulated instruction plus CBI, simulated instruction can take place more frequently while CBI will prepare students to use the skills in the community.

---

streets and CBI on public streets; Pattavina, Bergstrom, Marchand, Martella, & Martella, 1992) and making cell phone calls when lost (i.e., simulated instruction included learning skills in the classroom before additional practice in a grocery store, public library, and a department store; Taber, Alberto, Hughes & Seltzer, 2002). Furthermore, in order to gauge a student's skill generalization, data must ultimately be collected in natural settings (e.g., Alberto, Hughes & Seltzer, 2005; Mechling & Cronin, 2006).

What are the Advantages of Simulated Instruction Paired with CBI?

First, using simulated instruction paired with CBI diminishes the need for teachers to spend time and money creating materials to replace opportunities for learning in the community because students will have exposure to the materials in the community. Second, using both methods diminishes the probability that a teacher will not expose students to unpredictable situations that are important to students' skill development. Third, simulated instruction paired with CBI alleviates the problems associated with the burden of teaching a skill in only a community setting such as transportation, permission, cost, and schedule limitations. Finally, pairing the two types of instruction will also allow teachers to instruct larger groups in the classroom and use more strategies that are most effective while maintaining natural ratios and using inconspicuous strategies and materials for community instruction. See Table 8.10 for three additional examples of instruction that pair CBI with simulated instruction.

Next Steps: Selecting Evidence-based Practices for Simulated Instruction and CBI

Three recommendations are especially important when planning and implementing instruction aimed to improve community participation. First, using constant time delay guarantees errorless learning. Second, designing task analyses breaks complex tasks into discrete steps. Third,

Table 8.10 Examples of instruction that pair CBI with simulated instruction

Instructional content	Simulated instruction	CBI
Providing personal information at a doctor's office and waiting to be seen	Role-play including telling name to secretary in school and being called to be seen	Visiting local doctor's office for an appointment
Finding your seat at a basketball game	Using a map of the arena to identify where your seat is and role-playing with teacher in appropriate manner to ask for assistance if needed at home	Attending a basketball game and finding seat with least-to-most prompting
Identifying aisle signs in the grocery store	Instruction via constant time delay for aisle sign words as well as additional practice in sorting items to be found in various aisles in the classroom	Going to grocery store to find items on a grocery list using aisle signs

Table 8.11

Ms. Shepherd made plans to implement simulated instruction paired with CBI for her students. The simulated instruction would include the role-play scenarios in the classroom on Monday through Friday each week. The CBI would take place in community settings each Friday. See Table 8.12 to see how Ms. Shepherd pairs simulated instruction with CBI to teach purchasing skills to her students.

Table 8.12 Ms. Shepherd's plan for a week of Simulated Instruction paired with CBI to teach purchasing skills

Monday	*Skill area: purchasing skills*

Group 1 (with Teacher): Sarah, James, and Nicole
    Activity: Given visual representation of price and verbal statement of price, the students will use "one-more-than" method to pay up to $9.99
    Materials: Ten one-dollar bills for each student, notecards with prices up to $9.99 written
Group 2 (with paraprofessional): Jeremy, Tamara, and Jamil
    Activity: Given role play using a children's cash register which displays price and a verbal statement of price, the students will use "one-more-than" method to pay up to $9.99
    Materials: Ten one-dollar bills for each student, cash register
Group 3 (Independent): Maria and Heather
    Activity: Computer-based instruction via laptop computer using video footage and still photographs (Mechling, 2004)
    Materials: CD-ROM and laptop for each student

Tuesday	*Skill area: purchasing skills*

Group 1 (with paraprofessional): Jeremy, Tamara, and Jamil
    Activity: Given visual representation of price and verbal statement of price, the students will use "one-more-than" method to pay up to $9.99
    Materials: Ten one-dollar bills for each student, notecards with prices up to $9.99 written
Group 2 (with teacher): Maria and Heather
    Activity: Given role play using a children's cash register which displays price and a verbal statement of price, the students will use "one-more-than" method to pay up to $9.99
    Materials: Ten one-dollar bills for each student, cash register
Group 3 (Independent): Sarah, James, and Nicole
    Activity: Computer-based instruction via laptop computer using video footage and still photographs (Mechling, 2004)
    Materials: CD-ROM and laptop for each student

Wednesday	*Skill area: purchasing skills*

Group 1 (with paraprofessional): Maria and Heather
    Activity: Given visual representation of price and verbal statement of price, the students will use "one-more-than" method to pay up to $9.99
    Materials: Ten one-dollar bills for each student, notecards with prices up to $9.99 written
Group 2 (with teacher): Sarah, James, and Nicole
    Activity: Given role play using a children's cash register which displays price and a verbal statement of price, the students will use "one-more-than" method to pay up to $9.99
    Materials: Ten one-dollar bills for each student, cash register
Group 3 (Independent): Jeremy, Tamara, and Jamil
    Activity: Computer-based instruction via laptop computer using video footage and still photographs (Mechling, 2004)
    Materials: CD-ROM and laptop for each student

Thursday	*Skill area: purchasing skills*

Follow plan for Monday

Friday	_Skill area: purchasing skills_

CBI location: Target on Seventh Avenue
Materials: Ten one-dollar bills for each student
Group 1 (with teacher): Maria and Sarah
Group 2 (with paraprofessional): Nicole and Jamil
Group 3 (with speech therapist): Heather and James
Group 4 (with volunteer): Jeremy

training for generalization facilitates learners' use of skills in the settings and situations where they need them, which is the whole point!

Constant Time Delay

How It Works

Constant time delay involves instruction that includes (a) initial trials in which a student receives both the target stimulus and the controlling stimulus simultaneously (i.e., 0-second delay) and (b) later trials in which a predetermined delay is inserted between the target stimulus and the controlling stimulus (e.g., 4-second delay). The 0-second delay trials provide an opportunity for errorless learning in that students are provided with the question or direction, as well as the appropriate response, at the same time. For example, to teach a student to read the word _caution_ using constant time delay, the teacher would point to the word in print and say, "What word? (i.e., the target stimulus) Caution" (i.e., the controlling stimulus). In later trials, a predetermined amount of time would be inserted between the target stimulus and the controlling stimulus. For example, the teacher would point to the word in print and say, "What word?" (i.e., the target stimulus), insert a wait time of 4 seconds to allow for student's unprompted response. If the student does not respond, the teacher would then say, "Caution" (i.e., the controlling stimulus). If a student provides the incorrect response, such as "Cause," the teacher would immediately provide the controlling stimulus, "Caution." In subsequent sessions, the teacher would implement 0-second delay trials again for this word.

How Can Constant Time Delay Be Used to Teach Community-Referenced Skills?

Given the errorless learning afforded to students via constant time delay instruction, constant time delay is a valuable strategy in and out of the classroom. Additionally, research indicates that time delay is effective for teaching a variety of skills important to community participation. First, Cuvo and Klatt (1992) successfully used constant time delay to teach sight words to teenagers with intellectual disabilities. The researchers taught nine words in groups of three using flash cards in a school setting, videotaped recordings in a school setting, and naturally occurring signs in the community. Second, Branham, Collins, Schuster, & Kleinert (1999) used a time-delay procedure to teach high school students with intellectual disabilities skills including banking, street crossing, and mailing in the community. Each participant showed an increase in the target behavior and generalized the skill to different settings. Finally, Morse and Schuster (2000) used constant time delay to teach grocery shopping skills to elementary school students with intellectual disabilities. A majority of participants reached their criterion after intervention.

Task Analysis

How It Works

Task analysis involves breaking complex tasks down into their component parts. To write a task analysis, a teacher must first identify a task to be completed. Second, the teacher will identify the observable steps required to complete the task. Third, the teacher will field test the task analysis to be sure that all steps in the task are included and listed in appropriate order. Finally, the task analysis is ready for use. During instruction, the students learn to demonstrate individual steps in the chain, which in turn, is progress towards completing the entire task.

How Can Task Analysis Be Used to Teach Community-Referenced Skills?

Task analysis is an essential tool for teaching complex skill sequences in the classroom (e.g., using a calculator) and in a variety of other settings (e.g., washing clothes, completing hygiene tasks, and bussing a table in a restaurant). Further, a wealth of research indicates that task analysis instruction is effective in teaching community-referenced skills. First, Vandercook (1991) taught high school students with multiple disabilities to perform leisure skills (i.e., bowling and pinball) in a bowling alley. Second, Haring, Breen, Weiner, Kennedy, & Bednersh (1995) used task analysis instruction to teach purchasing skills to students with severe intellectual disabilities and autism in a variety of community settings (i.e., bookstores, convenience stores, drug stores, gift shops, grocery stores, hobby shops, record stores).

Training for Generalization

Training for generalization involves teaching students to use skills in situations and settings beyond the initial training settings and situations. Training for generalization includes a number of different strategies, including, but not limited to, the following: (a) program common stimuli, (b) mediate generalization, (c) teach functional target behaviors, (d) train loosely, (e) use natural maintaining contingencies, and (f) train sufficient exemplars (Stokes & Baer, 1977).

Program Common Stimuli

To program common stimuli, teachers will attempt to precisely re-create conditions from the generalization setting and present them in the initial teaching environment. In other words, during instruction, teachers should use materials that are the same as those the student will use in generalized settings. One challenge in implementing this strategy can be difficulty in creating the materials.

Mediate Generalization

To mediate generalization, teachers provide instruction on a co-behavior that can assist the student in generalizing target skills to new settings. Specifically, the co-behavior serves as an intermediary between performing the skill in the initial training setting and performing it in the generalization setting.

Teach Functional Target Behaviors

By teaching skills that are needed and used on a day-to-day basis, teachers are supporting students in using skill that are more likely to be reinforced in the natural environment, which, in turn, will support skill generalization. Conversely, when skills are taught that are not essential for everyday life, these skills are not likely to occur in new situations and settings.

Train Loosely

By training loosely, teachers allow naturally occurring situations to prompt and reinforce students' performance as opposed to intervening to provide precise prompts and specific types of reinforcement. To train loosely, teachers do not strictly control the instructional conditions since the conditions under which we perform skills vary across settings and situations.

Use Natural Maintaining Contingencies

To employ natural maintaining contingencies, teachers select skills for instruction that will later be reinforced naturally in the environment in which the behavior typically occurs. Conversely, skills that will typically be reinforced via artificial means (e.g., candy, sticker) will pose challenges for facilitating generalization.

Train Sufficient Exemplars

Using sufficient exemplars in training involves teaching students in a manner that prepares them to perform a target skill in the wide array of situations where it is needed. To represent the various situations in which students must perform the skill, teachers can evaluate the numerous settings and situations in which students will be expected to perform the skill and systematically represent these characteristics in instruction.

When teachers plan life-skills instruction, they should also make a plan for supporting generalization by selecting one of these strategies. Given that these strategies are evidence-based, students are more likely to generalize the skills to new environments, that is, to perform skills in the variety of settings in which the skills are needed. See Table 8.13 for an example of how each generalization strategy can be used to support community-referenced instruction.

Conclusions

As a special educator, you have an enormous responsibility to teach valuable content and employ effective strategies. Although federal mandates place an emphasis on academic learning for students with disabilities, historically poor post-school outcomes among students with disabilities highlight the need for life-skill instruction. By finding a balance between academics and life skills and selecting evidence-based instructional strategies, special educators can support

Table 8.13 Facilitating generalization of community-referenced skills

Strategy	Example
Program common stimuli	Use real money instead of fake bills during purchasing role-play activities in the classroom since these materials are present in authentic purchasing situations.
Mediate generalization	Teach students to use a list to collect items needed for a task in the classroom and groceries in the grocery store.
Teach functional target behaviors	Teach students to use language for a purpose (e.g., requesting a drink) rather than when directed.
Train loosely	Use a variety of clerks and checkout aisles at the store on twice weekly trips to different grocery stores. Don't intervene to provide precise prompting and reinforcement. Let the situation prompt and reinforce.
Use natural maintaining contingencies	Teach purchasing skills in the school cafeteria. Natural maintaining contingencies are the food items purchased and eaten.
Train sufficient exemplars	When teaching ATM skills, to use many ATMs rather than one particular ATM.

students with disabilities as they move from high school to all arenas of adult life, including postsecondary education, employment, and independent living. The instructional decisions you make will have an everlasting impact on your students. To be confident your impact is a positive one, provide life-skills instruction via research-based strategies.

References

Alberto, P. A., Cihak, D. F., & Gama, R. I. (2005). Use of static picture prompts versus video modeling during simulation instruction. *Research in Developmental Disabilities, 26*, 327–339.

Algozzine, B., Browder, D., Karvonen, M., Test, D. W., & Wood, W. M. (2001). Effects of interventions to promote self-determination for individuals with disabilities. *Review of Educational Research, 71*, 219–277.

Berg, W. K., Wacker, D. P., Ebbers, B., Wiggins, B., Fowler, M., & Wilkes, P. (1995). A demonstration of generalization of performance across settings, materials, and motor responses for students with profound mental retardation. *Behavior Modification, 19*, 119–143.

Branham, R. S., Collins, B. C., Schuster, J. W., & Kleinert, H. (1999). Teaching community skills to students with moderate disabilities: Comparing combined techniques of classroom simulation, video-tape modeling, and community-based instruction. *Education and Training in Mental Retardation and Developmental Disabilities, 34*, 170–181.

Bullis, M., Davis, C., Bull, B., & Johnson, B. (1995). Transition achievement among young adults with deafness: What variables relate to success? *Rehabilitation Counseling Bulletin, 39*, 130–150.

Cihak, D. F., Alberto, P. A., Kessler, K. B., & Taber, T. A. (2004). An investigation of instructional sched-uling arrangements for community-based instruction. *Research in Developmental Disabilities, 25*, 67–88.

Clark, G. M., Field, S., Patton, J. R., Brolin, D. E., & Sitlington, P. L. (1994). Life skills instruction: A necessary component for all students with disabilities: A position statement of the Division on Career Development and Transition. *Career Development for Exceptional Individuals, 17*, 125–134.

Cronin, M. E. (1996). Life skills curricula for students with learning disabilities: A review of the literature. *Journal of Learning Disabilities, 29*, 53–68.

Cuvo, A. J., & Klatt, K. P. (1992). Effects of community-based, videotape, and flash card instruction of community-referenced sight words on students with mental retardation. *Journal of Applied Behavior Analysis, 25*, 499–512.

Davies, D., Stock, S., & Wehmeyer, M. L. (2003). Application of computer simulation to teach ATM access to individuals with intellectual disabilities. *Education and Training in Developmental Disabilities, 38*, 451–456.

Davis, C. A., Brady, M. P., Williams, W. E., & Burta, M. (1992). The effects of self-operated auditory prompting tapes on the performance fluency of persons with severe mental retardation. *Education and Treatment in Mental Retardation, 27*, 39–50.

Denny, P., & Test, D. (1995). Using the one-more-than technique to teach money counting to individuals with moderate mental retardation: A systematic replication. *Education & Treatment of Children, 18*, 422–32.

Ferguson, B., & McDonnell, J. (1991). A comparison of serial and concurrent sequencing strategies in teaching generalized grocery item location to students with moderate handicaps. *Education and Training in Mental Retardation, 26*, 292–304.

Field, S., Martin, J., Miller, R., Ward, M., & Wehmeyer, M. (1998). *A practical guide for teaching self-determination*. Reston, VA: Council for Exceptional Children.

Gibb, G. S., & Dyches, T. T. (2007) *Guide to writing quality individualized education programs*. (2nd ed.). Boston, MA: Pearson.

Halpern, A. (1985). Transition: A look at the foundations. *Exceptional Children, 51*, 479–486.

Halpern, A. (1992). Transition: Old wine in new bottles. *Exceptional Children, 58*, 202–211.

Haring, T. G., Breen, C. G., Weiner, J., Kennedy, C. H., & Bednersh, F. (1995). Using videotape modeling to facilitate generalized purchasing skills. *Journal of Behavioral Education, 5*, 29–53.

Heal, L. W., Khoju, M., & Rusch, F. R. (1997). Predicting quality of life of youths after they leave special education high school programs. *The Journal of Special Education, 31*, 279–299.

Heal, L. W., Khoju, M., Rusch, F. R., & Harnisch, D. L. (1999). Predicting quality of life of students who have left special education high school programs. *American Journal on Mental Retardation, 104*, 305–319.

Heal, L. W., & Rusch, F. R. (1994). Prediction of residential independence of special education high school students. *Research in Developmental Disabilities, 15*, 223–243.

Heward, W. L. (2009). *Exceptional Children: An introduction to special education* (9th ed.). Upper Saddle River, NJ: Merrill/ Prentice Hall.

Individuals with Disabilities Education Improvement Act of 2004 (IDEA), 20 U.S.C.

Mechling, L. C., & Cronin, B. (2006). Computer-based video instruction to teach the use of augmentative and alternative communication devices for ordering at fast food restaurants. *The Journal of Special Education, 39*, 234–245.

Mechling, L. C., Gast, D. L., & Langone, J. (2002). Computer-based video instruction to teach persons with moderate intellectual disabilities to read grocery aisle signs and locate items. *The Journal of Special Education, 35*, 224–240.

Mithaug, D., Martin, J. E., & Agran, M. (1987). Adaptability instruction: The goal of transitional programming. *Exceptional Children, 53*, 500–505.

Montague, M. (1988). Job-related social skills training for adolescents with handicaps. *Career Development for Exceptional Individuals, 11*, 27–41.

Morse, T. E., & Schuster, J. W. (2000). Teaching elementary students with moderate intellectual disabilities how to shop for groceries. *Exceptional Children, 66*, 273–288.

Newman, L., Wagner, M., Cameto, R., & Knokey, A. M. (2009). *The post-high school outcomes of youth with disabilities up to 4 years after high school. A report from the National Longitudinal Transition Study–2 (NLTS2)* (NCSER 2009–3017). Menlo Park, CA: SRI International.

Nietupski, J., Hamre-Nietupski, S., Clancy, P., & Veerhusen, K. (1986). Guidelines for making simulation an effective adjunct to in vivo community instruction. *Journal of the Association for Persons with Severe Handicaps, 11*, 12–18.

Pattavina, S., Bergstrom, T., Marchand-Martella, N. E., & Martella, R. C. (1992). "Moving on": Learning to cross streets independently. *Teaching Exceptional Children, 25*(1), 32–35.

Polloway, E. A., Patton, J. R., & Serna, L. (2008). *Strategies for teaching learners with special needs* (9th ed.). Upper Saddle River, NJ: Prentice Hall/Merrill.

Shafer, M. S., Inge, K. J., & Hill, J. (1986). Acquisition, generalization, and maintenance of automated banking skills. *Education and Training of the Mentally Retarded, 21*, 265–272.

Sitlington, P. L., Neubert, D. A., & Leconte, P. J. (1997). Transition assessment: The position of the Division on Career Development and Transition. *Career Development for Exceptional Individuals, 20*, 69–79.

Smith, T. E. (2004). *Teaching students with special needs in inclusive settings* (4th ed.). Boston, MA: Allyn and Bacon.

Souza, G., & Kennedy, C. H. (2003). Facilitating social interactions in the community for a transition-age student with severe disabilities. *Journal of Positive Behavior Interventions, 5*, 179–182.

Stokes, T. F., & Baer, D. M. (1977). An implicit technology of generalization. *Journal of Applied Behavior Analysis, 10*, 349–367.

Storms, J., O'Leary, E., & Williams, J. (2000). *Transition requirements: A guide for states, districts, schools, universities and families.* Stillwater, OK: National Clearinghouse of Rehabilitation Training Materials.

Taber, T. A., Alberto, P. A., Hughes, M., & Seltzer, A. (2002). A strategy for students with moderate disabilities when lost in the community. *Research and Practice for Persons with Severe Disabilities, 27*, 141–152.

Test, D. W., Fowler, C. H., Richter, S. M., Mazzotti, V., White, J., & Walker, A. R. (2009). Evidence-based practices in secondary transition. *Career Development for Exceptional Individuals, 32*, 115–128.

Test, D. W., Mazzotti, V. L., Mustian, A. L., Fowler, C. H., Kortering, L. J., & Kohler, P. H. (2009). Evidence-based secondary transition predictors for improving post-school outcomes for students with disabilities. *Career Development for Exceptional Individuals, 32*, 160–181.

Thoma, C. A., Held, M. F., & Saddler, S. (2002). Transition assessment practices in Nevada and Arizona: Are they tied to best practices? *Focus on Autism and Other Developmental Disabilities, 17*, 242–250.

Vandercook, T. (1991). Leisure instruction outcomes: Criterion performance, positive interactions, and acceptance by typical high school peers. *The Journal of Special Education, 25*, 320–339.

Walker, A. R., Uphold, N. M., Richter, S., & Test, D. W. (2010). A review of the literature on community-based instruction across grade levels. *Education and Training in Autism and Developmental Disabilities, 45*, 242–267.

Wehmeyer, M. L., & Palmer, S. B. (2003). Adult outcomes for students with cognitive disabilities three years after high school: The impact of self-determination. *Education and Training in Developmental Disabilities, 38*, 131–144.

Will, M. (1984). *OSERS programming for transition of youth with disabilities: Bridges from school to working life.* Washington, DC: U.S. Department of Education.

Wissick, C. A., Gardner, J. E., & Langone, J. (1999). Video-based simulations: Considerations for teaching students with developmental disabilities. *Career Development for Exceptional Individuals, 22*, 233–249.

9

Preparing Students for the 21st Century Workforce

Cheryl Hanley-Maxwell

UNIVERSITY OF WISCONSIN

Margaretha Vreeburg Izzo

THE OHIO STATE UNIVERSITY

Historically, the purpose of education in the United States is to prepare youth to become productive members of society, including maintaining employment, being good citizens, paying taxes, and contributing to our economy (Hanley-Maxwell & Collet-Klingenberg, 2012). The success of schools in fulfilling this purpose has been called into question as the global economy has challenged America's ranking as a world leader in the "high skills-high wages" race (Taskforce on the Future of American Innovation, 2005). Preparing youth for employment in this rapidly changing job market requires schools to reconsider both what and how we teach so our youth will have the skills to successfully compete for 21st century jobs. As a result, significant questions remain how to best prepare our youth for successful transitions to unknown future employment. These questions encompass the preparation of youth with and without disabilities.

Unfortunately, youth with disabilities face a more uncertain future than do their peers without disabilities (Newman, Wagner, Cameto, & Knokey, 2009). Rates of unemployment and underemployment are higher and access to postsecondary education, frequently required for better paying jobs, is more uncertain. According to a 2009 report from the National Longitudinal Transition Study (NLTS–2), 53% of out-of-school youth with disabilities were employed at the time of the interview, as compared to 66% of youth in the general population (Newman et al., 2009). Enrollment in postsecondary education evidenced a similar pattern; 45% of youth with disabilities were enrolled in some type of postsecondary program, as compared with 53% of youth in the general population (Newman et al., 2009). Although the NLTS reveals inequities, data related to overall employment rates for adults with disabilities reveal an even darker picture. For adults living in the community, the employment rate for individuals with disabilities is only 36.2% compared with a rate of 75% for individuals without disabilities (Rehabilitation Research and Training Center on Disability Statistics and Demographics, 2009).

Lower employment rates reflect a variety of issues that confront job-seeking adults with disabilities. These issues involve systems-related problems that range from financial disincentives and difficulty finding transportation services to employer biases (Wehman, Brooke, & Inge, 2001). Of more concern is that individuals with disabilities also face educator and adult service providers' negative assumptions and beliefs about their employability (Szymanski, Enright, & Hershenson, 2003). These lowered expectations result in restricted access to certain types of training and experiences (Szymanski et al., 2003). Consequently, poor employment rates may reflect the fact that students do not receive access to curricula and experiences that provide them with opportunities to establish transition goals based on their interests and abilities and ultimately prepare them for employment.

The continuation of poor employment outcomes for adults with disabilities is especially distressing given that over thirty years of legislation and research have focused on improving employment outcomes. Numerous commissions, alliances, and legislative mandates have established transition to employment for youth as a priority. Some of the more notable initiatives include the career education programs of the 1970s, the secondary and transition initiatives of the 1980s, the transition services mandates of the 1990s, the Secretary's Commission on Achieving Necessary Skills (SCANS, 1993), Taxonomy for Transition Programming (Kohler, 1996), the National Alliance for Secondary Education and Transition (NASAT, 2005), and the Partnership for 21st Century Skills (2010). Additionally, the U.S. Department of Education, Office of Special Education Programs funded two technical assistance centers that specifically address the transition process: National Secondary Transition Technical Assistance Center and the National Post-School Outcomes Center.

Current education legislation mandates that high schools ensure all students have the skills necessary for employment (No Child Left Behind Act of 2001, NCLB (PL 107–110); Goals 2000: Educate America Act of 1994 (PL 103–227):). The Individuals with Disabilities Education Improvement Act of 2004 defined transition services as a "coordinated set of activities that is designed within a results-oriented process, that is focused on improving the academic and functional achievement of the child with a disability to facilitate the child's movement from school to post-school activities including post-secondary education, vocational education, integrated employment (including supported employment), continuing and adult education, adult services, independent living, or community participation" (IDEA, 2004, Sec. 602). NCLB mandated that state and local education agencies improve the quality of secondary education, deliver standards-based instruction for all students, *and ensure that students are prepared to enter college and the workforce with the skills to succeed.*

Both IDEA (2004) and NCLB (2001) reflect an emphasis on academic proficiency, standards-based reform, and high-stakes testing for an increasingly technologically driven world. This new era of accountability mandates that schools provide students with disabilities an individualized education program (IEP) that identifies measurable postsecondary goals for employment, further education and training, and independent living. The IEP outlines the delivery of a coordinated set of transition services/activities including instruction, community experiences, related services, and adult linkages that prepare students with disabilities for employment (IDEA of 2004). These mandates generate a philosophical challenge for educators: How do we teach standards-based education and deliver individualized transition services to prepare each student for the 21st century workforce? What content must we teach to assure each student is prepared for the 21st century? What process, settings, and experiences best prepare youth to become productive members of the workforce? The purpose of this chapter is to address these questions by providing a framework that utilizes evidence-based research for integrating academic, career, and transition skills through authentic learning experiences that synthesize 21st century skills youth need to engage in meaningful and productive employment.

Twenty-first Century Skills Defined

While Congress and educators focused on schools' roles in preparing youth for the workforce, in 1990 the U.S. Department of Labor established the Secretary's Commission on Achieving Necessary Skills (SCANS) that included representatives from businesses, unions, government, and schools. The purpose of this Commission was to identify the type and level of skills our youth need to succeed in a high-performance economy characterized by high-skill, high-wage employment (U.S. Department of Labor, n.d). The foundation skills and basic competency areas identified by SCANS include basic academic skills, thinking skills, personal qualities, and basic competencies related to the use of resources, technology, information, interpersonal skills, and systems thinking (SCANS, 1993). Although developed in the 1990s, the SCANS skills and competencies serve as an important framework that provides a comprehensive overview of the skills youth should acquire to become contributing members of the workforce (Workplace Essential Skills: Resources Related to the SCANS Competencies and Foundation Skills Release Date: 2000).

SCANS skills have been affirmed and expanded by recent work in the area of 21st century skills, defined as proficiency in core subjects such as English, mathematics, sciences, history, languages; life and career skills such as self-direction, productivity, social and cross–cultural skills; and information, media and technology skills (Partnership for 21st Century Skills, 2011). Information technology is defined as the skills needed to find, retrieve, analyze, and use information (American Association of College and Research Libraries, 2011). The Partnership for 21st Century Skills (2011) recommends that educators (a) emphasize core subjects that incorporate 21st century tools and skills; (b) use 21st century tools to develop learning skills in current standards, curricula, and assessments of core subjects; (c) teach and learn in a 21st century context and content (i.e., real-world applications and examples); and (d) use 21st century assessments to measure 21st century skills.

Technological influences have irrevocably redefined our world and created an environment in which future job demands will reflect the accelerating pace of technological change, requiring future employees to be proficient using computer hardware and software programs. For example, Jeff is a high school student with severe disabilities who works at West Hospital as an intern stocking patient rooms with medical supplies. He walks up to the computerized locked supply cabinet and enters his user name and password into the locked supply cabinet. He places his finger on the finger scan to confirm his identity. The hospital supply cabinet unlocks. He loads his supply cart with the syringes, medical tape, and dressings he needs to restock patient rooms. Once he obtains the supplies, he logs off to automatically relock the cabinets.

Schools across the nation are engaging in redesign and reform efforts to offer educational experiences that integrate rigorous academic instruction with relevant learning experiences, with an emphasis on career and transition skills (Bassett & Kochhar-Bryant, 2006; Izzo, Torres, & Johnson, 2005; Joselowsky, 2007). Schools that are initiating these reforms are adopting evidence-based practices and pedagogical approaches to deliver content in authentic settings to engage students with disabilities who acquire the 21st century skills needed to transition to the 21st century workforce as productive members of society.

Content: Academic, Career, and Transition Skills

The skills associated with 21st century employment make it clear that work preparation begins earlier than the secondary education years, and extends beyond high school. In fact, employment skills represent the culmination and combination of the skills and knowledge children, adolescents and adults acquire throughout their development. Not all students must have highly developed skills in all academic, career, and transition areas. But all must have some skill developed in each area or have the supports or assistive technology needed to compensate for missing skills.

Changing economies, globalization, and resulting changes in labor markets dictate that future employees leave formal schooling with a set of marketable, flexible skills, useful across occupational clusters. Future employees will need to be prepared to be able to change job roles and functions, requiring them to be able to self-assess, set goals, and identify, obtain, and organize additional education/training needed to pursue their changing goals (Partnership for 21st Century Skills, 2011).

Although there is some debate as to whether or not anyone can identify a set of skills that applies to all occupations, there is consensus on a core set of skills. Using a Career and Life Skills lens that promotes authentic learning emphasizing value beyond school, Table 9.1 provides an overview of skills needed for 21st century jobs and the evidence-based practices that can be used to ensure that students acquire these skills.

This section reorganizes and further describes the core set of skills, using an organizational model proposed by Hanley-Maxwell and Collet-Klingenberg (2012). For purposes of discussion, the skills are grouped within three categories: foundation skills, integrative skills, and application skills. In reality, youth and adults combine and recombine skills in these areas as they apply them in employment settings.

Foundation Skills

Foundational skills are the simple-to-complex skills that provide the underpinning for a variety of occupations later in life (Steere, Rose, & Cavaiulo, 2007). Foundation skills include skills in four general areas: personal care, communication, academics, and technology.

Table 9.1 Content and skills needed for the 21st century workforce

Foundation	Integrative	Application
LIFE SKILLS	**SOCIAL SKILLS**	**CAREER PLANNING**
Personal care	Hygiene	Interest assessment
Transportation	Dresses appropriately	Self assessment
Physical/mental health	Daily living skills	Vocational training
Safety	Follows social rules	Mentoring
Communication		Career exploration
		Post-graduation/IEP planning
CORE ACADEMIC SKILLS	**SELF-DETERMINATION**	Career portfolios
English	Self-knowledge	
Mathematics	Self-direction	
Sciences	Plans and sets goals	**JOB SEARCH**
History	Self-regulates	Community-based instruction
CAREER SKILLS	Problem solving	Work experience
Abilities	Self-advocacy	Service learning
Interests		Job clubs
Limitations		Apprenticeships and internships
Values		
Accommodation needs		
INFORMATION, MEDIA, TECHNOLOGY SKILLS	**PERSONAL VALUES**	
Find & analyze Information	Responsible	
Computer & internet skills	Respectful	
Using media	Collaborates	
Work technologies	Cooperates	
Communication technologies	Ethical	
	Continuously learns	

Personal Care

At the most basic level, future employees must be able to take care of their everyday needs or have supports in place to help them meet their personal-care needs. These daily living skills support employment (Schloss, Schloss, & Schloss, 2007), as opposed to being directly related to employment, and include dressing, grooming, hygiene, eating, mobility and use of transportation alternatives, and other activities needed to function in everyday life, as well as to prepare for work. In addition to addressing the traditional personal-care areas, skills in this area incorporate maintaining physical and mental health, including prevention and intervention. Future employees need to understand how their physical and mental health can affect job performance by impacting stamina, attendance, attention to task, independence, etc. (Partnership for 21st Century Skills, 2011).

Communication

Communication skills are built around expressing and receiving (verbally and nonverbally) information and include responding to directions or questions, asking for help, contributing information, decoding the meaning of nonverbal communication, and interacting in social situations (Hanley-Maxwell & Collet-Klingenberg, 2012). Deficits in communication skills are, in part, a defining characteristic of many disabilities such as autism spectrum disorder, intellectual disabilities, learning disabilities, and emotional or behavioral disorders (Cartledge, 2005; Downing, 2005). Alwell and Cobb (2009) reported strong support for teaching communication interventions with transition-age youth that used prompting, videotape modeling, differential feedback, role-playing, and rehearsal to teach conversation and social skills. Roessler, Brolin, & Johnson (1990) reported that students with high social skills were more likely to be engaged in post-school employment.

Within the context of 21st century jobs, communication takes on new forms and meanings, requiring employees to interact with diverse individuals in a professional and respectful manner, using proper etiquette, and when appropriate, communicating expectations to others through behaviors. It also includes knowing how to use various forms of communication, including media and digital technologies. Successful digital communications require the user to know how to create, transmit, and obtain information/ideas, applying appropriate constructions or conventions related to their use. Sophisticated media and digital communication also include understanding the purposes of those communications and the impact of these communications on the individuals involved (Partnership for 21st Century Skills, 2011). For example, Emma works at West Hospital as a patient care assistant. She wears a Vocera®, an employee communication and location device, around her neck just like all the other employees at West Hospital. She uses her Vocera® to keep in touch with her supervisor and report any emergencies. Initially Emma used the Vocera® to interrupt others' work with off-task remarks. Emma's job coach taught her how to use the Vocera® correctly. Now Emma asks questions and receives direction from her job coach and worksite supervisor using the communication device, saving valuable time and effort.

Academic Skills

Academic skills or knowing how to use accommodations and assistive technology in the areas of reading, math, science, and writing is essential to succeeding in work environments (Schloss et al., 2007). Skills in these three areas range from functional usage to technical and creative applications.

Emerging occupations demand that future employees obtain information by reading in various formats (words, pictures, symbols, figures), and use that information to be creative and innovative by synthesizing, analyzing, and predicting (Partnership for 21st Century Skills,

2011). Like reading, math skills step beyond functional use to using mathematical data to inform decisions and guide actions. At the lowest level, writing skills are needed to complete job applications, create resumes and application letters, and sign legal documents. They are also needed for creating communications related to job tasks (e.g., memos, invoices) and fulfilling jobs expectations in careers related to writing (e.g., journalism, editing, authoring). Employees also need to be facile with various forms of written communication (e.g., e-mails, blogs, electronic scheduling), integrating reading and writing skills with higher-order thinking skills as they appropriately use the related technologies.

Knowledge in the various core academic subjects also influences employability in that jobs in the 21st century will reflect the increasingly complicated world in which jobs exist. Worldwide economies and networks demand that future employees develop competence related to global and civic issues. Additionally, skills from the various content areas will need to be combined to ensure that future employees understand how various financial and economic issues affect business and entrepreneurial endeavors, as well as communities and their governmental structures, and themselves. Finally, to access the high technology jobs of the future, employment candidates will need varying levels of skill in the areas of science, technology, engineering, and math (Hilton, 2008). Consequently, special educators must hold high academic expectations for students with disabilities (Benz, Lindstrom, & Yovanoff, 2000), incorporating higher-order thinking skills into academic content knowledge. Rapidly changing and emerging jobs as well as the increasing use of technology require future workers to use higher-order thinking skills that are flexible and adaptable, readily learning and performing new and modified skills (Luecking & Fabian, 2000).

Academic content should be taught authentically, enhancing relevance by helping the student connect the content to present and future uses (especially within the context of work). Providing students with instruction and experience in applying academic skills to their chosen career empowers students to gain needed academic skills and set realistic goals. Izzo and Lamb (2002) recommend that teachers integrate theoretical learning with applied, experiential learning, connecting school- and work-based learning. These connections have a positive impact on students' self-determination and transition skills as evidenced by increased motivation, persistence, and decision-making (Eisenman, 2001). Furthermore, community-focused and functionally oriented curricula, and community work experiences contribute significantly to post-school employment (Benz et al., 2000).

Information, Media, and Technology

Numerous researchers are calling for an increase in the development and use of accessible electronic texts, online curricula, and digitized resources to improve access to, and achievement in, the general curriculum (Anderson-Inman & Horney, 2007; Boone & Higgins, 2007; Rose & Meyer, 2006). The use of information, media, and technology can serve as powerful learning tools that compensate for deficits in reading, writing, and information-processing skills (Fried-Oken, 2007). Students with disabilities who use assistive technology such as text-to-speech (TTS), organizational software, and voice recognition applications are able to read information, organize, and write their thoughts more clearly (Forgrave, 2002). Izzo, Yurick, et al. (2009) reported that TTS improved students' quiz performance in an online curriculum. Boone, Burke, Fore, & Spencer (2006) recommended using computer technology to provide simulated life situations by incorporating photographs depicting actual scenarios, as well as an interactive format that provides content and feedback to students. Stock, Davies, Secor, & Wehmeyer (2003) used a multimedia computer program that included video clips, audio recordings, and digitized content about specific job options for adults with intellectual disabilities and reported that participants expressed job preferences based on the information provided. Mazzotti, Test, Wood, & Richter (2010) reported that computer-assisted instruction was an effective strategy for teaching students with intellectual disabilities about their post-school options for employment, independent living, and postsecondary education.

Effectively using various information, media, and technology tools is critical to success in many employment settings (Izzo, Murray, & O'Hanlon, 2005). Numerous businesses accept online job applications and deliver required trainings via password-protected internet sites or computer-assisted instructional programs, so learning information technology skills is essential to gaining and maintaining employment.

Integrative Skills

Integrative skills develop across an individual's life and are often taught within the context of other skills. They are important to the acquisition and application of foundational skills as well as the continued learning of the individual. These skills are interrelated and include the "covert cognitive skills that underlie functional skill usage" (Hanley-Maxwell & Collet-Klingenberg, 2012, p. 544). Inclusion of this category highlights the need to assist students in acquiring the skills in three primary categories: social skills, self-determination, and personal values.

Social Skills

Social competence is defined as a person's ability to influence the behavior of those around him or her and adjust that behavior to match social norms in varied settings (Janney & Snell, 2006). In a systematic review of interventions to improve social and communication skills of secondary students with disabilities, Alwell and Cobb (2009) reported that social-skill training interventions improved targeted social skills. They concluded that promoting the acquisition, performance, and generalization of prosocial behaviors ultimately improves transition outcomes for youth.

Social skills are a crucial component of job success. Current projections for 21st century jobs focus on growth in the service sector and in professional/technical careers. Careers in both sectors require employees to have good social skills. Even in highly independent technical careers, employment projections highlight the need for employees to be able to work in teams, cooperating, considering others' perspectives, problem solving, and negotiating conflict in multicultural environments (Hilton, 2008).

Social skills can be viewed on the "micro-level" as the skills needed to engage in interpersonal interactions (e.g., turn-taking in conversations, eye contact, understanding interpersonal space). They also play out in the variety of communication and collaboration skills needed to work within groups, and to use digital media and communication effectively. All local or distant interactions require the individual employee to negotiate meaning and differences of opinion, communicate successfully across varying cultural and technological milieus, and appropriately exhibit leadership and responsibility. In an increasingly global environment, social skills also require that employees understand their rights and responsibilities as employees and citizens (Partnership for 21st Century Skills, 2011).

Self-Determination

Emphases on helping students with disabilities develop self-determination skills are in concert with the demands of 21st century jobs. At the core, self-determination skills build on self-knowledge and the sense of self, to create a person who exhibits a culturally appropriate degree of autonomy by being self-directed, self-regulated, and self-efficacious (Wehmeyer, 2003). The degree to which an individual engages in self-determined behavior is shaped by the learning and development of that person, and the opportunities, supports, and accommodations available to that individual (Shogren et al., 2007).

Self-determined behavior related to employment requires individuals to have knowledge of their own interests, skills, and needs; job types and their associated requirements; and the resources available to them (e.g., training opportunities, college programs, legal rights). Goal setting and attainment combine and apply knowledge in these areas as the individual works towards his/her desired employment outcomes. Embedded in the planning and execution processes are skills related to choice making, problem solving, decision-making, self-regulation and self-advocacy or leadership (Wehmeyer, 2003). Additionally, individuals must consider the risks and benefits of various courses of actions as they make and enact decisions (Hanley-Maxwell & Collet-Klingenberg, 2012). Ultimately, self-determination skills help employees enhance their own productivity and may drive their own continued learning.

Personal Values

Personal values such as respect, responsibility, perseverance, integrity, ethics, and commitment are critical employment skills (Partnership for 21st Century Skills, 2011). To ensure that future employees develop the values, flexibility, and self-direction skills needed to survive and prosper in 21st century jobs, they must be given opportunities to learn and practice increasing levels of autonomy. Early experiences help students develop self-esteem and self-determination skills. Additionally, early responsibilities such as home and school responsibilities/chores, neighborhood jobs (e.g., lawn mowing, dog walking), and participating in school and community groups, sports, and clubs help students develop effective work behavior. Early responsibilities also help to develop work support values and behaviors such as attendance, punctuality, effort, time management, independence, and cooperation (Steere, Rose, et al., 2007).

Personal values are also entwined with accessing and using media, information, and technology during and after work. With increasing access to information and dissemination tools, future employees need to understand the associated legal, ethical, and privacy issues and engage in access and use behaviors that reflect their understanding of these issues (Partnership for 21st Century Skills, 2011).

Application Skills

Application skills combine fundamental and integrative skills for use in specific jobs, career planning, and job seeking, and eventually in specific jobs. Application skills may also require additional postsecondary education or training. Student interests, abilities, and needs, as well as the demands of targeted job types and community expectations, determine the combinations of fundamental and integrative skills when they are applied in job settings.

Hilton (2008) predicts that future jobs will increasingly be in the service industry (mostly manual tasks) and high-skilled professions (mostly abstract tasks), already accounting for approximately half of all jobs in 2006. She also predicts that the lines between job types will gradually blur, requiring employees to blend technical and service skills and knowledge with strong social and higher-order thinking skills. These emerging requirements make the task of identifying application skills even more difficult. However, because of these flexible and emerging job descriptions and the recreation of job characteristics, it may be possible to create additional job opportunities for persons with disabilities, capitalizing on their assets.

Current occupations for adults with disabilities are limited mostly to service industry jobs (e.g., restaurant and food services, janitorial), other manual labor occupations (e.g., construction, production, and stocking), retail/sales, and office-related work (Morgan, Ellerd, Jensen, & Taylor, 2000). Skills associated with these job types consist of keyboarding, word processing, and data entry; filing, telephone answering, copying, collating/stapling, mail prep; packaging, pricing, delivery, and light assembly; and cleaning tasks (Johnson & Wehman, 2001).

These job clusters and their related skills do not represent all the possible employment opportunities for individuals with disabilities. Instead, they reflect, in part, educators' and human service providers' assumptions and expectations about the learning and performance characteristics of persons with disabilities. Consequently, it is important that educators use student interests and goals to guide potential career selections instead of using historical employment patterns. Starting with student interest and goals creates an interactive approach to preparing students for employment rather than preparing them for a job (Hanley-Maxwell & Collet-Klingenberg, 2012). Interests and goals interact with experiences and the divergent thinking of the educator to identify or create multiple employment opportunities that are unique to the individual student. The commonalities in these opportunities can be used to identify and assist students in developing skills that cut across occupational areas, identify needed accommodation and adaptations, identify needed and available supports, and shape potential jobs to better fit with students' assets.

Career planning and job search are application skills that allow students to respond to their changing interests and goals, growing through their career exploration and work experiences. Skills in these areas should be taught in conjunction with the skills related to targeted job clusters, providing students with applied planning and search experiences.

Career Planning

Career planning applies self-determination skills (e.g., self-knowledge, self-awareness, planning) to preparing for employment. Career planning uses self-knowledge related to interests, aptitudes, values, personal strengths and limitations to make informed choices about careers that match a person's personal preferences and attributes. It combines self-knowledge with occupational knowledge, knowing what jobs or job types are available or likely to be available, and the requirements of these jobs/job types (Benz et al., 2000; Eisenman, 2001) to identify potential career opportunities and to assist the student in planning to reach career goals. Izzo, Yurick, Nagaraja, & Novak (2012) reported that online curricula significantly increased students' knowledge of how to set career goals, find jobs, complete online job applications, and select colleges that match their career goal, as compared to students in traditional high school classes.

Job Search

Teaching job search skills is identified as an evidence-based practice associated with improving transition outcomes (Benz et al., 2000; Nelson, Smith, & Dodd, 1994; Test, Fowler, et al., 2009). Locating available jobs and contact information and obtaining general information about potential jobs are important first steps. Future employees also need to know how to apply for jobs (e.g., online, in person, paper applications) and how to interview for jobs (formally and informally). Beyond knowing the purposes and process of interviewing, future employees need to know how to begin and close an interview. They also need to know how to present information about their disabilities, work histories, relevant skills and experiences; obtain information about the job (e.g., wage, benefits, hours, requisite skills, job tasks); and address other relevant topics in a way that reflect best on the interviewee (Hanley-Maxwell & Collet-Klingenberg, 2012). These skills help employees enhance their own productivity and may drive their own continued learning.

Processes for Preparing Students for Work

The National Alliance for Secondary Education and Transition (NASET, 2005a) published national standards and quality indicators that provide guideposts to assist all students in navigating the transition process. Building upon the three components authorized in the School-to-Work Act of 1994 (i.e., school-based learning, work-based learning, and connecting activities to link the content learned in school to workplace applications), NASET created five guideposts: (1) school-based preparatory experiences, (2) career preparation and work-based learning experiences, (3) youth development and leadership, (4) family involvement, and (5) connecting activities. Standards and indicators for each of these guideposts provide a universal approach for preparing all youth for employment. In the previous sections we discussed school-preparatory experiences. In this section, we focus on career preparation and work-based learning experiences to connect students to post-school jobs. Family involvement is addressed by another chapter of this text so we refer you to Chapter 9 for information about this essential topic.

Career Exploration

Career exploration begins in early childhood through the development of career fantasies. Nurturing career fantasies by allowing students to explore "what they want to be when they grow up" assists students in beginning to compare their interests and skills with potential careers. This is the beginning of a process in which students identify career interests, explore how these interests fit with their vision of the future, and progressively narrow their interests through a variety of experiences. The process is enhanced when children have home and neighborhood jobs and chores, observe appropriate work models, explore various career opportunities (e.g., field trips, career days, job shadowing, job sampling), and use interest assessments and career exploration tools (e.g., career software programs and other electronic resources). Through these experiences, students progressively move toward career options that represent real job opportunities and closer interest/skill matches (Szymanski, Enright, et al., 2003).

Career exploration opportunities also include participating in rehabilitation agency-sponsored job clubs (Johnson & Wehman, 2001) and occupationally related school clubs (Steere et al., 2007). In addition, vocational training and work experiences provide a greater depth of occupational knowledge, further refining the student's career interests and goals.

Work Experience

Work experience includes home and community jobs, service learning, vocational training programs and apprenticeships, paid work experiences, work-based training (Schloss et al., 2007), and internships (Rutkowski, Daston, et al., 2006). The purpose of these experiences is to provide students with the information about themselves and potential jobs that they need to make career choices (Steere et al., 2007). These experiences also help students refine their proficiency in the use of fundamental and integrative skills, with special emphasis on developing work-support behaviors related to self-determination, attitudes and values, career planning, and job-seeking skills (Hanley-Maxwell & Collet-Klingenberg, 2012). Regardless of the form they take, throughout these experiences educators need to assist students in considering how their evolving interests, needs, and abilities match targeted work environments or occupational clusters (Schloss et al., 2007; Steere et al., 2007). These experiences also help students develop work histories that can be used in career portfolios and resumes, as well as provide sources for recommendations and potential job leads.

Early employment-related experiences may be unpaid service learning. However, later experiences should include paid jobs because paid employment during high school, including summer jobs, school-year jobs associated with high school programs, and jobs students have obtained on their own, improves employment outcomes (Benz et al., 2000). Determining when to move from unpaid and/or unstructured experiences to paid employment is a decision that should be made in conjunction with the individual student and her/his family. In addition to the desires of students and their families, students' developmental levels, work histories, work-related skills development, and age in proximity to school-leaving will influence when a student moves into paid employment and the type of employment sought.

Vocational Training

Work experiences can be obtained through vocational training programs, which include vocational classes, site-based programs, occupational programs, employer-provided programs (e.g., mentoring, apprenticeship), and blended occupational-academic programs. Cooperative education, youth apprenticeship, school-based enterprises, career academies, work-study, and tech-prep are commonly available vocational training models (Rusch & Millar, 1998). Most but not all vocational training programs include opportunities to learn, practice, and refine actual job skills in several community-based settings. Some include certification or other formal recognition (associate degree) related to the program (e.g., tech-prep) (U.S. Department of Labor, n.d.).

Work experiences should reflect the students' changing interests and needs, taking into consideration the students' learning needs, moving from helping them to learn and adjust to work-related settings to assisting them to develop job-seeking and selection skills. Along the way, information gained from these job experiences should be used to shape the selection of subsequent work experiences as well as identify additional career exploration needs, highlighting aspects of jobs that appeal to the students and those aspects that are unwanted in future employment. Work experiences should culminate in helping students obtain paid employment, ideally within an occupational area that matches students' interests and abilities and has potential for career growth.

Vocational training through simulated work experiences completed in special education classrooms is more accessible to students with disabilities. In these experiences, students complete tasks such as collating a school mailing or cooking a meal, with teachers providing employability instruction on work habits, quality, and quantity of work produced. Unfortunately, generalization of these skills to real community-based jobs is questionable.

Some schools provide vocational training via the school-based enterprise model. In this model, well-developed career and technical programs provide job training within a lab setting, using simulated and real work in various occupations such as business, automotive, and health. Students with high-incidence disabilities such as learning disabilities and attention deficit disorders often are included in these programs and are able to move successfully into community jobs within the same occupations. Students with severe disabilities have more difficulty generalizing learned skills to community employment and often end up being on waiting lists for adult service programs, losing the skills they may have learned.

Another popular program is work-study, a model that combines classroom instruction with actual work experience. The positions are often community jobs in traditional worksites such as restaurants and grocery stores and are limited to a few hours per day (Rutkowski et al., 2006). Other options such as Cooperative Education programs, Youth Apprenticeships, and Career Academies include part-time employment as part of their preparation programs. All three options target specific job types usually reflecting in-demand occupations, with the structure of job experiences ranging from the minimal structure of Cooperative Education programs to the highly structured experiences associated with youth apprenticeships. The highly structured work experiences of youth apprenticeships are typically last two years in which the employer guides the workplace learning of the apprentice while school personnel and the employer connect and integrate academic learning to the vocational applications. These experiences often include a postsecondary education component, culminating in awarding the students with occupational and academic skills mastery credentials (Test et al., 2006).

Participation in vocational training has been correlated with improved postsecondary job success (Benz et al., 2000), with blended academic-occupational programs identified as producing better results in teaching work-related skills (e.g., self-determination, academic skills) than academic or vocational only programs (Eisenman, 2001).

Connecting Services

Selecting employment experiences and providing connecting and planning services are based on early and ongoing assessment. Results of these assessments are reflected in planning, job development and placement, and on-the-job training.

Assessment

IDEA requires the IEP team to summarize the age-appropriate assessments that were conducted to determine the student's interests, abilities, and needed transition services and activities (IDEA,2004, Section 614). Assessment is the foundation of establishing post-school employment goals, individualizing the work preparation program/sequence, and identifying the academic and social skills the student will need to successfully transition to employment. The assessment process includes the student, school and agency personnel, and family members who collaborate to identify potential jobs, and current and future support needs and resources. Assessment should be ongoing and interactive, helping shape future actions and experiences to respond to emerging skills, interests, and challenges.

Student assessment includes general interest assessment, identification of potential career goals, review of learning patterns and needs, identification of potential assets and barriers, determination of skill needs, and identification of previous vocational-related experiences (home and community jobs, volunteer experiences, etc.). Although initial interest assessment may precede work experience, it should not be the sole source of information. Assessments during and after work experiences may reveal skills, needs, and preferences that were not observed in other settings.

To ensure future flexibility and self-direction, students should be taught to conduct self-assessments. Through self-assessment students monitor their work performance, assess their developing needs and interests, assess their job satisfaction, etc. They should then use the information to set goals, plan and access continued education or training, look for a new job, modify job performance, and identify support needs.

Job analysis in assessing targeted jobs, job types, or career clusters generally focuses on identifying the requirements of the job, including potential skill analyses. Job analysis is a useful tool when a student's targeted job or job type is known or the educator is building a bank of work experience sites. Through observation and interviews with knowledgeable persons, job analysis identifies the essential job functions and the social, job-task, and job-related skill requirements of the job or job type. Additionally, job analysis identifies natural supports, employer-provided training, and employment variables such as wages, hours, benefits, work culture, schedule variations, etc. When jobs are analyzed with specific students in mind, job restructuring and accommodation needs may also be identified (Hanley-Maxwell, Maxwell, Fabian & Owen, 2010). All job analyses do not have to be originally created. Vocational educators, rehabilitation counselors, and supported employment providers may be excellent sources of information about specific jobs.

If a student will be entering customized or supported self-employment, job analyses include other aspects. For customized employment, job analysis includes identifying job components and related skill needs across multiple positions/job roles. These components and skills are then reconfigured to match the assets and needs of the individual. In supported self-employment, job analysis focuses on creating a job in an area of interest to the individual job seeker. In this case, individual job interests are considered within the context of economic viability. Business structures and plans, locations, start-up costs, sources of financial support, business connections, personnel needs, and organization supports are also identified (Hagner & Davies, as cited in Hanley-Maxwell et al., 2010).

Support assessment is also important to identify relationships that could support or inhibit job success for some students with disabilities. Support systems include agency-mediated supports (e.g., job coaches, assistive technology, personal attendants, work-setting modifications), business-mediated supports (e.g., employer or co-worker provided, existing employer-provided programs), government-mediated supports (e.g., work incentives, Plans for Achieving Self-support), or family/community-mediated supports (e.g., family members, friends, neighbors) (Wehman & Bricout, 2001). Emphases should be placed on identifying supports that are generally available to non-disabled employees, utilizing resources that are normally available in work, home, and community settings. While most support-system assessment focuses on developing and sustaining support networks, it is important to note that some "supports" can interfere with job performance. Consequently, it is important to work with students to identify what support systems are active in the students' lives, what roles these supports play in the present, and what roles they may play in the future. Once identified, plans to access and utilize those supports can be created (Hanley-Maxwell et al., 2010).

Planning and connecting: In addition to transition planning within the context of the IEP, students with disabilities may work with guidance counselors, peers, parents, and/or teachers to create post-graduation plans and develop career portfolios. Through these activities, adults and students collaborate to identify post-school employment goals, identify and select the resources needed to meet those goals, and create plans to attain or modify the students' goals. They should also collaborate to develop curricular career exploration and work experience plans, gradually moving planning and execution responsibilities to the students (as appropriate).

Educators should also connect students and, as appropriate, their families/support sources with the services and programs that will assist students in securing and maintaining their career goals (e.g., rehabilitation counselor, adult service provider, postsecondary education transition coordinator). In addition to connecting, educators need to ensure that students and their families know how to access and manage these resources. IEP team members should also identify potential assistive technology, adaptation, and accommodation needs and create plans to access these sources of assistance, as well as how to instruct the students in their use.

As school departure gets closer, IEP team members may need to consider how students will get additional training related to a specific job, and, if needed, how to pay for this training and/or for support needs and accommodations. Planning for post-school training and support should consider employer-provided programs and supports, job coaching, vocational counseling, union apprenticeship programs, technical college programs, etc. Funding may come from employers, state departments of vocational rehabilitation, mental health programs, state developmental disability programs/developmental disability councils, Medicaid waivers, and Ticket-to-Work and work program vouchers (Hanley-Maxwell et al., 2010).

Job development and placement: Some students will go directly to employment, with many of these students beginning their jobs before leaving school. Securing a job at this time helps ensure that students will continue to be eligible for disability-related services with no gaps in the services. Assisting students in getting jobs prior to leaving school means educators need to engage in locating and securing jobs and/or work with adult service providers to do so. Job development for some students will focus on creating customized jobs within these employment settings or developing the structures needed to start a self-employment business. Job development may also occur when educators and/or adult service providers identify jobs that will be used for work experience reasons only.

One example of a job development and placement program is Project SEARCH. This program, which combines real-life work experience, training in employability and independent living skills, and placement assistance through an active collaboration of the education, vocational rehabilitation and employment systems, has more than doubled post-school employment outcomes for students with significant disabilities. Students in Project SEARCH are completely immersed in the workplace, spending their entire school day as interns completing real-work tasks for approximately 20 hours per week. Program outcomes for 23 recent graduates from 2003 to 2005 resulted in a 78% placement rate at the end of the program at average hourly earnings of $7.89 (Rutkowski et al., 2006). Similar programs hosted in employment sites such as the Marriott Bridges program (Tilson, Luecking, & Donovan, 1994) have reported significantly improved employment outcomes over the traditional school-based transition programs.

Regardless of the reason for job development, educators and adult service providers must collaborate with the student, and when appropriate her/his family, when selecting a job or developing a new job for that student. Educators should assist students in identifying jobs that match their interests and skills as well as needs (Schloss et al., 2007; Steere et al., 2007) because a good job–employee match results in higher job satisfaction. Assisting students in developing and using career portfolios and resumes to make these matches can connect self-knowledge with career interests (Szymanski et al., 2003) and build self-determination skills. Matching should also consider which jobs allow for career advancement or that build skills that can be generalized. These types of jobs are particularly desirable because first jobs typically are not permanent; they are steps in the development of careers (Hanley-Maxwell et al., 2010).

How educators and adult services providers develop jobs and assist students in acquiring their first jobs can affect the outcomes. Mank, Cioffi, & Yovanoff (as cited in Hanley-Maxwell et al., 2010) report that job development and placement practices that mirror those used by persons without disabilities produce better wages and benefits. Consequently, teaching students with disabilities how to access and use services such as the One-Stop Career Centers should be part of any work preparation program (Hanley-Maxwell & Collet-Klingenberg, 2012).

Conclusion

Just over a decade into the 21st century, legislators, educators and business leaders are recognizing that utilizing the potential of all of our youth by designing education programs that prepare youth with and without disabilities to become productive members of the 21st century workforce is every bit as important a natural resource as land, oil, and capital. It is clear that renewed investments in education are needed to maintain our country's economic leadership. All students must be engaged in rigorous, relevant academic content that translates into student readiness to succeed in a knowledge-based, high tech, global economy. Administrators and educators must ensure access to academic rigor in the context of critical thinking, real-world applications, and contemporary tools to truly prepare students to gain and maintain employment in this increasingly global, high-tech world.

References

Alwell, M., & Cobb, B. (2009). Social and communicative interventions and transition outcomes for youth with disabilities: A systematic review. *Career Development for Exceptional Individuals*, *32*(2), 94–107.

American Association of Colleges and Research Libraries. (2011). What is information literacy? Accessed January 21, 2011, Issues and Advocacy, Information literacy, Overview, Introduction to information literacy, What is information literacy, http://www.ala.org/ala/mgrps/divs/acrl/issues/infolit/overview/intro/index.cfm

Anderson-Inman, L., & Horney, M. (2007). Supported etext: Assistive technology through text transformations. *Reading Research Quarterly*, *42*, 153–160.

Bassett, D. S., & Kochhar-Bryant, C. A. (2006). Strategies for aligning standards-based education and transition. *Focus on Exceptional Children*, *39*(2), 1–19.

Benz, M. R., Lindstrom, L., & Yovanoff, P. (2000). Improving graduation and employment outcomes of students with disabilities: Predictive factors and student perspectives. *Exceptional Children*, *66*, 509–529.

Boone, R. T., Burke, M. D., Fore, C. III, & Spencer, V. G. (2006). The impact of cognitive organizers and technology-based practices on student success in secondary social studies classrooms. *Journal of Special Education Technology*, 21(1), 5–15.

Boone, R., & Higgins, K. (2007). The role of instructional design in assistive technology research and development. *Reading Research Quarterly*, *42*, 135–139.

Cartledge, G. (2005). Learning disabilities and social skills: Reflections. *Learning Disability Quarterly*, *28*, 179–181.

Downing, J. E. (2005). Teaching communication skills to students with severe disabilities. (2nd ed.). Baltimore: Paul Brookes.

Eisenman, L. (2001). Conceptualizing the contribution of career oriented schooling on self-determination. *Career Development for Exceptional Individuals*, *24*, 3–17.

Forgrave, K. E. (2002). Assistive technology: Empowering students with learning disabilities. *Assistive Technology*, *73*, 122–126.

Fried-Oken, M. (2007). Assistive technology in communication disorders. In R. Paul, & P. W. Cascella (Eds.), *Introduction to clinical methods in communication disorders* (2nd ed.) (pp. 303–320). Baltimore, MD: Paul H. Brookes Publishing Co.

Goals 2000: Educate America Act of 1994 (PL 103–227), 20 U.S.C. §§ 5801 et seq.

Hanley-Maxwell, C., & Collet-Klingenberg, L. (2012). Curricular choices related to work. In P. Wehman & J. Kregel (Eds.), *Functional curriculum for elementary, middle, and secondary age students with special needs* (3rd ed. pp. 529–578). Austin, TX: PRO-ED.

Hanley-Maxwell, C., Maxwell, K., Fabian, E., & Owens, L. (2010). Supported employment. In E. M. Szymanski & R. M. Parker (Eds.), *Work and disability: Issues and strategies in career development and job placement*, 3rd ed. (pp. 415–453). Austin, TX: PRO-ED.

Hilton, M. (2008). Skills for work in the 21st century: What does the research tell us? *The Academy of Management Perspectives* (formerly The Academy of Management Executive) (AMP), 22 (4), 63–78.

Individuals with Disabilities Education Improvement Act, 20 U.S.C. §1400 et seq. (IDEA) (2004). Sec. 101. Amendments To The Individuals With Disabilities Education Act, Part B: Assistance for Education of All Children with Disabilities, Sec. 614 Evaluations, Eligibility, Determinations, Individualized Education Programs, and Educational Placements. Retrieved January 21, 2011 from U.S. Department of Education, Office of Special Education Programs' (OSEP's) IDEA website, Statute, http://idea.ed.gov/explore/view/p/,root,statute,I,B,614

Izzo, M. V & Lamb, M. (2002). *Self-determination and career development: Skills for successful transition to post-secondary education and employment*. A white paper for the Post-School Outcomes Network of the National Center on Secondary Education and Transition (NCSET) at the University of Hawaii at Manoa. Available online at: http://www.ncset.hawaii.edu/Publications/

Izzo, M. V., Murray, A., & O'Hanlon, N. (2005). Enhancing academic achievement and transition outcomes using technology. *Information Brief: Addressing Trends and Developments in Secondary Education and Transition*, *4*(5). Minneapolis, MN: National Center on Secondary Education and Transition.

Izzo, M. V., Torres, K., & Johnson, G. (2005). *Guide to meeting the education and transition needs of all students with Project Discovery*. Louisville, KY: Education Associates.

Izzo, M. V., Yurick, A., & McArrell, B. (2009). Supported eText: Effects of text-to-speech on access and achievement for high school students with disabilities. *Journal of Special Education Technology*, *24*(3), 9–20.

Izzo, M. V., Yurick, A., Nagaraja, H. N., & Novak, J. A. (2012). Effects of a 21st-Century curriculum on students' information technology and transition skills. *Career Development for Exceptional Individuals, 33*(2), 95–105.

Janney, R., & Snell, M. E. (2006). *Teachers' guides to inclusive practices: Social relationship and peer support* (2nd ed.). Baltimore: Paul Brookes.

Johnson, S., & Wehman, P. (2001). Teaching for transition. In P. Wehman (Ed.), *Life beyond the classroom*, 3rd Ed. (pp. 145–170). Baltimore: Paul H. Brookes.

Joselowsky, F. (2007). Youth engagement, high school reform, and improved learning outcomes: Building systemic approaches for youth engagement. *NASSP Bulletin, 91*, 247–257.

Kohler, P. D. (1996). *Taxonomy for transition programming: A model for planning, organizing, and evaluating transition services and programs*. Urbana-Champaign, IL: University of Illinois.

Luecking, R. G., & Fabian, E. S. (2000). Paid internship and employment success for youth in transition. *Career Development for Exceptional Individuals, 23*, 205–219.

Mazzotti, V. L., Test, D. W., Wood, C. L., & Richter, S. (2010). Effects of computer-assisted instruction on students' knowledge of postschool options. *Career Development for Exceptional Individuals, 33*(1), 25–40.

Morgan, R. L., Ellerd, D. A., Jensen, K., & Taylor, M. (2000). A survey of community employment placements: Where are youth and adults with disabilities working? *Career Development of Exceptional Individuals, 23*(1), 73–86.

National Alliance for Secondary Education and Transition (NASAT). (2005). *Handbook for implementing a comprehensive work-based learning program according to the Fair Labor Standards Act*. Minneapolis: University of Minnesota, National Center on Secondary Education and Transition.

Nelson, J. R., Smith, D. J., & Dodd, J. M. (1994). The effects of learning strategy instruction on the completion of job applications by students with learning disabilities. *Journal of Learning Disabilities, 27*, 104–110.

Newman, L., Wagner, M., Cameto, R., & Knokey, A.-M. (2009). *The Post-High School Outcomes of Youth with Disabilities up to 4 Years After High School. A Report of Findings from the National Longitudinal Transition Study–2 (NLTS2) (NCSER 2009–3017)*. Menlo Park, CA: SRI International. Available at www.nlts2.org/reports/2009_04/nlts2_report_2009_04_complete.pdf

No Child Left Behind Act of 2001 (NCLB), PL 107–110. Stat 1425 (2002)

Partnership for 21st Century Skills. (2011). *P21 common core toolkit: A guide to aligning the common core state standards with the framework for 21st century skills*. Washington, DC. Retrieved August 9, 2011 from http://www.p21.org/images/p21_toolkit_final.pdf

Rehabilitation Research and Training Center on Disability Statistics and Demographics. (2009). *Annual compendium of disability statistics compendium: 2009*. Rehabilitation Research and Training Center on Disability Demographics and Statistics, Hunter College, Retrieved 10/10/09 from http://www.disabilitycompendium.org

Roessler, R. T., Brolin, D. E., & Johnson, J. M. (1990). Factors affecting employment success and quality of life: A one year follow-up of students in special education. *Career Development for Exceptional Individuals, 13*, 95–107.

Rose, D. H., & Meyer, A. (2006). *A practical reader in universal design for learning*. Cambridge, MA: Harvard Education Publishing Group.

Rusch, F. R., & Millar, D. (1998). Emerging transition best practices. In F. R. Rusch and J. Chadsey-Rusch (Eds.). *Beyond high school: Transition from school to work*. (pp. 36–59). Pacific Grove, CA: Brooks/Cole Publishing.

Rutkowski, S., Daston, M., Van Kuiken, D., & Riehle, E. (2006). Project SEARCH: A demand-side model of high school transition. *Journal of Vocational Rehabilitation, 25*, 85–96.

Schloss, P. J., Schloss, M. A., & Schloss, C. N. (2007). *Instructional methods for secondary students with learning and behavior problems*, 4th ed. (pp. 277–293). Boston: Allyn and Bacon.

Secretary's Commission on Achieving Necessary Skills, U.S. Department of Labor (SCANS) (1993). Teaching the SCANS competencies. Washington, D. C.: Author.

Shogren, K. A., Wehmeyer, M. L., Palmer, S. B., Soukup, J. H., Little, T. D., Garner, N. et al. (2007). Examining individual and ecological predictors of the self-determination of students with disabilities. *Exceptional Children, 73*, 488–509.

Steere, D. E., Rose, E., & Cavaiuolo, D. (2007). *Growing up: Transition to adult life for students with disabilities*. Boston: Pearson Education, Inc.

Stock, S. E., Davies, D. K., Secor, R. R., & Wehmeyer, M. L. (2003). Self-directed career preference selection for individuals with intellectual disabilities: Using computer technology to enhance self-determination. *Journal of Vocational Rehabilitation, 19*, 95–103.

Szymanski, E. M., Enright, M., & Hershenson, D. B. (2003). Career development theories, constructs, and research: Implications for people with disabilities. In E. M. Szymanski & R. M. Parker (Eds.), *Work and disability: Issues in career counseling and job placement* (2nd ed.). Austin, TX: PRO-ED.

Taskforce on the Future of American Innovation. (2005). *Benchmarks of our innovation future: The knowledge economy: Is the United States losing its competitive edge?*

Test, D. W., Aspel, N. P., & Everson, J. M. (2006). *Transition methods for youth with disabilities.* Upper Saddle River, NJ: Pearson.

Test, D. W., Fowler, C. H., Richter, S. M., Mazzotti, V., White, J., Walker, A. R., et al. (2009). Evidence-based practices in secondary transition. *Career Development for Exceptional Individuals, 32*, 128–155.

Tilson, G. P., Luecking, R. G., & Donovan, M. R. (1994). Involving employers in transition: The Bridges Model. *Career Development for Exceptional Individuals, 17*(1), 77–88.

U.S. Department of Labor (n.d.) Retrieved 12/15/09 from http://wdr.doleta.gov/SCANS/

Wehman, P., & Bricout, J. (2001). Supported employment: New directions for the new millennium. In P. Wehman (Ed.), *Supported employment in business: Expanding the capacity of workers with disabilities* (pp. 3–22). St. Augustine, FL: TRN Publications.

Wehman, P., Brooke, V., & Inge, K. J. (2001). Vocational placements and careers. In P. Wehman (Ed.), *Life beyond the classroom*, 3rd ed. (pp. 211–246). Baltimore: Paul H. Brookes.

Wehmeyer, M. L. (2003). Self-determination, vocational rehabilitation, and workplace supports. *Journal of Vocational Rehabilitation, 19*, 67–69.

10

Career Development and Vocational Instruction

Jeanne B. Repetto

UNIVERSITY OF FLORIDA

W. Drew Andrews

DUVAL COUNTY SCHOOLS

> The direction in which education starts a man will determine his future life.
> (Plato (427 BC–347 BC), *The Republic*)

> The universe is change; our life is what our thoughts make it.
> (Marcus Aurelius Antoninus (121 AD–180 AD), *Meditations*)

These two quotes suggest that man has known since ancient times the impact education and self-discovery can have on a person's future. Each of us is a compilation of our own history, made up of a series of events and our reactions to them. These encounters trigger a self-evaluation, causing us to learn a bit more about who we are with each new event. This self-discovery is at the heart of career development, helping us to define our choice of employment, friends, community interactions, and all of our other life roles. This life-long development helps us to become more clearly ourselves (Hall, 1989).

This process of self-discovery begins the second a child enters the world and cries in reaction to a gentle slap, and lasts throughout life. During the toddler years, early interventionists encourage parents to provide a rich environment full of experiences and literature to prepare children for learning. In fact, research shows that children who are read to are more likely to enter school ready to learn (Buss, Van Ijzendoom, & Pellegrini, 1995; Torgeson, 1998). Elementary curriculum continues to foster student self-discovery by providing activities that assist students to make connections between academics and functional skills (e.g., learning addition by counting money). As students progress to middle and high school, academics shift from skill development to content learning. This shift changes the curriculum focus from students learning about themselves and their abilities to learning specific knowledge. This change in the focus of academic content comes at a time when young adolescents are starting to explore their relationship to the larger world (Juvonen, Le, Augustine, & Constant, 2004; National Middle School Association, 2010). Therefore, middle and high school educators need to provide curriculum that teaches content but also allows students to continue their self-discovery through career development and vocational education (National Middle School Association, 2010; Repetto, Webb, Neubert, & Curran,

2006; Sitlington, Neubert, & Clark, 2010). Figure 10.1 represents this interconnection between academics, career development, and vocational education.

Maintaining the connection between learning and self-discovery through career development and vocational education is important because it helps students understand that the information they are learning in school impacts their future outcomes. Among the reasons students give for dropping out of school is not feeling what they are learning is preparing them for their future, along with disliking school and having poor self-esteem (Dunn, Chambers, & Rabren, 2006; National Longitudinal Transition Study 2, 2005). School completion rates for all students with disabilities is 72%, with rates for specific disability categories ranging from 95% for students who are blind or have low vision to 56% for students with emotional disturbance (National Longitudinal Transition Study 2 [NLTS2]). Students who complete high school are more likely to attend postsecondary education programs, be employed, have checking accounts, postpone parenthood, and participate in community activities than students who drop out (NLTS2).

Providing a curriculum that includes career development and vocational education is critical in the middle and high school grades for students with disabilities between the ages of 14 and 16 who are asked to make decisions regarding their educational paths. Current legislative mandates focusing on improved student outcomes require students to pass high-stakes tests in order to graduate from high school (Individuals with Disabilities Education Improvement Act, 2004; No Child Left Behind Act, 2001). Students with disabilities are offered needed accommodations, as outlined on their Individualized Education Program (IEP), to support their test taking (IDEA, 2004). However, there are students who will not successfully pass the high-stakes tests even with accommodations. In many states these students can choose to obtain an alternative school diploma, a decision made during their IEP meetings. Alternate diplomas (e.g., special diplomas, certificates of attendance) require a prescribed set of coursework or experiences in order to receive the diploma (Johnson, Stout, & Thurlow, 2009; Thurlow, Cormier, & Vang, 2009). Usually decisions about which diploma type a student will pursue are

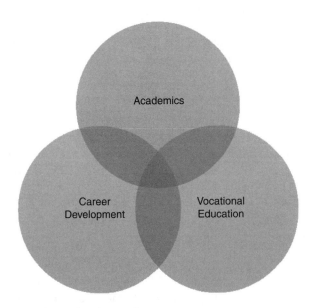

Figure 10.1 Interconnecting school experiences

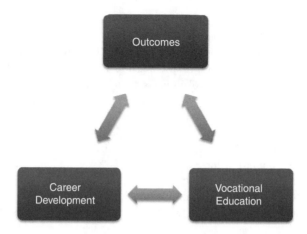

Figure 10.2 The relationship of career development and vocational education to outcomes

made between the ages of 14 and 16. This decision has a huge impact on the post-school life of students with disabilities by focusing their preparation for universities, vocational programs, employment, or supported employment upon graduation. This *tracking* of students at such a young age increases the importance of offering students with disabilities career development and vocational education programs throughout their school careers, not only when they are in high school. They need to have a sense of self and where they want to go prior to making the decision about which diploma type best meets their future goals.

In this chapter career development and vocational education will be discussed separately even though they are both part of a framework for life-long self-discovery. A life-long relationship between career development and vocational education to outcomes exists as shown in Figure 10.2. Each time we switch careers, move to another city, or change relationships we re-evaluate our vocational and career development needs. This relationship is noted when Sears (1982) defines career development as:

> The total constellation of psychological, sociological, educational, physical, economic, and change factors that combine to shape the career of any given individual over a life span.
> (p. 139)

Career Development

According to Kochhar-Bryant and Greene (2009), career development is one of the five theoretical foundations of transition, along with the theories of general systems, adolescent development, social and cognitive development, and self-determination. Similar to the other theories, career development began in general education and was adapted for use with students with disabilities (Flexer, Baer, Luft, & Simmons, 2008; Kochhar-Bryant & Greene, 2009). The concept of career development is rooted in the work of John Dewey (1916), who advocated for an educational system reflective of the larger society and did not isolate academics from life skills. This foundational concept espouses that all meaningful learning grows from activities rooted in the real world (Herschbach, 2001). In the 1970s, career development (in this chapter career development and career education will be used interchangeably) was embraced as a means to solve social concerns including high dropout rates, poor preparation for higher education, and poor life skills preparation in U.S. schools (Brolin, 1996; Herschbach, 2001; Kolstoe,

1996). Federal demonstration grants were funded to encourage general education school programs to develop career education curriculum. Unfortunately, most of the demonstration programs were ended as funding was terminated, but the foundation for transition was laid. Although no one definition of career education evolved from this period, one definition that helped to shape the concept of career development for students with disabilities is:

> Career education is the totality of experiences through which one learns about and prepares to engage in work [e.g., employee, patent, friend, consumer] as part of his or her way of living.
> (Hoyt, 1975, p. 4)

Understanding the factors that promote positive employment outcomes can help develop educational programs that better prepare students for the future (Doren, Lindstrom, Zane, & Johnson, 2007). An article by Evans and McClosky (2001), first published in 1973 and republished in 2001, discusses a rationale for career education. Career education is presented as an "emerging concept" that is part of the process used by educational systems to prepare students to earn incomes, pursue leisure, and fulfill the obligations of citizenship. It is noted that the components of career education already exist in schools but need to be merged into a coherent whole, extending from early childhood through retirement. Five components of career education to consider in this merger include (a) practice in career decision-making, (b) motivation to learn academics, (c) preparation for work, (d) the changing needs of workers, and (e) the importance of work to society. When introducing the reprint of this article, Herschbach (2001) commented that much of this discussion is "strikingly relevant today."

In the 1980s and 1990s, career development became part of transition programming for students with disabilities, a movement advanced by the 1983 Amendments to the Education of Handicapped Act (PL 98–199). This merger is evident in the definition of transition in 1994 by the Division on Career Development and Transition (Halpern, 1994).

> Transition refers to a change in status from behaving primarily as a student to assuming emergent adult roles in the community. These roles include employment, participating in postsecondary education, maintaining a home, becoming appropriately involved in the community, and experiencing satisfactory personal and social relationships. The process of enhancing transition involves the participation and coordination of school programs, adult agency services, and natural supports within the community. The foundation for transition should be laid during the elementary and middle school years, guided by the broad concept of career development. Transition planning should begin no later than age 14, and students should be encouraged, to the full extent of their capabilities, to assume a maximum amount of responsibility for such planning.
>
> (p. 117)

As transition was defined and redefined over the past thirty years, so have the career development theories that are foundational to transition planning and programs. The career development theory chosen as the foundation for a program impacts the methods of transition assessment and planning employed. For example, in the developmental theory, transition planning would occur over the life span and include the many roles a person plays (e.g., student, citizen, worker). In contrast, in the person-environment or work-adjustment theory, the students and work factors are evaluated for "fit." Since it is more than likely the career development theory used by most transition programs is an integration of many theories, it is important to have an understanding of the various theories (Flexer et al., 2008; Kochhar-Bryant, & Greene, 2009). For this reason, a brief overview of several career development theories is given below.

Structural Theories

In structural theories (Holland, 1992), an individual's traits are matched to work environments and, based on matches, appropriate occupational choices can be made. For example, structural theorists believe an occupational choice is made by examining the relationship between the individual (e.g., aptitudes, abilities, limitations) and the occupation (e.g., requirements, advantages, disadvantages).

Sociological Model

This is an ecological model (Szymanski & Hershenson, 1998) that takes into account environmental factors beyond the individual that impact career choices. For example, in this model expectations of others are taken into consideration along with the career needs of the individual when choosing an occupation.

Developmental Theory

This theory is grounded in the concept that as people mature, they become better able to compare their needs and abilities to situations to make career choices (Super, 1957). These choices occur over time as a result of interactions between the individual and the environment.

Work Adjustment Theory

In this theory, the satisfaction of the individual worker and the work site are considered (Dawis, 1996). The satisfaction measures are for a specific job to determine the individual's adjustment to that particular job.

Learning Theory

This theory is based on social learning, believing a person's career choice is influenced by previous learning experiences. When forming an opinion on which career is the best choice for them, individuals interpret their learning experiences.

These theories are used in transition planning, career counseling, and vocational rehabilitation for occupational planning. Various assessment instruments have been developed specific to the individual theories. For example, based on structural theory, the *Self-Directed Search* (Holland, Fritzche, & Powell, 1994) is designed to identify a person's dominant personality type to match it to occupations. However, rather than selecting one theory or assessment tool, an integrative approach is advocated as the foundation for transition planning (Flexer et al., 2008; Kochhar-Bryant, & Greene, 2009).

Life-centered Career Education

One model that integrates components of several theories and is commonly infused into transition programming is the Life Centered Career Education (LCCE) Model (Brolin, 1996; Brolin & Loyd, 2004; Sitlington et al., 2010). The four stages of career development that frame LCCE are (a) career awareness, (b) career exploration, (c) career preparation, and (d) career assimilation. Along with the career development stages, LCCE includes a set of competencies clustered in three domains: (a) daily living skills, (b) personal-social skills and (c) occupational guidance and preparation. This career-development model defines "career" as encompassing the various roles one plays throughout life (e.g., employee, friend, consumer, exerciser, parent, traveler).

The LCCE stages are meant to be developmental, spanning from elementary grades through adulthood. At the same time they are fluid, allowing a person to move up and down the continuum when learning new competencies or adapting to a new setting. For example, a person wanting to switch careers would be in the exploration stage as they explore possible jobs. Similarly, traveling to a new country where you need to learn about new currency might cause you to be at the awareness stage, learning the value of the various coins. The developmental stages, described below, build upon one another, allowing students to progress through the stages as they learn about careers and plan for transition.

Career Awareness

Typically this stage starts in the elementary grades with students learning about careers roles and tasks (e.g., firefighters put out fires, architects build buildings, friends help each other).

Career Exploration

This stage usually begins in middle school when students start to compare the tasks of various careers to their own skills and likes. These comparisons are often made through job shadowing, work samples, service learning, and other hands-on job exploration. Interest inventories may also be given at this age to assist students to begin to match their talents and likes to the right occupation. During this time students are also exploring non-occupational roles such as who they are as friends and members of the community.

Career Preparation

High school is typically the time frame for this stage where students choose an initial career path when deciding to prepare for postsecondary education or employment. Students who want to continue their education after high school may enroll in Advanced Placement (AP) courses to begin their college preparation. Other students may decide that they want to work after high school and begin preparation for employment through work-study programs, on-the-job training, vocational programs, or supported employment. Still other students might enter Tech Prep, requiring two years of high school with two years of technical college to complete. This transition preparation is guided by the postsecondary goals set by the transition team in a student's Individualized Education Program (IEP).

Career Assimilation

This stage is the transition from high school into postsecondary settings such as technical schools, work, universities, or supported employment.

In addition to the four stages in the LCCE model, *continuing education* is included as a stage of career development by Kokaska, Gruenhagen, Razeghi, & Fair (1985). At this stage, students continue to gather knowledge from opportunities provided within the community. In this manner, they become life-long learners as they adjust to new situations.

Revised Comprehensive Transition Model

Another model comprising components from the various career-development models and presented as a transition model rather than a career-development model is the Revised

Comprehensive Transition Model (Sitlington et al., 2010). This model is similar to LCCE in that it has stages and competencies. However, the stages begin in infancy and the competencies are broader (e.g., self-determination, health and fitness, further education and training). In addition, this model indicates service delivery systems and supports for schools to incorporate into their transition programs (e.g., general education with related and support services, community colleges, apprenticeship programs).

To summarize, beginning in elementary school, career development is crucial to transition planning (Weidenthal & Kochhar-Bryant, 2007). It is important to offer students the opportunities to explore their interests and preferences to help them make realistic career choices (Storm, O'Leary, & Williams, 2000). The more information students gather on various career paths in relationship to their personal satisfaction and identity the better prepared they will be for transition planning (Kochhar, West, & Taymans, 2000). In this manner, students begin to create an identity profile promoting an understanding of their abilities and future goals (Weidenthal & Kochhar-Bryant, 2007).

Vocational Education

Vocational education is more limiting than career development because its focus is learning about occupations and the skills needed to be successful as a worker. The definition of work in vocational education is more traditional, focusing on a job and the necessary competencies for employment. Vocational education programs first became part of the school system in the early 1900s as the U.S. changed from an agrarian to a manufacturing society (Gordon, 1999; Scott & Sarkees, 1996). This shift required students to learn new skills to be successful in manufacturing trades. In 1917, the Smith-Hughes Act (PL 347) was passed, funding secondary vocational school programs for general education students in agriculture, trade and industry, and home economics. Legislation mandating the inclusion of students with disabilities was not passed until the 1968 Amendments (PL 90–210) to the Vocational Education Act of 1963 (PL 88–210). These amendments expanded programs to include business education and cooperative work-study along with mandating "set-aside funding," within the state grant for vocational education, for special populations defined as youths with disabilities (10%) and youths with disadvantages (15%) (Cobb & Neubert, 1998). During this time, students with disabilities made up 2.1% of vocational enrollment with 70 % of these students in separate classes (Hagerty, Halloran, & Taymans, 1981). The Education Amendments of 1976 (PL 94–482) focused on expanding this enrollment and increasing the number of students with disabilities in general vocational education classes. This act increased set-aside funding and mandated coordination of vocational education programming with other federal education programs. This coordination ensured interdisciplinary assessment, training, and employment activities (Neubert, 1997). Between 1976 and 1982, enrollment of students with disabilities in vocational education programs increased by 95% (Conway, 1984).

The Carl D. Perkins Vocational Education Act of 1984 (PL 98–524) continued to mandate the inclusion of individuals with disabilities in vocational education and expanded support services to ensure their success. While supplemental services continued for students with disabilities, the Carl D. Perkins Vocational Education Act of 1990 (PL 101–392) eliminated set-aside funding and emphasized the integration of academic and vocational content. This linkage between academic and vocational programs was strengthened in the Carl D. Perkins Vocational and Applied Technology Act Amendments of 1998 (PL 105–332) and 2006 (PL 1009–270). In these acts, secondary programs are linked to postsecondary programs and greater accountability for student outcomes is established through a state performance accountability system. Vocational education is redefined in these Acts as Career and Technical Education (CTE).

Career and Technical Education (CTE)

Career and Technical Education is a broadening of the traditional outcome for vocational education from entry-level jobs requiring less than a four-year baccalaureate program to career pathways designed to link secondary and postsecondary education. The change in vocational education is reactive to the rapid change in jobs due to the move towards a global economy and emerging technology (National Center for Career and Technical Education, 2010). Students complete CTE programs at different times (e.g. high school graduation, postsecondary graduation) depending on the skills needed for the job they choose. In addition, CTE is designed to reinforce academic skills (National Center for Career and Technical Education, 2010). The three purposes for CTE at the secondary level are to:

- Support students in the acquisition of rigorous core knowledge, skills, habits, and attitudes needed for success in postsecondary education and the high-skilled workplace;
- Engage students in specific career-related learning experiences that equip them to make well-informed decisions about further education and training and employment opportunities; and
- Prepare students who may choose to enter the workforce directly after high school with levels of skill and knowledge in a particular career area that will be valued in the marketplace. (Association for Career and Technical Education, 2006, p.1)

Students exit CTE programs at various points within career clusters; each career cluster is a grouping of many occupations with similar skills and characteristics. Career clusters include a range of occupations with varied skill levels so that exit points might be after high school or after postsecondary education depending on the requirements of the chosen occupation within the career cluster. The National Career Technical Education Foundation (NCTEF) established the States' Career Clusters Initiative (SCCI) to serve as a clearinghouse for research and technical assistance related to career clusters. The definition of a career cluster used by SCCI is as follows:

> Career Cluster is a grouping of occupations and broad industries based on commonalities. The 16 Career Clusters organize academic and occupational knowledge and skills into a coherent course sequence and identify pathways from secondary schools to two- and four-year colleges, graduate schools, and the workplace. Students learn in school about what they can do in the future. This connection to future goals motivates students to work harder and enroll in more rigorous courses.
> (http://www.careerclusters.org/aboutus.php?define=CC)

Sixteen career clusters are identified by SCCI that shape the career paths offered by CTE programs, which are part of the later career development stages of preparation and assimilation. In addition, these 16 clusters can provide broad career areas to promote student awareness and exploration as they progress through the early stages of career development. These clusters include:

- Agriculture, Food, and National Resources
- Architecture and Construction
- Arts, A/V Technology, and Communication

- Business, Management, and Administration
- Education and Training
- Finance
- Government and Public Administration
- Health Science
- Hospitality and Tourism
- Human Services
- Information Technology
- Law, Public Safety, Corrections, and Security
- Manufacturing
- Marketing, Sales, and Service
- Science, Technology, Engineering, and Mathematics
- Transportation, Distribution, and Logistics.

(http://www.careerclusters.org/16clusters.cfm)

Instructional programs developed around these 16 clusters include Tech Prep, career academics, work-based learning programs, high school programs, service learning, and magnet programs. One example is the Government and Public Administration Academy at Charles E. Shea Senior High School in Pawtucket, Rhode Island, which is a learning academy for high school seniors (http://sheahighschool.webs.com/aboutus.htm). Students enrolled in this academy experience a variety of work-based learning experiences, including internships with the Rhode Island state government and collaborative student projects. The projects address pressing issues in government and public administration. One of their projects is collaboration with the Watson Institute for International Studies at Brown University focused on terrorism and immigration.

Students with Disabilities in Vocational Programs

When Wagner and her colleagues examined the "holding power" of secondary programs for students with disabilities (Wagner, Blackorby, & Hebbeler, 1993), several school-related factors were identified. These factors included individualized tutoring, completing homework, attendance, and an ongoing focus on school; and during the last two years of school (a) participation in vocational education classes, and (b) participation in community-based work experience programs. The importance of students with disabilities taking career and technical courses is supported by data indicating a 61.3% enrollment of students with disabilities in these courses compared to 79.5% of students without disabilities (Wagner, Newman, Cameto, Levine, & Marder, 2003). The following are real-life case studies of students with disabilities who enrolled in various career cluster programs.

Health Service (Cosmetology)

Brenda is a student with specific learning disabilities who was good in math but had difficulty with reading. She lost interest in school but managed to pass the state comprehensive academic test required for graduation. Due to the lack of credits earned, Brenda enrolled in a class that would prepare her for the General Education Development test (GED) and planned to receive her diploma through the GED Exit Option. She also applied to enter the cosmetology program at the career technical center. Once she started the high school cosmetology program, her interest in school increased. She completed the cosmetology program and passed her state licensing certification before graduating from high school. She has since graduated and is currently employed in a local salon.

Science, Technology, Engineering, and Mathematics (Welding)

Tucker is a young man with a learning disability and low vision. He enrolled in the welding program at the career technical center. With the use of filter lens magnification, he has become a successful welder. He has earned completion points and received an American Welding Society (AWS) certification.

Architecture and Construction (Masonry)

Donald is in the Academy of Building Construction at the career technical center. He has reached completion points to receive two certifications from the National Center for Construction Education and Research (NCCER). He receives support services from a reading teacher, as indicated on his IEP, to assist him in learning job preparedness skills. Reading in this program is taught using the construction curriculum. Donald will exit the program with two professional certifications, but students who do not meet the standards for professional certification exit the program with a certificate of program completion from the career technical center.

Health Science (Academy of Health Science)

Janet is a young woman who became a quadriplegic as a result of an injury while she was in elementary school. She is enrolled in the Health Occupation Program and has completed Health 1, Health Careers 2 and 3, which are a sequence of courses articulated with the local college. After completing these courses, she will take an exam that will allow her to have earned three college-level credits. The program coordinators are working to expand the program to include a health coordinator certification so that Janet can leave high school with certification. Currently, Janet plans on attending the local college after graduation to continue her education and exiting the Health Science program with a professional certificate requiring an Associate Degree, which she anticipates earning after two years of college.

Another student in the Academy of Health Science, an adult who is deaf, completed both the Certified Nursing Assistant Program and the phlebotomy program. He currently works as a lab technician in a local doctor's office. One simple accommodation that was provided was a special stethoscope. The Career Center allows adults to work alongside high school student CTE programs.

Transportation, Distribution, and Logistics (Diesel Mechanics)

Will is a young man with Traumatic Brain Injury (TBI) who is enrolled in the Diesel Mechanics Program at the career technical center. To meet Will's learning needs, Modified Occupational Completion Points (MOCPs) are being used. MOCPs are selected sets of student performance standards that fall between established occupational completion points as identified in vocational job preparatory course descriptions. These selected standards guide the student in completing a modified program and developing marketable skills (http://www.fldoe.org/workforce/programs/ss5.asp). Certification in the program is through the National Institute for Automotive Service Excellence (ASE). Will hopes to someday have his own garage.

During this time of increased accountability and pressure to document special education's impact on students with disabilities, the importance of vocational education and training is a critical element in the transition-planning process. Indicators identified for Part B State Performance Plans (SPP) and Annual Performance Reports (APR) that focus on transition include indicator 1 (graduation), 2 (dropout), 13 (IEPs) and 14.

Indicator 14 is the percentage of youth who had IEPs, were no longer in secondary school and have been competitively employed, enrolled in some type of postsecondary school, or both, within one year of leaving school. Vocational technical training is, in fact, an area that spans secondary to postsecondary. The question bank for collecting post-school outcome data used to address Indicator 14, includes the question: "What type of school or training program are you currently attending?" Choices include (a) GED program or Adult Basic Education, (b) vocational technical training, (c) community education class(es), (d) two-year community college, (e) four-year college or university, or (f) other (http://www.nsttac.org/indicator13/TransitionResourceGuide.aspx). For many students, career technical education is an appropriate post-school education option. The Northwest Policy Center (2001) projected that 60% of the job opportunities that provide a living wage in 2010 will require a combination of (a) basic literacy and computer skills, (b) occupationally specific instruction and on-the-job training, and (c) work experience (Flallery, Yovanoff, Benz, & McGrath, 2008). This combination of necessary skills can be addressed through CTE programs that prepare students in career clusters through job-specific skill training and on-the-job training (http://www.betterhighschools.com/docs/NHSC_TransitionsOutFactSheet.pdf).

In summary, CTE (vocational education) provides work-related education to high school and postsecondary students organized around 16 career clusters. Programs support student learning of technical and employment skills that are linked to academic instruction in several formats including Tech Prep, work experience, service learning, career academies, and apprenticeship. Students with and without disabilities are eligible for these programs, which they may exit upon graduation from high school, or postsecondary programs depending on the requirements of their chosen occupation.

Summary

Current State

Career development and vocational education programs support students in reaching their transition goals and offer them career-related work experiences, two factors shown to improve graduation rates and positive employment outcomes (Benz, Lindstrom, & Yovnoff, 2000). School programs fostering work-related goal planning are linked to positive employment outcomes for students (Nurmi, Salmela-Aro, & Koivisto, 2002) in light of the fact that student post-school outcomes are one measure of the success of school systems (Doren, Lindstrom, Zane, & Johnson, 2007). Current legislation (IDEA, 2004) mandates access to general education, preparation for adult living, postsecondary education, and employment to ensure students with disabilities have positive post-school outcomes. Although the high school reform movement supports rigorous curriculum, it also calls for a connection with the necessary preparation to enter employment (Barton, 2006).

For students with disabilities, a connection between school and work is crucial because individuals with disabilities have post-school outcomes that are less positive than their peers without disabilities. Data from the 2004 National Organization on Disability/Harris Survey of Americans with Disabilities indicated 35% of people with disabilities were employed compared to 78% of people without disabilities. This discrepancy is further supported by NLTS2 data showing that two years out of high school, 42.9% of students with disabilities are employed whereas 55% of their nondisabled peers are employed (Wagner, Newman, Cameto, Garza, & Levine, 2005). In U.S. society, employment is central to positive adult outcomes, emphasizing the need to prepare students for employment or postsecondary employment preparation. This sentiment is evident in the following statement by Rogan, Grossi, & Gajewski (2002):

Work is a central component of a quality adult life. Employment provides a source of income, enhances self-esteem, provides important social connections, and allows people to fulfill their duties as contributing, tax-paying citizens.

(p. 104)

Students with disabilities continue to leave high school programs unprepared for their postsecondary experience. Their outcomes might be improved by expanding programs to include additional components such as (a) job seeking skills along with opportunities to practice these skills (McDonnall & Crudden (2009)); and (b) work-based learning involving hands-on employment experience (Luecking & Mooney, 2002). A study by Guy, Sitlington, Larsen, & Frank (2009) focused on patterns that exist in the employment preparation courses offered to students with disabilities. They investigated (a) numbers of courses offered, (b) subject areas in which these courses were offered, (c) percentage that were classroom based, (d) percentage that were work based, and (e) percentage that were a combination of classroom and work based. Data from districts participating in their study reported only 31.6% of the classes they offered focused on preparing students for employment (Guy et al., 2009). This is somewhat disheartening because research indicates the knowledge and skills needed by youth to effectively transition to employment should focus on (a) occupational awareness and exploration, (b) employment-related knowledge and skills, and (c) specific occupational knowledge and skills (Brolin & Loyd, 2004; Clark, Carlson, Fisher, Cook, & D'Alonzo, 1991; Sitlington & Clark, 2006).

The successful transition of youth with disabilities to employment has consistently been associated with work experience while in school (Stodden, Dowrick, Gilmore, & Galloway, 2001). Unfortunately, employment-preparation programs are decreasing even though they have been shown to be effective in preparing youth for employment after high school (Guy et al., 2009). In another study, Carter, Trainor, Cakiroglu, Sweeden, & Owens (2010) studied the availability of career development and vocational activities to students with disabilities. Data collected showed that although schools offered a wide range of career development and vocational activities, only limited participation in these activities was reported for youth with disabilities.

Future Directions

Three areas should be considered as career development/CTE continues a role in the school system. First, the relationship between career development/CTE and academics needs to be expanded especially for students with disabilities and those at risk of dropping out. Studies have shown that students who understand the link between what they are learning in school and their future needs are more likely to remain engaged in their learning (Benz et al., 2000; Nurmi et al., 2002). Since career development and CTE programs promote this linkage, research needs to be conducted on effective ways to strengthen the relationship between academic and career development and CTE. The importance of the connection between academics and career development and CTE is further supported by the Northwest Policy Center's (2001) projections that 60% of the jobs in 2010 will require both job-specific and academically related skills (Flallery et al., 2008). Second, effective accommodations to support individuals with disabilities as well as an ever-expanding diverse school population need to be studied. Research conducted by the National Center for Self-Determination and 21st Century Leadership indicates an increasingly diverse population of youth who are in transition, including youth who are culturally and linguistically diverse and young adults in the foster-care system (Gil-Kashiwabara, Hogansen, Geenen, Powers, & Powers, 2007). Finally, vocational education has historically been reactive to the needs of society. For this reason, CTE programs need to continually reinvent themselves to stay abreast of workplace trends. One example is the expansion of CTE programs to meet the needs of green industries (Arenas, 2004).

Preparing individuals with disabilities to function effectively and experience success in the many roles they will have as adults is central to positive student outcomes. The preparation is challenging because of the changing nature of the needs of the workplace and school programs that are not always able to accommodate these changing needs (Benz et al., 1997). Therefore, providing students with the skills necessary to react to the changing needs of society and work is crucial; career development and CTE programs support the development of these skills.

References

Arenas, A. (2004). School-based enterprises and environmental sustainability. *Journal of Vocational Education Research*, *28* (2), retrieved on May 2, 2010 from http://scholar.lib.vt.edu/ejournals/JVER/v28n2/arenas.html

Association for Career and Technical Education. (2006). *Reinventing the American High School for the 21st Century*. Alexandria, VA: Author.

Barton, P. (2006). *High school reform and work: Facing labor market realities*. Princeton, NJ: ETS.

Benz, M., Lindstrom, L., & Yovnoff, P. (2000). Improving graduation and employment outcomes of students with disabilities: Predictive factors and student perspectives. *Exceptional Children 66* (4), 509–29.

Brolin, D. (1996). Reflections on the beginning . . . and future directions. *Career Development for Exceptional Individuals*, *19*(2), 93–100.

Brolin, D., & Loyd, R. (2004). *Career development and transition services: a functional life skills approach* (4th ed.). Upper Saddle River, NJ: Pearson.

Buss, A., Van Ijzendoom, M., & Pellegrini, A. (1995). Joint reading makes for success in learning to read: A meta-analysis on intergenerational transmission of literacy. *Review of Educational Research*, *65*, 1–21.

Carl D. Perkins Vocational Education Act of 1990, Public Law 101–392, 20 U.S.C., 2301.

Carl D. Perkins Vocational Education Act of 1984, Public Law 98–524, 98 STAT, 24345-2491.

Carl D. Perkins Vocational and Applied Technology Act Amendments of 1998 (Pl 105–332) and 2006 (PL 1009-270).

Carter, E., Trainor, A., Cakiroglu, O., Sweeden, B., & Owens, L. (2010). Availability of and access to career development activities for transition-age youth with disabilities. *Career Development for Exceptional Individuals*, *33*(1), 13–24.

Clark, G. M., Carlson, B. C., Fisher, S., Cook, I. D., & D'Alonzo, B. J. (1991). Career development for students with disabilities in elementary schools: A position statement of the Division on Career Development and Transition. *Career Development for Exceptional Individuals*, *14*, 109–120.

Cobb, B., & Neubert, D. (1998). Vocational education: Emerging vocationalism. In F. Rusch & J. Chadsey (Eds.), *Beyond high school: Transition from school to work* (pp. 101–126). Boston, MA: Wadsworth.

Conway, C. (1984). *Vocational education and handicapped students. Programs for the handicapped: Clearinghouse on the handicapped*. Washington, DC: Office of Special Education and Rehabilitation Services.

Dawis, R. (1996). The theory of work adjustment and person-environment-correspondence counseling. In D. Brown, L. Brooks, & Associates (Eds.). *Career choice and development* (3rd ed., pp. 75–120). San Francisco: Jossey-Bass.

Dewey, J. (1916). *Democracy and education*. New York: Macmillan.

Doren, B., Lindstrom, L., Zane, C., & Johnson, P. (2007). The role of program and alterable personal factors in postschool employment outcomes. *Career Development for Exceptional individuals*, *30* (3), 171–183.

Dunn, C., Chambers, D., & Rabren, K. (2006). Variables affecting students' decision to drop out of school. *Remedial and Special Education*, *27* (5), 314–323.

Evans, R., & McCloskey, G. (2001). Rationale for career education. *Journal of Industrial Teacher Education*, *39*(1), Retrieved from http://scholar.lib.vt.edu/JITE/v39n1/evans.html

Flallery, K., Yovanoff, P., Benz, M., and McGrath, K. (2008). Improving employment outcomes of individuals with disabilities through short-term postsecondary training. *Career Development for Exceptional Individuals*, *31* (1), 26–36.

Flexer, R., Baer, R, Luft, P., & Simmons, T. (2008). *Transition planning for secondary students with disabilities*. Upper Saddle River, NJ: Pearson.

Gil-Kashiwabara, E., Hogansen, J., Geenen, S., Powers, K., & Powers, L. (2007). Improving transition outcomes for marginalized youth. *Career Development for Exceptional Individuals*, *30* (2), 80–91.

Gordon, H. (1999). *The history and growth of vocational education in America*. Needham, MA: Allyn & Bacon.

Guy, B., Sitlington, P., Larsen, M., & Frank, A. (2009). What are high schools offering as preparation for employment? *Career Development for Exceptional Individuals, 32* (1), 30–41.

Hagerty, G., Halloran, W., & Taymans, J. (1981). Federal perspectives on the preparation of vocational personnel on the preparation of vocational personnel to serve handicapped students. In C. A., MacMarthur & C. Allen (Eds.), *Vocational education for the handicapped: Models for preparing personnel* (pp. 5–22). Urbana-Champaign, IL: Leadership Training.

Hall, L. (1989). *Where have all the tigers gone?* New York: Scribner.

Halpern, A. (1994). The transition of youth with disabilities to adult life: A position statement of the Division on Career Development and Transition, the Council for Exceptional Children. *Career Development for Exceptional Individuals, 17,* 115–124.

Herschbach, D. (2001). The 1970's. *Journal of Industrial Teacher Education, 39*(1), Retrieved from http://scholar.lib.vt.edu/JITE/v39n1/1970.html

Holland, J. (1992). *Making vocational choices: A theory of vocational personalities and work environment* (3rd ed.). Odessa, FL: Psychological Assessment Resources.

Holland, J., Fritzche, B., & Powell, A. (Eds.). (1994). *Self-directed search manual.* Odessa, FL: Psychological Assessment Resources.

Hoyt, K. (1975). *Career education: contributions to an evolving concept.* Salt Lake City, UT: Olympus.

Individuals with Disabilities Education Improvement Act of 2004 (IDEA), 20 U.S.C. § 1400 et seq.

Johnson, D., Stout, K., & Thurlow, M. (2009). Diploma options and perceived consequences for students with disabilities. *Exceptionality, 17*(3), 119–134.

Juvonen, J., Le, V-N., Augustine, C., & Constant, L. (2004). *Focus on the wonder years: Challenges facing the American middle school.* Santa Monica, CA: Rand Corporation.

Kochhar, C. A., West, L. L., & Taymans, J. M. (2000). *Successful inclusion: Practical strategies for a shared responsibility.* Upper Saddle River, NJ: Prentice Hall.

Kochhar-Bryant, C., & Greene, G. (2009). *Pathways to successful transition for youth with disabilities.* Upper Saddle River, NJ: Pearson.

Kokaska, C. J., Gruenhagen, K., Razeghi, J., & Fair, G. W. (1985, October). Division on Career Development's position statement on transition. In D. E. Brolin (Ed.) *Proceedings of the International Conference on the Decade of the Disabled: Transition to Work and Adult Life,* p. 28. Las Vegas, NV.

Kolstoe, O. (1996). From a perspective of forty years in the field: Retrospective and prospective. *Career Development for Exceptional Individuals, 19*(2), 111–120.

Luecking, R. G., & Mooney, M. (2002). Tapping employment opportunities for youth with disabilities by engaging effectively with employers. In *Research to Practice Brief 1*(3). Minneapolis: National Center on Secondary Education and Transition, University of Minnesota. Retrieved from http://ncset.org/publications/viewdesc.asp?id=716

McDonnall, M. C., & Crudden, A. (2009) English Article (EJ) 13 *Journal of Visual Impairment & Blindness,* v103 n6 329–341 June.

National Center for Career and Technical Education. (2010). *Professional development for career and technical education: Implications for change.* Louisville, KY: Author.

National Longitudinal Transition Study 2 (NLTS2). (2005). *Facts from NLTS2: High School Completion by Youth with Disabilities.* Menlo Park, CA: SRI International. Retrieved from www.nlts2.org/fact_sheet_2005_11.pdf

National Middle School Association. (2010). *In this we believe: Keys to educating young adolescents.* Westerville, OH: Author.

National Organization on Disability. (2004). *2004 N.O.D./Harris survey of Americans with disabilities.* Washington, DC: Author. Retrieved May 17, 2010 from http://www.nod.org/index.cfm?fuseaction=Feature.showFeature&FeatureID=1422

Neubert, D. (1997). Time to grow: The history and future of preparing youth for adult role in society. *Teaching Exceptional Children, 29*(5), 5–17.

No Child Left Behind Act of 2001, 20 U.S.C. §6301(2001).

Northwest Policy Center. (2001). *Northwest Job Gap Study: Searching for work that pays.* Seattle, WA: Author.

Nurmi, J. E., Salmela-Aro, K., & Koivisto, P. (2002). Goal importance and related achievement beliefs and emotions during the transition from vocational school to work: Antecedents and consequences. *Journal of Vocational Behavior, 60,* 241–261.

Repetto, J, Webb, K, Neubert, D, & Curran, C. (2006). *The middle school experience: successful teaching and transition planning for diverse learners.* Austin, TX: PRO-ED.

Rogan, P., Grossi, T. A., & Gajewski, R. (2002). Vocational and career assessment. In C. L. Sax & C. A. Thoma (Eds.). *Transition assessment: Wise practices for quality lives* (pp. 103–117). Baltimore: Paul H. Brookes.

Scott, J. & Sarkees, M. (1996). *Overview of vocational and applied technology education.* Homewood, IL: American Technical Publishers.

Sears, S. (1982). A definition of career guidance terms: A national vocational guidance perspective. *Vocational Guidance Quarterly (31),* 137–143.

Sitlington, P. L., & Clark, G. M. (2006). *Transition education and services for students with disabilities* (4th ed.). Boston, MA: Allyn & Bacon.

Sitlington, P., Neubert, D., & Clark, G. (2010). *Transition education and services for student with disabilities.* Boston, MA: Merrill.

Stodden, R. A., Dowrick, P., Gilmore, S., & Galloway, L. M. (2001). *A review of secondary school factors influencing postschool outcomes for youth with disabilities.* Honolulu: National Center for the Study of Postsecondary Educational Supports, University of Hawaii at Manoa. Retrieved from http://www.rrtc.hawaii.edu/documents/products/phase1/043-H01.pdf

Storm, J., O'Leary, E., & Williams, J. (2000, May). *The Individuals with Disabilities Education Act of 1997. Transition requirements: A guide for states, districts,* States' Career Cluster Initiative. Retrieved May 3, 2010 from http://www.careerclusters.org/index.php

Super, D. (1957). *The psychology of careers: An introduction to vocational development.* New York: Harper & Brothers.

Szymanski, E., & Hershenson, D. (1998). Career development of people with disabilities: An ecological model. In E. M. Szymanski & R. M. Parker (Eds.). *Rehabilitation counseling: Basics and beyond* (3rd ed., pp.327–378). Austin, TX: PRO-ED.

Thurlow, M., Cormier, D., & Vang, M. (2009). Alternative routes to earning a standard high school diploma. *Exceptionality, 12*(3), 135–149.

Torgeson, J. (1998). Catch them before they fall. *American Educator, 22,* 32–39.

Vocational Education Act of 1916, PL 347, 6th Congress.

Vocational Education Act Amendments of 1968, PL 90–210, U.S C., 1263(b). (f), (1970).

Vocational Education Act Amendments of 1976, PL 94–482, U.S.C., 2310 (a), (b), (1982).

Wagner, M., Blackorby, J., & Hebbeler, K. (1993). *Beyond the report card: The multiple dimensions of secondary school performance of students with disabilities.* Menlo Park, CA: SRI International.

Wagner, M., Newman, L., Cameto, R., Garza, N., & Levine, P. (2005). *After high school: A first look at the postschool experiences of youth with disabilities. A report from the National Longitudinal Transition Study-2 (NLTS2).* Menlo Park, CA: SRI International.

Wagner, M., Newman, L., Cameto, R., Levine, P., & Marder, C. (2003). *Going to school: Instructional contexts, programs, and participation of secondary school students with disabilities. A report from the National Longitudinal Transition Study-2 (NLTS2).* Menlo Park, CA: SRI International.

Weidenthal, C., & Kochhar-Bryant, C. (2007). An investigation of transition practices for middle school youth. *Career Development for Exceptional Individuals, 30,* 147–157.

11

Self-Determination and Adolescent Transition Education

Michael L. Wehmeyer

UNIVERSITY OF KANSAS

Sharon Field

WAYNE STATE UNIVERSITY

Colleen A. Thoma

VIRGINIA COMMONWEALTH UNIVERSITY

Over the past two decades, promoting the self-determination of students with disabilities has become a best practice in secondary education and transition services (Wehmeyer, Abery, Mithaug, & Stancliffe, 2003; Wehmeyer, Agran, Hughes, Martin, Mithaug, & Palmer, 2007). This chapter will provide an overview of the major theoretical models that have been developed and validated to drive intervention development, examine research that documents the importance of promoting self-determination during the adolescent transition period, and discuss instructional and assessment models that have been shown to be effective for use in promoting self-determination. Finally, we conclude the chapter with a discussion of the role of families in promoting self-determination and the importance of teachers' self-determination.

What is Self-determination?

The self-determination construct has its roots in 19th and 20th Century discussions in philosophy and psychology about determinism and free will. Determinism is the philosophical doctrine positing that events, such as human behavior, are effects of preceding causes. Self-determination, as proposed by psychological theorists, is a general psychological construct within the organizing structure of theories of human agentic behavior. An agentic person is the "origin of his or her actions, has high aspirations, perseveres in the face of obstacles, sees more and varied options for action, learns from failures, and overall, has a greater sense of well being" (Wehmeyer & Little, 2009 p. 868). Theories of human agentic behavior are organismic in that they view people as active contributors to, or *authors* of, their behavior, which is self-regulated and goal-directed *action*. Such actions are motivated by biological and psychological needs, directed toward self-regulated goals linked to these needs, precipitate self-governance of behavior, and require an explicit focus on the interface between the self and the context. Self-determination as a psychological construct, then, refers to self- (vs. other-) caused action—to people acting volitionally, based on their own will. Volition is the capability of conscious choice, decision, and *intention*. Self-determined behavior is volitional, intentional, and self-caused or self-initiated action. There are several theoretical models of self-determination that have emerged from research and practice in the field of special education, the most widely adopted of which in the field of transition are detailed in the following section.

Models of Self-determination

A Functional Model of Self-determination

Wehmeyer and colleagues (Wehmeyer et al., 2003; Wehmeyer et al., 2007) proposed a functional model of self-determination in which self-determination is conceptualized as a dispositional characteristic (enduring tendencies used to characterize and describe differences between people) based on the *function* a behavior serves for an individual. Self-determined behavior refers to "volitional actions that enable one to act as the primary causal agent in one's life and to maintain or improve one's quality of life" (Wehmeyer, 2005, p. 117). Self-determination refers to self (vs. other) caused action; to a person acting volitionally, based upon his or her own will. The word volitional is defined as the act or instance of making a *conscious* choice or decision. Conscious means intentionally conceived or done; deliberate. Volitional behavior, then, implies that one acts consciously . . . with intent. Self-determined behavior is volitional and intentional, not simply random and non–purposeful.

The concept of causal agency is central to this perspective. Broadly, *causal agency* implies that it is the individual who makes or causes things to happen in his or her life. Causal agency implies more than just causing action; it implies that the individual acts with an eye toward causing *an effect* to *accomplish* a *specific end* or to *cause* or *create change*.

One frequent misinterpretation of self-determination is that it means "doing it yourself." When self-determination is interpreted this way, however, there is an obvious problem for most students with special educational needs, who frequently have limits to the number and types of activities they can perform independently. However, the *capacity* to *perform* specific behaviors is secondary in importance to whether one is the *causal agent* (e.g., caused in some way to happen) over outcomes such behaviors are implemented to achieve. Thus, students who may not be able to "independently" make a complex decision or solve a difficult problem may be able, with support, to participate in the decision-making process, and thus have the opportunity to be the causal agent in the decision-making process and, consequently, act in a self-determined manner.

The functional model sees self-determination as an integral part of the process of individuation and adolescent development. Self-determination emerges across the life span as children and adolescents learn skills and develop attitudes and beliefs that enable them to be causal agents in their lives. These skills and attitudes are the *component elements* of self-determined behavior, and include choice making, problem solving, decision making, goal setting and attainment, self-advocacy, and self-management skills.

This model has been empirically validated (Shogren, Wehmeyer, et al., 2008; Wehmeyer, Kelchner, & Richards, 1996); operationalized by the development of an assessment linked to the theory (Wehmeyer, 1996); served as the foundation for intervention development, particularly with regard to the development of the *Self-Determined Learning Model of Instruction* and related efforts (Wehmeyer, Palmer, Agran, Mithaug, & Martin, 2000); and provided impetus for a variety of research activities (see Wehmeyer et al., 2007).

A Five-step Model of Self-determination

Field and colleagues (Field & Hoffman, 2001; Hoffman & Field, 2005) proposed a five-step model for promoting self-determination. As described in this model, self-determination is either promoted or discouraged by factors within the individual's control (e.g., values, knowledge, skills) and variables that are environmental in nature (e.g., opportunities for choice making, attitudes of others). The model addresses both internal, affective factors and skill components that promote self-determination. The model has five major components: *Know Yourself and Your Environment, Value Yourself, Plan, Act, and Experience Outcomes and Learn.* The first two components describe internal processes that provide a foundation for acting in a self-determined manner. The next two components, *Plan and Act,* identify skills needed to act on this foundation. One must have internal awareness as well as the strength and ability to act on that internal foundation to be self-determined. To have the foundation of self-awareness and self-esteem but not the skills, or the skills but not the inner knowledge and belief in the self, is insufficient to fully experience self-determination. To be self-determined, one must know and value what one wants and possess the necessary skills to seek what is desired. The final component in the self-determination model is *Experience Outcomes and Learn.* This step includes both celebrating successes and reviewing efforts to become self-determined so that skills and knowledge that contribute to self-determination are enhanced.

As stated above, self-determination is affected by environmental variables as well as by the knowledge, skills, and beliefs expressed by the individual. Field and Hoffman identified nine indicators of environments that support the expression of self-determination (Field & Hoffman, 2001), including:

1   Knowledge, skills and attitudes for self-determination are addressed in the curriculum, in family support programs, and in staff development.
2   Students, parents, and staff are involved participants in individualized educational decision making and planning.
3   Students, families, faculty, and staff are provided with opportunities for choice.
4   Students, families, faculty, and staff are encouraged to take appropriate risks.
5   Supportive relationships are encouraged.
6   Accommodations and supports for individual needs are provided.
7   Students, families, and staff have the opportunity to express themselves and be understood.
8   Consequences for actions are predictable.
9   Self-determination is modeled throughout the school environment.

The five-step model was developed over a three-year effort (Field & Hoffman, 1994) that included: (a) reviewing the literature, (b) conducting interviews, (c) observing students in a variety of school settings, (d) considering internal expertise, and (e) considering external expertise. The model-development process included over 1,500 student observations and interviews with more than 200 individuals. The model was reviewed by panels of experts (including consumers, parents, educators, and adult service providers) in three states and revised based on their input. In addition, a national review panel of experts provided input on the model and oversaw the model-development process. The model has provided the framework for intervention development, particularly the Steps to Self-Determination curriculum (Hoffman & Field, 2005) and its related assessment tools (Field & Hoffman, 2007).

An Ecological Model of Self-determination

Abery and colleagues (Abery & Stancliffe, 1996) proposed an ecological model of self-determination that defines the self-determination construct as "a complex process, the ultimate goal of which is to achieve the level of personal control over one's life that an individual desires within those areas the individual perceives as important" (p. 27). The ecological model views self-determination as driven by the intrinsic motivation of all people to be the primary determiner of their thoughts, feelings, and behavior. It may involve, but is not synonymous with, independence and autonomy. Rather, it entails the person determining in what contexts and to what extent each of these behaviors/attitudes will be manifested. Self-determination, accordingly, is the product of both the person and the environment—of the person using the skills, knowledge, and beliefs at his/her disposal to act on the environment with the goal of obtaining valued and desired outcomes. The ecological model was derived from Bronfenbrenner's ecological perspective (1979, 1989), within which people develop and lead their lives is viewed as consisting of four levels: the *microsystem, mesosystem, exosystem*, and *macrosystem* (see Wehmeyer et al., 2003 for more detail). The ecological model has been empirically evaluated (Abery, McGrew, & Smith, 1994; Abery, Simunds, & Cady, 2006; Stancliffe, Abery, & Smith, 2000), operationalized in the development of assessments (Abery, Simunds, & Cady, 2002; Abery, Stancliffe, 1995a, 1995b), and has also provided a foundation for intervention (Abery, Arndt, Greger, Tetu, Eggebeen, Barosko, 1994; Abery & Eggebeen, 1995) and research (Abery, Simunds, & Cady, 2006).

Self-determination as Self-regulation

Mithaug (Wehmeyer et al., 2003) hypothesized that self-determination is an unusually effective form of self-regulation markedly free of external influence in which people who are self-determined regulate their choices and actions more successfully than others. Mithaug suggested that individuals are often in flux between existing *states* and *goal* or desired states. When a discrepancy between what one has and wants exists, an incentive for self-regulation and action becomes operative. With the realization that a discrepancy exists, the person may set out to achieve the goal or desired state. The ability to set appropriate expectations is based on the person's success in matching his or her *capacity* with present *opportunity*. Capacity is the person's assessment of existing resources (e.g., skills, interests, motivation), and opportunity refers to aspects of the situation that allow the individual to achieve the desired gain. Mithaug referred to optimal prospects as "just-right" matches in which people are able to correctly match their capacity (i.e., skills, interests) with existing opportunities (e.g., potential jobs). The experience generated during self-regulation is a function of repeated interaction between capacity and opportunity. Further, Mithaug (1998) suggested that "self-determination always occurs in a social context" (p. 42) and that the social nature of the construct is worth reviewing because the distinction between self-determination and other-determination is nearly always in play when assessing an individual's prospects for controlling their life in a particular situation" (p. 42).

The Importance of Promoting Self-determination in Adolescent Transition

The emphasis on promoting self-determination was introduced both in response to calls from people with disabilities for greater control in their lives, as well as to findings that transition and rehabilitation outcomes for adolescents with disabilities (e.g., employment, independent living, community integration, etc.) were not as positive as desired. The proposal that self-determination is an important focus if students with disabilities are to achieve more positive transition-related outcomes is predicated on an assumption that self-determination and positive transition-related outcomes are, in fact, causally linked—an assumption supported by a growing literature base.

To begin with, this literature base has established the need for intervention to promote self-determination, documenting that students with intellectual disability (Wehmeyer et al., 2007), learning disabilities (Field, Sarver, & Shaw, 2003; Pierson, Carter, Lane, & Glaeser, 2008), emotional and behavioral disorders (Carter, Lane, Pierson, & Glaeser, 2006; Pierson et al., 2008) and autism (Wehmeyer & Shogren, 2008) are less self-determined than their non-disabled peers.

Second, given the documented need for such instruction, a number of studies have documented that if provided instruction to promote self-determination, students with disabilities benefit. In a meta-analysis of single-subject and group subject design studies, Algozzine, Browder, Karvonen, Test, & Wood (2001) found evidence for the efficacy of instruction to promote component elements of self-determined behavior, including self-advocacy, goal setting and attainment, self-awareness, problem-solving skills, and decision-making skills. Cobb, Lehmann, Newman Gonehar, & Alwell (2009) conducted a narrative metasynthesis—a narrative synthesis of multiple meta-analytic studies—covering seven existing meta-analyses examining self-determination, and concluded that there is sufficient evidence to support the promotion of self-determination as effective. Recently, Wehmeyer, Palmer, Shogren, Williams-Diehm, & Soukup (in press) conducted a randomized-trial, placebo control group study of the effect of interventions to promote self-determination on enhanced self-determination, finding that students in the treatment group who received instruction to promote self-determination obtained better self-determination outcomes than did their peers who did not receive such instruction.

Third, self-determination status has been linked to the attainment of more positive academic (Fowler, Konrad, Walker, Test, & Wood, 2007; Konrad, Fowler, Walker, Test, & Wood, 2007; Lee, Wehmeyer, Soukup, & Palmer, 2010) and transition outcomes, including more positive employment and independent living outcomes (Martorell, Gutierrez-Rechacha, Pereda, & Ayuso-Mateos, 2008; Wehmeyer & Palmer, 2003; Wehmeyer & Schwartz, 1997), and more positive quality of life and life satisfaction (Lachapelle et al., 2005; Nota, Ferrari, Soresi, & Wehmeyer, 2007; Shogren, Lopez, Wehmeyer, Little, & Pressgrove, 2006; Wehmeyer & Schwartz, 1998).

For example, Wehmeyer and Schwartz (1997) measured the self-determination of students with cognitive disabilities, and then examined their adult outcomes one year after they left high school. Students in the high self-determination group were more than twice as likely as young people in the low self-determination group to be employed, and earned, on average, more per hour. Wehmeyer and Palmer (2003) conducted a second follow-up study, examining the adult status of 94 students with cognitive disabilities one and three years post-graduation. One-year after high school, students in the high self-determination group were disproportionately likely to have moved from where they were living during high school, and by the third year they were still disproportionately likely to live somewhere other than their high school home and were significantly more likely to live independently. For employed students, those scoring higher in self-determination made statistically significant advances in obtaining job benefits, including vacation, sick leave, and health insurance, an outcome not shared by their peers in the low self-determination group. Sowers and Powers (1995) showed that instruction on multiple components related to self-determination increased the participation and independence of students with severe disabilities in performing community activities.

Wehmeyer and colleagues recently conducted a randomized-trial, placebo control group study of the effect of the *Self-Determined Learning Model of Instruction* (discussed subsequently) on outcomes including student self-determination (Wehmeyer, Shogren, Palmer,

Williams-Diehm, Little, & Boulton, in press), access to the general education curriculum, and transition and academic goal attainment (Shogren, Palmer, Wehmeyer, Williams-Diehm, & Little, in press), and determined that students involved in such instruction became more self-determined, had greater access to the general education curriculum, and had higher rates of goal attainment than did students in the control group.

Summary

In summary, then, research has documented that students with disabilities are less likely to be self-determined than their non-disabled peers; that if provided instruction to promote self-determination, they can become more self-determined; and that enhanced self-determination is causally linked to more positive school and transition-related outcomes. The following sections introduce strategies with regard to planning and assessment pertaining to educational efforts to promote self-determination, and overview methods, materials, and strategies that have been shown to be effective in promoting self-determination.

Planning and Assessment to Promote Self-determination

Promoting the self-determination of students with disabilities takes more than simply teaching skills leading to self-determination. Certainly, students need skills, but they also need opportunities to use and improve those skills and the experiences that demonstrate to them clearly that such action has an impact on their lives in a positive way. Such instructional outcomes require thoughtful planning and assessment.

A variety of materials, methods, and strategies, discussed in a subsequent section, have been developed to promote self-determination, and many of these have criterion-referenced assessments to accompany them. These assessments are designed to identify existing self-determination skills as well as those that were missing from an individual student's repertoire. This assessment information could then be linked to educational goals and lesson plans that teachers can use in classroom settings to teach one or more of these skills.

In addition to these curriculum-based assessments, there have been some other, stand-alone assessments developed during that time, including The Arc's Self-Determination Scale (Wehmeyer & Kelchner, 1995), the AIR Self-Determination Scale (Wolman, Campeau, DuBois, Mithaug, & Stolarski, 1994), and the Self-Determination Assessment Battery (Hoffman, Field, & Sawilowsky, 2004). Descriptions of these assessments and the information they can provide to guide planning for the promotion of self-determination skill development follow below.

The Arc's Self-Determination Scale (Wehmeyer & Kelchner, 1995) consists of a combination of four sections that students complete independently or with assistance if needed with reading. Questions in each section are presented in different formats. The *autonomy* section consists of a series of Likert-scaled questions that students use to rate the likelihood that they would engage in certain behaviors, from "I do not do this even if I have the chance" to "I do this every time I have the chance." The *self-regulation section* presents the beginning and end of a series of scenarios and asks the student to describe the middle part of the story. The third section, *psychological empowerment*, provides two different options and requires that a student choose the option that best describes them. The last section, *self-realization*, asks the student to agree or disagree with each statement. Following the directions provided in the manual, teachers convert the scores to percentile ranks and uses the information to complete a student profile.

The AIR Self-Determination Scale (Wolman et al., 1994) consists of three similar assessment tools completed by the student, educator, and teacher respectively. Each of these components is designed to determine a student's self-determination knowledge and skills. Information about a student's opportunity to use and improve those skills at school and home is also part of this assessment. The use of three different but similar versions completed by people who know the student provides an opportunity to triangulate the information collected, thus minimizing the challenge of using self-reported data. A graphic profile is used to illustrate student performance on the assessment and their overall self-determination score.

A third example of a self-determination assessment is the *Self-Determination Assessment Battery* (Hoffman et al., 2004). This assessment also provides opportunities for students, educators and parents to participate in completing components of the assessment. The battery includes an observational checklist, a knowledge scale, student scale, teacher perception scale, and parent perception scale. Using the directions in the manual, educators compile this information to score each assessment and identify student needs for skill development as well as opportunities to use existing knowledge and skills.

Assessment of current skills and abilities is a critical first step in the teaching process. The assessment process should provide information about what a student can do, as well as information about the context of the setting in which the skill is assessed. It's important to remember that a specific component skill such as self-advocacy might be demonstrated in one situation and not in others, making it imperative that the assessment process include multiple settings and multiple perspectives. Discrepancies between settings and/or evaluator perspectives provide valuable information that can guide further assessment to determine the aspects of the setting, the situation and/or the individuals with whom the student interacts that support or act as barriers to self-determination. This information can then be used to identify the strategies that promote the development and use of self-determination for that individual.

Interventions to Promote Self-determination

There have emerged, over the past twenty years, numerous interventions, from curricular programs to instructional models, developed to promote self-determination. For purposes of the current overview, we turn to the National Secondary Transition Technical Assistance Center's (NSTTAC) (http://www.nsttac.org) review of evidence-based practices in transition as a framework for identifying those evidence-based practices that promote self-determination or skills leading to enhanced self-determination.

The NSTTAC (Test, Fowler, Kohler, & Kortering, 2010) established a moderate level of evidence for teaching skills related to self-determination and identified self-determination as one of 16 evidence-based predictors of post-school employment, education and independent living success (Test, Mazzotti, Mustian, Fowler, Kortering, & Kohler, 2009). The NSTTAC evaluation, was based primarily on a meta-analysis of interventions to promote self-determination and component elements thereof (based upon the functional model of self-determination described previously) conducted by Algozzine et al. (2001). This meta-analysis covered 51 intervention studies evaluating efforts to teach self-advocacy, goal setting and attainment, self-awareness, problem solving, decision making, choice making, and self-regulation skills, as well as Individualized Education Program (IEP) participation. These intervention studies evaluated role-playing, modeling, task analysis, corrective feedback, direct instruction, learning strategy instruction, and self-instruction interventions conducted with 992 participants across every Individuals with Disabilities Education Act (IDEA) special education categorical area. Single subject and group experimental design studies were analyzed separately, indicating a strong positive effect for interventions from single-subject design studies, and an effect size of 1.38 from the group design studies.

Subsequent to the Algozzine et al. study on which the NSTTAC evaluation was based, several studies have been published that make the case for a strong level of evidence for the effectiveness of teaching skills leading to self-determination. The Cobb et al. (2009) narrative metasynthesis covering seven existing meta-analyses examining self-determination concluded that there is sufficient evidence to support the promotion of self-determination as effective. Additionally, several studies have subsequently documented the positive impact of efforts to promote student involvement in educational and transition planning to increase the likelihood of more positive transition and self-determination related outcomes (Martin, Van Dycke, Christensen, Greene, Gardner, & Lovett, 2006; Mason, Field, & Sawilowsky, 2004; Test, Mason, Hughes, Konrad, Neale, & Wood, 2004) The establishment of a "strong" level of evidence requires the publication of research that establishes a clear causal relationship between an intervention and anticipated outcomes. A series of recent studies has begun to provide such evidence. To establish a causal relationship between interventions to promote self-determination and enhanced student self-determination, Wehmeyer, Palmer, Shogren, Williams-Diehm, & Soukup (in press) conducted a randomized-trial, placebo control group study of 371 high school students receiving special education services under the categorical areas of intellectual disability or learning disabilities. Students were randomly assigned to an intervention or control group (by high school campus), with students in the intervention condition receiving multiple interventions to promote self-determination. Latent growth curve analysis showed that although all students in the study showed improved self-determination over the three years of the study as a function of typical development, students in the intervention group showed significantly greater growth, indicating the efficacy of the interventions.

Wehmeyer, Shogren, Palmer, Williams-Diehm, Little, & Boulton (in press) conducted a group-randomized, modified equivalent control group design study of the efficacy of the Self-Determined Learning Model of Instruction (SDLMI), to promote self-determination. Data on self-determination using multiple measures were collected with 312 high school students with cognitive disabilities in both a control and treatment group and used to examine the relationship between the SDLMI and self-determination using structural equation modeling. After determining strong measurement invariance for each latent construct, Wehmeyer et al. (2010) found significant differences in latent means across measurement occasions and differential effects attributable to the intervention across disability category, providing causal evidence of the positive impact of the intervention on student self-determination.

Shogren et al. (in press) conducted a cluster-randomized trial control group study to examine the effect of the SDLMI on transition and academic goal attainment and access to the general education curriculum. Though patterns varied by type of disability, the study established a causal effect for the SDLMI on student attainment of educational goals and access to the general education curriculum. Finally, Wehmeyer, Palmer, Williams-Diehm, Shogren, Davies, & Stock (2011) conducted a randomized-trial, control group study of the impact of technology use on student self-determination, establishing that the implementation of educational technology results in enhanced self-determination for students with disabilities.

In addition to the SDLMI, which is a model of teaching, the literature has identified an evidence-base for a number of curricular programs developed to promote self-determination, as reviewed below [Note: A number of programs designed to promote student involvement in transition planning have been found to have a positive impact on self-determination, but those are detailed in Chapter 6.]. Test, Karvonen, Wood, Browder, & Algozzine (2000) conducted an extensive review of curricular materials to promote self-determination and located 60 such products. Reviews and information about most of these procedures are available online at http://www.uncc.edu/sdsp and, as such, readers are referred to that resource for greater detail on the array of materials available.

It is important to emphasize that the first line of intervention to promote self-determination involves infusion of instructional strategies, such as those highlighted by the Algozzine et al. (2001) meta-analysis (e.g., modeling, role-playing, direct instruction, self-instruction, etc.)

across multiple content areas and across the school day. Students can learn problem-solving, goal-setting, or decision-making skills (as well as other component elements of self-determined behavior) in math, science, or social studies as well as through community-based instruction and functional skills instruction.

Curricula to Promote Self-determination

The ChoiceMaker Curriculum (with The Self-Directed IEP materials) (Martin, Marshall, Maxson, & Jerman, 1993) consists of three sections: (1) Choosing Goals, (2) Expressing Goals and (3) Taking Action. Each section contains from two to four teaching goals and numerous teaching objectives addressing six transition areas. Included are: (a) an assessment tool; (b) Choosing Goals lessons; (c) the Self-Directed IEP, and (d) Taking Action lessons. The program includes a criterion-referenced self-determination transition assessment tool that matches the curricular sections. The Choosing Goals lessons enable students to learn the necessary skills and personal information needed to articulate their interests, skills, limits, and goals across one or more self-selected transition areas. The Self-Directed IEP lessons, described in more detail in Chapter 6, enable students to learn the leadership skills necessary to manage their IEP meeting and publicly disclose their interests, skills, limits, and goals identified through the Choosing Goals lessons.

The *Taking Action* materials enable students to learn how to break their long-range goals into specific goals that can be accomplished in a week. Students learn how they will attain their goals by deciding: (1) a standard for goal performance; (2) a means to get performance feedback; (3) what motivates them to do it; (4) the strategies they will use; (5) needed supports; and (6) schedules. There have been four studies examining the efficacy of the ChoiceMaker materials (Allen, Smith, Test, Flowers, & Wood, 2001; Cross, Cooke, Wood, & Test, 1999; Snyder, 2002; Snyder & Shapiro, 1997) documenting positive effects on student self-determination, skills in goal setting and leadership, and student involvement in educational planning.

Steps to Self-Determination (2nd ed.)(Hoffman & Field, 2005) involves lessons using modeling, cooperative and experiential learning, lectures, and discussions through which students complete an hour-long orientation session, a six-hour workshop, and 16 classroom-based lessons focused on content related to self-determination, including setting and attaining goals, self-advocacy, and decision making. The package includes assessment tools, objectives, preparation guidelines, lesson plans, overhead and handout masters, and teacher information. The materials were primarily designed for students with mild to moderate learning and behavior difficulties, including students with learning disabilities and mild intellectual disability. Four percent of students received instruction using this curriculum (61% students with LD, 39% students with MR) and completed all 16 classroom-based lessons.

Self-determined Learning Model of Instruction

Like all educators, special education teachers use a variety of teaching models, defined as "a plan or pattern that can be used to shape curriculums (long-term courses of study), to design instructional materials, and to guide instruction in the classroom and other settings" (Joyce and Weil, 1980, p. 1). Such models are derived from theories about human behavior, learning, or cognition, and effective teachers employ multiple models of teaching, taking into account the unique characteristics of the learner and types of learning. The teaching model most frequently adopted by special educators is the contingency management model, drawing from operant psychology. The *Self-Determined Learning Model of Instruction* (Wehmeyer et al., 2007) is a model of teaching based on the component elements of self-determination, the process of self-regulated problem solving, and research on student-directed learning. It is appropriate for use with students with and without disabilities across a wide range of content areas, and enables teachers to engage students in the totality of their educational program by increasing opportunities to self-direct learning and, in the process, to enhance student self-determination.

Implementation of the model consists of a three-phase instructional process. Each instructional phase presents a problem to be solved by the student. The student solves each problem by posing and answering a series of four Student Questions per phase that students learn, modify to make their own, and apply to reach self-selected goals. Each question is linked to a set of Teacher Objectives. Each instructional phase includes a list of Educational Supports that teachers can use to enable students to self-direct learning. In each instructional phase, the student is the primary agent for choices, decisions, and actions, even when eventual actions are teacher-directed.

The Student Questions in the model are constructed to direct the student through a problem-solving sequence in each instructional phase. The solutions to the problems in each phase lead to the problem-solving sequence in the next phase. Teachers implementing the model teach students to solve a sequence of problems to construct a means–ends chain—a causal sequence—that moves them from where they are (an actual state of not having their needs and interests satisfied) to where they want to be (a goal state of having those needs and interests satisfied). Its function is to reduce or eliminate the discrepancy between what students want or need and what students currently have or know. That means–ends sequence is constructed by having students answer the questions that connect their needs and interests to their actions and results via goals and plans. To answer the questions in this sequence, students must regulate their own problem solving by setting goals to meet needs, constructing plans to meet goals, and adjusting actions to complete plans. Thus, each instructional phase poses a problem the student must solve (What is my goal? What is my plan? What have I learned?) by solving a series of problems posed by the questions in each phase. The four questions differ from phase to phase, but represent identical steps in the problem-solving sequence. That is, students answering the questions must: (1) identify the problem, (2) identify potential solutions to the problem, (3) identify barriers to solving the problem, and (4) identify consequences of each solution. These steps are the fundamental steps in any problem-solving process and they form the means–ends problem-solving sequence represented by the *Student Questions* in each phase and enable the student to solve the problem posed in each instructional phase.

The Student Questions are written in first-person voice in a relatively simple format with the intention that they are the starting point for discussion between the teacher and the student. Some students will learn and use all 12 questions as they are written. Other students will need to have the questions rephrased to be more understandable. Still other students, due to the intensity of their instructional needs, may have the teacher paraphrase the questions for them. The first time a teacher uses the model with a student, the initial step in the implementation process is to read the question with or to the student, discuss what the question means and then, if necessary, change the wording to enable that student to better understand the intent of the question. Such wording changes must, however, be made such that the problem-solving intent of the question remains intact. The Teacher Objectives within the model are just that—the objectives a teacher will be trying to accomplish by implementing the model. In each instructional phase, the objectives are linked directly to the Student Questions. These objectives can be met by utilizing strategies provided in the Educational Supports section of the model. The Teacher Objectives provide, in essence, a road map to assist the teacher that enables the student to solve the problem stated in the student question.

The emphasis in the model on the use of instructional strategies and educational supports that are student-directed provides another means of teaching students to teach themselves. As important as this is, however, not every instructional strategy implemented will be student-directed. The purpose of any model of teaching is to promote student learning and growth. There are circumstances in which the most effective instructional method or strategy to achieve a particular educational outcome will be a teacher–directed strategy. Students who are considering what plan of action to implement to achieve a self-selected goal can recognize that teachers have expertise in instructional strategies and take full advantage of that expertise.

The fundamental purpose of any model of instruction is to promote student learning. Teachers use models of instruction to drive curriculum and assessment development and to design instructional methods, materials and strategies, all with the intent of improving the quality of the instructional experience and, presumably, enhancing student achievement. Thus,

Table 11.1 Empirical validation of the self-determined learning model of instruction

Study	Design	Subjects	Dependent variables	Outcomes
Wehmeyer, Palmer, Agran, Mithaug, & Martin (2000)	Pre-post no control group	40 HS students: 13 w/ MR, 17 w/ LD, 10 w/ EBD	SD, GAS, goal skills, locus of control	Progress on 80% of educational goals, enhanced SD and perceptions of control.
Agran, Blanchard, & Wehmeyer (2000)	Delayed multiple baseline across groups	19 MS/HS students w/ severe MR	GAS, % correct on transition goals linked to functional needs	Students attained transition-related goals using model.
McGlashing-Johnson, Agran, Sitlington, Cavin, & Wehmeyer, (2003)	Multiple baseline across subjects	4 HS students with severe MR	% correct on job tasks, GAS	
Palmer & Wehmeyer (2003)	Pre-post no control group	50 K-3rd grade students: 21 w/ LD, 6 w/ MR, 5 w/ Speech Imp, 2 w/ OHI, 16 w/ DD	Goal attainment and skills	Students achieved goals at greater than expected level and acquired goals knowledge and skills.
Palmer, Wehmeyer, Gibson, & Agran (2004)	Interrupted time series w/ switching replication	22 MS students with MR	SD, Problem solving skills, GAS	Students able to achieve goals linked to general education curriculum using model
Agran, Cavin, Wehmeyer & Palmer (2006)	Multiple-baseline across subjects	3 MS students with moderate MR	Academic goals linked to district standards	Students mastered skills linked to standards in science, geography.
Agran, Wehmeyer, Cavin, & Palmer (2008)	Multiple baseline across subjects	3 junior high students with cognitive disabilities.	Goals linked to active participation in general education classroom	Students mastered classroom participation skills.
Lee, Wehmeyer, Palmer, Soukup, and Little (2008)	Group-randomized pre-post control group	42 HS students (20 treatment/ 22 control) (6 w/ ADHD/OHI, 3 w/ EBD, 32 w/ LD, 1 w/ Aut	Interval time sample data on access, self-determination, goal attainment	Treatment group achieved significantly higher rate of goal attainment, self-regulation predicted access.

the first requirement of any model of instruction is that teachers can use the model to "teach" students educationally valued skills or concepts. We have proposed that the Self-Determined Learning Model of Instruction has the added benefit of enhancing student self-determination. As such, evaluation activities have focused on ensuring that students with disabilities achieve educationally valued goals when provided instruction using the model and examining the impact of the model on student self-determination. Table 11.1 presents a summary of published studies using the SDLMI. In general, these studies show that students provided instruction using the SDLMI achieve transition and academic achievement goals at levels greater than expected and gain skills related to self-determination.

As mentioned previously, Wehmeyer and colleagues (Shogren et al., in press; Wehmeyer et al., in press) have reported findings from a randomized-trial, placebo control group study of the SDLMI. Since the SDLMI is a model of teaching, the first level of evaluation was on the impact of instruction with the SDLMI on educational outcomes. In this case, Shogren et al. examined the impact of the SDLMI on academic and transition goal attainment and on access to the general education classroom. The study involved 312 high school students with intellectual or learning disabilities. Half of the students were assigned to a control group and half to a treatment group for one year, with students in the treatment group receiving the SDLMI. During the second year, all students received the SDLMI. Using a multilevel modeling analysis, Shogren et al. (in press) found that students who received instruction using the SDLMI showed significantly higher goal attainment, though for students with ID this was for transition goals only and for students with LD it was for academic goals only. Both groups showed higher access to the general education curriculum when receiving the intervention. Wehmeyer and colleagues (in press) reported the impact of the SDLMI on student self-determination within this same sample using structural equation modeling procedures and determined that students with disabilities receiving the SDLMI intervention were significantly more self-determined after one year of instruction. These studies establish a causal relationship between intervention with the model, increased self-determination, goal attainment, and access to the general education curriculum.

Self-determination and the Transition to Post-secondary Education

Much of this chapter has focused on promoting the self-determination of children and youth with disabilities and the role of K-12 educators in that process. There is growing awareness, however, of the need to focus on the promotion of self-determination in the transition to post-secondary educational settings (Thoma & Wehmeyer, 2005). Research has only begun to examine and validate the positive impact that enhanced self-determination has on the success of students with disabilities in postsecondary settings (e.g. Getzel & Thoma, 2006, 2008; Thoma & Getzel, 2005). This section of the chapter will examine the role of promoting self-determination in the transition to (and subsequent success for) postsecondary education.

Recent research on postsecondary education has focused on understanding the skills and experiences that students with disabilities identify as being most helpful in promoting their transition to and success in college (Getzel & Thoma, 2006; Getzel & Thoma, 2008; Thoma & Getzel, 2005). The critical skills as identified by students who participated in the focus groups included problem-solving, self-awareness, goal-setting, self-management, and self-advocacy skills.

When students were asked what they thought an effective advocate did to ensure he or she stays in school and gets the supports needed, the most common answer was problem-solving skills. Problem solving was important in making decisions about self-disclosure and in identifying supports beyond those provided through offices for students with disabilities. Other students talked about using problem-solving skills to overcome barriers to college admissions, receive appropriate support services, and manage the logistics of completing a program of study.

In addition, students spoke about interpersonal problem-solving opportunities that college provides.

Students also felt that it was critically important to understand their own strengths, preferences, interests and needs in order to make good decisions about college admissions, majors, friends, and services. Students believed that educators and college personnel may not consider that a student with a disability can be successful. It is imperative that students learn as much as possible about themselves, how the disability impacts their learning, and the supports, services, and accommodations that can help them be successful. Further, students who were successful in getting admitted and staying in college reported that their abilities to set and measure progress toward achieving goals had a significant impact on their success. They indicated that both long-range (I want to succeed in this course because it's required for the career I want to have) and short-term goals (I will finish the research for this paper by Friday so that I will have time to write the paper itself by the due date) were important.

Self-management skills, including the ability to organize one's time, materials, and tasks to keep up with studying and keeping up with all aspects of class including class notes, materials, assignments, quizzes and exams, are obviously critical. In particular, students noted that this aspect of self-management was critical in determining when additional supports and services were needed, as well as when it was acceptable to participate in some of the other experiences of college life.

Finally, students discussed the importance of advocating for themselves and spoke of the relationships forged with faculty, support staff, and peers as the three most important aspects of self-advocacy. Developing support systems on campus such as study groups, mentorship relationships, and even social groups can help ease the sense of isolation and hopelessness that can be a barrier to staying in college. Successful students identified and then made use of any and all supports and services that were available, often long before there was a problem. They urged others to do that as well, rather than waiting until after failing an exam or a course grade.

Of course, acquiring self-determination skills to support the transition to and success in postsecondary education needs to begin long before a student arrives on a college campus.

During high school, most students who are planning to continue their education at postsecondary settings visit a variety of colleges and universities to help with making a decision about which one to attend. For students with disabilities, it can be argued that this process is even more critical. Besides learning about the academic programs and financial aid options offered by a specific college or university, students with disabilities must also learn about the supports offered at the university to find a good match between their support needs and the ability of the college or university to accommodate them.

One of the most important resources for students with disabilities is the college or university office that provides and coordinates access to services. Students and their transition team members need to research the typical services available through these offices for each postsecondary setting being considered to be sure that the supports an individual student needs will actually be available. Unlike a student's public school experiences, not every accommodation and/or support necessary for success needs to be provided. Instead, postsecondary institutes need to adhere to the requirements of the Americans with Disabilities Act (ADA, 1990) and the Rehabilitation Act of 1973 (PL 93–112) which require that they do not discriminate against otherwise qualified individuals and that they provide equal access to the physical and learning environments.

It is also important to discuss documentation of one's disability, as this is a growing concern in the transition from high school to postsecondary educational settings (Reilly & Davis, 2005). In public schools, students have an initial evaluation to determine whether they qualify as having a disability and need supports to benefit from their education. Under IDEA, students then are re-evaluated every three years, unless the team determines that this re-evaluation is not necessary. More and more high schools are now waiving that re-evaluation when a student is in high school, believing that they have qualified for services for many years and a re-evaluation at that point would not provide any additional, relevant information. However, if a student is going on to a postsecondary educational setting, this re-evaluation is crucial to qualify for services there. Most universities and colleges will not accept an IEP document as sufficient documentation of proof that he or she has a disability. In addition, they will not accept a re-evaluation or initial evaluation report that is more than three to five years old. Many students are therefore caught with having to arrange and pay for their own evaluation to prove that they qualify to receive supports through a university's office for students with disabilities, even if they received special education services for their entire K-12 public school experience.

There are obviously many issues to examine when a student with a disability decides to transition from high school to postsecondary educational settings. The benefits of organizing this transition are well documented: students who attend colleges, even if they do not earn a degree, are more likely to find work they enjoy and earn better wages and benefits than those who have no postsecondary educational experience (Gajar, Goodman, & McAfee, 1995). And students with disabilities who score higher on measures of self-determination have also been shown to be more successful in employment, community living, finances, and in postsecondary education.

The Role of Families and Educators in Promoting Student Self-determination

Research has demonstrated that self-determination flourishes in a context of strong, positive relationships (Ryan & Deci, 2000). Both family members and educators play important roles in helping students develop competencies that lead to increased self-determination. Family members and educators can play an important role in students' self-determination by:

- Providing a foundation of security for self-determination through strong, positive relationships;
- Directly teaching knowledge and skills for self-determination;
- Providing opportunities for students to practice their self-determination skills; and
- Serving as role-models of self-determination.

The Unique Role and Needs of Families

Turnbull and Turnbull (1996) identified four features of families that affect student self-determination.

- Family characteristics including factors such as characteristics of the disability, cultural values, beliefs and expectations, and coping styles;
- Family interactions such as role expectations, relationships, cohesion, and adaptability;
- Family functions, including economic, daily care, recreation, socialization, affective, educational/vocational, and self-definition needs;
- Family lifespan issues, including developmental stages of family interactions and functions over time, transitions or changes in family characteristics, composition, cohesion, and function.

Because each of these factors is unique for each student and family, it is important to develop an understanding of the strengths and needs of each family and tailor a system of self-determination supports that addresses the family's unique needs. Turnbull and Turnbull (1996) stated:

> Having a prototypical "ideal family" in mind and judging all families against that prototype is a strategy that brings only frustration and failure. A key for success is not only recognizing family diversity, but indeed honoring it and taking it fully into account when designing self-determination training, supports and services. (p. 216)

When designing self-determination instruction and supports, different approaches to the concept of self-determination may need to be considered to honor a family's cultural background. For example, within some cultures, group achievement is more highly valued than individual accomplishment. For these students, depending on their specific needs and values and those of their families, it may be important to support students in establishing their goals within the context of a group rather than as an individual. In addition, to it is important to recognize that families will have varying capacities to engage with the school and their sons and daughters around self-determination instruction and supports. Some parents may not be able to participate in classroom activities during the school day, but can do individual activities with their sons and daughters during the evening. Others may be able to participate at school if child care for younger siblings is provided.

Self-determination Support Strategies for Families

There are many different ways schools can help parents learn to support student self-determination. First, many self-determination curricula provide opportunities for parents to engage in the curriculum with their sons and daughters. This allows parents to learn more about the concept of self-determination while they are, at the same time, enhancing their relationships with their sons and daughters. For example, *Steps to Self-Determination* (Hoffman & Field, 2005) offers opportunities to include parents, with their sons and daughters, in a self-determination workshop that introduces the concept of self-determination. The workshop also includes activities that parents and their children complete together in areas such as self-awareness and acceptance. Several optional activities are provided for students and their parents to complete as homework. The *Self-Determined Learning Model for Early Elementary Students: A Parent's Guide* (Palmer & Wehmeyer, 2002) offers instructional activities parents can use with their children to help them learn how to use the self-determined learning model of instruction. Parent/child activities are provided for problem-solving, communication and self-advocacy skills and self-management. A list of children's books that parents can read with them to help teach self-determination concepts is provided. The Take Charge curriculum (Powers, Turner, Westwood, Matuszewski, Wilson, & Phillips, 2001) includes monthly community-based workshops for youth, parents, and mentors as well as telephone and home visit support for parents. The curriculum includes a video, also titled *Take Charge*, which offers a personal look at parents' reactions to their sons and daughters becoming more self-determined as well as providing insight on ways parents can encourage self-determination.

Many schools offer programs and services specifically for parents that help them to learn more about self-determination and how they can support their sons and daughters to be more self-determined. An instructional program that was designed specifically to help parents learn about the concept of self-determination and apply those concepts to their parenting is *Self-Determined Parenting* (Field, Hoffman, & Les, 2006). *Self-Determined Parenting* focuses on helping parents apply self-determination skills in their lives so they can be more effective parents and role-models of self-determination for their children. The program also provides some suggestions for ways in which parents can support development of knowledge and skills for self-determination in their daughters and sons.

Many of the parent support programs that are typically offered within schools can be modified to include an emphasis on self-determination. For example, many schools offer workshops on building strong family relationships or parent effectiveness skills. Given the importance of relationships and families to increased self-determination, self-determination concepts and strategies could be easily infused within these activities. In addition, self-determination can be modeled and infused in one-to-one interactions between parents and school personnel.

The Unique Role and Needs of Educators

Educators also play a key role in students' lives. With the exception of family members, there are few adults that students interact with as consistently as they do with teachers. Teachers serve as important role-models for students. Teachers' efforts to build and express a sense of self-determination in their own lives can contribute to increased student self-determination. Powers (1997, p. 1) suggested "modeling is a critical ingredient for bolstering self-determination and it is essential that teachers have the information, skills, and supports necessary to function as instructors and role models for youth." Martin (1997) stated "Teacher self-determined behavior does indeed impact student self-determination. This comes through in every-day student-teacher interactions, plus in how the teachers model their own self-determination" (p. 2).

In addition to serving as role-models of self-determination, teachers need to focus on self-determination because it will help them be more effective and efficient in their jobs. The ability to be self-determined is essential to designing and implementing effective instruction and to effectively participating in the school improvement process. Finally, student self-determination is maximized when educators share a strong philosophical foundation about the need to promote self-determination throughout the culture of the school (Wehmeyer & Field, 2007).

Wehmeyer & Field (2007) suggested specific steps that educators can take to increase their self-determination. These steps include:

- Learn more about self-determination and how it applies to you.
- Discover your strengths, weaknesses, needs and preferences on a daily basis.
- Set some goals. Move into action.
- Don't go it alone. Find your sources of support.

By becoming more self-determined, educators can become more effective in their work and life while they are at the same time serving as important role-models for their students.

References

Abery, B. H., Arndt, K., Greger, P., Tetu, L., Eggebeen, A., Barosko, G., et al. (1994). *Self-determination for youth with disabilities: A family education curriculum*. Minneapolis MN: University of Minnesota, Institute on Community Integration.

Abery, B. H., & Eggebeen, A. (1995). *Findings from a field-test of a self-determination capacity building curriculum* (Technical Report No. 3). Minneapolis, MN: University of Minnesota, Institute on Community Integration.

Abery, B. H., McGrew, K., & Smith, J. (1994). *Validation of an ecological model of self-determination for children with disabilities* (Technical Report No. 2). Minneapolis, MN: University of Minnesota, Institute on Community Integration.

Abery, B. H., Simunds, E., & Cady, R. (2002). *The Minnesota Health Care Self-Determination Scales.* Minneapolis, MN: University of Minnesota, Institute on Community Integration.

Abery, B. H., Simunds, E., & Cady, R. (2006). *The Impact of health care coordination on the lives of adults with physical disabilities* (Technical Report #2). Minneapolis, MN: University of Minnesota, Institute on Community Integration.

Abery, B. H., & Stancliffe, R. J. (1996). The ecology of self-determination. In D. J. Sands & M. L. Wehmeyer (Eds.), *Self-determination across the life span: Independence and choice for people with disabilities* (pp. 111–145). Baltimore, MD: Paul H. Brookes.

Abery, B. H., Stancliffe, R. J., Smith, J., McGrew, K., & Eggebeen, A. (1995a). *Minnesota Opportunities and Exercise of Self-Determination Scale – Adult Edition.* Minneapolis, MN: University of Minnesota, Institute on Community Integration, Research and Training Center on Community Living.

Abery, B. H., Stancliffe, R. J., Smith, J., McGrew, K., & Eggebeen, A. (1995b). *Minnesota Self-Determination Skills, Attitudes, and Knowledge Evaluation Scale – Adult Edition.* Minneapolis, MN: University of Minnesota, Institute on Community Integration, Research and Training Center on Community Living.

Agran, M., Blanchard, C., & Wehmeyer, M. L. (2000). Promoting transition goals and self-determination through student-directed learning: The Self-Determined Learning Model of Instruction. *Education and Training in Mental Retardation and Developmental Disabilities, 35,* 351–364.

Agran, M., Cavin, M., Wehmeyer, M. L., & Palmer, S. (2006). Participation of students with severe disabilities in the general curriculum: The effects of the Self-Determined Learning Model of Instruction. *Research and Practice for Persons with Severe Disabilities, 31,* 230–241.

Agran, M., Wehmeyer, M. L., Cavin, M., & Palmer, S. (2008). Promoting student active classroom participation skills through instruction to promote self-regulated learning and self-determination. *Career Development for Exceptional Individuals, 31,* 106–114.

Algozzine, B., Browder, D., Karvonen, M., Test, D. W., & Wood, W. M. (2001). Effects of interventions to promote the self-determination for individuals with disabilities. *Review of Educational Research, 71,* 219–277.

Allen, S. K., Smith, A. C., Test, D. W., Flowers, C., & Wood, W. M. (2001). The effects of "Self-Directed IEP" on student participation in IEP meetings. *Career Development for Exceptional Individuals, 4,* 107–120. Bronfenbrenner, U. (1979). *The ecology of human development: experiments by nature and design.* Cambridge, MA: Harvard University Press.

Bronfenbrenner, U. (1989). Ecological systems theory. *Annals of Child Development, 6,* 187–249.

Carter, E. W., Lane, K. L., Pierson, M. R., & Glaeser, B. (2006). Self-determination skills and opportunities of transition-age youth with emotional disturbance and learning disabilities. *Exceptional Children, 72*(3), 333–346.

Cobb, B., Lehmann, J., Newman-Gonchar, R., & Alwell, M. (2009). Self-determination for students with disabilities: A narrative metasynthesis. *Career Development for Exceptional Individuals, 32*(2), 108–114.

Cross, T., Cooke, N. L., Wood, W. M., & Test, D. W. (1999). Comparison of the effects of MAPS and ChoiceMaker on students' self-determination skills. *Education and Training in Mental Retardation and Developmental Disabilities, 34,* 499–510.

Field, S., & Hoffman, A. (1994). Development of a model for self-determination. *Career Development for Exceptional Individuals, 17,* 159–169.

Field, S., & Hoffman, A. (2001). *Teaching with integrity, reflection, and self-determination.* Detroit, MI: Wayne State University.

Field, S., & Hoffman, A. (2005). *Steps to Self-Determination,* 2nd ed. Austin, TX: ProEd.

Field, S., & Hoffman, A. (2007). Self-determination in secondary transition assessment. *Assessment for effective intervention, 32*(3), 181–190.

Field, S., Hoffman, A. & Les, B. (2006). *Self-determined parenting.* Detroit, MI. Center for Self-Determination and Transition, College of Education, Wayne State University.

Field, S., Sarver, M. D., & Shaw, S. F. (2003). Self-determination: A key to success in postsecondary education for studnets with learning disabilities. *Remedial and Special Education, 24*(6), 339–349.

Fowler, C. H., Konrad, M., Walker, A. R., Test, D. W., & Wood, W. M. (2007). Self-determinatoin interventions' effects on the academic perfromance of students with developmental disabilities. *Education and Training in Developmental Disabilities, 42*(3), 270–285.

Gajar, A., Goodman, L., & McAfee, J. (1995). *Secondary schools and beyond: Transition of individuals with mild disabilities.* New York: Macmillan/McGraw-Hill.

Getzel, E. E. & Thoma, C. A. (2006). Voice of experience: What college students with learning disabilities and attention deficit/hyperactivity disorders tell us are important self-determination skills for success. *Learning Disabilities: A Multi-disciplinary Journal, 14*, 33–39.

Getzel, E. E. & Thoma, C. A. (2008). Experiences of college students with disabilities and the importance of self-determination in higher education settings. *Career Development for Exceptional Individuals, 31*(2), 77–84.

Hoffman, A., & Field, S. (2005). *Steps to self-determination* (2nd ed.). Austin, TX: ProEd.

Hoffman, A., Field, S., & Sawilowsky, S. (2004). *Self-Determination Assessment Battery user's guide* (3rd ed.). Detroit, MI: Center for Self-Determination and Transition, College of Education, Wayne State University.

Individuals with Disabilities Education Improvement Act (IDEA) of 2004, PL 108–446, 20 U.S.C. ss 1400 *et seq.*

Joyce, B., & Weil, M. (1980). *Models of teaching* (2nd ed.). Englewood Cliffs, NJ: Prentice Hall.

Konrad, M., Fowler, C. H., Walker, A. R., Test, D. W., & Wood, W. M. (2007). Effects of self-determination interventions on the academic skills of students with learning disabilities. *Learning Disabilities Quarterly, 30*(2), 89–113.

Lachapelle, Y., Wehmeyer, M. L., Haelewyck, M. C., Courbois, Y., Keith, K. D., Schalock, R. et al. (2005). The relationship between quality of life and self-determination: An international study. *Journal of Intellectual Disability Research, 49*, 740–744.

Lee, S. H., Wehmeyer, M. L., Palmer, S. B., Soukup, J. H., & Little, T. D. (2008). Self-determination and access to the general education curriculum. *The Journal of Special Education, 42*, 91–107.

Lee, S. H., Wehmeyer, M. L., Soukup, J. H., & Palmer, S. B. (2010). Impact of curriculum modifications on access to the general education curriculum for students with disabilities. *Exceptional Children, 76*(2), 213–233.

McGlashing-Johnson, J., Agran, M., Sitlington, P., Cavin, M., & Wehmeyer, M. L. (2003). Enhancing the job performance of youth with moderate to severe cognitive disabilities using the Self-Determined Learning Model of Instruction. *Research and Practice for Persons with Severe Disabilities, 28*, 194–204.

Martin, J. (1997). *Self-determination is for teachers too.* Presentation to the Division on Career Development International Conference, Scottsdale, AZ.

Martin, J. E., Marshall, L., Maxson, L. L., & Jerman, P. (1993). *Self-directed IEP.* Longmont, CO: Sopris West.

Martin, J. E., Van Dycke, J. L., Christensen, W. R., Greene, B. A., Gardner, J. E., & Lovett, D. L. (2006). Increasing student participation in IEP meetings: Establishing the Self-Directed IEP as an evidenced-based practice. *Exceptional Children, 72*(3), 299–316.

Martorell, A., Gutierrez-Recacha, P., Pereda, A., & Ayuso-Mateos, J. L. (2008). Identification of personal factors that determine work outcome for adults with intellectual disability. *Journal of Intellectual Disability Research, 52*(12), 1091–1101.

Mason, C., Field, S., & Swailowsky, S. (2004). Implementation of self-determination activities and student participation in IEPs. *Exceptional Children, 70*, 441–451.

Mithaug, D. (1998). Your right, my obligation? *Journal of the Association for Persons with Severe Disabilities, 23*, 41–43.

Nota, L., Ferrrari, L., Soresi, S., & Wehmeyer, M. L. (2007). Self-determination, social abilities, and the quality of life of people with intellectual disabilities. *Journal of Intellectual Disability Research, 51*, 850–865.

Palmer, S. & Wehmeyer, M. L. (2002). *Self-Determined Learning Model for Early Elementary Students: A Parent's Guide.* Lawrence, KS: Beach Center on Disability, Schiefelbusch Institute for Lifespan Studies, University of Kansas.

Palmer, S., & Wehmeyer, M. L. (2003). Promoting self-determination in early elementary school: Teaching self-regulated problem-solving and goal setting skills. *Remedial and Special Education, 24*, 115–126.

Palmer, S. B., Wehmeyer, M. L., Gibson, K., & Agran, M. (2004). Promoting access to the general curriculum by teaching self-determination skills. *Exceptional Children, 70*, 427–439.

Pierson, M. R., Carter, E. W., Lane, K. L., & Glaeser, B. C. (2008). Factors influencing the self-determination of transition-age youth with high-incidence disabilities. *Career Development for Exceptional Individuals, 31*(2), 115–125.

Powers, L. (1997). Self-determination is for teachers too. Presentation to the Division on Career Development International Conference, Scottsdale, AZ.

Powers, L. E., Turner, A., Westwood, D., Matuszewski, J., Wilson, R., et al. (2001). A controlled field-test of Take Charge: A multi-component intervention to promote adolescent self-determination. *Career Development for Exceptional Individuals, 24*, 89–104.

Rehabilitation Act of 1973, PL 93–112, 29 U.S.C., SS 794.

Reilly, V. J. & Davis, T. (2005). Understanding the regulatory environment. In E. E. Getzel & P. Wehman (Eds.). *Going to college: Expanding opportunities for people with disabilities* (pp. 25–48). Baltimore: Paul H. Brookes.

Ryan, R. M., & Deci, E. L. (2000). Self-determination theory and the facilitation of intrinsic motivation, social development, and well-being. *American Psychologist*, *55*(1), 68–78.

Shogren, K. A., Lopez, S. J., Wehmeyer, M. L., Little, T. D., & Pressgrove, C. L. (2006). The role of positive psychology constructs in predicting life satisfaction in adolescents with and without cognitive disabilities: An exploratory study. *The Journal of Positive Psychology*, *1*, 37–52.

Shogren, K., Palmer, S., Wehmeyer, M. L., Williams-Diehm, K., & Little, T. (in press). Effect of intervention with the Self-Determined Learning Model of Instruction on access and goal attainment. *Remedial and Special Education*.

Shogren, K. A., Wehmeyer, M. L., Palmer, S. B., Soukup, J. H., Little, T., et al. (2008). Understanding the construct of self-determination: Examining the relationship between The Arc's Self-Determination Scale and the American Institute for Research Self-Determination Scale. *Assessment for Effective Instruction*, *33*, 94–107.

Snyder, E. P. (2002). Teaching students with combined behavioral disorders and mental retardation to lead their own IEP meetings. *Behavioral Disorders*, *27*, 340–357.

Snyder, E. P., & Shapiro, E. S. (1997). Teaching students with emotional/behavioral disorders the skills to participate in the development of their own IEPs. *Behavioral Disorders*, *22*, 246–259.

Sowers, J., & Powers, L. (1995). Enhancing the participation and independence of students with severe physical and multiple disabilities in performing community activities. *Mental Retardation*, *33*, 209–220.

Stancliffe, R. J., Abery B. H., & Smith, J. (2000). Personal control and the ecology of community living settings: Beyond living-unit size and type. *American Journal on Mental Retardation*, *105*, 431–454.

Test, D. W., Fowler, C., Kohler, P., & Kortering, L. (2010). *Evidence-based practices and predictors in secondary transition: What we know and what we still need to know.* Charlotte, NC: National Secondary Transition Technical Assistance Center.

Test, D. W., Karvonen, M., Wood, W. M., Browder, D., & Algozzine, B. (2000). Choosing a self-determination curriculum: Plan for the future. *Teaching Exceptional Children*, *33*, 48–54.

Test, D. W., Mason, C., Hughes, C., Konrad, M., Neale, M., & Wood, W. M. (2004). Student involvement in individualized education program meetings. *Exceptional Children*, *70*(4), 391–412.

Test, D. W., Mazzotti, V. L., Mustian, A. L., Fowler, C. H., Kortering, L. J., & Kohler, P. H. (2009). Evidence-based secondary transition predictors for improving post-school outcomes for students with disabilities. *Career Development for Exceptional Individuals*, *32*, 160–181.

Thoma, C. A. & Getzel, E. E. (2005). Self-determination is what it's all about: What post-secondary students with disabilities tell us are important considerations for success. *Education and Training in Mental Retardation and Developmental Disabilities*, *40*, 35–48.

Thoma, C. A., & Wehmeyer, M. L. (2005). Self-determination and the transition to postsecondary education. In E. E. Getzel & P. Wehman (Eds.), *Going to college: Expanding opportunities for people with disabilities* (pp. 49–68). Baltimore: Paul H. Brookes.

Turnbull, A. P., & Turnbull, H. R. (1996). Self-determination within a culturally responsive family systems perspective. In L. E. Powers, G. H. S. Singer, & J. Sowers (Eds.), *On the road to autonomy: promoting self-determination in children and youth with disabilities* (pp. 195–220). Baltimore, MD: Paul H. Brooks.

Wehmeyer, M. L. (1996). A self-report measure of self-determination for adolescents with cognitive disabilities. *Education and Training in Mental Retardation and Developmental Disabilities*, *31*, 282–293.

Wehmeyer, M. L. (2005). Self-determination and individuals with severe disabilities: Reexamining meanings and misinterpretations. *Research and Practice for Persons with Severe Disabilities*, *30*, 113–120.

Wehmeyer, M. L., Abery, B., Mithaug, D. E., & Stancliffe, R. J. (2003). *Theory in Self-Determination: Foundations for Educational Practice.* Springfield, IL: Charles C Thomas Publisher, LTD.

Wehmeyer, M. L., Agran, M., Hughes, C., Martin, J., Mithaug, D. E., & Palmer, S. (2007). *Promoting self-determination in students with intellectual and developmental disabilities.* New York: Guilford Press.

Wehmeyer, M. L. & Field, S. L. (2007). *Self-determination instructional and assessment strategies.* Thousand Oaks, CA: Corwin Press.

Wehmeyer, M. L. & Kelchner, K. (1995). *The Arc's Self-Determination Scale: Procedural guidelines.* Arlington, TX: Author.

Wehmeyer, M. L., Kelchner, K., & Richards, S. (1996). Essential characteristics of self-determined behavior of individuals with mental retardation. *American Journal on Mental Retardation*, *100*, 632–642.

Wehmeyer, M. L., & Little, T. D. (2009). Self-Determination. In S. Lopez (Ed.), *The Encyclopedia of Positive Psychology* (Vol. 2, pp. 868–874). Boston: Blackwell Publishing.

Wehmeyer, M. L., & Palmer, S. B. (2003). Adult outcomes from students with cognitive disabilities three years after high school: The impact of self-determination. *Education and Training in Developmental Disabilities, 38*, 131–144.

Wehmeyer, M. L., Palmer, S. B., Agran, M., Mithaug, D. E., & Martin, J. E. (2000). Promoting causal agency: The *Self-Determined Learning Model of Instruction. Exceptional Children, 66*(4), 439–453.

Wehmeyer, M. L., Palmer, S., Shogren, K., Williams-Diehm, K., & Soukup, J. (in press). Establishing a causal relationship between interventions to promote self-determination and enhanced student self-determination. *Journal of Special Education.*

Wehmeyer, M. L., Palmer, S. B., Williams-Diehm, K., Shogren, K. A., Davies, D., & Stock, S. (2011). The impact of technology use in transition planning on student self-determination. *Journal of Special Education Technology, 26*(1), 13–24.

Wehmeyer, M. L., & Schwartz, M. (1997). Self-determination and positive adult outcomes: A follow up study of youth with mental retardation or learning disabilities. *Exceptional Children, 63*, 245–255.

Wehmeyer, M. L., & Schwartz, M. (1998). The relationship between self-determination and quality of life for adults with mental retardation. *Education and Training in* Mental Retardation and Developmental Disabilities, 33, 3–12.

Wehmeyer, M. L., & Shogren, K. (2008). Self-determination and learners with autism spectrum disorders. In R. Simpson & B. Myles (Eds.), *Educating Children and Youth with Autism: Strategies for Effective Practice* (2nd Ed.)(pp. 433–476). Austin, TX: ProEd Publishers, Inc.

Wehmeyer, M. L., Shogren, K., Palmer, S., Williams-Diehm, K., Little, T., & Boulton, A. (in press). Impact of the Self-Determined Learning Model of Instruction on student self-determination: A randomized-trial placebo control group study. *Exceptional Children.*

Wolman, J. M., Campeau, P. I., DuBois, P. A., Mithaug, D. E. & Stolarski, V. S. (1994). *AIR Self-Determination Scale and user guide.* Stanford, CA: American Institutes for Research.

12

Structured Work Experiences

Lauren Lindstrom, Bonnie Doren, and K. Brigid Flannery

UNIVERSITY OF OREGON

Michael R. Benz

TEXAS A & M UNIVERSITY

Introduction

According to the Individuals with Disabilities Education Improvement Act of 2004, the fundamental purpose of a free appropriate public education is to prepare youth with disabilities for "further education, employment, and independent living" (IDEA, 2004 Sec 601 (d) (1) (A)). Students with disabilities need comprehensive transition planning, structured instruction, individual supports, and community-based experiences to adequately prepare them to transition into adult roles in the community. Structured work experience is a critical component of these transition best practices and an effective tool for preparing youth for future employment options (Benz, Lindstrom, & Yovanoff, 2000; National Alliance for Secondary Education and Transition (NASET), 2005; Test et al., 2009).

The purpose of this chapter is to summarize current research and describe effective practices for implementing structured work experience opportunities. Throughout the chapter, the umbrella term "structured work experience" is used to refer to a variety of work-based activities that connect students to work, build employability skills, and increase career options and opportunities. The chapter is organized into three major sections. The first section provides a summary of the current work experience literature, including a number of challenges and special considerations. Next, a framework for developing work experience options is outlined. The chapter concludes with detailed descriptions of effective structured work experience options.

What Do We Know About Work Experience?

> We must not lose sight of the purpose for our efforts—to provide all youth, including youth with disabilities and other special needs, a more meaningful education and better opportunities for economic self sufficiency and responsible productive adulthood.
>
> (Benz & Kochhar, 1996)

Importance of Work in High School and Early Transition Years

Obtaining and maintaining meaningful employment is an important goal for most adults in our society. However, the literature suggests that the benefits accrued from having a stable, fulfilling job have gone largely unrealized by people with disabilities (National Organization on Disability (NOD), 2004; U.S. Bureau of Labor Statistics, 2009). Overall employment rates for people with disabilities continue to lag behind those without disabilities. The 2004 NOD/*Harris Survey of Americans with Disabilities* reported that 35% of people with disabilities were employed full or part-time compared with 78% of people without a disability (NOD, 2004).

Historically, young adults with disabilities have not achieved the same level of post-school employment success as their peers without disabilities (Benz, Yovanoff, & Doren, 1997; Benz et al., 2000; Johnson, Stodden, Emanuel, Luecking, & Mack, 2002). For the past two decades, there has been a national effort to create effective transition services and improve post-school employment outcomes of youth with disabilities. These efforts have resulted in modest gains in the overall employment rates for youth with disabilities (Newman, Wagner, Cameto, & Knokey 2009). Despite these gains, the National Longitudinal Transition Study-2 (NLTS-2) reported lower employment rates and hourly wages and less job stability for youth with disabilities who have been out of school for up to four years compared with youth in the general population. In addition, the NLTS-2 study noted several significant differences in employment outcomes based on type of disability, gender, level of household income, and race/ethnicity.

One of the most consistent predictors of post-school employment reported over the past two decades for students with disabilities is participation in work experience during high school. Numerous studies have found that students with disabilities who held paid jobs during their high school career were significantly more likely to be engaged in post-school employment than students who did not hold jobs (Benz et al., 1997; Benz et al., 2000; Hasazi, Johnson, Hasazi, Gordon, & Hull, 1989; Luecking & Wittenburg, 2009; Rabren, Dunn, & Chambers, 2002). In addition, research suggests that the impact of participation in work experience during high school holds true for both males and females (Doren & Benz, 1998) and for both youth with and without disabilities (Benz et al., 1997), highlighting the importance of work experience for all youth. Beyond high school, the early transition years can be particularly challenging for young adults with disabilities. Young adults with disabilities face unique challenges as they move from the structured environment of high school to post-school environments where the type and level of support are quite different. Programs that offer continued services beyond secondary schooling, including work experiences, have resulted in positive post-school employment outcomes (Benz et al., 2000; Izzo, Cartledge, Miller, Growicki, & Rutkowski, 2000). In addition, the inclusion of structured work experiences in postsecondary occupational training programs has emerged as an important element in post-school employment success (Flannery, Yovanoff, Benz, & McGrath-Kato, 2008).

Structured work experiences provide students with disabilities opportunities to explore a variety of career options, develop and practice specific vocational skills and work behaviors, and integrate academic knowledge in applied settings (Doren, Lindstrom, Zane, & Johnson, 2007; Lindstrom & Benz, 2002). Early career exploration activities that include job shadows, job sampling, or volunteer work can increase career expectations and career options considered by youth. This is especially important for young women, youth from low-income families, and minority youth with disabilities who tend to have lower career expectations and a restricted range of potential career options (Blustein, et al., 2002; Fabian, 2007; Lindstrom, Benz, & Doren, 2004). Longer-term, occupationally specific work experiences through internships, apprenticeships, or postsecondary training can provide young adults with specific skills to enter higher skill and higher wage occupations. Work experiences also provide a real-world context to develop a whole host of knowledge and skills that facilitate post-school living, learning, and working including self-management and social skills (Doren et al., 2007; Lindstrom & Benz, 2002; Trainor et al., 2007; Scholl & Mooney, 2003).

Challenges and Special Considerations

A number of critical issues face education personnel who are striving to develop effective, efficient, and sustainable work experience opportunities for youth with disabilities. Work-based learning options are influenced by and operate within the larger context of current educational policies, changing school system requirements, and other cultural and systemic barriers (Benz, Lindstrom, et al., 2004; NASET, 2005; Trainor, Lindstrom, et al., 2008). These complex challenges and contextual factors need to be taken into consideration in order to build successful work programs. Three of the most salient issues to consider include: (a) school reform and accountability standards, (b) changing workplace demands, and (c) issues of equity and access.

School Reform and Accountability

The 2002 No Child Left Behind Act placed new emphasis on increasing academic standards and performance expectations for all youth. Under the provisions of this legislation, schools are expected to offer a challenging curriculum and promote high expectations. School districts must also demonstrate that all students, including students with disabilities, English-language learners, youth from low-income families, and other at-risk youth are making adequate yearly progress as measured by standardized assessments. All students are required to participate in accountability systems designed to insure student achievement over time (NASET, 2005).

In addition, the Individuals with Disabilities Education Act of 2004, requires states to provide students with disabilities access to the general education curriculum including a definition of how such access is provided, participation in standardized assessments, and public reporting of assessment results (Guy, Sitlington, Larsen, & Frank, 2009; NASET, 2005). These new special education requirements have resulted in increasing time in general education classrooms for high school students with disabilities and a greater emphasis on remedial instruction to improve academic performance.

Secondary school reform efforts designed to promote rigor and increase academic performance have oftentimes produced unintended and potentially negative consequences for youth with disabilities preparing for adult roles in the community (Benz, Lindstrom, & Yovanoff, 2000; Furney, Hasazi, Clark-Keefe, & Harnett, 2003). As school personnel face increasing pressure to meet high-stakes testing requirements, there has been a corresponding reduction in the amount of time available to provide functional skills instruction. In addition, many schools have reduced the number of career and technical courses, school-sponsored work experiences, and elective options available (Baer et al., 2003; Guy et al., 2009).

Workplace Demands

In addition to meeting accountability standards within the school system, special education and transition personnel need to be aware of the changing demands of the current workplace. Rapid technological advances and increasingly global competition have created increasingly high-performance work organizations (Grubb, 2001). Workers at all levels now need to be able to understand data, communicate clearly, learn rapidly, use technology, and work well in teams. Employers desire high school graduates who possess solid academic, social, and occupational skills (Benz et al., 1997; National Collaborative on Workforce and Disability, 2009). However, the specific work-based training needed to prepare youth to enter high-skill high-wage jobs is not always available within the confines of existing high school programs (Baer et al., 2003).

Equity and Access

A final challenge that must be addressed in developing work experience options is the critical need to provide equal access and insure positive outcomes for youth from historically marginalized and vulnerable groups (Gil-Kashiwabara, Hogansen, Geenen, Powers, & Powers, 2007). Students with disabilities from culturally diverse backgrounds, young women, and youth from low-income families all face significant barriers to post-school employment and have not benefited equally from participation in school and work-based transition programs (Lindstrom et al., 2004; Trainor et al., 2008).

A number of recent studies have documented that youth from culturally diverse groups have differing educational experiences and poorer post-school outcomes than their dominant culture peers (Fabian, 2007; Newman, Wagner, Cameto, & Knokey, 2009). For example, African-American youth are more likely to be identified with an emotional or cognitive disability and are less likely than European-American youth to spend the greatest part of their school day in general education settings (U.S. Department of Education, 2004). Youth with disabilities from culturally diverse backgrounds also do not achieve equitable post-school employment outcomes. The National Longitudinal Transition Study (NLTS-2) documented that 74% of European-American youth with disabilities had been employed since high school compared with 65% of Latino youth and 62% of African Americans. Wages also differed across groups, with 90% of European-American youth earning above minimum wage compared with 77% of African-American and 69% of Latino youth (Wagner, Newman, Cameto, & Levine, 2005).

Youth with disabilities from lower-income households ($25,000 per year or less) also experience lower levels of engagement in postsecondary education and employment than those from higher-income families. Students from lower-income households are more likely than youth from higher-income households to participate in low-skill low-wage employment and earn *less* than $5.15 per hour (Wagner, Newman, Cameto, Levine, & Garza, 2006). Blustein's 2002 study describing the role of social class in school-to-work transition also found that family socioeconomic status (SES) was an especially strong predictor of later access to career opportunities and options. Youth from higher socioeconomic backgrounds often aspired to higher-status/prestige occupations, were more likely to value work as a source of personal satisfaction, and had greater access to external supports in the employment preparation process (Blustein et al., 2002).

Finally, previous research has documented a number of gender differences in work experience opportunities and employment outcomes (Hogansen, Powers, Geenen, Gil-Kashiwabara, & Powers, 2008; Lindstrom & Benz, 2002). Although young women with disabilities have made gains in overall employment rates, recent national longitudinal data show that young women who were out of school for up to two years earned significantly lower average wages, worked fewer hours per week, and were less likely to be employed in skill-based jobs than their male peers (Wagner et al., 2005). Young women with disabilities are also less likely than their male peers to be engaged in vocational training or work experience during their high school careers and those who do enroll in work-based learning options tend to participate in lower-wage, lower-skill, traditionally female-oriented programs such as child care (Doren & Benz, 1998). In addition, young women with disabilities are less likely than young men with disabilities to take a concentration or sequence of occupational coursework leading to higher-skill occupations (Lindstrom & Benz, 2002; Luecking & Fabian, 2002).

Developing a Framework for Work-Based Leaning

> It has become evident that the diverse and complex needs of youth cannot be met by any one school district, school, community service agency, or family regardless of their hard work or good intentions.
>
> (NASET, 2005)

Given the numerous and complex challenges described above, it is clear that school personnel must tread carefully, think creatively, and work collaboratively to develop effective work-based opportunities. Work-experience models should ideally be structured to fit within the current educational climate of higher standards and increasing rigor while at the same time preparing youth to excel in highly competitive workplaces. Employment and training needs for diverse youth, youth from low-income families, and young women need to be addressed to increase equity in service delivery and outcomes.

Meeting the multiple needs of individual youth, school systems, and employers calls for a systemic approach, taking into consideration existing school and community programs while striving to build partnerships within communities (Benz et al., 2004; Hamilton, M. & Hamilton, 1997; Luecking 2009). A three-stage approach will assist in developing a broad framework of work experience options for all youth with disabilities:

1 Taking stock of existing opportunities and resources;
2 Reaching out to the community;
3 Building an integrated system of options;
   Each of these three components is described briefly here.

Taking Stock

The first step is simply to develop a clear understanding of existing school programs and services. What are the current career, vocational, or technical preparation opportunities within your high school? Are there any existing courses that include career awareness or work-based learning options? Can students with disabilities get connected with any volunteer, service learning, or school-based businesses that might build work skills while providing academic credit? Who provides the supervision, training, and monitoring for these experiences? Gaining a clear understanding of the various requirements and opportunities within the school system provides a helpful foundation for addressing needs, coordinating services, and taking advantage of existing opportunities offered within the high school. At this stage, it is also important to consider various post-school work experience options such as occupational training through community colleges, private vocational schools, or publicly funded programs such as Job Corps. These post-school options can meet an important need for students who are enrolled in general education classes and not able to participate in extensive work experience during high school.

Reaching Out

Reaching out requires school personnel to gather additional information to understand potential employment and training resources and build connections beyond the high school. As noted previously in this chapter, the most effective way to develop work skills and increase post-school employment outcomes is to connect students with employment experiences in the community (Benz et al., 2000; Fabian, 2007). School staff need to identify and recruit local employers as partners and invest time in understanding the needs of businesses that may serve as training or placement sites for young people (Benz & Lindstrom, 1997; Carter et al., 2009). Postsecondary education programs, vocational or trade schools, or other short-term training programs can provide additional opportunities for youth to develop work skills leading to higher-wage occupations (Flannery, Lindstrom, & Toricellis, 2009). Finally, during this phase school personnel should make a commitment to reach out to underserved populations, such as culturally diverse youth and youth from low-income families, to insure they are being adequately served and benefiting equally from these efforts. Work experience options should ideally broaden the opportunities and options for vulnerable youth and prepare them for economic self-sufficiency (Lindstrom & Benz, 2002).

Building A System

For work-based learning to succeed, no single stand-alone approach is adequate. Instead schools must adopt a "systems change" approach that focuses on building collaborative comprehensive systems versus programs or individual services (Benz & Lindstrom, 1997; Northwest Regional Educational Laboratory, 1994). Such systems are ideally "integrated internally and connected externally," linking school and work-based preparation to higher education and the labor market (Hamilton, M. & Hamilton, 1997). A system-level approach to collaboration may include creating written agreements that structure the roles of participating agencies along with professional training to support collaborative activities (Benz et al., 2004). Identifying and funding designated individuals who can develop and support work experience options over time is another important element that is crucial to long-term success. Administrative support and shared funding for employment or transition specialist positions may be needed to build and maintain a comprehensive menu of options (Flannery et al., 2009; Benz et al., 2004).

Using these three stages as a framework, school personnel can move beyond the typical scenario of a single teacher in a single classroom placing a young person into an individual structured work experience. Those placements certainly offer short-term rewards. However, in the long term it is

Table 12.1 Case study: Sunnydale High School

Site case study: Sunnydale High School

Sunnydale is a rural community that was hit hard by the economic recession. The high school served about 800 students, many from low-income families. In addition, many of the high school students with disabilities had no means of transportation, no prior job experience, and were at risk of dropping out of high school. In the past, resources to provide individualized job training and support services were simply not available. The Special Education Director remembered, "And so we really floundered for a couple of years. We didn't know how to make transition happen. And we didn't feel we had the staffing to make it happen."

About ten years ago, one innovative school administrator and a long-time special education teacher decided to focus their efforts on developing a range of transition services to improve outcomes for Sunnydale High students. First, they examined high school and community programs to understand the existing resources that might be utilized. With support from education assistants, some students with disabilities were able to enroll in vocational courses such as welding and drafting at the high school. Others were connected to community college options for occupational training and continuing education programs. Sunnydale staff also understood the importance of reaching out to the community. They collaborated with the local office of Vocational Rehabilitation, and worked out an arrangement for the rehabilitation counselor to conduct intake appointments at the high school on a regular basis. In addition, staff made a concerted effort to connect with community employers, attending Chamber of Commerce meetings and developing individual relationships with a number of key employers.

To meet the needs of youth with no prior work experience, staff created a number of training opportunities within the school building. They developed partnerships with a variety of existing school services including the print shop, mail room, cafeteria, custodial, and laundry services. Students were placed into these worksites and then provided supervision, training, and ongoing monitoring to learn specific tasks as well as general work skills and behaviors. The following year, transition staff decided to further expand the in-school training options by developing a school-based business. A portable coffee cart was purchased and placed at the high school. Students who were interested in working at the cart were enrolled in a formal curriculum called "Espresso Adventure" that included money handling, customer service, and food preparation skills. Upon completion of the training, students worked a number of shifts each week at the coffee cart with supervision from school personnel. Several students were promoted to the role of coffee cart managers, allowing them further opportunities for leadership and vocational skill development.

In addition to the in-school training options, staff worked to help students obtain and maintain community-based employment opportunities. The VR counselor assigned to work with this school commented, "The real goal, of course, is to get them into on-the-job training where they are earning some wages and learning job skills." Paid community employment offered opportunities for increasing job skills and building valuable work experiences. A final goal was to assist each student to enter either paid employment or post secondary training at the time of high school completion. Over 75% of students with disabilities from Sunnydale High were successfully engaged in the community after high school graduation, either working in community jobs or continuing their training through post secondary training programs.

---

more beneficial to create a range of work experience options designed to build career skills and increase opportunities for all youth with disabilities. The case study in Table 12.1 illustrates this type of integrated approach to creating comprehensive work-based learning options.

Structured Work Experience Options

> Workplaces are no more magical than schools: simply placing young people
> in them does not guarantee that they will learn.
>
> (Hamilton, M. & Hamilton, 1997)

Work-based learning is an effective tool for preparing youth for future employment opportunities (Benz, Lindstrom, & Yovanoff, 2000; National Collaborative on Workforce and Disability, 2009; Rabren et al., 2002). To reap these benefits, young people with disabilities need to participate in a range of structured work-experience options that include less intensive experiences (e.g., job shadowing), as well as more extensive longer-term training opportunities (e.g., internships, apprenticeships, postsecondary training). Early exploratory experiences can increase career awareness and help open up a range of possible options for all youth including those from marginalized groups (Lindstrom et al., 2004). More extensive training offers an ideal venue to prepare youth for high-wage high-skill occupations. Work experiences may unfold quite differently for those students with disabilities who are earning a regular diploma than for students participating in a modified diploma or life skills curriculum. Some youth may engage in multiple internships or paid jobs while in high school, while others who are accessing the general education curriculum will participate in structured work-experiences only as part of a postsecondary or vocational training program after high school graduation.

In this section, we provide information about a variety of work-experience opportunities. The umbrella term "structured work experience" is used here to refer to a variety of work-based activities that connect students to work, build employability skills, and increase career awareness. Table 12.2 provides definitions and benefits for nine different structured work-experience options. Although they vary in intensity, scope, and duration, all of these experiences are designed to be *intentional* and *experiential* (Hamilton, S. & Hamilton, 1997). Merely placing students into a work site does not constitute a structured work experience—school staff must consider the purpose of the placement, determine the skills or learning goals to be demonstrated, and provide clear support to address these goals. The work–experience options in Table 12.2 are presented in a continuum from less to more extensive; however, it is important to understand that students do not necessarily need to complete these activities in any prescribed order. This list of options is not a checklist to complete but instead a menu of possible choices. School staff need to provide the

Table 12.2 Structured work experience options

Type	Definition	Purpose & benefits
Job shadowing	Opportunity to observe or "shadow" a professional in a specific occupation	• Increase career awareness • Observe work environments and requirements
Service-learning	Hands-on volunteer service projects in community settings. Connected to academic content and skills	• Link academic skills to community settings • Increase personal and social development • Build citizenship and community engagement
School-based enterprise	Student-run businesses operated within a school setting	• Learn and practice hands-on work and business skills • Create opportunities for student leadership • Provide goods or services to the school or community
Internship	Paid or unpaid placements in an established business setting for a predetermined time. Supervision and training provided by school employee	• Develop and refine work habits and behaviors • Offer opportunity for structured feedback and supervision on the job
Paid employment	Standard job with public or private employer that may occur after school, on weekends or in the summer	• Learn and practice general employability skills and work habits • Provide wages
Apprenticeship	Individualized pairing with experienced worker designed to teach occupational skills related to a specific trade	• Provide in-depth training in specific occupational skills (e.g., welding, electrician, etc.) • Meet competencies determined by industry • Lead to a certificate
Community college work programs	Postsecondary programs including cooperative work experience and short-term occupational skills training	• Offer hands-on training in employment setting • Create access to higher wage employment options
Trade school	School that offers training to prepare for employment in a specific occupations (e.g., beauty school)	• Lead to employment in specific career • Provide extensive skill training
Job corps	Federally funded no cost job training program for youth 16–24 years of age	• Provide employability and independent living skills training • Offer training in specific career area

Sources: Guy et al., 2009; Hamilton, S. & Hamilton, 1997; Luecking, 2009; National School-to-Work Office, 1997

variety and intensity of work experience options that will meet the individualized transition needs of each student (Luecking, 2009).

Job Shadowing

Job shadowing is a commonly used introductory work-based learning activity. A job shadow provides an opportunity for an individual student to spend an extended period of time (often a full work day or several days) with someone who is actually performing that job (Luecking, 2009). For example, a student with a disability who is interested in a medical career may spend a day at a hospital shadowing a certified nursing assistant or lab technician. Student activities are limited to observation as well as opportunities to interact and ask questions of an employer/host. Job shadowing helps introduce students to the expectations of various careers by allowing them to observe the daily routines, activities, and requirements of an occupation (Luecking, 2009; National School-to-Work Office, 1997).

Although a job shadow is usually a short-term, onetime event, it does require both planning and commitment on the part of students, school staff, and employers. Students are typically required to: (a) select an appropriate employer and set up the job shadow date, time, and location; (b) arrange transportation to the job shadow; (c) ask relevant and thoughtful questions; and (d) complete an evaluation, reflection, or other appropriate assignments related to the experience. The employer's responsibilities include: (a) explaining the job requirements in detail; (b) providing a tour and/or opportunity to observe in their place of business; (c) discussing the education and training needed to perform the job; and (d) answering student questions. School staff provide support by helping to facilitate the initial connections to the employer, creating the needed evaluation forms, and monitoring the overall experience.

One final important aspect of any job shadow experience is the reflection and evaluation component. Once students have completed a job shadow, they should have an opportunity to debrief and describe what they learned through the experience. Specific questions (e.g.: What was a typical day like for the individual in this career? Were there any job requirements or experiences that surprised them?) can be used to begin this reflection process. While job shadowing can potentially provide insights into possible career options after high school, these experiences in the field can also help students gain insights about jobs they may *not* want to pursue, thus clarifying their career goals and interests (Lindstrom & Benz, 2002). Job shadowing is an especially appropriate work-experience option for students with limited access to job settings or those who may have only considered a restricted range of career options.

Service-Learning

Service-learning is another work-experience option that can offer multiple benefits for youth with disabilities. Defined as "a teaching and learning strategy that integrates meaningful community service with instruction and reflection to enrich the learning experience, teach civic responsibility, and strengthen communities" (National Commission on Service Learning (NCSL), 2002), service-learning provides an opportunity for youth to participate in the community while gaining valuable teamwork and leadership skills. Typically, groups of students participate in service-learning projects which are tied to academic coursework or competencies. Some high schools require service-learning hours as a condition of graduation, while others may offer service-learning as one component of existing academic or career-related classes (Luecking, 2009; NCSL, 2002).

Service-learning has a number of unique characteristics (Hamilton, S. & Hamilton, 1997). First, service-learning projects are linked to the school curriculum and driven by specifically defined learning goals. For example, students in a science class may analyze water quality in a wetlands project, while language arts students use writing and publishing skills to create flyers for a community event. Second, service-learning projects should be designed to meet a real need in the community. Third, service-learning projects should offer avenues for youth decision making and leadership. School staff can facilitate opportunities for students to be involved in designing, implementing, and evaluating all aspects of the projects. Finally, service-learning also includes reflection and analysis, which may take place through classroom discussions or more formal written assignments that help students link academics with applied work (NCSL, 2002; O'Connor, 2009).

Specific service-learning projects can vary greatly based on community needs and resources and may include activities ranging from volunteering at a homeless shelter to raising awareness of a critical community issue. Teachers are usually responsible for exploring possible options within their local neighborhood and working with students to establish the specific location and scope of the project. Many service-learning projects fall into the following four broad categories:

1   **Environmental projects**: such as participating in wetlands or stream clean-up tasks, designing recycling projects, or building community gardens;
2   **Cultural or regional history projects**: such as collecting and documenting information about members of a tribe or other community group, participating in cultural fairs or exhibitions, or creating murals or other permanent artwork;
3   **Addressing social problems**: such as volunteering in a soup kitchen, collecting food or clothing for low-income families, or tutoring younger children;
4   **Advocacy and civic engagement**: such as researching information on child maltreatment, preparing summary information for political or advocacy groups, or participating in voter registration. (O'Conner, 2009)

Utilizing service-learning available through high school coursework can help students meet required graduation competencies while at the same time learning basic work skills. Students engaged in service-learning projects also gain specific information about possible occupations, meet and interact with working professionals, and obtain information related to career goals (NCSL, 2002).

School-Based Enterprises

School-based enterprises are student-operated businesses that produce goods or services as part of an ongoing school program (National School-to-Work Office, 1997). For example, students may operate a food services cart or work in a small manufacturing company based in a high school. These school-based business ventures can provide an ideal opportunity to teach work skills to students with disabilities in a supervised setting prior to entering a more intensive internship or paid job in a community setting (Lindstrom, Benz, & Johnson, 1997). In addition, some communities may not have the resources available for students to gain extensive work-based experiences in the private sector. School-based enterprises can be utilized to fill this void for hands-on training as well as provide a supplement to traditional classroom instruction (Kentucky Office of Career and Technical Education, 2009).

School-based enterprises offer a variety of experiences for students and a range of services to consumers. These enterprises also provide students with opportunities to develop a more in-depth understanding of specific occupations and the requirements of operating a business. As important, these school-based enterprises provide an opportunity for students to learn transferable skills for any job (e.g., attendance, social skills) even if the specific enterprise is unrelated to the student's post-school career goal. Ideally, students can be involved in all aspects of the business and will rotate among the various positions and tasks involved in the designated business venture (Hamilton, S. & Hamilton, 1997; Kentucky Office of Career and Technical Education, 2009). Although businesses can be created to fit any niche or need, many high schools have developed retail, service, or manufacturing enterprises. These enterprises can:

- Be created in urban or rural communities;
- Provide a training site that is easily accessible for students;
- Offer a range of goods or services that is needed in the community;
- Generate profits to help support student wages or other program needs;
- Teach valuable work and business skills (Benz & Lindstrom, 1997; Lindstrom et al., 1997).

School-based businesses require an initial and ongoing time commitment from school staff as well as fiscal resources for "start up" costs. Teachers or other school staff who plan to create a school-based enterprise need to engage in a series of steps including: (a) developing a business plan, (b) assigning or reassigning staff to manage business operations, (c) addressing liability, licensure, and accounting procedures within a school district, (d) recruiting and scheduling students to participate, (e) establishing learning goals related to skills that are needed to be learned, and (f) providing ongoing training and supervision to students (Lindstrom et al., 1997). Although these steps may be time-consuming, this upfront investment typically leads to multiple benefits for students to gain skills, confidence, and preparation for the workforce. School-based enterprises are a prime example of a longer-term work experience approach that requires resources but can also create systems change within a school building.

Internships

Internships are paid or unpaid placements in community employment settings. Sometimes referred to as "cooperative work experiences" or simply "work experiences," internships provide students with longer-term, structured job experiences in an established business setting (National School-to-Work Office, 1997). These internships are dependent on successful partnerships with community employers and can also be enhanced by collaboration with local agencies such as vocational rehabilitation or other federal job training programs. Structured internships also offer a mechanism for placing young women, youth from low-income families, and youth from diverse groups into on-the-job experiences that may lead to higher-wage employment over time (Fabian, 2007; Lindstrom et al., 2004).

Unlike service-learning or school-based enterprises, internships are individualized work experiences connected with specific learning goals. Students may be placed into any number of employment settings, based on career goals, strengths, and interests (Benz & Lindstrom, 1997). Depending on the nature of the job, students can complete internships ranging from several weeks to a full academic year. Supervision and monitoring are provided by school staff in cooperation with the employer and the cooperating business has no obligation to hire the student at the conclusion of the internship (Fabian, 2007; Luecking, 2009).

Internships focus on learning and practicing employment skills in applied settings. Prior to an internship, teachers or other school staff should develop a written training agreement that outlines the expectations for the internship, which can be used to monitor student performance on the job. Students in internships are responsible for: (a) working with school staff to locate an appropriate internship site; (b) meeting performance and attendance criteria set by the school and work site; (c) arranging transportation to and from work setting; (d) arriving and departing as scheduled; (e) displaying appropriate on-the-job social skills; (f) learning and asking questions as needed; and (g) completing evaluation documentation as required by the school. Employers at the internship site are asked to: (a) conduct a formal interview to determine if the student is a good match for the site; (b) identify a site supervisor; (c) provide initial on-the-job training and ongoing supervision; and (d) complete an evaluation of the internship experience (Benz & Lindstrom, 1997; Luecking, 2009).

There are several key characteristics of successful internship programs including:

- Students are carefully screened and evaluated before placement.
- Programs use a systematic planned approach to build interpersonal and employability skills necessary for success.
- Clear guidelines and procedures exist for the evaluation of student interns, remediation of work-related problems, and transfer or termination.
- Students are under the supervision of a certified, trained educator as required by state law and district policy.
- Employers are recognized and celebrated for their contributions (Benz & Lindstrom 1997; The Principal's Partnership, 2009).

Paid Employment

Paid employment in local community settings can provide another venue for youth with disabilities to gain work experience and build work skills. These paid jobs may occur after school or on the weekends and are not typically connected to school programs or academic goals (Luecking, 2009). Although they do not offer the same structure and support as internships or apprenticeships, typical "first jobs" such as fast food, child care, or other service industry jobs can still offer some important lessons including personal and social competence, reliability, responsiveness to supervision, customer relations, and other basic work habits (Hamilton, S. & Hamilton, 1997; Lindstrom, Doren, Metheny, Johnson, & Zane, 2007).

Summer jobs provide another often underutilized work-experience option (Carter et al., 2009; Trainor, Carter, Owens, & Sweeden, 2008). Working in the summer has several advantages. Many communities have numerous short-term work opportunities that open up during the summer season. Unlike work experience during the school year, summer jobs do not compete with academic coursework requirements or extracurricular commitments and students may have more flexibility and availability to commit to these activities (Carter, Sweeden, & Trainor, 2009). For many students with disabilities, summer work can provide an important training ground for specific occupational and social skills while engaging in productive activities.

Apprenticeships

Apprenticeships are one of the most elaborate and intensive types of structured work experiences (Hamilton, S. & Hamilton, 1997; Luecking, 2009). An apprenticeship pairs a novice worker with a highly skilled employee for the purpose of learning a specific trade such as carpentry, electrical contracting, or plumbing. Although apprentices are paid for their work, the focus is on skill-building and attaining specific trade competencies. All apprenticeship programs must meet federally approved standards and be registered with the Bureau of Apprenticeship and Training, U.S. Department of Labor, or a local state apprenticeship agency or council (Yates, 1996).

Minimum requirements vary by industry area but most apprenticeship programs require applicants to be at least 18 years of age, and have a high school diploma or GED certificate. Some occupations may also require completion of specific subjects such as algebra, blueprint reading, or related shop work. The apprenticeship can last for two to five years depending on the requirements of the chosen industry. Apprentices attend related classroom training along with on-the-job training experience. As with all aspects of an apprenticeship, the training requirements vary according to the standards of the industry. Typically programs require approximately 144 hours of school per year (e.g., one or two evenings per week during the academic school year). The credits earned in an apprenticeship can often be applied towards an associate degree at a community college. Although apprenticeships are not commonly available to high school students, these experiences can offer skill development and a clear path to higher wage post-school employment options (Luecking, 2009; Hurd, 2004).

Community College Programs

Community colleges can provide multiple options for skill building that involve hands-on learning and intensive structured work experiences. Because of their mission to serve the local community, open enrollment policies, low cost, and flexible scheduling, community colleges offer an under-utilized option for students with disabilities interested in pursuing further training (Flannery et al., 2008). Students in community colleges may explore a variety of occupations while being exposed to work procedures and equipment that would not be available in a classroom. Cooperative work experience and short-term occupational training are two examples of work-experience programs that are open to any students who choose to enroll in a community college.

Cooperative Work Experience

Cooperative Work Experience Programs (CWE), located on community college campuses, were developed to build a bridge from college to career by providing on-the-job training opportunities and additional resources for career success. These programs integrate student academic and career interests with productive work experience. The program faculty, CWE program instructors, and training-site supervisors work together with the student to develop an experience that will enhance the student's skills and expose the student to authentic work conditions. Typically, students are able to earn credit while working full- or part-time in jobs related to their college program.

Students in Cooperative Work Experience gain hands-on learning and an understanding of employer expectations. Benefits to students include:

- Exploring jobs and careers related to their area of college studies;
- Improving professional confidence and job skills;
- Gaining experience to put on their resume;
- Earning academic credit toward graduation;
- Earning wages to help pay college expenses;
- Making valuable employer contacts and networking in a field of interest;
- Increasing chances for a full-time job after graduation.

Short-Term Training Certificate Programs

Short-term skills training programs are available in most community colleges. These programs are designed to provide individuals with the specific competencies and technical skills necessary for high-skill, high-wage employment, as well as basic academic competencies and transferable or "soft skills" such as problem-solving, communications, and teamwork (Grubb, 1996; Grubb, 2001). These competency-based training programs result in students learning practical occupational skills at their own pace. Students who learn best when a major portion of the information is provided "hands-on" at a training site benefit from this kind of skill training option. In many skills training programs, the student is placed on a training site in their career area for up to 40 hours per week. An individualized curriculum based on skills needed for the job is developed by the college staff and the training-site supervisor and monitored by the college staff (Flannery et al., 2009; Flannery et al., 2008).

Trade Schools

A vocational or trade school is an educational setting that focuses on skills needed to perform a specific occupation. Admissions requirements vary, but the majority of vocational schools require students to have completed either a high school diploma or General Educational Development test (GED). Trade schools can prepare students for positions such as beautician, truck driver, medical technician, automotive repair, or heavy equipment operator. After graduating from a trade school, an individual should be able to immediately enter the job market and receive a high rate of compensation. Most trade schools require a six-month to two-year time commitment. Students leave the trade school certified and eligible to take any state administered tests needed for the occupation. Many trade schools receive assistance from the government so that they can offer housing, child care, nutrition education, and other options to disadvantaged students, usually for free or at a minimal price (http://www.wisegeek.com/what-is-a-trade-school.htm).

Job Corps

Job Corps is a no-cost education and vocational training program funded by Congress and administered by the U.S. Department of Labor. The purpose of Job Corps is to provide employability and independent living skills to at-risk youth and to place them in meaningful jobs or further education. Job Corps is available to individuals 16 through 24 years of age. Besides career training, the Job Corps offers GED programs, health and dental care, and a basic living allowance. There are over 100 Job Corps centers nationally that provide training in specific career areas, including automotive and machine repair, construction, finance and business services, health care, hospitality, information technology, manufacturing, and renewable resources. Job Corps provides both classroom and practical learning experiences that integrate a set of core competencies in academic, vocational, employability skills, and social competence (U.S Department of Labor, 2009).

Final Thoughts

Structured work experiences offer an important avenue for hands-on learning and exposure to the realities of work. These benefits are well documented in the transition literature, and have been reinforced by practitioners in the field (Lindstrom et al., 2007). As illustrated by the case studies in Table 12.3, work experiences have multiple benefits as youth prepare to transition to the world of work.

In order to successfully prepare for the transition from high school to adult roles in the community, students with disabilities need multiple opportunities over time to explore career options and gain work skills. Education personnel should work closely with local employers and

Table 12.3 Case studies

MICHELLE

Michelle grew up in a low-income family in a small rural community. Diagnosed with a learning disability in the areas of reading, writing, and math, she participated in the general curriculum and received supplemental special education services throughout her school years.

Starting in her junior year of high school, Michelle began working with a Transition Specialist who provided career exploration, transition planning, and job search assistance. Michelle also completed two work experiences in high school. Working as a dishwasher in a local café helped her gain basic work skills and also motivated her to look for work outside of the food service industry. Michelle's second work experience was a federally subsidized summer internship in a fish hatchery, which sparked an interest in non-traditional employment. After high school graduation, her Transition Specialist arranged for a number of job shadows in high-wage, non-traditional occupations. Three months after high school graduation, Michelle was hired as a production worker in a manufacturing company. She earns approximately $14.50 per hour, has an excellent benefits package, and looks forward to taking advantage of opportunities for advancement with her current employer.

JACK

Jack had a fairly unstable childhood living in a rundown trailer park with his mother and unemployed stepfather. Throughout his school years, Jack received special education services due to a learning disability. By the time he reached adolescence, Jack's reading, math, and writing skills were several years behind those of his peers, and he was acting out and causing behavior problems in school.

In high school, Jack participated in woodshop, automotive, and welding classes. He also held a variety of paid jobs primarily to supplement the family income. Paid employment helped Jack gain work skills and confidence, as well as develop relationships with stable adult mentors. He also gained a growing interest in working in the automotive field. After high school graduation Jack enrolled in a one-year, short-term occupational training program in auto body repair, in cooperation with a large automotive dealership and the local community college. Community college faculty worked with Jack's employer to develop a skills-training curriculum, and his Vocational Rehabilitation counselor subsidized his wages throughout the first year and purchased tools that he needed for work.

Jack has been working in a major automotive dealership as an auto body technician for several years now. He makes over $17.00 per hour, receives benefits, and occasionally fills in for the manager. He feels confident about his skills and is proud of his successful employment outcome.

other key partners to explore, design, and coordinate a variety of structured work experience opportunities. The strategies and examples presented in this chapter will help prepare students for an array of meaningful future employment opportunities.

References

Baer, R., Flexer, R., Beck, S., Amstutz, N., Hoffman, L., & Brothers, J. (2003). A collaborative follow-up study on transition service utilization and post school outcomes. *Career Development for Exceptional Individuals, 26*(1), 7–25.

Benz, M., & Kochhar, C. (1996). School to work opportunities for all students: A position statement of the Division on Career Development and Transition. *Career Development for Exceptional Individuals, 19*(1), 31–48.

Benz, M., & Lindstrom L. (1997). *Building school-to-work programs: Strategies for youth with special needs.* Austin, TX: PRO-ED.

Benz, M., Lindstrom, L., Unruh, D., & Waintrup, M. (2004). Sustaining secondary and transition programs. *Remedial and Special Education, 25*(1), 39–50.

Benz, M., Lindstrom, L., & Yovanoff, P. (2000). Improving graduation and employment outcomes of students with disabilities: Predictive factors and student perspectives. *Exceptional Children, 66*(4), 509–529.

Benz, M., Yovanoff, P., & Doren, B. (1997). School to work components that predict success for students with and without disabilities. *Exceptional Children, 63,* 151–163.

Blustein, D. L., Chaves, A. P., Diemer, M. A., Gallagher, L. A., Marshall, K. G., Sirin, S. et al. (2002). Voices of the forgotten half: The role of social class in the school-to-work transition. *Journal of Counseling Psychology, 49,* 311–323.

Carter, E. W., Owens, L., Sweeden, B., Trainor, A., Thompson, C., Ditchman, N. (2009). Conversations that matter: Engaging communities to expand employment. *Teaching Exceptional Children, 41*(6), 38–46.

Carter, E. W., Sweeden, B., & Trainor, A. (2009). The other three months: Connecting transition age youth with disabilities to meaningful summer experiences. *Teaching Exceptional Children, 41*(6), 18–25.

Doren, B., & Benz, M. (1998). Employment inequality revisited: Predictors of better employment outcomes for young women with disabilities in transition. *The Journal of Special Education, 31,* 425–442.

Doren, B., Lindstrom, L., Zane, C., & Johnson, P. (2007). Post-school employment outcomes: The role of program and alterable personal factors. *Career Development for Exceptional Individuals, 30*(3), 171–183.

Fabian, E. S. (2007). Urban youth with disabilities: Factors affecting transition employment. *Rehabilitation Counseling Bulletin, 50,* 130–138.

Flannery, B., Lindstrom, L., & Toricellis, M. (2009). High school and community college partnerships with vocational rehabilitation. In D. K. Unruh & H. B. Clark (Eds.) *Transition of young people with emotional or behavioral difficulties: An evidence based handbook.* Baltimore, MD: Brookes Publishing.

Flannery, K. B., Yovanoff, P., Benz, M. R., & McGrath-Kato, M. (2008). Improving employment outcomes of individuals with disabilities through short-term training. *Career Development for Exceptional Individuals, 31*(1), 56–64.

Furney, K., Hasazi, S., Clark-Keefe, K. & Harnett, J. (2003). A longitudinal study of shifting policy landscapes in general and special education reform. *Exceptional Children, 70*(1), 81–94.

Gil-Kashiwabara, E., Hogansen, J., Geenen, S., Powers, K., & Powers, L. (2007). Improving transition outcomes for marginalized youth. *Career Development for Exceptional Individuals, 30*(2), 80–91.

Grubb, W. N. (1996). *Working in the middle.* San Francisco, CA: Jossey-Bass Publishers.

Grubb, W. N. (2001). From isolation to integration: Postsecondary vocational education and emerging systems of workforce development. *New Directions for Community Colleges, 2001*(115), 27–37.

Guy, B., Sitlington, P., Larsen, M., & Frank, A. (2009). What are high schools offering in preparation for employment? *Career Development for Exceptional Individuals, 32*(1), 30–41.

Hamilton, M. A., & Hamilton, S. F. (1997). When is work a learning experience? *Phi Delta Kappan,* 682–689.

Hamilton, S. F., & Hamilton, M. A. (1997). When is learning work based? *Phi Delta Kappan,* 677–681.

Hasazi, S. B., Johnson, R. E., Hasazi, J. E., Gordon, L. R., & Hull, M. (1989). Employment of youth with and without handicaps following high school: Outcomes and correlates. *The Journal of Special Education, 23,* 243–255.

Hogansen, J., Powers, K., Geenen, S., Gil-Kashiwabara E., & Powers, L. (2008). Transition goals and experiences of females with disabilities: Youth, parents and professionals. *Exceptional Children, 74*(2), 215–234.

Hurd, B. (2004). Manufacturing and production technician youth apprenticeships. In R. Luecking (Ed.). *In their own words: Employer perspectives on youth with disabilities in the workplace.* Minneapolis, MN: University of Minnesota, Institute on Community Integration. National Center on Secondary Education and Transition.

Individuals with Disabilities Education Improvement Act of 2004 (IDEA), 20 U.S.C. 1400 et seq. (re-authorization of the Individuals with Disabilities Education Act of 1990).

Izzo, M.V., Cartledge, G., Miller, L., Growicki, B., & Rutkowski, S. (2000). Increasing employment earnings: Extended transition services that make a difference. *Career Development for Exceptional Individuals, 16,* 107–121.

Johnson, D., Stodden, R., Emanuel, E., Luecking, R., & Mack, M. (2002). Current challenges facing secondary education and transition services: What research tells us. *Exceptional Children, 68*(4), 519–531.

Kentucky Office of Career and Technical Education (2009). *School based enterprises.* Retrieved September 8, 2009 from kytech.ky.gov/pawblschoolenter.doc

Lindstrom, L., & Benz, M. (2002). Phases of career development: Case studies of young women with disabilities entering the workforce. *Exceptional Children, 69*(1), 67–83.

Lindstrom, L., Benz, M., & Doren, B. (2004). Expanding career options for young women with learning disabilities. *Career Development for Exceptional Individuals, 27*(1), 43–63.

Lindstrom, L., Benz, M., & Johnson, M. (1997). From school grounds to coffee grounds: An introduction to school-based businesses. *Teaching Exceptional Children, 29*(4), 18–22.

Lindstrom, L., Doren, B., Metheny, J., Johnson, P., & Zane, C. (2007). Transition to employment: Role of the family in career development. *Exceptional Children, 73* (3), 348–366.

Luecking, R. (2009). *The way to work: How to facilitate work experiences for youth in transition.* Baltimore, MD: Brookes Publishing.

Luecking, R., & Fabian, E. (2002). Paid internships and employment success for youth in transition. *Career Development for Exceptional Individuals, 23*(2), 205–221.

Luecking, R. G., & Wittenburg, D. (2009). Providing supports to youth with disabilities transition to adulthood: Case descriptions from the Youth Transition Demonstration. *Journal of Vocational Rehabilitation, 30,* 241–251.

National Alliance for Secondary Education and Transition (NASET) (2005). *National standards and quality indicators: Transition toolkit for systems improvement.* Minneapolis, MN: University of Minnesota, Institute on Community Integration.

National Collaborative on Workforce and Disability for Youth. (2009) *Work based learning jump start.* U.S. Department of Labor Office of Disability Policy. Washington, DC: Author.

National Commission on Service Learning (NCSL). (2002). *Learning in deed: The power of service-learning for American schools.* Retrieved from http://www.servicelearning.org/what-service-learning

National Organization on Disability (NOD). (2004). *2004 N.O.D./Harris survey of Americans with disabilities.* Retrieved October 2009 from http://www.nod.org/index.cfm?fuseraction=Feature. showFeature&FeatureID=1422

National School-to-Work Office. (1997). *School to work glossary of terms.* Washington, DC: Author.

Newman, L., Wagner, M., Cameto, R., & Knokey, A. M. (2009). *The post-high school outcomes of youth with disabilities up to 4 years after high school. A report of findings from the National Longitudinal Transition Study-2 (NLTS2)* (NCSER Report No. 2009–3017). Menlo Park, CA: SRI International. Available at www.nlts2.org/reports/2009_04/nlts2_report_2009_04_complete.pdf

Northwest Regional Education Laboratory (October 1994). *School to work: Meeting student needs, workplace demands.* Portland, OR: Author.

O'Connor, M. P. (2009). Service works! Promoting transition success for students with disabilities through participation in service learning. *Teaching Exceptional Children, 41*(6), 12–17.

The Principal's Partnership: A Program of Union Pacific Foundation. (2009). *Research brief: Internships for high school students.* http://www.principalspartnership.com

Rabren, K., Dunn, C., & Chambers, D. (2002). Predictors of post high school employment among young adults with disabilities. *Career Development for Exceptional Individuals, 25,* 25–40.

Scholl, L., & Mooney, M. (2003). Youth with disabilities in work-based learning programs: Factors that influence success. *The Journal of Vocational Special Needs Education, 26*(2), 4–16.

Test, D. W., Fowler, C. H., Richter, S. M., White, J., Mazzotti, et al., (2009). Evidence-based practices in secondary transition. *Career Development for Exceptional Individuals, 32*(2), 115–128.

Trainor, A., Carter, E. W., Owens, L., & Sweeden, B. (2008). Special educator's perceptions of summer employment and community participation opportunities. *Career Development for Exceptional Individuals, 31*(3), 144–153.

Trainor, A., Lindstrom, L., Simon-Burroughs, M., Sorrells, A., & Martin, J. (2008). From marginalized to maximized opportunities for diverse youth with disabilities: Position paper of the Division on Career Development and Transition. *Career Development for Exceptional Individuals, 31*(1), 56–64.

U.S. Department of Education (2004). Twenty-sixth annual report to Congress on the implementation of the IDEA. Washington, DC: Author.

U. S. Department of Labor. (2009). *Job Corps Informational Web Site.* http://www.jobcorps.gov/Home. aspx

Wagner, M., Newman, L., Cameto, R., and Levine, P. (2005). *Changes over time in the early postschool outcomes of youth with disabilities. A report of findings from the National Longitudinal Transition Study (NLTS) and the National Longitudinal Transition Study-2 (NLTS2).* Menlo Park, CA: SRI International.

Wagner, M., Newman, L., Cameto, R., Levine, P., and Garza, N. (2006). *An overview of findings from wave 2 of the National Longitudinal Transition Study-2 (NLTS2).* Menlo Park, CA: SRI International.

Yates, D. (1996). *Apprenticeship survival guide for the trades: Surviving your apprenticeship with style, grace and humor.* Portland, OR: Day Publications.

13

School Completion and Adolescent Transition Education

Larry Kortering

APPALACHIAN STATE UNIVERSITY

Youth with disabilities have a difficult time completing high school. The Office of Special Education's (OSEP) Annual Report (2006), using district reported data, shows that for the 2001–02 school year, 373,407 students age 14 to 21 exited school. For this group of exiting youth, 61% left as school completers (51% left with a standard or non-standard diploma and 10% exited with a certificate) while 21% left as official dropouts and 16% having "moved but not known to have continued" in school. This latter category, as suggested in an earlier OSEP Annual Report (U.S. Department of Education, 1987), likely represents a large proportion of school dropouts. The completion rate (diploma or certificate) varies by disability from a high of 78% for youth with hearing impairments to a low of 38% for youth with emotional/behavior disorders (EBD). These data, an illustration of impact, suggest that about 450 youth with disabilities exit as "official" dropouts each school day and others who leave under "unknown" circumstances would raise this total. On a positive note, the overall rate, using data from the annual reports, shows improvement of nearly 15% since the 1993–2004 school year. The rate, however, remains well below the national completion rate of 89%, including via the General Education Development (GED) program, among 18–24-year-olds (Cataldi, Laird, & KewalRamani, 2009).

The importance of school completion can perhaps be best understood by considering the impact it has on an individual and society. From an individual youth's perspective, school completion greatly affects opportunities to become a productive adult (Bullis, 2004). For instance, U.S. Census Bureau (2005b) data showed that the typical "employed" dropout earned around $19,200 per year as compared to the typical employed high school graduate ($28,600), one with some college ($32,000) and one with a bachelor's degree only ($51,600). Over the soon-to-be standard of 45 years of adult employment, the respective lifetime earning difference ranges from $423,000 (versus a high school graduate) to $1,908,000 (versus a college graduate). These statistics were for the "employed" dropout who participates in census data collection. There were many more dropouts who were not employed or who were imprisoned. A related statistic shows that an "employed" dropout requires 11 years to find "stable" employment (defined as two or more years at the same or a related job) as compared to 5 and 2 years for the average high school and college graduate, respectively (Yates, 2005). Moretti (2005) further noted: "It is well known that individuals with lower levels of education are over-represented in the criminal justice system" (p. 3). Specifically, his research demonstrated that a single year of additional schooling reduces the odds of imprisonment by 10% for Caucasian youth to a high of 37% for African American youth.

Another national data source showed that at any given time some 144,000 youth offenders are in "prison or related facilities and some 40% to 70% of these youth have been classified as having a disability" (Snyder & Sickmund, 2006). Similarly, estimates from 1997 showed that at least 40% of all inmates lacked any form of a high school credential (Harlow, 2003).

Aside from a general understanding of how school completion affects an individual, an overview of general social costs seems in order. Consider, for instance, that in 2001 annual operating expenses for an inmate were just over $22,600 (Stephan, 2003), well above the $12,525 annual cost of educating a student with a disability during the 1999–2000 school year (Chambers, Shkolnik, & Perez, 2003). In an earlier study, Cohen (1998) estimated that we would spend $1 million to $1.5 million for one youth who embarks on a life of criminal activity. Today this estimate would be much higher and does not consider the monetary impact crime has on victims. Health care presents another social cost, with the Alliance for Excellent Education (2006) calculating some $13,706 in lifetime Medicaid costs for the typical school dropout. If you consider the estimated 1.2 million dropouts each year, this cost becomes a staggering $17 billion (Muenning, 2006). Similarly, Muenning (2006) noted that dropouts represent 25% and 28% of all state Medicaid recipients and uninsured citizens, respectively, while college graduates account for 1% and 6%, respectively. Finally, the lost tax revenue associated with dropping out of school is even more compelling. Rouse (2007) reported national data that showed the average dropout in 2004 paid $1,302 in federal tax revenues, or less than half and a third of that paid by a high school graduate ($3,085) and college graduate ($5,954), respectively. Of course, this annual figure would need to be multiplied by the years of employment. One might also want to consider the corresponding impact on social security and state tax returns. In summary, Levin and Belfield (2007) perhaps put it best by documenting that the average high school graduate will generate $139,100 more in taxes across his or her lifetime than will a peer who never completes high school.

A final consideration relative to school completion is that existing special education services are often a final opportunity for youth with disabilities to secure education and training to prepare them for a productive adulthood. For instance, a promising statistic is that more than 45% of all dropouts earn a high school diploma or its equivalent (e.g., GED) within eight years of leaving school (U.S. Department of Education, 2004; Scott, McGuire, & Shaw, 2003). As for youth with disabilities, national data for GED completion are unavailable but, given the increasing rigor and limited proportion of accommodations provided (General Educational Testing Service, 2009), it seems reasonable to suggest they have a much lower success rate. Youth with disabilities who fail to complete school seldom get connected with adult services like Vocational Rehabilitation (Kortering & Braziel, 1999a) or enroll in postsecondary schooling (Brinckerhoff, McGuire, & Shaw, 2002). In a practical sense, leaving an individual educational program (IEP) without completing school puts a person at a serious disadvantage in an increasingly competitive and education-driven workforce (Friedman, 2005).

The need to establish interventions that improve school completion rates for youth with disabilities is compelling. It is in the best interest of every educator, parent, and taxpayer that we improve this rate. Accordingly, this chapter provides an overview of what we have learned about students who fail to complete school, discusses an emerging conceptualization of school completion that serves as a framework for guiding future interventions, and reviews nine guiding principles. The chapter concludes with a look at emerging issues affecting future efforts to improve school completion rates.

Research on Factors Affecting School Completion

The research on youth with disabilities who fail to complete high school is limited relative to the amount of research targeting peers from general education. Nonetheless, a structured review of existing research sets the foundation for a conceptual model to guide interventions that help more students to complete high school. Accordingly, the following section highlights research that is instructive in understanding the school completion challenge. This research is put into one of three areas: descriptive and comparative studies, student perceptions of school completion, and intervention research.

Descriptive and Comparative Studies

Descriptive and comparative studies help us to better understand key features of youth with disabilities and the environment that may affect school completion. Seidal and Vaughn (1991) found non-completers with specific learning disabilities (SLD) (*n* of 17) perceived a higher rate of social alienation in school relative to SLD peers who graduated (*n* = 37) from a large metropolitan school district. A study of urban students with high-incidence disabilities (i.e., SLD, EBD, mild intellectual disability or ID) showed that peers who had not graduated (*n* = 462) averaged three times as many school-initiated transfers and ten times as many releases as a dropout than did peers who were graduated (*n* = 291) (Blackorby, Edgar, & Kortering, 1991). This comparative study also showed non-completers were significantly more likely to be a minority (62% vs. 50%), identified as EBD (18% vs. 8%), and come from a non-intact family (33% vs. 20%). In contrast, the groups were comparable across measures of grade at referral, IQ (full-scale and verbal and performance subscales), gender, and reason for referral. Another comparison of urban youth with SLD included 100 graduates and 113 non-completers. This study found that a statistical procedure using just three pieces of data, including school-initiated transfers (50% higher for non-completers), number of previous releases from school (nearly 300% higher), and family intactness (20% less likely), classified individuals into one of two groups with 73% accuracy (Kortering, Haring, & Klockars, 1992). Other variables including family socio-economic status (SES), reading ability, and student ethnicity showed little if any differences between the groups. In a study of urban youth with EBD who had graduated (*n* = 22) or dropped out from high school (*n* = 81), the two groups were comparable on measures of information at referral (i.e., age, grade level, full-scale IQ, family intactness, reason, and source for referral), gender, and race (Kortering & Blackorby, 1992). Significant differences again emerged for school history, with non-completers having more than five times as many school-initiated transfers and previous releases from school as a dropout and 50% more changes in service placements (e.g., moved to a self-contained from a resource setting). Finally, Karpinski, Neubert, & Graham (1992) conducted a follow-up study involving interviews with rural youth with high-incidence conditions who had graduated (*n* = 52) or dropped from school (*n*=34). They found the groups to be comparable across grade at referral and enrollment in one or more vocational course, but dropouts had a much higher rate of absenteeism in their final year (34 and 24 days, respectively) and lower rate of working during high school (59% vs. 90%, respectively). The dropouts also reported leaving school due to discipline problems (32%), academic problems (24%), boredom (12%), and pregnancy (12%), a pattern sharply different from that reported by the school (attendance—38%, employment—15%, personal choice—15%, and no reason—32%).

More recent studies include Reschley and Christenson's (2006) documentation of a connection between measures of school engagement and school completion. This study used data from the National Educational Longitudinal Study, which included some 1,064, 338, and 96 parent-identified students with SLD or EBD. The resulting data showed that after controlling for socio-economic status, grade retention, and test scores, student engagement variables (including measures of attendance, behavior, skipping, preparation, extracurricular participation, and homework) were significant predictors for school completion. Another study involving interviews with 45 school completers and 31 non-completers, all identified as SLD, yielded surprising results. Specifically, no significant differences emerged when comparing the groups relative to intelligence and achievement measures and their self-reported levels of satisfaction with their reading skills, behavior in school, self-worth, and teachers (Bear, Kortering, & Braziel, 2006). Finally, Mellard and Patterson's (2008) study involved 311 adult education learners, 90 (29%) of whom reported having SLD. Using a structured interview, along with various assessments, they found the SLD group had significantly lower levels of reading ability, suggesting a need for concentrated instruction to prepare them for adult literacy programs.

Student Perspectives of School Completion

Research involving the perceptions of school completion from the perspective of youth with disabilities has been an emerging focus. The idea is that they, as a consumer of services, have insight into the school completion process. Lichenstein (1993) was among the first researchers to provide information to help us better understand the process of leaving high school without completing from the perspective of actual students. His qualitative study, spanning two years of contact with four youth identified as having an SLD, highlighted how these youth eventually decided that "further academic efforts would be anxiety provoking and humiliating" (p. 340). Noticeably absent in their educational program was their participation in activities or services that might have kept them in school, including formal vocational assessments (especially given the role employment played in their lives), the IEP process, and the involvement of adult services.

Kortering and Braziel (1999a) interviewed 44 dropouts from a rural and small-city setting who had been identified as having a high-incidence disability. Two-thirds of these former students reported that changes would have helped them to stay in school. The top changes were "teachers improving their attitude and relationships with students" and the "students themselves improving their own attitude and behavior." In a second study involving student interviews, Kortering and Braziel (1999b) sought to understand school completion from a group of 185 ninth and tenth graders with high-incidence disabilities. One hundred (54%) students felt a school-based change would help them to stay in school, with the dominant themes being more individual academic or personal assistance, changes in school rules relating to discipline, putting students in classes they saw as more relevant and enjoyable, and improved teacher attitudes toward students. Personal changes that would help them to stay in school came from 133 (72%) of the students, with half reporting a need to improve their work habits and grades and another 20% suggesting a need to change their own attitude. Another series of interviews with 33 students identified with EBD found 64% reporting a school-based change falling into one of three themes (i.e., putting a student in elective classes like Reserve Officers' Training Corps (ROTC) or vocational courses, offering more learning and behavior support, and changing disciplinary rules) and 48% suggesting changes they needed to make, with the dominant theme being their behavior in school. Dunn, Chambers, & Rabren (2004) used data from a post-school survey to compare 228 non-completers and 228 completers who had been identified as having a high-incidence disability. Their findings included the feature that those who did not get a diploma reported not being prepared for life after high school, not having access to a helpful person while in school, and not having had a helpful class. These features were the keys to distinguishing between the two groups.

Intervention-based Research

Intervention-based research on school completion is limited to a pair of literature reviews and investigations of the Check & Connect Model. Cobb, Sample, Alwell, Alwell, & Johns (2006) used a systematic review of scientifically based studies that led them to identify cognitive behavioral interventions as a promising intervention for reducing problem behavior (e.g., aggressive behavior, off-task behavior) associated with school completion. Their study, examining 25 years of research, identified 16 examples of evidence supporting the use of these interventions with half taking place in traditional public-school settings. All of the interventions involved some aspect of cognitive behavioral training including a formal curriculum often adapted to meet the unique needs of the setting. Test and his colleagues (2009) used Kohler's Taxonomy (Kohler, 1996) to categorize their review of the research involving evidence-based practices that show promise for enhancing school-completion rates. Their review yielded 11 articles, including two experimental studies involving the Check & Connect Model (Sinclair, Christenson, Evelo, & Hurley, 1998; Sinclair, Christenson, & Thurlow, 2005), offering recommendations falling into one or more of the following categories: student-focused planning (e.g., student involvement in their IEP), student development (e.g., life skills instruction, helping students find jobs during high school), interagency collaboration (e.g., collaborating with potential employers, developing interagency agreements), family involvement (e.g., supporting families with referrals to community agencies), and program structures (e.g., vocational instruction and community-based programming).

The Check & Connect Model, as implemented by Sinclair and her colleagues, evaluates one approach to school completion with students having disabilities. Their first study (Sinclair et al., 1998) examined the impact of a sustained school-engagement procedure (later referred to as Check & Connect) on 94 seventh and eighth graders identified as EBD who received dropout-prevention interventions in an urban district. Upon entering high school, the initial group was evenly split into a control group and treatment group. The treatment group received ongoing contact with an adult who monitored student engagement in school (the "check" component) and provided connections that would help the student stay in school (the "connect" component). In terms of impact, measures of school performance (e.g., continued enrollment at the end of school year, completed course assignments, credits earned) were significantly higher for students participating in the treatment condition. In contrast, no differences emerged on comparisons of measures of school identification (e.g., perceptions of the importance of school) and teacher ratings of student academic competence and level of problem behavior. In a second study involving 144 youth identified as EBD in an urban setting, Sinclair and colleagues (2005) examined the impact of key "check" and "connect" components including the following: routine monitoring of student engagement, individualized and timely interventions, relationship-building activities, following transferring students, problem-solving sessions, prevailing message that someone at school cared about their success (persistence plus), and efforts to promote school affiliation. As for impact (and most important), treatment participants were less likely to have dropped out of school than their control peers after four (39% vs. 58%) and five years (42% vs. 94%). Less clear were eventual school-completion outcomes given student mobility in and out of and between schools and the feature that more than a third of treatment participants were still in some form of schooling at the end of five years.

In summary, the previous research involving school completion and youth with disabilities is limited but three patterns are worth noting. First, a consistent finding is the presence of "educational mobility" as youth who fail to complete high school tend to change schools and settings while dropping in and out of school. This feature may well be the dominant trait that best distinguishes between completers and non-completers. Second, their initial referral to special education suggests, based on measures of academic achievement or school behavior, future difficulty meeting the academic demands, which become even greater at the high school level. Interestingly, the limited data suggest that in terms of the academic "tools for success" (e.g., measures of intelligence and achievement) meeting academic demands of those who are graduated are on par with those who do not complete school. Third, school settings can be changed so as to have an impact on measures likely to affect one's likelihood for having graduated from school. This feature holds considerable promise for interventions that keep youth in school.

Learning and School Engagement: A Key to School Completion Rates

In contrast to a traditional focus on dropping out of school after the fact or "fixing" students in some way (Kortering & Christenson, 2009), the construct of learning and school engagement affords a proactive approach that focuses on alterable features of our schools. Engaging youth with disabilities in learning and school, as eloquently defined by Christenson and her colleagues (Appleton, Christenson, & Furlong, 2008), includes a two-prong approach: "1) helping students acquire the skills to meet the demands of the high school environment and 2) creating relationships with students to facilitate their active involvement in school and learning" (Kortering & Christenson, 2009; p. 7).

Learning and School Engagement as a Construct

The earlier work of Finn (1989) and the existing research on school completion for youth with disabilities set the stage for a re-visioning of the school-completion process. Finn suggested two models to explain why students fail to complete high school: frustration–self esteem and participation–identification. Both these models help us to better understand the importance of engaging students in learning and school. For instance, previous research has chronicled the frustration and self-esteem issues endured by youth with disabilities, including academic failure (Murray, 2003), grade retention (Reschley & Christenson, 2006), alienation (Seidal & Vaughn, 1991) and frustrating relationships with teachers (Kortering & Braziel, 1999a; 1999b). Likewise, researchers have established the importance of helping students with disabilities to participate and, in turn, identify with their high school. For example, research shows youth demonstrate improved test scores, grades, and graduation rates when they engage in general after-school activities (Cooper, Nye, & Valentine, 1999; Eccles & Baber, 1999) and specifically high school sports (Eccles & Barber, 1999; Kleitman & Marsh, 2002; Mahoney & Cairns, 1997).

The construct of student engagement, focusing on learning and the school itself, can be characterized as having four interrelated subtypes (Sinclair et al., 2005). The first subtype is academic engagement as represented by such indices as time on task and credits earned. A second subtype involves behavioral engagement including attendance, participating in extra-curricular activities, disciplinary issues, and overall preparation for classes. Cognitive and psychological engagement are the third and fourth subtypes. The former refers to the perception by students that their high school education is relevant to their future and, in turn, their goal setting, self-regulatory behavior, and autonomy. The latter entails one's relationships with teachers and peers, which contribute to a sense of belonging. In combination, these subtypes provide points of emphasis for interventions that help youth to complete high school. As we target these areas of emphasis, Kortering and Christenson (2009) highlighted the need to focus on "facilitators" or alterable contextual features that influence the degree of one's engagement in school and learning. These facilitators of engagement, while alterable in the sense that educators can influence their use, range from individual informal behaviors of teachers as they interact with students to formal school polices affecting discipline and attendance.

A final aspect of using engagement as a construct to better understand school completion is that it offers a natural evolution of the IEP process to incorporate strategies and activities that facilitate a youth's engagement in school and learning. In other words, engagement becomes an effective venue for meeting the IEP goals and objectives that target standards for graduation, remediation of deficits, and postsecondary ambitions. These features of engagement blend with self-determination and empowerment by turning a focus to setting features and strategies that help youth take on an active role in their learning and school environment.

Core Elements for Interventions

The idea behind "core elements" is that they are universal. They can be infused into any existing or emerging approach to engage youth in learning and school. An appreciation for the elements begins with three assumptions. First, in the case of ninth and tenth graders, the period during which most drop out (Kortering & Braziel, & Tompkins, 1999b; 2002), nearly all these youth report a strong motivation to get a high school education (Kortering, Braziel, et al., 2002; Kortering, deBettencourt, & Braziel, 2005). They make the connection between a high school education and an improvement in their opportunities as an adult. This motivation shows that a high school education has incredible value, even in the face of the academic and social challenges they may endure as a student. Second, we see youth as having an important role to play in their completion of high school (Bridgeland, Dilulio, & Morrison, 2006; Kortering & Braziel, 1999a; 1999b; 2002). Their role includes having the option to walk away from their "special educational opportunity," a feature that demands attention to their perceptions of school. Their perspective, while influencing their thoughts and actions in school, is central to their engagement. Third, the ambition behind the original passage of PL 94–142 (the Education of All Handicapped Children Act) was that truly "special" education programs would prepare these youth for being productive taxpayers (U.S. States Congress and Administration, 1973). This ambition is more pronounced given that today's taxpayers fully expect such efforts to prepare youth for a productive adulthood. To best achieve this objective, we must prepare youth to succeed in tomorrow's labor market, characterized as increasingly knowledge-based, complex, and competitive (Friedman, 2005). A "meaningful education" in the sense of providing the knowledge and skill set required in postsecondary settings and careers with suitable wages, promotion potential, and benefits lies in general education classrooms. With these

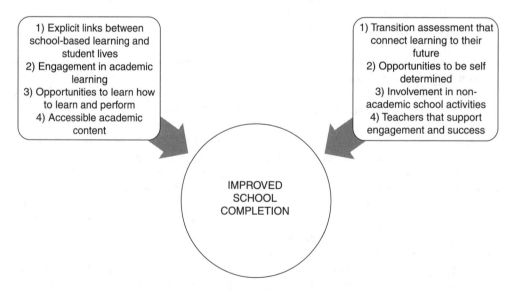

Figure 13.1 Elements of School Completion

assumptions in mind, the following elements set the stage for engaging youth along two inter-related dimensions: helping youth meet the demands of the school environment and providing access to relationships that engage youth in school and learning.

Meeting the Academic Demands of High School

In an era of high-stakes testing and accountability, youth with disabilities face increased pressure to meet challenging academic demands. These demands, inclusive of various content exams (e.g., End of Course or EOC exams for academic classes) and general competency evaluations (e.g., exit exams), have raised the standards that must be met for high school graduation (Thurlow, Cormier, & Vang, 2009; Zhang, 2009). Youth are struggling to pass these standards, as evidenced by Zhang, Katsiyannis, & Kortering (2007) who found that youth with high-incidence disabilities passed EOC exams, a requirement for graduation, at less than half the rate of their general-education peers. This trend was over a four-year period on one state's EOC exams in Algebra, Biology, English 1, and Economics.

Explicit Links between School-Based Learning and their Lives

Youth consistently suggest that they see limited relevance in what they are doing in high school (Pope, 2001; Willingham, 2009) and youth with disabilities are no different in this regard (Higgins, Boone, & Lovitt, 2002; Kortering & Braziel 1999a, 1999b). Cushman (2003) illustrated this point by using youth voices to document their need to understand why they need to know what we are trying to teach them and their requests that educators do a better job at connecting learning to the lives of their students. Other evidence includes the recent *Silent Epidemic* report, which chronicles similar suggestions from a national sample of school dropouts (Bridgeland, Dilulio, & Morrison, 2006).

In the local school, efforts to connect learning to the lives of students begin with an understanding of them as well as the academic content. This understanding includes knowing about their interests, ambitions, learning styles, and life outside of school. For example, a young woman identified as having SLD demonstrates an interest and talent in working as a carpenter. This understanding then offers her Algebra teacher a unique opportunity—connecting algebraic concepts to the field of carpentry. Another example would be the young woman with SLD who shows an established interest in social careers or those involving working with and for others in some way. This student would perform best in classroom settings allowing work with her peers in a cooperative learning-type structure and be an ideal candidate for service-learning activities. Other local efforts might include the regular use of student feedback (e.g., interviews, online surveys) to establish information on how youth perceive school in terms of meeting their needs, specific courses, and ideas for improvement (Kortering & Braziel, 1999a; 1999b; Kortering, deBettencourt, & Braziel, 2005). This feedback then provides an evidence base for contemplating general and specific school improvement driven by a better understanding of students.

Engagement in Academic Learning

Csikszentmihalyi and Larson (1984) conducted an intriguing study that demonstrated that engaged youth enjoy what they are doing while being more successful at it. The downside is that this engagement seldom happens while youth are in their academic classes. This earlier work finds support in research by Lan and Lanthier (2003) and Black (2003), which again showed how high school students are often dissatisfied with school and unmotivated to engage in traditional learning activities. A similar thread runs through Wagner's (2008) report on why our schools are failing to teach children what they need to learn.

In contrast to a lack of engagement, Moses (2001) illustrated how even the most challenging academic content can be structured in a local setting to engage youth; in this case with inner-city youth participating in the Algebra Project. He documented how Algebra content becomes engaging by having youth access real life and hands-on experiences. Other practical ideas for engaging youth in academic learning include recognition that today's youth live in a world of engaging media and most will undoubtedly be in a work environment driven by technology. This suggests adopting educational technology and related tools to replace more traditional lecture formats (Foreman, 2003).

Opportunities to Learn How to Learn and Perform

Opportunities that help youth learn how to learn and demonstrate their learning, to perform if you will, would seem a natural response to the demands of the high school general-education classroom (Schumaker & Deshler, 2005). These opportunities become especially compelling given the limited academic achievement levels that characterize youth with disabilities, especially in reading (Saenz & Fuchs, 2002) and math (Kortering, deBettencourt, et al., 2005) along with their limited knowledge of learning strategies (Chen et al., 2009; deBettencourt & Sabornie, 2008).

In terms of the local classroom, Chen et al. (2009) suggested that youth need "instruction involving specific learning strategies that help them comprehend, compose, study, and learn" (p. 158). They further call for this instruction to involve general education teachers who are well versed in their subject's content. In addition, traditional approaches like after-school tutoring programs (see e.g., Houck, Pulvers, & Deshler, 2001), strategy instruction (see Boyle & Wsihaar, 2002; Fontana, Scruggs, & Mastropieri, 2007; Lenz, Adams, Bulgren, Pouliot, & Laraux, 2007; Meltzer, Katzier-Cohen, Miller, & Roditi, 2001), and test-taking interventions (Lancaster, Schumaker, Lancaster, & Deshler, 2009) warrant consideration. The evolving learning technologies and digital learning environments also demand attention to effective assessments of their technology-related proficiency and opportunities to learn about these technologies (Parker & Banejee, 2007). An intriguing development in learning how to learn involves technology-based tools that help youth offset difficulties in reading (Marino, 2009) and performance (Maccini, Gagnon, & Hughes, 2002). Other examples include pending innovations related to specific tools like NimbleTools® (Russell, Hoffman, & Higgins, 2009) and more generic ones like eText (Anderson-Inman, 2009; Izzo, Yurick, McArrell, 2009).

Accessible Academic Content

The high school environment remains dominated by the "Stand and Deliver" model, assigning and reading a text as the dominant forms of instruction. In contrast, the concept of Universal Design for Learning (UDL) suggests improving the accessibility of academic content by adhering to three principles: multiple means of representation of content; multiple options for student expression and control; and multiple means for engagement and motivation (Rose & Meyer, 2002). UDL as a concept for content-area teaching holds promise as evidenced in a study of student perceptions of Algebra and Biology interventions using UDL.[1] In this study, students participating in UDL interventions expressed higher levels of satisfaction, including more than 90% reporting a desire to have their teachers use more of these interventions as well as engagement in comparison with their other academic classes (Kortering, McClannon, & Braziel, 2009).

Relationships that Foster Engagement

A recent meta-analysis of the research demonstrates that supportive interactions between teachers and students moderate the challenges and failures youth endure in high school (Boster & Strom, 2007). These interactions are the foundation for relationships characterized by adults who listen to youth, communicate a sense of caring, and promote the youth's involvement in their education. In the academic classroom, these relationships prove especially important for youth who struggle. Helping these youth persist in the face of daily academic and corresponding struggles they encounter in and outside the classroom is central to fostering their interest and, it is hoped, some level of enthusiasm for school.

Transition Assessments that Connect School to their Future

The most important motivation youth report for being in school relates to the concept of personal development (Kortering & Konold, 2005; Kortering, Konold, & Glutting, 1998). This motivation, defined as a perception that education prepares students for a productive adulthood, is a key to engagement. By helping youth understand their talents and limitations, one enhances their motivation for personal development by linking what they do in school to their future ambitions, which begins to foster their positive relationships with others. This process also provides educators with insight to better understand student success and failure in school, including why specific students experience difficulty with certain classroom structures, teacher personalities, and academic content.

At the local level, an ongoing transition assessment process begins with an initial background survey on factors influencing a youth's skill development and interests, including work and educational histories of family members, perceptions of school, and general ambitions (Clark, Patton, & Moulton, 2000; Kortering, Braziel, & Sitlington, 2010). Next, a basic interest inventory followed by a formal assessment of a youth's preferences, including learning styles, is appropriate. Based on a youth's established interest, turn to a general (i.e., measuring several areas) or specific (i.e., measuring a single area) aptitude test to evaluate one's actual (as opposed to self-reported) level of talent in an expressed area or areas of interest. For example, a young man showing an established interest in mechanical occupations would benefit from a test of his mechanical skills. Finally, the recent Indicator 13 language mandates that IEPs for students age 16 and up include an age-appropriate transition assessment that provides a basis for appropriate postsecondary goals and identifying the supports necessary for helping students achieve those goals.

Opportunities to Be Self-Determined

Self-determination has a long-established history in special education. Relating to school completion, Zhang and Law (2005) use a review of the literature to connect interventions focusing on self-determination and improved outcomes associated with school completion. Similarly, Eisenman (2007) reinforced this connection with the suggestion that interventions to promote self-determination provide a foundation for school completion as youth begin to take an active role in their education while pursing educational goals based on their strengths and interests. Finally, Murray and Naranjo (2008) found that a strong sense of self-determination was a consistent theme to help explain school completion among a sample of high-risk urban youth with an SLD.

As adults we can relate to the concept that when we have some level of self-determination over what we do in life and work, we tend to be more engaged and successful. Youth are no different and often complain about the lack of freedom they experience while in high school (Cushman, 2003). Local school-based opportunities for developing the behaviors necessary for self-determination and empowerment range from formal curricula like the Steps to Self-Determination (Hoffman & Field, 2006) to the simple deployment of opportunity structures that allow youth control over their learning (e.g., providing options for learning, choosing which set of problems to do, options for demonstrating their learning of key content). Finally, simply asking youth about what they want to learn and improve at in school offers a starting point to incorporating their goals into the IEP process (Agran & Hughes, 2008).

Involvement in Non-Academic School Activities

Research has demonstrated that youth engaged in the non-academic side of schooling, including participation in athletics, musical groups like band or choir, school groups like Reserve Officer Training Cadets (Price, 2007), and other activities, are more likely to complete high school. The influence of this element stems from giving students an opportunity to be affiliated with the school while doing something that does not involve success with academic performance, a feature these youth have probably struggled with for the duration of their schooling. Such involvement also affords youth an opportunity for more positive teacher/student relationships as something other than academic learning becomes the focus of their interaction (Finn, 1989).

In terms of one's local high school, non-academic school activities range from team sports, including being a manager or a participant, and service-learning opportunities to joining various school clubs or groups. As students enter the ninth grade, one can begin to identify potential means for engagement. These activities then serve important social and educational functions (Ream & Rumbuger, 2008), including facilitating a sense of belonging or school membership (Finn, 2006).

Teachers Who Support Engagement and Success

Last, and most important, engaging youth in learning and school is facilitated by having access to a caring educator, someone who helps students persist in school. Research on the Check & Connect Model for school completion clearly documents the importance of relationships that promote engagement in school and learning (see Anderson, Christenson, Sinclair, & Lehr, 2004). Similarly, Murray and Naranjo (2008) found that teachers who conveyed a sense of caring while providing ongoing involvement and support, instrumental support, and a powerful presence in the classroom were key to the school-completion process for at-risk youth with an SLD.

At the local-school level, Price (2007), drawing on his experience with the military and its training of incoming recruits and cadets, suggested that young people who struggle in school often yearn for access to an adult they see as valuing them and believing in their potential for success. Along with a sense of valuing and believing in youth, key features of a relationship that proves supportive for students include listening to them, dedicating time for problem solving, and celebrating their successes (Mihalas et al., 2009).

Conclusion

This chapter provides a conceptualization of school completion relative to the importance of engaging youth in learning and school. This conceptualization reflects on previous models of school completion and incorporates the emerging research on student engagement. Central to this chapter is the idea that we *must* do a better job of helping more youth with disabilities to complete high school and that there are things we *can* do in our local school. A lack of effective action will leave our former students without access to a decent wage in a work world where 85% of current jobs and more than 90% of the fastest-growing jobs are projected to require a postsecondary education (Wagner, 2008), a scenario likely to undermine the future of all of us.

Note

1 The Center for Applied Special Technology (http://www.cast.org) offers access to a variety of resources related to UDL and content accessibility in the local high school classroom, including online training modules, archived resources, and various teacher tools. Another specific example of making content more accessible via UDL is the Virtual History Museum for teaching social studies (Bouck, Courtad, Okolo, & Englert, 2009). The Museum offers a free web-based environment for learning about history, including interactive exhibits, artifacts, and activities (see http://www.vhm.msu.edu). Other examples include the National Instructional Media Accessibility Standards, which offers digitized formats for textbooks and the ever-changing field of simulated learning that use interactive online tools (Cavanaugh Okolo, & Englert, 2009) and gaming technology to help students to better understand academic content (Gee, 2003).

References

Agran, M., & Hughes, C. (2008). Asking student input: Students' opinions regarding their individual education program involvement. *Career Development for Exceptional Individuals, 31*, 69–76.

Alliance for Excellent Education (2006). *Who's counted? Who's counting? Understanidng high school graduation rates*. Washington, DC: Author. Accessed online August 9, 2011 at http://www.all4ed.org/files/WhosCounting.pdf

Anderson-Inmann, L. (2009). Supported eText: Literacy scaffolding for students with disabilities. *Journal of Special Education Technology, 24*(3), 1–8.

Anderson, A. R., Christenson, S. L., Sinclair, M. F., & Lehr, C. A. (2004). Check & Connect: The importance of relationships for promoting engagement with school. *Journal of School Psychology, 42*, 95–113.

Appleton, J., Christenson, S., & Furlong, M. (2008). Student engagement with school: Critical conceptual and methodological issues of the construct. *Psychology in the Schools, 45*, 369–386.

Bear, G., Kortering, L., & Braziel, P. (2006). School completers and non-completers with learning disabilities: Similarities in academic achievement and perceptions of self and teachers. *Remedial and Special Education, 27*, 293–300.

Black, S. (2003). *Engaging the disengaged*. Retrieved July 12, 2005, from http://www.asbj.com/2003/12/1203research.html

Blackorby, J., Edgar, E., & Kortering, L. (1991). A third of our youth? The problem of high school dropout among mildly handicapped youth. *Journal of Special Education, 25*, 102–113.

Boster, J. F., & Strom, R. E. (2007). Dropping out of high school: A meta-analysis assessing the effects of messages in the home and in school. *Communication Education, 56*, 433–452.

Bouck, E. C., Courtad, C. A., Heutsche, A., Okolo, C. M., & Englert, C. S. (2009). The Virtual History Museum: A universally designed approach to social studies instruction. *Teaching Exceptional Children, 42*(2), 14–21.

Boyle, J. R., & Wsihaar, M. (2002). The effects of strategic note taking on the recall and comprehension of lecture information for high school students with learning disabilities. *Learning Disabilities Research, 16*, 133–141.

Bridgeland, J. M., Dilulio, J. J., & Morrison, K. B. (2006). *The silent epidemic: Perspectives of high school dropouts*. Seattle, WA: Bill & Melinda Gates Foundation.

Brinckerhoff, P., McGuire, J., & Shaw, S. (2002). *Postsecondary Education and Transition for Students with Learning Disabilities* (2nd ed.). Austin, TX: PRO-ED.

Bullis, M. (2004). Hard questions and final thoughts regarding the school-to-community transition of adolescents with emotional or behavior disabilities. In D. Cheney (Ed.) *Transition of students with EBD: Current approaches for positive outcomes*. Arlington, VA: Children with Behavior Disorders and Division on Career Development and Transition.

Cataldi, E. F., Laird, J., & KewalRamani, A. (2009). *High school dropout and completion rates in the United States: 2007*. Washington, DC: National Center for Education Statistics, Institute for Educational Sciences, U.S. Department of Education.

Chambers, J. G., Shkolnik, J., & Perez, M. (2003). *Total expenditures for students with disabilities, 1999–2000: Spending variation by disability*. Washington, DC: Special Education Expenditure Project.

Chen, H. Y., Courtad, C. A., Englert, C. S., Jocks-Meier, B. S., Mariage, T. V., Moxley, K. D., et al. (2009). The learning to learn strategies of adolescent students with disabilities: Highlighting, note taking, planning and writing expository texts. *Assessment for Effective Intervention, 34*, 147–161.

Clark, G. M., Patton, J. R., & Moulton, L. R. (2000). *Informal assessments for transition planning*. Austin, TX: PRO-ED.

Cobb, B., Sample, P. L., Alwell, M., & Johns, N. R. (2006). Cognitive-behavioral interventions, dropout and youth with disabilities. *Remedial and Special Education, 27*, 259–273.

Cohen, M. A. (1998). The monetary value of saving a high risk youth. *Journal of Quantitative Criminology, 14*, 5–33.

Cooper, H., Lindsay, J. J., Nye, B., & Valentine, J. C. (1999). Relationships between five after-school activities and academic achievement. *Journal of Educational Psychology, 91*, 369–378.

Csikszentmihalyi, M., & Larson, R. (1984). *Being adolescent: Conflict and growth in the teenage years.* New York: Basic Books, Harper Collins.

Cushman, K. (2003). *Fires in the bathroom.* New York: The New Press.

deBettencourt, L., & Sabornie, E. (2008). *Teaching students with mild and high incidence disabilities at the secondary level* (2nd ed.). Columbus, OH: Pearson. Deschler and Schumaker 2006.

Dunn, C., Chambers, D, & Rabren, K. (2004). Variables affecting students' decisions to drop out of school. *Remedial and Special Education, 25*, 314–325.

Eccles, J. S., & Baber, B. L., (1999). Student council, volunteering, basketball, or marching band: What kind of extra-curricular involvement matters? *Journal of Adolescent Research, 14*, 10–43.

Eisenman, L. T. (2007). Self-determination interventions: Building a foundation for school completion. *Remedial and Special Education, 28*, 2–8.

Finn, J. (1989). Withdrawing from school. *Review of Educational Research, 59*, 117–142.

Finn, J. D. (2006). *The adult lives of at-risk students: The role of attainment and engagement in high school.* Washington, DC: National Center on Educational Statistics.

Fontana, J. L., Scruggs, T., & Mastropieri, M.A. (2007) Mnemonic strategy instruction in inclusive secondary social studies classes. *Remedial and Special Education, 28*, 345–355.

Foreman, J. (2003). NEXT-generation: Educational technology versus the lecture. *Educause, July–August*, 12–22.

Friedman, T. (2005). *The world is flat: A brief history of the twenty-first century.* New York: Farrar, Straus, and Giroux.

General Educational Testing Services (2009). *2007 GED Testing Program Statistical Report.* Washington, DC: American Council on Education.

Harlow, C. (2003). *Education and Correctional Populations.* Washington, DC: Bureau of Justice Statistics.

Higgins, K., Boone, R., & Lovitt, T. (2002). Adapting challenging textbooks to improve content area learning. In M. R. Shinn, H. M. Walker, & G. Stoner (Eds.). *Interventions for academic and behavior problems II: Preventive and remedial approaches* (pp. 758–790). Bethesda, MD: National Association of School Psychologists.

Hoffman, A., & Field, S. (2006). *Steps to self-determination.* Austin, TX: PRO-ED.

Houck, M. F., Pulvers, K. A., & Deshler, D. D. (2001). The effects of an after-school tutoring program on the academic performance of at-risk students and students with LD. *Remedial and Special Education, 22*, 172–186.

Izzo, M.V., Yurick, A., & McArrell, B. (2009). Supported eText: Effects of text to speech on access and achievement for high school students with disabilities. *Journal of Special Education Technology, 24*(3), 9–20.

Karpinski, M. J., Neubert, D. A., & Graham, S. (1992). A follow-along study of postsecondary outcomes for graduates and dropouts with mild disabilities in a rural setting. *Journal of Learning Disabilities, 25*, 376–385.

Kleitman, S. & Marsh, H. (2002). Extracurricular school activities: The good, the bad, and the nonlinear. *Harvard Educational Review, 72* (4), 1–31.

Kohler, P. (1996). *Taxonomy for transition planning: Linking research to practice.* Champaign, IL: University of Illinois at Champaign-Urbana.

Kortering, L., & Blackorby, J. (1992). High school dropout and students identified with behavioral disorders. *Behavioral Disorders, 18*, 24–32.

Kortering, L., & Braziel, P. (1999a). Dropout prevention: A look at what dropout youths have to say. *Remedial and Special Education, 20*, 78–83.

Kortering, L., & Braziel, P. (1999b). Staying in school: The perspective of ninth graders. *Remedial and Special Education, 20*, 106–113.

Kortering, L., & Braziel, P. (2002). Improving high school programs: What youths with LD have to say. *Learning Disabilities Quarterly, 25*, 177–188.

Kortering, L, Braziel, P., & Tompkins, J. (2002). The challenge of school completion among youth with behavior disabilities: Another side to the story. *Behavioral Disabilities, 27*, 142–154.

Kortering, L., deBettencourt, L. & Braziel, P. (2005). Improving performance in high school algebra: What students with learning disabilities are saying. *Learning Disabilities Quarterly, 28*, 191–204.

Kortering, L. & Christenson, S. (2009). Engaging students in school and learning: The real deal for school completion. *Exceptionality, 17*, 5–15.

Kortering, L., Braziel, P., & Sitlington, P. (2010). Age appropriate transition assessments for youths with EBD. In D. Cheney (Ed.) *Transition of students with EBD: Current approaches for positive outcomes* (2nd ed.). Arlington, VA: Children with Behavior Disorders and Division on Career Development and Transition.

Kortering, L., & Christenson, S. (2009). School completion: The right stuff. *Exceptionality, 17*, 5–15.

Kortering, L., Haring, N., & Klockars, A. (1992). The identification of learning disabled high school dropouts: The utility of a discriminant analysis function. *Exceptional Children, 58*, 422–436.

Kortering, L., & Konold, T. (2005). Coming to school: A comparison of youth with and without LD. *Journal of At-Risk Students. 13*, 12–22.

Kortering, L., Konold, T., & Glutting, J. (1998). Why come to school: An empirical investigation of what youth have to say. *Journal of At-Risk Issues, 5*, 10–16.

Kortering, L., McClannon, T., & Braziel, P. (2009). Universal design for learning: What students have to say. *Remedial and Special Education 29*, 352–363.

Lan, W., & Lanthier, R. (2003). Changes in students' academic performance and perceptions of school and self before dropping out of schools. *Journal of Education for Students Placed at Risk, 8*, 309–332.

Lancaster, P. E., Schumaker, J. B., Lancaster S. J., & Deshler, D. D. (2009). Effects of a computer program on use of the test-taking strategy by secondary students with disabilities. *Learning Disability Quarterly, 32*, 165–179.

Lenz, K. R., Adams, G. L., Bulgren, J. A., Pouliot, N., & Laraux, M. (2007). Effects of curriculum maps and guiding questions on the test performance of adolescents with learning disabilities. *Learning Disability Quarterly, 30*, 235–244.

Levin, H. M., & and Belfield, C. R. (2007). Educational interventions to raise high school graduation rates. In C. R. Belfield & H.M. Levin (Eds.) *The price we pay: Economic and social consequences of inadequate education* (177–199). Washington, DC: Brookings Institute Press.

Lichtenstein, S. (1993). Transition from school to adulthood: Case studies of adults with learning disabilities who dropped out of school. *Exceptional Children, 59*, 336–348.

Maccini, P., Gagnon, J., & Hughes, C. (2002). Technology-based practices for secondary students with learning disabilities. *Learning Disability Quarterly, 25*, 247–260.

Mahoney, J. L., & Cairns, R. B., (1997). Do extracurricular activities protect against early school dropout? *Developmental Psychology, 33*, 241–253.

Marino, M. T. (2009). Understanding how adolescents with reading difficulties utilize technology-based tools. *Exceptionality, 17*, 88–102.

Mellard, D. F., & Patterson, M. B. (2008). Contrasting adult literacy learners with and without SLD. *Remedial and Special Education, 29*, 133–144.

Meltzer, L., Katzier-Cohen, T., Miller, L., & Roditi, B. (2001). The impact of effort and strategy use on academic performance: Student and teacher perceptions. *Learning Disability Quarterly, 24*, 85–95.

Mihalas, S., Morse, W. C., Allsop, D. H., & McHatton, P. A. (2009). Cultivating caring relationships between teachers and secondary students with emotional and behavioral disorders: Implications for practice. *Remedial and Special Education, 30*, 108–125.

Moretti, E. (2005). *Does education reduce participating in criminal activities?* Berkeley, CA: University of California, Berkeley, Department of Economics.

Moses, R. P. (2001). *Radical Equations: Civil rights from Mississippi to the Algebra Project.* Boston, MA: Beacon Publishing.

Muenning, P. (2006). *State-level health cost-savings associated with improvements in high school graduation rates.* Washington, DC: Alliance for Excellent Education.

Murray, C. (2003). Risk factors, protective factors, vulnerability, and resilience. *Remedial and Special Education, 24*, 1–16.

Murray, C., & Naranjo, J. (2008). Poor, black, learning disabled, and graduating: An investigation of factors and process associated with school completion among high-risk urban youth. *Remedial and Special Education, 29*, 145–160.

Parker, D. R., & Banejee, M. (2007). Leveling the digital playing field: Assessing the learning technology needs of college-bound students with LD and/or ADHD. *Assessment for Effective Intervention, 33*, 5–14.

Pope, D. C. (2001). *Doing school: How we are creating a generation of stressed, materialistic and miseducated students.* New Haven, CT: Yale University Press.

Price, H. B. (2007). *Demilitarizing what the Pentagon knows about developing young people: A new paradigm for educating students who are struggling in school and life.* Washington, DC: Center on Children and Families.

Ream, R. K., & Rumburger, R. W. (2008). Student engagement, peer social capital, and school dropout among Mexican American and non-Latino white students. *Sociology of Education, 81*, 109–139.

Reschley, A. L., & Christenson, S. L. (2006). Prediction of dropout among students with mild disabilities: A case for the inclusion of student engagement variables. *Remedial and Special Education, 27*, 276–292.

Rose, D. H., & Meyer, A. (2002). *Teaching every student in the digital age: Universal design for learning.* Alexandria, VA: Association for Curriculum and Instruction.

Rouse, C. E. (2007). Consequences for the labor market. In C. R. Belfield & H.M. Levin (Eds.) *The price we pay: Economic and social consequences of inadequate education* (pp. 99–124). Washington, DC: Brookings Institute Press.

Russell, M., Hoffman, T., & Higgins, J. (2009). NimbleTools: A universally designed test delivery system. *Teaching Exceptional Children, 42*(2), 6–13.

Saenz, L. M., & Fuchs, L. S. (2002). Examining the reading difficulty of secondary students with learning disabilities: Expository versus narrative text. *Remedial and Special Education, 23*, 31–41.

Schumaker, J. B., & Deshler, D. D. (2005). Teaching students to be strategic learners. In D. D. Deshler & J. B. Schumaker (Eds.), *Teaching adolescents with disabilities: Accessing the general education curriculum* (pp. 64–84). Thousand Oaks, CA: Corwin Press.

Scott, S. M., McGuire, J. M., & Shaw, S. F. (2003). Universal design for instruction: A new paradigm for adult instruction in postsecondary education. *Remedial and Special Education, 24*, 369–379.

Seidal, J., & Vaughn, S. (1991). Social alienation and the learning disabled school dropout. *Learning Disabilities Research, 6*, 152–157.

Sinclair, M. F., Christenson, S. L., Evelo, D. L., & Hurley, C. M. (1998). Dropout prevention for youth with disabilities: Efficacy of a sustained school engagement procedure. *Exceptional Children, 65*, 7–21.

Sinclair, M. F., Christenson, S. L., & Thurlow, M. L. (2005). Promoting school completion of urban secondary youth with emotional or behavior disabilities. *Exceptional Children, 71*, 465–482.

Snyder, H. N., & Sickmund, M. (2006, November). *Juvenile offenders and victims: 2006 national report.* Washington, DC: National Center on Juvenile Justice.

Stephan, J.J. (2003). *State prison expenditures, 2001.* Washington, DC: U.S. Department of Justice, Bureau of Justice Statistics.

Test, D. W., Fowler, C. H., Richter, S. M., Mazzotti, V., White, J., Walker, A. R., et al. (2009). Evidence-based practices in secondary transition. *Career Development for Exceptional Individuals, 32*, 155–128.

Thurlow, M. L., Cormier, D. C., & Vang, M. (2009). Alternative routes to earning a standard high school diploma. *Exceptionality, 17*, 135–149.

U.S. Census Bureau (2005a). Current Population Survey. *Educational Attainment in the U.S.: 2005* (pp. 133–183). Washington, DC: Census Bureau.

U.S. Census Bureau (2005b). *School Enrollment=NSocial and Economic Characteristics of Students: October 2005: Detailed Tables*: Table 1. Accessed August 9, 2011 at http://www.census.gov/population/www/socdemo/school/cps2005.html

U.S. Congress and Administration (1973). *Aid to Education of the Handicapped Act approved.* (pp. 651–656). St. Paul, MN: West Law Reporter.

U.S. Department of Education (1987). *7th Annual Report to Congress on the implementation of the Individuals with Disabilities Education Act, 2004.* Washington, DC: Office of Special Education Programs.

U.S. Department of Education (2004). Educational attainment of high school dropouts 8 years later. *Issue Brief*, November, Washington, DC: National Center for Educational Statistics.

Wagner, T. (2008). *The global achievement gap: Why even our best schools don't teach the new survival skills our children need and what we can do about it.* New York: Basic Books.

Willingham, D. T. (2009). *Why don't students like school? A cognitive scientist answers questions about how the mind works and what it means for the classroom.* San Francisco: Jossey-Bass Publishing.

Yates, J. A. (2005). The transition from school to work: Education and work experiences. *Monthly Labor Review*, February, 21–32.

Zhang, Y. (2009). *State high school exit exams: Trends in test programs, alternative pathways, and pass rates.* Washington, DC: Center on Educational Policy.

Zhang, D., Katsiyannis, A., & Kortering, L. (2007). Performance on exit exams by students with disabilities: A four-year analysis. *Career Development for Exceptional Individuals, 30*, 48–57.

Zhang, D. & Law, B. H. (2005). Self-determination as a dropout prevention strategy. *Journal of At-Risk Issues, 11*(2), 25–31.

14

Social Skills, Supports, and Networks in Adolescent Transition Education

Laura T. Eisenman

Sarah A. Celestin

UNIVERSITY OF DELAWARE

Laying a foundation for adult social relationships in the community, further education, and at work is a central task of transition services for adolescents with disabilities. Halpern (1994) noted that developing "effective *personal and social relationships* may be the *most important* of all the transition goals" (p. 120, italics in original). In the special education literature, approaches to developing personal and social relationships often focus on increasing students' *social skills* and *social competence* (see for example, Alwell & Cobb, 2007; Gresham, Sugai, & Horner, 2001). Social skills refer to particular behaviors that individuals employ to participate in a social interaction. Shaking hands, initiating a conversation, or requesting assistance are examples of social skills. Social competence refers to using such skills in ways that are valued by others within a specific culture or context. Knowing with whom and when to shake hands as well as moderating the strength of one's handshake to avoid negative judgments from others are both examples of social competence.

Youths' social skills and competence are recognized as making important contributions to their *social acceptance* and *social inclusion* (Chadsey & Shelden, 1998; Devine & Lashua, 2002). Others are more likely to acknowledge and engage someone if that person displays social behaviors that are seen as normative social interactions with the person are viewed positively (or at least not negatively), or the person holds a valued social role, such as friend or colleague (Wolfensberger, 2000). Because people typically encounter many different social groups across different environments (e.g., school, work, leisure), their social acceptance and inclusion may vary by context. Being seen as a socially competent or valued member in one community does not ensure the same in another. Also, social inclusion is not entirely dependent on a person's skill and competence. Inclusion within a group may be accorded to an individual in spite of some skill limitations because of other strengths or attributes that are more highly valued by the group. Further, social skills and competence can be formally or informally mediated by others in ways that support and strengthen otherwise weak social relationships, thus providing opportunities for social inclusion that might be unavailable to the person without those supports.

Social capital (Bourdieu, 1986; Putnam, 2000; Trainor, 2008) is a concept that encompasses the ideas of social relationships, skill, competence, acceptance, and inclusion by focusing attention on the ways that social networks influence personal opportunities, success, and well-being.

Social networks may be thought of as the multiple relationships that create bonds within groups or bridges between diverse groups. Social networks thrive on reciprocity and trust. Social capital is an asset that individuals can accrue and leverage—or lack—based on the qualities of their connections to others. Having diverse social networks (a variety of reciprocating connections with many types of people) may have both a protective and empowering function for people with disabilities. Being known and valued by networks of people that include both intimates and acquaintances decreases the likelihood of a person becoming isolated and vulnerable and increases a person's opportunities to effect personally meaningful changes in community, work, and education settings. The transition from school to adult life is a time to systematically invest in developing youths' social capital.

Importance of Social Relationships in Postsecondary Environments

Prior research suggests that limitations in the social skills, supports, and networks of youths with disabilities negatively affect their success in employment, postsecondary education, and independent living or community participation. Conversely, in each of these new environments, youths' social relationships can provide them with access to new opportunities and the supports they need for success.

Employment

Appropriate social behaviors as well as the establishment of social supports and relationships are directly connected to employment outcomes of youth with disabilities; finding and maintaining employment may both be problematic due to limited social skills and supports (Chadsey & Shelden, 1998). However, the process of finding employment can be facilitated by the social relationships acquired during school years and the acquaintances that formed during vocational and recreational experiences. When seeking employment, social networks with many "weak ties" (i.e., acquaintances) influence knowledge of and access to employment choices (Eisenman, 2007). Integrated employment opportunities, such as supported employment, also have been found to increase the richness of young adults' social networks (Forrester-Jones, Jones, Heason, & Di' Terlizzi, 2004). Unfortunately, many young people with disabilities have social networks that are constricted and have few interconnections (Knox & Parmenter, 1993). Especially if their school experiences have been primarily in segregated environments, they may feel less socially supported in inclusive environments and rely primarily on peers with disabilities and family members for social support.

Social relationships are important during employment as well. People with disabilities must have the competence to navigate the culture of the workplace and make connections with co-workers. Workplace culture refers to the unspoken rules and customs within the workplace (Elksnin & Elksnin, 1998). For example, during break times, do co-workers tend to talk about recreational activities and family events or maintain an all-business conversation? Is it acceptable to eat at your desk or workstation, or is food only allowed in the break room? While these examples are not strictly social in nature, the consequence of not understanding the culture can have a direct effect on an individual's social relationships and acceptance within the workplace. Understanding the culture may be difficult initially but is important for establishing social relationships and gaining opportunities for social supports (Butterworth, Hagner, Helm, & Whelley, 2000; Devine & Lashua, 2002; Elksnin & Elksnin, 1998; Hagner & DiLeo, 1993). This socialization process in the workplace is the way in which people are incorporated into the organization and become accepted as insiders rather than outsiders (Szymanski & Parker, 1996).

Further Education

As more adolescents with disabilities choose to go on to further education, the importance of social relationships in that setting emerges. The act of socially navigating a college campus can be overwhelming as there are so many differences between that and high school (Brinckerhoff, 1996). The need to find assistance independently and the level of personal freedom often represent major changes from the secondary environment. Developing social networks and mentoring support in college settings is essential for navigating personal and institutional barriers (Garrison-Wade & Lehmann, 2009). For example, a student new to a college campus may be interested in joining clubs or organizations but is unaware or unsure of how to do so. Peer mentors can assist with learning about which groups match a student's interests, when organizations meet, what they do, and how to become a member. Formal or informal peer-support groups also can help to alleviate the stress of the new postsecondary social scene. The act of sharing personal experiences with people who have had similar experiences can foster self-realization and promote a sense of unity and community, which will aid in the transition and retention of students in postsecondary settings (Brinckerhoff, 1996; Getzel & Thoma, 2008; Lovitt & Emerson, 2008).

In addition to supports from social networks and mentors, young adults in postsecondary school environments need self-advocacy skills (Getzel & Thoma, 2008; Mull, Sitlington, & Alper, 2001). They must recognize when and how to secure accommodations. This understanding involves willingness to take initiative to find services on campuses and social competence to form relationships with professors, and actively develop support systems through friends, mentors, and support groups. Through the process of building social relationships and becoming a self-advocate, the postsecondary environment can become less overwhelming and lead to success.

Independent Living and Community Participation

In addition to employment and further education, social relationships play a key role in successful independent living and community participation. Many youth with disabilities continue to have regular communication with friends in post-school settings. However, more than half do not engage in community group activities, and a small number (about 6%) have no contact with friends apart from occasional organized activities. Young adults with intellectual, physical, or multiple disabilities tend to be less engaged in community activities than their peers (Newman, Wagner, Cameto, & Knokey, 2009).

Often, a major source of social support post-school lies within the individual's family (Eisenman, Tanverdi, Perrington, & Geiman, 2009; Knox & Parmenter, 1993). Although families may play a central role, this is not always the case. People with intellectual or psychiatric disabilities may see themselves as having fewer supportive ties and being less central in their families, and over time, they tend to have fewer spouses, partners, or children and thus, limited family-based social capital (Widmer, Kempf-Constantin, Robert-Tissot, Lanzi & Carminati, 2008).

The community can be a resource for social supports outside of the family. Rural communities sometimes act as an informal support system with the whole community participating in a supportive role (Irvine & Lupart, 2006). For young people who live in urban or suburban environments, social supports may need to be built through small communities or circles of support to bolster independence. Relationships are needed and desired to further develop youths' social networks and help them become an active part of the community. Individuals with disabilities and their families may find support through informal social networks and community groups such as church or clubs (Eisenman et al., 2009; Walker & O'Connor,

1997). Having a supportive social network enhances resilience and provides a way to overcome barriers and decrease vulnerability during transitions (Gerber, Ginsburg, & Reiff, 1992; Murray, 2003).

Further, because "disability" is sometimes viewed negatively by others, people with disabilities may view themselves negatively (Devine & Lashua, 2002). Active construction of mutually supportive social interactions can counter the negative views and support a positive self-image. Perceiving oneself as socially accepted is critical to many people when participating in community leisure activities (Devine & Lashua, 2002). An individual's self-determination skills and social competence, particularly social cognitive problem-solving abilities, play a role in sustaining relationships and increase the chance of postsecondary success (Murray, 2003). Students who are socially competent or who have established social supports will be less vulnerable in new social situations such as negotiating living arrangements with roommates or experiencing intimate relationships.

Participation in community groups and clubs can provide opportunities for young adults to practice negotiation and advocacy skills in a safe environment. Youth with disabilities who participate in extracurricular activities tend to be those with more friends and larger social networks (Wagner, Cadwallader, & Marder, 2003). Therefore, involving students in extracurricular activities while in the secondary setting may lead to both greater social skill capacity and an increase in friends and social supports.

Learning Opportunities that Promote Youths' Social Transition

Creating learning opportunities for youth who are transitioning into new adult social roles can be viewed through three dimensions: development, environments, and relationships. First, a career-development framework is familiar to many people involved in transition services and can be useful, too, for thinking about transition-related social development. Opportunities for occupational awareness, exploration, and preparation help to pave the way into later employment by assisting young adults to formulate employment goals and plans that are based on solid information and experiences about themselves and the world of work. Likewise, new and meaningful post-school social roles and relationships can be facilitated by youths' earlier opportunities to engage in social awareness, exploration, and preparation activities.

Second, for students in transition, opportunities to engage in these developmental tasks (social awareness, exploration, and preparation) must be considered as they apply across and within the major postsecondary life domains of employment, education, and independent living/community participation. Across domains, some knowledge and skills will be useful in general. For example, knowing some general strategies for conflict resolution will be useful in the workplace, in schools, at home, and in the neighborhood. However, the utility and acceptability of specific conflict-resolution strategies will vary from workplace to workplace and community to community. Youth with disabilities must become aware of that environmental variability, explore how and why to use strategies in different environments, and gain some experience with using those strategies in the post-school environments they plan to inhabit.

Third, as discussed earlier, it is important to recognize and address the multiple facets of social relationships, including social skills and competence, supports for social acceptance and inclusion, and social networks. As represented in Figure 14.1, regardless of postsecondary environment or developmental focus, learning opportunities should promote needed skills, access to supports, and creation of networks.

This multidimensional perspective is critical for transitioning students given the known limitations of typical approaches that focus on social skills training within school contexts. Social-skills training interventions for secondary school-age youth with disabilities have been

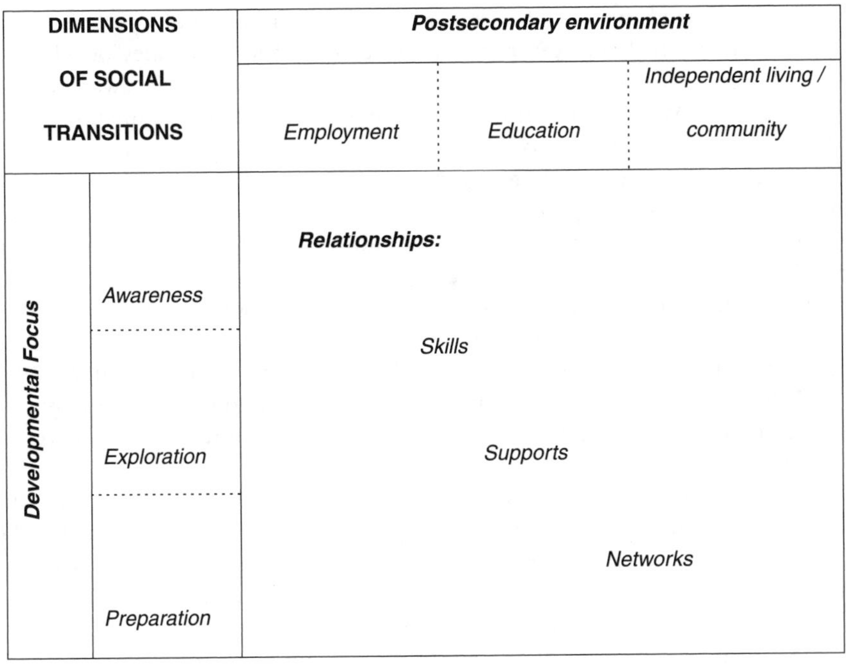

DIMENSIONS	Postsecondary environment		
OF SOCIAL			Independent living /
TRANSITIONS	Employment	Education	community

Relationships:

Skills

Supports

Networks

Developmental Focus: Awareness, Exploration, Preparation

Figure 14.1 Three Dimensions of Learning Opportunities to Promote Social Transitions

shown to have moderate effects (Alwell & Cobb, 2007). Yet, the impact of such training may be reduced by insufficient frequency or intensity of training as well as lack of opportunities for generalizing skills in natural environments (Black & Langone, 1997; Gresham, Sugai, & Horner, 2001). This is especially important for students whose social interaction difficulties are a primary manifestation of disability. Teaching students the social skills they need to succeed in a school setting is important but inadequate if the goal is to become a socially engaged adult.

This is not to say that social interactions with other school-age peers who have disabilities cannot be formative, too. Interacting socially with others who have common disability-related experiences may enhance youths' confidence and social awareness. Targeted interventions conducted by supportive educators within a familiar social environment can be an effective way to bolster students' specific knowledge and skills. These include opportunities that involve sharing and evaluating one's social interactions, role playing, counseling, video modeling, assertiveness training, practicing management and leadership of group work, and testing strategies for responding to teasing or other negative acts (Black & Ornelles, 2001; Devine & Lashua, 2002; Elksnin & Elksnin, 1998; Hughes & Carter, 2000; Irvine & Lupart, 2006; Wang & Spillane, 2009). The challenge for teachers is to identify ways to help students generalize their knowledge and skills for use in post-school settings by creating connections to activities and adults in those environments.

Teachers have a central role in promoting students' social competence and relatedness in ways that affect students' autonomy and postsecondary outcomes (Deci, Vallerand, Pelletier, & Ryan, 1991; Eisenman, 2007). Teachers can identify opportunities afforded by the classroom, school, or community for students' access to adult and peer role models, engagement with peers and adults in supportive relationships, and participation in socially meaningful activities. They can critically examine and, as needed, alter school structures or processes that limit opportunities for youth with disabilities to experience valued and positive peer social interactions, such as beliefs about which students should participate in which school and community activities (Farmer, Pearl, Van Acker, 1996). Teachers can ensure that all social activities include a "stretch" component of encouraging students to ask questions regarding their social awareness, exploration, and preparation: What am I learning about the social world beyond my immediate situation? What am I learning about my social interests and abilities? What social experiences might help me to become a member of new groups?

Recognizing that the school setting is not always conducive to helping students to establish connections beyond the school walls, students, families, and other Individualized Education Program (IEP) team and community members must be enlisted to identify work, volunteer, and leisure activities in the community where new social relationships can be explored. The community activities and locations should be places where youth can be present and participate with those who have mutual interests or goals. These may be formal or informal activities where, in addition to learning about specific social activities, youth have an opportunity to experience a variety of reciprocating social roles (e.g., giving and receiving support, companionship) (Butterworth et al., 2000).

Leake and Cholymay (2004), in a discussion of the challenges facing culturally and linguistically diverse youth with disabilities in postsecondary education, suggested that cultural brokers can be an important key to facilitating youths' social engagement. Brokers are people with or without disabilities who have bonds to multiple social groups and who are skilled at creating bridges between groups. They are willing to establish relationships with youth who have disabilities, to introduce them to others, and to provide guidance and support as these youth learn to navigate new social territory and establish bonds within a new group. Similar strategies are part of social interventions that may be familiar to educators, such as peer buddies (Copeland et al., 2002) and ambassador programs (e.g., Autism Ambassadors, n.d.), which promote positive interactions and acceptance among youth with and without disabilities. Another way to create social bridges is with peer-to-peer support programs (e.g., Hillier, Fish, Cloppert, & Beversdorf, 2007) that match people with disabilities who have found success in new social environments with those who aspire to participate in or have recently entered those environments.

Mentorship is another familiar model of cultural brokering, especially as it applies to career development. As people make the transition into the world of work, it is helpful to receive guidance and support from someone who is well established in the social culture of the workplace and who has an interest in furthering the development of the mentee. Enlisting co-workers who may befriend and provide natural supports has long been recognized as an effective way to integrate people with disabilities into workplace cultures (Hagner & DiLeo, 1993; Szymanski & Parker, 1996). Similarly, youth may benefit from mentors or other cultural brokers who are familiar with diverse postsecondary education settings and who will venture with them into exploring specific social opportunities. Mentors can assist students to learn about activities that might be of interest given their prior experiences, the array of social activities available, clues to look for to determine whether a "welcoming" environment exists, pros and cons of revealing one's disability, and formal supports or accommodations one might need to participate (Eisenman & Mancini, 2009). It is within the context of brokered social relationships that youth with disabilities can further develop their social skills, identify useful supports, and enlarge their social networks in ways that help them bridge school and post-school environments.

Embedding Social Goals into Transition Planning

Facilitating new social relationships for adolescents in transition means looking beyond secondary school settings and into the postsecondary environments where students' post-school goals are likely to take them. As noted previously, research indicates that postsecondary social skills, supports, and networks are of concern for many youth with disabilities; students' social competencies and connections can make or break their success in each postsecondary domain. For purposes of transition planning, that means IEP teams should consider the roles of social skills, supports, and networks to students' success in employment, further education, and independent or community living, and as suggested in Figure 14.1, students' goals could address awareness (e.g., recognizing unspoken rules of the workplace), exploration (e.g., learning how to negotiate for accommodations in higher-education settings), or preparation (e.g., joining community groups).

As with other transition-related goals, social goals for transition should be based upon transition assessments that assist the IEP team to understand a student's current situation, become familiar with future environments, and develop a plan for moving toward post-school goals. Many formal and informal transition assessments include relevant components on social skills and community activities within and across post-school goal areas (Clark, 1998; Hughes & Carter, 2000; Sitlington, Neubert, Begun, Lombard, & Leconte, 2007). These assessments can be the basis for identifying areas of student needs and developing transition-focused instruction and support plans related to social goals. Regardless of the assessment approach or tool used, the fact that students' relationships are in transition must also be considered. The IEP team should identify the family and community relationships that are likely to remain with the student post-school, which relationships may fall away, and where new relationships must be built.

Assessment of current and future social relationships can be incorporated into the transition-planning process through the use of informal social network interviews and social network mapping conducted by or with the student and family members. Interview techniques used by researchers to determine the extent of individuals with disabilities' social networks (Butterworth et al., 1993; Eisenman, 2007; Hagner, Butterworth, & Keith, 1995) can be adapted for use in transition assessments. Table 14.1 presents sample questions from a social network interview. Likewise, methods used to diagram a person's circle of support as part of a person-centered planning process can be adapted to help IEP teams consider the diversity and durability of students' social networks within and across post-school domains (Amado & McBride, 2001). Network interviews and mapping with people in the community also can be conducted to help IEP team members understand the social relationships that are central to the student's future environments. Social network interviews and maps can be regularly updated and re-evaluated as part of transition assessments to determine whether transition services are leading to multiple important outcomes of (a) enhanced social skills, (b) access to social supports, and (c) a growing diversity of social connections.

The results of these assessments also can be analyzed in a variety of ways to identify sources of support and opportunities for growth. One such analysis might focus on social "bonds" and "bridges."

- What are the social groups with which the young person is affiliated or identifies?
- How are or could these groups be connected to the person's post-school goals?
- What new groups might the youth affiliate with to further his or her goals?
- Who is familiar with those new groups and would welcome the person in?

A second point of analysis is to consider the types of relationships represented in the student's current and future networks (e.g., acquaintances, friends, family, colleagues, professionals). If the student's relationships are of only one or two types, is there a need to increase the variety of relationships in order to reduce social vulnerability and increase access to opportunities? Does the student accurately recognize the role others ascribe to him or her? A further point of exploration is to develop individually referenced definitions of these relationships. What does "friend" mean to the student? What kinds of friendships are important to the student? Does the

Table 14.1 Sample social-network questions

- In what activities do you regularly participate at (home/community/work/school)? How often? Where?
- With whom do you typically interact in these activities? How?
- What is your relationship with (identified individuals)?
- How long have you known (identified individuals)? How did you meet him/her?
- Who else is involved in these activities? What is your relationship to them?
- Who else do you talk to on the phone (or email/text) regularly? What do you talk about?
- Which of the people you've named do you consider most important to you?
- Is there anyone else whom you haven't named who is very important to you or whose opinions mean a lot to you?
- Who else do you know that could tell others about you (e.g., what you like to do, what you are good at doing)?
- Which of these activities and people will you continue to be in contact with later/after you leave school?
- If you were doing (an activity) at (home/school/work/community) and needed help getting something done, whom would you ask?
- If you were at (home/school/work/community) and wanted some advice, whom would you ask?
- If you were at (home/school/work/community) and wanted to do something fun, whom would you ask to join you?

student understand what an "acquaintance" is and why acquaintances are equally as important as having friends?

A third take on relationships is to consider whether the young person's level of social engagement in current and future activities is or will be sufficient to promote a sense of belonging and the recognition by others that the young person is an integral and valued part of the activity. Who would miss the young person if he or she were not present during the activity? What degree of presence and participation is personally meaningful to the young person? What variety of social roles are available within the activity? What kinds of supports (e.g., accommodations, assistive technology, personal assistance) would promote the young person's inclusion in the activity? Wolfensberger (2000) reminds those who work with people who have disabilities, especially intellectual disabilities, that it is important to attend to messages of "valuing" and "devaluing" of an individual that are being conveyed in social activities on multiple levels: physical context and environment; social context and environment; behaviors and activities; language used with and about people; and individuals' personal appearance. Teaching young disabled people strategies for proactive and reactive construction of social acceptance can assist them to be agents in their own social development (Devine & Lashua, 2002).

Conclusion

As youth with disabilities begin their transitions from school to adult life, they also must begin to develop new social relationships that enhance the social capital they will need for success in the adult world. Beyond learning social skills that have relevance in post-school environments, they also must begin to identify and explore new forms of social supports in those environments. Mentors and other cultural brokers can facilitate the bonding and bridging needed to extend youths' networks of supportive relationships across environments. Further, youth can learn self-advocacy, problem-solving and other strategies that prepare them to take advantage of opportunities within their emerging adult networks and become self-determined, fully participating members of their communities.

References

Alwell, M., & Cobb, B. (2007). Social/communicative interventions and transition outcomes for youth with disabilities: A systematic review. *What works in transition: Systematic review project.* Colorado State University. Available at http://www.nsttac.org/pdf/social_communications_skills_full_text.pdf

Amado, A. N., & Mc Bride, M. (2001). *Increasing person-centered thinking: Improving the quality of person-centered planning: A manual for person-centered planning facilitators.* Minneapolis: University of Minnesota, Institute on Community Integration.

Autism Ambassadors. (n.d.). Available at http://www.autismambassadors.org

Black, R. S., & Langone, J. (1997). Social awareness and transition to employment for adolescents with mental retardation. *Remedial and Special Education, 18*(4), 214–222.

Black, R. S., & Ornelles, C. (2001). Assessment of social competence and social networks for transition. *Assessment for Effective Intervention, 26*(4), 23–39.

Bourdieu, P. (1986). The forms of capital. In J. Richardson (Ed.), Handbook of theory and research for the sociology of education (pp. 241–258). New York: Greenwood.

Brinckerhoff, L. C. (1996). Making the transition to higher education: Opportunities for student empowerment. Journal of Learning Disabilities *29*, 118–136.

Butterworth, J., Hagner, D., Heikkinen, B., Faris, S., DeMello S. & McDonough, K. (1993). Social network interview guide. In *Whole life planning: A guide for organizers and facilitators.* Boston: University of Massachusetts, Institute for Community Inclusion.

Butterworth, J., Hagner, D., Helm, D. T., & Whelley, T. A. (2000). Workplace culture, social interactions, and supports for transition-age young adults. *Mental Retardation, 38*(4), 342–353.

Chadsey, J., & Shelden, D. (1998). Moving toward social inclusion in employment and postsecondary school settings. In F. Rusch & J. Chadsey (Eds.) Beyond high school: Transition from school to work (pp. 406–437). Belmont, CA: Wadsworth.

Clark, G. (1998). *Assessment for transitions planning.* Austin, TX: PRO-ED.

Copeland, S. R., McCall, J., Williams, C. R., Guth, C., Carter, E. W., Presley, J. A. (2002). High school peer buddies: A win-win situation. *TEACHING Exceptional Children, 35*(1), 16–21.

Deci, E., Vallerand, R., Pelletier, L., & Ryan, R. (1991). Motivation and education: The self-determination perspective. *Educational Psychologist, 26*(3 & 4), 325–346.

Devine, M., & Lashua, B. (2002). Constructing social acceptance in inclusive leisure contexts: The role of individuals with disabilities. *Therapeutic Recreation Journal, 36* (1), 65–83.

Eisenman, L.T. (2007). Self-determination interventions: Building a foundation for school completion. *Remedial and Special Education, 28*(1), 2–8.

Eisenman, L. T., & Mancini, K. (2009). College perspectives and issues. In M. Grigal & D. Hart (Eds.), *Think college: Post-secondary education options for students with intellectual disabilities* (pp. 161–187). Baltimore: Paul H. Brookes.

Eisenman, L. T., Tanverdi, A., Perrington, C., & Geiman, A. (2009). Community and social activities of youth with significant intellectual disabilities. Education and Training in Developmental Disabilities, *44*, 168–176.

Elksnin, N. & Elksnin, L. K. (1998). *Teaching occupational social skills.* Austin, TX: PRO-ED.

Farmer, T. W., Pearl, R., & Van Acker, R. (1996). Expanding the social skills deficit framework: A developmental synthesis perspective, classroom social networks, and implications for the social growth of students with disabilities. *Journal of Special Education, 30*(3), 232–256.

Forrester-Jones, R., Jones, S., Heason, S. & Di'Terlizzi, M. (2004). Supported employment: A route to social networks. Journal of Applied Research in Intellectual Disabilities, *17*, 199–208.

Garrison-Wade, D. F., & Lehmann, J. P. (2009). A conceptual framework for understanding students' with disabilities transition to community college. Community College Journal of Research and Practice, *33*(5), 417–445.

Gerber, P., Ginsberg, R., & Reiff, H. (1992). Identifying alterable patterns in employment success for highly successful adults with learning disabilities. Journal of Learning Disabilities, *25*, 475–487.

Getzel, E., & Thoma, C. (2008). Experiences of college students with disabilities and the importance of self-determination in higher education settings. Career Development for Exceptional Individuals, *31*(2), 77–84.

Gresham, F., Sugai, G., & Horner, R. (2001). Interpreting outcomes of social skills training for students with high-incidence disabilities. *Exceptional Children, 67*(3), 331–344.

Hagner, D., Butterworth, J., & Keith, G. (1995). Strategies and barriers in facilitating natural supports for employment of adults with severe disabilities. *Journal of the Association for Persons with Severe Handicaps, 20*, 110–120.

Hagner, D., & DiLeo, D. (1993). *Working together: Workplace culture, supported employment, and persons with disabilities.* Cambridge, MA: Brookline Books.

Halpern, A. S. (1994). The transition of youth with disabilities to adult life: A position statement of the Division on Career Development and Transition. Career Development for Exceptional Individuals, *17*, 115–124.

Hillier, A., Fish, T., Cloppert, P., & Beversdorf, D. (2007). Outcomes of a social and vocational skills support group for adolescents and young adults on the autism spectrum. *Focus on Autism and Other Developmental Disabilities, 22*(2), 107–115.

Hughes, C., & Carter, E. (2000). *The transition handbook: Strategies high school teachers use that work!* Baltimore: Paul H. Brookes.

Irvine, A., & Lupart, J. (2006). Social supports in inclusive settings: An essential component to community. *Developmental Disabilities Bulletin, 34*(1–2), 107–126.

Knox, M., & Parmenter, T. (1993). Social networks and support mechanisms for people with mild intellectual disability in competitive employment. International Journal of Rehabilitation Research, *16*, 1–12.

Leake, D., & Cholymay, M. (2004). Addressing the needs of culturally and linguistically diverse students with disabilities in postsecondary education. *Information Brief, 3*(1). National Center on Secondary Education and Transition, University of Minnesota. Available at http://www.ncset.org/publications/viewdesc.asp?id=1411

Lovitt, T., Emerson, J. (2008). Foster youth who have succeeded in higher education: Common themes. Information Brief, 7(1). Minneapolis: University of Minnesota, National Center on Secondary Education and Transition. Institute on Community Integration. Available at http://www.ncset.org/publications/viewdesc.asp?id=4195

Mull, C., Sitlington, P. L. & Alper, S. (2001). Postsecondary education for students with learning disabilities: A synthesis of the literature. Exceptional Children, *68*(1), 97–118.

Murray, C. (2003). Risk factors, protective factors, vulnerability, and resilience: A framework for understanding and supporting the adult transitions of youth with high-incidence disabilities. Remedial and Special Education *24*(1), 24–26.

Newman, L., Wagner, M., Cameto, R., & Knokey, A. -M. (2009). Social and community involvement of out-of-high school youth with disabilities (Chapter 6). In The post-high school outcomes of youth with disabilities up to 4 years after high school. A report of findings from the National Longitudinal Transition Study-2 (NLTS2) (NCSER 2009-3017). Menlo Park, CA: SRI International. Available at www.nlts2.org/reports/2009_04/nlts2_report_2009_04_complete.pdf.

Putnam, R. (2000). Bowling alone: The collapse and revival of American community. New York: Simon & Schuster.

Sitlington, P., Neubert, P., Begun, W., Lombard, R., & Leconte, P. (2007). *Assess for success: A practitioner's handbook on transition assessment* (2nd ed.). Thousand Oaks, CA: Corwin.

Szymanski, E., & Parker, R. (Eds.) (1996). *Work and disability: Issues and strategies in career development and job placement.* Austin, TX: Pro Ed.

Trainor, A. (2008). Using cultural and social capital to improve postsecondary outcomes and expand transition models for youth with disabilities. Journal of Special Education, *42*, 148–162.

Wagner, M., Cadwallader, T., & Marder, C. (with Cameto, R., Cardoso, D., Garza, N., Levine, P., & Newman, L.). (2003). Life outside the classroom for youth with disabilities. A report from the National Longitudinal Transition Study-2 (NLTS2) (Executive Summary). Menlo Park, CA: SRI International. Available at http://www.nlts2.org/reports/2003_04-2/nlts2_report_2003_04-2_execsum.pdf

Walker, P., & O'Connor, P. (1997). Not just a place to live: Building community in Toronto. (ED412683). Syracuse, NY: Center on Human Policy, Syracuse University.

Wang, P., & Spillane, A. (2009). Evidence-based social skills interventions for children with autism: A meta-analysis. *Education and Training in Developmental Disabilities, 44*(3), 318–342.

Widmer, E. D., Kempf-Constantin, N., Robert-Tissot, C., Lanzi, F., Carminati, G. G. (2008). How central and connected am in my family? Family-based social capital of individuals with intellectual disability. Research in Developmental Disabilities: A Multidisciplinary Journal, *29*(2), 176–187.

Wolfensberger, W. (2000). A brief overview of social role valorization. *Mental Retardation, 38*(2), 105–125.

15

Assistive Technology in the Transition Education Process

Karen B. Patterson

UNIVERSITY OF NORTH FLORIDA

Terrence Cavanaugh

UNIVERSITY OF NORTH FLORIDA

The future is here. It's just not widely distributed yet.

(William Gibson)

Assistive and adaptive technology, both with and without the use of computers, is quickly becoming an integral part of our education system and society; many of our society's contributing members, such as Stephen Hawking, could not function without such technology. Assistive technology (AT) is primarily designed to allow individuals with disabilities access to information. With the use of adaptive technologies, computers can become the eyes, ears, voices, and hands for many individuals. Special education programs in American public schools provide resources such as AT and AT services to students with special needs. Many consider the use of the AT to be the great leveler or equalizer for those students with disabilities (Flippo, Inge, & Bareus, 1995).

Essentially, assistive technology is a tool that provides access and promotes independence for individuals with disabilities across all facets of life.

Assistive technology is defined as: ". . . any item, piece of equipment or product system, whether acquired commercially off the shelf, modified, or customized, that is used to increase, maintain, or improve functional capabilities of individuals with disabilities." An assistive technology service is defined as: ". . . any service that directly assists an individual with a disability in the selection, acquisition, or use of an assistive technology device," 20 U.S.C. § Chapter 33, Section 1401 (p. 250).

The broadness of the legal definition of AT and AT services allows for a wide array of devices and services, as long as these devices and services improve functionality. Assistive technology tools can make a significant difference for individuals with disabilities in educational, employment, family, and community settings because AT and AT services provide access to information and activities that otherwise could be inaccessible.

In an educational setting, AT has the potential for promoting independence, increasing participation in educational activities, and simultaneously advancing academic standing for individuals with disabilities. Through the use of AT devices, many students with disabilities can decrease their isolation and become active participants in classrooms. Further, students who are not physically present in the learning environment can still participate fully through the use of technological or electronic supports.

Educational technology is instrumental in solving instructional and performance problems when combined with other concepts like the application of research, learning theories, emergent technology and psychology. This interdisciplinary overlap is known as Assistive Educational Technology (AET). AET is the theory and practice of design, development, utilization, management, and evaluation of processes and resources that are used to increase, maintain, or improve functional capabilities of individuals for learning (Cavanaugh, 2000). The complexity and importance of AET cannot be overemphasized as students and their transition teams develop the transition segments of Individualized Education Plans (IEPs). Students must practice using AT and AT services; therefore middle school and high school years should be used to refine their needs as they practice using AT and AT services.

The use of AT is typically individualized and tailored for the uniquely personal needs of the student. Subsequently, many AT and AT services intervention studies are single-subject research design and include small numbers of study participants; research-based practices regarding the use of AT are limited as research results may not be generalizable to other settings and individuals. This scenario may contribute to the concern voiced by experts in the field about the dearth of AT research (Campbell, Milbourne, Dugan, & Wilcox, 2006; Salminen, 2008). For example, the National Center for Technology Innovation, during the AT Outcomes Summit, identified one of the challenges concerning the integration of technology into general practice as being the absence of an AT outcomes research base to steer policy (National Center for Technology Innovation, 2005).

Legislation and Assistive Technology

Federal requirements and support for special education and AT began with Section 504 of the Rehabilitation Act of 1973. The passage of this legislation is significant because it impacts *all* students with disabilities, even those who are not eligible for special education services and do not have IEPs. This is important to students who, though they may not have an IEP, are entitled to educational accommodations, including AT and AT services, in order to access educational opportunities (Dell, Newton, & Petroff, 2008; Copenhaver, 2004).

In 1975, the Education for All Handicapped Children Act (EHA) began the process of (a) ensuring equal access for children with disabilities, (b) funding educational opportunities and programs from which many students had been excluded, and (c) started identifying assistive devices and services to support students' education. In 1986, public law 99-457 reauthorized the EHA, changing its name to the Individuals with Disabilities Education Act (IDEA). The IDEA regulation states:

> Each state must establish procedures to assure that, to the maximum extent appropriate, children with disabilities . . . are educated with children who are not disabled, and that special education, separate schooling, or other removal of children with disabilities from the regular educational environment occurs only when the nature or severity of the disability is such that education in regular classes with the use of supplementary aids and services cannot be achieved satisfactorily. (20 U.S.C. § 1412(5)(B))

Although the Individuals with Disabilities Education Improvement Act 2004 (IDEIA, or commonly referred to as IDEA) is the most recent reauthorization of the federal law that regulates the education of students with disabilities in P-12 settings, it was the 1997 reauthorization that changed the role of AT. This reauthorization clearly defined AT and required consideration of the AT needs of every student receiving special education services. IDEA 1997 also adopted the definition of AT established by the Technology-Related Assistance for Individuals with

Disabilities Act of 1988 (Tech Act). This law was passed by Congress to provide funding for the development of consumer information and training programs for individuals with disabilities. Consequently, this action led to an increase in the number of students and a broader range of disabilities that were considered for technology-related services.

IDEIA regulations have significantly impacted the responsibilities of schools when considering a student's AT needs. While each case is individualized, AT is generally considered if it will increase student participation in the "free and appropriate public education" (FAPE) environment and if it can help maintain students in their "least restrictive environment" (LRE). Furthermore, this technology can extend from school to home if a need is determined. The following federal legislations described in Table 15.1 have all impacted the use of computers/technology in education and transition to adulthood:

Table 15.1 Laws impacting assistive technology

Law	Date	Content that applies to assistive technology
Rehabilitation Act 93–112	1973	Reasonable accommodations and LRE mandated in federally funded employment and higher education; AT devices and services required
Vocational Rehabilitation Act, Section 504	1973	AT can be used as an accommodation to enhance student participation in school activities
Education for All Handicapped Children Act (EHA) 94–142	1975	Reasonable accommodations and LRE were extended to all school-age children; IEPs mandated; AT played a major role in gaining access to educational programs
Preschool and Infant/ Toddler Program – amendments to EHA	1986	Reasonable accommodations and LRE were extended to children from age 3 to 5; expanded emphasis on educationally related assistive technologies
Technology Related Assistance for Individuals with Disabilities Act (Tech Act) 100–407	1988	First federal legislation directly related to assistive technology; defined AT devices and services; stressed consumer-driven systems and systems changes
Individuals with Disabilities Education Act (IDEA) 101–496	1990 & 1997	Specifically defined assistive technology devices and services as well as delineated how they apply to education and transition services; reauthorization required AT needs be considered in an IEP
Assistive Technology Act ATA 105–394	1998	(Re-authorization of the Tech Act) Under Title I in the new ATA, states and funded territories are required to conduct the following activities: 1 Support a public awareness program designed to provide information related to the availability and benefits of assistive technology devices and assistive technology services. 2 Promote inter-agency coordination that improves access to assistive technology devices and services for individuals of all ages with disabilities. 3 Provide technical assistance and training including the development and implementation of laws, regulations, policies, practices, procedures, or organizational structures that promote access to assistive technology devices and services. 4 Provide outreach support to statewide community-based organizations that provide assistive devices or services to individuals with disabilities or assist individuals in using assistive technology devices and services including focusing on individuals from underrepresented and rural populations.

Assistive Technology and the Individualized Education Program

The Individualized Education Program (IEP) is a written legal document that is developed for any child with a disability who is eligible for services. This document is important for children with disabilities, their educators and other stakeholders, including those persons who may be responsible for providing or paying for AT and AT services. IEP components include:

- A statement of the student's present levels of academic achievement and functional performance;
- A statement of measurable annual goals;
- A description of how the student's progress toward meeting the annual goals will be measured;
- A statement of the special education and related services and supplementary aids, based on peer-reviewed research to the extent attainable, that are to be provided to the student and a statement of the program modification or supports for the school personnel that will be provided to enable the student to be included in the general education curriculum and advance appropriately toward the established goals;
- An explanation of the extent, if any, to which a student will not participate with nondisabled students in inclusive settings;
- An explanation of the need for the student to take an alternative assessment instead of a state or district assessment;
- The projected date for the beginning of the services and modifications and the anticipated frequency, location, and duration of special education and related services, supplementary aids and services, and modifications and supports (U.S. Department of Education's Office of Special Education Programs, 2009).

IEP standards must reflect scientifically based instructional practices, cognitive behavioral interventions, and early intervention services, as appropriate. They must also include plans for the use of AT. Decisions about the use of technology should be made in collaboration with the team that develops the student's IEP. Moreover, IDEIA amendments require that AT devices and services be considered on an individualized basis as the use of AT or services to achieve success is based on each student's needs. The IDEIA statements concerning the need and application of AT require that the IEP team ask a series of questions about AT devices and/or services. For example:

- Will AT enable the student to meet the goals set for the education program that cannot be met because of his/her disability?
- Does the student need assistive technology to be involved in the general curriculum, including participation in state- and district-wide assessments?
- Does the student need AT for augmentative communication?
- Does the student need to use the device at home or in the community to achieve the goals of the IEP?

If the answer to any of the above questions is yes, then needed AT devices and/or services must be provided to the student (Florida Department of Education, 2000).

IEPs and Transition

A transition plan must be included in all IEPs for students at age 16, or for younger students if appropriate, and transition services must include instruction, community experiences, development of employment, and other post-school adult-living objectives (Kirk, Gallagher,

Coleman, & Anastasiow, 2012). However, as students prepare to transition to postsecondary educational settings, it is important to note that the AT currently being used by the student will not automatically transfer to the new setting. This is often a surprising fact to the user, parents, and other personnel who may assume that AT devices or services will transition with the individual. Careful attention and planning are required across the lifespan of individuals with disabilities and the area of transition is a critical juncture. Behnke and Bowser (2010) identified six best practices identified by the Quality Indicators in Assistive Technology (QIAT Consortium, 2005) as characteristics of exemplary transition planning for AT:

1   Transition plans address AT needs of the student, including the roles and training needs of team members, subsequent steps in AT use, and follow-up after transition takes place.
2   Transition planning empowers the student using AT to participate in the transition-planning process at a level appropriate to age and ability.
3   Advocacy related to AT use is recognized as critical and planned for by the teams involved in the transition.
4   AT requirements in the receiving environment (e.g., environmental requirements, skill demands, and needed support) are identified during the transition-planning process by representatives from both the sending and receiving environments.
5   Transition planning for AT proceeds according to an individualized timeline with clear action steps and specific target dates identified.
6   Transition plans address specific equipment, training, and funding issues such as transfer or acquisition of AT, manuals, and provisions for ongoing maintenance and technical support.

AT can be applied in many situations within the school, classroom, employment, community, and other educational or personal settings as students transition to postsecondary education. Among the areas of application are existence (necessary to sustain life), communication (oral and written expression, as well as visual and auditory reception and social interaction), positioning (body support), mobility (navigation), physical education (adaptive materials that enable participation in physical activities), and environmental interaction (activities associated with daily living) (Poel, 2007). While these areas are all part of AT, their functions and the way in which they are implemented vary considerably.

For example, some AT tools may be more appropriate accommodations for students in the middle and secondary grade levels because of the educational focus and the goals and objectives identified on the IEP. As students transition to postsecondary adult settings, the focus should broaden to include other aspects of daily living, necessitating the needs for other tools (U.S. Department of Education's Office of Special Education Programs, 2009) that could include:

Computer access
- Alternative mouse and/or keyboard
- Narration tool for voice output
- Speech recognition software

Classroom Interaction and Lecture
- Sign language interpreter
- Notetaking assistant or other notetaking tools
- FM amplification or captioning system

Personal Organization
- Talking watch
- Scheduling software
- Phone/page reminder service/software

Studying/Learning
- Graphic organizer software
- Digital recorder
- Computer files provided by professor

Test-taking
- Extended time or oral testing
- Low-distraction testing environment
- Use of computer for testing

Mathematics
- Talking or large key calculator
- High-contrast graph paper or geoboard
- Visual graphing software

Reading
- Audio book or digital text version for text-to-speech
- Large-print, Braille material or computer Braille display
- Screen magnifier

Writing
- Computer or portable word processor
- Electronic spell checker and dictionary
- Speech recognition software.

AT Classification, Resources and Support

When AT needs are being considered, one must evaluate the environment, the individual, and the characteristics and levels of the technology being incorporated (Lee, 2008). While it is common for many to think of AT as being sophisticated, complicated, and computer-driven, that is not always the case. Assistive technology can be classified as low-, middle-, or high-tech (Kirk, Gallagher, et al., 2012).

- Low-tech devices are usually easy to use, have low cost, and typically do not require a power source. Devices may include non-electronic devices like pencil grips, adaptive spoon handles, and picture boards.
- Middle-tech are also easy to operate but do typically require a power source. Examples include things like audio books, word-processing computers, and tape recorders.
- High-tech devices are usually complex and programmable. They are typically specifically designed to support an individual's needs and may include speech recognition software, electronic communication devices, and mobility technologies for guiding wheel chairs.

An example of the application of technology could range from having a voice input word processor (high tech) to a student using an adapted pencil grip (low tech) to assist a student in writing (Dell, Newton, et al., 2008).

Along with considering the level of the technology needed, one must also consider how the AT devices or services could be applied into the classroom environment. Consideration should be given to whether a device is *personally, developmentally,* or *instructionally* necessary when needs are determined (Assistive Technology Categories, 2000). Personally necessary items are devices that are used by an individual to effectively interact with his or her environment; personally necessary items are not typically shared (Assistive Technology Categories, 2000). Developmentally necessary devices and/or services may be shared among individuals; these devices help to meet an educational need based on a developmental delay, which is likely to not exist in the future, thereby eliminating the need for future use (Assistive Technology Categories, 2000). Lastly, instructionally necessary devices and/or services are ones that have modified the instructional process to promote user success (Assistive Technology Categories, 2000).

The following are examples of the range of AT categories that are frequently considered when planning for an individual's needs (Assistive Technology Categories, 2000):

Aids for Daily Living/Self Care
- Aids to improve self-help skills and encourage independence in activities such as cooking, eating, dressing, toileting, and home maintenance. Examples include: modified utensils

Communication/Augmentative Communication
- Electronic and non-electronic devices that enhance communication skills for persons who are semi-intelligible or non-verbal. Examples include: communication board/book with pictures/objects/letters/words, eye gaze board/frame, voice output device, and devices with speech synthesis for typing.

Computer Access
- Devices that enable persons with disabilities to use a computer. Examples include: input and output devices (voice, Braille), alternative access aids (headsticks, light pointers), modified or alternative keyboards, switches, and special software.

Environmental Controls
- Electronic systems that enable someone without mobility to control various devices such as appliances, electronic aids, and security systems in her or his room, home or other surroundings.

Computer Based Instruction
- Computer-based instruction can directly provide instruction or can allow alternative ways of responding. Examples of direct instruction include instructional software and distance learning; alternative responding software provides tools for written expression, spelling, and calculation.

Instructional Material Aids
- Tools that can substitute for or assist with instructional classroom applications; subcategories can include composing written materials, reading, math, learning and studying. Examples include: handwriting tools, audiotape players, Braille displays, print magnifiers, and calculators.

Leisure time or Recreational Adaptations
- Structural adaptations to promote participation in cultural events and leisure time activities for individuals with disabilities. Examples include: use of battery interrupters and switches to operate devices, universal cuff to hold crayons, markers, paint brush, adaptive sporting equipment, and drawing or graphic programs on a computer.

Mobility Aids
- Vehicles used to increase personal mobility. Examples include: manual and electric wheel-chairs, mobile bases for custom chairs, walkers, three-wheel scooters, scooters, modifications of vans for travel, and canes used by pedestrians who are blind or have low vision.

Prosthetics and Orthotics Replacements
- Substitution or augmentation of missing or malfunctioning body parts with artificial limbs or other orthotic aids (splints, braces, etc.).

Seating and Positioning Aids
- Aids that assist people in maintaining body alignment and control so they can perform a range of daily tasks. Examples include: adapted seating, standing tables, seat belts, braces, transfer aids, cushions and wedges to maintain posture, and devices for trunk alignment.

Sensory Aids (visual aids/assistive listening)
- Devices for people who are blind, have low vision or are hard of hearing. Examples include: talking electronic device/software to pronounce challenging words, scanner with OCR and auditory output, audio books, close captioning, light or audio warnings, and personal amplification systems.

The use of AT devices promotes independence, self-confidence, freedom, and meaningful participation in daily activities. With the advances in technology, AT devices are no longer confined to any one setting so individuals with disabilities can make seamless transitions across settings without losing existence, communication, positioning, mobility, physical education, and/or environmental interaction. Such transitions are only possible, however, with adequate AT resources and support.

Several states provide technological assistance to users of AT devices. For example, Florida Alliance for Assistive Services and Technology and Oregon's Statewide Assistive Technology Program (http://www.accesstechnologiesinc.org) provide information and referrals about devices and services to individuals with disabilities. Some states also have AT libraries that can provide short-term device loans, device demonstrations, device exchange and recycling programs, and funding resources for AT. A list of state organizations that provide such services is available from the RESNA Catalyst Project (see http://www.resnaprojects.org/scripts/contacts.pl).

Assistive Technology and Transition to Postsecondary Education

The attainment of postsecondary education has been shown to improve the chances for meaningful employment, increased vocational options, and better lifetime earnings (Heward, 2003). The National Center for the Study of Postsecondary Education Supports (2000) recommended that (a) students have opportunities during secondary education to understand themselves and their disability in relation to needed services and supports and (b) secondary programs develop models of assistance that are individualized to meet the needs of the student with a disability in the postsecondary setting.

The manner in which AT is managed may change as the student moves from the PK-12 arena to a postsecondary education setting. As discussed multiple times in this handbook, the AT and AT services students receive under IDEIA are entitlements; in other words, students receive AT and AT services as accommodations mandated by their IEPs. In postsecondary settings, these same AT and AT services must be requested by the adult student, the need must be documented by a licensed professional, and services must be approved by the disability service office at the postsecondary education institution.

While a substantial body of literature currently exists within the field of special education that describes the importance of technology in elementary and secondary curriculum (Blackhurst & MacArthur, 1986; Smith, 2000), the research at the postsecondary level tends to be less comprehensive and limited to specific aspects or applications of technology (Michaels, Prezant, Morabbito, & Jackson, 2002). Effective and appropriate implementation of technology will require that colleges and universities develop comprehensive and systematic plans for AT services and delivery (Raskind & Higgins, 1998). However, when 977 postsecondary institutions were surveyed, less than 50% reported that they had a policy or an institution-wide planning process for the purchase and use of new technology. Of those institutions with policies in place, only half reported they consider the needs of students with disabilities and/or that they would request input from the Office for Students with Disabilities before making technology decisions (U.S. Department of Education, 1999; Michaels, Prezant, et al., 2002). As indicated by the Tech Act, AT promotes:

> (a) individuals to have greater control over their own lives, (b) participate in and contribute more fully to activities in their home, school and work environments, and in their communities, (c) interact to a great extent with non-disabled individuals, and (d) otherwise benefit from opportunities that are taken for granted by individuals who do not have disabilities.
>
> (p.1044)

When the appropriate AT is carefully aligned with the necessary environment modifications and the needs of an individual, the likelihood exists for improvement in the overall quality of life for individuals. However, certain barriers exist when moving from secondary education to postsecondary education that could be prevented with careful attention to AT instruction and infrastructure, transition practices, and self-determination. For example, Houchins (2001) identified the following barriers: lack of early transition planning by high schools; insufficient AT training in high schools; lack of collaboration between high school and postsecondary institutions; lack of AT assessment/evaluation; insufficient AT training in high schools for students; postsecondary faculty is unaware of AT; high schools lack knowledge of AT; lack of follow-up once the student has AT equipment; postsecondary faculty is unaware of general adaptations; and rural areas have limited services. The following statement emphatically underscores the importance of the effective and efficient use of AT in meeting the needs of individuals with disabilities:

AT is a lifespan issue. Whether the individual is in a secondary, postsecondary, or adulthood setting, AT can significantly alter their quality of life. To negate the AT needs of individuals, disabilities at any stage in their lives, is to deny them their dignity, independence, self-determination, and potentially their very existence. (Houchins, 2001, p. 85)

In a study that addressed the perceptions of postsecondary service providers to students with disabilities, Michaels, Prezant, et al. (2002) had the following recommendations for improving the access and delivery of AT and instructional technology (IT) services to students with disabilities in postsecondary educational environments:

1   The actual achievement of AT access, training, awareness, and usage must be brought into closer alignment with the perceived importance.
2   There is a need for administrative, programmatic and fiscal support and collaboration to address the limited availability of AT on college campuses as well as the high costs associated with rapid changes and upgrades.
3   Access to IT must be considered more frequently and by the entire college community.
4   Providing full access to both AT and IT services requires the consideration of technology needs across academic programs and departments.

While colleges and universities are required to provide auxiliary aids and services at no cost to the student as a reasonable accommodation, they are not required to provide individualized or requested AT directly to the student. Auxiliary aids and services refer to the devices and services that allow the student with disabilities to function within the institution's environment. It is also acceptable for a higher educational institution to provide a different technology product from the one originally requested by the student. Table 15.2 shows examples of obligations under the Americans with Disabilities Act (ADA) for higher educational institutions and students with disabilities. Table 15.3 compares the requirements and procedures of the (ADA) and the Individuals with Disabilities Education Act (IDEA).

Table 15.2 Colleges' and students' obligations under the ADA

College obligations under the ADA	Student obligations under the ADA
Ensure that qualified applicants and students have access to the college's programs	Self-identify that she/he has a disability (by following the specific college's stated policies and procedures); provide appropriate documentation of disability
Provide reasonable accommodations for the student's documented disabilities	Request specific accommodation(s)
Demonstrate a good faith effort to provide the student with meaningful access	Follow the agreed-upon procedures for using accommodations

Table 15.3 Comparison of the Requirements and Procedures of the Americans with Disabilities Act (ADA) and the Individuals with Disabilities Education Act (IDEA)

	IDEA (K-12)	ADA (College)
Rights guaranteed by the law	Free, appropriate public education (FAPE)	Prohibits discrimination on the basis of disability
Who is covered	Every child; concept of zero reject	Students who are "otherwise qualified"
Identification and evaluation of students with disabilities	District is responsible for identifying students with disabilities, evaluating them, and covering costs	College has no such responsibility; student must self-identify and provide appropriate documentation and if an evaluation is needed, the expense is the student's responsibility
Determining services	Individualized education plan (IEP) developed by team; curriculum modifications and special programs are common	Reasonable accommodations, including auxiliary aids; student must request services; academic adjustments that equalize opportunity for participation are required; substantial modifications to curriculum and lowering standards are not required
Personal devices and services (wheelchairs, hearing aids, and personal care attendants)	Provided by district if determined to be necessary (and included in IEP)	Colleges are not required to provide personal devices/services
Role of parents	Parents must be included in decision-making	College students are over 18 and are considered adults; parent consultation is not required
Appeals process	Right to due process as defined by law	College grievance procedure; file a complaint with the USDOE Office of Civil Rights

Source: Used with permission from "Transition: There are no IEPs in college" by A. Dell. Retrieved from http://www.tcnj.edu/~technj/2004/transition.htm

Assistive Technology and the Transition to Employment

The transition from an educational setting, secondary or postsecondary, to employment is rarely without its challenges. Individuals with disabilities, especially those who rely on assistive technology, face even greater challenges than the average job seeker due to the stigma encircling their disability and their need for workplace supports; employment is a domain that exhibits a visibly wide gap between the general population and individuals with disabilities (Johnson, Stodden, Emanuel, Luecking, & Mack, 2002). Assistive technology can be utilized as a tool to reduce this gap, if all stakeholders (individuals, families, teachers, employers, etc.) are made aware of the technology available to individuals with disabilities and potential employers (Burgstahler, 2003).

Use of assistive technology in preparation for employment is a critical discussion for many students to have with their families, agencies, and school personnel. Several studies have indicated that usage of assistive technology is directly related to employment outcomes. McDonnall and Crudden (2009) reported that use of assistive technology, along with work experience and self-determination, were associated with employment for transition-age youths who were blind or had low vision. In another study, parents of high school students with disabilities believed their sons or daughters who used assistive technology were 1.5 times more likely to eventually have a paid job than the parents of those who did not use assistive technology (Kelly, 2011).

Assistive technology devices, sometimes known as ATDs, can facilitate the performance of the tasks the individual wants to complete, thus giving the individual confidence and authentic connection to employment performance (Scherer, Elias, & Weider, 2010). For example, Burke and colleagues (2010) used a performance cue system consisting of an iPhone application that was adapted to teach social-vocational skills to six young adults with Autism Spectrum Disorder. Five of the adults reached expectations using the cue system, results that have implications for future study in other employment settings. Scherer, Elias, et al. (2010) used ATDs to assist individuals with Traumatic Brain Injury with short-term memory and executive skills. By using ATDs to help structure daily routines, appointments, and tasks, they reported that individuals had an enhanced quality of life and higher employment performance.

Employers are not always very familiar with assistive technology as evidence by relating literature. For example, in a study on the perceptions of employers in regard to hiring individuals with disabilities, employers stated "we do not have experience in this area" or "it [applying advanced technology to employment of people with disabilities] has not become important" (Greenan, Wu, & Black, 2002, p. 32). Those that were aware of assistive technology were reluctant to use AT in their business or even hire an individual that required AT due to the high cost of the technology and/or the cost to implement the technology (Greenan, Wu, et al., 2002). This resistance due to cost is another example of lack of awareness on the part of the general population. Though the cost of assistive technology falls to individuals or business, there is funding available to both groups to defer some or all of the costs. If the need for AT is medically related, Medicare is a good resource for locating funding (see http://www.medicare.gov); if the need for AT is more of a lifestyle issue, Vocational Rehabilitation provides services and funding (see Florida's Division of Vocational Rehabilitation, http://www.rehabworks.org/).

Overall, employers seem to have a positive outlook on assistive technology in the workplace, believing that AT could be used in their business (Greenan, Wu, et al., 2002). For those employers that already provide accommodations like alternative trainings or job restructuring to nondisabled employees for the sake of employee productivity, utilizing assistive technology is not that large a leap (Luecking & Mooney, 2002). This leap must be facilitated by practices at the start of the transition from education to employment; however, the connection between educational institutions and the business sector must be strengthened with an exchange of knowledge and joint benefits (Burgstahler, 2003). Students with disabilities must also be involved in all stages of assistive technology selection and application so they develop the self-advocacy skills needed to retain assistive technology in the workplace (Burgstahler, 2003).

As students, families, and professionals incorporate Assistive Technology Devices into transition planning, they must be cognizant of the purposes and ultimate outcomes that any assistive devices offer, namely performance and communication. Murphy (2009) cautioned that using assistive technology in work environments, especially augmentative and alternative communication is about human communication, rather than the specific technology.

AT Professional Development and Ethical Considerations

An important consideration is for school leaders to provide and participate in effective professional development opportunities so that school personnel understand the role of AT in helping students with disabilities to be effective and successful learners. Meaningful, standards-based professional development should be connected to how AT is utilized to promote successful learning outcomes within the general education curriculum (Dyal, Carpenter, & Wright, 2009). Another important consideration refers to the ethical conduct of school personnel within all aspects of operating a school. Individuals with disabilities are protected under special laws because of historical illegal and unethical treatment of persons with disabilities (Dyal et al., 2009). Additionally, students with disabilities remain vulnerable to mistreatment even within the school environment (Dyal et al., 2009). Therefore, all school personnel must understand and practice ethical codes of behavior.

Future Directions

The future is here. Technology is rapidly changing and this change will provide access for a greater number of individuals with disabilities to live meaningful lives. With the increase in options, information, and needs, several challenges are inherent. However, the need still exists for students to be self-advocates as they transition to postsecondary settings, for greater collaboration with families and professionals, and for a stronger focus on developing or restructuring a seamless service delivery system that guarantees access.

References

Americans with Disabilities Act (ADA), P. L. 101–336 (1990).

Assistive Technology Act (ATA), P. L. 105–394 (1998).

Burgstahler, S. (2003). The role of technology in preparing youth with disabilities for postsecondary education and employment. *Journal of Special Education Technology, 18*(4), 7–19.

Burke, R. V., Andersen, M. N., Bowen, S. L., Howard, M. R., & Allen, K. D. (2010). Evaluation of two instruction methods to increase employment options for young adults with autism spectrum disorders. *Research in Developmental Disabilities: A Multidisciplinary Journal, 31* (6), 1223–1233.

Cavanaugh, T. (2000). *Defining assistive educational technology*. Retrieved from http://www.drscavanaugh.org/assistive/define_AIT.htm

Cavanaugh, T. (2000). *Assistive Technology Categories*. Retrieved from http://www.drscavanaugh.org/assistive/define_AIT.htm

Dell, A. (N.D.). *Transition: There are no IEPs in college*. Retrieved from http://www.tcnj.edu/ technj/2004/transition.htm

Dyal, A., Carpenter, L. B., & Wright, J. V. (2009). Assistive technology: What every school leader should know. *Education, 129*(3), 556–560.

Education for All Handicapped Children Act, P.L. 94–142 (1975).

Florida Department of Education. (2000). *Developing quality Individual Education Plans: A guide for instructional personnel and families.* Tallahassee, FL: Author.

Greenan, J. P., Wu, M., & Black, E. L. (2002). Perspectives on employing individuals with special needs. *Journal of Technology Studies, 28*(1/2), 29–37.

Heward, W. L. (2003). Exceptional children: An introduction to special education (7th ed). Upper Saddle River, NJ: Merrill/Prentice Hall.

Houchins, D. E. (2001). Assistive technology barriers and facilitators during secondary and postsecondary transitions. *Career Development for Exceptional Individuals, 24*(1), 73–88.

Individuals with Disabilities Education Act (IDEA), P.L. 99–457 (1990).

Johnson, D. R., Stodden, R. A., Emanuel, E. J., Luecking, R., & Mack, M. (2002). Current challenges facing secondary education and transition services: What research tells us. *Exceptional Children, 68*(4), 519–531.

Kelly, S.M. (2011). The use of assistive technology by high school students with visual impairments: A second look at the current problem. *Journal of Visual Impairment & Blindness, 105*(4), 235–239.

Kirk, S., Gallagher, J., Coleman, M. R., & Anastasiow, N. (2012). Educating exceptional children. Belmont, CA: Wadsworth.

Lee, H. (2008). Ensuring equal access to technology: Providing assistive technology for students with disabilities. *Theory into Practice, 47*(3), 212–219.

Luecking, R. G. & Mooney, M. (2002). Tapping employment opportunities for youth with disabilities by engaging effectively with employers. *Research to Practice Brief, 1*(3). Retrieved from www.ncset.org

McDonnall, M. C., & Crudden, A. (2009). Factors affecting the successful employment of transition-age youths with visual impairments. *Journal of Visual Impairment & Blindness, 103*(6), 329–341.

Murphy, P. (2009). Starting somewhere: Folks with unique communication needs make their way to work. *Exceptional Parent, 39*(10), 36–38.

National Center for Technology Innovation. (2005). *AT outcomes summit 2005.* Retrieved from http://www.nationaltechcenter.org/index.php/2005/12/15/at-outcomes-summit-2005/

National Center for the Study of Postsecondary Education Supports. (2000). *National survey of educational support provision to students with disabilities in postsecondary education settings.* Retrieved from www.rrtc.hawaii.edu/documents/products/phase1/037-H01.pdf

Oregon's Statewide Assistive Technology Program. Retrieved from http://www.accesstechnologiesinc.org

Poel, E. W. (2007). Enhancing what students can do. *Educational Leadership, 64*(5), 64–66.

QIAT Consortium (2005). *Quality indicators for assistive technology services.* Retrieved from http://natri.uky.edu/assoc_projects/qiat/documents/6%20QIAT%20QIs%20Transition.pdf

Raskind, M. H., & Higgins, E. L. (1998). Assistive technology for postsecondary students with learning disabilities: An overview. *Journal of Learning Disabilities, 31*, 27–40.

Rehabilitation Act, P.L. 93–112 (1973).

Salminen, A. (2008). European research related to assistive technology for disabled children. *Technology and Disability, 20*(3), 173–178.

Scherer, M., Elias, E., & Weider, K. (2010). TBI-ROC part seven: Traumatic brian injury-technologies to support memory and cognition. *Exceptional Parent, 40* (11), 29–30.

Smith, R. O. (2000). Measuring assistive technology outcomes in education. *Assessment for Effective Intervention, 25*(4), 273–290.

Technology-Related Assistance for Individuals with Disabilities Act (Tech Act) (1988), P.L. 100–407.

Technology-Related Assistance for Individuals with Disabilities Act Amendments, P.L. 103–218 (1994).

U.S. Department of Education, Office of Educational Research and Improvement, National Center for Education Statistics. (1999). *An institutional perspective on students with disabilities in postsecondary education* (NCES Publication No. 1999046). Retrieved from http://nces.ed.gov/pubsearch/pubsinfo.asp?pubid=1999046

U.S. Department of Education's Office of Special Education Programs, The Family Center on Technology and Disability. (2009). *Family information guide to assistive technology and transition planning.* Retrieved from http://www.fctd.info/assets/assets/8/FCTD-AT-Transition-Guide.pdf?1281716039

Section IV
Adolescent Transition Education Program Structure

16

Adolescent Transition Education and School Reform

Diane S. Bassett

UNIVERSITY OF NORTHERN COLORADO

Carol A. Kochhar-Bryant

GEORGE WASHINGTON UNIVERSITY

Change efforts in general and special education have followed parallel but separate tracks. Unfortunately, general education reform efforts too frequently reflect limited attention to the unique needs of students with disabilities, and special educators have not systematically been invited into the dialogue. We discuss recent reforms in secondary education and explore their implications for efforts to improve outcomes for youth as they transition to postsecondary education and employment. We examine how the federal government and states have responded to these reforms and explore initiatives to align secondary education with transition services. Recommendations will be made for advancing the alignment of transition services with secondary education reforms.

A Brief History of Secondary Education Reform

The advancement of secondary education has its roots as far back as the year 1635 with the establishment of Latin Academies for the elite sons of wealthy American landowners. It was Benjamin Franklin who first proposed secondary public schools that would teach useful subjects such as geometry, English, astronomy, navigation, gardening, and good citizenship to American youth beyond the aristocracy. By the 1850s, comprehensive "academies" for both genders were established that sought to broaden the educational opportunities for youth who could afford to pay tuition fees. Over 6,000 of these academies were established that taught the classics and vocational subjects such as surveying, agriculture, geology, and bookkeeping (George, McEwen, & Jenkins, 2000).

Massachusetts was the first state, in 1827, to pass a law requiring towns of more than 4,000 to establish free public high schools. The state established two "tracks": one built on the classics to prepare youth for college, and the other vocational, designed for those students who would directly enter the world of business and commerce (George et al., 2000). As the mandate of public high schools spread to other states, goals of "social efficiency and social mobility" were established that would "instill the values of ambition, hard work, delayed gratification, and earnestness—students would become sober, law-abiding, and respectable citizens" (Reese, 1995, p. 57). In 1892, the National Education Association appointed the Committee of Ten on

Secondary School Studies. Because it was composed primarily of college presidents and professors, its recommendations (naturally) called for a return to a classical education and academic training. It also called for the establishment of each subject taught for one hour across a five-day week, a vestige of which is evident still in high schools today.

The beginning of the 20th century saw millions of youth attending high schools due to increasing prosperity, the advent of child labor laws, and burgeoning immigration. This growth changed the course of American high schools as they struggled to meet the needs of all students through academic and vocational tracks. Despite this influx, 97% of students failed to graduate, leading some scholars to call for even stronger tracking that would match students' economic and perceived intellectual "probable destiny" (George et al., 2000, p. 11).

By 1920, America had evolved from an agrarian society to an industrial one. No longer were as many youth needed on farms so that many were able to pursue high school. Tracked systems prevailed throughout the decades beyond WWII. The USSR's *Sputnik* launch on October 8, 1957, however, changed the face of American education, and in particular, high school curricula. Suddenly, education was perceived as a means of providing "safety" through a renewed call for intellectual development and scientific and academic achievement. "Carnegie Units" for measuring academic rigor were created (which remain today) and students were channeled into a strict, standardized curriculum that included many hours of homework.

This approach changed radically in the 1960s and 1970s. Issues of racial and socioeconomic equality, reactions to an unpopular war, and student activism led to many changes in the way secondary education was addressed. Critics such as A.S. Neill, Goodman, Silberman, Rogers, and Holt argued for more diverse educational opportunities. Ironically, the continued use of tracking led to student cliques known all too well today: the jocks, the druggies, the slow learners, the dropouts. In 1983, *A Nation at Risk* detailed the "educational inadequacies" (George et al., 2000, p. 28) of the American school system. Citing a "rising tide of mediocrity," the report called for strengthened graduation requirements, extension of the school day and year, increased scrutiny of individual student academic progress, and stronger preparation of teachers (with concomitant salary increases). Also for the first time, business and industry joined the national debate in an attempt to prepare a more qualified workforce.

In 1996 the National Association of Secondary School Principals developed a comprehensive report entitled *Breaking Ranks: Changing an American Institution* (1996). Unlike previous reports that relied heavily on the recommendations of higher education professionals, *Breaking Ranks* argued that purposeful reform must come from those who practice it daily: high school practitioners. The report outlined a vision incorporating nine themes that should guide high schools in the 21st century:

1   A community committed to demonstrable academic achievement;
2   An experience in transition to the next stage in life for every student with the understanding that "ultimately each person needs to earn a living;"
3   A gateway to multiple options;
4   A place to prepare lifelong learners;
5   A provision of the necessities for developing good citizens for "full participation in the life of a democracy;"
6   A place where students are helped to develop as social as well as academic beings;
7   A place where students learn to be comfortable in a technological society;
8   A place where students become equipped for life in an internationally interdependent world;
9   A place that "unabashedly advocates in behalf of young people" (p.2).

Breaking Ranks was followed by *Breaking Ranks II* (National Association of Secondary School Principals, 2004), which offered specific strategies to improve student performance. These strategies included (a) an advancement of core knowledge, (b) interactions and connections with students, (c) a comprehensive advisory program for students, (d) use of a variety of instructional strategies and assessments, (e) flexible use of scheduled time, (f) structural leadership changes, and (g) continuous professional development for educational professionals. These strategies were infused into three core areas: collaborative leadership and personal learning communities; personalization of the school environment; and curriculum, instruction, and assessment. The goal of the *Breaking Ranks* reports was to return to the ideals of a democratic citizenry tempered by equality, social efficiently, and social mobility for all (George et al., 2000).

Transition-related Historical Reforms for Students with Disabilities

In parallel efforts, policy and practices have been aimed at improving access to education and improved outcomes for students with disabilities as well. Numerous large-scale initiatives to improve the performance of high schools in the United States have been undertaken in the past twenty years by government agencies, foundations, non-profit organizations, and independent developers for both typical students and those with disabilities. Because high schools are the final level of compulsory schooling, they must prepare students for different postsecondary destinations. They must provide the skills and knowledge to help them successfully attain more advanced credentials in the higher education system and to provide the knowledge and skills to adequately prepare them to enter the workforce (Rumberger, 2009). For both destinations, high schools should prepare all students for a successful transition to adulthood. Three generations of reform efforts illustrate these endeavors.

First Generation of Reform: Practical Skill Development

The federal government assumed an important role in the expansion of "vocational" and technical education, with the creation of the Commission on National Aid to Vocational Education (1914) and passage of the Smith-Hughes Act (P.L. 64–347, 1917), which provided the basis for the vocational education movement. Vocational rehabilitation programs for individuals with disabilities were also built into this Act (Meers, 1980). The career education movement in the United States gained additional momentum in the 1960s when it became a high priority of the then U.S. Office of Education's Bureau of Adult, Vocational and Technical Education (Halpern, 1985, 1999). In 1963 the Vocational Education Act of 1963 (P.L. 88–210) was passed to maintain, extend, and improve upon existing programs of vocational education, as well as to use funds for persons who have academic, socioeconomic, or other disadvantages that prevent them from succeeding in regular vocational education (Gordon, 1999). In 1971 the U.S. Commissioner of Education, Sidney Marland, Jr., proclaimed career education as a major educational reform. Marland believed that the high dropout rate in the United States was due, in part, to the failure of the educational system to provide students with a "relevant" education that was aligned with their future goals and potential (Kokaska & Brolin, 1985).

During this period, federal involvement in youth development was primarily characterized by an ad hoc approach to policy making in which special population groups that had previously been left out were added into existing programs. Many youth advocates view this era of policy making as aimed at leveling the playing field and providing leverage to state and local educational and human service agencies to build their own foundations for equity and productivity (Horne & Morris, 1999).

In 1984 the Carl D. Perkins Vocational Education Act of 1984 (P.L. 98-524) was passed and named for House Representative Carl D. Perkins, a civil rights supporter who introduced the bill, which still bears his name. During the 1970s and 1980s, policies increased education and training resources that provided extra help to all youth, particularly those special populations who faced severe disadvantages in schools and the workplace. These special populations included students with disabilities, students who were limited English proficient or economically disadvantaged, teen parents, and school-age youth in correctional settings. Educators cautioned policy makers that students with disabilities continued to experience limited access to educational and employment programs. The work of Gary Clark greatly influenced practice and policy related to the career development of children and youth with disabilities. His lifespan approach to career development represents a major contribution building upon the early development of the concept of career development (Clark, Carlson, Fisher, Cook, & D'Alonzo, 1991).

Thus, the first generation of transition services (1960s to 1980s) was characterized by early definition of transition services, establishment of services and supports, and emerging evidence of the relationships between transition planning and successful student transition to postsecondary education and employment.

Second Generation of Reform: Accountability for Student Achievement

In the 1990s, partly in reaction to public concerns about the eroding quality of education in the United States and weakening economic competitiveness, policy makers turned their attention to improving student academic achievement. Policy initiatives reflected the belief that improving education depended upon the creation of national standards that defined what every student should know and be able to do (Jennings, 1995, 2000). The standards-based reform movement led to a shift in the attention of educators from work and career-preparation to academic performance outcomes (Halloran, 1993; Kochhar-Bryant & Vreeburg-Izzo, 2006; Vreeburg-Izzo, Hertzfeld, Simmons-Reed, & Aaron, 2001).

The second generation of transition services that began in the 1990s was characterized by federal policy initiatives that further defined transition services and provided resources to build capacity in the states and local communities. In 1990 the amendments to the Individuals with Disabilities Education Act (IDEA) (P.L. 101–476) defined transition services and activities, and the relationship between the individualized education program (IEP) and needed transition services. IDEA 1990 mandated formal agreements with school-linked agencies to share the responsibility for long-range transition planning; it also described the responsibility of state and local educational agencies to monitor and sustain the provision of such linkages. Five additional events contributed to expansion of transition services: (a) the passage of the Americans with Disabilities Act (P.L. 101–336), which prohibited workplace discrimination against individuals with disabilities, (b) an identified shortage of prepared adults in the workforce, (c) research findings that demonstrated the relationship between transition services and postsecondary success for youth, (d) federal initiatives to promote state development of transition services, (e) amendments to the Rehabilitation Act to promote coordination with secondary schools to improve transition services, and (f) the School to Work Opportunities Act of 1994 (P.L. 103–239). Although the ad hoc nature of policy making among government agencies contributed to an uncoordinated patchwork of youth programs and initiatives, transition practices have expanded. These initiatives were based on early research evidence of the relationship between transition planning and student postsecondary outcomes and evidence of underdeveloped implementation of the legal requirements for transition services in the states. Educators and advocates hoped that IDEA would provide more specific guidance for implementation that would help expand transition services.

Third Generation of Reform: Equity and Accountability

Since the 1980s, educational improvement legislation, including IDEA 2004 and the No Child Left Behind Act of 2001 (NCLB) (P.L.107–110), has sought to improve public school programs for all students (National Center on Secondary Education and Transition, 2004). These laws promote comprehensive planning to enable all students to achieve high academic standards while holding educators responsible for the progress of students. The Elementary and Secondary Education Act (ESEA) of 1994 (Improving America's Schools Act of 1994, P.L. 103–227, sec 3(4) encouraged the states to adopt two types of voluntary standards: (a) content standards which identify what students are to learn in one subject, and (b) performance standards that define the quality of the performance considered satisfactory (sec.3 (9)). When ESEA was re-authorized in 2001 as the No Child Left Behind Act, it strengthened the focus on standards, requiring states and districts to develop challenging state academic content standards, state assessments, and new curriculum standards (Kochhar-Bryant & Bassett, 2002). Students with disabilities are expected to be included, to the extent possible, in the general education curriculum and in standardized assessments. To support these goals, educational laws reflect stronger mandates for collaboration between general and special education teachers; teachers and related services professionals; teachers, families and students; preschool and elementary schools; elementary and middle schools; middle and high schools; high schools and postsecondary institutions (colleges and universities); and school and community agencies. Under NCLB (now ESEA) and IDEA 2004, children with disabilities must be considered to be general education students first. States are responsible for implementing a single accountability system for all students based on strong academic standards for what every child should know and learn, including children with disabilities.

The third generation of transition services (2000s) has been characterized by more explicit definition and guidance in IDEA 2004 for developing a comprehensive and systematic transition-planning process that is individualized for each student. In secondary education, so that students with disabilities will have meaningful access to the general education curriculum, transition planning and services must be tailored to individual needs and preferences, relevant to postsecondary goals, and use flexible curricula and environments. Such a transition program recognizes different pathways to graduation for students, incorporates the concept of integrated transition planning and participation in a general education course of study, and employs flexible combinations of academic, career-technical education classes, and community-based work experiences to achieve different pathways to graduation.

The third generation is also characterized by efforts to validate effective transition practices—i.e., what works? For example, research related to transition has demonstrated that effective high schools are characterized by strong professional collaboration and interagency coordination for postsecondary planning (Deshler & Schumacher, 2006; McLaughlin & Talbert, 2001). Written agreements among agencies are essential for interagency coordination, and are a defining characteristic of model transition programs (Harley, Donnell, & Rainey, 2003; Research and Training Center on Service Coordination, 2001). Results from case studies showed that in model sites (those that demonstrated the best results for youth), one or more persons known as transition facilitators were designated to implement transition services. Participation in work-based learning is also associated with successful outcomes for youth with disabilities.

Relationships between students' involvement in their own individualized educational planning and transition goal-setting have been associated with improved postsecondary outcomes (Bremer, Kachgal, & Schoeller, 2003; Martin, Marshall, & DePrey; Repetto, Webb, Neubert, & Curran, 2006). Students show a greater ability to advocate for themselves after high school if they have gained an understanding of their strengths and disability in high school. When they are better prepared to make decisions and choices about their future, they are more likely to enroll in and complete advanced education and to enter and sustain employment (NCSET, 2004; U.S. Government Accountability Office, 2003; Wehmeyer, Field, Doren, Jones, & Mason, 2004). Several professional and research organizations and federal agencies have contributed to strengthening transition services through research (e.g., National Secondary Transition and Technical Assistance Center; Center on Postsecondary Education and Disability; National Center on Accessing the General Education Curriculum; National High School Center, Office for Vocational and Adult Education, U.S. Department of Education; Manpower Demonstration Research Corporation; Council for Exceptional Children, Division on Career Development and Transition; Institute for Community Inclusion).

Finally, transition coordination can increase the likelihood that incarcerated youth will be re-enrolled in their home school, complete high school, and become gainfully employed in their communities (Stephens & Arnette, 2000). Studies of service coordination strategies for young offenders have shown that these services can improve positive adjustment, decrease negative behaviors and reduce the likelihood of re-incarceration (Stephens & Arnette, 2000).

Content Standards, Common Curriculum, and Assessment Practices

There is a growing movement in many states to not only specify the number and types of courses needed for high school graduation but also the content standards and sequence of courses needed to become "college and workplace ready." The American Diploma Project (ADP) is leading this effort. In its report, *Ready or Not: Creating a High School Diploma that Counts* (2004), the document argued that all students, no matter what their future destination, should take the same academic curriculum in high school:

> Successful preparation for both postsecondary education and employment requires learning the same rigorous English and mathematics content and skills. No longer do students planning to go to work after high school need a different and less rigorous curriculum than those planning to go to college. In fact, nearly all students will require some postsecondary education, including on-the-job training, after completing high school. Therefore, a college and workplace readiness curriculum should be a graduation requirement, not an option, for all high school students.
>
> (pp. 8–9)

The report suggested that states should support and encourage different approaches or "multiple pathways" to help students meet these standards, including vocational programs, project-based learning, charter schools, and advanced coursework, such as Advanced Placement and International Baccalaureate Programs. Some states have gone further, mandating a broader curriculum for all students that includes career and technical education (ADP, 2007).

Despite the call for multiple pathways to meeting course standards, students in many states must also pass a high school exit exam. In the 1970s several states began using minimum competency tests, typically in a multiple-choice format, to assure that students had mastered basic skills before receiving a high school diploma. With the growth of the accountability movement and standards-based reform in the 1990s, assessments were used to ensure that students had mastered more rigorous, grade-level content standards. In 1979 New York became the first state to require an examination before a student could receive a diploma (Warren, Jenkins, & Kulick, 2006). In the 1980s, twelve additional states added exam requirements, and four more added exam requirements in the 1990s. By 2006, 22 states required that students pass some sort of exit exam before being awarded a diploma (Snyder, Slauson, & Carpenter, 2009). All of the exams are limited to core academic subjects, such as English and math, with some states also including science and history. However, the fact that these exams have not been correlated with specific transition outcomes (e.g., postsecondary enrollment, employment, access to adult services, etc.) and that these outcomes are not systematically tracked within and across states remains a challenge that cannot inform secondary schools of their educational efficacy (Academy for Educational Development, 1999; National Alliance for Secondary Education and Transition, 2005; National Council on Disability, 2004).

General Secondary Educational Reforms and Transition

Approaches to Improving High School Performance

Although there are a variety of specific approaches to improving high school performance, they fall into four basic categories: targeted, comprehensive, collaborative, and systemic (Müller & Burdette, 2007; National Association of Secondary School Principals, 2005). The first category represents targeted approaches, which involve strategies for improving particular facets of the school. The three most common facets are instructional interventions (designed to improve classroom teaching and student achievement), student support programs (designed for students who may need extra support), and school restructuring (designed to alter the organizational structure of the school). Targeted approaches generally attempt to alter one particular facet of the school, rather than all, under the assumption that at least some aspects are functioning adequately so that reforming a single facet of the school may be sufficient to bring about the desired improvement in school performance.

The second category represents comprehensive approaches, which involve altering all aspects of the school, under the assumption that the school itself is not performing adequately for most students. Two strategies within this category are reforming existing high schools by developing a comprehensive set of practices and programs locally or by adopting an externally developed comprehensive school reform model or creating new schools, by either developing a new school locally or by adopting an externally developed whole-school model. Both of these strategies can be used to create comprehensive high schools to serve all students or to create specialized high schools to serve specific populations of students, such as students who are at risk or have already dropped out of school.

The third category represents collaborative approaches, which involve attempts to create partnerships between schools and local government and community agencies, under the assumption that schools alone cannot successfully address the needs of students and improve their performance in school. Instead, schools are more likely to be successful if they work with outside agencies to provide more support to students and to all the institutions—families, schools, communities—that serve them.

The first three categories all represent school reform strategies because schools are the focus of change. The fourth category represents systemic approaches, which involve making changes to the entire state educational system, under the assumption that such changes can transform how all schools function in the system, a sort of "systemic school reform" (Smith & O'Day, 1991). State and federal accountability systems represent the one recent example of systemic reforms (Elmore, 2004). One of the reform principles for high schools is to create smaller, more personalized learning environments for students and teachers. A reform strategy is to restructure large schools into small learning communities or create new, small schools, both of which are difficult to implement (Kennelly & Monrad, 2007). High schools are also difficult to reform because teachers are trained and credentialed in specific subjects, and many schools have departmental structures, both of which make it difficult for teachers to collaborate on instructional reform (Corcoran & Silander, 2009). Finally, students vary greatly in their academic preparation, which requires a broad array of instructional offerings and student-support services.

Given the seeming philosophical alignment between general education and transition initiatives, one might assume that the alignment of general education and special education for youth with disabilities would be seamless. Indeed, a number of proposals exist that would help to integrate the needs of youth with disabilities into public and private initiatives. Waves of legislation and experimental policy initiatives at national, state, and local levels have emerged to help high school youth prepare for changing work environments and to make a successful transition to adult life. Over the past forty years, numerous federal, state and privately driven initiatives have been aimed at improving high schools to increase student achievement. These are reviewed below with a discussion of their implications for supporting transition services.

Federal Programs Aimed at School Reform

Vocational Education

The federal government has supported high school reform since the initial passage of the Smith-Hughes Act in 1917, which provided federal aid to vocational education in high schools. The purpose of vocational education is to develop the academic and career-technical skills of secondary and postsecondary students. A comprehensive review of the impact of vocational education was completed in 2004 (Silverberg, Warner, Fong, & Goodwin, 2004), demonstrating the value-added effects of high school vocational education on a number of student outcomes: academic achievement, high school completion, postsecondary enrollment and completion, and short- and medium-run earnings. The most consistent positive finding was that students who completed an extra vocational course earned about three percent more in their jobs after completing school than students without the extra course (Rumberger, 2009).

Comprehensive School Reform Program and the School Improvement Fund

The Comprehensive School Reform Program (CSR) was first authorized as a demonstration program in 1998 and then embedded as a part of the No Child Left Behind Act (Cross, 2004). The federal CSR program was aimed to improve all aspects of a school's operation and performance. It studied eight models of reform in 650 elementary and middle schools and 21 districts across 17 states (Aladjem et al., 2006). In 2004 a Comprehensive School Reform Quality Initiative was launched to provide funds over a four-year period (2004–08) to support eight non-profit organizations, institutions of higher education, and consortia to increase capacity building for CSR providers, provide technical assistance, and evaluate progress (Rumberger, 2009). The School Improvement Fund replaces the Comprehensive School Reform Program and will be funded under the American Recovery and Reinvestment Act of 2009.

Forty percent of these funds will target middle and high schools.

School Dropout Prevention Program

The School Dropout Prevention Program was funded from 2004 to 2006 to support dropout prevention and reentry programs in middle and high schools. The program builds on the earlier program—the School Dropout Assistance Program, which operated from 1989 to 1991 and from 1991 to 1996. An evaluation of 20 programs found two common characteristics: (a) supports to assist students to overcome personal, family, and social barriers to school achievement, and (b) smaller, more personal settings for students (Dynarsky, 2004). Unfortunately, only three of the eight high schools lowered the dropout rate, and most of these by increasing General Educational Development test (GED) completion rates.

Smaller Learning Communities Program

This high-school targeted program, funded for nine years to support the implementation of "smaller learning communities," included innovative features such as freshman academies, multi-grade academies aligned with career areas, cohort groups of high school students, schools-within-schools models, student advisories, and mentoring programs. An evaluation of 119 such schools was completed in 2008 and found that most schools adopted Career Academies (55 schools) that integrated academic and career-related classes, and Freshman Academies (58 schools) that bridge middle and high school. Furthermore, schools adopted additional strategies such as block scheduling, career pathways, teacher teams, and mentoring arrangements. Features of such programs that contributed to their success included strong school leadership, adequate professional development, adequate resources, and willingness of teachers to reform their pedagogical practices (Rumberger, 2009). Student outcomes included improved student involvement in extracurricular activities, significant increases in 9th and 10th grade promotion rates, and reduced violence, but there were no significant improvements in statewide academic assessments or college entrance exams.

These reforms have yielded promising practices for secondary education for the general student population but have not reflected the special needs of students with disabilities. The challenge for secondary schools and school-linked agencies is to collaborate to ensure that secondary reforms are inclusive and incorporate the full range of transition services and supports for all students.

Private Efforts Aimed at Reform

A number of large-scale school reform efforts have been mounted outside federal and state governments, some focusing on high schools and some focusing on all levels of public schools.

National High School Center

The National High School Center provides the latest research and resources regarding high school improvement issues to help build statewide capacity. It includes a link to issues regarding students with disabilities in high school settings, including those students with mental health issues, access to general education, significantly struggling learners, strategies for dropout prevention, and access to academic and career readiness. It is administered by the American Institutes for Research, the Office of Elementary and Secondary Education, and the Office of Special Education Programs.

The International Center for Leadership in Education

The Center is a private, not-for-profit organization that seeks to provide technical assistance to those interested in high school reform. Among its many resources, it offers a Special Education Institute and various products to assist professionals in working with secondary students with disabilities. (Müller & Burdette, 2007).

The National Community of Practice in Support of Transition

This resource is sponsored by the IDEA Partnership at the National Association of State Directors of Special Education. It works collaboratively with state and local education agencies to improve interagency transition-focused initiatives and to promote the role of youth and high school reform issues (Müller & Burdette, 2007).

Gates Foundation High School Grants Initiative

Perhaps the most ambitious effort to reform America's high schools is being conducted by the Bill & Melinda Gates Foundation. The initiative is driven by the view that the U.S. system of public education is fundamentally obsolete, as stated emphatically by Bill Gates at the 2005 National Education Summit on High Schools:

> America's high schools are obsolete. By obsolete, I don't just mean that our high schools are broken, flawed, and under-funded—though a case could be made for every one of those points. By obsolete, I mean that our high schools—even when they're working exactly as designed—cannot teach our kids what they need to know today . . . This isn't an accident or a flaw in the system; it is the system.
>
> (Gates, 2005b)

The basic strategy was to provide grants to intermediary organizations that would start new high schools or redesign existing high schools. The evaluation of the Gates initiative documented an evolving theory of change, beginning with one that focused simply on creating not only small high schools (with no more than 100 students per grade level), but also schools with a number of essential attributes:

- Common focus by students and teachers on a few important goals;
- High expectations to complete a rigorous course of study to prepare for college, career, and citizenship;
- Personalized relationships between students and teachers;
- Respect and responsibility;
- Time for staff to collaborate;
- Performance-based advancement with adequate student support; and
- Technology as a tool (p. 3).

Carnegie Schools for a New Society

In 2000 the Carnegie Corporation of New York started a major reform initiative focused on redesigning high schools in urban communities. The initiative, Schools for a New Society, provided grants of $60 million (with support from the Bill & Melinda Gates Foundation) to seven cities. The initiative has several critical components:

- Encouraging and supporting partnerships between businesses, universities, parent and student groups, and community organizations;
- Holding all schools accountable for helping every student to meet high standards;
- Transforming large, impersonal high schools into small learning communities;
- Improving teaching by providing intensive professional development (Nichols-Solomon & Feist, 2006, p. 3).

To date, no summative evaluation of the impact of this initiative has been completed although an evaluation in one site found uneven impacts on reform efforts and student achievement (Reyes, Phillips, Alexander, & Fuller, 2007).

These private reforms efforts have also yielded promising outcomes and new directions in secondary education reform for the general student population but have not reflected the special needs of students with disabilities.

New Directions for Transition in the Context of Secondary Reform

The mandate for the provision of transition planning and services has been part of the American educational landscape since 1990 with the reauthorization of IDEA. Leaders such as Will (1984) and Halpern (1985) envisioned a time when secondary school students would transition seamlessly into productive adulthood and education, employment, and independent living opportunities. Although there have been improvements, full realization of these goals continues to elude us. There is some good news: according to the National Longitudinal Transition Study Two (2009) and *Twenty-five Years of Educating Children with Disabilities* (2002), youth with disabilities are more engaged in school and community, dropout rates are decreasing, employment and wages are increasing, and postsecondary enrollment and community engagement are also increasing (Newman, Wagner, Cameto, & Knokey, 2009). Access to the general education curriculum and activities has also increased; 70% of all students with disabilities take at least one academic class and there is a dramatic increase in students taking academic courses over the last fifteen years (Wagner, Newman, Cameto, Levine, & Marder, 2003). Nevertheless, it is universally acknowledged that we still have a long way to go to increase postsecondary enrollment and completion, stem the tide of dropouts, guarantee post-school careers with competitive salaries and associated benefits, and ensure a place for young adults with disabilities as contributing members of their communities.

The parallel tracks of No Child Left Behind (NCLB)/ESEA and IDEA have assured us that "all means all:" students with disabilities participate in access to a standards-based education and are counted in assessment practices. State departments of education and local education agencies are now required to demonstrate compliance on indicators measuring appropriate transition planning, post-school outcome data collection, dropout prevention, and family involvement. University-based special education programs must demonstrate they are teaching the knowledge and skills regarding provision of transition services. Families are becoming stronger advocates for youth with disabilities. However, all of these efforts aimed at youth with disabilities are not yet considered an integral part of general education reform.

The field of transition for youth with disabilities has been using many "best practices" for over twenty years that general education reform could embrace for all students: planning for transition to employment or further schooling, active student participation and advocacy, job development and career planning, contextual teaching practices in academic environments, early warning systems for dropout prevention, collaboration with teachers, families and students, and personalized postsecondary planning within the secondary setting. Why have these practices remained separate and parallel efforts, with minimal integration for all students?

Both the special and general education systems share responsibility. By not engaging with general education in these critical initiatives, youth with disabilities have been subjected to separate and unequal treatment in secondary schools. They are too often relegated to general education courses without benefit of support (Wagner, Newman et al., 2003). They too frequently continue to receive sub-standard opportunities for employment (Wagner et al., 2005). Although more students are attending postsecondary education, few graduate in comparison with typical young adults (Wagner et al., 2005). If youth with disabilities are to "blend seamlessly" into the mainstream of society, it must begin with our engagement and active participation in high school reform efforts.

Marlene Simon-Burroughs, Associate Division Director responsible for secondary education, transition, and postsecondary projects for OSEP, recently outlined issues affecting the provision of transition services within the context of high school reform efforts (Simon-Burroughs, 2009). She listed the following areas that warrant further scrutiny:

- Increasing literacy skills;
- Aligning with high school reform efforts;
- Measuring teacher effectiveness;
- Mandating teachers who are highly qualified;
- Increasing time for collaboration;
- Decreasing low-performing schools;
- Developing career standards;
- Utilizing comprehensive data systems;
- Mandating early childhood education for all students;
- Increasing high school graduation rates in "dropout factories;"
- Improving college matriculation and completion;
- Increasing technology use.

Past presidents of the Division for Career Development and Transition were informally polled regarding their top five issues for the field of transition. Twenty-eight separate issues were listed, reflecting in large part the disparity with which professionals in transition view the field. Broadly combined, these issues included self-determination, personnel preparation, job and career development, and compliance with transition planning. Only two respondents cited the need for collaborative work with general education regarding reform efforts. Given the premises that (a) the field of transition has a rich experience in working toward the post-school outcomes of youth and (b) general education reform is seeking ways to increase positive high school reform as it reflects positive post-school outcomes, and (c) each field can benefit from the expertise of the other, the following recommendations for blended reform are suggested.

1. Leaders in the field of transition need to participate actively in general high school reform efforts and in defining measurements for high school performance

The NCLB/ESEA's mechanism for measuring school performance, Adequate Yearly Progress (AYP), currently does not adequately measure the dual purpose of high schools: (a) that all students graduate from high school with a regular diploma, and (b) that students acquire the necessary content knowledge and skills for postsecondary education and career success (Tucci, 2009). To make AYP more meaningful at the high school level, federal policy should support efforts to develop common national standards and assessments that are aligned to postsecondary transition to college and career readiness outcomes. Active participation must include teachers in school and district planning meetings, local transition leaders and educational administrators, state departments that combine general and special education initiatives, colleges and universities working in concert with content area preparation, and federal and private initiatives that directly target funds addressing the needs of youth with and without disabilities. Professionals in the field of transition must be key participants in secondary education redesign at all levels (Jorgensen, 1998; Lehmann, Cobb, Tochterman, 2001; Müller & Burdette, 2007; West & Whitby, 2008).

2. Leaders in the field of transition need to extend its empirical base and advocate for parity in education, employment, and community living opportunities for secondary youth with disabilities

Youth with disabilities still need strong and informed advocates who can help them to navigate the many pathways they seek into the postsecondary world. Efficacy-based practices should be promoted that are unique to students with disabilities. They should be advocated for in the context of general education, in sustaining transition programs in schools and districts, and in providing specific and positive direction toward the goals of postsecondary education, employment, and community involvement (Benz, Lindstrom, Unruh, & Waintrup, 2004; Test, Mazzotti, Mustian, Fowler, & Kortering, 2009).

3. Transition professionals should provide the pedagogy for relevant and contextually centered general education curriculum in concert with general education content educators

If secondary students are to participate in general education settings, the curriculum itself must provide relevance and accessibility so that content may be mastered by all students. It is becoming increasingly evident that academics in high school prepare youth equally for postsecondary education and employment. Transition educators must work actively and collaboratively with content specialists to ensure that the material is clear, relevant, and challenging while also being accessible. It is critical that youth with disabilities master academic skills to ensure future success (Bassett & Kochhar-Bryant, 2006; Kochhar-Bryant & Bassett, 2002; Lee, Wehmeyer, Soukup, & Palmer, 2010; Stodden, Galloway, & Stodden, 2003; Wilson, Hoffman, & McLaughlin, 2009).

4. Self-determination for students with disabilities should be strengthened and explicitly cued in general education and community-based settings

Many students now participate in their IEP development but may not participate in other authentic choice-making opportunities. The field of transition can make huge inroads into secondary reform as youth with disabilities demonstrate their strengths and interests and advocate for their needs. Student self-determination can bridge the gap for secondary educators who feel that youth with disabilities display only learned helpless and lackluster behaviors (Carter, Lane, Pierson, & Stang, 2008; Mason, Field, & Sawilowsky, 2004; Palmer, Wehmeyer, Gipson, & Agvan, 2004; Test, Mason, Hughes, Konrad, Neale, & Wood, 2004; Wehmeyer, Field, Doren, Jones, & Mason, 2004).

5. Teacher preparation programs must improve their education of both pre-service special educators and general educators regarding transition-focused strategies

Transition-focused constructs and competencies must be infused in all pre-service special education and general education coursework. Secondary content teachers often lack the knowledge or context to understand the needs of students with transition IEP goals. Further, content teachers cannot cue students to use transition-focused strategies (i.e., self-advocacy, learning strategies, etc.) if they do not understand the transition process themselves. Given the dearth of transition certification and degree program content in the United States, it is not surprising that misperceptions and misgivings regarding transition for youth with disabilities exist (Anderson et al., 2003; Blalock et al., 2003; Wandry, Webb, Williams, Bassett, Asselin, & Hutchinson, 2008).

6. While actively working within general education reform, transition professionals must continue their own research and practice in ways that inform both special and general education professionals

The field of transition must continue empirically based studies and practice in a wide range of areas including: (a) data collection and comprehensive data systems, (b) integrated service delivery models, (c) transition education in middle grades, (d) cultural diversity and competence, (e) tiered approaches to the provision of transition services, (f) career development and maintenance, (g) uses of technology, (h) agency coordination of services, and (i) increased post-secondary matriculation and graduation. While this list is by no means exhaustive, it does illustrate the many areas that warrant further investigation and study (Benz et al., 2004; Carter et al., 2008; Kochhar-Bryant & Bassett, 2002; Palmer et al., 2004; Repetto et al., 2006; Stodden et al., 2003; Test et al., 2009).

Conclusion

Two central goals in the United States are to preserve democracy and build our national economy by promoting full participation of all citizens in the work of the nation. To increase the likelihood that all youth can and will prepare for participation in their communities, governmental and educational institutions are providing direct assistance to youth with disabilities as they navigate the transition from school to adult life and constructive citizenship. The challenge for secondary schools and school-linked agencies is to collaborate to ensure that secondary reforms are inclusive and incorporate the full range of transition services and supports for all students.

References

Academy for Educational Development. (1999). *Positive youth development: AED makes young people a priority.* Washington, DC: Author.

Aladjem, D. K., LeFloch, K. C., Zhang, Y., Kurki, A., Boyle, A., Taylor, J. (2006). *Models matter: The final report of the National Longitudinal Evaluation of Comprehensive School Reform.* Washington, DC: American Institutes for Research.

American Diploma Project (ADP) (2004). *Ready or not: Creating a high school diploma that counts* (2004). Washington, D.C.: Achieve, Inc.

American Diploma Project (ADP) (2007). *Closing the expectations gap 2007: An annual 50-state progress report on the alignment of high school policies with the demands of college and work.* Washington, D.C.: Achieve, Inc.

Americans with Disabilities Act of 1990, P.L.101–336, 104 Stat. 327; 42 U.S.C. 12101 et seq.

American Recovery and Reinvestment Act of 2009, PL. 111–5; [pg. 123 STAT. 115].

Anderson, D., Kleinhammer-Trammill, P.J., Morningstar, M., Lehmann, J., Bassett, D., Kohler, P., (2003). What's happening in personnel preparation in transition? A national survey. *Career Development for Exceptional Individuals, 26,* 27–44.

Bassett, D.S., & Kochhar-Bryant, C.A. (2006). Strategies for aligning standards-based education and transition. *Focus on Exceptional Children, 39*(2), 1–19.

Benz, M.B., Lindstrom, L, Unruh, D., & Waintrup, M. (2004). Sustaining secondary transition programs in local schools. *Remedial and Special Education, 25*(2), 39–50.

Blalock, G., Kochhar-Bryant, C., Test, D., Kohler, P., White, W., Lehman, J., et al. (2003). The need for comprehensive personnel preparation in transition and career development: A position statement of the Division on Career Development and Transition. *Career Development for Exceptional Individuals, 26,* 91–110.

Bremer, C., Kachgal, M., & Schoeller, K. (2003). *Self-determination: Supporting successful transition.* Research to Practice Brief: Improving Secondary Education and Transition Services Through Research, *2,*91.

Carl D. Perkins Vocational Education Act of 1984. P.L. 98–524. U.S.C. 29 USC Section 721.

Carter, E. W., Lane, K. L., Pierson, M. R., & Stang, K. K. (2008). Promoting self-determination for transition-age youth: Views of high school general and special educators. *Exceptional Children, 75*(1), 55–70.

Clark, G., Carlson, B., Fisher, S., Cook, I., & D'Alonzo, B. (1991). Career development for students with disabilities in elementary schools: A position statement of the Division on Career Development. *Career Development for Exceptional Individuals, 14,* 109–120.

Commission on National Aid to Vocational Education, 1914. (1974). In M. Lazerson & W. N. Grubb (Eds.). *American education and vocationalism: A documentary history 1870–1970* (pp. 116–132). New York: Teachers College Press.

Corcoran, T., & Silander, M. (2009). Instruction in high schools: The evidence and the challenge. *Future of Children, 19*(1), 157–183.

Cross, C. (2004). *Putting the Pieces Together: Lessons from Comprehensive School Reform Research.* Washington, D.C: National Clearinghouse for Comprehensive School Reform.

Deshler, D. D., & Schumaker, J. B. (2006). *Teaching adolescents with disabilities: Accessing the general education curriculum.* Thousand Oaks, CA: Corwin Press.

Elementary and Secondary Education Act (ESEA) (Pub.L. 89-10, 79 Stat. 27, 20 U.S.C. ch.70).

Elmore, R. (2004). *School reform from the inside out: Policy, practice, and performance.* Cambridge, MA: Harvard Education Press.

Gates Foundation High School Grants Initiative (2005a). Seattle, WA: Bill and Linda Gates Foundation. http://www.gatesfoundation.org/learning/Documents/Year4EvaluationAIRSRI.pdf

Gates, W. (2005b, Feb.). *What's wrong with U.S. high schools–and how we can make them better.* Speech delivered at the National Governors Association, National Summit on High Schools, Washington, DC.

George, P. S., McEwen, K. C., & Jenkins, J. M. (2000). *The exemplary high school.* Ft. Worth, TX: Harcourt Brace.

Gordon, H. (1999). *History and growth of vocational education in America.* Boston, MA: Allyn & Bacon.

Halloran, W. D. (1993). Transition services requirement: Issues, implications, challenges. In R. C. Eaves & P. J. McLaughlin (Eds.), *Recent advances in special education and rehabilitation* (pp. 210–224). Boston, MA: Andover Medical.

Halpern, A. (1985). Transition: A look at the foundations. *Exceptional Children, 5*(6), 479–486.

Halpern, A. (1999). *Transition: Is it time for another rebottling?* Paper presented at the 1999 Annual OSEP Project Directors' Meeting, Washington, DC.

Harley, D. A., Donnell, C., & Rainey, J. A. (2003). Interagency collaboration: Reinforcing professional bridges to serve aging populations with multiple service needs. *Journal of Rehabilitation, 69*(2), 32–37.

Horne, R., & Morris, S. (1999). *Transition of youth with disabilities.* Liaison Bulletin, *28*(4).

Improving America's Schools Act of 1994, P.L. 103–227, 20 U.S.C. § 5801.

Individuals with Disabilities Education Act of 1990 (IDEA), Pub. L.101–476, 20 U.S.C. 1400.

Individuals with Disabilities Education Act of 2004, 20 U.S.C. §1400 et seq.

Jennings, J. (1995). *A brief history of the federal role in education: Why it began and why it is still needed.* Washington, DC: Center on Education Policy.

Jennings, J. (2000). *The future of the federal role in elementary and secondary education.* Washington, DC: Center on Education Policy.

Jorgensen, C. M. (1998). *Restructuring high schools for all students: Taking inclusion to the next level.* Baltimore, MD: Paul H. Brookes Publishing.

Kennelly, L., & Monrad, M. (2007). *Easing the transition to high school: Research and best practices to support high school learning.* Washington, DC: National High School Center. American Institute for Research.

Kochhar-Bryant, C., & Bassett, D. (2002). *Aligning Transition and Standards-Based Education.* Columbus, OH: Merrill/Prentice Hall.

Kochhar-Bryant, C., & Vreeburg-Izzo, M. (2006). The summary of performance as transition "passport" to employment and independent living. *Assessment for Effective Intervention, 32*(3).

Kokaska, C. J., & Brolin, D. E. (1985). Career *education for handicapped individuals* (2nd ed.). Columbus, OH: Merrill.

Lee, S.-H., Wehmeyer, M. L., Soukup, J. H., & Palmer, S. (2010). Impact of curriculum modifications on access to the general education curriculum for students with disabilities. *Exceptional Children, 76*(2), 231–233.

Lehmann, J., Cogg, B., & Tochterman, S. (2001). Exploring the relationship between transition and educational reform initiatives. *Career Development for Exceptional Individuals, 24*(2), 185–198.

Martin, J., Marshall, L., & DePry, R. (2002). Participatory decision-making: Innovative practices that increase student self-determination. In R. Flexer, T. Simmons, P. Luft, & R. Baer (Eds.), *Transition planning for secondary students with disabilities* (2nd ed., pp. 246–275). Columbus, OH: Merrill.

Mason, C., Field, S., & Sawilowsky, S. (2004). Implementation of self-determination activities and student participation in IEPs. *Exceptional Children, 70*(4), 441–452.

McLaughlin, M. W., & Talbert, J. E. (2001). *Professional communities and the work of high school teaching.* Chicago: University of Chicago Press.

Meers, G. (1980). *Introduction to special vocational needs education.* Rockville, MD: Aspen Publications.

Müller, E., & Burdette, P. (2007). *High school reform: Integration of special education.* In Forum, December. Alexandria, VA: National Association of State Directors of Special Education, Washington, DC, 1–9.

National Alliance for Secondary Education and Transition. (2005). *National standards and quality indicators: Transition toolkit for systems improvement.* Minneapolis, MN: National Center on Secondary Education and Transition, University of Minnesota.

National Association of Secondary School Principals. (1996). *Breaking ranks: Changing an American institution* (1996). Reston, VA: Author.

National Association of Secondary School Principals. (2004). *Breaking ranks II: Strategies for leading high school reform* (2004). Reston, VA: Author.

National Association of Secondary School Principals. (2005). *High school reform.* Reston, VA: Author.

National Center on Secondary Education and Transition (NCSET). (2004). *Current challenges facing secondary education and transition services for youth with disabilities in the United States.* University of Minnesota, National Center on Secondary Education and Transition Web site. Retrieved May 26, 2005, from http://www.ncset.org/publications/ discussionpaper/default.asp

National Council on Disability. (2004). Improving educational outcomes for students with disabilities. Retrieved February 11, 2008, from http://www.ncd.gov/ newsroom/publications/2004/education-outcomes.htm

Newman, L., Wagner, M., Cameto, R., & Knokey, A-M. (2009). *The post-high school outcomes of youth with disabilities up to 4 years after high school: A report from the National Longitudinal Transition Study-2 (NLTS2)* (NCSER 2009-3017). Menlo Park, CA: SRI International.

Nichols-Solomon, R., & Feist, M. (2006). High schools for the future: Lessons from reforming schools. *Carnegie schools for a new society: Reflections on a national, district wide high school reform initiative.* Washington, DC: Academy for Education Development.

No Child Left Behind Act of 2001, P.L. 107–110, 20 U.S.C.§ 6301 et seq.

Palmer, S., Wehmeyer, M. L., Gipson, K., & Agran, M. (2004). Promoting access to the general curriculum by teaching self-determination skills. *Exceptional Children, 70*(4), 427–440.

Reese, W. (1995). *The origins of the American high school.* New Haven: Yale University Press.

Repetto, J., Webb, K., Neubert, D.A., & Curran, C. (2006). *The middle school experience: Successful teaching and transition planning for diverse learners.* Austin: PRO-ED, Inc.

Research and Training Center on Service Coordination. (2001). *Data report: Service coordination policies and models.* Farmington, CT: Author.

Reyes, P., Phillips, J. C., Alexander, C., & Fuller, E. (2007). *Houston Schools for a New Society evaluation. Summative* Austin: University of Texas, Study of High School Restructuring. Houston, TX.

Rumberger, R. (2009). *What the federal government can do to improve high school performance.* Washington, DC: Center on Education Policy.

School to Work Opportunities Act of 1994, P.L. 103–239, 20 U.S.C. § 6101 et seq.

Silverberg, M., Warner, E., Fong, M., & Goodwin, D. (2004). *National assessment of vocational education: Final report to Congress.* U.S. Department of Education. Washington, DC: Government Printing Office.

Simon-Burroughs, M. (2009, October). *Remarks regarding Office of Special Education (OSEP) issues.* Presented at the Division on Career Development and Transition International Conference, Savannah, GA.

Smith, M., and O'Day, J. (1991). *Putting the pieces together: Systemic school reform.* CPRE Policy Brief. New Brunswick, NJ: Eagleton Institute of Politics.

Smith-Hughes Act of 1917, P.L. 64–347, 20 U.S.C., Vol. 20 § 1145, 16–28.

Snyder, J., Slauson, G., & Carpenter, D (2009). Action plan to increase IS enrollment based on recent survey evidence. *Information Systems Education Journal, 7* (65). http://isedj.org/7/65/

Stephens, R. D., & Arnette, J. L. (2000). *From the courthouse to the schoolhouse: Making successful transitions.* Washington, DC: U.S. Department of Justice.

Stodden, R. A., Galloway, L. M., & Stodden, N. J. (2003). Secondary school curricula issues: Impact on postsecondary students with disabilities. *Exceptional Children, 70*(1), 9–25.

Test, D. W., Mason, C., Hughes, C., Konrad, M., & Wood, W. M. (2004). Student involvement in individualized education program meetings. *Exceptional Children, 70*(4), 391–412.

Test, D. W., Mazzotti, V. L., Mustian, A. L., Fowler, D. H., Kortering, L., et al. (2009). Evidence-based secondary transition predictors for improving postschool outcomes for students with disabilities. *Career Development for Exceptional Individuals, 23*(3), 160–181.

Tucci, T. (2009). *Whole-school reform: Transforming the nation's low-performing high schools.* Policy Brief, July. Washington, D.C.: Alliance for Excellent Education.

Twenty-five years of educating children with disabilities: The good news and the work ahead. (2002). Washington, DC: American Youth Policy Forum and Center on Education Policy. Accessed August 10, 2011 at http://www.aypf.org/publications/special_ed.pdf

U.S. Government Accountability Office. (2003). *Federal actions can assist state in improving postsecondary outcomes for youth* (GAO-03-773). Washington, DC: U.S. Government Printing Office.

Vocational Education Act of 1963, P.L. 88–210. 20 U.S.C., §1241 et seq.

Vocational Education Amendments of 1968, P.L. 90–576. 20 U.S.C. 2301.

Vreeburg-Izzo, M., Hertzfeld, J., Simmons-Reed, E.,& Aaron, J. (2001). Promising practices: Improving the quality of higher education for students with disabilities. *Disability Studies Quarterly, 21*(1). Retrieved January 25, 2008, from http://www.dsq-sds. org/_articles_pdf/2001/Winter/dsq_2001_Winter_03.pdf

Wagner, M., Newman, L., Cameto, R., Levine, P., & Marder, C. (2003). *Going to school: Instructional contexts, programs, and participation of secondary school students with disabilities. A Report from the National Longitudinal Transition Study-2 (NLTS2).* Menlo Park, CA: SRI International.

Wagner, M., Newman, L., Cameto, R., Garza, N., & Levine, P. (2005). *After high school: A first look at the postschool experiences of youth with disabilities. A report from the National Longitudinal Transition Study-2 (NLTS2).* Menlo Park, CA: SRI International.

Wandry, D., Webb, K., Williams, J., Bassett, D., Asselin, S., & Hutchinson, S. (2008). Identifying the barriers to effective transition planning and implementation: A study of teacher candidates from five teacher preparation programs. *Career Development for Exceptional Individuals, 31*(1), 14–25.

Warren, J. R., Jenkins, K. N., & Kulick, R. B. (2006). High school exit examinations and state-level completion and GED Rates, 1975 through 2002. *Educational Evaluation and Policy Analysis 28*(2), 131–152.

Wehmeyer, M. L., Field, S., Doren, B., Jones, B., & Mason, C. (2004). Self-determination and student involvement in standards-based reform. *Exceptional Children, 70*(4), 413–426.

West, J. E., & Whitby, P. J. S. (2008). Federal policy and the education of students with disabilities: Progress and the path forward. *Focus on Exceptional Children, 41*(5), 1–16.

Will, M. (1984). *OSERS programming for the transition of youth with disabilities: Bridges from school to working life.* Washington, DC: Office of Special Education and Rehabilitation Services, U.S. Office of Education.

Wilson, M. G., Hoffman, A. V., & McLaughlin, M. J. (2009). Preparing youth with disabilities for college: How research can inform transition policy. *Focus on Exceptional Children, 41*(7), 1–12.

17

Middle School Transition Education Planning and Services

Jeanne B. Repetto

UNIVERSITY OF FLORIDA

> There is something that is much more scarce, something finer far, something rarer than ability. It is the ability to recognize ability.
>
> (Elbert Green Hubbard, 1901, p. 163)

The experience students have in middle school may be the most important factor of successful post-school outcomes. This may seem to be an over-enthusiastic statement made by a zealous middle school advocate, but there is growing evidence on the impact middle school education can have on keeping students in school until they graduate. Research has shown that students likely to drop out of school before graduating can be identified as early as the sixth grade and that schools can impact school retention through the use of identified promising practices (Institute of Education Sciences, 2008; Jerald, 2006). Students who graduate from school with a diploma are more likely to go on to postsecondary education and fulltime employment (National Longitudinal Transition Study 2, 2005). Therefore, middle schools play an important role in keeping students engaged in school until they enter and graduate from high school, thus improving their postsecondary outcomes (Alliance for Excellent Education, 2009).

Although it may be a leap to say middle schools are the most important factor of successful post-school outcomes, they do play an important role. Although transition planning is no longer mandated until the age of 16 (Individuals with Disabilities Education Act, 2004), middle schools are an important component of transition planning. Good middle school programs not only keep students engaged in school, they also guide young adolescents' exploration of their abilities in school and in the community, helping them to find their talents.

Middle School

History

Historically, young adolescents have presented school systems with a challenge to meet their unique needs, which differ from elementary and high school students. Until the 1960s, schools that educated students in seventh through ninth grades were called junior high schools. Established in 1909, when the first junior high school opened its doors in Columbus, Ohio (Manning, 2000), the junior high school was established to meet the needs of early adolescents. The idea for a separate education system for this age group began with the 1890s work of the

National Education Associations' Committee of Ten, composed of university presidents, and the elementary-education-focused Committee of Fifteen. These two groups worked together to standardize admission standards to universities and establish 18 as the age students enter college. The recommendation from these two committees was to reorganize the current eight-year elementary and four-year high school system by separating grades seven and eight into a unique program in which to start college preparation (Dickinson, 2001). Although this initiative failed, it laid the foundation for junior high schools, prompting educators to begin addressing the varied different needs of elementary, middle, and high school students (Manning, 2000; Wiles & Bondi, 2001).

Around this time America was experiencing an increase in immigrant children entering school systems. Many of these students left school before graduating from eighth grade to work in factories with their parents. One solution offered to keep these students engaged in school longer and assist them to better assimilate into society was a separate seventh- and eighth-grade school system that offered academics along with job training curriculum (Dickinson, 2001; Powell, Farrar, & Cohen, 1985). This recognition that the eight-year elementary and four-year high school system was not meeting the needs of a changing society further contributed to the establishment of junior high schools (George & Alexander, 1993).

In the 1950s and 1960s junior high schools began to be replaced by middle schools that spanned sixth, seventh, and eight grades. This transition took place because junior high schools focused on curriculum change to meet societal needs and failed to take into account the needs of the young adolescent (Manning, 2000). Middle schools were developed to address the unique interests and requirements of young adolescents by providing professionals educated to teach young adolescents using a curriculum responsive to their needs (McEwin, Dickinson, & Jenkins 1996). Such a curriculum includes teaching in interdisciplinary teams and integrating themes taught through differentiated and exploratory curricula (George, 2001; Wiles & Bondi, 2001).

Today middle school education is delivered by various grade groupings with the most popular being sixth, seventh, and eighth grouped together (Juvonen, Le, Kaganoff, Augustine, & Constant, 2004). Middle school grades act as a bridge between elementary school and high school. Their intent is to meet the unique needs of young adolescents while providing a safe environment for them to explore their academic and social place in the world. In their 2010 position statement titled *This We Believe: Keys to Educating Young Adolescents*, the National Middle School Association (NMSA) states that an education for middle school students must be developmentally responsive, challenging, empowering, and equitable (p. 15). The four essential attributes are achieved through 16 characteristics such as valuing students, providing challenging curriculum, using multiple learning approaches, fostering a safe school environment, and collaborating with families (see http://www.nmsa.org/AboutNMSA/ThisWeBelieve/tabid/1273/Default.aspx).

Effective middle school programs are impacted by four key elements: (a) student, (b) teacher, (c) environment, and (c) subject matter. Therefore, each of these four areas will be discussed in the following sections.

Student

Young adolescents (10–15 years old) are often described using adjectives such as gangly, temperamental, frustrating, hungry, clumsy, wild, contrary, inquisitive, and immature. These terms are testimony that young adolescence is a time of great change in all areas of life (mental, physical, emotional, and social). Often one only has to look at a young adolescent's face to see the inner conflict all this change is causing. This is a period of betrayal, when everything you are sure of as a child changes and no longer seems to fit. This change can be evident enough that during this time parents will remark, "Where did my child go?" At the same time, the young adolescent might express frustration with this change by making statements like: "I don't feel right" or "I just don't know what to do." An example of the impact of this change is the student who has always been very self-assured and able to make choices but all of a sudden keeps saying, "I don't know, what do you think?" because he or she is truly no longer able to make choices that once seemed so evident. This student's inability to choose is not only frustrating to him or her but to teachers who are confused about what happened to the self-assured student. In an effort to get back to feeling "normal," young adolescents are forced to explore new ways to make their lives work again. This transformation is necessary to build the foundation for an adulthood based on individual needs, wants, and abilities. In this manner, the frustration and confusion of young adolescence is crucial to success and happiness as an adult. This physical, cognitive, social/emotional change is real, not concocted by young adolescents to frustrate parents and teachers.

Physical Change

During the ages of 10–15 years, individuals change physically, becoming a mature, sexual human being. This physical change happens over several years causing uneven physical growth and hormone levels (NMSA, 2010; Walker & Lirgg, 1995). Uneven physical growth characterized by long legs and arms compared to the torso, or large feet compared to height, can cause clumsiness until students get used to their changing bodies or the body's development evens out. Hormone levels that have not leveled off can spike, causing irritability and moodiness, which improves as students get used to hormone levels and the levels begin to stabilize.

Cognitive Change

Cognitive development in a middle school student is expanding from concrete to abstract thinking (Mitchell, 1998; Piaget, 1972; Repetto, Webb, Neubert, & Curran, 2006; Wavering, 1995). An increase in abstract thinking allows students to think about the future and what role they may play in their own future. They can begin to evaluate their preferences and abilities in relationship to schoolwork, future jobs, etc. If given opportunities in class, they are able to address Bloom's higher-order thinking competencies such as drawing inferences, discussing relationship among topics, or inventing more efficient ways to complete a task (Bloom, 1956; Olson, Platt et al., 2008). Testing out their theories, exploring their place in the world, or simply being able to be more reflective helps to foster growth in self-esteem and self-confidence (Lipka, 1997; NMSA, 2010). This growth can be uneven, causing students to be a bit unsure of their actions and decisions until they become more confident in their new skills.

Social/Emotional Change

Socially, middle school students define themselves by what clique they do or don't belong to; this can change on a daily or even hourly basis. Young adolescents are working at defining who they are so they "try on" many groups for fit. Although they are learning about their uniqueness, they want to belong by being part of "group think," dressing and even talking like everyone else in the clique (Newman & Newman, 2001; NMSA, 2010). During this time, a group of friends often becomes more important to them than the family unit as they start to break away to become their own person although their families are still important (Ames, Ilg, & Baker, 1988; NMSA). Often parents will remark, "My daughter did not pay any attention to me and was even rude to me until it was time to go to bed, when she wanted me to tuck her in." This is typical and speaks to a powerful theme of this age group: CONFLICT.

Teacher

Parents don't have a choice but to hold on and enjoy the changes happening right before their eyes. Teachers are different; they chose this age group to teach. Teaching students in the middle of a huge learning curve can be thrilling, allowing teachers to have a true sense of impact every time a student has an "Aha!" moment (Repetto et al., 2006). Experiencing this moment is the ultimate pay off for a teacher, as described by one middle school teacher who thought his work with a student who seemed unmotivated had not made a difference until one day she came to school all dressed up and he asked why:

> She said, completely unexpectedly, "Thanks to you I have a job interview. I went to the animal hospital myself and they told me that someone had just quit and they needed some help. I told them I would be available over the summer and they told me that I could probably work there and that I should come in for an interview." Now what could I possibly say to all of *that*? I was flabbergasted and elated for her. Mary said then, in a moment I will never forget, "I want to give you half of my first paycheck for helping me do this. Thank you." I was already paid in more ways than she would ever know.
>
> (Repetto et al., p. 13)

Even though teaching middle school students can be frustrating, difficult, and confusing, it can be very rewarding. As one teacher put it, " . . . I can be as crazy as the kids are and nobody notices" (Repetto et al., p. 23). Another teacher likens the experience to being a rodeo clown: "You've got to be ready when they come out of the chute, step in when you are needed, catch their attention immediately, and guide them where they need to go. Of course, all this needs to be done with a bit of humor and laughter" (Repetto et al., p. 85).

Besides a sense of humor, what skills do middle school teachers need? It seems clear the skills needed differ from the skills needed to teach elementary students because central to working with middle school students is a working knowledge of young adolescent cognitive, physical, and social/emotional development along with the appropriate curriculum and instructional techniques to teach this age group (Jackson & Davis, 2000; NMSA, 1995; 2010). As Wormeli (2001) notes, middle-level teachers need to have the ability to mend a broken heart, make peace, laugh instead of cry, enthrall students, celebrate success, guide the lost, and tolerate conflict.

Teachers and principals across the United States validated and rank ordered a set of characteristics for middle school teachers (Arth, Lounsbury, McEwin, & Swain, 1995). Identified characteristics focused on the importance of student-centered teaching grounded in effective practices. Although the group rankings differ, each set of the top five necessary middle school teacher characteristics includes student-centered, teacher-centered, and instruction-centered themes. The majority of the characteristics reflect the student-centered philosophy of the middle school model ensuring (a) respect for student diversity, (b) developmentally appropriate teaching, (c) success in learning for all students, and (d) development of self-respect and love of learning. In addition, effective middle school teachers are (a) self-confident when challenged and (b) role models and advocates for middle school students. Principals felt it is important for teachers to maintain a safe and caring environment while focused on individualizing instruction with the use of varied strategies.

These same skills are present in NMSA reports (2001; 2010) characterizing an effective middle-level teacher as knowledgeable about their subject matter as well as the developmental needs of young adolescents. In addition, effective teachers (a) like teaching young adolescents, (b) understand the developmental need of this age group, (c) share their school's vision, (d) hold high expectations for all students, (e) advocate for every student, (f) promote a positive, supportive, and safe environment, (g) engage students in active earning, and (g) foster family and community partnerships.

Environment

One of the foundational principles of middle school is the provision of a safe and supportive environment in which students can explore and learn. Middle schools are the bridge between elementary and high school. During this time students are expected to learn how to function in a high school setting that is subject-centered and requires students to travel between class periods on their own. In the high school setting, students need to be independent learners, self-determined, and confident in their ability to function independently. These are skills learned throughout middle school as students mature and explore ways to function in an environment that is less structured than elementary school but more so than high school. Typically, in middle school students start and end the day in homeroom but move throughout the school building for their other classes and electives. However, they typically move with the students in their homeroom among a core group of teachers. This provides a safe community in which to explore and learn.

School environment has a relationship to student learning because it comprises the conditions under which students learn. Juvonen et al. (2004) conducted a review of the literature to study the conditions in which middle school students learn focusing on (a) social-emotional well-being, (b) engagement, (c) school context, and (d) climate. Examining the relationship between social–emotional well-being and academic performance, the authors found evidence-based practices supporting a link between a student's psychosocial and academic functioning. This link suggests that attempts to improve academics in young adolescents must also address ways to improve social-emotional concerns. Further, reviewed practices relating to school alienation and school engagement suggests that students who feel disengaged and alienated tend to be poor school performers and are at risk to be retained a grade, a factor in school drop-out (Jerald, 2006; Juvonen et al., 2004). Therefore, engaging students in school can have life-long consequences for students and society.

A relationship seems to exist between school safety and school functioning. For example, students who feel safe at school function at higher levels than students who are stressed by witnessing or experiencing bullying. This conclusion is stated in a 1995 National Center on Educational Statistics report noting that student energy spent on avoiding harm could be used on learning (Chandler, Nolin et al., 1995). When asked about school safety, middle school students reported a safe and orderly environment as being very important (National Association of Secondary School Principals & Phi Delta Kappa, 2007). They ranked discipline issues higher than teaching, teachers, and administrative or school structure issues as the biggest problem facing middle schools. Specifically identified discipline concerns in rank order from most to least include bullies/gangs, inappropriate student behaviors, social pressure, fights, and illegal activities. Such ratings from students indicate that they feel schools need to be safer, leading to the assumption that safety issues are distracting them from learning.

Subject Matter

In this section a broad view of subject matter will be discussed, taking into account the infrastructure as well as content of middle school coursework. Effective middle school infrastructure elements include interdisciplinary teaming, mentoring; or advisement programs, and flexible structures (Manning & Bucher, 2001; NMSA, 2010). Elements of effective content for middle school coursework include providing exploratory curriculum through required coursework and electives; building on prerequisite skills learned in elementary grades; offering core curriculum in language arts, social studies, mathematics, and science as prerequisites for high school courses; requiring physical education; and providing transition assessment and exploration (Manning & Bucher; NMSA; Repetto et al., 2006; Sitlington, Neubert, Begun, Lombard, & Leconte, 2007; Wiles & Bondi, 2001).

Infrastructure

The infrastructure elements, such as a flexible schedule and interdisciplinary teams, are designed to foster a sense of community within which students and teachers work as a team to support learning (NMSA, 2010). Flexible scheduling can support longer class periods during which teachers and students get to know each other better and have time to explore a content area, perhaps discussing its application across several disciplines. Interdisciplinary teams encourage the teachers working with a particular group of students to have a common planning period to discuss the needs of their group. These foundational elements in the concept of middle schools are promising practices that need further research to establish their effectiveness (Juvonen et al., 2004).

Content

Middle school coursework is meant to provide a bridge connecting elementary and high school curriculum. This bridge builds on skills learned in elementary school to ensure the readiness of students for the level of skill development required in high school. In addition, middle school educators must prepare their students to make adequate yearly progress on state standardized tests (No Child Left Behind (NCLB), 2001). It is troubling that the 2007 National Assessment of Education Progress data indicated a decline in the proficiency levels for reading and math from fourth to eighth grades (United States Department of Education, 2008) pointing to the need to further study evidence-based practices for teaching content to middle school students.

Beyond learning subject content, students also need to become independent learners to prepare for high school work. Also, middle school students are cognitively becoming more abstract thinkers, which allows them to explore how their learning connects to the world around them and to their own lives. Therefore, middle school teachers need to address content needs to prepare students for high school coursework and to pass state standardized tests (NCLB, 2001) while at the same time guide their students in exploring the connection between what they are learning to the world outside of school.

Middle School Model

One model that brings all the elements of effective middle school education together is the MidEx Model (Repetto et al., 2006). Central to the MidEx Model are the characteristics of the middle school student such as concrete to abstract thinking, asynchronous growth, and peer orientation. In the MidEx Model the student is connected to middle school practices (e.g., being responsive, developmentally appropriate, interdisciplinary) and effective teacher characteristics (e.g., partnering, bridging transitions, being knowledgeable). These three central components (student, practices, and teacher) constitute the core of the Model and are constantly interacting with each other. The six outer components (school, family, community, mission, reflection, and engagement) continually provide input and support to the three core components.

For example, students who are taking a general education math course may need to improve their study skills to pass the course. To address this need, teachers could teach students a learning strategy for studying and ask parents to monitor home practice of the new strategy. Once the strategy is learned the teacher would work with the students to explore its application across coursework and in everyday life. Another example would be the teacher who works with the school's business partner to start an entrepreneur program that helps students apply academic skills to a real-world business model.

Transition Education

Central to the mission of middle school education is preparation of students for their future. Middle school is all about transitions; it is sandwiched between two important vertical transitions, moving from elementary to middle school and from middle school to high school. In addition, young adolescents experience many other transitions including (a) moving from course to course, (b) growing in family and peer relationships, (c) budding physically, and (d) maturing cognitively. Added to this already impressive list of transitions is the necessity for young adolescents to begin thinking about their transitions from high school to the world, helping them to choose the correct high school program to match their future plans. How students navigate all these transitions impacts their future (Jerald, 2006; National Longitudinal Transition Study 2, 2005). During this time, it is easy for students to get lost, frustrated, or confused, causing them to drop out, act out, or simply shut down. Therefore, perhaps the biggest challenge for middle school educators is to help students navigate through all their transitions. In this section we will discuss promising strategies to assist students through their transitions.

Academic Strategies

Academically, students are moving from learning how to read, spell, write, and compute math to application of these skills in content-based curriculum. Academic coursework focuses more on learning content to build the foundation for high school courses. For example, in math students are no longer learning how to compute basic functions but rather how to apply these math functions to algebra or geometry, or in language arts students are no longer being taught how to write a paragraph but rather how to write a paper on the meaning of a poem. Some students still need help to remember the basic math functions or how to write a paragraph. Providing these students with strategies to support their learning will assist them in learning the course content. Research findings indicate student use of learning strategies positively affects learner outcomes (Deshler, Ellis, & Lenz, 1996; Snoeren, Repetto, & Miller, 2007). Researchers at the University of Kansas have developed a series of evidence-based learning strategies for use by students, starting in middle school, to assist them in becoming independent learners able to understand information and solve problems (Deshler et al., 1996). Learning strategies have been developed for (a) reading, (b) studying and remembering information, (c) writing, (d) improving assignment and test performance, (e) effectively interacting with others, (f) motivation, and (g) math (Center for Research on Learning, 2009). An example of a writing strategy is the *Paragraph Writing Strategy* which gives specific steps to follow when planning and writing a paragraph. The following six steps are for the SCRIBE paragraph-learning strategy:

Step 1: **S**et up a diagram.
Step 2: **C**reate the title.
Step 3: **R**eveal the topic.
Step 4: **I**ron out the details.
Step 5: **B**ind it together with a clincher.
Step 6: **E**dit your work.

(Schumaker & Lyerla, 1993, p. 326)

Another important academic strategy for teachers to employ when designing and teaching courses is considering the varied ways students learn (NMSA, 2010). Teachers can meet the different learning needs of students through the application of the universal design principles of employing multiple formats for representing and expressing information and engaging students (Nolet & McLaughlin, 2000). For example, to accommodate students with various learning styles, use a variety of formats including discussions, graphs, demonstrations, and the internet.

Life Skills Strategies

The overriding goal of middle school students is to become more independent not only in academic coursework but in skills that they need to function in and out of school (e.g., cooking, shopping, hanging out with friends, going to the movies). Being successful in these activities requires life skills learned in and out of school (e.g., reading a recipe, making change, conversing with friends, deciding on a movie).

A comprehensive set of life skills taught to students that may be embedded in existing course content, taught in a separate course, or infused into school activities is Life Centered Career Education (LCCE). This evidence-based curriculum lists necessary competencies to perform tasks that most adults encounter in various life roles (e.g., work, family, education, recreation). The LCCE Model is a set of 22 competencies grouped under the headings of daily living skills (e.g., manage personal finances, food preparation, leisure activities), personal/social skills (e.g., self-awareness, communication skills, decision-making), and occupational guidance and preparation skills (e.g., work habits, maintaining employment, specific job skills) (Brolin, 1997). Another set of life skills developed by Cronin and Patton (1993) has six domains (Employment and Education; Home and Family; Leisure Pursuits; Community Involvement; Physical and Emotional Health; Personal Responsibility and Relationships) with Subdomains and Life Demands under each Domain. For example, under the Community Involvement Domain a Subdomain is *citizenship* with the Life Demand of *understand legal rights*. Both sets of skills can be used to expand student learning by engaging them in the application of content to real-life situations.

Self-determination

Middle schools are the perfect environment to foster self-determination in students. Self-determination is defined as a person's ability to identify and set goals, act on those goals, and evaluate their actions (Field, Martin, Miller, Ward, & Wehmeyer, 1998). This is exactly what young adolescents are trying to do. They want to take control over their lives. Think about taking a group of eighth graders on a field trip to Epcot. Once students are organized into small groups with a chaperone, the teacher can (a) have all the groups stay together and give a little talk about what they are learning as they go from country to country or (b) set country-based learning goals with the students before the trip and give the groups the freedom to explore as they want. Chances are the students from Group (a) will get frustrated, act-out, and learn very little while the students from Group (b) will have fun and meet the pre-set learning goals. The difference is Group (b) students helped to identify the goals, decided how they wanted to achieve the goals, and evaluated when they had met them. Group (b) students are practicing their self-determination skills while Group (a) students are being told what, how, and when they learned the teacher's goal. Good middle school teachers have the ability to help students become self-determined by advocating for them to set goals, take calculated risks, self-manage learning, and make decisions (Deshler & Schumaker, 2006; Repetto et al., 2006).

Exploration Strategies

What is so wonderful about working with young adolescents is their openness to try new experiences, perhaps similar to when they were two years old and exploring their world as they learned to walk and talk. The difference is that young adolescents are exploring an expanded world that goes beyond their neighborhoods and schools into communities reaching as far as they can imagine. Like the two-year-old, they are learning their place in this new and expanded world, figuring out what they like and dislike, and how they can contribute now and in the future. This exploration takes place while going to school, surfing the internet at home, playing football, seeing the dentist, shopping at the mall, and visiting family members at Thanksgiving. Young adolescents are always working on how they fit in socially and how they can excel. What students learn about themselves through their exploration impacts what they decide to do as adults. Therefore, it is important for middle school programs to incorporate opportunities for exploration into their curricula. The following are two ways in which schools can provide avenues for students to explore who they are and what they want to do.

Service Learning

Service learning gives students a chance to explore their social and academic abilities while participating in a community project (Billing, 2002). The community projects can be activities sponsored by the school, community organizations, non-profit organizations, or student-initiated projects in response to a need (Bohnenberger & Terry, 2002). Service learning extends community service by connecting it to academic leaning. An example of the connection between service and academics is the eighth-grade social studies class in Massachusetts that worked with a museum to tape oral histories from retired tool-industry employees (Scales, Blyth, Berkas, & Kielsmeier, 2000). A key to connecting service learning to academics and to student self-exploration is the inclusion of a reflective activity (e.g., journal). Participation in service-learning activities can positively impact social responsibility and academic outcomes (Scales et al., 2000).

Career Exploration

Since the IDEA 2004 increased the age to begin transition planning from 14 to 16, most transition assessment takes place at the high school level. However, middle school students need to make decisions impacting their post-school futures regarding the types of high school diploma they will receive (e.g., a standard or special diploma) and the type of high school program they will enter (e.g., general education, honors academic magnet, tech prep program). A young adolescent's readiness to explore careers, along with the need to gather information on which to base decisions about their high school paths, makes career exploration a very important part of a middle school curriculum. Through career exploration, students can evaluate their unique interests and abilities in relationship to a variety of careers. Students should not narrow their searches to just one career, but should rather begin to focus on areas of interest. For example, they may explore jobs in the medical field but not a specific kind of medicine, or they may look at careers in technology but not decide on a specific type of computer programming. This concept is illustrated by a middle school student who insisted he wanted to be a doctor but, upon completing a career exploration activity requiring him to list all the reasons why he wanted to be a doctor, decided that what he really liked about being a doctor was getting to help people, wear a white coat, and eat hospital food. There are many jobs besides being a doctor in the medical field that would fit his interests. Taking a closer look at the specific components of a job and matching them to student interests and skills may broaden rather than narrow job opportunities.

If you ask a middle school student what they want to do for a job, chances are you will be told a singer, dancer, football player, doctor, teacher, etc. Their answers are based on careers they are familiar with or activities they like to do. During middle school these options need to be expanded to include a variety of careers in many fields. Exploration can be done through a combination of internet searches, job shadowing, field trips, guest presenters, work samples, connecting curriculum to careers, creating a class company, and job try-outs (Repetto et al., 2006). Through these activities students learn about new jobs by asking questions: What skills are needed? What education is necessary? How much do workers earn? Do you need to travel for the job? Matching the answers to these questions to their own interests and skills helps students further define their future job and the high school and diploma path they need to take.

Individualized Education Program (IEP)

The IEP is the planning process used to develop educational programs for middle school students with disabilities as mandated by the Individuals with Disabilities Education Act (IDEA, 2004). Since the IDEA 2004 raised the age for transition planning from 14 to 16, middle school IEPs are no longer mandated to address transition. However, some states (e.g., Florida) have state regulations in place that still require transition planning to begin at age 14. In either case, it is important to consider the young adolescents' future dreams, interests, preferences, and strengths when planning programs. This is crucial to ensure that they are offered the best middle school opportunities to help them choose the appropriate high school program and diploma type. The IEP meeting is also a good time to address any concerns that parents may have about their child's future in high school and post-school.

Summary

This chapter provides a brief summary of the history of middle school education along with effective practices for middle school programs. An in-depth discussion is provided on curriculum components that are designed to meet the unique needs of young adolescents. The many transitions middle school students encounter are discussed along with several key curriculum components fostering their social and academic growth along with their independence as they navigate these transitions. In addition, exploratory curriculum is discussed and its importance in guiding students in choosing future paths.

Middle school is a crucial period in a student's academic career because choices made during these years will impact the future. Schools that are able to engage students in learning and provide them with a caring community can have a lasting impact on the lives of their students by encouraging them to stay in school until they graduate. Middle schools providing students with strategies to become independent learners and to explore how they fit in the world help improve the quality of life that each of their students will have as adults.

References

Alliance for Excellent Education (November, 2009). The nation's path to economic growth: The economic benefits of reducing the dropout rate. Washington, DC: Author. Retrieved November 24, 2009 from http://www.all4ed.org/publication_material/EconMSA

Ames, L., Ilg, F., & Brown, S. (1988). *Your ten-to fourteen-year-old*. New York: Delacorte Press.

Arth, A., Lounsbury, J., McEwin, C. K., & Swain, J. (1995). *Middle level teachers: Portraits of excellence*. Westville, OH: National Middle School Association and National Association of Secondary School Principals.

Bloom, B. (1956). *Taxonomy of educational objectives, handbook 1: Cognitive domain.* New York: David McKay Co., Inc.

Bohnenberger, J. E., & Terry, A. W. (2002). Community problem solving works for middle level students. *Middle School Journal, 34*(1), pp. 5–12.

Brolin, D. E. (1997). *Life centered career education: A competency based approach* (5th ed.). Reston, VA: Council for Exceptional Children.

Center for Research on Learning. (2009). *Learning strategies.* Lawrence, KS: The University of Kansas. Retrieved December 1, 2009 from http://www.ku-crl.org/sim/strategies.shtml

Chandler, K., Nolin, M., & Davies, E. (1995). *Student strategies to avoid harm at school.* Washington, DC: U.S. Government Printing Office, NCES 95–203.

Cronin, M. E., & Patton, J. R. (1993). *Life skills instruction for all students with special needs: A practical guide for integrating real-life content into the curriculum.* Austin, TX: PRO-ED.

Deshler, D., Ellis, E., & Lenz, B. (1996). *Teaching adolescents with learning disabilities: Strategies and methods.* Denver, CO: Love Publishing Company.

Deshler, D., & Schumaker, J. (2006). *Teaching adolescents with disabilities: Accessing the general curriculum.* Thousand Oaks, CA: Corwin Press.

Dickinson, T. S. (Ed.) (2001). *Reinventing the middle school.* New York: RoutledgeFalmer.

Field, S., Martin, J., Miller, M., Ward, M., & Wehmeyer, M. (1998). Self-determination for persons with disabilities: A position statement of the Division on Career Development and Transition. *Career Development for Exceptional Individuals, 21*(2), 113–128.

George, P. S. (2001). The evolution of middle schools. *Educational Leadership, 58*(4), 40–44.

George, P. S., & Alexander, W. M. (1993). *The exemplary middle school.* Fort Worth, TX: Harcourt Brace Publishers.

Hubbard, E. H. (1901). *A message to Garcia and thirteen other things.* East Aurora, NY: Roycrafters.

Individuals with Disabilities Education Act of 2004 (IDEA), 20 U.S.C. § 1400 et seq.

Institute of Education Sciences (2008). *IES practice guide: Dropout prevention* (NCEE 2008-4025). What Works Clearinghouse, U.S. Department of Education. Washington, DC.

Jackson, A. W., & Davis, G. A. (2000). *Turning points 2000: Educating adolescents in the 21st century.* New York: Teachers College Press.

Jerald, C. (2006). *Identifying potential dropouts: Key lessons for building an early warning system.* Achieve, Inc. Retrieved November 26 from http://www.achieve.org/measuresthatmatter

Juvonen, J., Le, V-N., Kaganoff, J., Augustine, C., & Constant, L. (2004). *Focus on the wonder years: Challenges facing the American middle school.* Santa Monica, CA: Rand Corporation.

Lipka, R. (1997). Enhancing self-concept/self-esteem in young adolescents. In J. L. Irvin (Ed.), *What current research says to the middle level practitioner* (pp. 31–39). Columbus, OH: National Middle School Association.

Manning, M. L. (2000). A brief history of the middle school. *The ClearingHouse, 73*(4), 192.

Manning, M., & Bucher, K. (2001). *Teaching in the middle school.* Columbus, OH: Merrill Prentice Hall.

McEwin, K., Dickinson, T., & Jenkins, D. M. (1996). *America's middle schools: Practices and progress.* Westville, OH: National Middle School Association.

Mitchell, J. (1998). *The natural limitations of youth: The predispositions that shape the adolescent character.* Stamford, CT: Anlex.

National Association of Secondary School Principals & Phi Delta Kappa. (2007). *Middle school poll.* Retrieved September 8, 2009 from http://www.principals.org/s_nassp/index.asp?CID=1138&DID=54609

National Longitudinal Transition Study 2. (2005). *Facts from NLTS2: High School Completion by Youth with Disabilities.* Menlo Park, CA: SRI International. Retrieved September 10, 2009 from http://www.nlts2.org/fact_sheets/

National Middle School Association (NMSA). (1995). *This we believe: Developmentally responsive middle level schools.* Columbus, OH: Author.

National Middle School Association (NMSA). (2001). *In this we believe . . . and now we must act.* Westerville, OH: Author.

National Middle School Association (NMSA). (2010). *In this we believe: Keys to educating young adolescents.* Westerville, OH: Author.

Newman, B., & Newman, P. (2001). Group identity and alienation: Giving the we its due. *Journal of Youth and Adolescence, 30*, 515–538.

No Child Left Behind Act of 2001, 20 U.S.C. §6301(2001).

Nolet, V., & McLaughlin, M. J. (2000). *The general education curriculum: Including students with disabilities in standards-based reform.* Thousand Oaks, CA: Crown Press.

Olson, J., Platt, J., & Dieker, L. (2008). *Teaching children and adolescents with special needs*. Columbus, OH: Merrill Publishing.

Piaget, J. (1972). Intellectual evolution from adolescence to adulthood. *Human Development, 15*, 1–12.

Powell, A. G., Farrar, E., & Cohen, D. K. (1985). *The shopping mall high school: Winners and losers in the educational marketplace*. Boston, MA: Houghton Mifflin.

Repetto, J., Webb, K., Neubert, D., & Curran, C. (2006). *The middle school experience: Successful teaching and transition planning for diverse learners*. Austin, TX: PRO-ED.

Scales, P., Blyth, D., Berkas, T., & Kielsmeier, J. (2000). The effects of service-learning on middle school students' social responsibility and academic success. *The Journal of Early Adolescence, 20*(3), 332–358.

Schumaker, J., & Lyerla, K. (1993). *Learning strategies curriculum: The paragraph writing strategy*. Lawrence, KS: University of Kansas.

Sitlington, P., Neubert, D., Begun, W., Lombard, R., & Leconte, P. (2007). *Assess for success: A practitioner's handbook on transition assessment*. Thousand Oaks, CA: Corwin Press.

Snoeren, F., Repetto, J., & Miller, D. (2007). *The relationship between self-determination, learning strategies and learning outcomes* [Data file]. Gainesville, FL: Author.

United States Department of Education. (2008). *Mapping America's educational progress 2008*. Retrieved August 24, 2009 from http://www.ed.gov/nclb/accountability/results/progress/nation.html

Walker, D., & Lirgg, C. (1995). Growth and development during middle school years. In M. J. Wavering (Ed.), *Educating young adolescents: Life in the middle* (pp. 53–78). New York: Garland.

Wavering, M. (1995). Cognitive development of young adolescents. In M. J. Wavering (Ed.), *Educating young adolescents: Life in the middle* (pp. 111–130). New York: Garland.

Wiles, J., & Bondi, J. (2001). *The new American middle school*. Upper Saddle River, NJ: Merrill Prentice Hall.

Wormeli, R. (2001). *Meet me in the middle: Becoming an accomplished middle-level teacher*. Portland, ME: Stenhouse Publishers.

18

Providing Transition Education to a Diverse Student Population

Sharon deFur

COLLEGE OF WILLIAM AND MARY

Audrey A. Trainor

UNIVERSITY OF WISCONSIN-MADISON

Special education researchers and practitioners alike often discuss the changing demography of the U.S. population, noting achievement and outcome gaps between groups of youth based on race/ethnicity. For example, concerns about the disparity in high school graduation rates between White youth with disabilities and their Black and Latino peers are often translated into a need to address "diversity." Actually, it has now been three decades since Fair and Sullivan (1980) noted that groups of youth with disabilities had limited access to career opportunities based on their group characteristics, such as race. More recently, researchers have focused on the need to think about cultural and linguistic diversity in transition planning (Geenen, Powers, Lopez-Vasquez, & Bersani, 2003). In fact, diversity has become something of a buzzword throughout education; student-teachers say that they have "done that diversity training" (Gay, 2002), researchers acknowledge the importance of including diverse populations in projects (August & Hakuta, 1997), and practicing teachers and transition specialists agree that we should improve our ability to be culturally responsive as we work with diverse populations (Leake & Black, 2005). Unfortunately, these words and phrases, as is often the case with buzzwords, have lost precision. In this chapter, we define diversity in the context of special education transition research and practice as we attempt to answer this central question: *What do we know about educating a diverse population of students with disabilities who are transitioning into adulthood?*

What is Diversity and Why does it Matter as a Transition Focus?

In the context of this discussion of special education transition, we use the term diversity to represent differences among and between members of groups of people based on race/ethnicity, disability, language, gender, and a myriad of other characteristics that contribute to individuals' cultural identities. Therefore, when we use the term diversity, we are focusing on the multicultural aspects of transition that include, for example, the perceptions and experiences of a 15-year-old White Christian male with ADHD to the same extent that they include an 18-year-old Black Muslim female with a physical disability. In other words, we do not use the term diversity synonymously with "people of color."

Further, we recognize that cultural identities are both fluid and dynamic (Gudykunst, 2003), making it impossible both to trace individuals' values and beliefs about life after high school to one aspect of their identities and to make assumptions about individuals based on group membership. For example, we understand that an English-language learner who has citizenship or residency documentation may experience the transition to employment quite differently than an English-language learner who does not have such documentation although they may be members of the same community or even the same family. We also recognize that despite the fact that the U.S. teaching force is majority White, female, and middle-class, teachers themselves represent a range of identities and related values and beliefs about education, disability, and the transition to adulthood. We also know that the face of America is changing and that race and ethnicity are likely to become increasingly blurred.

That the U.S. society is pluralistic, composed of many peoples, all of whom have complex cultural identities, is not new. Historically, diversity has been a defining characteristic of who we are as Americans. However, differences among and between people extend beyond neutral preferences, habits, and mores regarding postsecondary education, career trajectories, and adult living arrangements. Unquestionably, economic and associated resources, power, and status are important factors in accessing education (Darling-Hammond, 2006). For example, transition specialists may need to help youth from low socioeconomic status (SES) backgrounds consider applying for subsidized health care options, where available, while such guidance may not be necessary for youth from middle and high SES backgrounds who may remain insured under their parents' policies during the initial years of young adulthood. From a different perspective, Allen (2009) argues that many recent immigrant Latino students and their families may not be familiar with the steps required to navigate the transition to postsecondary education in the United States, an increasingly important path to employment for youth with and without disabilities. Furthermore, the traditional 20th century conceptualization of family as being two parents (husband and wife) and their children living separate from other family members may not always be representative of the families with whom we work.

In sum, diversity is actually an inclusive term rather than one that refers to specific segments of the American population. We underscore the reality that diversity occurs across *and* within groups, making overgeneralizations and stereotypes unhelpful. At the same time cross-cultural considerations are critical to successful secondary to postsecondary transitions. Researchers, practitioners, and policy-makers must cultivate knowledge, understanding, and skills to expand culturally responsive practices.

In the remainder of this chapter, we begin by presenting a viable model that helps explain how our cultural identities and the cultural systems in which we interact influence postsecondary outcomes. Then we use nationally representative outcome data to depict the state of postsecondary transition for groups based on disability, race/ethnicity, SES, and gender. We also draw attention to some of the limitations of available outcome data. Next, we review the extant research on transition education of youth with disabilities from diverse backgrounds and we outline implications for practice. Last, we suggest questions that should be examined further by transition practitioners and researchers.

An Ecological Model of Interactions Influencing Transition Outcomes

Given the persistent disparity of outcomes across disability, race/ethnicity, and gender, key stakeholders in special education have been concerned with understanding and addressing obstacles that impede successful transitions for youth with disabilities. Theories of adolescent and career development have long been frames of reference for the postsecondary transition of adolescents with disabilities as they approach adulthood. During the 1980s and into the

1990s, scholars, practitioners, family members, and individuals with disabilities began to reflect on personal experiences and examine initial waves of postsecondary outcome data. Concerns unique to having a disability fueled the expansion of these models beyond conceptualizing transition as preparation for employment. Transition models also needed to include the capacity to explain the important roles of community involvement (Halpern, 1985) and self-determination (Field & Hoffman, 1994) in successful postsecondary transitions.

Existing transition models, however, rarely depict or explicate what roles one's cultural identities or the systemic cultures in which one interacts play during postsecondary transition. To better understand diversity in transition, an ecological theoretical perspective is instructive because it allows us to understand how both individuals and systems, all of whom have multiple and interacting identities and practices, exert influence on planning and engaging in transition education (Gil-Kashiwabara, Hogansen, Geenen, Powers, & Powers, 2007; Trainor, Lindstrom, Simon-Burroughs, Martin, & Sorrells, 2008). We find socio-ecological theory (Bronfenbrenner, 1979) particularly useful because its focus on interactions affords us a way to make meaning of the power and influence leveraged by various individuals and systems over time.

The model for ecological development has four essential dimensions. First, the *microsystem* is composed of individuals and their interactions with one another. In postsecondary transition for youth with disabilities, this system has been heavily scrutinized. For example, researchers and practitioners are keenly aware that an adolescent's relationship and interactions with key individuals (e.g., a parent, a peer, a teacher) influence their career choices and interests (Morningstar, Turnbull, & Turnbull, 1995; Rojewski, 1996). Adopting a culturally responsive stance requires transition service providers within the microsystem to attend to cross-cultural communication and interaction, acknowledging and attending to, for example, a collectivist approach to decision-making whereby youth and parents reach decisions about the future only after consulting important elders in their community.

The *mesosystem*, or the interactions between multiple microsystems including those comprising home and school, is the second essential component. For instance, much of the extant literature on transition planning emphasizes the importance of home–school interactions, particularly parent participation in transition planning (Geenen et al., 2003; Harvard Family Research Project [HFRP], 2007; Hogansen, Powers, Geenen, Gil-Kashiwabara, & Powers, 2008). If, for example, schools foster relationships and interactions that include parents of students with disabilities in planning for postsecondary education, networking opportunities among teachers and other parents may bolster the quantity and quality of support students receive through the college application process.

The *exosystem* reflects a third level of essential interaction: systems-level interactions in which individuals may not be present or may exert little direct control. For example, federal educational policies such as the Individuals with Disabilities Education Improvement Act of 2004 (IDEA) and the No Child left Behind Act of 2001(NCLB) have set specific guidelines for secondary curricular requirements for school-age youth heavily steeped in core academic knowledge and skills such as reading and math, creating both barriers and opportunities for adolescents with disabilities as they decide to prepare for postsecondary education, employment, or both (Kochhar-Bryant & Bassett, 2002). Finally, the *macrosystem*, the fourth essential component, reflects societal-level interactions. For example, social and economic forces associated with financial recession or expansion affect youths' opportunities and attitudes about employment and other aspects of adult living such as whether to remain in the family home following high school or to move to a separate household.

Systemic and Contextual Influences on Post-School Outcomes

It is no secret that youth with disabilities experience more challenges than their typically developing age peers as they move through school and enter the adult world. Disability, by its very definition, suggests an obstacle or obstacles that potentially challenge academic or performance success. At the macro- and exosystemic levels, requirements of various federal and state laws and policies such as the provision of reasonable accommodations and modifications, individualized education programs, specialized instruction, inclusion in the general accountability system, and access to programs represent Congressional attempts to address the structural deficits of disability (e.g., the IDEA, the Americans with Disabilities Act [ADA], and the No Child Left Behind Act [NCLB]). Furthermore, Congress included transition policy mandates beginning with the 1990 IDEA and subsequent re-authorizations as an attempt to mediate ability differences and focus education on improving post-school outcomes for all young adults with disabilities.

The National Council on Disability (NCD, 2008) examined the impact of NCLB and IDEA on the outcomes of students with disabilities. In this report, the authors concluded that these policies target academic improvement for subgroups of the population, (e.g., students with disabilities, students from historically marginalized groups, students from low SES backgrounds as required under NCLB), have, as intended, heightened attention to addressing the needs of these subgroups, particularly students with disabilities. At the same time, the NCD (2008), like many others (Darling-Hammond, 2006, 2007), cited unintended consequences of the NCLB and IDEA accountability requirements. For example, Darling-Hammond (2007) expressed concern that the NCLB punished the neediest schools and students where such sanctions have created an environment that excludes diverse learners whose test scores threaten school accreditation.

IDEA 2004 requires State Education Agencies (SEA) to collect and publicly report performance data for students with disabilities, including indicators of post-school outcomes. These data offer program evaluation benchmarks for schools to examine system efforts relative to transition. For example, the SEA reports illustrate graduation rates, dropout rates, achievement rates based on standardized and high stakes assessments, as well as the existence of measurable transition goals and post-school outcomes. Coupled with NCLB accountability data, comparison data across subgroups offer insight into the effect of policy intervention for diverse youth with disabilities. Transition policy-makers, practitioners, and researchers can monitor progress and identify areas for further exploration to explain student outcomes.

Transition Outcomes for Diverse Students with Disabilities

Undeniably, structural and systemic challenges continue for youth and young adults with disabilities in spite of targeted systems-change policies. In part, special education research has yet to identify the best evidence-based practices for leveling the playing field that might raise academic skills, enable school completion, and thus increase transition outcomes for young adults with disabilities. While the field continues to seek strategies to improve academic performance or bypass any handicap of disability, well-intentioned policy or even evidence-based practices still cannot mandate changes in personal attitude or expectations.

Microsystem and mesosystem interactions often perpetuate inappropriate attitudes, practices, and low expectations based on race/ethnicity and other variables. For example, Sleeter (2008) claims that "students of color—especially Black and Latino students—are much more likely than White students to be taught by teachers who question their academic ability, are uncomfortable around them, or do not know how to teach them well" (p. 559). Sleeter asserts that many White teachers make assumptions that families from Black or Latino backgrounds do not value education, and thus these teachers often fail to establish relationships with families whose race/ethnicity differs from their own. Oftentimes, people fail to recognize their own attitudes and practices, so educators commonly deny having such biases or disconnection from their students.

The stigma of disability, as well as racial, ethnic, gender, sexual orientation, or social class biases, continues to perpetuate deficit-based attitudes for youth and young adults who learn or look differently from the traditional concept of U.S. youth and young adults. Sadly, this orientation continues to interfere with expectations of success by educators, families, and even young adults with disabilities themselves. Furthermore, transition researchers like secondary educators are predominantly White, which may contribute to superficial understandings of cultural differences and associated implications of power and bias. Transition professionals cannot overlook the implicit or explicit challenges of being disabled and culturally or linguistically diverse in a society where ableism, racism, sexism, etc., continue to exist. Confronting this reality may be one of the biggest challenges of providing transition services or researching culturally diverse youth with disabilities and their families that can support successful postsecondary outcomes in employment, education, and independent living.

School Completion

According to the National Longitudinal Transition Study-2 (NTLS2) (Newman et al., 2009), the majority of youth with disabilities completed school either through a range of diploma options or by staying through the age of eligibility. Other sources report much lower completion rates (about 48%) when standard diplomas are used as the criteria (Martin & Halperin, 2006). Furthermore, school completion varies by disability and by race/ethnicity. Citing the 26th Annual Report to Congress on IDEA, the National High School Center (2007) identified that more than half of American Indian/Alaska Native students with disabilities do not complete school. Black and Latino students with disabilities dropped out of school at similar rates (45% and 44% respectively). The report cited that 34% of White students with disabilities dropped out of school as did 28% of Asian/Pacific Islander youth with disabilities. About half of students identified as having an emotional disability in the NLTS2 completed school through traditional means (diploma or aging out); this percentage has remained consistent since the first National Longitudinal Transition Study (NLTS1) completed in 1989. Furthermore, Martin and Halperin (2006) reported that high school students (irrespective of disability status) from families with low income drop out of school at six times the rate of their peers.

Given the overrepresentation of Black and Latino youth identified as having emotional disabilities and a recent report from the National High School Center (2007) that only half of Black or Latino males with or without disabilities graduate from high school, concerns emerge regarding the transition outcomes for these youth. Murray and Naranjo (2008) identify various risk factors that contribute to the potential for dropping out for Black males (in particular) with learning disabilities. These include peer pressure, a family history of dropping out, community acceptance of dropping out as an option, personal conflicts with teachers, as well as poverty and perceived racial discrimination. Regardless of disability or other demographics, school completion remains a major factor associated with positive transition outcomes.

Engagement and Post-Secondary Education

Education can celebrate the progress of the past twenty years noting many positive outcomes for young adults with disabilities. According to reports from the second National Longitudinal Transition Study (NTLS2), young adults with disabilities reported being engaged in multiple ways in postsecondary education, employment, or independent living and at rates that are somewhat parallel (although not equal) to those of their typically developing young adult peers (Newman, Wagner, Cameto, & Knokey, 2009; Wagner, Newman, Cameto, & Levine, 2005). For example, an increasing number of young adults with disabilities attended postsecondary education, and young adults with disabilities accessed two-year colleges at about the same rate as young adults without disabilities. An examination of postsecondary enrollment based on racial/ethnic background illustrates that although enrollment in postsecondary education across vocational, two-year, and four-year settings was not statistically significant, nearly 16% of White and 15% of Latino young adults with disabilities enrolled in four-year colleges; far fewer Black young adults (5%) made similar choices (Newman et al., 2009). Also, an examination of SES and enrollment does reveal statistically significant differences. For instance, 40% of young adults from families with incomes of more than $50,000 enrolled in two-year colleges as compared with 22% of young adults from families with incomes of less than $25,000. In fact, young adults with disabilities from families whose income exceeded $50,000 scored higher on tests of achievement, were more likely to complete school, to have a driver's license, were more likely to be employed or attend school, and were more likely to report some type of overall engagement after school exit (Newman et al. 2009).

Many young adults with disabilities reported having friends and being engaged in their community. Eighty-nine percent (89%) of White young adults said they had been engaged in some way since leaving high school; significantly, only 67% of Black young adults reported having similar engagement. National and state policies focusing on improving post-school outcomes can claim some credit for the increased academic participation for students with disabilities and students from racially/ethnically diverse backgrounds. At the same time the outcome disparities for Black young adults suggest that the policies by themselves cannot ameliorate the marginalization that occurs based on racial attitudes or contextual experiences.

Employment

Newman et al. (2009) reported average wages to be $8.20 per hour for all young adults (1–4 years post high school) with disabilities compared with $9.20 hourly for youth without disabilities. Youth with other health impairments (68%) or learning disabilities (64%) experienced higher employment rates than youth with orthopedic impairments, mental disability, or emotional disturbance (27% to 42%). In addition, young women with disabilities tended to work fewer hours per week.

Based on the NLTS2 interviews, young adults with disabilities from Black or Latino backgrounds reportedly found themselves under-employed more frequently than their White peers. White youth were more likely to have held jobs that required skilled employment than their racial/ethnic counterparts. In addition, White youth with disabilities reported higher rates of employment than their Black peers (63% compared with 35%), as well as a significantly higher employment history (80% compared with 47%) since leaving high school. Employment disparities based on race perpetuate marginalization for these young adults.

Developmental Barriers in the Microsystem

In 1995 the Carnegie Council on Adolescent Development identified eight developmental needs for healthy adolescent development. These needs cross race/ethnicity, SES, ability, and gender. Youth need to be able to (a) find a valued place in a constructive group, (b) learn how to form close, durable human relationships, (c) feel a sense of worth as a person, (d) achieve a reliable basis for making informed choices, (e) know how to use the support system available to them, (f) express constructive curiosity and exploratory behavior, (g) find ways of being useful to others, and (h) believe in a promising future with real opportunities. Taylor and Whittaker (2009) cited Wire and Barocas's assertion that attributes academic achievement as a positive outcome of successful identity development whereas youth whose identity development is thwarted or delayed may experience underachievement and lowered self-esteem. When the school or family or community experiences of youth with disabilities are unable to create environments that support these developmental needs, or when adolescents themselves reject the efforts of adults in their lives to support such needs, youth and young adults often seek alternative ways to have their needs met. These decisions are not always in the student's best self-interest.

Disclosing Disability

Knowing how to access the available support systems and making informed choices is a critical skill for young adults with disabilities. Newman et al. (2009) reported that, upon graduation, about half of the young adults with disabilities interviewed actually argued that they did not have a disability. In tandem with this notion, only 40% of the young adults interviewed who enrolled in postsecondary education ever disclosed their disability; they never applied for post-school educational supports even though these youth had identified IDEA disabilities during their high school years. Even fewer young adults with disabilities seemed willing to admit to needing supports in their work environment. Interestingly, Newman et al. reported that only 5% of Latino and 6% of Black young adults disclosed their disability to their employers. On the other hand, White youth were more likely to let employers know of their disability and needs for accommodations although only 24% of employed White youth confided in their employer that they might need supports. Given these findings, one might hypothesize that all young adults with disabilities recognize disclosing their disability in college or as employees as a high-risk action and that the risk may seem maximized to a student with a disability from Black or Latino backgrounds.

Another argument might be that the majority of young adults with disabilities, regardless of race/ethnicity, lack the self-awareness and self-advocacy skills to talk about their disabilities and their accommodation needs with confidence. In a qualitative study with ninth-grade students from an urban setting, Scanlon et al. (2008) found that few youth with disabilities (regardless of race/ethnicity) could adequately describe their disability or their need for special education services; this descriptor of students with learning disabilities has been persistent.

Social Skills and Behavior

Youth and young adults with disabilities need to find a place in a group, close relationships, a feeling of worth, and to engage in curiosity and exploratory behaviors. Extracurricular activities, school and community groups, friendships and adult mentors, community service and experiences, and opportunities to experience physical and intellectual challenges traditionally serve to support these developmental transition needs for the majority of youth. These settings and experiences often exert influence that in some cases keep students coming to school (Martin & Halperin, 2006). Unfortunately, without access to (or sometimes interest in) socially acceptable options, youth with disabilities across races and ethnicities often turn to alternative ways of meeting these developmental needs. Newman et al. (2009) found that four years after school exit, 20% of young adults with disabilities (more likely to be males) were on probation or parole from some involvement with the criminal-justice system. Young adults who had dropped out of school were much more likely to have been arrested than school completers.

Youth with emotional disabilities were more frequently involved with criminal activity than other youth with disabilities (as were youth with Other Health Impairments [OHI] and learning disabilities [LD]), although the NTLS2 did not identify race or ethnicity as disproportionately involved with the justice system, a report by the Children's Defense Fund (2007) noted that nationally a third of Black and a sixth of Latino boys born in 2001 may face prison at some point in their lifetime. The convergence of data (e.g., school completion, achievement outcomes, post-school employment) suggests that the social and systemic experiences of diverse youth (including race/ethnicity, gender or poverty) contribute to a risk of involvement in the criminal-justice system. Transition planning must face this reality and assume a prevention or intervention focus for all youth with disabilities, but in particular those who may be at highest risk due to the degree of marginalization they face. Using the Carnegie Council's list of adolescent needs can serve as one way of assessing the effectiveness of the transition-education environment in offering needed developmental support.

Diversity and Evidence-based Transition Practices

Transition research amassed over the past three decades has provided evidence in support of positive predictors of post-school success in the areas of employment, postsecondary education, and independent living. These practices may serve to ameliorate or address transition-education needs of youth with a range of disabilities. For example, career awareness and early work experiences, access to the general education curriculum, interagency collaboration, parental involvement, and self-determination represent only a handful of the 16 evidence-based predictors recently identified by the National Secondary Transition Technical Assistance Center following systematic reviews of experimental and correlational research (Test, Fowler et al., 2009a; Test, Mazzotti et al., 2009b). Because these reviews are focused on quality indicators of the interpretation of quantitative data rather than the studies' holistic designs, conclusions about the predictive strength of specific factors on the positive or negative post-school outcomes of specific subgroups of the U.S. youth based on variables such as race/ethnicity or SES are not possible. This is unfortunate because post-school outcomes of youth from historically marginalized groups are significantly worse than the outcomes of youth with disabilities from the majority group. Further, research itself is a cultural practice (Arzubiaga, Artiles, King, & Harris-Murri, 2008). In other words, the construction of a knowledge base or body of evidence in any discipline requires scholars to make decisions about how studies are designed, who gets included in studies, and to what extent the analysis of results can be generalized across groups. So while evidence may be mounting about factors predictive of positive post-school outcomes, we must interpret these findings with the understanding that there are many unanswered questions about the applicability of these findings for the subgroups of youth who constitute our diverse society.

Simply put, our understanding of evidence-based practices, as defined by extant research, as in the work by Test and colleagues (2009a, 2009b), or those that have been identified through reviews of "gold-standard" research (i.e., randomized controlled trials; Odom et al., 2005, p. 138), does not sufficiently address essential questions about transition outcomes for subgroups of our population based on race/ethnicity, SES, gender, or even disability, much less on the intersections of these demographic characteristics. Nevertheless, transition research provides insight regarding the state of transition for youth with disabilities, including young people from historically marginalized groups. Using the frame of the ecological model presented earlier in the chapter, we outline three of the predictor variables (e.g., family involvement, self-determination, and access to the general education curriculum) identified by Test and colleagues (2009b), and we discuss the relevancy that each has on the transition of youth in a culturally diverse population.

Family Involvement

Although the evidence is that effective transition planning and services make a difference for post-school outcomes, it is important to realize that not all cultures share the future-orientation that informs transition education. Hodgkinson (2000) claimed that such a future-orientation actually reflects a minority view in the world. He argued that the U.S. work ethic puts a high premium on "doing things"—being pragmatic— at the expense of being and becoming. Furthermore, many parents (principal players in youths' microsystem), particularly parents from groups who have been historically marginalized, feel ill-informed about transition. For example, Gil-Kashiwabara and colleagues (2007) interviewed parents of high-school youth, two-thirds of whom were people of color. They found that these parents were not familiar with transition planning or its legal requirements. Barriers to their participation in transition planning included work-related barriers (e.g., time off from work), communication barriers (e.g., language differences) and personal barriers (e.g., feelings of inadequate preparation). Similar findings have been reported by other researchers (deFur, Todd-Allen, & Getzel, 2001; Morningstar, Turnbull, & Turnbull, 1995).

Perceptions of family involvement by transition specialists, teachers, administrators, and agencies often reflects a traditional middle-class filter. Researchers (Ankeny, Wilkins, et al., 2009; Trainor, 2005, 2007; deFur, et al. 2001) have found that youth and their families, regardless of cultural background, consistently express hopes and expectations to experience fulfilling adult lives. Oftentimes, families have multiple stressors, economic as well as emotional, which challenge the way schools perceive these families' level of involvement in their son's or daughter's transition education. Structural barriers, such as economic and social welfare inequity, biases, and prejudices create barriers to well-known correlates to school success such as perceived active family involvement or holding high expectations for achievement. In a comprehensive review on collaboration with Culturally and Linguistically Diverse (CLD) families, Harry and Klingner (2006) concluded that service providers' deficit view of families blinds the providers to family strengths and values, and noted that such attitudes by service providers block the emergence of mutual respect. Similarly, Spradlin and Parsons (2008) argued that negative interactions with schools over time serve to marginalize families who have limited resources or whose cultural and linguistic differences differ from the majority culture.

Regardless of ability, economic status, or race/ethnicity, family involvement in education remains one of the strongest predictors of transition success for all youth, including young adults with disabilities. In a synthesis of seven years of empirical research, the Harvard Family Research Project (HFRP, 2007) identified parenting styles, home–school relationships, and responsibilities for learning outcomes as ways to organize family-involvement processes. This project concluded that warm, demanding parents who also supported and monitored their teens' behavior typically had a positive influence on their adolescent sons or daughters. However, parenting styles may vary based on culture, ethnicity, or contextual environment, and adolescents' responses to a particular style are complex. For example, the HFRP found that high parental monitoring resulted in greater engagement in school for at-risk, inner-city adolescent boys. On the other hand, adolescent girls were more engaged when there was a high level of monitoring and strong family cohesion. Supporting family involvement in the transition process requires deep understanding of family culture and resources, coupled with a true commitment and knowledge of the student.

Home–school relationships (key to the mesosystem) include communication as well as parent participation or volunteering in school events (HFRP, 2007). For families whose culture or schooling experiences differ from the majority of transition-service providers, the transition process and the expectations of parental involvement may amplify these differences. For example, some family members from diverse backgrounds may have felt marginalized as students themselves, some may view the school as a system or agency not to be trusted, some may have legitimate fears such as legal citizenship, and still others may experience disrespect and marginalization as a result of school personnel biases, and thus view the inquiry central to transition planning as difficult or onerous (Harry & Klingner, 2006; Lareau & Horvat, 1999; Rueda, Monzo, Shapiro, Gomez, & Blacher, 2005). In addition, views of disability, what constitutes a natural transition event, or family decision-making structures vary and, for some families, contradict the focus on transition to independence that policy and the majority tradition count as success (Geenen et al., 2003). Transition-service providers must recognize that the authority of their positions carries perceived hierarchical expert power that can interfere with the intended transition goal of collaborative planning and decision-making with families. Not only could this power role minimize family contribution to transition planning, but it potentially can create conflict that reinforces mistrust (deFur, 2009).

Self-Determination

Student self-determination is considered a key lever in the successful transition of students with disabilities (see chapter 13 for a robust discussion of this topic). In education research, self-determination is "a combination of skills, knowledge, and beliefs that enable a person to engage in goal-directed, self-regulated, autonomous behavior. As such, self-determination includes an understanding of one's strengths and limitations, together with a belief of oneself as capable and effective"(Field, Martin, Miller, Ward, & Wehmeyer, 1998, p. 2), and "acting as the primary causal agent in one's life and making choices and decisions regarding one's quality of life free from undue external influence or interference" (Wehmeyer & Schwartz, 1997, p. 246). In addition to the multiple types of evidence (i.e., correlational, experimental, descriptive), increasing student involvement in and ownership of decision-making, goal-setting, self-reflection, and self-assessment makes sense because people are likely to work toward goals that they themselves prioritize.

Important to consider when we focus on the diverse population of youth with disabilities, however, is that the ways in which individuals think about disability, adulthood, and success in life are culturally constructed. For instance, Rueda and colleagues (2005) found that Latina mothers' views of independence of their children with developmental disabilities favored family interdependence and responsibility. Rather than seeking independent and separate residences as their children entered adulthood, these mothers preferred for their sons and daughters to remain in the family home. This study provides an illustration of the ways in which microsystemic interactions can influence transition. The preferences of these Latina mothers are likely communicated within the microsystem to at least two important stakeholders—their children with disabilities and teachers. This is not to say that the mothers' preferences for interdependence will result in a lack of self-determination; rather, their preferences will likely shape the parameters in which the youths' self-determination develops or the self-determination opportunities for practice that teachers present.

In another example, both Trainor (2007) and Hogansen and colleagues (2008) found that young women with disabilities identified parenting as one aspect of successfully transitioning to adulthood, a priority that has not been documented in research with young men with disabilities (Trainor, 2005). At the microsystemic level, for example, how parents talk to their children about becoming parents themselves or how teachers prepare youth for life after high school likely influences the decisions and choices of adolescents. Yet in the frame of an ecological model, other systemic interactions are also important. At both the exo- and macrosystems the gender roles of young men and women may influence whether young adults make choices that position themselves as parents. Similarly, generational cultures influence whether such decisions are considered to be socially acceptable. Therefore, becoming a young parent despite financial risks may speak more to confluence of self-determination with mores about child bearing and rearing than it says about the individual development of self-determination in microcontexts.

While conceptualized largely at the level of the microsystem, self-determination is also embedded in a context of social interactions in which the power of adults, for example, may act as a lever in adolescents' opportunities to practice and develop self-determination. Similarly, meso-, exo- and macrosystemic interactions influence self-determination. For example, disregard or ignorance of families' needs or values (Geenen et al., 2003) and assumptions about postsecondary goals based on group membership rather than individual experience thwart the development of self-determination for youth with disabilities (Trainor, 2005). Acts of prejudice and discrimination are complex and involve social, political, and historical factors reflective of the exo- and macrosystems, but they are likely to impact the extent to which individuals experience self-determination at the microsystemic level. For instance, Goff and colleagues (2007) asserted that in a racialized society the "burden of acting White," a phenomenon first identified by John Ogbu and colleagues in the 1980s (cited in Goff, Martin, and Thomas, 2007) in which Black students find academic achievement incompatible with their Black identities, can be offset by increased self-determination. These authors further asserted that White teachers are largely unaware of this phenomenon and how to address its deleterious effects through self-determination instruction. Indeed, cross-cultural ignorance and misunderstandings have the potential to impact mesosystemic factors. Teacher-education programs continue to struggle to prepare teachers to work with youth from historically marginalized groups, balancing differentiation, equitable expectations, and high-quality academic instruction (Delpit, 2006; Sleeter, 2008).

Although only a handful of studies have addressed self-determination as it relates to diverse youth and cultural values and beliefs, the work of Martin and colleagues (2004, 2006a, 2006b) has provided ample evidence that youth with disabilities across racial/ethnic, gender, and SES groups experience precious few opportunities to practice self-determination in the context of individual education program (IEP) meetings. This is most unfortunate because these meetings are one of the few formal vehicles for youth, families, and professionals to come together to address transition planning and education. Even though these studies did not disaggregate data according to groups based on race/ethnicity and other markers of diversity, we need to be aware that students who are most vulnerable to prejudice and discrimination may have fewer opportunities than their White peers from middle- and high-SES backgrounds to develop self-determination, an essential set of knowledge, skills, and attitudes associated with postsecondary success.

Access to the General Education Curriculum

Interestingly, diversity considerations regarding family involvement and self-determination as predictors of positive postsecondary outcomes involve practices heavily steeped in individuals' cultural values and beliefs about disability, education, and adulthood. Access to the general education is also a cultural practice but from the perspective of an institution—that of schools and the U.S. system in which they exist. In fact, the IDEA mandates that students with disabilities have access to general education curriculum, a vestige of the historic struggle to provide equal educational opportunities to youth with disabilities and to consider inclusive educational settings rather than allow separate settings to function as a default. However, such access has never been clearly defined or delineated (Wehmeyer, 2002). When access is constructed as learning the same curriculum as students without disabilities, researchers have posited that for adolescents without high-incidence disabilities (e.g., LD and emotional and behavioral disabilities [EBD]), such access is a necessary prerequisite to participating in higher education and employment (Maccini, Strickland, Gagnon, & Malmgren, 2008). Again, from an ecological perspective, macrosystemic institutional cultures that prioritize normalized educational practices (i.e., inclusion and access to general curricula) and individualization may be important drivers of the types of transition education to which adolescents with disabilities gain access, but little is known about how this interacts with issues related to diversity.

We do know, however, that access to the general curriculum is stratified across disability and race/ethnicity. Black students across disability categories are more likely to be educated in separate and less-inclusive settings than their peers from any other racial/ethnic group (U.S. Department of Education, 2007). Further, Black males are more likely than others to be identified as students with EBD compared to youth from other groups. This is problematic in the context of transition because only 35% of adolescents with EBD graduate with regular diplomas, one indication of access to general education curricula (U.S. Department of Education, 2007). Much is known about the microsystemic challenges faced by adolescents with EBD across racial/ethnic backgrounds as they interact with teachers and other adults. Additional mesosystemic factors such as home–school interactions and methods of collaboration for families with children with EBD have also been documented (Harry & Klingner, 2006; Trainor, 2010; Zionts, Zionts, Harrison, & Bellinger, 2003). Unfortunately, much less is known about the extent to which cultural, social, and historical contexts influence exo- and macrosystemic variables.

Implications for Research, Practice, and Advocacy

Diversity coupled with transition education becomes a complicated topic. Although the notion that U.S. classrooms are diverse is factual and indisputable, the values and beliefs that underlie the significance with which we associate this diversity are impacted by the historical, social, and political contexts that embed conceptualizations of education, disability, and adulthood. In this section, we highlight some key implications in research, practice, and advocacy. Although reviews of scholarship commonly include implications for research and practice, we include advocacy as a third major area in need of attention to explicitly acknowledge that many of the issues that surface in any discussion of diversity also engage inequities that must be addressed through advocacy.

Research

An increasing body of research integrates factors of diversity as part of the research questions. In fact, the American Psychological Association (APA) guides scholars to position cultural considerations in the fore of research design and dissemination (APA, 2008). Research goals must be expanded to identify and document transition practices that uniquely foster transition education by developing both descriptive and intervention studies which include factors and variables that denote diversity across youth and young adults with disabilities (August & Hakuta, 1997; Trainor et al., 2008).

Culturally competent transition researchers must examine their own biases and develop research questions, designs, and analyses that consider the cultural context for the subjects of their research (Arzubiaga et al., 2008). While qualitative research places significant importance on the researcher biases and positionality, and critical theorists openly adopt a position relative to their perspective of social justice, other research paradigms have not addressed potential research biases across methods. We agree with Arzubiaga and colleagues that attention must be paid to these issues. Simultaneously, we concur with Test and colleagues (2009a, 2009b) that experimental and correlational research designs are effective means to identify promising transition practices. Hence, we believe that all research, whether qualitative, quantitative, or mixed methods, follow the ethical and quality guidelines for research with participants from both dominant and historical minority populations. In addition to the APA guidelines, researchers in special education should follow quality indicators for research (Odom et al., 2005).

Given these guidelines, several areas in need of research should be prioritized. For the correlational and experimental work that has been used to identify predictors of post-school success, we must test and measure these predictors for populations who have previously been omitted from data collection or data analysis. Further, we need to employ research methods that allow us to learn more about the social validity of transition education approaches for a range of individuals based on disability, race/ethnicity, SES, and gender. This is complicated, of course, because the number of possible variable combinations is extensive. For example, why do post-school outcomes differ for youth with EBD or LD? And, within the subgroup of youth with EBD, do students from different racial/ethnic backgrounds experience unique barriers or facilitators? Or, what drives gender-based differences in transitions to employment? To illustrate, an example research question might be: Given special education disproportionality (i.e., the association of race, gender, and EBD), what are the specific transition-related preferences, strengths, and needs of Black adolescent males who have been identified with EBD? In addition, how do we prepare teachers to implement culturally responsive instruction in ways that facilitate and support positive post-school outcomes for members of this group who experience some of the worst post-school outcomes? Research provides solutions in incremental steps; considerations for diversity are complex but essential if we are to solve some of the most challenging and enduring problems in our field.

Practice

For the past several decades, personnel preparation programs throughout the United States have struggled to develop teacher education that yields professionals skilled in working with the diversity of students they might teach. Although programs increasingly attempt to respond to this need, their efforts often get diluted because of competing demands, limited faculty experience, and uncertainty regarding culturally appropriate ways to engage in dialogue about the issues (Trent, Kea, & Oh, 2008). Cultural competence requires an acceptance and respect for difference, an ongoing assessment of one's own culture and biases, attention to the dynamics of difference, a commitment to continuous expansion of cultural knowledge and resources, and a willingness to change one's practice with deepening understanding (deFur & Williams, 2002).

DeFur and Williams (2002) said "Adding to this complexity *(of transition planning)* is the fact that concepts of success and the dreams that families hold for their children are interwoven with cultural perspectives" (p.107). For example, transition assessment encourages IEP teams to ask questions of youth such as "where do you want to live?" after finishing high school. In many cultures, adult children continue to live with a parent until the young adult marries. Even then, some cultures expect that one child will always live with a parent to care for a mother or father. Many parents of adult children with developmental disabilities see living away from family as a far-off goal not a graduation goal (deFur, 2009). IDEA requires that IEP transition teams set employment goals with students, yet many students may have not even observed family members working. Perhaps the IEP team suggests trying out another job or work less time to accomplish academic goals; the IEP team may not realize that the youth's pay provides financial support for the family. By law, transition IEPs must discuss postsecondary education options, but many students may be the first in their family to attend college and perhaps the family lacks knowledge of how to access higher education. Culturally responsive transition professionals develop deep cultural understanding of students and their families. They seek support from the community when needed to assist in the development of trust with families. Using this frame of reference and paired with high expectations and strategies for successful post-school outcomes, the culturally responsive professional facilitates a shared vision with the family for the young adult's future (deFur, 2009).

Transition assessments, school curriculum, and community experiences must also be examined to discern the degree to which these reflect the diversity of youth in transition. For example, are the transition assessments inclusive of various race and ethnicities? Do the transition curriculum materials (books, media, posters, etc.) reflect the cultural diversity of the country? Are there school policies that demonstrate that racism, ableism, or sexism will not be tolerated with clear consequences when people violate these policies? Does the school track students and does this tracking separate students by race/ethnicity and contribute to lower standards—if so, what steps can be taken to change this? Are disciplinary procedures administered consistently and fairly regardless of race/ethnicity, ability, or gender? Do dropout prevention efforts include students with disabilities and consider culturally responsive practices? Transition practitioners and administrators must be proactive in addressing these questions to ensure culturally responsive school-based transition practices.

Advocacy

Howard (1999) reminds us that "diversity is not a choice, but responses to it certainly are" (p. 2). In the context of transition education and planning for youth with disabilities, the multiple facets of diversity paired with a lack of understanding of family and student cultures could potentially paralyze proactive transition planning and preparation. Transition educators or systems may choose to respond to this complexity by ignoring the structural challenges that exist for diverse youths and young adults. Furthermore, Weissglass (1997) claimed that biases regarding race, ethnicity, class, and gender are institutionalized (we would argue the same is true for people with disabilities) and achieving equity goes beyond addressing personal prejudices. Clearly, there are risks in addressing the systemic bias and discrimination that pervade our society and schooling, but the risk of doing nothing is even greater (as evidenced by transition outcome gaps based on the demographic characteristics of students). Aligning our professional efforts with efforts to advocate for the rights of all people with disabilities (both youth and adults) is key to sustaining opportunities to live, learn, and work in our communities.

There are multiple avenues to begin advocating for culturally responsive transition policy, research, and practice for youth and young adults with disabilities; the ethical choice is whether to begin.

References

American Psychological Association Task Force on Evidence-Based Practice for Children and Adolescents. (2008). Disseminating evidence-based practice for children and adolescents: A systems approach to enhancing care. Washington, DC: American Psychological Association.

Ankeny, E. M., Wilkins, J., & Spain, J. (2009). Mothers' experiences of transition planning for their children with disabilities. *Teaching Exceptional Children, 41,* 28–36.

Allen, R. (2009, August). Preparing Latino students for college success. *Education Update, 51*(8), 1–2, 6.

Arzubiaga, A. E., Artiles, A. J., King, K. A., & Harris-Murri, N. (2008). Beyond research on cultural minorities: Challenges and implications of research as situated cultural practice. *Exceptional Children, 74,* 309–327.

August, D., & Hakuta, K. (1997). Priorities for research. In D. August & K. Hakuta (Eds.), *Improving schooling for language-minority children: A research agenda* (pp. 343–362). Washington, DC: National Academy Press.

Bronfenbrenner, U. (1979). *The ecology of human development.* Cambridge, MA: Harvard University Press.

Carnegie Council on Adolescent Development. (1995). *Great transitions: Preparing adolescents for a new century.* Carnegie Foundation of New York. Retrieved from http://www.carnegie.org/sub/pubs/reports/great_transitions/gr_intro.html

Children's Defense Fund (2007). *America's cradle to prison pipeline.* Washington, DC: Author. Retrieved from http://www.childrensdefense.org/child-research-data-publications/data/cradle-prison-pipe-line-report-2007-full-highres.pdf

Darling-Hammond, L. (2006). Securing the right to learn: Policy and practice for powerful teaching and learning. *Educational Researcher, 35,* 13.

Darling-Hammond, L. (May 2, 2007). Evaluating No Child Left Behind. *The Nation.*

deFur, S. H. (2009). Parents as collaborators: Building collaborative partnerships with school-based and community-based providers. In D. Wandry & A. Pleet (Eds.) *Engaging and empowering families in secondary transition – a practitioner's guide.* Arlington, VA: Council for Exceptional Children.

deFur, S., Todd-Allen, M., & Getzel, L. (2001). Parent participation in the transition planning process. *Career Development for Exceptional Individuals, 24,* 71–88.

deFur, S., & Williams, B. T. (2002). Cultural considerations in the transition process and standards-based education. In C. Kochhar-Bryant & D. S. Bassett (Eds.). *Aligning transition and standards-based education: Issues and strategies.* Arlington, VA: Council for Exceptional Children.

Delpit, L. (2006). Lessons from teachers. *Journal of Teacher Education, 57,* 220–231.

Fair, G. W., & Sullivan, A. R. (1980). Career opportunities for culturally diverse handicapped youth. *Exceptional Children, 46,* 626–631.

Field, S., & Hoffman, A. (1994). Development of a model for self-determination. *Career Development for Exceptional Individuals, 17*(2), 159–169.

Field, S., Martin, J., Miller, R., Ward, M, & Wehmeyer, M. (1998). *A practical guide for teaching self-determination.* Reston, VA: Council for Exceptional Children.

Gay, G. (2002). Preparing for culturally responsive teaching. *Journal of Teacher Education, 53,* 106–116.

Geenen, S., Powers, L. E., Lopez-Vasquez, A., & Bersani, H. (2003). Understanding and supporting the transition of minority youth. *Career Development for Exceptional Individuals, 26,* 27–46.

Gil-Kashiwabara, E., Hogansen, J. M., Geenen, S. J., Powers, K. M., & Powers, L. E. (2007). Improving transition outcomes for marginalized youth. *Career Development and Exceptional Individuals, 30,* 80–91.

Goff, C., Martin, J. E., & Thomas, M. K. (2007). The burden of acting White: Implications for transitions. *Career Development and Exceptional Individuals, 30,* 134–146.

Gudykunst, W. B. (2003). Issues in cross-cultural communication research. In W. B. Gudykunst (Ed.), *Cross-cultural and intercultural communication.* Thousand Oaks, CA: SAGE Publications, Inc.

Halpern, A. S. (1985). Transition: A look at the foundations. *Exceptional Children, 51,* 479–486.

Harry, B., & Klingner, J. K. (2006). *Why are so many minority students in special education? Understanding race and disability in schools.* New York: Teachers College Press.

Harvard Family Research Project (HFRP). (2007, Spring). *Family involvement in middle and high school students education* (No. 3). Cambridge, MA: Author.

Hodgkinson, H. (2000). *Secondary schools in the new millennium: Demographic certainties, social realities.* Reston, VA: National Association of Secondary School Principals.

Hogansen, J. M., Powers, K. M., Geenen, S., Gil-Kashiwabara, E., & Powers, L. E. (2008). Transition goals and experiences of females with disabilities: Youth, parents, and professionals. *Exceptional Children, 74,* 215–234.

Howard, G. R. (1999). *We can't teach what we don't know.* New York: Teachers College Press.

Individuals with Disabilities Education Improvement Act of 2004 (IDEA), 20 U.S.C. § 1400 et seq. (2004).

Kochhar-Bryant, C. A., & Bassett, D. S. (2002). Challenge and promise in aligning transition and standards-based education. In C. A. Kochhar-Bryant & D. S. Bassett (Eds.), *Aligning transition and standards-based education: Issues and strategies* (pp. 1–23). Arlington, VA: Council for Exceptional Children.

Lareau, A., & Horvat, E. M. (1999). Moments of social inclusion and exclusion: Race, class, and cultural capital in family-school relationships. *Sociology of Education, 72,* 37–53.

Leake, D., & Black, R. (2005, October). *Cultural and linguistic diversity: Implications for transition personnel.* National Center on Secondary Education and Transition. Minneapolis, MN: Institute on Community Integration Publications.

Maccini, P., Strickland, T., Gagnon, J. C., & Malmgren, K. (2008). Accessing the general education math curriculum for secondary students with high-incidence disabilities. *Focus on Exceptional Children, 40*(8), 1–32.

Martin, J. E., Huber Marshall, L., & Sale, P. (2004). A 3-year study of middle, junior high, and high school IEP meetings. *Exceptional Children, 70*(3), 285–297.

Martin, J. E., Van Dycke, J. L., Christensen, W. R., Greene, B. A., Gardner, J. E., & Lovett, D. L. (2006a). Increasing student participation in their transition IEP meetings: Establishing the self-directed IEP as evidenced-based practice. *Exceptional Children, 72*(3), 299–316.

Martin, J. E., Van Dycke, J. L., Greene, B. A., Gardner, J. E., Christensen, W. R., & Woods, L. L. (2006b). Direct observation of teacher-directed secondary IEP meetings: Establishing the need for student IEP meeting instruction. *Exceptional Children, 72*, 187–200.

Martin, N., & Halperin, S. (2006). *Whatever it takes: How twelve communities are reconnecting out-of-school youth.* Washington, DC: American Youth Policy Forum.

Morningstar, M., Turnbull, A. P., & Turnbull, H. R. (1995). What do students with disabilities tell us about the importance of family involvement in the transition from school to adult life? *Exceptional Children, 62*, 249–260.

Murray, C., & Naranjo, J. (2008). Poor, black, learning disabled, and graduating: an investigation of factors and processes associated with school completion among high-risk urban youth. *Remedial and Special Education, 29*, 145–160.

National Council on Disability (NCD). (2008). *The No Child Left Behind and the Individuals with Disabilities Education Act: A progress report.* Washington, DC: Author.

National High School Center. (2007, May). *Dropout prevention for students with disabilities: A critical issue for State Education Agencies.* Clemson, SC: Author. Retrieved from http://www.betterhighschools.org/docs/NHSC_DropoutPrevention_052507.pdf

Newman, L., Wagner, M., Cameto, R., & Knokey, A.-M. (2009). *The post-high school outcomes of youth with disabilities up to 4 years after high school.* Menlo Park, CA: SRI International.

No Child left Behind Act of 2001, 20 U.S.C. § 6301 et seq. (2001).

Odom, S. L., Brantlinger, E., Gersten, R., Horner, R. H., Thompson, B., & Harris, K. (2005). Research in special education: Scientific methods and evidence-based practices. *Exceptional Children, 71*, 137–148.

Rojewski, J. W. (1996). Educational and occupational aspirations of high school seniors with learning disabilities. *Exceptional Children, 62*, 463–476.

Rueda, R., Monzo, L., Shapiro, J., Gomez, J., & Blacher, J. (2005). Cultural models of transition: Latina mothers of young adults with developmental disabilities. *Exceptional Children, 71*, 401–414.

Scanlon, D., Saxon, K., Cowell, M., Kenny, M. E., Guladron-Muhrib, L., & Jernigan, M. (2008). Urban adolescents' post-school aspirations and awareness. *Remedial and Special Education, 29*, 161–174.

Sleeter, C.E. (2008). Preparing white teachers for diverse students. In M. Cochran-Smith, S. Feiman-Nemser, & J. McIntyre (Eds.). *Handbook of research in teacher education: Enduring issues in changing contexts, 3rd Ed.* (pp. 559–582). New York: Routledge.

Spradlin, L. & Parsons, R. (2007). *Diversity matters: Understanding diversity in schools.* New York: Wadsworth Publishing.

Taylor, L.S., & Whittaker, C.R. (2009). *Bridging multiple worlds: Case studies of diverse educational communities* (2nd ed.). Boston, MA: Pearson Education, Inc.

Test, D. W., Fowler, C. H., Richter, S. M., White, J., Mazzotti, V., & Walker, A. R. (2009a). Evidence-based practices in secondary transition. *Career Development and Exceptional Individuals, 32*, 115–128.

Test, D. W., Mazzotti, V., Mustian, A. L., Fowler, C. H., Kortering, L., & Kohler, P. D. (2009b). Evidence-based secondary transition predictors for improving postschool outcomes for students with disabilities. *Career Development and Exceptional Individuals, 32*, 160–181.

Trainor, A. A. (2005). Self-determination perceptions and behaviors of diverse students with LD during the transition planning process. *Journal of Learning Disabilities, 38*(3), 233–249.

Trainor, A. A. (2007). Perceptions of adolescent girls with LD regarding self-determination and postsecondary transition planning. *Learning Disability Quarterly, 30*(1), 31–45.

Trainor, A. A., Lindstrom, L., Simon-Burroughs, M., Martin, J. E., & Sorrells, A. (2008). From marginalized to maximized opportunities for diverse youth with disabilities: A position paper of the Division on Career Development and Transition. *Career Development for Exceptional Individuals, 31*, 56–64.

Trainor, A. A. (2010). Reexamining the promise of parent participation in special education: An analysis of cultural and social capital. *Anthropology & Education Quarterly, 41*, 245–263.

Trent, S. C., Kea, C. D., & Oh, K. (2008). Preparing preservice educators for cultural diversity: How far have we come? *Exceptional Children, 74*, 328–350.

U.S. Department of Education (2007). *Twenty-seventh annual report to Congress on the implementation of the Individuals with Disabilities Education Act, 2005.* Washington, DC: U.S. Department of Education.

Wagner, M., Newman, L., Cameto, R., & Levine, P. (2005). *Changes over time in the early postschool outcomes of youth with disabilities.* Menlo Park, CA: SRI International.

Wehmeyer, M. L. (2002). Transition and access to the general education curriculum. In C. A. Kochhar-Bryant & D. S. Bassett (Eds.), *Aligning transition and standards-based education: Issues and strategies* (pp. 25–40). Arlington, VA: Council for Exceptional Children.

Wehmeyer, M. L., & Schwartz, M. (1997). Self-determination and positive adult outcomes: A follow-up study of youth with mental retardation or learning disabilities. *Exceptional Children, 63*, 245–255.

Weissglass, J. (1997). Deepening our dialogue about equity. *Educational Leadership (54)*, 78–81.

Zionts, L. T., Zionts, P., Harrison, S., & Bellinger, O. (2003). Urban African American families' perceptions of cultural sensitivity within the special education system. *Focus on Autism and Other Developmental Disabilities, 18*(1), 41–50.

19

Transition to Postsecondary Education

Elizabeth Evans Getzel

VIRGINIA COMMONWEALTH UNIVERSITY

Kristine W. Webb

UNIVERSITY OF NORTH FLORIDA

> You need to be independent in college. You need to know that if you don't study, it's
> not going to get done. I had to grow up. I had to study because I wanted to study, not
> because someone told me to.
>
> (Kochhar-Bryant, Bassett & Webb, 2008, p. 156)

This quotation from a college student with a disability provides an important perspective on the transition from high school to college. Students with disabilities need to prepare not only for the transition to postsecondary education, but must also prepare to remain and persist in college. There are several decisions and preparations for college that are the same for all students, including students with disabilities. Every student needs to consider the size and location of the college, the programs and majors available, extracurricular offerings, the diversity of students, and the availability of scholarships or financial aid. However, students with disabilities must explore additional areas when determining an appropriate college or university program. Some of these include the availability of support services, campus accessibility, and documentation requirements to obtain services.

Research has shown a connection between higher earnings for young adults with disabilities and further education after high school even when a degree is not earned (Grigal & Hart, 2010; Wehman, 2006); however, participation by youth with disabilities in higher education, particularly four-year institutions, is significantly lower when compared to that of the general college population. Youth without disabilities are four times more likely to attend a four-year school when compared to a similar age group of young adults with disabilities (Newman, Wagner, Cameto, & Knokey, 2009). This chapter will highlight some of the important planning and preparation needs of students with disabilities who are considering postsecondary education as a transition goal. Information and resources will be provided on applying for college, the differences between two- and four-year colleges, disclosure of a disability, and the differences between high school and college. Knowing the characteristics of successful college students with disabilities is critical to the transition and retention of students with disabilities. Such topics as the willingness to disclose, previous coursework, entrance exams, and the rigor of high school courses will be discussed. The importance of work experiences and internship opportunities while in college is an important part of retention and persistence of students with disabilities in college, and this topic will be discussed in the chapter. Student voice is one of the most crucial components of the transition to, and retention in college, and we are including student voices throughout this chapter to ensure that the reader understands the important role this plays in the student's involvement in the planning, preparation, and decision-making involved in determining the postsecondary program which is the *right fit*. We conclude with current and emerging challenges as we work with students with disabilities who seek postsecondary education options.

Preparing for the Transition to College

> You need to learn to manage your own time. You are taking care of yourself now and for some people that is a very scary thought.
>
> (Kochhar-Bryant et al., 2008, p. 157)

Differences Between High School and College

The transition to college must begin early in the educational experiences of students with disabilities. Academic preparation needs to begin in middle school by taking demanding courses in English, math, science, history, or a foreign language. Middle school students need to learn about high school programs that will help them pursue academic and career interests and work to develop strong study skills and learning strategies (Getzel, 2005). Preparation for college includes learning the skills necessary to deal with the academic and social challenges that students face in college. There are a number of differences between high school and college, and students need to be aware of these differences and plan accordingly. Examples of the most significant differences include: (a) less contact with instructors, (b) expectations of higher levels of academic capability, (c) fewer tests covering greater amounts of material, (d) changes in the support systems that students had in high school, (e) higher expectations to achieve independently, and (f) changes in social and independent living demands (Getzel, 2005, 2008; Kochhar-Bryant et al., 2008; Shaw, Madaus, & Dukes, 2010). Kochhar-Bryant and colleagues (2008) emphasized that students with disabilities in college compete with other students who did reasonably well in high school as compared with students competing against one high school student body. The more informed and involved students are in the planning process, the smoother the transition will be from secondary to postsecondary education. It is extremely helpful for students with disabilities, their family members, and teachers to work together to assist students to understand these differences, in their academic preparation as well as developing skills in such areas as self-management (i.e., organizational/time management) and self-determination (i.e., self-advocacy, knowledge of effective learning strategies) to meet the challenges in college.

College Environments

The internet provides a wealth of information through specific college websites or general websites on colleges that provide specialized programs for students with disabilities. Shaw and colleagues (2010) suggest such websites as Collegenet.com, Collegeview.com, and Collegelink.com for students with disabilities to view programs, where the college is located geographically, majors, tuition fees, financial aid, and other information. Resource books that compile information on a number of colleges and universities also are available in bookstores, state departments of education, and agencies. All aspects of the college experience should be explored during the process of selecting a college; however, it is critical to carefully review the require-ments in specific majors that students are interested in pursuing. Remember, preparing for the transition to college is one step in the process; staying in college and completing a degree or certificate program is equally important. For example, students with disabilities may be accepted to a specific college without taking many foreign language courses, but then face difficulties meeting the college's foreign language requirement for graduation (Madaus, 2003; Shaw et al, 2010). We cannot assume that courses, such as a foreign language or math, will be substituted at the college level because they were accepted in secondary education. It is important to under-stand the policies and procedures for course substitutions at specific colleges and the degree requirements for earning a college diploma.

Virtual tours are useful for determining what colleges a student may want to visit, in preparing for an onsite visit, or serving as a substitution for a campus visit should time or finances be concerns (Shaw et al., 2010). If a campus tour is possible, visiting potential schools to learn about the academic program offerings, the services and supports provided to all students, and those services specifically for students with disabilities can greatly assist in the decision-making process. Prior to visiting a campus, students should contact the office that is responsible for determining accommodations for students with disabilities. Talking with the office staff about the process for receiving accommodations once a student is enrolled is a critical step in getting the services and supports needed. When requesting a meeting with this office, students should ask to speak with a current college student with a disability. Talking with someone already enrolled at the college can provide tremendous insight into what it takes to be successful on campus. Webb and Peller (2004) developed a college exploration worksheet which asks students to investigate a variety of areas that make up the college experience. This tool is a helpful resource not only to document information during the exploratory process, but it can help guide students about the critical considerations when exploring colleges or universities. This worksheet can be found on pages 76–79: http://www.fldoe.org/ese/pdf/dream_adults.pdf

When exploring college environments, students should understand some of the differences between attending a two-year college versus a four-year college or university. Program consider-ations that meet students' career goals, level and type of support services provided, level of academic preparedness required, and general atmosphere, size and diversity of the student body are impor-tant for students to explore (Getzel, 2005). Two-year colleges offer both vocational programs and academic studies, associate's degrees and certificates in various occupational fields, and courses that prepare students to continue their studies at a four-year institution (Rioux-Bailey, 2004).

Admission requirements to community colleges may differ from four-year institutions. Community colleges generally enroll students who have a high school diploma or the equiva-lent (i.e., General Educational Development test or GED), offer opportunities for students to attend higher education programs at a more affordable tuition rate, and provide students who may not have a strong grade point average (GPA), Scholastic Aptitude Test (SAT), lack course-work required by a four-year college, or achieved low standard entrance exam scores (i.e., SAT or ACT) opportunities to prepare for entrance into a four-year program.

For students to be admitted to community colleges, they must be able to pass basic skills testing or they will be enrolled in basic skills remedial courses, often for no credit (Shaw et al., 2010).

Admission to four-year colleges and universities is more competitive and all students must have the appropriate college preparatory classes in order to apply. Higher education programs usually require SAT or ACT scores, references, and a personal statement. The personal state-ment or letter is used to provide college admission officers a personal picture of the applicant. Some students choose to discuss their disabilities in personal statements to explain deficits in grades or standardized test scores. Harris and Robertson (2001) advised that an essay or letter should focus on such areas as a student's coping skills, motivation, and maturity. The decision to disclose a disability in a personal statement is an individual decision and should be thoroughly considered in the transition process in high school. A helpful tool to assist students with disabilities, families, and secondary education in the transition to college is www.going-to-college.org (Virginia Commonwealth University, 2009).

Financial Aid

Many college-bound students seek financial resources beyond what their families can provide to cover tuition, room and board, books, and other expenses (Getzel, 2005; Getzel et al., 2008; Shaw et al., 2010). Financial aid may be available from programs through a state's vocational rehabilitation agency or from the Social Security Administration (Miller, O'Mara, & Getzel, 2009). There are four types of financial aid that students with disabilities can consider, namely: (a) grants (funds that usually do not need to be repaid), (b) loans (funds that are borrowed to cover costs and repaid over time), (c) work study (employment that helps students earn money to cover costs), and (d) scholarships (e.g., awards based on specific criteria such as academic achievement, career goals)(Rioux-Bailey, 2004). Some suggested resources on financial aid are FASTWEB: http://www.collegegold.com/index.phtml, or Federal Student Aid U.S. (Department of Education, 2011): https://studentaid2.ed.gov/xap_pack/Default.asp

Disclosing a Disability

Often students enter college unprepared to disclose their disability or lack understanding of how to access services on campus. Students must self-identify to the university to request accommodations and supports; yet, national data show that more than half (55%) of students identified as having a disability in high school do not consider themselves as having a disability when entering postsecondary programs (Newman et al., 2009). Another 8% of youth know they have a disability, but decide not to disclose (Newman et al., 2009). Nearly two-thirds of students who enter collegiate programs do not disclose and face the challenges of coursework without accommodations. Some students are anxious for a *new start* and avoid dealing with labels. Others wait to disclose until they experience academic problems or are uncomfortable disclosing due to attitudes on campus (Burgstahler & Doe, 2004; Getzel & McManus, 2005; Kochhar-Bryant et al., 2008; Shaw et al., 2010). Another reason that students are not disclosing may be that they are truly prepared for the rigors of college. For some students, this might be true; however, data of college graduation rates of students with disabilities are troubling. Results from a national study found that when students left postsecondary education, only three in ten reported graduating or completing their programs (Newman et al., 2009). Preparations for the transition to college also involves ensuring that students with disabilities understand information, and that they need to persist, including obtaining and implementing accommodations.

Disclosing a disability at the college level to receive accommodations can be very confusing to young adults because of the significant differences between secondary and postsecondary education services and supports. In high school, assessments are conducted to determine if a student has a disability that requires services. If the student needs special education, the student is entitled to these services through federal regulations under the Individuals with Disabilities Improvement Act (IDEIA)(2004). In college, young adults are responsible for providing documentation of their disabilities. This documentation must be provided by students to determine if they are eligible for accommodations provided by the university. If a student is eligible for accommodations in college, these are based on ensuring access to materials, information, and programs on campus. The Americans with Disabilities Act Amendments Act (ADAAA)(2004) and Section 504 of the Rehabilitation Act (1973) are the laws that cover higher education institutions, and they do not focus on providing individualized programs for students. These laws have provisions to ensure that institutions (a) cannot discriminate, and (b) provide access to education (Eckes & Ochoa, 2005). Since the IEP is no longer a legal document at the college level, students are fully responsible for self-disclosing disabilities and providing documentation on the impact of their disabilities. Unfortunately, families and students are unaware of these changes until after the student enrolls in a college program (Getzel, 2005; 2008; Kochhar-Bryant et al., 2008).

An important part of the college exploration process is learning about the services and supports provided on campus for students with disabilities. If students and family members are taking a campus tour, they should schedule an appointment with this office to discuss eligibility for services. Examples of the types of questions to ask concerning services and supports include: (a) what specific documentation does your campus require to be eligible for services? (b) what types of support services are typically provided to students (i.e., learning disability, attention–deficit/hyperactivity disorder, low vision)? (c) how recent does the documentation need to be in order to receive accommodations (i.e., every three years)? (d) What is the process for accessing support services? and (e) how are instructors notified of a student's disability? (Deschamps, 2003). Further information is provided in the "Current and Emerging Issues" portion of this chapter.

Understanding how to access accommodations in college is an important self-determination skill. Self-determination is a set of personal or interpersonal skills that include (a) acceptance of a disability and how it impacts learning, (b) awareness of what support services are needed, (c) knowing how to describe one's disability and the need for specific supports to services providers, and (d) having the determination to overcome obstacles that may be presented (Getzel, 2008; Thoma & Wehmeyer, 2005). The development of self-determination skills in students with disabilities should begin in preschool or elementary level, but often these skills are not included in the academic experience of students until middle or secondary school. Tools are needed to assist students with disabilities to understand who they are, to become more involved in their Indiividualized Education Program (IEP) planning process, and to discover their own "voice" in this process. One tool is called the *One Pager* (Virginia Department of Education, nd), and it provides an opportunity for students to describe their strengths, interests, preferences, and needs. Students can prepare and distribute this document prior to an IEP meeting. A second tool is the *My Good Day Plan* (Virginia Department of Education, n.d.). This activity allows students to describe what happens on a good day, identify positive behaviors, assess if it is happening, problem solve what actions are needed to reach goals, and identify who can assist in this process. Rather than teaching students problem solving and goal setting in abstract terms, these tools use students' experiences. Both tools can be found at https://php.radford.edu/~imdetermined/

Characteristics of Successful College Students with Disabilities

In response to the increased numbers of students with disabilities (National Center for Education Statistics, 2006), postsecondary education institutions are required to provide services to a wide array of students. This section will discuss indicators for success and characteristics of college students with disabilities, thus giving high school students and their facilitators ideas about planning and preparation for higher education pursuits.

Academic Readiness for Postsecondary Education

Educational readiness is thought to be the prime factor as students transition to higher education institutions. Information is typically collected on high school courses taken, high school grade point averages (GPAs), and scores on college entrance exams (Conley, 2007). These data have been prevalent measures of all college-bound students, including those who have disabilities. Rugsaken, Robertson, & Jones (1998) reported that scores on entrance exams and high school rank were accurate predictors of academic performance during the first semesters of college work among students in the general population.

According to the National Center for Education Statistics (NCES, 2005), students with disabilities lag behind their non-disabled peers in college entrance scores, GPAs, and class ranks. Many researchers have investigated if these same factors of academic readiness are predictors of success among students with disabilities. A considerable amount of this research initially focused on college students with learning disabilities because this group entered postsecondary education in great numbers beginning in the 1970s.

Vogel and Adelman (1992) investigated the connection between college entrance exam scores, high school GPAs, and college GPAs for college students with learning disabilities and their non-disabled peers. They found that college entrance exam scores were not related with college GPAs for both groups, but they did find a relationship with students' high school GPAs and performance in college. They reported that students with learning disabilities had significantly lower scores on the ACT and ACT subtests. They advised the field to supplement these scores with high school grades, academic achievement levels, results from IQ tests, psychoeducational reports, case histories, letters of recommendation, and student interviews. Almost two decades later, Jorgensen, Fichten, & Havel (2009) also reported that high school graduates with disabilities had lower college entrance exams scores than the scores achieved by their non-disabled peers. Those students with disabilities who did achieve high GPAs when they graduated from high school had a higher probability of earning a high GPA in postsecondary education (DaDeppo, 2009). DeDeppo urged professionals to consider academic and social integration rather than focusing on isolated characteristics like GPAs, or SAT and ACT scores.

Transition professionals are able to locate a wealth of literature about the value of students with disabilities taking classes with their peers (e.g., Eisenman, Pleet, Wandry, & McGinley, 2011). These studies are valuable because they provide valuable data about the inclusion of students in rigorous courses with their peers. In 2003, Baer and his colleagues found students who enrolled in academic classes with their peers were five times more likely to attend a postsecondary education institution. Oakes and Saunders (2007) confirmed the value of rigorous high school classes to both postsecondary education attendance and persistence.

Non-Academic Readiness

Non-academic factors are important when considering transition program components (Pickering, Calliote, & McAuliffe, 1992). Attributes such as self-advocacy (Skinner, 2004), students' self-awareness of their disabilities (Kurtz & Hick-Coolick, 1997), and students' knowledge about their accommodations (Eckes & Ochoa, 2005) are critical. In 2009, Milsom and Dietz asked professionals in special education, higher education, and counseling to rate the importance of knowledge, skills, attitudes, and other attributes for college students with learning disabilities. They reported confidence, persistence, perseverance, resilience, self-determination skills, and self-discipline were the characteristics most highly rated by the experts. The sense of belonging to the place of learning, involvement on campus, a strong sense of purpose, and self-determination were identified by Belch (2005) as important factors affecting retention for college students with disabilities.

Halpern, Yovanoff, Doren, & Benz (1995) conducted a study to determine what elements influenced enrollment in postsecondary education. They reported student and parent satisfaction with high school experiences, along with effective transition planning, student achievement, and appropriate instruction in high school were convincing predictors of postsecondary education enrollment. Earlier, Fairweather and Shaver (1991) described the levels of education of parents and socio-economic status as being notable predictors of postsecondary attendance.

Interagency collaboration is repeatedly listed as a component of transition planning (Johnson, Stodden, Emanuel, Luecking, & Mack, 2002). Bullis and his colleagues (1995) reported that students who received support from three to six community agencies were more likely to have employment or postsecondary education experiences than students who had less assistance. Repetto, Webb, Garvan, & Washington (2002) examined the relationships between transition programs and postsecondary education attendance. When they compared transition services offered by 67 Florida school districts with outcome data from the Florida Education and Training Placement Information Program, they found agency services, referrals, and interagency agreements positively correlated with the number of students who attended postsecondary education institutions.

Internships or Other Career-Related Experiences

Internships or other career-related experiences are included in this chapter because as students with disabilities enter postsecondary education, they must be aware of the career-related programs and activities they need for a profession. Prior to entering college, students should understand the career services and resources on campus and in the community. All too often, students have limited career development or meaningful work experiences to assist them in choosing a career (Briel & Getzel, 2005, 2009; Roessler, Hennessy, & Rumril, 2007). It is critical for students with disabilities to fully prepare for the global marketplace in light of recent estimates showing 29% of youth with disabilities between the ages of 20 and 24 are employed compared with 61% of their counterparts without disabilities (U.S. Department of Labor, 2011).

Programs exist on college campuses to assist all students in building career-related skills for employment. These programs may include job clubs, employment workshops, and work experience programs including internships, job shadow opportunities, and informational interviews, mentors, and career counseling (Getzel & Briel, 2008). Contacts with employers or professionals through internships, job shadowing, informational interviews or mentoring has impact on the career development of students with disabilities (Briel & Getzel, 2001; Getzel & Briel, 2008; Hagner, McGahle, & Cloutier, 2001).

Like their non-disabled peers, college students with disabilities have challenges as they seek careers in their professional fields; however, there are some unique differences in the career development needs of students with disabilities. These differences include: (a) direct exposure to the variety of career opportunities potentially available to them, (b) an understanding of their disability and how it influences career choices and work performance, (c) an awareness of rights and responsibilities at work, (d) risks and benefits of disclosing a disability to employers, and (e) understanding of which accommodations improve performance and how to request them from an employer (Briel & Getzel, 2001; Briel & Wehman, 2005; Gerber & Price, 2003; Getzel & Briel, 2008; Hennessy, Richard, Cook, Unger, & Rumril, 2006; Michaels & Barr, 2002).

Resources on campus and in the community can assist students with career preparation and planning process. Colleges and universities have career centers that provide a wealth of information and activities for students. Some postsecondary schools locate their career services center and office for services for students with disabilities to ensure close collaboration. Community agencies or organizations can also play an important role including vocational rehabilitation or independent living centers.

Internships or other career-related experiences help students with disabilities connect their learning to careers. As students with disabilities stated after participating in a business mentoring program, "It put my school in a real life application," and, "I learned about an interesting job that I was unaware existed" (Getzel & Briel, 2008). These comments provide insight into the importance of career-related experiences and awareness of these resources by students with disabilities as they enter and persist in higher education settings.

What College Students Tell Us: The Importance of Listening to Students' Voices

Scholars must continue to collect data about the transition of young adults to postsecondary education, but in order to get a complete picture of this process, we believe inquiry must include the voices of students who have made transitions to postsecondary education settings. Their ideas are based on experiences, navigation of processes, and wisdom. As a college student advised, "Begin to treat students as they will be treated in college. Learn to balance holding their hand and letting them fly alone" (Kochhar-Bryant et al., 2008, p.158).

Accommodations

Kurth and Mellard (2006) gathered students' ideas about the accommodation process and barriers that limited access to higher education. Students were frustrated with choosing from a menu of accommodations, a scenario they believed was not built on what they needed. Cawthon and Cole (2010) asked college students with disabilities their perspectives on accommodations and obstacles when accessing learning. Their results indicated that students used accommodations from high school and relied on service providers in the campus disability office, rather than resources on campus. These findings are consistent with cautionary words from Getzel (2008), who stated that after being educated under the entitlement programs in IDEA, students become accustomed to services at hand, rather than advocating for needed supports and services. Postsecondary education service providers facilitate access to education; however, these providers must not be viewed as the only campus support system for students. Accommodations should be selected based on contextual and individual needs, and advocacy for these accommodations should be initiated by students in higher education. A college student with a disability offered, "Learn to speak for yourself. It will be your job to tell professors and administrators what you need. Nothing looks more unprofessional than using a parent or friend as a mouthpiece . . . Accountability is key. Excuses are pointless" (Kochhar-Bryant et al., 2008, p.162).

Outside of the Classroom

When college students with and without disabilities were asked to share their perceptions on five benchmarks of student engagement and institutional performance, students with disabilities perceived their student faculty relationships more favorably than their peers (Hedrick, Dizen, Collins, Evans, & Grayson, 2010). The students with disabilities were less engaged in social or non-academic activities and relationships and did not see their campus as a supportive environment, whereas the students without disabilities had favorable opinions about these aspects. The authors suggested that students with disabilities may have opportunities to interact with faculty because they may discuss accommodations and academic performance, but they feel disenfranchised from more social components of college life.

College students with disabilities believed they needed more training and information on the development and enhancement of advocacy skills (Stodden, Whelley, Chang, & Harding, 2001). Several years later, college students with disabilities who reported they had self-determination, family involvement and previous involvement, in their IEPs seemed to have higher levels of psychological empowerment, hope, and internal loci of control during their college years (Morningstar et al., 2010). Engagement with peers, self-determination, advocacy skills, and student involvement in planning are critical needs and should be included as elements in comprehensive skill building before students graduate from high school.

Current and Emerging Challenges

Documentation and Summary of Performance

The documentation of a disability can be a perplexing process for college-bound students with disabilities. Because students are responsible for self-disclosing, providing evidence of the disability and accommodations, evaluating accommodations, and arranging logistics of the transition to postsecondary education, students must be active participants in this process (Madaus, 2010). The mandates (e.g., IDEA vs. ADA and Section 504) governing secondary and postsecondary schools are fundamentally different in who is responsible for evaluation. Since postsecondary education institutes have varying requirements for documentation (e.g., recency of evaluation, source of evaluation), careful planning, along with investigation of postsecondary requirements must happen early in the transition process (Madaus, Benerjee, & Hamblet, 2010).

The Association on Higher Education and Disability (AHEAD) compiled a list of *Seven Essential Elements of Quality Disability Documentation* (AHEAD, 2010). The following elements are sound guidelines for students and their transition facilitators as they prepare to submit documentation that includes: (a) the credentials of a licensed or credentialed professional, (b) a diagnostic statement that identifies the disability, (c) descriptions of the criteria, evaluation methods, tests and dates, and narrative about the student's disability, (d) a report of the functional limitations and how a major life activity is substantially limited, (e) progression or stability of the disability, (f) history of accommodations, services, or medications, and (g) recommendations for accommodations, assistive and adaptive devices, effective strategies, and recommended services.

Summary of Performance

The Individuals with Disabilities Improvement Act (IDIEA)(2004) provided language about a summary document that would give students with disabilities information about their academic and vocational skills and abilities. This document also provides information on students' post-school goals and recommendations to reach these goals. The document is called the Summary of Performance (SOP) and is defined in the legislation as, "The public agency provides a summary of academic and functional performance, including recommendations to assist the student in meeting postsecondary goals, for students whose eligibility terminates because of graduation with a regular high school diploma or because of exceeding the age eligibility for FAPE under State law" (300.305 (e) (3)). The legislation does not specify how the summary should be developed, but it does identify three areas to be addressed—academic achievement, functional performance, and recommendations to assist the student in reaching postsecondary goals (Getzel, Deschamps, & Thomas, 2010; Kochhar-Bryant, 2007).

There is great variation across states on the length and amount of detail provided on a student's Summary of Performance (Getzel, Deschanps, et al., 2010). If developed by a team with student involvement, the summary provides a tool to record the history of student progress and reminds them of the next steps needed to reach their goals (Getzel et al., 2010). Secondary educators have expressed the need of a tangible tool that includes information for students as they apply for jobs, seek services, or enter postsecondary education

(Deschamps & Getzel, 2007). This summary does not guarantee that students with disabilities will be eligible for accommodations in higher education (Kochhar-Bryant et al., 2008). Students must understand and participate in the development of their summaries in order to discuss the summary content with colleges. Students also need to ask college disability support personnel if the Summary of Performance will be used as part of the documentation of a disability.

The Summary of Performance can serve as a bridge for students as they transition from secondary to postsecondary education by documenting strategies, services, and accommodations that have worked for them in the past (Kochhar-Bryant, 2007); yet further research and evaluation is needed on its effectiveness. As we determine what formats or information prove helpful to colleges and universities, secondary and postsecondary educators need to work collaboratively to design and implement summaries that can assist students with disabilities to obtain needed services and supports in college.

Technology

Students with disabilities are entering postsecondary programs unaware of existing technologies that can assist them in college (Getzel, 2008; Shaw, Glaser et al., 2010). Introducing students to the use of technology and software that assists them in organizing reading materials or the development of a paper; text-to-speech software for reading, writing and taking exams; or hand-held technologies to assist in time management or organization is essential. Access to technology that enables success in higher education increases the likelihood of improved career outcomes (Burgstahler, 2005; Fichten, Asuncion, Barile, Fossey, Robillard, & Wolforth, 2001; Getzel, 2008; Kim-Rupnow & Burgstahler, 2004).

Students with disabilities must be prepared to use technology for access and accommodations, but students, along with their IEP teams, need to learn how technology is used for instructional purposes (Shaw et al., 2010). "Awareness and development of skills and strategies for tech-blended and online learning is imperative if students with disabilities are to become successful college graduates" (Shaw et al., 2010, p.134).

Services for Diverse Populations of Students with Disabilities

Data from the Cooperative Institutional Research Program, an ongoing national study of fall semester freshmen, indicated that 6% of students in their sample reported a disability, totaling 66,000 students nationally (Henderson, 2001). Students with disabilities were grouped as: (a) hearing disabilities—9%, (b) speech—3%, (c) orthopedic disabilities—7%, (d) health-related disabilities—15%, (e) blind or low vision—16%, and other disabilities—17%). The largest group was students with learning disabilities—40% were included in this group.

During the last decade, other groups of students with disabilities have entered college in increasing numbers, and these groups are receiving more attention from researchers. Students with autism, attention deficit disorders, psychological disorders and mental health issues, chronic illnesses, and medical conditions have entered postsecondary institutions in greater numbers. Students with intellectual disabilities have also gained entry into postsecondary education (see Chapter 25 of this publication). In the following section, we will discuss these relatively new groups of students who are enrolling in postsecondary education settings.

Autism Spectrum Disorders

Increasing numbers of students with autism spectrum disorder (ASD), especially those diagnosed with Asperger's Syndrome (ASD) are attending postsecondary education institutions

(Wenzel & Rowley, 2010). Because of the many children diagnosed with autism spectrum disorders during the 1990s, postsecondary education settings are now viewed as viable options for many of these students, and they are entering college in surprising numbers (Shaw, 2010; VanBerquejik, Klin, & Volkmar, 2008).

Students with ASD may face unique challenges that include difficulty with social cues, perceptions, and interpersonal difficulties (Miyahara, Ruffman, Fujita, & Tsjujii, 2010). Further, Kanne, Christ, et al., (2009) reported that college students with ASD had more significant difficulties with depression, anxiety, interpersonal relationships, overall psychiatric difficulties and adjustment to college than their peers. Shaw (2010) listed specific difficulties with motivation, perspective, organization, rigidity, and impulse control as characteristics that may impede the success of college students with ASD. He urged high school personnel to "identify the supports and accommodations that each student finds helpful in adjusting to what often seems like a confusing and hostile environment" (p. 275).

Young adults with autism have ongoing difficulties with language, especially with their peers in college. Furthermore, because language patterns of adolescents and young adults tend to be spoken quickly with somewhat overstated and metaphorical references, along with a given understanding of other people's perspectives, college environments may be especially demanding for students with ASD (Brinton, Robinson, & Fujiki, 2004).

In response to the unique needs of students with ASD, the Center for Students with Disabilities at the University of Connecticut instituted a first-year experience course for students with ASD. The program focuses on the distinctive needs of this population by teaching the students skills and strategies for college success (Wenzel & Rowley, 2010). Other researchers also have advocated for coaching students with ASD about academic functioning, independent living, social skills, vocational planning and personal counseling on campus (VanBerquejik, Klin, et al., 2008). These researchers urged careful transition planning, appropriate accommodations, and individually designed support. Taylor (2005) stressed the critical need for preparation by students with ASD as they made transitions to higher education, but also urged institutions of higher education to be prepared for the special needs of this population.

Attention Deficit Disorder and Attention Deficit Hyperactivity Disorder

> They have this fit mold, like this cut gingerbread mold, and here's me. I am Santa Claus and they want Gingerbread Man, and I don't fit in the Gingerbread Man cut out because I'm different.
>
> (Perry & Franklin, 2006, p. 94)

This student's response was from a study of college students with Attention Deficit Hyperactivity Disorder (ADHD) or attention deficit disorder (ADD). Perry and Franklin reported that low self-esteem and self-doubt were commonly expressed by the study participants. Recommendations included education about rights and disability laws, intensive instruction about self-determination, self-advocacy, self-accommodation, and knowledge of learning style and needs. A more recent study of female young adults with ADHD confirmed the themes of low self-esteem discussed earlier, but offered that these women seemed to be involved in fewer romantic relationships and experienced depression during young adulthood, information that could certainly impact the transition of young women with ADHD (Babinski et al., 2011).

Current researchers are proposing that ADHD may be a complex dysfunction of the cognitive management system also known as executive functioning (Brown, 2007). College students with ADHD and learning disabilities reported that they attributed their academic goal acquisition to executive function coaching, rather than to more typical formats of academic supports on campus (Parker & Boutelle, 2009). The students who were interviewed stated the coaching helped them develop and manage their autonomy and promoted self-management, self-confidence, and independent learning—all strategies that could be incorporated in high school.

Students with Psychological Disorders and Mental Illnesses

The 2007 tragedy at Virginia Tech heightened awareness about college students with psychological disorders or mental illnesses (Fallahi, Austad, Fallon, & Leishman, 2009). One can find an abundance of literature about prevention, proactive steps, and other emergency campus measures; however, as Webber and Plotts (2008) reported, little evidence-based information can be found on "specific approaches to dealing with important issues such as career preparation, sex-related problems, and drug abuse" (p. 350).

The lack of information about transition for students with psychological disorders or mental illnesses may be particularly challenging for college-bound students, their families, and the professionals who facilitate the transition process. College years are stressful for all students as they step on college campuses, and this new environment may cause anxieties that can exacerbate the onset or recurrence of mental illness (Speer, McFaul, & Mohatt, 2009). Many college students diagnosed with mental illness are intellectually capable, but they may isolate themselves, complain of physical ailments, and experience shame and stigma, ultimately resulting in academic difficulties (Bertram, 2010). Bertram urged professionals to offer tools to students to enable them to understand the emotional, intellectual, and psychological elements of issues and integrate these elements into their lives. Shaw (2010) contended that the less structured environment of college and the absence of the support systems of home, community, and school may justify a supported educational array of services that include such components as mentors, time management, and interpersonal skills, along with stress management and counseling. These recommendations and knowledge of the student's unique mental health needs are critical factors when planning the transition to postsecondary education settings.

Chronic Illnesses or Medical Conditions (Contributed by Kelsey A. Alderfer)

College students with chronic illnesses or medical conditions face immense challenges including absences from classes, extreme fatigue, and *mental fog*. Chronic illnesses and medical conditions are long-term illnesses or conditions that severely impact an individual's daily life and result in frequent and/or extended hospital visits (Shaw, Glaser, Stern, Sferdenschi, & McCabe, 2010; Shiu, 2001), and many of these are not visible (Edelman, Schuyler, & White, 1998; Jung, 2002). These illnesses or conditions may wax and wane thus requiring frequent adjustments to lifestyle (Royster & Marshall, 2008; Shiu, 2001). They often suffer from exhaustion (e.g., after undergoing chemotherapy treatments) and must block time each night to sleep and regain strength. Many have restricted diets and have to plan mealtimes. These students may also have to deal with severe daily pain. Others contend with infectious diseases, such as HIV/AIDS, and must take appropriate precautions. Because of these scenarios, students with chronic illnesses or medical conditions may experience mild cognitive complications. Learning to keep a detailed planner of medication and daily activities is a helpful tool for many students.

Students with chronic illnesses or medical conditions have more to handle than the typical *freshman 15* pounds. These students may be unqualified for insurance, unable to complete college courses due to medical relapses (Royster & Marshall, 2008), are and not able to complete their programs of studies within the same time period as their non-disabled peers

(Stodden, Whelley, Chang, & Harding, 2001). Approximately 17.3% of college students had a health impairment in 2006 (Horn, Nevill, & Griffin, 2006), and the number of individuals with chronic illnesses and medical conditions is rising (Perrin, Bloom, & Gortmaker, 2007), increasing the percentage of students with chronic illnesses or medical conditions enrolled in postsecondary education every year.

To be eligible for accommodations and other services, students must provide medical/psychological documentation of their disabilities to the postsecondary institution (Barnard-Brak, Lechtenberger, et al., 2010; Edelman, Schuyler, & White, 1998); this process may be deeply personal for some students. Many students with chronic illnesses or medical conditions choose not to disclose because they do not believe they have a disability or need special assistance (Barnard-Brak, Lechtenberger, & Lan, 2010; Jung, 2002). Once the student has registered with the campus disability office, accommodations are considered based on individual needs, often on a course-to-course basis (Shaw, 2009). Students must decide how they will coordinate their needs with the campus health office and physicians in the community. The importance of having these supports in place is a critical—sometimes a life-and-death scenario—and students must plan this segment of transition to postsecondary education accordingly.

Conclusions

> Give them positive supports and preparation so they feel like they can do it. Encourage them during this preparation. "When I went to college, I wasn't scared of it."
> (Kochhar-Bryant et al., 2008, p. 163)

With planning, preparation, anticipating, rehearsing, and making self-determined and informed choices, all college-bound students will have a seamless transition to postsecondary education without fear.

References

Americans with Disabilities Act Amendments Act (ADAAA) of 2008. PL 110-325, 42 U.S.C. §§ 12101 et seq.

Association on Higher Education and Disability (AHEAD). (2010). *Seven essential elements of quality disability documentation.* Retrieved from http://www.ahead.org/resources/best-practices-resources/elements

Babinski, D. E., Pelham, W. E., Jr., Molina, B. S., Gnagy, E. M., Waschbusch, D. A., Yu, J. et al. (2011). Late adolescent and young adults outcomes of girls diagnosed with ADHD in childhood: An exploratory investigation. *Journal of Attention Disorders, 15*(3), 204–211.

Baer, R. M., Flexer, R. W., Beck S., Amstutz, N., Hoffman, L., Brothers, J. et al. (2003). A collaborative followup study on transition service utilization and post-school outcomes. *Career Development for Exceptional Individuals, 26,* 7–25.

Barnard-Brak, L., Lechtenberger, D. & Lan, W. Y. (2010). Accommodation strategies of college students with disabilities. *The Qualitative Report, 15*(2), 411–429.

Belch, H. A. (2005). Retention and students with disabilities. *Journal of College Student Retention, 6*(1), 3–22.

Bertram, M. (2010). Student mental health: Reframing the problem. *About Campus, 15,* 30–32.

Briel, L. W. & Getzel, E. E. (2001). Internships in higher education: Promoting success for students with disabilities. *Disability Studies Quarterly, 21,* 1–12.

Briel, L. W., & Getzel, E. E. (2005). Internships and field experiences. In E. E. Getzel & P. Wehman (Eds.), *Going to college: Expanding opportunities for students with disabilities* (pp. 271–290). Baltimore: Paul H. Brookes Publishing Co.

Briel, L. W., & Getzel, E. E. (2009). Postsecondary options for students with autism. In P. Wehman, M. D. Smith, & C. Schall (Eds.). *Autism & the transition to adulthood: Success beyond the classroom* (pp. 189–208). Baltimore: Paul H. Brookes Publishing Co.

Briel, L. W., & Wehman, P. (2005). Career planning and placement. In E. E. Getzel & P. Wehman (Eds.), *Going to college: Expanding opportunities for students with disabilities* (pp. 291–305). Baltimore: Paul H. Brookes Publishing Co.

Brinton, B., Robinson, L. A., & Fujiki, M. (2004). Description of a program for social language intervention: "If you can have a conversation, you can have a relationship." *Language, Speech, and Hearing Services in the Schools, 35,* 283–290.

Brown, T. E. (2007). A new approach to attention deficit disorder. *Educational Leadership, 64*(5), 26–27.

Bullis, M., Davis, C., Bull, B., & Johnson, B. (1995). Transition achievement among young adults with deafness: What variables relate to success? *Rehabilitation Counseling Bulletin, 39,* 130–150.

Burgstahler, S. (2005). The role of technology in preparing college and careers. In E. E. Getzel & P. Wehman (Eds.), *Going to college: Expanding opportunities for students with disabilities* (pp. 179–198). Baltimore: Paul H. Brookes Publishing Co.

Burgstahler, S., & Doe, T. (2004). Improving postsecondary for students with disabilities: Designing professional development for faculty. *Journal of Postsecondary Education and Disability, 18,* 135–147.

Cawthon, S. W., & Cole, E. V. (2010). Postsecondary students who have a learning disability: Student perspectives on accommodations access and obstacles. *Journal of Postsecondary Education and Disability, 23*(2), 112–128.

Conley, D. (2007). *Toward a more comprehensive conception of college readiness.* Eugene, OR: Educational Policy Improvement Center. Retrieved January 20, 2011 from http://www.collegiatedirections. org/2007_Gates_CollegeReadinessPaper.pdf

DaDeppo, L. M. W. (2009). Integration factors related to the academic success and intent to persist of college students with learning disabilities. *Learning Disabilities Research & Practice, 24*(3), 122–131.

Deschamps, A. (2003). Traveling the road from high school to college: Tips for the journey. *Transition Times, 9,* 1–2.

Deschamps, A., & Getzel, E. E. (October, 2007). *Summary of performance: One state's perspective on its implementation.* Presentation at the Division on Career Development & Transition International Conference, Orlando, FL.

Eckes, S. E., & Ochoa, T. A. (2005). Students with disabilities: Transitioning from high school to higher education. *American Secondary Education, 33*(3), 6–20.

Edelman, A., Schuyler, V. E. & White, P. H. (1998). Maximizing success for young adults with chronic health-related illnesses: Transition planning for education after high school. *HEATH Resource Center.* Retrieved April 17, 2011, from http://www.eric.ed.gov/PDFS/ED418562.pdf

Eisenman, L. T., Pleet, A. M., Wandry, D., McGinley, V. (2011). Voices of special education teachers in an inclusive high school: Redefining responsibilities. *Remedial and Special Education, 32* (2), 91–104.

Fairweather, J. S., & Shaver, D. M. (1991). Making the transition to postsecondary education and training. *Exceptional Children, 57,* 264–270.

FASTWEB. (2011). College gold: The step-by-step guide to paying for college. Retrieved from http:// www.collegegold.com/index.phtml

Fallahi, C. R., Austad, C. S., Fallon, M., & Leishman, L. (2009). A survey of perceptions of the Virginia Tech tragedy. *Journal of School Violence, 8*(2), 120–135.

Fichten, C. S., Asuncion, J. V., Barile, M., Fossey, M. E., Robillard, C., & Wolforth, J. (2001). Computer technologies for postsecondary students with disabilities II: Resources and recommendations for postsecondary service providers. *Journal of Postsecondary Education and Disability, 15,* 59–83.

Gerber, P. J., & Price, L. A. (2003). Persons with learning disabilities in the workplace: What we know so far in the American with Disabilities Act era. *Learning Disabilities Research and Practice, 18,* 132–136.

Getzel, E. E. (2005). Preparing for college. In E. E. Getzel & P. Wehman (Eds.), *Going to college: Expanding opportunities for students with disabilities* (pp. 69–87). Baltimore: Paul H. Brookes Publishing Co.

Getzel, E. E. (2008). Addressing the persistence and retention of students with disabilities in higher education: Incorporating key strategies and supports on campus. *Exceptionality, 16*(4), 207–219.

Getzel, E. E., & Briel, L. W. (June, 2008). Experiences of college students with disabilities and the importance of a business mentoring program. In P. Wehman, J. Kregel, & V. Brooke, Eds.), *Promoting an employer driven approach to employment of people with disabilities* (pp. 157–167). Richmond, VA: Virginia Commonwealth University, Rehabilitation, Research & Training Center on Workplace Supports and Job Retention.

Getzel, E. E., Deschamps, A., & Thoma, C. A, (2010). Transition individualized education planning and summary of performance. In C. A. Thoma & P. Wehman (Eds.), *Getting the most out of IEPs: An educator's guide to the student-directed approach* (pp.173–188). Baltimore: Paul H. Brookes Publishing Co.

Getzel, E. E., & McManus, S. (2005). Expanding support services on campus. In E. E. Getzel & P. Wehman (Eds.), *Going to college: Expanding opportunities for Students with Disabilities* (pp. 139–161). Baltimore: Paul H. Brookes Publishing Co.

Grigal, M., & Hart, D., (2010). *Think college! Postsecondary options for students with intellectual disabilities.* Baltimore: Paul H. Brookes Publishing Co.

Hagner, D., McGahle, K., & Cloutier, H. (2001). A model career assistance process for individuals with severe disabilities. *Journal of Employment Counseling, 38,* 197–206.

Halpern, A. S., Yovanoff, P., Doren, B., & Benz, M. R. (1995). Predicting participation in postsecondary education for school leavers with disabilities. *Exceptional Children, 62,* 151–164.

Harris, R., & Robertson, J. (2001). Successful strategies for college-bound students with learning disabilities. *Preventing School Failure,* 45, 125–131.

Hedrick, B., Dizen, M., Collins, K., Evans, J., and Grayson, T. (2010). Perceptions of college students with and without disabilities and effects of STEM and non-STEM enrollment on student engagement. *Journal of Postsecondary Education and Disability, 23*(2), 129–136.

Henderson, C. (2001). College Freshmen with Disabilities, 2001: A Biennial Statistical Profile. Washington, DC: HEATH Resource Center.

Hennessey, M. L., Richard, R., Cook, B., Unger, D., & Rumril, P. (2006). Employment and career development concerns of postsecondary students with disabilities: Service and policy implications. *Journal of Postsecondary Education and Disability,* 19, 39–55.

Horn, L., Nevill, S. & Griffin, J. (2006). *Profile of undergraduates in U.S. postsecondary education institutions: 2003=N04 with a special analysis of community college students.* Washington, DC: U.S. Department of Education, National Center for Education Statistics, Institute of Education Sciences. Retrieved April 17, 2011, from http://nces.ed.gov/pubs2006/2006184_rev.pdf

Individuals with Disabilities Education Improvement Act (IDEIA) of 2004, PL 108–446, 20 U.S.C. §§ 1400 et seq.

Johnson, D. R., Stodden, R. S., Emanuel, E. J., Luecking, R., & Mack, M. (2002). Current challenges facing secondary education and transition services: What research tells us. *Exceptional Children, 68,* 519–531.

Jorgensen, S., Fichten, C. S., & Havel, A. (2009). Academic success of graduates with and without disabilities: A comparative study of university entrance scores. *Pedagogie Collegiale, 22*(5), 26–29.

Jung, K. E. (2002). Chronic illness and educational equality: The politics of visibility. *NWSA Journal, 14*(3), 178–200.

Kanne, S. M., Christ, S. E., & Rejersen, A. M. (2009). Psychiatric symptoms and psychosocial difficulties in young adults with autistic traits. *Journal of Autism and Developmental Disorders, 39* (6), 827–833.

Kim-Rupnow, W. S., & Burgstahler, S. (2004). Perceptions of students with disabilities regarding the value of technology-based support activities on postsecondary education and employment. *Journal of Special Education Technology,* 19, 43–56.

Kochhar-Bryant, C. (2007). The summary of performance as transition "passport" to employment and independent living. *Assessment for Effective Intervention, 32,* 160–170.

Kochhar-Bryant, C., Bassett, D. S., & Webb, K. W. (2008). *Transition to postsecondary education.* Thousand Oaks, CA: Corwin Press.

Kurth, N., & Mellard, D. (2006). Student perceptions of the accommodation process in postsecondary education. *Journal of Postsecondary Education and Disability,* 19, 71–83.

Kurtz, D. P., & Hick-Coolick, A. (1997). Preparing students with learning disabilities for success in postsecondary education: Needs and services. *Social Work in Education,* 19, 31–42.

Madaus, J. W. (2003). What high school students with learning disabilities need to know about college foreign language requirements. *Teaching Exceptional Children, 36,* 32–37.

Madaus, J. W. (2010). Let's be reasonable: Accommodations at the college level. In S. F. Shaw, J. W. Madaus, & L. L. Dukes, (Eds.), *Preparing students with disabilities for college success: A practical guide to transition planning* (pp.37–63). Baltimore: Paul H. Brookes.

Madaus, J. W., Banerjee, M., & Hamblet, E. C. (2010). Learning disability documentation decision making at the postsecondary level. *Career Development for Exceptional Individuals, 33*(2), 68–79.

Michaels, C. A., & Barr, V. M (2002). Best practices in career development programs for post- secondary students with learning disabilities: A ten-year follow-up. *Career Planning and Adult Development, 18,* 61–79.

Miller, L. A., O'Mara, S., & Getzel, E. E. (2009). Saving for post-secondary education: Strategies for individuals with disabilities. *Journal of Vocational Rehabilitation, 31,* 167–174.

Milsom, A., & Dietz, L. (2009). Defining college readiness for students with Learning disabilities: A Delphi study. *Professional School Counseling Journal, 12*(4), 315–323.

Miyahara, M., Ruffman, T., Fujita, C., & Tsujii, M. (2010). Young people with Asperger's Disorder recognize threat and learn about affect in faces?: A pilot study. *Research in Autism Spectrum Disorders, 4*(2), 242–248.

Morningstar, M. E., Frey, B. B., Noonan, P.M., Ng, J., Clavenna-Deane, B., Graves, P. et al. (2010). A preliminary investigation of the relationship of transition preparation and self-determination for students with disabilities in postsecondary educational setting. *Career Development for Exceptional Individuals, 33*(2), 80–94.

National Center for Education Statistics (NCES) (2006). *Profile of undergraduates in U.S. postsecondary education institutions: 2003–2004.* Retrieved November 30, 2010, from http://nces.ed.gov/pubsearch/pubsinfo.asp?pubid-226184

National Center for Education Statistics (NCES) (2005). *Dual enrollment of high school students at post-secondary institutions: 2003–2003.* Washington, DC: U.S. Department of Education.

Newman, L., Wagner, M., Cameto, R., & Knokey, A. M. (2009). The post-high school outcomes of youth with disabilities up to 4 years after high school. *Report of findings from the national longitudinal transition study 2 (NCSER 2009–3017).* Menlo Park, CA: SRI International. Retrieved March 30, 2010 from www.nlts2.org/reports/2009_04nlts2_report_2009_04_complete.pdf

Oakes, J., & Saunders, M. (2007). Multiple pathways: High school reform that promises to prepare all students for college, career, and civic responsibility. *Multiple perspectives on multiple pathways: Preparing California's youth for college, career, and civic responsibility.* Los Angeles: University of California.

Parker, D. R., & Boutelle, K. (2009). Executive function coaching for college students with learning disabilities and ADHD: A new approach for fostering self-determination. *Learning Disabilities Research & Practice, 24*(4), 204–215.

Perrin, J. M., Bloom, S. R. & Gortmaker, S. L. (2007). The increase of childhood chronic conditions in the United States. *JAMA, 297*(24), 2755–2759.

Perry, S. N. & Franklin, K. K. (2006). I'm not the gingerbread man! Exploring the experiences of college students diagnosed with ADHD. *Journal of Postsecondary Education and Disability, 19*(1), 94–107.

Perry, S. N., & Franklin, K. K. (2006). I'm not the gingerbread man! Exploring the experiences of college students diagnosed with ADHD. *Journal of Postsecondary Education and Disability, 19*(1), 94–109.

Pickering, J., Calliote, J., & McAuliffe, G. (1992). The effects of noncognitive factors on freshman academic performance and retention. *Journal of the Freshman Year Experience, 4*, 7–30.

Rehabilitation Act of 1973, PL 93–112, 20 U.S.C. §§701 et seq.

Repetto, J. B., Webb, K. W., Garvan, C. W., & Washington, T. (2002). Connecting student outcomes with transition practices in Florida. *Career Development for Exceptional Individuals, 25*, 123–139.

Rioux-Bailey, C. (2004). *Students with disabilities and access to communitycollege: Continuing issues and new directions.* Washington, DC: George Washington University.

Roessler, R. T., Hennessy, M. T., & Rumril, P. D. (2007). Strategies for improving career services for postsecondary students with disabilities: Results of a focus group study of key stakeholders. *Career Development for Exceptional Individuals, 30*, 158–170.

Royster, L. & Marshall, O. (2008). The chronic illness initiative: Supporting college student with chronic illness needs at DePaul University. *Journal of Postsecondary Education and Disability, 20*(2), 120–125.

Rugsaken, K. T., Robertson, J. A., & Jones, J. A. (1998). Using the learning and study strategies inventory scores as additional predictors of student academic performance. *NACADA Journal, 18*(1), 20–26.

Shaw, S. F. (2009). Transition to postsecondary education. *Focus on Exceptional Children, 42*(2), 1–16.

Shaw, S. F. (2010). Planning for the transition to college. In S. F. Shaw, J. W. Madaus, & L. L. Dukes, (Eds.), *Preparing students with disabilities for college success: A practical guide to transition planning* (pp.257–279). Baltimore: Paul H. Brookes.

Shaw, S. F., Madaus, J. W., & Dukes, L. L. (2010). *Preparing students with disabilities for college success: A practical guide to transition planning.* Baltimore: Paul H. Brookes.

Shaw, S. R., Glaser, S. E., Stern, M., Sferdenschi, C. & McCabe, P. (2010). Responding to students' chronic illnesses. *Principal Leadership, 10*(7), 12–16.

Shiu, S. (2001). Issues in the education of students with chronic illness. *International Journal of Disability, Development and Education, 48*(3), 269–281.

Skinner, M. E. (2004). College students with learning disabilities speak out: What it takes to be successful in postsecondary education. *Journal of Postsecondary Education and Disability, 17*, 91–104.

Speer, N., McFaul, M., & Mohatt, D. (2009). Nourishing students' mental health in a difficult economy. *Chronicle of Higher Education, 55*(36), 25.

Stodden, R. A., Whelley, T., Chang, C. & Harding, T. (2001). Current status of educational support provisions to students with disabilities in postsecondary education. *Journal of Vocational Rehabilitation*, *16*(1), 189–198.

Taylor, M. J. (2005). Teaching students with autistic spectrum disorders in HE. *Education & Training*, *47* (7), 484–495.

Thoma, C. A., & Wehmeyer, M. L. (2005). Self-determination and the transition to postsecondary education. In E. E. Getzel & P. Wehman (Eds.), *Going to college: Expanding opportunities for students with disabilities* (pp. 49–68). Baltimore: Paul H. Brookes.

U.S. Department of Education. (2011). *My FAFSA*. Retrieved May 12, 2011 from https://studentaid2. ed.gov/xap_pack/Default.asp

U.S. Department of Labor. (2011) *Youth employment rate*. Retrieved May 12, 2011 from http://www.dol. gov/odep/categories/youth/youthemployment.htm

VanBerquejik, E., Klin, A. & Volkmar, F. (2008). Supporting more able students on the autism spectrum: College and beyond. *Journal of Autism and Developmental Disorders*, *38*(7), 1359–1370.

Virginia Commonwealth University. (2009). *Going to college*. Retrieved from http://www.going-to-college.org/overview/index.html

Virginia Department of Education. (nd). *I'm determined*. Richmond, VA: Author. Retrieved on April 5, 2011 from www.imdetermined.org

Vogel, S., & Adelman, P. (1992). The success of college students with learning disabilities: Factors related to educational attainment. *Journal of Learning Disabilities*, *25*, 430–441.

Webb, K. W., & Peller, J. (2004). *Dare to dream for adults*. Tallahassee, FL: Bureau of Instructional Support and Community Services, Florida Department of Education.

Webber, J., & Plotts, C. A. (2008). *Emotional and behavioral disorders: Theory and practice*. Boston, MA: Pearson.

Wehman, P. (2006). *Life beyond the classroom: Transition strategies for young people with disabilities* (4th ed.). Baltimore: Paul H. Brookes Publishing Co.

Wenzel, C., & Rowley, L. (2010). Teaching social skills and academic strategies to college students with Asperger's Syndrome. *Teaching Exceptional Children*, *42*(5), 44–50.

20

Effective Strategies for Interagency Collaboration

Patricia M. Noonan

Mary E. Morningstar

UNIVERSITY OF KANSAS

A common denominator among adolescents with disabilities making the transition from school to adult life is the complexity of their support needs, especially when it comes to employment, living independently, and postsecondary education and training (Certo et al., 2003; Morningstar, Kleinhammer-Tramill, & Lattin, 1999). Often, a major barrier impacting the transition to adulthood is the fragmentation, duplication, and inadequacy of adult services and supports (Sitlington, Clark, & Neubert, 2009). Across the board, young adults with disabilities have continued to experience dramatically lower adult outcomes than youth without disabilities (deFur & Patton, 1999; U.S. Department of Education, 2001; Newman, Wagner, Cameto, & Knokey, 2009). While post-school outcomes have improved over the past twenty years, youth with disabilities still do not fare as well as their non-disabled peers given their: (a) poor graduation rates from high school, (b) higher rates of unemployment, (c) lower enrollment in postsecondary education while those who are enrolled do not receive appropriate accommodations, and (d) limited social engagement (Newman et al., 2009; Wagner, Newman, Cameto, Levine, & Garza, 2006).

Interagency collaboration has been ironically described as "an unnatural act between two non-consenting adults" (Agran, Cain, & Cavin 2002); irrespective of this, transition stakeholders strive to achieve this elusive act. Unfortunately, evidence-based models of interagency collaboration have not yet been found within transition research (Test, Fowler, White, Richter, & Walker, 2009). Barriers to collaboration have included poor or inaccurate perceptions of outside agencies and nonexistent or ineffective procedures throughout referral, eligibility, determination, and transition planning processes (Agran et al., 2002; Benz, Johnson, Mikkelsen, & Lindstrom, 1995; Li, 2004). Other limitations have been identified that are inherent to public school systems (i.e., locus of service delivery and staffing patterns) or among adult agencies (i.e., discrepancies between entitlement vs. eligibility and differing services (Certo, Pumpian, Fisher, Storey, & Smalley, 1997).

Interagency collaboration is a predictor of success for improving post-school outcomes (Test, Mazzotti, Mustian, Fowler, Kortering, & Kohler, 2009). For employment outcomes, Rabren, Dunn, & Chambers (2002) identified assistance from vocational rehabilitation, mental health, and developmental disabilities agencies prior to and during the transition from school as a critical factor. Bullis and colleagues also found that students who received assistance from multiple agencies prior to exiting high school were more likely to be employed or enrolled in postsecondary educational settings (Bullis, Davis, Bull, & Johnson, 1995). Similar findings have emerged from the transition-integrated service model (Certo et al., 1997, 2003) that included schools, vocational rehabilitation, and adult employment agencies collaborating in the provision of services prior to students exiting school. By minimizing the disruptions typically experienced when moving from school to outside agencies, the students with significant disabilities involved in the integrated model achieved and maintained higher rates of employment.

In terms of postsecondary education, Repetto, Webb, Garvan, & Washington (2002) found that services (i.e., agencies and organizations within a community) and supports (i.e., percentage of agency referrals, case management, and transportation) were significantly and positively correlated with the rate of enrollment in postsecondary education. These authors also identified that interagency transition councils had a positive impact on post-school outcomes. In other words, the stronger the linkages with adult services and supports before exiting high school, the greater the likelihood that students would be enrolled in postsecondary education.

Accordingly, interagency collaboration is a linchpin during transition for improved employment and postsecondary education outcomes. However, transition practitioners struggle to operationally define and integrate it into daily practice (Benitez, Morningstar & Frey (2009)). Effective transition requires resources and expertise of multiple agencies and professionals.

Legal Requirements for Interagency Collaboration

Legislative mandates for agency partnerships offer clear direction for continued efforts to understand effective strategies. Transition at its core is an interagency event, with multiple agencies, the family, and the student highly involved in the planning and implementation of services (Noyes & Sax, 2004). Mandates requiring schools, community organizations, and governmental agencies to work together are specified in the Individuals with Disabilities Education Act (IDEA), the Vocational Rehabilitation Act, and the Workforce Investment Act (WIA), (Timmons, Cohen, & Fesko, 2004). Federal legislation for youth with disabilities includes specific provisions not only to provide services but to collaborate among agencies to ensure seamless transitions (Luecking & Certo, 2002).

Transition was first mandated under the 1990 reauthorization of IDEA to include post-secondary education, vocational training, integrated employment, adult education, adult services, and independent living or community participation. IDEA has promoted interagency collaboration by: (a) articulating critical interagency linkages, (b) including students, parent, and community agencies during IEP planning, and (c) coordinating services both in school and with outside agencies (Morningstar, Kleinhammer-Tramill, & Lattin, 1999). The transition IEP plan can serve to articulate coordinated services as well as staff and agency responsibilities, thereby avoiding disruption of services (Wehman & Wittig, 2009). The interagency linkages requirement of IDEA reflects the sentiment that "improved post-school outcomes are the driving force and focal point of a free appropriate public education for students with disabilities" (Benz, Lindstrom, & Yovanoff, 2000).

Along the same lines, the Vocational Rehabilitation Act specifies the empowerment of individuals with disabilities to maximize employment, economic self-sufficiency, independence, and full integration into society. Interestingly, the Rehabilitation Act emphasizes collaboration both at the local and state levels, thereby taking the lead among state agencies. The role of rehabilitation services during transition is initially for planning services upon exiting school. However, Title I of the Rehabilitation Act encourages partnerships with educational agencies by using the same definition of transition services as IDEA and allowing agencies to share resources to provide services. Transition services offered by rehabilitation agencies include consultation, technical assistance, and participation in IEP meetings prior to opening a VR case.

Similar to the Rehabilitation Act, the Workforce Investment Act (WIA) contains provisions for serving youth with disabilities and mandating a broad array of programs for at-risk youth. WIA promotes partnerships between education and adult agencies to address employment needs (Timmons et al., 2004). Three of the core principles of Title I of WIA impacting youth include: (a) universal access, (b) streamlined services by One-Stop Centers, and (c) youth activities which strengthen linkages between academic and occupational learning (John J. Heldrich Center for Workforce Development, 2000). In this respect, WIA is intended to serve youth and adults with multiple barriers to employment through a broad array of services delivered in a one-stop format.

Defining Interagency Collaboration

Interagency collaboration should be considered as developmental in nature and involving multiple agencies such as business, health, social service, and education working collaboratively (Johnson, Zorn, Tam, Lamontagne, & Johnson, 2003). Each agency participates within its own system, at its own pace, yet continually develops toward providing better services in collaboration with others (Timmons et al., 2004). Interagency collaboration has been defined as a "mutually beneficial and well-defined relationship entered into by two or more individuals or organizations to achieve common goals" (Parent Advocacy Coalition for Educational Rights, 1994, p. 2). This definition is characterized by a commitment to: (a) identify mutual relationships and goals, (b) jointly develop structures for shared responsibility, (c) jointly develop authority and accountability for success, and (d) share resources and rewards (Mattessich, 2003). Interagency collaboration in transition needs to be sustained and systemic, and can be operationalized by: (a) key positions jointly funded by education and adult agencies, (b) regular and ongoing interagency planning, (c) cross-agency training opportunities, and (d) development of student-focused services that promote post-school outcomes (Benz et al., 2000; Certo et al., 2003; Test, Mazzotti et al., 2009). One model of interagency collaboration uses three essential tools: (a) case conferencing, (b) information sharing, and (c) cross-agency training (Rado, Hamner, & Foley, 2004) to promote state and local-level collaboration among employment providers (e.g., VR, WIA, SSA). Through teamwork, efforts to use these tools expanded the levels of communication and sustained efforts to improve services. Additionally, Harley, Donnell, & Rainey (2003) proposed strategies for "crossing professional borders" (p. 35) to promote integrated service delivery systems. Finally, the development of state and local interagency agreements can enhance systems change because they concentrate resources (i.e., funding, personnel) as well as articulate agency intent (Metzel, Foley, & Butterworth, 2005).

To facilitate interagency collaboration, transition services must be designed to be equally administered by all participants, consumer-driven, and focused on post-school outcomes. Effective interagency collaboration often requires a change in behavior among participants and increased attention to both the process of collaboration and its goal while maintaining a focus on outcomes. Collaboration has been characterized by Hill and Lynn (2003) as "voluntary participation in inter-organizational relationships that involve agreements or understandings concerning allocation of responsibilities and rewards among the collaborators" (p. 65). Given this characterization, it stands to reason that collaborative planning and service delivery require knowledge of complex service issues and community resources, how to work with others, a willingness to share knowledge and resources, and the ability to carry out agreed-upon plans (deFur & Patton, 1999). It is also clear that deliberate actions made on the part of professionals can promote interagency collaboration (Johnson et al., 2003; Timmons et al., 2004). Examples of such actions undertaken by educators and agency staff include: (a) developing a proactive approach to communication, (b) being upfront with the issues, (c) creating frequent opportunities for communication, and (d) involving upper management (Johnson et al., 2003). These actions can be accomplished through strategies such as: (a) cross-training, (b) frequent meetings to increase communication, and (c) focusing on relationship building (Timmons et al., 2004). The end result of such actions may be higher levels of trust and a sense of mutual responsibilities.

In summary, interagency collaboration can promote maximized service delivery systems and reduced operational costs since specialized agencies and disciplines work together to remedy deficiencies in current service systems and to promote transition outcomes (Certo et al., 2003; Johnson et al., 2003). The ultimate goal of collaboration is to produce the seamless transition from one life stage to the next, thereby ensuring needed supports with minimum disruptions (Halpern, 1994). Given this, interagency collaboration for transition can be defined as a broad concept that encompasses formal and informal relationships between schools and adult agencies in which resources are shared to achieve common transition goals. A deeper understanding of strategies to improve interagency collaboration at local and state levels is certainly warranted.

Local-level Strategies for Increased Interagency Collaboration

Noonan, Morningstar, & Gaumer-Erickson (2008) identified local and state-level strategies for interagency collaboration through a qualitative analysis of high-performing school districts in multiple states reporting data reflecting high levels of interagency collaboration. The strategies targeted both local and state activities resulting in high levels of collaboration leading to positive outcomes for young adults with disabilities. Quotations in the following section are directly from research participants—namely transition coordinators at the local and state levels performing interagency collaboration effectively.

Key strategies for effective interagency collaboration at the local level can be categorized as: school-based, bridging school and community, and community-based. These strategies are most likely to involve local educational agency (LEA) staff and a variety of community agencies, organizations, and other stakeholders (e.g., employers, parents, students).

School-based Strategies

Local school-based strategies critical for interagency collaboration to occur include: (a) scheduling and staffing, (b) agency meetings with students and families, and (c) training for students and families. These strategies often occur within the walls of the school to create an environment in which interagency collaboration can transpire.

Create Flexible Scheduling and Staffing

Flexible scheduling and adequate staffing in schools create a foundation for interagency collaboration to transpire. A primary responsibility of the school transition coordinator is to work closely with numerous agencies and parents in order to initiate and secure adult services for youth with disabilities prior to exiting high school. This requires high levels of knowledge about eligibility requirements, services, and funding. To make this happen, transition coordinators need to be given adequate time and resources. During the interviews, one transition coordinator stated, "There is no way you can sit in a classroom and teach *and* coordinate and network in the community. You can't do both, and that's why your transition coordinator serves a role different than a classroom teacher." Another commented, "You can't advocate for your student if you don't know what's out there."

Flexible schedules are necessary in order to collaborate with agencies and parents and to provide community-based experiences. One transition coordinator reflected: "One of the most important issues is to help people in public education get out of the 8am–4pm workday . . . I go to meetings all the time in the evenings and on Saturdays . . . I think the job needs to be done and the families can't be taking days off work all the time."

In addition to scheduling, it is important to be flexible and innovative in the location of services. Flexible location of services ensures collaboration through a shared workspace: "Our rehabilitation counselor is just down the hallway from me . . . she has an office in our facility, so that makes communication real easy."

Not surprisingly, administrative support for flexibility is an essential ingredient. Administrative support included allowing flexible scheduling and offering compensation time, paid summer training, as well as substitutes when needed. As one transition coordinator noted, "When special education directors aren't involved, collaboration doesn't happen." An administrator illustrating high levels of support described it this way:

> I pay people in summer. I pay people for orientation programs. If I want them to go to meetings, I give them an alternate currency . . . if they participate in things [evening and weekend training and meetings] they can build up comp time as an alternate currency other than money.

Another administrator noted, "It takes a lot of administrative support . . . pay for subs and let your teachers collaborate."

Facilitate Meetings with Agencies, Students, and Families

In addition to annual IEP meetings, LEA transition coordinators facilitated frequent meetings between adult agencies and students and families. These meetings should not be limited to Vocational Rehabilitation but occur with a diverse group of adult agencies based on the needs and post-school goals of each student.

It was critical that a good relationship was established between the adult agency and the student. One transition coordinator reflected, "We involve mental health . . . when we're working out behavior plans, they're there. They now come to these meetings and want to come . . . they are a part of it." Districts engaged in early and ongoing relationships between students and agencies and promote high levels of agency presence at high schools. Noted one transition coordinator, "They're [adult agencies] there [in schools] and they know they're a part of what we're doing especially as they move closer to transition and the kids are getting ready to really be more independent."

In addition to meetings between agencies and students, adult agencies should meet regularly with families. Transition coordinators facilitated parent and student questions by setting up meetings with adult agency staff in the family's home. Transition coordinators often set appointments for groups of parents to meet and tour adult agencies. This was an especially effective approach in rural communities with limited services. The importance of establishing meetings was highlighted by one transition coordinator: "We've had greater luck with post-school outcomes if we can get that relationship [between agencies and parents] established before graduation."

Provide Information and Training to Students and Families

LEAs provided information and training to students and families regarding adult agency services, employment, and postsecondary education. Information for students was incorporated into school-based classes, agency presentations, and community-based experiences, for example:

(a) agency staff visited a 10th grade class to discuss services; (b) One-Stop Work Center staff presented to a class on a quarterly basis; (c) employers provided training sessions at a corporate site for students twice a year; (d) agencies (mental health and a center for independent living) provided a life skills course for all students; and (e) a university sponsored a two-week summer camp for youth with disabilities.

Empowering families was seen as a key element in securing agency services and linkages. As one transition coordinator reflected:

> I think in terms of making the connection work . . . helping the parents develop the confidence . . . they can take the assignment and run with it, and they understand who to connect with . . . they build a confidence along with their students to advocate for themselves.

Information can be provided to families through transition fairs or conferences, parent visits to agencies, and agency-sponsored parent training. LEAs can invite agencies to evening workshops or host a monthly agency night for staff and families. Many parent-training sessions are co-sponsored by multiple agencies. For example, one annual transition fair for families is co-sponsored by the local center for independent living, a developmental disability organization, and the LEA. Districts often offered childcare for families to attend transition events.

Other ways to train students and families include: (a) family weekend training, (b) videotaping agency presentations for ongoing use, (c) coordinated parent visits to agencies, and (d) inclusive events for the entire school population. One transition coordinator described how she "will take parents and ask them to take a day off work and go with them to see 4 or 5 programs and talk to the directors of the programs. It's at that point that the parents start to educate themselves." Another noted: "It's pretty productive and parents are usually pretty anxious . . . we block in some time for lunch and reflect on what we've seen."

Strategies for Bridging School and Community

Local strategies for bridging school and community included using a variety of funding sources and relationship building. These strategies are largely for the purpose of bridging services for students and can be considered the glue between school and community-based strategies.

Use a Variety of Funding Sources

Securing additional funding was an essential part of interagency collaboration. External grant opportunities helped to fund efforts to improve collaboration. Funding was used to pay transition staff, develop innovative transition programs, and purchase key equipment. LEAs can share funds and resources with other agencies (e.g., mental health, social services, vocational rehabilitation, workforce investment) to make dollars stretch. Some examples include: (a) LEA and Vocational Rehabilitation (VR) share costs of a summer work program for 30–36 students; (b) LEA shares costs with VR and Mental Health for community-based work sites; (c) LEA and the Workforce Investment Act (WIA) provider share costs for a staff person for a community employment program; (d) LEA and VR hire blended staff position, and (e) LEA and Center for Independent Living (CIL) share costs of a transition fair.

Build Relationships

Building collaborative, trusting relationships with adult providers is critical for interagency collaboration. One transition coordinator explained, "We attend their meetings; we sit on some of the boards that they sit on . . . we get to know them on a personal basis. I think that is probably the key." For interagency collaboration to occur, LEAs need to: (a) accommodate adult agencies, (b) learn their needs and limitations, (c) share resources, and (d) work as a team. An administrator summarized the benefits to strong relationships with adult agencies by saying:

> Once a community reaches that level [high collaboration], you get to a culture of commitment and all of a sudden, agencies are making suggestions [to LEA], employers are making suggestions, and it goes far beyond the scope of one individual. It feeds on itself.

Relationships can be developed through shared problem solving and goal setting, joint training, and high levels of effort from all sides. The main relationship building capacity identified was positive attitudes toward collaboration. LEAs must understand adult agency priorities and needs. When asked for advice for districts struggling with collaboration, a transition coordinator suggested, "To me, the best thing is going to their [adult agencies] turf and finding out what their perceptions are . . . It's hard going and it takes time . . . You've got to stay on top of it." Relationship building with the general community was also identified: "It's not always them coming forward, it's us going forward . . . making sure I'm part of the Boys and Girls Club, community members team, the DSS [disability support services] teams."

Relationship longevity between agencies and LEAs was identified as indicative of positive collaboration. Interagency collaboration grew out of prior joint efforts, and relationships evolved over the years. The history or length of time of a relationship enhanced the ability of LEAs and agencies to maintain high levels of trust. Specific relationship-building strategies included joint advocacy efforts and ongoing meetings. LEA staff often advocated for adult linkages by working closely with adult agencies to develop new programs for unmet community needs. Ongoing meetings were also important to building relationships: "Ongoing meetings have been extremely helpful to educate each other about what the expectations are in each of our systems. There was a lot of misinformation, and a lot of lack of information."

Community-based Strategies

Local community-based strategies included: (a) joint training of staff, (b) community transition teams, and (c) broad dissemination of information. These strategies occur in the community and are critical for interagency collaboration to occur. All of the strategies are highly interrelated and can often be viewed in relation to each other.

Jointly Train Staff

LEA and agency staff indicated they attended and participated in joint training opportunities. This strategy was most often operationalized by a variety of participants representing education, adult agencies, parent groups, regional groups, students and families who planned and co-sponsored training events. Common elements of joint training included: (a) school-sponsored events frequented by multiple agencies, (b) LEA staff attending adult agency training, and (c) jointly planned and supported training events. Statewide transition conferences were an essential aspect of joint training.

Meet with Agency Staff through Community Transition Teams

Meetings among LEA and adult agency staff varied from weekly to monthly to quarterly; however, the variety of agencies involved in such ongoing meetings was consistent. Often, the purpose of these meetings was to share information or focus on planning for an individual student (i.e., case conferencing). Examples elicited included a VR counselor meeting weekly with school staff to discuss specific students and services or the mental health provider meeting regularly to discuss student behaviors and jointly plan supports.

Community transition teams facilitate ongoing meetings between transition coordinators, adult agencies, community organizations, parents, and students and are an important mechanism for interagency collaboration. Blalock and Benz (1999) identified a framework for selecting and orienting members, team maintenance, and mission and goal setting through five basic development steps: (1) team building, (2) needs assessment, (3) program planning, (4) program implementation, and (5) program evaluation and repetition of cycle. Community transition teams consistently work to identify needs, plan and implement new programs, and evaluate their efforts in order to modify and improve services for youths with disabilities.

One transition coordinator noted, "Being part of the transition team really helped us learn about how important interagency collaboration was, and is, and will continue to be." Community transition teams keep lines of communication open and help develop relationships as joint problem solvers. Effective teams have a shared vision, are action-oriented, and contain a variety of stakeholders. A transition coordinator described teaming as, "I call it putting them to work, getting them involved, having them on the council not just to talk, but actually do something . . . it makes a difference if you have them involved doing things." Examples of jointly planned activities included: youth transition conferences, transition fairs, parent training, and resource guides.

Disseminate Transition Information

All high-performing districts provided information about adult–agency contacts, types of available services, and strategies for securing services in easily understood formats for parents and students. Products were developed specifically targeting students and families, such as: (a) agency resource guides, (b) manuals on navigating the adult service systems, (c) checklists of potential agencies to contact, and (d) websites for families, students, and agencies.

LEAs also disseminated information through interagency groups, mailings, and presentations. Examples include: (a) mass mailings twice a year inviting parents and students to a training on connecting with agencies, (b) a presentation by the transition team to community organizations, (c) resource manuals for students and families via CD-ROM, paper, and websites, and (d) videotaped agency presentations to share with students and families. Additionally, it was critical to share information throughout the LEA. Many districts employed a "train the trainer model," and sent representatives to regional or state training with expectations that staff will share new information with LEA staff.

In summary, strategies critical for collaboration at the local level are categorized as: (a) school-based (i.e., creating flexible scheduling and staffing; facilitating meetings with agencies, students and families; providing information and training to students and families), (b) bridging school and community (i.e., using a variety of funding sources and building relationships), and (c) community-based (i.e., jointly training staff, meeting through community transition teams, and disseminating transition information).

State-level Strategies for Increased Interagency Collaboration

Noonan et al. (2008) also discovered critical roles for state education agency (SEA) support in facilitating interagency collaboration. State-level strategies identified as necessary for promoting interagency collaboration included: (a) state transition teams, (b) funding, (c) legislative support,

(d) local input, (e) interagency agreements, and (f) disseminating information. These strategies allowed SEAs to collaborate with outside agencies and national experts by using funding and legislative support mechanisms.

State Transition Teams

State transition teams consist of state-level policy-makers representing the broad array of agencies impacting students and adults with disabilities. Activities among state members included sharing resources, networking, and jointly planning policies and state activities (e.g., conferences, Memorandum of Understanding [MOU], legislative advocacy, and responding to LEA needs). State transition teams jointly plan activities such as cross-agency training, conferences, and statewide transition projects (e.g., dropout prevention initiative).

SEA staff indicated that state collaboration was not always easy and required a commitment to identifying common goals: "It is hard because sometimes what you have to do is give up your own system or what you see as your particular perspective to look at what is the perspective coming across from the larger group." Furthermore, it is important for SEA staff to participate and serve on other interagency teams.

Apply for External Funding

Funding was identified as an indispensable strategy to support new state and local initiatives as well as new and ongoing training. SEAs worked to secure additional funds for transition technical assistance by writing federal grants and partnering with university researchers. Additionally, SEAs sometimes shared funding with adult agencies to match and draw down additional federal dollars (e.g., SEA and Rehabilitation Services) to co-fund transition-related staff working within district programs. Such jointly funded staff represented multiple agency roles. Additionally, state agency staff responsible for transition were knowledgeable of other agency funding streams and state-level partnership opportunities (e.g., Department of Labor and Social Security Administration interagency efforts).

The level of state collaboration depended upon both federal and state mandates. Some states operated with specific mandates for state interagency teams. Additionally, legislative advocacy was important to maintain high levels of collaboration by increasing funding in identified areas of need as well as broadening services for certain populations.

Listen to Local Input

SEA transition staff considered the needs of transition counselors, secondary teachers, and communities when planning technical assistance and training. For effective interagency collaboration, information flowed from the state to the local level and also from local to state levels. One SEA staff explained:

> If you look at it [flow of info from LEAs to SEA] . . . It's like a big cycle that keeps going up and down. We're looking at needs from the bottom coming up . . . and [we're] trying to work back through it at the state level and trying to help them . . . we start to look at building policies and procedures . . . we go right back to the grassroots saying, "What is the effect of this?"

Additionally, local and state needs were analyzed before developing action plans for professional development In some states, district teams completed needs assessments to identify priority areas for training and support. Professional development was then addressed based on these results through state transition conferences as well as regional and local professional development. Additionally, action planning was used to facilitate LEA team goal setting for targeted improvements. One SEA coordinator commented: "Half of the time at the conference spent together is devoted to teams in their own work sessions with a trained facilitator moving forward on their action plans . . . It's much more powerful than just going to sessions."

Develop Memorandum of Understanding (MOU)

Memoranda of Understanding (MOUs) were a key strategy for state-level interagency collaboration. MOUs are formal documents that outline the relationships between state agencies (e.g., SEA and VR). MOUs were used to establish and maintain relationships and for promoting activities such as shared funding and joint training. State MOUs provided guidance for sharing local resources. In one state, an MOU was developed between two agencies to form a new service provision to provide at-risk students and students with mild disabilities vocational training and assessment through community colleges across the state. In another state, the SEA transition coordinator commented:

> We have very clearly set the expectation [for interagency collaboration] through our Memorandum of Understanding . . . these relationships are improving dramatically . . . and there's an expectation of cooperation from the highest level right on through the system.

Additionally, state-level MOUs were developed as a major activity of the state transition team. The development process served as a key activity for relationship building in which participants shared information and worked on common goals. In one state, the MOU team directed the provision of joint regional training and the development of resources to improve local collaboration.

Disseminate Information

Dissemination was seen as an effective strategy for sharing information about adult agency programs and policies, joint training opportunities, and transition resources. One SEA coordinator commented, "We've got the technology with telephone conferencing, video conferencing, email, and listservs to really be much more interactive and participative across and among states." State websites were extensive and often contained state guidance documents, training, publications, links to adult agencies, and resources for families. States disseminated information in a variety of ways including interagency groups, websites, listservs, conference calls, videoconferencing, online chats, mailings, and email. SEAs utilized technology (e.g., wikis, blogs, discussion boards, webinars, conference calls) to reach more stakeholders. Additionally, states collected examples of LEA initiatives and projects and widely shared this information.

In summary, state-level strategies which were critical for interagency collaboration to occur included: (a) state transition teams, (b) external funding, (c) listening to local input, (d) Memoranda of Understanding (MOU), and (e) dissemination. State transition teams composed of state-level professionals from multiple agencies often worked to jointly plan and deliver agreed-upon activities. With the assistance of experts, SEA transition coordinators listened to LEA needs and trained and disseminated information. SEA transition coordinators worked to understand and implement federal legislation as well as to secure funding for interagency collaboration through grants and legislative advocacy.

Implications for the Field

Effective interagency collaboration requires complex and system-wide change. Several key strategies for increasing and enhancing interagency collaboration have been identified across local and state levels. Interestingly, many of the identified strategies involved the formal role of a transition coordinator. Furthermore, the results indicated that in order to achieve effective transition linkages, transition coordinators needed to possess skills to build effective relationships with adult agencies. Therefore, the role of the transition coordinator is an essential element necessary for interagency collaboration.

The Need for Well-trained Transition Coordinators

High-performing districts relied on the formalized role of the transition coordinator to ensure interagency collaboration. On the local level, transition coordinators employed many strategies when collaborating with outside agencies. Furthermore, high-performing LEAs had the capacity to support this collaboration because transition coordinators were allowed the flexibility in their work schedule needed to build relationships and creating linkages for youths with disabilities.

Since 1990 and with subsequent amendments in 1997 and 2004, the transition provisions of the Individuals with Disabilities Education Act (IDEA) have been a strong impetus for special educators to assume a coordinated approach to delivering transition services. Effective transition planning requires that students with disabilities receive instruction and experiences in order to assume their emergent adult roles. This requires secondary special education teachers to know about and employ evidenced-based practices that are responsive to students with disabilities. However, research examining transition implementation illustrates that service delivery is highly variable (Johnson, Stodden, Emanuel, Lucking, & Mack, 2002; Sitlington, 2003). Unfortunately, one reason students with disabilities face challenges during transition may be due to secondary special education teachers feeling unprepared to deliver transition services (Li, 2004; Wolfe, Boone, & Blanchett, 1998).

Secondary special educators often feel poorly prepared to address transition needs of their students (Blanchett, 2001; Prater, Sileo, & Black, 2000). Researchers have found a connection between teachers' perceptions of their knowledge base and the transition-related activities they were implementing with their students (Knott & Asselin, 1999). Similar conclusions were made by Benitez, Morningstar, & Frey (2009) from a national sample of over 600 secondary special educators—teachers who feel less prepared are least likely to implement transition activities. These same researchers are currently working to identify that a significant factor influencing a teacher's ability to implement transition practices is transition personnel development and coursework. Emergent research supports the contention that training does matter and that quality personnel development positively impacts teacher competencies and skills, as well as influences changes in programs and practices (Morningstar & Clavenna-Deane, 2010).

Given that all secondary special educators should be involved, to varying degrees, in transition planning and service delivery, they must possess the core knowledge and skills that enable them to effectively plan and deliver transition services. However, not all special educators believe that they possess high levels of competence and have reported possessing little understanding of and experience with interagency and adult services or how best to support families (Benitez et al., 2009). More importantly, only those teachers who perceive that they are well prepared are likely to implement effective transition-related activities.

Effectively preparing personnel requires focusing on specific transition competencies that are often beyond the current curricular scope of most special education teacher preparation programs (Anderson et al., 2003; Morningstar & Clark, 2003). For many programs, transition content that covers the unique needs of adolescents with disabilities is relegated to a few hours of lecture time during one or two courses (Anderson et al., 2003; Razeghi, 1996). Despite the availability of national standards for preparation of transition specialists (see Division of Career Development and Transition, 2000), most states' teacher licensure or certification policies do not make provisions for certification of transition personnel (Kleinhammer-Tramill, Gieger, & Morningstar, 2003).

In terms of possessing state-of-art knowledge of effective transition interventions, research is emerging that links certain transition strategies (e.g., student-focused planning, student skill development) with improved transition-related outcomes (Cobb & Alwell, 2007; Test, Mazotti et al., 2009). However, not enough evidence yet exists to ascertain the effectiveness of strategies such as interagency collaboration or family involvement. It is interesting to note that these are two of the transition practices in which teachers feel the least prepared (Benitez et al., 2009; Blanchett, 2001; Knott & Asselin, 1999). Therefore, developing comprehensive models of professional development—from teacher education training to on-the-job training—is a critical next step for supporting the capacity of programs to engage in high quality interagency collaboration.

Multi-tiered Models of Collaboration for Transition

While we have provided detailed descriptions of strategies for interagency collaboration at both the local and state levels, a systems perspective is needed if communities are to achieve enhanced levels of interagency collaboration. Indeed, one transition coordinator commented that the list of strategies and capacities should not be used as a laundry list for interagency collaboration. He indicated that such strategies are insufficient if implemented only at the local level by the transition coordinator or any individual person. Instead, in high-performing districts, the identified strategies represented a complex and interrelated system of support, knowledge, relationships, and funding.

In essence, effective interagency collaboration requires complex and system-wide change. Systems change is often discussed, but difficult to achieve. The North Central Educational Laboratory (1995) defines systems change as:

> Change that occurs in all aspects and levels of the educational process and that affects all of the people included in this process—students, teachers, parents, administrators, and community members. It is a dynamic process that requires constant communication (p. 1).

In order for systems change to occur, critical stakeholders must participate and the school climate must accommodate change (Ellsworth, 2000; Fullan and Stiegelbauer, 1991; Fixsen, Naoom, Blase, Friedman, & Wallace, 2005). Fullan and Stiegelbauer (1991) identified critical stakeholders as: (a) teacher, (b) principal, (c) student, (d) administrator, (e) consultant, (f) parent/community, and (g) government. More recently, Fixsen and his colleagues at the National Implementation Research Network synthesized a wide range of implementation research to identify a list of core implementation components and stages of implementation (Fixsen et al., 2005). The seven components are: staff selection, preservice and in-service training, ongoing coaching and consultation, staff evaluation, program evaluation, facilitative administrative support, and systems interventions (Fixsen et al., 2005, p. 29). The components are not uniform across implementations: in some contexts, strengths in certain of the components compensate for weaknesses in others.

In recent years, multi-level models of school reform have emerged as one approach to comprehensive school change. A recent analysis of multi-tiered models of school reform (i.e., High

Schools That Work, Response to Intervention, Professional Learning Communities, Schoolwide Positive Behavioral Supports, and Professional Learning Communities) indicated that collaboration was one of nine essential elements (Jenson, 2008). Commitment to a shared vision is essential for success and requires effective leadership and collaboration throughout all levels (state, district, and building) and across key stakeholders in a collaborative environment that supports and encourages continuous discussion, sharing, reflection, and problem solving about and toward a common goal (Jenson, 2008). It follows that interagency collaboration could be viewed across multiple tiers of student needs to enhance service capacity, prevent duplication of services, and promote high effectiveness of a variety of school roles (e.g., special education, general education, guidance and counseling, administration, English Language Learners (ELL)).

All multi-tiered models share an overall conceptual framework of intervention. As students demonstrate differing responsiveness to the general curriculum and consequently exhibit differing levels of need, the intensity of supports increases or decreases. All tiers of support are provided within the general school context, and student movement between levels of support should be seamless, with decisions regarding levels of needed supports based upon data.

In a multi-tiered model of interagency collaboration, mechanisms for collaboration are established and directed at each tier moving from universal and broad-based collaboration to more intensive strategies for collaboration directed toward students with significant transition support needs.

Tier 1 is the universal level comprising core, evidence-based strategies and supports available to all students. Collaboration at Tier 1 should be considered to be grounded in principles of systems collaboration within schools (general education, special education, career/ technology programs; related services and school support staff) as well as outside agency involvement (workforce development, business community, family organizations, cultural organizations, social service systems, juvenile and adult justice). To effectively engage all

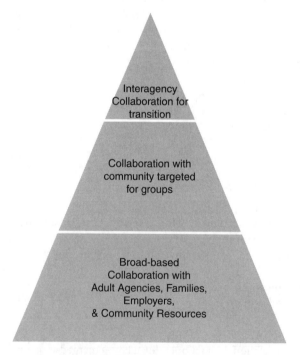

Figure 20.1 Multi-Tiered Model of Interagency Collaboration

students, teachers make meaningful linkages to real life throughout the curriculum. Additionally, schools partner and work closely with the community, employers, families, and various agencies to capitalize on available resources. Interagency collaboration directed at the universal level is broad-based (diverse stakeholder perspectives) and contains an overarching shared vision. The collaborative process is often data-driven, as partners focus efforts in response to school/district need. Examples of Tier 1 interagency collaboration mechanisms include: formalized school–business partnerships, job/college fairs for all students (partnership with employers and higher education), bullying prevention programs (partnership with community mental health, higher education, parent group), alcohol and drug prevention (partnership with community mental health and parent group), and co-funded school resource officers (partnership with Juvenile Justice, Corrections, and Foster Care). While adopting mechanisms such as those described above, successful collaboration must include local-level strategies included earlier in the chapter in order to form and sustain quality collaborations (e.g., building relationships, providing information and training to students and families, and applying for external funding).

Tier 2 comprises the core instruction plus timely, targeted instruction for students needing additional instructional supports. When schools (a) implement quality curriculum and instruction with fidelity and (b) engage in systematic progress monitoring, they are able to identify students demonstrating needs for additional supports. Students who are struggling to make progress in the core curriculum are provided with supports for targeting specific areas of need. Often, this supplemental instruction is provided in small groups. The supplemental interventions must retain the integrity of being evidence-based and involve ongoing progress monitoring. Interagency collaboration to enhance supplemental services is often directed at specific types of students (e.g., students who are culturally or linguistically diverse, at-risk of failing and dropout, and/or receiving special education services). A strategy to ensure culturally responsive practices throughout Tier 2 instruction is to include a wide variety of stakeholder input. Examples of Tier 2 interagency collaboration mechanisms include: co-funded Social Worker/Guidance group counseling (partnership with Community Mental Health, professional organization, employer for neutral setting); participation in community organizations such as Business Advisory Councils, Job Board, Chamber of Commerce, and board membership of agencies; co-funded wrap-around services (partnership with Behavioral/Mental Health); and Dropout Prevention Coach (co-funded career-technical education and postsecondary education). Tier 2 transition mechanisms must include local-level strategies included earlier in the chapter in order to engage in high-quality collaboration (e.g., using a variety of funding sources, jointly training staff, and broad dissemination of information).

In **Tier 3**, the core instruction is complemented with intensive, individualized supports. While receiving Tier 1 and then Tier 2 supports, some students may demonstrate a unique and specialized need for intensive supports. For students continuing to struggle despite Tier 2 support, more individually focused problem solving is required. Individualized, evidence-based interventions, in addition to focused progress monitoring, are characteristics of Tier 3 supports. To best serve students with the most intense support needs, professionals from diverse roles should work together to provide high-quality educational programming directly related to real life. School staff work directly with outside agency staff to develop individualized linkages for postsecondary outcomes. Relationship building between staff is critical for the success of students in living independently as possible, postsecondary education/training, and employment. Examples of Tier 3 interagency collaboration mechanisms include: community-based 18–21 program (located at a community college, apartment or home, or elsewhere in the community) and community transition team model (representation from Vocational Rehabilitation, Independent living centers, Workforce Investment One-Stop Centers, developmental disability organizations, healthcare, employers, employment service providers, parents, adults with disabilities, etc.). As discussed earlier, strategies for high-quality collaboration at the local level are a foundation for the success of Tier 3 transition activities (e.g., community transition team, flexible scheduling and staffing, and facilitating meetings with agencies, students and families).

Conclusion

Interagency collaboration is the critical foundation for providing high-quality transition education and services. In a time of decreasing resources, it is important to dedicate the time and resources necessary to capitalize on staff abilities, relationships, and partnerships. Interagency relationships can assist in meeting the needs of all students if purposefully initiated and viewed through tiered-levels of support.

References

Agran, M., Cain, H. M., & Cavin, H. (2002). Enhancing the involvement of rehabilitation counselors in the transition process. *Career Development for Exceptional Individuals, 25* (2), 141–155.

Anderson, D., Kleinhammer-Trammil, P. J., Morningstar, M. E., Lehmann, J., Bassett, D., Kohler, P. et al. (2003). What's happening in personnel preparation in Transition? A national survey. *Career Development for Exceptional Individuals, 26* (2), 145–160.

Benitez, D. T., Morningstar, M. E., & Frey, B. B. (2009). A multistate survey of special education teachers' perceptions of their transition competencies. *Career Development for Exceptional Individuals, 32,* 6–16.

Benz, M. R., Clark, G. M., & Neubert, D. A. (2009).*Transition Education and Services for Students with Disabilities* (5th ed). Boston, MA: Prentice Hall.

Benz, M. R., Cohen, A., & Fesko, S. L. (2004). Merging cultural differences and professional identities: Strategies for maximizing collaborative efforts during the implementation of the Workforce Investment Act. *Journal of Rehabilitation, 70*(1), 19–27.

Benz, M. R., Donnell, C., & Rainey, J. A. (2003). Interagency collaboration: Reinforcing professional bridges to serve aging populations with multiple service needs. *The Journal of Rehabilitation, 69* (2), 32–38.

Benz, M. R., Foley, S. M. & Butterworth, J. (2005). State-level Interagency Agreements for Supported Employment of People with Disabilities. *Journal of Disability Policy Studies, 16*(2), 102–114.

Benz, M. R., Fowler, C. H., White, J., Richter, S. & Walker, A. (2009). Evidence-based secondary transition practices for enhancing school completion. *Exceptionality, 17*(1), 16–29.

Benz, M. R., Hamner, D., & Foley, S. (2004). State agency systems collaboration at the local level: Gluing the puzzle together. *Research to Practice, 10*(1).

Benz, M. R., Johnson, D. K., Mikkelsen, K. S., & Lindstrom, L. E. (1995). Barriers to school and VR collaboration. *Career Development for Exceptional Individuals, 18* (2), 133–156.

Benz, M. R., Kleinhammer-Benz, M. R., & Lattin, D. L. (1999). Using successful models of student-centered transition planning and services for adolescents with disabilities. *Focus on Exceptional Children, 31*(9), 2–20.

Benz, M. R., Lindstrom, L., & Yovanoff, P. (2000). Improving graduation and employment outcomes of students with disabilities: Predictive factors and student perspectives. *Exceptional Children, 66* (4), 509–529.

Benz, M. R., Mazotti, V. L., Benz, M. R., Fowler, C. H., Benz, M. R., & Kohler, P. H. (2009). Evidence-based secondary transition predictors for improving post-school outcomes for students with disabilities. *Career Development for Exceptional Individuals, 32,* 160–181.

Benz, M. R., & Patton, J. R. (1999). *Transition and school based services: Interdisciplinary perspectives for enhancing the transition process.* Austin, TX: PRO-ED.

Benz, M. R., Sileo, T. W., & Black, R. S. (2000). Preparing educators and related school personnel to work with at-risk students. *Teacher Education and Special Education, 23*(1), 51–64.

Benz, M. R., Stodden, R. A., Benz, M. R., Luecking, R., & Mack, M. (2002). Current challenges facing secondary education and transition services: What research tells us. *Exceptional Children, 68* (4), 519–532.

Benz, M. R., Webb, K. W., Benz, M. R., & Washington, T. (2002). Connecting student outcomes with transition practices in Florida. *Career Development for Exceptional Individuals, 25*(2), 123–139.

Benz, M. R., Zorn, D., Tam, B. K., Lamontagne, M., & Johnson, S. A. (2003). Stakeholders' views of factors that impact successful interagency collaboration. *Exceptional Children, 69* (2), 195–209.

Blalock, G. & Benz, M. R. (1999). *Using community transition teams to improve transition services.* Austin, TX: PRO-ED.

Blanchett, W. J. (2001). Importance of teacher transition competencies as rated by special educators. *Teacher Education and Special Education, 24* (1), 3–12.

Bullis, M., Davis, C., Bull, B., & Johnson, B. (1995). Transition achievement among young adults with deafness: What variables relate to success? *Rehabilitation Counseling Bulletin, 39,* 103–150.

Certo, N. J., Mautz, D., Pumpian, I., Sax, C., Smalley, K., Wade, H. A. et al. (2003). Review and discussion of a model for seamless transition to adulthood. *Education and Training in Developmental Disabilities, 38* (1), 3–17.

Certo, N., Pumpian, I., Fisher, D., Storey, K., & Smalley, K. (1997). Focusing on the point of transition. *Education and Treatment of Children, 20,* 68–84.

Cobb, B. & Alwell, M. (2007). *Social/Communication Interventions and Transition Outcomes for Youth with Disabilities: A Systematic Review.* Colorado Springs: CO: Colorado State University, What Works in Transition: Systematic Review Project.

Division of Career Development and Transition. (2000, March). *Transition specialist competencies* (Fact sheet). Arlington, VA: Council for Exceptional Children.

Ellsworth, J. B. (2000). *Surviving change: A survey of educational change models.* Syracuse, NY: ERIC Clearinghouse on Information and Technology (ED No. 443417).

Fixsen, D. L., Naoom, S. F., Blase, K. A., Friedman, R. M. & Wallace, F. (2005). *Implementation research: A synthesis of the literature.* Tampa, FL: University of South Florida, Louis de la Parte Florida Mental Health Institute, The National Implementation Research Network (FMHI Publication #231). Retrieved July 27, 2009, from http://www.fpg.unc.edu/~nirn/resources/publications/Monograph/pdf/Monograph_full.pdf

Fullan, M., and Stiegelbauer, S. (1991). *The New Meaning of Educational Change.* New York, NY: Teachers College Press.

Halpern, A. S. (1994). The transition of youth with disabilities to adult life: A position statement of the Division on Career Development and Transition, The Council for Exceptional Children. *Career Development for Exceptional Individuals, 17* (2), 115–124.

Hill, C. J., & Lynn, L. E., Jr. (2003). Producing human services: Why do agencies collaborate? *Public Management Review, 5,* 63–81.

Jenson, R. (2008). Missouri Integrated Model Blueprint. Retrieved July 20, 2010 from http://www.mimschools.org

John J. Heldrich Center for Workforce Development. (2000). *The Workforce Investment Act of 1998: A primer for people with disabilities.* New Brunswick, NJ: Rutgers.

Kleinhammer-Tramill, P. J., Geiger, W., & Morningstar, M. (2003). Policy contexts for transition personnel preparation: An analysis of transition-related credentials, standards, and course requirements in state certification and licensure policies. *Career Development for Exceptional Individuals, 26* (2), 185–206.

Knott, L., & Asselin, S. B. (1999). Transition competencies: Perceptions of secondary special education teachers. *Teacher Education and Special Education, 22* (1), 55–65.

Li, J. (2004). *Interagency collaboration in transition practice: An initial model.* Greeley: University of Northern Colorado.

Luecking, R., & Certo, N. (2002). Integrating service systems at the point transition for youth with significant disabilities: A model that works. *National Center on Secondary Education and Transition (NCSET), Information Brief, 1*(4).

Mattessich, P. (2003). *Can this collaboration be saved? Twenty factors that can make or break any group effort.* Montclair, NJ: National Housing Institute. Retrieved October 2, 2004 from, http://www.nhi.org

Morningstar, M. E., & Clark, G. M. (2003). The status of personnel preparation for transition education and services: What is the critical content? How can it be offered? *Career Development for Exceptional Individuals, 26*(2), 227–237.

Morningstar, M. & Clavenna-Deane, B. (2009). *Evaluation of KU TransCert Program Graduates.* Lawrence, KS: University of Kansas, Department of Special Education.

Newman, L., Wagner, M., Cameto, R., & Knokey, A.-M. (2009). *The post-high school outcomes of youth with disabilities up to 4 years after high school. A report of findings from the National Longitudinal Transition Study–2 (NLTS2) (NCSER 2009–3017).* Menlo Park, CA: SRI International. Available at www.nlts2.org/reports/2009_04/nlts2_report_2009_04_complete.pdf

Noonan, P., Morningstar, M. E., & Gaumer Erickson, A. S. (2008). Improving interagency collaboration: Effective strategies used by high performing local districts and communities. *Career Development for Exceptional Individuals, 31,* 132–143.

North Central Regional Educational Laboratory. (1995). Facilitating systemic change in science and mathematics education: A toolkit for professional developers. Retrieved November 14, 2004, from http://www.ncrel.org/sdrs/

Noyes, D. A. & Sax, C. L. (2004). Changing systems for transition: Students, families, and professionals working together. *Education and Training in Developmental Disabilities, 39*(1), 35–44.

Parent Advocacy Coalition for Educational Rights [PACER]. (1994). *Interagency collaboration and transition.* Salt Lake City, UT: Center for Expertise. Retrieved May 21, 2003, from http://www.pacer.org

Rabren, K., Dunn, C., & Chambers, D. (2002). Predictors of post-high school employment among young adults with disabilities. *Career Development for Exceptional Individuals, 25*(1), 25–40.

Razeghi, J. A. (1996). The important role of career development in preventing special education dropouts. *Career Development for Exceptional Individuals, 19,* 145–158.

Sitlington, P. L. (2003). Postsecondary education: The other transition. *Exceptionality, 11*(2), 103–113.

U.S. Department of Education (2001). *Twenty-third annual report to congress on implementation of the Individuals with Disabilities Education Act,* Washington, DC: Author.

U.S. General Accounting Office. (2003, July). *Special education: Federal actions can assist states in improving postsecondary outcomes for youth.* Report to the Ranking Minority Member, Committee on Health, Education, Labor and Pensions, U.S. Senate (GAO–03–773). Retrieved October 10, 2003, from http://www.gao.gov

Wagner, M., Newman, L., Cameto, R., Levine, P., & Garza, N. (2006). An overview of findings from Wave 2 of the National Longitudinal Transition Study–2 (NLTS2). Menlo Park, CA: SRI International. *Retrieved September 28,* 2010, from www.nlts2.org/reports/2006_08/nlts2_report_2006_08_complete.pdf

Wehman, P., & Wittig, K. (2009) *Transition IEPs* (3rd edn). *A curriculum guide for teachers planning and designing transition programs.* Austin, TX: PRO-ED.

Wolfe, P. S., Boone, R. S., & Blanchett, W. J. (1998). Regular and special educator's perceptions of transition competencies. *Career Development for Exceptional Individuals, 21*(1), 87–106.

21

Innovative Employment Support Models

Wendy Parent-Johnson

UNIVERSITY OF KANSAS

Lucy is 21 and excited about leaving school this year. Both she and her parents are interested in Lucy going to work once she completes her school year. In preparation for Lucy's life after school, her transition coordinator scheduled a meeting with Lucy, her mother, case manager, rehabilitation counselor, teacher, and paraprofessional to make the final arrangements. As soon as the meeting began, the case manager stated that there was a waiting list for developmental disability services so there were no options available to her. Immediately everyone around the table talked about budget cuts, the poor economy, and the dismal prospects for employment in the community. The meeting ended with no provisions or plan for Lucy's post-school outcome. The team talked about her completing the school year and staying home with her mother until another opportunity for services became available.

Sarah is 21 and is counting down the days until she completes high school. Her team led by her transition coordinator and including her rehabilitation counselor, case manager, mother, teacher, and benefits specialist, has arranged a meeting to determine what Sarah will be doing next year. Sarah really wants a job and her mother is expecting her to go to work. The meeting starts out with introductions and Sarah is asked what she likes, specifically "What are your passions?" During her school-work experiences, Sarah realized how much she liked working with people and her love for flowers. The team brainstormed ideas for jobs in their small rural town, such as a florist, an event caterer, a floral shop in a grocery store, a satellite floral stand in a hospital or coffee shop, a self-employment floral delivery business, or a special events order taker. Sarah was thrilled with the possibilities and the team identified action steps to explore each one more thoroughly. Based upon their findings and the needs of Sarah and the business community, the idea of creating a job with the grocery store in the nearby city was pursued. Sarah would pick up their flowers and set up a mini flower shop in a variety of local businesses on a rotating schedule. The use of Social Security Work Incentives and vocational rehabilitation dollars in collaboration with the school-based job coach made Sarah's employment outcome a reality.

It is obvious that Lucy and Sarah face very different futures despite the similarities of their present situations. Both young women want to work, have family support, an interagency transition team, and participated in community-based work experiences while in school, all important elements for successful transition (Wehman, 2006). What distinguishes the two is the nature of their planning meeting and the expectations and actions of participants. The enthusiasm and creativity of Sarah's team is contagious and promotes a "can do" attitude that drives the transition process, staying focused on employment and not accepting anything less than the desired outcome.

What are the Possibilities?

Transition is a time to have high expectations for employment, explore options, decide on a work outcome, and promote a work ethic. All too often these elements are overlooked as a result of not knowing what is possible for employment or what resources and supports could potentially be available. Perceptions that individuals cannot work or that they must meet arbitrary criteria before being ready to work can frequently interfere with implementing what we know to be best practices that contribute to students becoming employed when they finish school. It is important to note that transition is a future-driven, outcome-oriented process and, as such, provisions for all students to have an employment or postsecondary goal and the steps for achieving it should be part of each individual's IEP-planning process (Wittig, 2009).

Advancements in how we support individuals in employment and the variety of employment situations that are available have opened new doors for students regardless of disability label or support needs (Griffin & Hammis, 2003; Luecking, Fabian, & Tilson, 2004; Wehman, Inge, Revell, & Brooke, 2007a). An array of strategies, made possible through supported and customized employment approaches, have expanded the options for young adults to be able to find the job niche that best matches their skills, interests, contributions, and support needs in relation to competitive labor market demands. Supported employment services are characterized by competitive employment in a community business with individualized assistance by a skilled job coach who helps a person find a job, learn how to do the job, and provides follow-along support to assist with keeping their job (Rusch, 1990; Wehman & Kregel, 1995; Wehman, Sale, & Parent, 1992). Examples of types of job supports include natural supports, natural cues, assistive technology, environmental modifications, rehabilitation engineering, compensatory strategies, and systematic instructional techniques.

Customized placement strategies involve negotiating a relationship between an individual and employer that meets the needs of both and results in individually designed services, supports, and jobs (Callahan & Rogan, 2004; Button, 2007). Customized employment builds on and expands the options available under supported employment practices, all of which are most often described as integrated employment. The critical elements shared by both include: (a) customer choice, (b) the belief that individuals should be viewed from an abilities versus disabilities perspective, (c) workplace integration, (d) jobs/careers of choice, (e) competitive/prevailing wages, and (f) consumer-directed services with individualized workplace supports (Wehman, Inge, et al., 2007b, p. 132).

As a result, created and "carved" jobs, resource ownership, self-employment, and business within a business are all viable, evidence-based options that expand the choices available to young adults as they graduate from school. More recently, employer-initiated models have become increasingly visible and offer additional opportunities for many more young adults interested in work (Katz & Luecking, 2009). It is unfortunate that despite the many illustrations of the effectiveness of these approaches, transition and employment outcomes for youth with disabilities remain poor and dramatically inferior to those achieved by their peers without disabilities (Newman, Wagner, Cameto, & Knokey, 2009). Often information about what is possible or the tools and resources for implementing these strategies are simply lacking for the majority of people most affected by their availability and outcomes. The purpose of this chapter is to provide an overview of innovative and creative employment options to bridge the information gap and enable more young adults with disabilities to benefit from their availability. First, a description of each strategy will be provided followed by an example and "how to" tips for implementation. Second, an employment team-meeting process for making decisions regarding the best approach and developing individual action plans will be presented. Throughout, specific techniques to be utilized by school personnel to promote employment outcomes for their students with disabilities will be discussed.

What are the Different Options and How do I Implement them?

Often, job placement decisions are made based upon an available opening, agency service provisions, pressure from others, funding streams, the local economy, or geographical location. While these elements may be part of the consideration, the importance of a good job match based upon the skills, interests, passions, and support needs of the individual in relation to the opportunities and business needs of the employer, cannot be overlooked. A critical component of the job-matching process is knowledge of the variety of employment configurations that can be accomplished through business development techniques aimed at finding that best fit for both the individual and the employer. The variety of possibilities for integrated, competitive employment has expanded the opportunities for negotiating a successful job match for all individuals including those with significant support needs and those with limited or no work history or unsuccessful past employment experiences. In addition, negotiating a business arrangement with an employer offers a viable alternative that can be a particularly attractive option during poor economic times or in rural areas where employers have specific needs but may not have the hiring flexibility to fill those positions. Typically, these are negotiated by a skilled job coach, employment specialist, job developer, paraprofessional, transition coordinator, or job placement person who has responsibility for assisting young adults with employment. The available tools offered to these professionals and the individuals they serve are highlighted below.

Created Jobs

These require establishing a new job or job duties that did not previously exist as a position within a business. As defined by the Department of Labor (Office of Disability Employment Policy, 2004), "A created job description is negotiated from unmet needs in the employer's workplace. This leads to a new job description based on unmet needs of the employment setting . . ." A created job is developed based upon knowledge of the industry and the specific company and presented as a business proposal to an employer with whom there is a relationship that offers them an alternative option which meets their needs and makes good economic sense. For example, Sally's position was created in the medical records department of a hospital to address the backlog of patient records by having her organize medical documents in sequential order for filing in patients' folders by medical records staff. The position was negotiated at 20 hours a week at $9.55 an hour with full benefits. Systematic instructional techniques by a job coach and modifications provided by a rehabilitation engineer assisted Sally with being able to perform her job within the quality and production standards of the company. Interestingly, the hospital had laid off personnel and did not have a Full-Time Equivalent (FTE) to hire someone in medical records. However, suggesting a new part-time position to arrange documents in order for more efficient filing by medical records staff was a cost-effective and doable solution to the ever-mounting problem faced by the department.

Carved Jobs

These are designed from the redistribution of job duties from one position to another, tailoring them to the job seeker's unique skills and abilities. Job carving is the "creation of a job description based on tasks derived from a single traditional job in an employment setting. The carved job description contains one or more, but not all, of the tasks from the original job description" (Office of Disability Employment Policy, 2004). It is important to note that job carving is not: pulling tasks that no one wants to do, used to devalue the worker, used to segregate from coworkers, used to create something "special," done in a way to violate the work culture because the employer should be nice, or made up and the first to go. For example, Gary works as an office assistant at a bank and performs a variety of duties that were chosen based upon what he likes and is good at and what the bank needed even though they were not the tasks typically assigned to someone in that position or outlined in the job description. These include: delivering mail, typing, sweeping, and stocking the kitchen and pop machine, vacuuming the vault, picking up recycling, encoding, cleaning the ATM lane, delivering paper, stuffing bank statements, and cleaning windows. Gary learned how to do his job with the help of instruction and advocacy provided by a job coach and compensatory strategies, such as a laminated checklist with multi-colored markers, down time job duties of choice, and supervisor approval of completed checklist to assist with keeping his job.

Resource Ownership

This involves the purchasing of equipment, machinery, or other items that an individual owns and brings to the workplace as part of their employment, offering an additional advantage to the employer. In this way, the individual brings to the business a resource that they own to fill an unmet need oftentimes leveling the playing field when competing against other applicants who may have more education or work experience. Funding sources can include vocational rehabilitation, Social Security Administration work incentives, Individual Development Accounts, and grants, state, or other specialized dollars. For example, Cindy purchased a computer and educational software with help from her rehabilitation counselor and was hired as a daycare assistant, a job where she used the equipment to instruct and entertain young children. Lee brought a riding lawn mower to the job in exchange for a part-time position and training after a friend of his family heard the recreation center was in need of an additional landscape crew member but could not afford the equipment as well as a position. In addition, Amy wanted to work in the catering business but had no experience so her job coach arranged for the purchase of an industrial-size refrigerator and a position was found with a small local catering company. Joe's passion was cars and his job coach found him a job with a new car detailing business that was interested in expanding to include a mobile component which Joe assisted with when he brought a detailing machine and trailer to the company upon his hire.

Self-employment

This involves becoming a small business owner and operator. Steps for starting a business include coming up with a business idea, developing a business plan, obtaining start-up funds, and arranging supports. It is important to note that the term implies supported self-employment where individuals receive assistance with learning how to run their business and the supports necessary to operate their business. Support for self-employment can be obtained from vocational rehabilitation, a supported employment provider, the business department of a high school, the Small Business Development Centers, and Start-Up USA (VCU Rehabilitation Research and Training Center on Workplace Supports, n.d.). One idea is to develop a start-up plan to get the business up and running followed by a second expansion plan that is designed to grow and maintain the business offering a competitive wage or higher for its owner. For example, Judy has started her own art business selling her designs on stationery, cards, magnets, pictures, necklaces, coffee cups, and t-shirts at arts/craft venues, professional conferences, local businesses, and website sales which have been international in scope. Judy started her business while still enrolled in high school and received assistance and support from her school, vocational rehabilitation, and case manager. Barbara started her own home-based linen service for hair salons with plans for expansion to include fitness centers and gyms. The supported employment provider, funded by vocational rehabilitation, helped Barbara with developing a business plan, providing job coach support, assisting with start-up, and making on-going marketing and quality assurance checks.

Business within a Business

This requires the development of a self-employment venture within an existing business setting. Similar to negotiating a job match, this arrangement becomes a win-win situation for the business and entrepreneur as a result of an established customer base for the small business and the addition of a product that the business does not currently offer but would enhance their market expanding the customers who patronize the larger company. For example, Cathie brought magazine racks, magazines, and books to a coffee shop where she sells them to coffee shop patrons. She receives assistance from coworkers and the owner, who ring up her sales for a small administration fee. Customers who come in for coffee and food tend to stay longer and make additional purchases due to the reading materials available to them. A disk refurbishing business was started by Leon in a rural town where only one other machine was available at the local video rental store. Leon purchased the machine and established his business within a pawnshop that felt Leon's presence would increase sales of movies and games while Leon benefited from the steady customer traffic, natural employer supports, and assistance with financial transactions.

Finding an employment niche requires becoming familiar with the business community and developing relationships with individual companies. Making employer contacts to explore the labor market and gain information about different industries including their hiring trends and future growth plans is a critical first step. Knowledge from a business' perspective allows us to suggest a good job match that is beneficial to the employer and makes good economic sense.

Employer-Initiated Models

These offer innovative options for expanding competitive employment opportunities using strategies such as universal design, modified training, and natural supports that are available for all employees of the company. Project SEARCH, an internship and employment program for youth with disabilities between the ages of 18 and 21, originated at Cincinnati Children's Hospital in 1996 and is currently located in 42 states and in a new federal model within the Department of Labor (http://www.cincinnatichildrens.org/svc/alpha/p/search/). Walgreens Distribution Center in Anderson, South Carolina, has hired 42% of its 800-person workforce, employees with physical and cognitive disabilities, using technology throughout the building to facilitate and support all employees who perform equal jobs and earn the same pay (http://abcnews.go.com/WN/story?id=4272981&page=1). AMC Theaters has initiated a pilot program focusing on increasing the number of individuals with disabilities in their companies through modifications in their application and interview process and increased job-learning time while maintaining the same performance standards (http://asa.confex.com/asa/2010/webprogram/Session5227.html). APSE HR Connect Staffing offers a collaborative model between staffing agencies and community rehabilitation providers which results in increased numbers of qualified individuals with disabilities being hired to fill the staffing agencies' job orders (http://www.apse.org/business/lead.cfm). The U.S. Business Leadership Network (BLN) is a business organization representing more than 5,000 employers who promote employment of people with disabilities to other employers by sharing their experiences, supporting best practices, and expanding its BLN affiliates (http://www.usbln.org). In addition, several corporations are employing their own diversity coordinators who assist with expanding their workforce to hire and support underrepresented populations including individuals with disabilities.

What can Help us Think Outside the Box?

Determining an employment option can be a challenging task particularly when attempting to make decisions in isolation of key pieces of information or resources. Our experience suggests conducting an Employment 1st Team Meeting as an effective strategy that bypasses these shortcomings and leads to a creative employment outcome (Parent, 2009). Participants ideally include the student, family member(s), teacher, transition coordinator, rehabilitation counselor, job coach, case manager, and benefits specialist; however, a meeting can be held if one or more representatives may be absent and any one person can take the lead to make the initial arrangements. While the people involved may be familiar, the agenda is unique because the purpose of the meeting is not to decide if the student can work or should work but rather that he or she will work and what the team can do to make that happen. A very different outcome occurs when employment, or postsecondary education in preparation for employment, is established up front as the only acceptable goal for students with disabilities transitioning from high school, forcing the team to come together and address any potential challenges. The meeting starts with asking the student about his or her passions. What does he like? What does she typically do? What has he shown an interest in? What excites her? and What would they like to do? These passions spark ideas and interestingly, the enthusiasm of the group fosters creativity and an energized forum for exploration and brainstorming. For example, one student with a passion for animals found out a variety of job possibilities when her team identified the following business ideas: pet wash, doggie daycare or resort, nature center, veterinarian's office, pet store, humane society, service dog trainer, dog biscuit maker, pet sitter or dog walker, animal caretaker, or pet food delivery. This was a significantly larger list than the humane society suggested during her previous traditionally run meeting.

It is not uncommon for a member of the team to know someone or have a previous experience related to each idea that is generated. Now comes the time to assign homework so everyone has at least one area to investigate further and bring back to the larger group. For example, one member may have a brother who is a veterinarian. Another may have worked at one time in a pet store. One may have a neighbor who owns her own small business. Still another may have used a pet sitter and dog walker service or the student may agree to take his dog to a pet washing salon, talk to a friend who works at a humane society, or visit a nature center. Additionally, questions may be raised regarding something the members have limited knowledge of, such as using Social Security Work Incentives, or due to a key person being absent from the group, warranting different assignments for participants. The result is a blueprint for moving forward with a scheduled date for coming back together to share everyone's findings, typically within two to four weeks.

The next meeting is the time to review the information, put the pieces together, and formulate a more specific employment direction, discussed and decided in the context of the information generated by this exploration phase. The new information will foster additional brainstorming as the group considers what ideas seem doable, what is and isn't available in the community, and what sounds best to the individual. For example, it may have been discovered that the community is saturated with pet-sitter businesses or the student may have figured out that pet washing was not an attractive option. Another member may have found out that pet food delivery was not a selling point to pet stores which rely on customer impulse buying but was to a farm store. Or the small business development center may have informed someone that four novelty pet stores had been opened in the community in the last ten years with no success. Additionally, the individual is certain to like and dislike some ideas and to be intrigued by others. It is likely that a few options will begin to emerge to everyone and become the main focus of the meeting.

Similarly, information about funding and support resource options are important pieces of the puzzle for consideration. For example, it may be determined that there is a waiting list for Medicaid Waiver services, that there are no job coaches in the individual's community, or that the state offers a unique pot of money for small business start-up. The team can use the information about resources, needs, and preferences to make decisions with the individual regarding a business arrangement that is most appealing. For example, if there are no job coaches, one option is to start a small business and hire an employee who can provide support. Another option is to use resource ownership to increase the chances of becoming employed in the desired position and receiving essential supports from the employer. Similar to a chess game, the team can move resources around in order to leverage others and address gaps in a most effective way. For example, if an individual needs to cover small-business start-up costs, job coaching services, and transportation assistance, perhaps the vocational rehabilitation counselor can offer to pay for start-up. The school then agrees to provide job coach support while Social Security Work Incentives are used to assist with transportation. Combining the pieces together in a workable solution will generally revolve around several important factors that influence decision-making. Questions for the individual to consider with his or her team are highlighted in Table 21.1.

The resulting discussions and information are compiled in a plan that outlines the road map for employment, including the action steps to get there, the persons responsible, and the timeline for completion. More information still may be needed and therefore should be included as a step in the action plan. For example, the individual may realize that she might like to work in a hospital so talking with her neighbor who is a nurse and visiting the local hospital are action

Table 21.1 Individual questions to be considered with the Employment 1st Team Meeting

1 What is available in your community in the field you are interested in? Do businesses already exist? Is there a need for a service or product that you have to offer?
2 What services are available in your community? Is there a supported employment provider? Do job coach services exist?
3 What types of support do you need and where would they best be available? Do you want to work independently or would you like other people around who could help?
4 How will regular employment, resource ownership, or self-employment affect your benefits? What benefits do you need?
5 What are your personal needs? Do you need a certain amount of income? Do you want a place to go every day once you graduate from school? Is health insurance something you are interested in?
6 What arrangement best meets your family's needs? Does your family want you to work full time or part time? Do they prefer you have a flexible or fixed schedule? Are they available to assist you?
7 What option do you like the most? Do you want to be your own boss? Do you want to work where your friends are working? Do you want one job now and another later as you pursue career advancement?
8 What funding resources are available to you? Are there disability-funded services that you can use? What non-disability funding options can you tap into? Are there special dollars for some of the options that you might want to take advantage of?

steps to help determine a specific employment arrangement. Similarly, an individual may know that he or she would like to do something with books but be uncertain as to what type of employment option would be most suitable (e.g. carved job, resource ownership, self-employment). For example, an individual wanting to start a business who is unsure if the idea is a good one might have an action plan that includes as a first step a visit to the Small Business Development Center to learn about self-employment. It is likely that some of the steps in the action plan may be a follow-up to questions raised from the previous homework experiences. For example, using work incentives may have been identified as an attractive option. However, contacting the PASS (Plan for Achieving Support) Cadre to help with that effort may be one of the steps. In addition, an individual may want to learn more about a specific business, such as a law office or an airport, so that a job shadowing or work experience arrangement in each of these settings becomes one of the action steps. Establishing a means of communication among the team, such as email, telephone, written correspondence, or another meeting date, and encouraging ongoing communication is critical to keep the plan moving forward as many of these questions are investigated and new information generated to guide activities and finalize the competitive employment outcome.

Those responsible for implementing the plan can begin to move forward by initiating business development activities, such as contacting specific employers, determining a market analysis, creating a business plan, making employer negotiations, and arranging funding/support arrangements. As business contacts are made, information to assist with deciding the specific employment outcome can be determined. For example, Maddy liked to sew and could run a machine with the use of assistive technology. The team brainstormed a variety of ideas such as working in a fabric store, starting a sewing repair business, working for a clothing manufacturer, running an embroidery machine, obtaining a job in a hobby or craft store, and developing a small business with sewn products for sale. The job coach contacted businesses in order to become familiar with the sewing industry in their small rural community. She realized that the fabric store was not hiring, clothing manufacturing did not exist, multiple people operated sewing and alteration businesses out of their homes, the sport store downtown was interested in expanding their product lines, and all team logo merchandise had to be shipped out of town with a delayed turn-around time. In addition, Maddy and her family were concerned about a home-based business with limited opportunities for coworker interactions and other social relationships. As a result of her findings, the job coach approached the sport store and proposed hiring a qualified employee who owned her own embroidery machine so that the business could increase its sales through the addition of embroidered merchandise with team logo items and uniforms. This resource ownership situation met a community need and made business sense to the employer while at the same time utilizing the talents and passions of Maddy in an environment that matched her interests. Final negotiations involved determining the specific job duties, hours, salary, benefits, and start date. The job coach made arrangements with the vocational rehabilitation counselor to purchase the industrial sewing machine and authorize hours for on-site training until Maddy was able to perform her duties and operate the machine at a competitive rate. The use of checklists, assistive technology, natural supports, and a cell phone, for on-going follow-along support increased Maddy's independence and overall job performance.

The advantages of the Employment 1st Team Meeting are numerous. First, no one person has to know it all. The actions of the group build on the expertise and exploratory labor of its members. Second, a wealth of resources contributes to getting the job done. All persons, including the student with a disability, are given homework assignments and share responsibility in implementing the specific action plan for employment. Third, a different way of thinking is offered that moves beyond the "yes but" or "can we" mentality. By relying on our creative energy, we can think beyond the status quo and look at a wide range of options typically available to all persons who leave school in anticipation of employment. Fourth, the process bypasses issues that impact disability service delivery systems. Problems that are identified are discussed and alternative plans offered based upon disability, generic, and natural supports in addition to different funding sources available to anyone. Fifth, opportunities for self-determination are promoted as a result of the very nature of the meeting format that puts individuals in the driver's seat, guiding and participating in the decision-making, problem-solving process. Finally, the foundation for employment activities lies in the business community, the very location where those outcomes occur.

Conclusion

This chapter presented an approach to be included in the transition process that promotes employment as the outcome for youth with disabilities as they exit from high school. Guided by an Employment 1st Team Meeting, creative decisions can be made from the starting point that integrated employment is the expected outcome for all youth and nothing less is acceptable. The additional resources offered by the team allow school personnel to expand options without having to know or do it all. As a result, a variety of employment models, such as carved and created jobs, resource ownership, self-employment, business within a business, and employer-initiated approaches, become viable options for their students. In addition, gaps in services and resource shortages are viewed as issues to be addressed by the team as part of the employment decision-making process rather than a closed door as is often the case in traditionally run meetings. It is suggested that the employment planning process be broken down into two components including what type of work the individual would like (e.g., animals, sports, office) and what business arrangement is the best option (e.g., carved job, resource ownership, self-employment). A combination of factors contributes to the employment configurations that can be developed in response to the passions and support needs of the individual and the demands of the business community. A "can do" attitude generated by knowledge of the possibilities and the creative energy of the group has a powerful impact on how employment is perceived and the action plan that guides those efforts, leading to quality competitive employment outcomes for graduating youth.

References

Benz, M.R., Fabian, E.S., & Tilson, G.P. (2004). *Working relationships: Creating career opportunities for job seekers with disabilities through employer partnerships.* Baltimore, MD: Paul Brookes Publishing Co.

Button, C. (2007). Customized employment: A new competitive edge. Retrieved from http://www.dol.gov/odep/alliances/ce.htm

Callahan, M., & Rogan, P. (2004). Customized employment—A discussion. *Choose Work, 15,* 2–3, 8.

Griffin, C., & Hammis, D. (2003). *Making self-employment work for people with disabilities.* Baltimore. MD: Paul Brookes Publishing Co.

Katz, E. & Luecking, R. (2009, October). Collaborating and coordinating with employers. In Brief (Issue Brief of the NTAR Leadership Center). Retrieved from NTAR Leadership Center: http://www.ntarcenter.org/research/research_products.php

Newman, L., Wagner, M., Cameto, R., & Knokey, A. (2009). The post-high school outcomes of youth with disabilities up to 4 years after high school: A report from the National Longitudinal Transition Study–2 (NLTS2). Arlington, VA: SRI International.

Office of Disability Employment Policy. (2004). Customized employment Q and A. Retrieved from http://www.dol.gov/odep/tech/employ.htm

Parent, W. (2009, June). *Turning passions into paychecks.* Workshop presented at Association for Community Living, Boulder, CO.

Rusch, F.R. (1990). *Supported employment: Models, methods, and issues.* Sycamore, IL: Sycamore Publishing Co.

VCU Rehabilitation Research and Training Center on Workplace Supports (n.d.). Self-employment, technical assistance, resources, and training. Retrieved from http://www.start-up-usa.biz/

Wehman, P. (2006). *Life beyond the classroom: Transition strategies for youngpeople with disabilities* (4th ed.). Baltimore, MD: Paul Brookes Publishing Co.

Wehman, P., Inge, K.J., Benz, M.R., & Brooke, V.A. (2007a). *Real work for real pay: Inclusive employment for people with disabilities.* Baltimore, MD: Paul Brookes Publishing Co.

Wehman, P., Inge, K.L., Benz, M.R., & Brooke, V.A. (2007b). Supported employment and workplace supports: Overview and background. In P. Wehman, K.J. Inge, W.G. Revell, & V.A. Brooke (Eds.), *Real work for real pay: Inclusive employment for people with disabilities* (pp. 117–138). Baltimore: Paul Brookes Publishing Co.

Wehman, P. & Kregel, J. (1995). Supported employment: At the crossroads. *Journal of the Association for Persons with Severe Handicaps*, 20(4), 286–299.

Wehman, P., Sale, P., & Parent, W. (1992). *Supported employment: Strategies for integration of workers with disabilities.* Stoneham, MA: Andover Medical Publishers, Inc.

Wittig, K.M. (2009). Setting transition IEP goals: How it all fits together. In P. Wehman & K.M. Wittig (Eds.), *Transition IEP's: A curriculum guide for teachers and transition specialists* (3rd ed., 29–56). Austin, TX: PRO-ED.

22

Job Development and Placement in Youth Transition Education

Richard G. Luecking

LaVerne A. Buchanan

TRANSCEN, INC.

Employment is both a desired outcome and an important component of secondary education for youth in transition. One of the chief indicators of whether youth have succeeded in the transition from school to adult life is whether or not they are employed after they exit school. Moreover, employment success is most likely when youth have experiences in authentic workplaces early and often during their secondary education years. When paid employment during secondary education is on a youth's resume, post-school employment is even more likely. This holds true for any student receiving special education services, regardless of disability label or intensity of the special education services (Luecking & Fabian, 2000; Wagner, Newman, Cameto, Garza, & Levine, 2006; Fabian, 2007). In other words, the culmination of special education services for all youth should be employment and a career path. To get there, youth will learn from work experiences and jobs as they prepare for school exit.

Work experiences and jobs, of course, do not happen without planning and developing effective matches that work for both the youth and the employer. Job development is therefore a critical activity as educators, transition professionals, rehabilitation counselors, and families help youth pursue opportunities to learn how to work and, ultimately, become employed. This chapter will provide an overview of key job-development activities, how they can lead to optimal work outcomes for youth, and what collaborative resources are available that contribute to these outcomes.

The Presumption of Employability

A key principle of any sincere job-development activity is the presumption of employability for all people with disabilities. Over recent decades there have been several key developments that support the notion that all people with disabilities can work, given the opportunity and the necessary support in the job search and on the job. These developments include enhancing legislation, policy initiatives, and the advancement of transition and employment methodology. Each of these has contributed to heightened expectations for all youth with disabilities as they prepare for and experience the transition to adult life.

Starting with the Education for All Handicapped Children Act of 1975 (PL 94–142) through recent reauthorizations of the Individuals with Disabilities Education Act (Individuals with

Disabilities Education Improvement Act) of 2004 (PL 108–446), there has been increasing emphasis on education services that are mindful of optimal post-school outcomes, especially employment. In addition, the reauthorizations of the Rehabilitation Act (Workforce Investment Act of 1998, PL 105–220) have a similar progressively strong emphasis on presumptive employ-ability, now making it unacceptable for the rehabilitation system to refuse or discontinue services on the basis of disability severity. The prospect of employability for people with disabil-ities is also reflected in the Ticket to Work and Work Incentives Improvement Act of 1999 (PL 106–170), which recognizes employment as a reasonable goal for individuals who, ironically, have had to prove they are too disabled to work in order to receive Social Security income support from SSA's Disability Insurance and Supplemental Security Income programs.

Major federal policy initiatives have also contributed to the recognition of employment as an achievable goal for individuals with disabilities as they exit publically supported education. Since 1984, when the U.S. Department of Education issued the first wave of transition initia-tives (Will, 1984), there have been several influential activities that have boosted the notion of employment as a key transition outcome. These include: state transition systems change grants where every state was encouraged to, among other things, bolster transition linkages that would lead to post-school employment for transitioning youth (Johnson & Guy, 1997); transi-tion demonstration grants whereby professionals and researchers have been encouraged to develop and test new transition methodologies that lead to employment for youth with disabil-ities in transition (U.S. Department of Education, 2007); and research to identify predictors of post-school employment outcomes for youth receiving special education services (Test et al., 2009).

Finally, key efforts have identified effective transition and employment methodology for youth with disabilities. These include publications by the National Alliance for Secondary Education and Transition (NASET) (2005) and the National Collaborative on Workforce and Disability/Youth (NCWD/Y) (2005). Both of these represent efforts to synthesize what is known about service features that lead to effective transition. Since they both drew upon a wide range of research and publications, as well as the expertise of well-informed leaders in the field, it is no surprise that they came to nearly identical conclusions. In the NASET Standards and Indicators for Effective Transition and in the NCWD/Y Guideposts for Success, five areas of intervention important to successful transition to employment include:

- *School-based preparatory activity*, that is, academic instruction and targeted curriculum that lead to effective transition to employment and careers;
- *Career preparatory and work experiences*, including vocational training, experience in authentic workplaces, and jobs;
- *Youth development and youth leadership*, especially as it relates to self-determined transition and career planning;
- *Family involvement*, including that which supports the pursuit of employment goals; and
- *Connecting activities*, or those activities that enable youth to be linked with organizations and services that complement their transition services and/or enable necessary post-secondary supports for finding and keeping employment.

These components of transition practice are universally accepted by education, transition, and youth-service professionals as useful and effective in helping youth achieve better education and employment outcomes. In the years since the publication of these guidelines, increasing efforts have promoted their adoption in everyday transition practice (Luecking, 2009). In fact, each of these transition components represents important influences on the ability of youth to reach for the gold standard of transition: a job and a clear career path.

All of these legislative, policy, and practice developments support the notion of presumptive employability. Said another way, it should be presumed that all youth can work given the opportunities and support to do so. Regardless of disability label, intensity of special education services, need for support and accommodations, or economic circumstances, job developers should assume that all youth can succeed in the workplace. For some youth this requires more intensive activity and support than it does for others. But it should be a foregone conclusion as soon as transition planning begins that employment can be in the post-school picture for every youth.

Frequent, quality experiences in the workplace and in jobs throughout the secondary school years are therefore critical for all youth receiving special education services. By being in authentic workplaces throughout their secondary and postsecondary education years, youth learn about work, how to work, what they like to do at work, what skills they have that are useful at work, and what supports and accommodations they need at work. Youth acquire this learning though various types of experiences in the workplaces of employers, which can include: job shadowing, work sampling, service-learning activities, internships, apprenticeships, and paid employment. A summary of the benefits of learning in the workplace is presented in Table 22.1.

These experiences ultimately point to job and career choices for the youth. Most important, they are a foundation for employment opportunities as they transition to adult life and ideally lead to a long-standing career of meaningful and self-determined employment. Job-development activity, where transition professionals link youth with employers, is therefore necessary for all of the interim work experiences and jobs that should occur in the workplaces of employers during the education experience and upon exit from school. Without the knowledge and skill of helping youth link to employers, transition professionals will struggle with this critical transition activity. Indeed, the effort to help youth achieve long-term employment will be sporadically successful at best without job-development acumen and skill. For these reasons, it is essential that transition practitioners be skilled in:

- Helping youth plan for work experiences and jobs;
- Counseling youth to identify the best ways to represent their disability and support needs to prospective employers;
- Identifying and recruiting employers who will host youth in their workplaces for work experiences or hire them for jobs;
- Negotiating for a good match that benefits both the youth and employer;
- Supporting youth once they are in the workplace;
- Engaging potential partners who can assist in the job-development and placement process.

Table 22.1 Benefits of work-based experiences

Students who participate in work-based experiences benefit by having the opportunity to:

- Identify career interests, skills, and abilities;
- Explore career goals;
- Identify on-the-job support needs;
- Develop employability skills and good work habits;
- Gain an understanding of employer expectations;
- Link specific classroom instruction with related work expectations and knowledge requirements;
- Develop an understanding of the workplace and the connection between learning and earning;
- Gain both general work experience as well as experience connected to specific job functions that can be added to a work portfolio or resume.

Source: Luecking, R. (2009). *The way to work: How to facilitate work experiences for youth in transition.* Baltimore: Paul H. Brookes Publishing Company. Reprinted by permission.

The remainder of this chapter will explore techniques and circumstances important for each of these areas of job–development activity.

Strategies for Developing Meaningful Work Experiences and Employment

From the time a youth begins considering the job search through the acquisition of a stable work experience or employment, several common approaches yield optimal placement outcomes. The process is not necessarily linear but common critical steps that job developers and youth take in preparing for and concluding the job search. These steps are represented in Figure 22.1 and discussed, in turn, below.

Planning the Search for Work Experiences and Jobs

All good job development starts with the individual. Given presumed employability for each youth, the operating principle in planning for job development should be that every youth has something to contribute in a workplace and to an employer's operation, regardless of disability label and regardless of the need for accommodations and support in the job search and on the job. Therefore, good job development starts with a solid knowledge of what youth are good at,

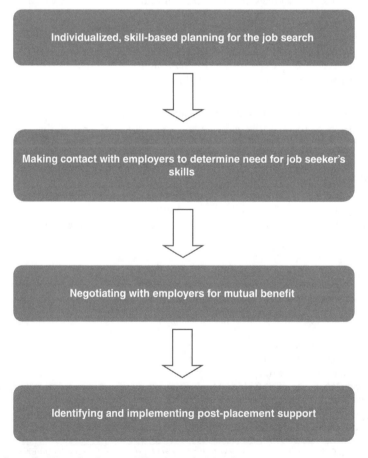

Figure 22.1 Steps for Developing an Effective Job Match

what they like to do, their preferences for work environments and related considerations, and what kind of support they will need to find the best job fit. For this, the effective job developer will access several sources of information.

Discovering Youth Strengths, Interests and Preferences

Formal assessments and school records are often used to gather information about youth competencies and interests. These sources of information can be useful in preparing for job development, provided they do not cause undue or unproductive focus on deficits or perceived disability-related barriers. Traditional and formal assessments, such as standardized tests and instruments available from commercial publishers, can provide a range of information related to general aptitude, adaptive behavior, cognitive or learning aptitude, occupational interests, personality/social skills, and learning styles. While this information can help inform a successful work experience or job search as a prelude to that search, it is less important than other tools for job-search planning, which will be discussed below. Nevertheless, job developers should be familiar with the range and uses of assessment instruments so that, when referencing student records, useful information for planning for and supporting of the job search can be obtained. Detailed summaries of various assessments and how they might apply in job development for transitioning youth include Sitlington, Neubert, Begun, Lombard, & Leconte (2007) and Timmons, Podmosko, Bremer, Lavin, & Wills (2004). Additional methods of job-development information gathering can include interviews, observations in various school and natural environments, situational assessments, and portfolio assessments (Rogan, Grossi, & Gajewski, 2002).

Successful job-development planning is first and foremost individualized and person-centered. The unique interests, talents, and need for support of each individual are what should drive job development, regardless of disability label or educational circumstance. Further, job-development planning cannot be considered individualized unless it features self-determination and informed choice. Each individual has preferences and each individual should be given an opportunity to express them. One tool that has been adopted for person-centered, individualized, and self-determined planning for job development is called the Positive Personal Profile (Tilson & Cuozzo, 2001; Luecking & Tilson, 2009).

The Positive Personal Profile is a tool for gathering information about a youth and his/her traits that will be useful to the youth and the job developer as they work together to plan for and find work experiences and jobs. As the name implies, the emphasis of the Profile is on affirming those traits and circumstances that help youth put their best foot forward to prospective employers as well as to acknowledge and plan for mitigating areas of support needs. Information for the Profile is gathered from interviewing and observing the youth and talking to family, friends, and other people who know the youth well. Records, files, and assessment documents provide other useful information and data. The components of the Profile include a compilation of basic information, including the youth's dreams and goals, interests, talents, skills, knowledge, learning styles, values, positive personality traits, environmental preferences, dislikes, life and work experiences, support system, specific challenges, creative solutions and accommodations, and creative possibilities and ideas for pursuing work experiences and jobs. Any format that helps the job developer gather this type of information can be a helpful basis for planning for and eventually identifying the best workplaces, tasks, and employers with whom the youth can be matched. Also, positive information about the youth's skills, interests, and relevant life and work experiences can often be translated into a resume or portfolio that can be presented to prospective employers as a representation of the youth's qualifications and interests.

Guiding Principles for Planning Job Development

The importance of the direct involvement of youth in job development is articulated by Sax and Thoma (2002); they contend that we "have no right to plan for another without their participation or permission" (p.14). This is one of the key building blocks of planning for the job search and job development for youth in transition. Based on the opinion and experience of prominent transition experts, job developers should incorporate several guiding principles in their work to help youth plan for the job search (Rogan et al., 2002; Sitlington et al., 2007; Wehman, 2006). Summarized by Luecking and Tilson (2009), these principles include the following:

- All youth have unique talents and gifts.
- Planning should focus on these unique attributes, not on deficits. Identified job-development challenges, such as unique or intensive need for job accommodations, should be seen in the context of how supports can minimize their impact on job performance.
- Youth should participate in job-development planning, empowered to provide the type of information about themselves that a Positive Personal Profile or similar planning document is designed to represent.
- Youth should be given necessary supports, accommodations, and modifications when participating in job-development planning activities.

These principles assume that youth are fully prepared and empowered to be directly involved in job-development planning. Often, this is not the case without specific preparation and support to learn how to assert their preferences and make informed choices. Many youth will not have the range of life experiences that have exposed them to options from which to make choices. Thus, it will sometimes be difficult to determine clear preferences during job-development planning. Regardless, the youth should be fully involved in the planning for developing work experience and jobs. Job developers have the responsibility to help youth be fully aware of what can be expected from any potential worksite to which they will be exposed. Indeed, every experience in the workplace is a way of building individual capacity to identify preferences and later employment choices. In any case, self-determination instruction and preparation are often an important prelude to moving from planning for job development to making contact with prospective employers.

Self-Determination in the Search for Work Experiences and Jobs

One definition of self-determination that has been supported by the Division on Career Development and Transition (DCDT) of the Council on Exceptional Children is as follows:

> Self-determination is a combination of skills, knowledge, and beliefs that enable a person to engage in goal directed, self-regulated, autonomous behavior. Self-determination is an understanding of one's strengths and limitations together with a belief in oneself as capable and effective. Then acting on the basis of these skills and attitudes, individuals have a great ability to take control of their lives and assume the roles of adults in society. (Field, Martin, Miller, Ward, & Wehmeyer, 1998)

When this level of self-understanding and self-belief is present, youth can be encouraged and expected to be the final voice in job-development planning. Self-determination can be both taught and reinforced through any number of activities that are common during the youth's transition years. Here are examples of activities that can be embedded in school curriculum and transition planning activities through which self-determination skills can be acquired that will serve as useful adjuncts to the entire job-development process:

- Facilitating youth to conduct and review self-assessments of skills and abilities;
- Preparing youth to be active participants, indeed leaders, during their Individual Education Program (IEP) meetings;
- Creating situations requiring students to self-advocate for specific need or preferences;
- Promoting opportunities for youth to have leading roles on school committees, teams, and extracurricular programs;
- Celebrating successes, large and small, as well as encouraging discussion of situations in which there was failure.

Ultimately, in the workplace, youth who are self-determined will likely experience reduced problem behaviors, better performance, effective decision making and problem solving, avoidance of abusive social interactions, and meaningful social linkages with co-workers (Wehmeyer & Palmer, 2003). Indeed, a well-planned job search is in evidence when these circumstances exist in the workplace. Luecking and Tilson (2009) suggest that youth are self-determined during the planning for work experiences and jobs when they:

- Are able to list activities and tasks that they perform well;
- Can list hobbies, favorite leisure opportunities, and areas of interest;
- Know what accommodations they might need and can ask for them, both during the planning process and in the eventual workplace;
- Can ask reasonable questions about what is expected at the prospective workplace;
- To the fullest extent possible, are able to express their preferences about aspects of the job search, e.g., location, schedules, tasks, accommodation needs, etc.
- Can list, discuss, and identify what they learned from any previous work experiences and jobs they may have had;
- Have decided whether they want to disclose disability, and, if so, how they will disclose it.

The last point has particular relevance in job development and placement for youth with disabilities. The nuances of the issue of disability disclosure are discussed in the next section.

Disability Disclosure in Job Development

The issue of disclosure of disability is pertinent to any job-development activity related to youth with disabilities. Disability disclosure has significant advantages. Proactive communication with a prospective employer about disability can sometimes show how necessary accommodations will enable and accentuate marketable skills. Disclosure also helps the individual implement self-determination and self-advocacy skills by learning how to present the need for accommodations and how to ask for them. Finally, when presented in the proper context of the employer's operation, later problems and misunderstandings can be prevented. Disclosure also poses significant risks. Negative stereotyping, deliberate or inadvertent discrimination, unfair treatment, excessive self-consciousness, and co-worker resentment, or even mistreatment, are all possible (Buchanan, 2003).

As with all other aspects of job-development planning, disclosure is a personal choice. The youth job seeker should have the final word on whether or not to disclose his or her disability. If the decision is to disclose, it is also the youth's decision as to when, how, and to whom to disclose. Many youth will decide that it is necessary or desirable for someone to represent them

Table 22.2 Self-determination and job choice

Self-determination and job choice
Melvin was given the opportunity to sample two jobs while he was in high school. These involved being in the workplace in an unpaid capacity so that he could sample job tasks. The intent was for him to experience what real workplaces were like, at what tasks he was adept, what tasks he liked and disliked, and what accommodations and support he might need as an eventual adult worker. In one job he helped clean tables and empty trash in a large shopping mall food court. In the other he worked in an office where he sampled collating, copying, and shredding tasks. He hated the first work experience and loved the second. When it was time, in his last year in school, to begin planning for the search for a paid job he would keep after he left school, he was in a position to express a clear preference about the kind of job he wanted. In fact, early in the job-search process the job developer found a vacancy in a fast food restaurant where Melvin might be assigned to clear tables and empty trash. However, when presented with this possibility, Melvin refused to go for an interview. The job developer soon realized how important it was for Melvin – and any other job seeker – to be the driver of the job-search planning process. The job developer learned that it was necessary to involve Melvin totally in the job-search process so that his preferences and his prior experiences were factors in determining where to look for potential job opportunities. It was clear that Melvin had some experience on which to build the job search and it was clear that he had preferences. Melvin accompanied the job developer on a series of informational interviews with employers who had office tasks that matched Melvin's previous experience. Melvin now works in a real estate investment office where his main assignment is to deliver documents from one department to another, in addition to copying and collating informational packets – a successful job search driven by a self-determined job seeker.

in finding and negotiating work experiences and jobs. This may be because of communication challenges, significant support needs, or simply lack of job-search experience or confidence. In such cases it is paramount that the job developer get the permission of the youth (and/or parent/guardian if necessary) to share personal information about disability before disclosing to a prospective employer.

By virtue of being a special education, transition, employment, or rehabilitation professional, many job developers are readily identified as "disability" professionals. Thus, anyone to whom these professionals introduce themselves already knows that they represent youth with disabilities. In that sense, some measure of disclosure has already taken place for youth represented by these professionals. A youth's association with a transition, school, or employment service may, however indirectly, identify him or her as having a disability. When this is the case, it is important that the youth understand the ramifications of this arrangement and approve of what and how much to disclose about their particular disability and its potential influence on their circumstances in a workplace.

Youth should be empowered to exercise control over what, how, and to whom information about their disability should be disclosed. Job developers who represent youth in the pursuit of and negotiation for jobs, as well as support them in the workplace, have an obligation to disclose information about youth's disabilities in a manner that is both respectful and appropriately presented, starting with a positive rendering of the youth's traits. Guidelines for helping youth with issues related to disability disclosure during job development are presented in Table 22.3.

Regardless of the decisions a youth makes concerning disclosure, hiring decisions by employers in the end are less likely to be influenced by the presence or absence of disability than by potential contribution of a job candidate to the company, especially when it is clear that value is being added to the employer's enterprise (Unger, (2002); Hernandez, 2000; Luecking,

Table 22.3 Guidelines for disability disclosure during job development

Disclosure dilemma	Guiding thoughts	Comments
Why disclose?	• Accommodations • Legal reasons • Background check • Safety and health reasons	Review the application and/or job description; determine whether there is a need to disclose; explore feelings about sharing personal information with others. If possible, find out about attitudes toward individuals who have been or are in a similar situation and have disclosed disabilities; weigh the benefits and risks of disclosure.
When to disclose? (now, later, never)	• Initial contact and application process • When arranging an interview • During the interview • After the interview, during the negotiation and hiring process • Anytime after employment / program has started • Never	The nature of the information to be disclosed will have an impact on when to disclose. For example: A person who is deaf may need to inform the employer/interviewer prior to the interview to receive accommodation at the interview; A youth with severe learning disabilities may need to discuss accommodations with his or her supervisor immediately following the job offer.
What to disclose?	• Remember the purpose for disclosing • Decide what is too little, too much, or just enough information	Be knowledgeable about the disability. Relate information to current situation. Know what accommodations are needed, where they can be obtained and cost, if applicable. Provide documentation. Be positive about what the youth can offer when accommodations are necessary.
Who needs to know?	• Person assisting in the job search • Person who can provide the needed accommodations • Person responsible for supervising staff • Person responsible for hiring and terminating	Not everyone at the job needs to know personal business. If the accommodation can be made and does not require any support from the employer or others, then personal information may be kept to oneself.
How to disclose?	• In writing • Verbally • Through a third party	Be honest, straightforward, factual and positive; speak or write clearly; describe positive strengths, skills and abilities; discuss how accommodations will enable and accentuate marketable skills.
Where to disclose?	• Discuss private information in a private/confidential setting	Only the person(s) intended to receive the information should be informed.

2004a; Luecking, 2004b). This has significant implications for planning for the job search and later for the actual contact and negotiation with employers. Successful presentation of the youth's skills, capabilities, and potential need for workplace accommodations during job-development activities requires youth's self-awareness of strengths and support needs and how these traits will be managed on the job. The goal is for youth to ultimately be considered by

Table 22.4 Disclosure and job development

Disclosure and job development
Vincent needs extensive workplace accommodations since he uses a motorized wheelchair and a specially designed computer keyboard. Therefore, it is necessary to disclose his disability to prospective employers. He worked with his transition teacher to develop a way to present his need for accommodation. He and his teacher agreed that she would say this to prospective employers: "Vincent is very interested in technology and knows many computer applications. He will bring his own keyboard to work, which will enable him to complete assigned tasks. I will help him set it up at his workstation so he can work efficiently." With this approach, the teacher communicated Vincent's positive traits and how these, along with the necessary accommodations, will help meet job expectations. After several employer contacts, the teacher helped Vincent get hired to assist with data entry by an employer with a backlog of data entry work.   On the other hand, Jason knows that his learning disability is accommodated well in school, but he is very uncomfortable disclosing his disability in other environments. Throughout his childhood, he was occasionally teased about his school performance and is very self-conscious about the label. He does not want people to think that he is "stupid." Consequently, he does not want anyone outside of school to know about his disability. He instructed his work-experience teacher to only represent him as a "high school student" looking for work experience. Jason has chosen to work without accommodations. Of course the risk he runs is that his oral processing disability will not be properly understood. After failing in two work experiences because he had trouble following directions, he and his job developer eventually found a work experience in which he could perform well. Jason remains uncomfortable about disclosing his disability to future employers, but at least he knows the risks of not doing so.

employers as potential contributors to the employer's enterprise. Armed with a thorough knowledge of the individual job seeker and his/her positive attributes, the youth's full participation in the job-search planning, and a clear plan for representing disability to prospective employers, the job developer should now be ready to begin fruitful contact with prospective employers.

Contacting and Recruiting Employers

As previously discussed, in policy and in practice, important and increasing emphasis has been placed on informed choice for individuals who are seeking employment. That is, the individual should drive the job-search process based on clear interests and preferences. Good job development does not happen without it. However, good job development also does not happen without knowledge and appreciation of what employers need and how they operate. Work experience and jobs for youth in transition are only possible to the extent that employers are willing and able to bring youth into their workplaces. After years of transition and employment experience, and parallel research, we know that employers are mostly interested in three things: making money, saving money, and/or operating more efficiently (Luecking, 2009). Ultimately, job-development success is dependent on the ability of transition professionals to develop and maintain partnerships with employers that benefit the employer as much as the youth. In other words, employers are as much an end user of transition and job-development services as are youth. There are three long-established techniques for developing relationships with employers who might later decide to hire youth with disabilities. They are: networking, learning business need, and appealing to employers' self-interest (Luecking, Fabian, & Tilson, 2004; Targett, 2006; Griffin, Hammis, & Geary, 2007).

Networking

The importance of an expansive and diverse network in successful job development has long been supported by research. As early as 1974, Granovetter found that the majority of job seekers find their jobs through personal contacts. Moreover, he found that the more people who are known to job seekers outside of immediate family and close friends, the more likely there will be a connection that resulted in a job. That is, the wider the circle of contacts, the more likely that acquaintances travel in different circles, leading to a more diverse and broader available job-development options. This is especially important for youth who have limited exposure to life outside of a small community of family and friends. What this means for many youth is that the job developer is key to expanding their universe of acquaintances that might connect them to employers. What it means for job developers is that building and expanding a network of employer contacts is a critical job-development activity. Indeed, many seasoned job developers would say that having a network of people who can put them in contact with many diverse employers is more important than any other method for identifying potential work experiences and jobs (Luecking, 2009).

Networks that connect the job developer to employers include:

- Family and friends of the youth job seeker;
- Family, friends, and acquaintances of the job developer;
- Family, friends, and acquaintances of colleagues of the job developer;
- Business people who belong to organizations in which the job developer also belongs (joining and participating in Chambers of Commerce, service clubs, and similar organizations are common avenues to expand a job developer's network of contacts);
- People who are encountered at church, the grocery store, cocktail parties—basically anyone the job developer ever meets.

It boils down to this: the more people the job developer knows, the better the foundation for good job development. Expanding one's network is a continuous process for the effective job developer. Then, as job search plans for individual youth dictate, the job developer is in a position to call on acquaintances to identify prospective employers and to determine if these employers have needs and circumstances that merit an introduction to the youth.

Learning Employer Needs

Employers have various operational and economic stakes in the success of programs that bring them in contact with youth with disabilities. From an employer's perspective, these programs can provide a source of workers for existing needs, they can provide a pipeline for future human resource needs, and they can enable employers to develop future workers in their respective industries (Luecking, 2005). Less important to employers is helping to meet a perceived community need; for example, helping youth develop into responsible adults. Regardless of their motivations for hiring these youth, employers still have to make sure they meet deadlines and satisfy their customers so that they make money, save money, and/or run their operation as smoothly as possible. Thus, as job developers help youth find work experiences and jobs, it is essential to understand employers' needs, circumstances, and perspectives. Indeed, employers who have hired or hosted youth in the workplace identify four expectations when interacting with transition programs and professionals representing youth with disabilities: competent and convenient assistance in receiving youth referrals; matching youth skills and interests to job tasks; support in training and monitoring the youth; and information on disability and accommodations if youth choose to disclose disability (Luecking, 2004b).

To meet the first two of these expectations, it is necessary for job developers to thoroughly understand employers' circumstances. What kinds of people do they hire? How do they operate? With whom do they conduct business? What is important to their customers? Do they have bottlenecks in their operation? Are there processes that could be improved? How do they train, supervise, and mentor new employees? By learning the particular operational needs of the employer, that is, how work gets done in the company, the job developer can better present candidates who can meet those needs. This is especially important in the case of youth job seekers who do not yet have the requisite skills, employment experience, or training to be considered by employers as viable employees, or who are just learning about the world of the workplace. Job developers can learn about employers and their operations through internet searches, dedicated websites, and a host of other print and electronic resources. However, meeting and talking to employers in person and on their own turf is the bedrock of effective job development. One especially helpful job-development strategy for determining employer needs is the informational interview (Luecking et al., 2004; Griffin et al., 2007).

Informational interviews serve many purposes. They are ways to meet new employers, thereby expanding those all-important networks discussed previously. They are especially good ways to learn about hiring and operational needs that might lead to a job opportunity for individual job seekers. And they are entrees for establishing long-standing partnerships with employers who come to regard the job developer as a valued partner for filling workforce needs. They are also an especially productive and non-threatening way to get one's foot in an employer's door. The object is not to "sell" employers on hiring a person with a disability. Rather, the purpose is to meet employers and learn more about them.

Once a contact person is identified in a company, job developers merely ask if they can set up a visit. Making the request an "easy ask" almost always opens doors for job developers. For example, "I'm interested in learning as much as I can about companies such as yours. Would it be possible for me to set up a brief visit to see firsthand how your company operates?" During the visit to the company, job developers ask questions and gather information about how the company conducts its business. This is an excellent opportunity to observe, listen, and learn. The most productive informational interviews feature a few targeted questions such as: what kind of people do you look for in your company? What are some of the hiring challenges? Are there operational challenges? How do you like to be approached by applicants or their representatives? Is it possible to tour the workplace? If there is a potential opportunity to negotiate for a position for an individual job seeker, effective job developers will ask to come back to learn more. At the very least, the job developer now knows more about the company than before the visit. Optimally, a budding working relationship has been established leading to future opportunities for youth job seekers.

Moreover, getting to know employer needs often yields opportunities where specific tasks can be re-assigned for better operational results, such as when a specific task that might be assigned to youth will make everyone's job easier. Hiring decisions are thus primarily the result of meeting a specific operational need rather than on the relative merits of job seekers with a particular label or the mission of a particular transition or employment program. In other words, there is no need to sell the employer on hiring someone with a disability. Instead, information gleaned from such employer encounters serve to provide a better understanding of employer needs, identify how those needs might be met by current or future job seekers represented by the job developer, and to ultimately identify if there are other value-added services the job developer can provide the employer. Also, the better the job developer knows the employer's needs and circumstances, the more likely a good match can be made between youth characteristics and employer need.

Table 22.5 Meeting a critical employer need

Meeting a critical employer need

During an informational interview and tour of a local store of a well-known retail chain, a job developer was able to recognize areas of operation that were causing some problems for the store manager. These included: frequent mismatching of the sizing tags on clothing with the size nubs on hangers, disorganization of the shoe department, and disarray in the stock room. In fact, these issues caused the store to be cited by national headquarters for failing to meet sales quotas as well as profit margins. The overtime paid to personnel each week for straightening the stock room did not help matters.

The job developer proposed that a list of specified tasks assigned to a youth she represented, who liked to work with people and excelled at detail work, could address these problems. These tasks included: weekly accuracy checks of tags to size nubs so that customers had fewer complaints, bi-weekly organization of the shoe department's stockroom area, and evening cleanup and preparation in the entire stock room for the morning shift to make sure all employees' jobs ran more smoothly. After the necessary training supports were organized for the youth, he began his work. Within a few weeks, the store increased its sales, decreased overtime for sales staff, and received recognition from national headquarters for improving its profit margins. The basis for this negotiation and hire was the store improvements that potentially could occur, not the fact that the job developer represented a special education student. The job developer learned about the store's needs and negotiated a solution that resulted in both a job for the student and added value to the employer.

As job developers meet and interact with employers, it is useful to adopt language that is more business-like and less special education jargon. Employers will not be interested in "IEPs," "vocational assessments," or "transition plans." They will, however, understand when job developers talk about "convenient access to potential employees," "youth who are prepared to work," or "careful matches to employer need and youth skills and interests." Employers, like potential partners in any kind of endeavor, are willing to do business with people they know, like, trust—and are easy to work with. Savvy job developers go where employers congregate, such as chamber of commerce meetings, and they visit workplaces in order to meet, talk to, and most of all *learn* about employers. Long-term, productive working relationships arise from frequent pleasant and positive interactions with employers. Unexpected opportunities for youth job seekers often spring from such relationships. Informational interviews, indeed any employer encounter, will ultimately lead to the identification of workplace and job opportunities for youth job seekers. Then, the task is to appeal to employer self-interest and successfully negotiate for youth placement (Luecking, 2009).

Negotiating for the Placement: Appealing to Employer Self-interest

Employers who have successfully brought youth with disabilities into the workplace cite three reasons for doing so (Luecking, 2005). In order of importance, they are:

1   To meet a specific company need, such as filling a job opening or addressing a production or service need;
2   To meet an industry-wide need, such as preparing potential new workers in a technology industry;
3   To meet a community need, such as helping youth become productive citizens.

Although many employers are willing and interested in hosting youth in the workplace out of good citizenship motivations, the order of these reasons suggests that it is more effective to appeal to employer self-interest than it is to appeal to their potential altruism in helping youth or helping people with disabilities. In other words, it is best to avoid appeals to employer benevolence. It is more important to find out what employers want and then determine if the job seeker can help them get it.

Each job seeker offers a potential range of competencies to any given workplace. Identifying those tasks that a job seeker is good at or can perform with accommodation or support is a critical first step. Then, successful job development hinges on proposing and negotiating task assignments based on how they will help the employer. Negotiations with employers are most successful when employers see what's in it for them. Job developers are in a position to negotiate for a possible hire when they see how an individual youth's task competency can benefit the employer's operation, such as making other workers' jobs easier, making things run more smoothly, addressing backlogged work, and so forth. It is not uncommon for such negotiation to lead to a successful employment proposal even when there are no job openings in the company. In fact, customizing assignments to match even a narrow set of tasks with youth skills often results in a successful and mutually beneficial hiring outcome. Ultimately, the decision by employers to hire youth or offer their workplaces for youth work experience of any kind is based on negotiation for mutual benefit. Employers should feel better off for having come in contact with the transition professional, and they should feel that they are getting at least as much from the relationship as they are giving (Luecking 2004a).

When negotiating a placement with an employer, an effective approach is to follow a sequence that emphasizes and re-emphasizes the benefit to the employer. Luecking (2009) offers a template for proposing a youth placement to an employer that includes these steps:

1   Recap the nature of the contact to date, as well as acknowledge the employer's time and the value of the contact.
2   Indicate what the job developer saw and heard during the employer contacts, such as what operational needs the job developer identified.
3   Offer suggestions about how these needs could be met by the youth job seeker.
4   Identify how such an arrangement will help the company: for example, how it will help other workers complete assignments, reduce backlogs, eliminate bottlenecks, etc.
5   Identify how the job developer and the transition program will support the youth, such as initial help with orientation, ongoing coaching, and follow-up help, etc.
6   Make the "ask," that is, ask if and when the youth can start.
7   Reiterate the benefits to the company from the arrangement (see 4 above).

Finally, in making and negotiating the match, the following negotiation points will also be important so the expectations of the arrangement are clear to all parties:

* Responsibilities and tasks to be assumed by the youth;
* Schedule and pay arrangements;
* Support strategies and supervision the youth will require;
* Productivity and outcome expectations;
* Responsibilities of all parties to orient, train, supervise, and give feedback to the youth.

The Employer as a Customer of Transition Services

In the end, placement negotiations are successful when all parties see the benefit of the arrangement. Effective job developers therefore adopt a dual-customer approach to job-development activities. That is, they regard both the youth job seekers and employers as end users and customers of transition services and their job-development initiatives. This notion has also been gaining momentum throughout the broader youth workforce development system (Marino & Tarr, 2004), but it has particular relevance to job development with youth with disabilities since relationships between employers and any initiative designed to connect individuals with perceived barriers to employment should be characterized by mutual benefit. Although special education and vocational rehabilitation have a long history of carefully assessing and understanding the needs of the job seeker customer, it is apparent to many transition and job-development experts that there continues to be an incomplete attempt to understand and incorporate employer perspectives in job-development approaches (Luecking, 2008). Thus, pursuing an effective dual-customer job-development strategy necessitates that employer perspectives be well understood and addressed. This is often referred to as a "demand-side" orientation since employers ultimately create the demand for their workforce. A demand-side orientation minimizes the "selling" to employers of potential candidates from categories of job seekers, such as youth with disabilities. Rather, it maximizes the importance of interactions that feature getting to know the particular circumstances of individual employers or the circumstances of specific industry clusters. This demand-side approach also means that, as with any successful marketing effort, it is better to find out what the employer customers want and need and then match it to what job developers and transition programs have to offer than it is to try to persuade them to "hire youth with disabilities" (Luecking, 2008).

A dual-customer approach ensures that job developers become cognizant of particular operational needs of the employer—that is, how work gets done in the company—so that the job developer can better present youth who can meet those needs. Especially in the case of youth who often do not yet have the requisite skills or training to apply for standard jobs in the company, getting to know employer circumstances often yields hidden job opportunities where specific tasks can be re-assigned for better operational results. Re-assignment of the task to deliver documents across company departments to a youth so that other workers can focus on more pressing tasks is one such example. Decisions to offer youth a work experience or to hire them for a job are thus primarily the result of meeting a specific operational need rather than on the relative merits of job seekers with a particular disability label or the stated mission of a transition or disability employment program.

After the Placement: Supporting the Youth and the Employer

The job developer's work is not done when the placement begins. Indeed, a dual-customer approach suggests that the job developer should remain involved as long as necessary to not only ensure that the youth is comfortable and performing on the job but also to make sure the employer customer is satisfied. Luecking and Tilson (2009) recommend a clear sequence of support activities that promote effective workplace support and that maximize youth workplace success and employer satisfaction. They are:

- Clarify the employer's requirements and performance expectations before, during, and after the negotiation for the job.
- Identify potential challenges and barriers that may affect performance.
- Determine the type, degree, and amount of support the youth may need to maximize performance and work behavior.
- Develop an individualized plan for providing support and stick to it. The support plan may include any number of useful interventions such as job coaching, identifying and supporting

workplace mentors, or high-tech accommodations. The support plan should be based on both the youth's need for support and the employer's environment.

- Build in regular opportunities to provide feedback to youth from both the transition program and the employer.
- Continuously evaluate the arrangement and adjust support as necessary.

The importance of an individualized support plan cannot be overstated. Without it, several potentially unfortunate scenarios are possible. The youth may not receive the support and help needed to perform and behave as expected. Consequently, youth success in the workplace is left to chance, or worse, doomed from the start. Thus, it is helpful to clearly identify the designated workplace supervisor or mentor, the frequency of on-site visits from school or transition program staff, the supports and accommodations necessary, and the respective responsibilities of the youth, the employer, and the job developer during the course of the work experience or job (Luecking, 2009).

Trouble can result when employers are left to manage a situation for which they are unprepared or about which they may be uncomfortable due to insufficient help and preparation for having the youth in the workplace. However, when clear plans for support are in place, the likelihood of success is increased. For their part, employers have consistently cited responsive post-placement support as critical to successfully hiring youth with disabilities (Luecking, 2004b; Luecking, Cuozzo & Buchanan, 2006). Consequently, effective job developers regularly solicit employer feedback in order to make sure the post-placement support arrangements are satisfactory for the employer. This strategy also ensures that when performance or social problems arise after placement, the transition professional is able to quickly help both the youth and the employer address the situation. Indeed, in the dual-customer paradigm of job development, the success of linking youth with work is as much about meeting employer needs as it is about serving youth job seekers.

Table 22.6 A responsive transition professional

A responsive transition professional

A hallmark of an effective transition professional or job developer is recognizing the importance of keeping employers happy. Indeed, in the dual customer paradigm employers' satisfaction is an important indicator of a successful placement. One transition teacher makes it a practice to consistently solicit feedback from every employer who hires students he represents. He asks regularly about what he can do to make sure he is providing the best guidance and support so the student performs to the employer's expectations. He also wants to know if there is anything he can do better to help when he asks: Are the students on time? Are they interacting with co-workers effectively? Are they completing their tasks according to expectations? Are they dressing appropriately? Does he need to stop by and check in on the student?

Such solicitousness can often head off potential problems, such as when a student was leaving the work floor frequently to call her friends on her cell phone. When the employer mentioned the problem after the transition teacher checked in, they were able to immediately counsel the student on the protocol at the work workplace for using the phone so that she rarely left the job station after that. More important to the employer, this level of careful attention to how the placement arrangement is working for the employer results in willingness to continue to work with the transition professional. This transition teacher recounts countless other circumstances where responsive attention to employers and their needs prevented such behaviors as mild as cell-phone use on the job and as serious as destruction of employer property, from impeding the relationship with employer partners who remained long-term "customers" of the transition program.

Disability Awareness and Employer Support

It is, of course, paramount that disability disclosure is a personal decision by each individual youth. However, when youth choose to disclose their disability, there is often the need to insure that the employer fully understands and is comfortable with both the disability and any attendant need for accommodation. Providing disability awareness information to supervisors and co-workers is often a useful strategy in order to diffuse potential confusion or discomfort at the workplace. Disability awareness information can be provided informally through conversation and demonstrating how accommodations can mitigate the effects of disability. There are many sources of written information about specific disabilities, their characteristics, and their potential accommodations that can be provided to employers when it becomes necessary or is requested. Many sources of information about how to offer disability awareness training to employers and co-workers can be very effective in defusing concerns and apprehension about disability (e.g., ADA Information Center of the Mid-Atlantic Region, 2004).

It is important for job developers to understand, however, that the absence of disclosure does not mean there is no need for support. Again, an individual support plan will help outline the parameters of responsibility for all parties involved with the youth so that performance expectations are met, youth preferences and skills are best matched with job tasks, and immediate attention is available as problems or challenges arise. In fact, identifying a workplace mentor can be a very effective strategy for insuring that youth have the benefit of experienced guidance and support at work (Gramlich, 1999). A well-matched mentor can help model and reinforce work behavior and performance, facilitate acceptance in the workplace by other co-workers, and help include the youth in the workplace's social network. Potentially, mentors also benefit from seeing the positive influence on the youth, as well as renewed enthusiasm for their own work. A seasoned job developer will look to exploit these possibilities when identifying youth supports, regardless of whether disclosure has taken place. As with any employer negotiation, mentorship relationships require making the proposition attractive to all parties.

Partners in the Job-development and Placement Process

In addition to the youth themselves, everyone on the youth's transition team can be a resource to help plan for and execute a job-development plan. Teachers and other school personnel, families, vocational rehabilitation counselors, and employment agency representatives can each contribute to the identification of youth characteristics that will help guide the job search. They can each help counsel the youth on disclosure decisions. They can each encourage self-advocacy and individual choice making. They can each identify networks that can connect them to prospective employers. And each can offer various kinds of support after placement into a worksite. In fact, a single job developer cannot be all things to all people, nor is it wise to work in isolation of so many other potential resources important to job-development and placement success.

Teachers are well positioned to support and contribute to the job-development process. They can provide important information about the youth's skills, interests, and need for accommodation. Teachers are also in a position to insure that job-development goals are an important component of the youth's Individual Education Plan (IEP). Indeed, schools have a responsibility to provide coordinated services that are designed to help the student to meet postsecondary goals (IDEA, PL 108–446). Since postsecondary goals will include employment for just about every student, activities to develop work experiences and jobs will be important adjuncts to the entire IEP. In this sense, anyone helping the youth develop work experience and job opportunities is contributing to the pursuit of IEP goals.

Similarly, educational goals are more effectively reached when the family is a recognized and involved partner (Wandry & Pleet, 2003). In fact, practitioner efforts to involve families have been shown to be as important to effective transition as family background variables such as income level, ethnicity, or marital status. In other words, when transition professionals work to include parents in planning for transition, the effects of other background characteristics are minimized (Pleet, 2000). Regardless of how challenging their circumstances, families are almost always in a position to know the youth the best, and they are therefore a critical source of information about youth characteristics that might influence the job-development plan.

Vocational rehabilitation (VR) and other disability employment services, often referred to as community rehabilitation providers (CRPs), may also become important participants in the job-development and placement process. Indeed, it is often the case that professionals affiliated with VR or CRPs are directly involved in the job-development process. VR may fund and/or provide adjunctive services, such as assistive devices, that may be necessary to the youth's performance on the job. CRPs may work with school personnel to directly assist youth in becoming connected to jobs. Indeed, the very job-development activities described throughout this chapter could be carried out by representatives of any of these partners. It has been widely recognized that successful employment outcomes are more likely when school personnel work in tandem with organizations and services that will continue to support youth as they exit secondary education (Wehman, 2006; Luecking, 2009). When the tandem effort is job placement and support, the benefits to the youth's transition success are clear.

In addition to these sources of job-development support, other potential partners and resources can contribute to effective job development. One such resource is the system of One-Stop Career Centers that was established by the Workforce Investment Act of 1998 (PL 105–220). Available in every community, these centers are mandated to provide services designed to help all citizens (including those with disabilities) access information, training, and other related support to obtain employment. Job developers and job seekers can glean information about the labor market, about specific job opportunities, and about services and training that can prepare job seekers for employment. Often, computers and internet access are available at One-Stop Centers to aid in

Table 22.7 Multiparty collaboration for job development

Multiparty collaboration for job development

Vladimir was in technical education classes to prepare for a career in auto body repair, an area that he was intensely interested in. Because of his hearing and learning disabilities, he received resource help for many of his classes. He needed a work-experience job to complement his coursework, but because of his academic and technical class schedules he had no time to participate in work-experience opportunities during the school year. Consequently, his transition teacher worked with the state vocational rehabilitation (VR) agency and the local One-Stop Career Center to refer him to a summer youth employment program. Through the program, youth received a stipend for working with cooperating employers. Finding the employers, however, was often a challenge.

The teacher and a representative from the VR agency worked with Vladimir to develop a profile that would present his interests and skills. The school contracted with a local community rehabilitation provider (CRP) to assist with the job development. All parties worked with the One-Stop Career Center program to identify potential employers to host him as a summer intern. Through the Career Center's roster of employers who participated in the summer youth employment program in previous years, they eventually located an auto body shop that was willing to offer a summer job to Vladimir. Initial job coaching was provided by the CRP job developer. By the end of the summer, the auto body shop realized they found someone with career potential. They hired Vladimir as a permanent employee. The collaboration of multiple parties contributed to this outcome.

---

resume development and job-search activities. In many communities, these centers also operate youth employment programs that provide job placement services and/or refer youth for summer jobs. The significance of One-Stop Career Centers for youth with disabilities in transition is that they represent a generic, that is, not disability-related, service where youth do not have to be concerned with the potential stigma of being associated with a "disability" program. However, if they choose to disclose their disability, the One-Stop Centers are obligated to provide physical and programmatic access to all of the services for which the youth is eligible. Thus, One-Stop Centers can be another ancillary resource for the job-development process.

Conclusion

In transition planning and services, employment is both an intervention and an ultimate outcome. Critical to pursuing both is effective job-development and placement strategies. This chapter provided an overview of the importance of work to youth with disabilities and the practices that constitute the foundations of good job development. Key among these strategies are those that feature individualized, self-determined job-search planning, careful considerations for disclosing disability, proactive employer recruitment, mutual benefit in negotiating with employers, and planning for support after the placement. Further, transition specialists can and should call on the many partners who can contribute to successful job development and placement. These are proven strategies to help all youth achieve the expectation of employment, regardless of disability label, intensity of support needs, or economic circumstances. As legislative intent, national policy, research, and practice continue to promote the value of work experience and jobs as components of secondary education for youth with disabilities, skilled job development will be an increasingly important component of educational and transition service.

References

ADA Information Center of the Mid-Atlantic Region (2004). *Workforce discovery: Diversity and disability in the workplace*. Rockville, MD: TransCen.

Buchanan, L. (2003). *The disclosure dilemma for advocates*. Washington, DC: George Washington University HEATH Resource Center.

Education for All Handicapped Children Act of 1975, PL 94–142, 20 U.S.C. §§ 241 et seq.

Fabian, E. (2007). Urban youth with disabilities: Factors affecting transition employment. *Rehabilitation Counseling Bulletin, 50*(3), 130–138.

Field, S., Martin, J., Miller, R., Ward, M., & Wehmeyer, M. (1998). Self-determination for persons with disabilities: A position statement of the Division on Career Development and Transition, Council for Exceptional Children. *Career Development for Exceptional Individuals, 21*, 113–128.

Gramlich, M. (1999). *How to facilitate workplace mentoring: A guide for teachers to support employers and student workers*. Rockville, MD: TransCen.

Granovetter, M. (1974). *Getting a job*. Chicago: University of Chicago Press.

Griffin, C., Hammis, D., & Geary, T. (2007). *The job developer's handbook: Practical tactics for customized employment*. Baltimore: Paul H. Brookes Publishing Company.

Hernandez, B. (2000). Employer attitudes towards disability and their ADA employment rights: A literature review. *Journal of Rehabilitation, 16*, 83–88.

Individuals with Disabilities Education Improvement Act of 2004, PL108-446, 20 U.S.C. §§ 1400 et seq.

Johnson, D. & Guy. B. (1997). Implications of the lessons learned from a state systems change initiative on transition for youth with disabilities. *Career Development for Exceptional Individuals, 20*, 191–199.

Luecking, R. (2009). *The way to work: How to facilitate work experiences for youth in transition*. Baltimore: Paul H. Brookes Publishing Company.

Luecking, R. (2008). Emerging employer views of people with disabilities and the future of job development. *Journal of Vocational Rehabilitation, 29*, 3–13.

Luecking, R. (2005). *Strategies for youth workforce programs to become employer-friendly intermediaries*. Washington, DC: Institute for Educational Leadership, National Collaborative on Workforce and Disability/Youth, *Info Brief, 12*, 1.

Luecking, R. (2004a). Employer perspectives on hiring and accommodating youth in transition. *Journal of Special Education Technology, 18,* 65–72.

Luecking, R., (Ed.) (2004b). *In their own words: Employer perspectives on youth with disabilities in the workplace.* Minneapolis, MN: University of Minnesota, Institute on Community Integration, National Center on Secondary Education and Transition.

Luecking, R., Cuozzo, L., & Buchanan, L. (2006). Demand-side workforce needs and the potential for job customization. *Journal of Applied Rehabilitation Counseling, 37,* 5–13.

Luecking, R., & Fabian, E. (2000). Paid internships and employment success for youth in transition. *Career Development for Exceptional Individuals, 23,* 205–221.

Luecking, R., Fabian, E., & Tilson, G. (2004). *Working relationships: Creating career opportunities for job seekers with disabilities through employer partnerships.* Baltimore: Paul H. Brookes Publishing Company.

Luecking, R., & Tilson, G. (2009). Planning for work experiences. In R. Luecking, *The way to work: How to facilitate work experiences for youth in transition.* Baltimore: Paul H. Brookes Publishing Co.

Marino, C., & Tarr, K. (2004). The workforce intermediary: Profiling the field of practice and its challenges. In R. Gilroth (Ed.), *Workforce intermediaries for the twenty-first century.* Philadelphia, PA: Temple University Press.

National Alliance for Secondary Education and Transition (NASET). (2005). *National standards and quality indicators: Transition toolkit for systems improvement.* Minneapolis, MN: University of Minnesota, National Center on Secondary Education and Transition.

National Collaborative on Workforce and Disability for Youth (NCWD/Y (2005). *Guideposts for Success.* Washington, DC: Institute on Educational Leadership.

Pleet, A. (2000). *Investigating the relationship between parent involvement in transition planning and post-school outcomes for students with disabilities.* Michigan: UMI Dissertation Services.

Rogan, P., Grossi, T., & Gajewski, R. (2002). Vocational and career assessment. In C. Sax & C. Thoma (Eds.), *Transition assessment: Wise practices for quality lives.* (pp. 103–117).

Sax, C., & Thoma, C. (2002). *Transition assessment: Wise practices for quality lives.* Baltimore: Paul H. Brookes Publishing Co.

Sitlington, P., Neubert, D., Begun, W., Lombard, R., & Leconte, P. (2007). *Assess for success: A practitioner's handbook on transition assessment* (2nd ed.). Thousand Oaks, CA: Corwin Press.

Targett, P. (2006). Finding jobs for young people with disabilities. In P. Wehman (Ed.), *Life beyond the classroom.* Baltimore: Paul H. Brookes Publishing Co.

Test, D., Mazzotti, V., Mustian, A., Fowler, C., Kortering, L., & Kohler, P. (2009). Evidence-based secondary transition predictors for improving postschool outcomes for students with disabilities. *Career Development for Exceptional Individuals, 32,* 160–181.

Ticket to Work and Work Incentives Improvement Act of 1999, PL 106–170, 42 U.S.C. §§ 1305 et seq.

Tilson, G., & Cuozzo, L. (2001). *Positive personal profile.* Rockville, MD: TransCen.

Timmons, J., Podmosko, M., Bremer, C., Lavin, D., & Wills, J. (2004). *Career planning begins with assessment: A guide for professionals serving youth with educational and career development challenges.* Washington, DC: National Collaborative on Workforce and Disability for Youth.

Unger, D. (2002). Employers' attitudes towards people with disabilities in the workforce: Myths or realities? *Focus on Autism and Other Developmental Disabilities, 17*(1), 2–10.

U.S. Department of Education (2007). Notice inviting applications. *Federal Register,* 72 FR 36682–36685.

Wagner, M., Newman, L., Cameto, R., Garza, N., & Levine, P. (2005). *After high school: A first look at the postschool experiences of youth with disabilities. A report from the National Longitudinal Transition Study 2 (NLTS2).* Menlo Park, CA: SRI International.

Wandry, D., & Pleet, A. (2003). *A practitioner's guide to involving families in secondary education.* Arlington, VA: Council for Exceptional Children.

Wehman, P. (2006). *Life beyond the classroom: Transition strategies for young people with disabilities* (4th ed.). Baltimore: Paul H. Brookes Publishing Co.

Wehmeyer, M., & Palmer, S. (2003). Adult outcomes for students with cognitive disabilities three years after high school: The impact of self-determination. *Education and Training in Developmental Disabilities, 38,* 131–144.

Will, M. (1984). *OSERS programming for the transition of youth with disabilities: Bridges from school to working life.* Washington, DC: Office of Special Education and Rehabilitative Services, U.S. Department of Education.

Workforce Investment Act of 1998, PL 105–220, 29 U.S.C., §§ 2801 et seq.

Section V

Disability Specific Adolescent Transition Education

23

Transition Education for Adolescents with Autism Spectrum Disorders

Brenda Smith Myles

AUTISM RESEARCH INSTITUTE AND OHIO CENTER FOR AUTISM AND LOW INCIDENCE

Daniel E. Steere

EAST STROUDSBURG UNIVERSITY

As detailed in previous chapters in this book, effective transition planning is essential to helping young people with disabilities achieve a satisfying and successful adult life. Although this chapter will address the unique concerns of students with autism spectrum disorders (ASD), we remind readers that the fundamentals of effective transition planning for all young people apply also to individuals with ASD (Steere, Rose, & Cavaiulo, 2007). These fundamentals include:

- A support network of family, friends, teachers, and other professionals who can assist the young person in transition planning;
- Accurate and comprehensive assessments of students' interests, strengths, needs, and abilities;
- Assistance to the young person in clarifying a vision of success in adult life;
- A planning process that translates the desired vision of success into transition goals or outcomes that will drive the transition-planning process;
- Curricular content that is challenging and that prepares the student to attain their desired post-school outcomes;
- Active student involvement in planning;
- Family and caregiver involvement in planning;
- Assistance from and collaboration with adult service agencies and sources of natural community support; and
- Ongoing refinement and adjustment of the transition plan as students gain experiences related to their desired post-school outcomes.

Students with ASD comprise a heterogeneous population of learners (Attwood, 2008; Hall, 2009) that includes students with autism, Asperger syndrome (AS), Rett syndrome, childhood disintegrative disorder, and pervasive developmental disorder not otherwise specified. The abilities and needs of these students are considered as a spectrum that ranges from more severe disabilities and intensive support needs to milder disabilities with less intensive support needs. These learners range from students with severe cognitive, speech, social, and behavioral deficits to students with AS who are of average intelligence, have no speech impairments, but experience challenges with social interaction, cognitive, and self-regulation skills. Because the type and intensity of support needs of these students are so varied, transition services for students with ASD must be responsive to these individual needs.

As established earlier in this book, transition planning and services are designed to help young people with disabilities achieve positive adult outcomes. These outcomes include a satisfying career, a home in the community, postsecondary education or training, and meaningful connections to one's community. The attainment of these outcomes for people with ASD has been particularly problematic. In particular, students with ASD have low rates of employment, with the majority being unemployed (Hendricks & Wehman, 2009; Myles, Grossman, Aspy, & Henry, 2009; Standifer, 2009; Steere & Cavaiuolo, in press). People with ASD typically have significantly restricted social networks of friends and other caring community members (Cadwallader & Wagner, 2003). In addition, they are under-represented in postsecondary education and training (Thomas, 2000). In general, then, transition outcomes for students with ASD have been poor and have not resulted in the attainment of a satisfactory quality of life (Geller & Cavanagh, 2005; Jobe & White, 2007).

In this chapter, we review strategies for planning for the successful transition of adolescents with ASD. In particular, we will focus on two specific planning models that identify the supports that students with ASD need to be successful. These models are effective across the lifespan (Myles, Smith, & Swanson, 2008). This chapter will discuss the application of these models in activities within the adult domains of employment, postsecondary education, and community living. These two models—the Ziggurat Model (Aspy & Grossman, 2008) and the Comprehensive Autism Planning System (CAPS) (Henry & Myles, 2007)— are reviewed in the next section (see Figure 23.1). We then provide examples of the use of these systems to plan effective supports for students with ASD who are in transition to adult life.

Before reviewing these two planning strategies, we should reiterate that there are a variety of approaches for helping young people who are in transition to identify their desired adult-transition goals or outcomes (cf., Held, Thoma, & Thomas, 2004; Mesibov, Thomas, Chapman, & Schloper, 2007; Steere et al., 2007). For example, for students with more significant disabilities, person-centered planning strategies have been demonstrated to be particularly useful in clarifying individuals' desired visions of success for their adult lives (cf., Madaus & Shaw, 2007; Miner & Bates, 1997; Steere, Gregory, Heiny, & Butterworth, 1995). There are also other approaches to increasing student self-determination abilities and student participation in the planning process, as described in Chapters 6 and 13 in this book. Because these approaches have been described earlier and in other sources, we will not focus on that aspect of transition planning for students with ASD. However, we do reiterate that the clarification of specific transition goals for adulthood is essential and provides the direction and context for the planning models that we describe below (Organization for Autism Research, 2006).

Ziggurat Model

The Ziggurat Model is a guide for designing comprehensive interventions for individuals with ASD. The premise of this model is that underlying needs and characteristics as well as strengths related to the spectrum must be identified and matched with interventions. This model is designed to utilize individual strengths to address true needs that result in social, emotional, and behavioral concerns. The Ziggurat approach centers on a hierarchical system, consisting

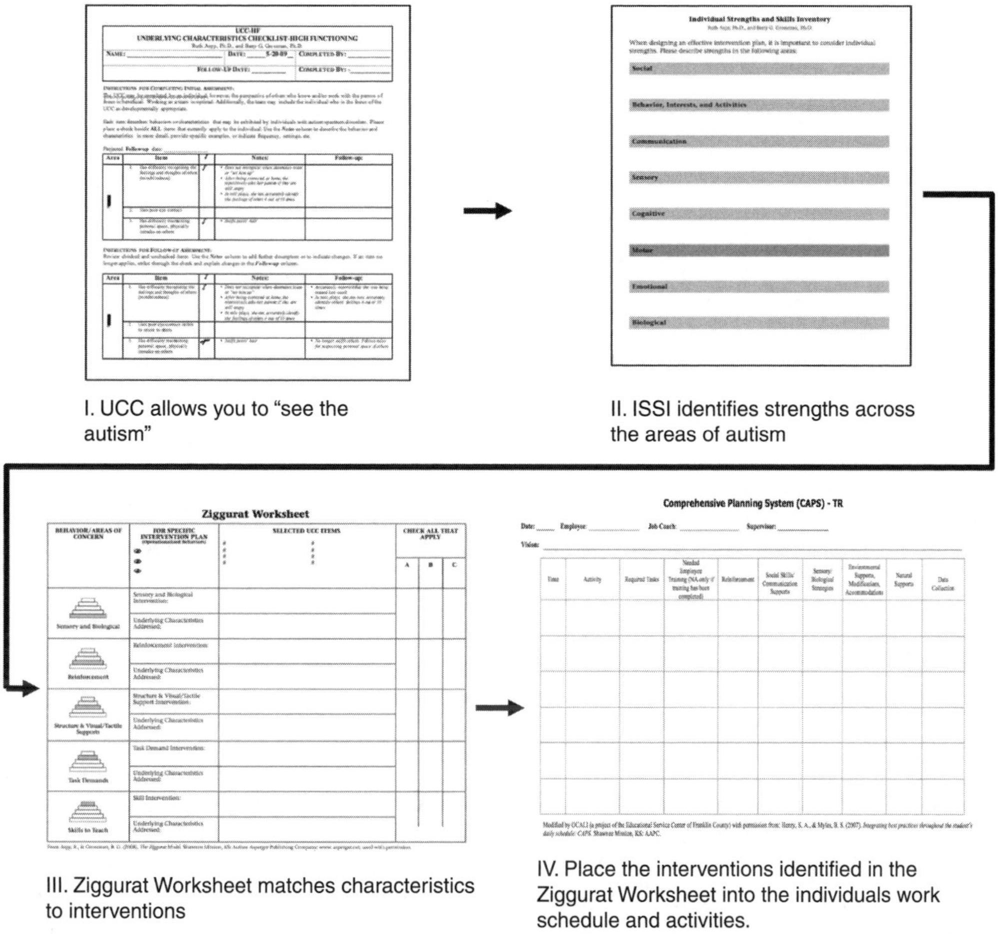
I. UCC allows you to "see the autism"
II. ISSI identifies strengths across the areas of autism
Ziggurat Worksheet
Comprehensive Planning System (CAPS) - TR
III. Ziggurat Worksheet matches characteristics to interventions
IV. Place the interventions identified in the Ziggurat Worksheet into the individuals work schedule and activities.

Figure 23.1 Overview of the comprehensive planning process
Source: From *Designing Comprehensive Interventions for Individuals with High Functioning Autism and Asperger Syndrome: The Ziggurat Model* by Ruth Aspy and Barry Grossman. Copyright 2008. Shawnee Mission, KS: AAPC Publishing. www.aapcpublishing.net.

of five levels that must be addressed for an intervention plan to be comprehensive (see Figure 23.2).

When designing a comprehensive program, it is essential to consider the context of the underlying ASD. This is overlooked all too often. Targeting underlying needs leads to identifying supports that are proactive and fundamental. In comparison, interventions that are solely designed to address surface behavior without consideration of the underlying ASD are potentially less effective and less likely to result in sustained employment and personal growth. Further, assessment of underlying characteristics provides insight into which skills should be taught and how to design instruction to facilitate learning and bring about meaningful and long-lasting change. The Underlying Characteristics Checklist (UCC) often serves as a basis for comprehensive program planning.

The Ziggurat model

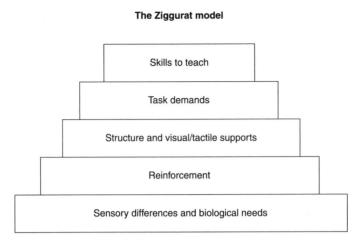

Figure 23.2 The Ziggurat model
Source: From *Textbook Support Materials* by AAPC Publishing. Copyright 2010. Shawnee Mission, KS: AAPC Publishing. <www.aapcpublishing.net/textbooksupportmaterials>. Reprinted with permission.

Underlying Characteristics Checklist

The UCC is an informal assessment designed to identify ASD characteristics for the purpose of intervention. There are three versions of the UCC: (a) UCC-HF for use with individuals who are high functioning, including those with AS; (b) UCC-CL for use with those with a more classic presentation in cognition and speech-language skills; and (c) UCC-EI that addresses the needs of those from 0 to 5 years of age. The UCC comprises eight areas. The first three represent the autism spectrum triad: social, restricted patterns of behavioral interests and activities, and communication. Characteristics often associated with ASD are addressed in the next four areas: sensory differences, cognitive differences, motor differences, and emotional vulnerability. The eighth underlying area is known medical and other biological factors.

Based on the results of completing the UCC, a comprehensive intervention plan is developed that targets ASD characteristics by incorporating each of the five levels of the Ziggurat. The UCC may be completed by the individual, service providers, job coaches, fellow employees, parents, or other service providers, individually or as a team.

Individual Strengths and Skills Inventory

The Individual Strengths and Skills Inventory (ISSI) was designed to accompany the UCC. The ISSI parallels the first seven areas of the UCC. The purpose of this tool is to ensure that underlying strengths and skills are incorporated in the intervention-design process. For example, one individual may have a strength in rote memory whereas another has an intense interest in and knowledge of animals. These assets can easily become key to identifying and developing supports in challenge areas. The UCC and ISSI can also help to determine a job match between individual skills and job requirements.

Intervention Ziggurat

The Intervention Ziggurat (IZ) is the centerpiece of the Ziggurat Model and is the framework on which comprehensive interventions are built. The IZ is composed of five critical levels structured into a hierarchy: Sensory Differences and Biological Needs, Reinforcement, Structure and Visual/Tactile Supports, Task Demands, and Skills to Teach (see Figure 23.2). The first level, Sensory Differences and Biological Needs, addresses basic internal factors that impact functioning. The second level addresses motivational needs prerequisite to skill development. The third level draws on individuals' strength of visual processing and addresses their fundamental need for order and routine. The final two levels of the IZ emphasize the importance of expectations and skill development in light of the characteristics of individuals with ASD.

The IZ helps ensure that critical areas that impact the effectiveness of any job placement are not overlooked. Each of the levels is essential and contributes to the effectiveness of the others. Thus, if needs on all levels are not addressed, interventions will not be as effective and skills will not develop as quickly. The following is a brief discussion of the five levels of the Intervention Ziggurat.

Sensory Differences and Biological Needs

The first level of the IZ represents what is, in one sense, the basis of all behavior—biology. Consideration of biological factors is especially important in the case of ASD due to the strong genetic, physiological, and neurological underpinnings of this disorder (Ashwood & Van de Water, 2004; Christensen et al., 2009; Hughes, 2008; Macefield, 2009). Unmet sensory and biological needs will result in changes in behavior, highlighting the importance of including strategies to address these needs. While sensory differences and biological needs are not included as core symptoms of ASD in the current diagnostic manual (American Psychiatric Association, 2000), they often present some of the greatest challenges for individuals on the spectrum (Ashburner, Ziviani, & Rodger, 2008; Myles et al., 2004).

Research exists on sensory and biological interventions for individuals with ASD. For example, Case-Smith and Arbeson (2008) identified 49 studies conducted on sensory and motor interventions. Much of the research on biological interventions has centered on the use of medications. There is support for several drug classes, including antidepressants (Namerow, Thomas, Bostic, Prince, & Monuteaux, 2003); antipsychotics (Erickson, Stigler, Posey, & McDougle, 2005); and stimulants (Di Martino, Melis, Chianchetti, & Zuddas, 2004).

Reinforcement

All employment plans ultimately target the development or use of a behavior or skill. This goal can only be accomplished by incorporating reinforcement into the comprehensive plan. The principles of effective reinforcement are well established in the research literature that has shown that without reinforcement, there is no intervention (Grindle & Remington, 2005; Higbee, Carr, & Patel, 2002; Kay, Harchik, Luiselli, 2006: Koegel, O'Dell, & Dunlap, 1988). Because of its fundamental nature, reinforcement is included as the second level of the IZ.

It may be necessary to think creatively about reinforcement for some adults with ASD. While social opportunities are often reinforcing for neurotypical individuals, these may be some of the most challenging situations for people with ASD. In seeking to identify effective reinforcers, it is often helpful to consider the special interests of students with ASD. Indeed, research has found that activities or objects related to interests or obsessions are often more effective than primary reinforcers, such as food (Charlop-Christy, Kurtz, & Casey, 1990; Winter-Messiers et al., 2007) for individuals on the autism spectrum.

Structure and Visual / Tactile Supports

The third level of the IZ is a direct response to the core characteristics of ASD. That is, individuals with ASD function best when predictability is established across the day, including schedules, routines, environments, behavioral and task-related expectations, and interpersonal interactions. If changes in routine occur, preparation for such change should be incorporated into the intervention plan. Because visual processing is often a strength for individuals with ASD, visual supports are critical aspects of intervention plans (Ganz, Bourgeois, Flores, & Campos, 2008; Wheeler, Baggett, Fox, & Blevins, 2006). Tactile supports are an additional alternative to verbal communication and should be considered, especially for those with ASD who also have a visual impairment.

The areas of structure and visual/tactile supports often overlap. Visual supports such as pictures, written schedules, and task strips may help clarify the structure of an activity. For example, visual schedules have been shown to be effective for improving transition speed (Dettmer, Simpson, Myles, & Ganz, 2000); decreasing behavior problems during transition (Dooley, Wilczenski, & Torem, 2001); and increasing on-task behavior (O'Reilly, Sigafoos, Lancioni, Edrisinha, & Andrews, 2005). There is substantial research support for other visual strategies, such as Social Stories™ (Sansosti, Powell-Smith, & Kincaid, 2004) and video modeling (Bellini & Akullian, 2007).

Task Demands

Task Demands with the IZ include job-related activities but go beyond, to include social, communicative, organizational, sensory, and other demands. An alternative term for Task Demands is *obstacle removal* (Eric Blackwell, personal communication July, 2006). For the purpose of designing quality interventions, expectations must be reasonable. One way to accomplish this is to ensure that obstacles are removed to the greatest extent possible to assist an individual in succeeding either independently or with assistance. The ways in which obstacles are removed are Task Demand Interventions. For example, an obstacle to completing tasks for an employee with ASD may be her difficulty processing verbal instructions. A Task Demand Intervention for this situation might be a picture schedule or written list of tasks to be completed.

Skills to Teach

The first four levels of the Ziggurat set the stage for skill acquisition. It is possible to resolve many behavioral concerns using strategies on the first four levels without ever teaching skills. Indeed, many improvements may be seen as a direct result of attending to an individual's biological needs, providing meaningful reinforcers, addressing the need for structure and predictability, and carefully matching demands to ability. As such, it is possible that teams may overlook this crucial last level. However, such a "partial" approach to intervention will have negative long-term outcomes because it does not allow for independence or promote generalization or growth. It is for this reason that the authors view Skills to Teach as essential to any intervention plan.

Several approaches to teaching skills to individuals with ASD have been supported in the literature, including priming (Zanolli, Daggett, & Adams, 1996); formal social skills instruction (Barry et al., 2003); and pivotal response training (Koegel, Koegel, & Carter, 1998).

Ziggurat Worksheet

The Ziggurat Worksheet guides the team through the development of a comprehensive intervention plan. With a new understanding of the needs of the individual based on completion of the UCC and the information on strengths and current skill level provided through completion of the ISSI, the next step is to prepare to design a plan that is targeted to individual needs. Areas of the UCC are prioritized and specific UCC items are selected. All interventions incorporated into the plan must address underlying needs from the UCC. This provides a safeguard from developing a plan that addresses only surface concerns or from recycling interventions that have been used with others without careful consideration of the individual on the spectrum. Further, the Ziggurat Worksheet promotes collaboration by helping all those who support the individual to understand her part in the larger intervention picture.

An intervention plan is truly comprehensive when interventions address each of the five levels of the Intervention Ziggurat (three points of intervention—antecedent, behavior, and consequence) and when each intervention strategy addresses underlying characteristics from the UCC. The Ziggurat Worksheet provides a structure for verifying that the intervention plan is indeed comprehensive. Interventions that are not comprehensive leave unnecessary holes where difficulties may occur and begin to undermine the effectiveness of the intervention techniques that are put into place. After completion of the Ziggurat Worksheet, the team is ready to complete the CAPS. While the Ziggurat Worksheet allows a team to know that the intervention plan is thorough and targeted, the CAPS provides a structure for implementation.

Comprehensive Autism Planning System-Transition

The Comprehensive Autism Planning System-Transition (CAPS-TR) (Coffin, Filler, & Owens, 2008; Henry & Myles, 2007) is a system that ties the type and intensity of supports that students require for their daily schedules of activities. The approach is designed to address the question: What supports will this individual require in order to successfully participate in or complete each activity on his daily schedule? Because adolescents with ASD typically have complex profiles of ability and support needs, the CAPS-TR model helps transition planning teams to pinpoint the type and nature of support and training that students will require in order to help them have a greater likelihood of attaining their desired transition outcomes.

The CAPS-TR planning template is organized around 10 key elements for planning a student's daily activities, as shown in Figure 23.1:

1   *Time and Activity:* The time of day and name of the required activity.
2   *Required Tasks:* Specific elements or task component duties that must be completed during this activity.
3   *Needed Employee Training:* A list of the specific training that the student needs in order to complete each of the required tasks.
4   *Reinforcement:* The type and amount of positive reinforcement that the student requires for success.
5   *Social Skills/Communication Supports:* Specific supports that are required for the successful completion of the required tasks.
6   *Sensory/Biological Strategies:* Strategies that assist students through sensory input or modification.
7   *Environmental Supports, Modifications, and Accommodations:* Supports and/or modifications that are built into the environment to complete the required tasks with greater independence.
8   *Natural Supports:* Supports that are provided by co-workers, community members, neighbors, and others who are not paid to provide services.
9   *Data Collection:* The type of data to be collected to document progress with the targeted activity.

As shown in Figure 23.1, the vision of success is listed at the top of the planning form. It is essential that the planning team remember that the completion of the daily activities listed on the CAPS-TR form should lead individuals toward greater independence and, in turn, the increased likelihood that they will attain their desired transition outcomes.

Case Studies

This section introduces two case studies of employees with autism spectrum disorders: Elle, a young woman with classic autism, and Phillip, who has been diagnosed as having AS. Both present with a high level of needs.

Elle

Elle is a young woman with autism, age 18, who lives with her family. Elle, her family, and a transition specialist worked together to find a job that Elle would both excel at and enjoy. To identify need—to actually "see her autism"—they completed an UCC-CL (see Table 23.1 for some of the UCC-CL items that match Elle's needs along with evidence) and an ISSI (see Figure 23.3). The completion of the UCC and ISSI allowed Elle, her parents, and her transition specialist to identify potential jobs of interests. Taking into consideration her special interest in DVDs and need for a highly structured environment, Elle found part-time employment at a local family-owned video store. The transition specialist, parents, and job coach completed a Ziggurat Worksheet and CAPS-TR (see Figures 23.4 and 23.5, respectively) to outline Elle's workday. As Elle began her job, the coach provided a brief orientation to employees and set out to help Elle become a part of the work environment. Elle travels to and from work using public

Table 23.1 Sample of selected UCC-CL items and supporting evidence that describe Elle's needs relative to her ASD

Area	Item	Notes
Social	Has difficulty making or keeping friends	Prefers being by herself
	Has difficulty joining an activity	Requires many verbal and physical prompts
	Has difficulty understanding nonverbal communication	Cannot interpret voice tone, gestures, expressions
	Appears to be unresponsive to others	Requires repeating several times
Communication	Has little to no speech	Nonverbal; uses AAC device
	Has difficulty expressing wants and needs	Uses AAC device inconsistently
	Fails to initiate or respond to greetings	Must be prompted to do these
	Communicates needs through behaviors	Vocalizes loudly, hits self, paces
	Has difficulty asking for help	Inconsistently accepts "help"
Sensory	Responds in an unusual manner to sounds	Gets upset at loud noises
	Seeks activities that provide movement	Paces
Emotional Vulnerability	Is anxious or easily stressed	In new situations or around new people
	Becomes stressed with new task situation	Begins to pace, vocalize, hit self
	Has difficulty tolerating mistakes – own and others'	Gets very upset; expects perfection in self

Individual Strengths and Skills Inventory

Ruth Aspy, Ph.D., and Barry G. Grossman, Ph.D.

Name	Elle Hoff

In designing effective intervention plans, it is important to be aware of individual strengths. Please describe strengths in the following areas:

Social
Is well liked by co-workers
Responds to praise from boss or job coach
Participates in community with family members

Behavior, interests, and activities
Enjoys family photo albums, colored markers, and watching DVDs
Responds well to routines
Independent with using vending machines

Communication
Is becoming more consistent with use of augmentative alternate communication device
Lets others know that her needs and wants are not being met

Sensory and biological
Enjoys work/activities which require movement
Likes wearing earplugs or head phones in environments that are loud
Has good stamina

Cognitive
Responds well to work tasks that are highly structured
Attends to tasks
Matches pictures, labels, etc. with very few errors

(*Continued*)

Motor
Can use both hands in a coordinated fashion to complete most work tasks
Likes activities/tasks that require movement (pacing)
Emotional
Likes to complete work tasks correctly
Holds high expectations for herself

Figure 23.3 Individual strengths and skills inventory (ISSI): Elle

Source: From *Textbook Support Materials* by AAPC Publishing. Copyright 2010. Shawnee Mission, KS: AAPC Publishing. <www.aapcpublishing.net/textbooksupportmaterials>. Reprinted with permission; Aspy, R., & Grossman, B. G. (2007). The Ziggurat Model. Shawnee Mission, KS: Autism Asperger Publishing Company.

transportation. During work, she is beginning to use an assistive technology device more consistently to express her needs and desires as well as to initiate conversation or respond to fellow employees. Elle receives support from a job coach on a consistent basis.

Phillip

Phillip is a 22-year-old man with AS. He lives with two other men in an apartment and receives supported-living services. To date, Phillip has held seven jobs, all of which ended with Phillip being fired. Because of his interest in catalogs, magazines, newspaper flyers, etc., Phillip requested that his rehabilitation counselor help him find a job that would incorporate his interest as well as allow him to "move up the job ladder." In order to provide a better job match and, hopefully, a long-term job, Phillip and his rehabilitation counselor completed a UCC (see Table 23.2) and ISSI (see Figure 23.6) to help further identify strengths, skills, and needs that

Table 23.2 Sample of summary of selected UCC-CL items and supporting evidence that describe Phillip's needs relative to his ASD

Area	Item	Notes
Social	Has difficulty recognizing the feelings and thoughts of others	Attempts to dominate all conversations with topics that interest him
	Has difficulty maintaining personal space	Gets very close to others when speaking, making others uncomfortable
	Has difficulty making or keeping friends	Has one friend to go out with
	Has difficulty understanding others' nonverbal communication	Does not understand body language including facial expressions
Emotional Vulnerability	Is easily stressed – worries obsessively	When he does not complete a task perfectly or unexpected change occurs
	Has difficulty tolerating mistakes	Paces, screams, will not move on
	Has low frustration tolerance	Expects perfection in self and others
	Has difficulty managing stress and/or anxiety	Paces and squeezes head

ZIGGURAT WORKSHEET: SENSORY AND REINFORCEMENT ONLY

Ruth Aspy, Ph.D., and Barry G. Grossman, Ph.D.

NAME	*Elle Hoff*

BEHAVIOR/AREAS OF CONCERN SOCIAL, COMMUNICATION, SENSORY, EMOTIONAL VULNERABILITY	FOR SPECIFIC INTERVENTION PLAN	PRIORITIZED UCC ITEMS	CHECK ALL THAT APPLY		
			A	B	C
	Operationalized Behaviors	# 10 Difficulty making or keeping friends # 11 Difficulty joining an activity # 15 Difficulty understanding non-verbals # 16 Appears unresponsive to others # 32 Has little speech # 33 Difficulty expressing wants/needs # 43 Fails to initiate/respond to greetings # 44 Communicates needs through behaviors	# 47 Has difficulty asking for help # 56 Responds in an unusual manner to sounds # 63 Seeks activities that provide movement # 92 Is anxious or easily stressed # 94 Becomes stressed when presented with new tasks # 99 Has difficulty tolerating mistakes			
	☺ ☺ ☺ ☺				
(ziggurat diagram)	Sensory/Biological Intervention	* Provide work experience that allows movement/pacing * Provide home base for when anxious or overwhelmed with noise or novel situation * Allow earplugs if environment becomes loud * Avoid vacuuming during hours that Elle is working * Keep intercom music to a medium to soft volume		X	X
Sensory/Biological Needs	Underlying Characteristics Addressed	#63 Seeks activities that provide movement #92 Is anxious or easily stressed			X

(Continued)

			X	
  Reinforcement	Reinforcement Intervention:	#94 Becomes stressed when presented with new tasks #56 Responds in an unusual manner to sounds		
		* Allow breaks: making purchases at the vending machine, looking at family photo albums * Reinforce Elle for responding to or initiating a greeting * Reinforce Elle for asking for help with her augmentative alternative communication device * Reinforce Elle for using her language board to express her wants or needs		
	Underlying Characteristics Addressed:	#92 Is anxious or easily stressed #33 Difficulty expressing wants/needs #94 Becomes stressed when presented with task #32 Has little speech #43 Fails to initiate/respond to greetings #44 Communicates needs through behavior #47 Difficulty asking for help		

Figure 23.4 Ziggurat worksheet sensory and reinforcement only: Elle

Source: From *Textbook Support Materials* by AAPC Publishing. Copyright 2010. Shawnee Mission, KS: AAPC Publishing. www.aapcpublishing.net/textbooksupportmaterials. Reprinted with permission.

Comprehensive Autism Planning System (CAPS)-TR (1ˢᵗ ACTIVITY ONLY)

Employee: *Elle Hoff* **Job Coach:** *Lori Carpenter/Jennifer Simms* **Date:** *March 2007* **Supervisor:** *Sarah Brown*

Vision: Ellie's vision is to be employed with support in a small family-owned video store that is highly structured and which matches her interests and skills.

Time/Activity	Required Tasks	Needed Employee Training	Reinforcement	Social Skills/ Communication Supports	Sensory/ Biological Strategies	Environmental Supports, Modifications, Accommodations	Natural Supports	Data Collection
10:00 am Arrival	Say good morning to supervisor	"Good morning" with AAC device	Verbal praise	Social narrative for greeting and responding to supervisor	Intercom music medium to soft volume	Slot labeled for time card separate from others' slots	Co-worker providing assistance when needed	Number of days per week Ellie greets supervisor upon arrival
	Punch in time clock	Use of time clock		AAC device for greetings and conversations		Job coach or supervisor prime Elle with changes in normal tasks		
	Put coat/lunch box in break room;	Finding "cubby" in break room for personal belongings					Co-worker modeling greetings and using time clock	Use of time clock and prompts needed
	Check in with supervisor for work assignments					AAC device; Picture work schedule for daily activities		

Figure 23.5 Comprehensive autism planning system–transition (CAPS-TR): Elle

Source: From *Textbook Support Materials* by AAPC Publishing. Copyright 2010. Shawnee Mission, KS: AAPC Publishing. www.aapcpublishing.net/textbooksupportmaterials. Reprinted with permission.

Individual Strengths and Skills Inventory

Ruth Aspy, Ph.D., and Barry G. Grossman, Ph.D.

Name	*Phillip Cullins*

In designing effective intervention plans, it is important to be aware of individual strengths. Please describe strengths in the following areas:

Social
Is beginning to form a relationship with one co-worker
Likes to share his interests with his co-workers

Behavior, Interests, and Activities
Enjoys looking at catalogs
Is very conscientious about completing tasks/activities before moving on to something else
Follows routines well

Communication
Likes to be involved in conversations around personal topics of interest
Can share extensive information about a topic of interest with co-worker
Follows 2-step directions consistently
Can ask for help when needed

Sensory and Biological
Enjoys activities that involve movement
Tolerates all types of fabrics/clothing (wears required uniform)
Likes wearing earplugs

Cognitive
Responds well to visual supports
Likes to practice skills over and over again
Asks for help when not sure what to do

Motor	
Moves quickly when working	
Able to manipulate packing labels, stickers, etc. independently	
Emotional	
Has an overall pleasant demeanor	
Regulates stress level by pacing and beginning to provide self with deep pressure	

Figure 23.6 Individual strengths and skills inventory (ISSI): Phillip
Source: From *Textbook Support Materials* by AAPC Publishing. Copyright 2010. Shawnee Mission, KS: AAPC Publishing. www.aapcpublishing.net/textbooksupportmaterials. Reprinted with permission; Aspy, R., & Grossman, B. G. (2007). The Ziggurat Model. Shawnee Mission, KS: Autism Asperger Publishing Company.

could be used to locate a potential job. Phillip and his counselor discovered a local catalog dissemination factory that they both thought would present an enjoyable, challenging, and somewhat structured work environment. Phillip interviewed for the job successfully following coaching and he and his counselor completed a Ziggurat Worksheet and CAPS-TR (see Figures 23.7 & 23.8) with the assistance of a job coach. Phillip currently works from 8:30 a.m. through 2:00 p.m. Monday through Friday. Even with support, Phillip struggles socially. He tends to be a perfectionist and expects that of others as well. He receives most of his support from his supervisor and co-workers.

Summary

In this chapter, we have described two planning strategies—the Ziggurat Model and the CAPS-TR—that can contribute to improved transition outcomes for students with ASD. These planning strategies must take place within the context of effective transition-planning practices, as detailed in earlier chapters of this book. Like all young people with disabilities, individuals with ASD need support in planning for a fulfilling and satisfying life that includes integrated employment, home living in the community, community participation, and perhaps postsecondary education (Hendricks & Wehman, 2009; Steere et al., 2007). Planning should be initiated as early as possible to provide sufficient time to explore options and to provide the experiences that will allow young people with ASD and their families the time that is necessary to plan a successful transition.

ZIGGURAT WORKSHEET: TASK DEMANDS AND SKILLS TO TEACH ONLY

Ruth Aspy, Ph.D., and Barry G. Grossman, Ph.D.

BEHAVIOR/AREAS OF CONCERN	FOR SPECIFIC INTERVENTION PLAN	PRIORITIZED UCC ITEMS	CHECK ALL THAT APPLY		
			A	B	C
SOCIAL, RESTRICTED PATTERNS OF BEHAVIOR, INTERESTS, ACTIONS, COMMUNICATION, SENSORY, EMOTIONAL VULNERABILITY	Operationalized Behaviors ⊚ ⊚ ⊚ ⊚	# 1 Difficulty recognizing others' feelings/thoughts # 19 Strong need for closure # 3 Difficulty maintaining personal space # 25 Difficulty with rules of conversation # 5 Lacks tact/appears rude # 31 Difficulty expressing thoughts/feelings # 9 Difficulty understanding others' nonverbal communication # 41 Responds unusually to loud sounds # 47 Seeks activities that provide movement # 12 Strong need for sameness # 76 Easily stressed # 14 Eccentric/intense preoccupations # 84 Difficulty making mistakes # 17 Displays repetitive motor movements # 85 Low frustration # 89 Difficulty managing stress & anxiety			
	Task Demand Intervention:	• Prime when job tasks will change • Educate supervisor about autism and Phillip's needs • Provide Phillip with a weekly schedule • Stress thermometer, coping cards • Social narrative for others' interests • Visual schedule for work day • Cartooning for proximity • Establish and train small group of co-workers to model appropriate ways to converse with others	X	X	
Task Demands	Underlying Characteristics Addressed:	• Difficulty recognizing thoughts/feelings of others • Difficulty with rules of conversation • Difficulty maintaining proximity/intrudes • Difficulty managing stress/anxiety • Low frustration			

Skills to Teach				
	Skill Intervention:	• Difficulty understanding others' nonverbals • Difficulty with making mistakes • Strong need for sameness • Teach Phillip to identify others' body cues/facial expressions • Teach Phillip how to appropriately respond when he or someone else makes a mistake • Teach Phillip how to express his feelings through words when he becomes anxious or upset • Teach Phillip what are "on-topic" statements and what are "off-topic" statements • Teach Phillip how to participate in conversations with coworkers by role playing • Teach Phillip how to appropriately request help when he doesn't know what to do or when overwhelmed • Conduct a social autopsy to understand what goes wrong with interactions among coworkers	X	X
	Underlying Characteristics Addressed:	• Difficulty recognizing thoughts/feeling of others • Difficulty understanding others' nonverbal communication • Low frustration • Difficulty with rules of conversation • Easily stressed • Difficulty managing stress and anxiety		

Figure 23.7 Ziggurat worksheet and task demands and skills to teach only: Phillip

Source: From *Textbook Support Materials* by AAPC Publishing. Copyright 2010. Shawnee Mission, KS: AAPC Publishing. www.aapcpublishing.net/textbooksupportmaterials. Reprinted with permission.

Comprehensive Autism Planning System (CAPS)-TR (ONE TASK ONLY)

Employee: <u>Phillip Cullins</u> **Job Coach:** <u>Tom Ceff</u> **Supervisor:** <u>John Davis</u> **Date:** September

Time/Activity	Required Tasks	Needed Employee Training	Reinforcement	Social Skills/ Communication Supports	Sensory/ Biological Strategies	Environmental Supports, Modifications, Accommodations	Natural Supports	Data Collection
Filling mail-orders	Reading orders;	How to read order forms;	Pacing, movement is reinforcing;	Power Card for when he or co-worker makes mistakes;	Ear plugs for noise level in factory;	Visual cue card for making mistakes;	Supervisor check-in;	Accuracy of orders and speed
9:00 to 10:15	Retrieving order from shelf;	Locating catalogs on shelves;	Catalogs	Visual for rules of conversation;	Coping cards for anxiety (change in task or mistakes);	Visual work schedule;	Coworkers in vicinity to provide support if needed	
10:30 to 11:30	Packaging order including order form;	Packaging catalogs correctly;		Cartooning for proximity and inappropriate comments;	Stress thermometer;	Supervisor or job coach forewarn if job is going to change unexpectedly;		
	Placing package with completed order in "completed order" bin;	How to respond if he doesn't finish work within time frame;			Work allows pacing and movement;	Bins labeled "incomplete order", "complete order";		
	Placing package with incomplete order in "incomplete order" bin	Who to go to for help;		Scripts for when working near co-worker				
		What to do if he finishes before time is up			Provide self with deep pressure			

Figure 23.8 Partial comprehensive autism planning system – transition (CAPS-TR): Phillip

Source: From *Textbook Support Materials* by AAPC Publishing. Copyright 2010. Shawnee Mission, KS: AAPC Publishing. www.aapcpublishing.net/textbooksupportmaterials. Reprinted with permission.

References

American Psychiatric Association. (2000). *Diagnostic and statistical manual of developmental disorders* (4th ed., text revision). Washington, DC: Author.

Ashburner, J., Ziviani, J., & Rodger, S. (2008). Sensory processing classroom emotional, behavioral, and educational outcomes in children with autism spectrum disorder. *American Journal of Occupational Therapy, 62*, 564–573.

Ashwood, P., & Van de Water, J. (2004). A review of autism and the immune response. *Clinical and Developmental Immunology, 11*, 165–174.

Aspy, R., & Grossman, B. (2008). *Designing comprehensive interventions for individuals with high-functioning autism and Asperger Syndrome: The ziggurat model.* Shawnee Mission, KS: Autism Asperger Publishing Company.

Attwood, T. (2008). An overview of autism spectrum disorders. In K. D. Buron & P. Wolfberg (Eds.), *Learners on the autism spectrum: Preparing highly qualified educators* (pp. 18–43). Shawnee Mission, KS: Autism Asperger Publishing Company.

Barry, T. D., Klinger, L. G., Lee, J. M., Palardy, N., Gilmore, T., & Bodin, S. D. (2003). Examining the effectiveness of an outpatient clinic-based social skills group for high-functioning children with autism. *Journal of Autism and Developmental Disorders, 33*, 685–701.

Bellini, S., & Akullian, J. (2007). A meta-analysis of video modeling and video self-modeling interventions for children and adolescents with autism spectrum disorders. *Exceptional Children, 73*, 264–287.

Cadwallader, T. & Wagner, M. (2003). Interactions with friends. In Wagner, M., Cadwallader, T., & Marder, C. (with Cameto, R., Cardoso, D., Garza, N. et al.), *Life outside the classroom for youth with disabilities. A report from the National Longitudinal Transition Study-2 (NLTS2).* Menlo Park, CA: SRI International. Available at www.nlts2.org/pdfs/life_outside_class_ch3.pdf

Case-Smith, J., & Arbeson, M. (2008). Evidence based review on interventions for autism used in occupational therapy. *The American Journal of Occupational Therapy, 62*, 417–429.

Charlop-Christy, M. H., Kurtz, P. F., & Casey, F. G. (1990). Using aberrant behaviors as reinforcers for autistic children. *Journal of Applied Behavior Analysis, 23*, 163–181.

Christensen, T. J., Ringdahl, Bosch, J. J., Falcomata, T. S., Luke, J. R., & Andelman, M. S. (2009). Constipation associated with self-injurious and aggressive behavior exhibited by a child diagnosed with autism. *Education and Treatment of Children, 32*, 89–103.

Coffin, A. B., Filler, C., & Owens, C. (2008). Comprehensive Autism Planning System: Transition. Unpublished document. Ohio Center for Autism, Columbus, OH.

Dettmer, S., Simpson, R. L., Myles, B. S., & Ganz, J. B. (2000). The use of visual supports to facilitate transitions of students with autism. *Focus on Autism and Other Developmental Disabilities, 15*, 163–169.

Di Martino, A., Melis, G., Cianchetti, C., & Zuddas, A. (2004). Methylphenidate for pervasive developmental disorders: Safety and efficacy of acute single dose test and ongoing therapy: An open-pilot study. *Journal of Child and Adolescent Psychopharmacology, 14*, 207–218.

Dooley, P., Wilczenski, F. L., & Torem, C. (2001). Using an activity schedule to smooth school transitions. *Journal of Positive Behavior Interventions, 3*, 57–61.

Erickson, C. A., Stigler, K. A., Posey, D. J., & McDougle, C. J. (2005). Risperidone in pervasive developmental disorders. *Expert Review of Neurotherapeutics, 5*, 713–719.

Ganz, J. B., Bourgeois, B. C., Flores, M. M., & Campos, B. A. (2008). Implementing visually cued imitation training with children with autism spectrum disorders and developmental delays. *Journal of Positive Behavior Interventions, 10*, 56–66.

Geller, L. L., & Cavanagh, J. M. (2005). *Falling through the cracks: Services for "higher-functioning" adults on the autism spectrum.* New York: Asperger Foundation International.

Grindle, C. F., & Remington, B. (2005). Teaching children with autism when reward is delayed: The effects of two kinds of marking stimuli. *Journal of Autism and Developmental Disorders, 35*, 839–850.

Hall, L. (2009). *Autism spectrum disorders: From theory to practice.* Upper Saddle River, NJ: Merrill-Pearson.

Held, M. F., Thoma, C. A., & Thomas, K. (2004). "The John Jones Show": How one teacher facilitated self-determined transition planning for a young man with autism. *Focus on Autism and Other Developmental Disabilities, 19*, 177–188.

Hendricks, D., & Wehman, P. (2009). Transition from school to adulthood for young with autism spectrum disorders. *Focus on Autism and Other Developmental Disabilities, 24*, 77–88.

Henry, S. A., & Myles, B. S. (2007) *The Comprehensive Autism Planning Systems (CAPS) for individuals with Asperger Syndrome, autism, and related disabilities. Integrating best practices throughout the student's day.* Shawnee Mission, KS: Autism Asperger Publishing Company.

Higbee, T. S., Carr, J. E., & Patel, M. R. (2002). The effects of interpolated reinforcement on resistance to extinction in children diagnosed with autism: A preliminary investigation. *Research in Developmental Disabilities, 23*, 61–78.

Hughes, J. R. (2008). A review of recent reports on autism: 1000 studies published in 2007. *Epilepsy and Behavior, 13*, 425–437.

Jobe, L. E., & White, S. W. (2007). Loneliness, social relationships and a broader phenotype in college students. *Personality and Individual Differences, 42*, 1479–1489.

Kay, S., Harchik, A. E., & Luiselli, J. K. (2006). Elimination of drooling by an adolescent student with autism attending public high school. *Journal of Positive Behavior Interventions, 8*, 24–28.

Koegel, R. L., Koegel, L K., & Carter, C. M. (1998). Pivotal responses and the natural language teaching paradigm. *Seminars in Speech and Language, 19*(4), 355–371.

Koegel, R. L., O'Dell, M., & Dunlap, G. (1988). Producing speech use in nonverbal autistic children by reinforcing attempts. *Journal of Autism and Developmental Disorders, 18*, 525–538.

Macefield, V. G. (2009). Developments in autonomic research: A review of the latest literature. *Clinical and Autonomic Research, 19*, 133–136.

Madaus, J., & Shaw, S. F. (Eds.). (2007). Transition assessment: Special issue. *Assessment for Effective Intervention, 32*.

Mesibov, G., Thomas, J. B., Chapman, S. M., & Schopler, E. (2007). *TEACCH Transition Assessment Profile – Second Edition.* Austin, TX: PRO-ED.

Miner, C., & Bates, P. (1997). The effect of person-centered planning activities on the IEP/transition planning process. *Education and Training in Mental Retardation and Developmental Disabilities, 32*, 105–112.

Myles, B. S., Grossman, B. G., Aspy, R., & Henry, S. A. (2009). Planning a comprehensive program for young children with Autism Spectrum Disorders. *International Journal of Early Childhood Special Education, 2*, 164–180.

Myles, B. S., Hagiwara, T., Dunn, W., Rinner, L., Reese, M., Huggins, A. et al. (2004). Sensory issues in children with Asperger syndrome and autism. *Education and Training in Developmental Disabilities, 3*, 283–290.

Myles, B. S., Smith, S., & Swanson, T. (2008). Supporting the transition years. In K. Buron & P. Wolfberg (Eds.), *Learners on the autism spectrum: Preparing highly qualified educators* (pp. 255–277). Shawnee Mission, KS: Autism Asperger Publishing Company.

Namerow, L. B., Thomas, P., Bostic, J., Prince, J., & Monuteaux, M. (2003). Use of citalopram in pervasive developmental disorders. *Developmental and Behavioral Pediatrics, 24*, 104–108.

O'Reilly, M., Sigafoos, J., Lancioni, G., Edrisinha, C., & Andrews, A. (2005). An examination of the effects of a classroom activity schedule on levels of self-injury and engagement for a child with severe autism. *Journal of Autism and Developmental Disorders, 35*, 305–311.

Organization for Autism Research. (2006). *Life journey through autism: A guide for transition to adulthood.* Arlington, VA: Author.

Sansosti, F. J., Powell-Smith. K. A., & Kincaid, D. (2004). A research synthesis of social story interventions for children with autism spectrum disorders. *Focus on Autism and Other Developmental Disabilities, 19*, 194–204.

Standifer, S. (2009). *Adult autism and employment; A guide for vocational rehabilitation professionals.* Columbia, MO: University of Missouri.

Steere, D., & Cavaiuolo, D. (in press). Transition planning for positive adult outcomes for individuals with autism spectrum disorders. In P. Gerhardt, (Ed.), *Critical issues for adolescents and adults with autism spectrum disorders.* Clifton, NJ: Routledge, Taylor & Francis.

Steere, D., Gregory, S., Heiny, R., & Butterworth, J. (1995). Lifestyle planning: Considerations for use with people with disabilities. *Rehabilitation Counseling Bulletin, 38*, 207–223.

Steere, D., Rose, E., & Cavaiuolo, D. (2007). *Growing up: Transition to adult life for students with disabilities.* Boston, MA: Allyn & Bacon.

Thomas, S. B., (2000), College students and disability law. *Journal of Special Education, 33*, 248–257.

Wheeler, J. J., Baggett, B. A., Fox, J., & Blevins, L. (2006). Treatment integrity: A review of intervention studies conducted with autism. *Focus on Autism and Other Developmental Disabilities, 21*, 45–55.

Winter-Messiers, M. A., Herr, C. M., Wood, C. E., Brooks, A. P., Gates, M.A.M., Houston, T. L. et al. (2007). How far can Brian ride the Daylight 4449 Express? A strength-based model of Asperger syndrome based on special interest areas. *Focus on Autism and Other Developmental Disabilities, 22*, 67–79.

Zanolli, K, Daggett, J., & Adams, T. (1996). Teaching preschool age autistic children to make spontaneous initiations to peers using priming. *Journal of Autism and Developmental Disorders, 2*, 407–422.

24

Transition Education for Adolescents with Learning Disabilities

Cari Dunn

AUBURN UNIVERSITY

Christina M. Curran

UNIVERSITY OF NORTHERN IOWA

A learning disability (LD) is a neurological disorder that affects an individual's ability to read, write, spell, reason, recall and/or organize information (Lerner & Johns, 2009). It was once believed that an LD was only a school-age problem; however, it is now recognized that an LD persists throughout an individual's life and the way in which it manifests itself varies at different stages of development (Gerber, 1998, Mercer & Pullen, 2005; NJCLD, 1991; Smith, 2004). In adulthood, LD can affect employment, education, personal relationships, and daily living.

Many youth with LD exit secondary schools with the skills, supports, and linkages they need to achieve their post-school goals (Carter, Trainor, Sun, & Owen, 2009; Chambers, Rabren, & Dunn, 2009), yet still a substantial number have significant difficulties attaining their postsecondary goals (Osgood, Foster, Flanagan, & Ruth, 2007). As young adults, these individuals frequently encounter problems related to employment (underemployment, low wages, dissatisfaction, and frequent job changes), participation and success in postsecondary settings, participation in community and leisure activities, and dependency on parents and others (Benz, Lindstrom, & Yovanoff, 2000; Blackorby & Wagner, 1996; Scanlon & Mellard, 2002).

Well-established recommended practices for improving the outcomes of youth with disabilities exist (e.g., early and active student involvement in transition planning and goal setting, paid employment/work experience) (Benz, Lindstrom, Unruh, & Waintrup, 2004; Test, Mazzotti, Mustian, Fowler, Kostering, & Kohler, 2009) along with a legal requirement for transition planning for youth with disabilities beginning at age 16, or younger if appropriate. Yet, transition planning for certain groups of individuals with disabilities has lagged behind that of other groups. Educators more frequently use research-based practices for students with moderate and severe disabilities (O'Connor, 2009). For students with LD, the transition-planning process often is not reflective of research and best practice. Reasons include (a) the assumption individuals with high-incidence disabilities do not need these services, (b) agency services and practices associated with effective planning for those with more significant disabilities are not in place for those with LD, and (c) students with LD are most frequently educated in general education classes in which little attention is devoted to transition (Dowdy, 1996; Lehman, Cobb, & Tochterman, 2001; Sitlington, 2008). This chapter explores the transition-planning needs and practices for students with LD in order to identify those practices that will assist individuals with LD transition successfully to adult roles and responsibilities.

Who are Adolescents with Learning Disabilities?

Learning disabilities are the largest disability category of students receiving special education services. During the fall of 2004, 1,741,127 adolescents ages 12 to 17 were served under the area of LD. Identification of LD is greatest in the age range of 9 to 14 years of age, with sharp decreases during the ages of 16 to 21, concomitant with an increased rate in the school drop-out rate for youth with LD (Lerner & Johns, 2009).

Like all adolescents, youth with LD are in a time of transition. However, middle and high school students with LD are a diverse group with distinctive cognitive, academic, social, and transition-related strengths and needs. Because adolescents with LD are a very heterogeneous group, the degree to which individuals exhibit one or more characteristics discussed below will vary widely across and within individuals (Dunn, 2008; Sabornie & deBettencourt, 2009).

Cognitive Characteristics

Intellectually, adolescents with LD exhibit average-to-above-average intelligence. Cognitively, however, they experience delays with executive function (Sabornie & deBettencourt, 2009). Executive function refers to the mental processes that support conscious control of a host of abilities related to academic, social, and life success. Skills involved in executive function include: inhibition, shift, emotional control, initiation, working memory, planning and organization, and self-regulation (Cooper-Kahn & Dietzel, 2008). Effective use of executive function requires metacognitive skills (i.e., thinking about learning and social tasks) and problem solving. Individuals with LD may have difficulty in the self-regulation of effective strategies in specific academic tasks related to reading, writing, and mathematics. They can display difficulty organizing tasks, developing learning or work plans, multitasking, and engaging in personal reflection and evaluation. They may also exhibit deficits with attention, having difficulty paying attention for extended periods of time and knowing what is most important to pay attention to (Dunn, 2008).

Academic Characteristics

Academic difficulties are a hallmark characteristic of adolescents with LD (Hallahan, Lloyd, Kauffman, Weiss, & Martinez, 2005). The breadth, depth, and complexity of academic content increase during middle and high school, with greater demand for complex literacy skill use, as well as social and academic independence. Literacy skills have profound impacts for adolescents' academic, social, economic, workplace, civic, and postsecondary school satisfaction and success (Alliance for Excellence in Education (AEA), 2009; National Joint Committee on Learning Disabilities (NJCLD), 2008). Reading difficulties are the most common area of academic difficulty for students with LD (Mercer & Pullen, 2005) with 80% of all students with LD experiencing problems in reading (Kavale & Forness, 1995). By high school, many students with LD have only mastered basic reading skills at the 4th–6th-grade level (Deshler, Ellis, & Lenz, 1996), demonstrating difficulties with word recognition, fluency, and comprehension tasks (Bender, 2008; Schloss, Schloss, & Schloss, 2007). In addition, they exhibit challenges in (a) learning, remembering, and understanding vocabulary; (b) selecting and using strategies to successfully address literacy tasks and different text structures; and (c) demonstrating motivation and persistence for reading-related tasks (Deshler & Schumaker, 2006; NJCLD, 2008). As youth leave high school, their literacy needs and challenges continue. Hock (2009) noted that the literacy challenges faced by adults with LD are even greater, with a significant number of adults with LD attending Adult Basic Education (ABE) classes. Many secondary students with LD also continue to demonstrate poor skills in written communication into the adult years (Harris, Graham, & Mason, 2003), exhibiting difficulty with the functional aspects of writing which include note taking, report writing, expository writing, and job-related writing tasks (Sabornie & deBettencourt, 2009).

Academic underachievement in mathematics is prevalent among at-risk adolescents. Goals in mathematics are found in the individualized education programs of 50% of students with LD (Lerner & Johns, 2009). Many secondary students with LD exhibit math performance at a 5th-grade level (Kortering, deBettencourt, & Braziel, 2005), demonstrating difficulties in basic operations, fractions, decimals, percentages, and measurement skills. Other learning characteristics such as memory, math anxiety, literacy, and information processing also impact mathematical learning (Lerner & Johns, 2009). Unfortunately, many students with LD do not experience access to highly valued mathematics content, critical for the workforce and necessary for high school graduation and/or postsecondary education and career training in math and science (National Mathematics Advisory Panel (NMAP), 2008). Only 12% report taking advanced mathematics classes (Blackorby & Wagner, 1996). Students with LD can succeed in advanced-level mathematics courses; however, effective course planning, strategic instruction, and universal design of content are essential for success.

Social-emotional Characteristics and Self-determination

Researchers estimate approximately one third of students with LD have difficulties in social skills (Lerner & Johns, 2009). They may experience problems related to social competence, including difficulties with social perception, social impulsivity, maintaining interpersonal relationships, and engaging in teacher- or adult-pleasing behaviors (Bryan, 1997; Lerner & Johns, 2009), which can lead to social rejection. Adolescents with LD also are at greater risk for depression and loneliness (Margalit & Levin-Alyagon, 1994) and may be more prone to engage in risk-taking behaviors (Bender, 2008). All of these can influence school, social, and vocational opportunities and outcomes.

Many adolescents with LD have experienced a history of academic failure and/or social rejection. They may have an external locus of control, attributing their successes and failures to factors outside of their control. They may also exhibit learned helplessness in approaching academic or life tasks. These behaviors or personal characteristics can influence their skills in self-determination, a set of skills essential for a higher quality of life (Wehmeyer & Field, 2007). Self-determination is defined as "one's ability to define and achieve goals based on a foundation of knowing and valuing oneself" (Field & Hoffman, 1994, p. 164). Skills that include personal awareness and acceptance, goal setting and goal-adjustment, and self-advocacy are all elements of self-determination.

What is the School Environment like for Adolescents with LD?

The educational programming students with disabilities receive and where they receive services have been given considerable attention over the years. These programmatic considerations have the potential to dramatically influence students' post-school outcomes.

Where Students with Learning Disabilities take Classes

The benefits of education in integrated settings have been documented and include access to the general education curriculum, high expectations, increased skill development, and socialization. Transition research literature also highlights the importance of integrated school and community activities to positive outcomes (Blackorby, Knokey, Wagner, Levine, Schiller, & Sumi, 2007; Wagner, Blackorby, Cameto, & Newman, 1993).

Students with LD are increasingly educated in the general education classroom (Newman, 2006). The most recent *29th Annual Report to Congress on the Implementation of the Education With Disabilities Education Improvement Act 2007* indicates that the majority of students with LD spend a significant portion of their day in general education. Specifically, approximately 54% spend less than 21% of their day outside the general education class, whereas only about 11% spend more than 60% of their time outside the general class.

While the benefits of inclusive settings have been acknowledged, inclusion at the secondary level is complex (Mastropieri & Scruggs, 2001; Wagner et al., 1993). The level and pace of the content, expectations for independent study skills, teacher attitudes, and high-stakes testing are important considerations. Simply placing students in general education classes without high expectations and appropriate support for success is counterproductive and could be detrimental. Also, the opportunity to acquire important life skills, such as self-determination and daily living, might not be emphasized in general education classes (Cronin, Lemoine, & Wheeler, 2008).

The Classes Students with Learning Disabilities Take

The secondary education programming in which students with disabilities participate is extremely important. It contributes to skill development essential for achieving postsecondary employment and education goals (McGuire, Madaus, & Currie, 2000) and indirectly influences those outcomes through the impact on students' school performance (Wagner et al., 1993).

A notable trend in course taking from 1987 to 2002 is the significant increase in the number of academic courses taken by students with LD, including those in math, science, social studies, and foreign languages (Newman, 2006; Wagner, Newman, & Cameto, 2004). This may be reflective of practices aimed at better encouraging and preparing students to pursue postsecondary education. Postsecondary education, however, is not a goal for all students with LD. Wagner, Newman, Cameto, Levine, & Marder (2003) noted vocational education plays a major role in the education of many students with LD. Approximately 60% of these students take a vocational class, typically in general education, any given semester (Wagner et al., 2003). The most common services are career skills assessments (50.9%) and career counseling (48%) (Wagner et al., 2003).

Instructional Practices Supporting Students with LD in General Education

Many students with LD require curriculum modifications or accommodations and supports in order to succeed in the general education class. Newman (2006) reports that while 35% of students with LD do not require curriculum modifications, 52% require only slight modifications and 13% require substantial modifications or a specialized curriculum.

Ninety-four percent of students with LD receive some accommodations and supports related to their general education participation (Newman, 2006). The most common accommodations are additional time for tests (76%) or assignments (67%). A substantial number of students with LD also have their progress monitored more closely by a special education teacher (63%) or receive more frequent feedback from the general education teacher (37%). More substantial accommodations, such as modified grading criteria, slower-paced instruction, or having tests modified or read, are received by one third, one fourth, and one fourth of the students with LD, respectively. Interestingly, only an approximate one fourth of the students actually receive direct instruction in skills such as learning strategies or study skills that would increase their independence and success in general education and postsecondary education.

Special Education Classes and Students with Learning Disabilities

While data from the National Longitudinal Transition Study-2 show that students with LD are taking more of their academic classes in the general education setting, there also has been an almost 28% increase of students taking any nonacademic class in a special education class. The greatest part of this increase can be attributed to the increase in taking life skills/study skills in the special education classroom. Oftentimes students with LD will need support and services of some type outside of the general education classroom in order to be successful in the general education setting. The types of supports and services students might need include remediation in basic skills, learning strategies instruction, and study skills instruction. Students with LD might also need to participate in classes designed to address transition skills such as self-determination, employment, social skills, and other important life skills areas since these topics are not typically being addressed in general education classes today (O'Connor, 2009).

What should Programming Look Like to Support Transition?

Transition planning for students with LD is challenging due to the heterogeneity of the population. Programming needs for some will be college-preparatory in general education classes with limited support whereas for others it might be career/technical training and life skills.

Benz et al. (2000) underscored the importance of providing a program that concomitantly focuses services on two goals—school completion and post-school preparation. They stressed that the support needs of youth with disabilities are complex in the transition from school to adult life and must consider "the full range of content related to the adult roles expected of youth when they leave school" (pp. 39–40). For students with LD, the full range of content is potentially vast and a broad array of services is required. A comprehensive transition program for students with LD should include content that will help students succeed in school and prepare them for their postsecondary roles, as well as processes that facilitate appropriate curriculum selection and implementation and postsecondary linkages.

Content Considerations

The decision about what to teach secondary students with LD should center on the skills each student needs to (a) succeed in school and (b) achieve his or her postsecondary goals. As such, there is no one curriculum that will meet the needs of all students with LD. Two major content considerations for those in secondary school are access skills and transition skills. Access skills can be thought of as skills other than the general education curriculum (e.g., study skills, self-determination) that students need in order to be successful in school. Transition skills are those skills that students need to transition to the next environment and to participate as successfully, independently and meaningfully as possible in integrated and community settings.

Developing Access Skills

When considering the diverse characteristics of adolescents with LD and of secondary education environments, it is not surprising that many students with LD have difficulty succeeding in school. Researchers have identified a number of setting demands or factors that interact with individual student characteristics to influence students' success in secondary school environments and curricula (Deshler, Schumaker, Harris, & Graham, 1999). They include organization, test-taking and study skills, social and behavioral skills, and cognitive as well as content literacy skills. An examination of these demands and skills suggests instructional consideration should be given in the areas of self-determination, learning strategies, study skills, survival skills, and basic skills remediation. These skills can be taught by directly embedding them within general education courses, or support personnel can teach these skills in an alternative setting such as a resource room and plan for generalization to other environments.

Self-Determination Skills

Facilitating the development of self-determination is now acknowledged as a best practice in the education of students with disabilities (Wehmeyer, 2007). Field (2008) noted that students with LD may face unique barriers to achieving self-determination. One such barrier relates to the fact that learning disabilities are hidden, and because having a disability is often viewed as stigmatizing in our society, many adolescents do not want to acknowledge that they have one or even understand the implications of their disability. This understanding and acceptance are critical to the development of self-determination skills. Field also noted that many of the skills that are linked to self-determination, such as decision making, problem solving, self-advocacy, and goal setting, are the very skills that are challenging for students with LD.

The lack of such skills observed in many students with LD and their relationship to positive adult outcomes highlights the need to consider self-determination in transition planning. A multipronged approach to the development of skills in this area should be employed. In addition to implementing curricula that address the development of self-determination skills across grade levels, teachers should use instructional strategies and environmental considerations, such as modeling, choice making, cooperative learning, opportunities for choice, coaching, attribution retraining, and appropriate behavioral strategies, to encourage self-determination (Field, 2008).

Learning Strategies

Students with LD are often described as inactive learners. They do not know how to effectively and actively approach learning tasks, and may remain on the periphery of academic and social tasks (Smith, 2004). "Learning strategy instruction is instruction in how to learn and perform in academic environments such that positive outcomes result" (Schumaker, 2009, p.3). Researchers at the University of Kansas Center for Research on Learning have developed the Learning Strategies Curriculum (LSC) throughout the last thirty years and there is much evidence to support their effectiveness with students with LD (Schumaker, 2009). Strategies in the LSC address three academic areas: acquiring information (e.g., reading), storing information (e.g., studying for tests), and expressing knowledge (e.g., completing assignments). Other researchers have developed strategies in areas such as writing (Harris & Graham, 1996), math (Miller & Mercer, 1991), and community-building skills.

Study Skills

Study skills are techniques and devices that help students acquire, remember, and demonstrate or express knowledge (Mercer & Mercer, 2005). Although study skills are deemed important, direct instruction in these skills is rarely provided (Mercer & Mercer, 2005). Important study skills to consider are reading, listening, time management, note taking, reports and oral presentations, graphic aids, test-taking, and reference use.

Survival Skills

Survival skills are those skills that are needed for successful functioning in high school (Lerner & Johns, 2009; Zigmond, 1990). Critical considerations for survival skills include (a) helping students stay out of trouble, and (b) assisting students in acquiring behaviors that result in positive perceptions by teachers and other adults. Mentors, graduation coaches, and service learning are possible strategies for helping students resist high-risk behaviors. Instruction in social skills can also help students acquire behavior that is more productive. Social skills can be classified along several dimensions including: peer relations (e.g., offering assistance, empathy), self-management (e.g., self-control, adhering to rules), academic (e.g., independent completion of work, task orientation), compliance skills (e.g., cooperating with others, following directions), and assertion (e.g., starting a conversation) (Caldarella & Merrell, 1997).

Academic Remediation

Basic literacy skills are essential to success in general education, postsecondary education, and independence in the community. As noted, many students with LD experience difficulties in literacy skills. Until recently, it was often assumed that secondary students with LD would not benefit from continued instruction in basic skills, so many middle and high school programs did not offer such instruction. Over the years evidence has accumulated that supports the practice of providing instruction in basic skills to secondary students with LD. For example, in a meta-analysis of interventions for adolescent struggling readers, Scammacca et al. (2007) concluded: "Adolescence is not too late to intervene, and older students who participate in [well-designed and effectively delivered] interventions can benefit" (p. 12). There are similar findings for writing (see Mason and Graham, 2008) and math (see Gersten, Chard, Jayanthi, Baker, Morphy, & Flojo, 2008).

Teaching Transition Skills

Increased standards and accountability for academic skills, coupled with the increased inclusion of students with LD in general education, have made it challenging to incorporate transition education into students' course of study (Benz et al., 2000; Dunn, 2008; O'Connor, 2009). Nonetheless, consideration should be given to employment, postsecondary education and training, social and emotional demands, and daily living skills.

Preparing for Employment

As Michaels (2008) wrote, one of the cornerstones of adulthood is productive work, which has the potential to positively or negatively influence various quality-of-life dimensions. Many students with LD will encounter difficulties related to employment for a number of reasons, including limited career maturity (Rosenthal, 1989), limited regular job preparation and lack of understanding of how their disability affects communication, daily life, and employment (Briel & Wehman, 2005). Kochar-Bryant and Greene (2009) suggested that students with LD have a greater need for transition services addressing career assessment, counseling, and employment than their peers without disabilities. As such, students with LD, even those planning on attending postsecondary education, need to be provided with numerous opportunities for career exploration, which will help them set realistic goals about which occupations to pursue (Getzel, Gugerty, McManus, 2006). Students should also have vocational and career assessment and counseling that assists them to (a) develop a better understanding of their work values, (b) assess their personal strengths and weaknesses, (c) cultivate realistic and informed career aspirations, and (d) expand their knowledge about the world of work (Michaels & Barr, 2002; Pierangelo & Giuliani, 2004).

Students who want to work after graduation will also need to participate in career/technical training (Benz et al., 2000) and work experiences while in high school (Benz et al., 2000; Rabren, Dunn, & Chambers, 2002). Many students with LD will also need training in related job skills such as job-seeking skills (e.g., writing résumés, locating jobs, filling out applications, and interviewing skills) and job-related academic skills and social skills (Elksnin & Elksnin, 1998).

Preparing for Postsecondary Education and Training

In today's economy a college education is increasingly important. Even though more students with LD are enrolling in postsecondary education, the number is comparatively low when compared to students without disabilities (Murray, Goldstein, Nourse, & Edgar, 2000). Students with LD also tend to take longer to complete their degrees and have a lower completion rate than their peers. Common difficulties faced by college students with LD include being unprepared for responsibilities, learning time management skills, making new friends, missing academic support from their parents, obtaining support of parents, telling others of disability, failing classes, and being realistic about how the disability affects goals and ambitions (Eaton & Coull, 1997). Finally, many students may need to take remedial coursework that does not count toward degree credit or core classes.

Several important curricular considerations for students planning to pursue postsecondary education and training have emerged. First, teachers and parents need to ensure that youth with LD understand what learning disabilities are and understand their own LD as it relates to needed supports and services (Brinkerhoff, 2008). Youth with LD also need to (a) understand changes in laws that will occur as they exit school (i.e., ADA and Section 504), (b) learn to advocate for their needs in postsecondary settings, and (c) know how to use compensatory strategies and accommodations related to their needs (Brinkerhoff, 2008).

Curriculum choices while in high school are also important. If students are to be adequately prepared for the rigor of postsecondary education, they must access and participate in college preparation coursework to acquire the content and concepts necessary for college success (Brinkerhoff, 2008; McGuire et al., 2000). Students will also need to identify and learn how to effectively use assistive technology that will enable them to access information and express themselves at levels commensurate with their intelligence in postsecondary education settings (Day & Edwards, 1996). Finally, teachers will want to assist students in obtaining a comprehensive psychoeducational evaluation in high school that will meet postsecondary institutions' requirements and facilitate linkages with postsecondary education services.

Preparing for Social and Emotional Demands

Social and emotional functioning is a critical component of an individual's quality of life (Wehman, 2006). Reiff and Gerber (1994) suggested that "the residual effects of learning disabilities, from frustration about schooling to a lack of satisfaction in one or a number of areas of adulthood, sometimes reverberate in the emotional sphere" (p. 72). Many adults with LD report they have problems dealing with frustration, controlling their temper, shyness, loneliness, dependence, and depression (Smith, 2004). Therefore, if needed, social and emotional skill development should be an important component of the secondary curriculum to assist students in understanding their disability and in developing positive coping and compensatory strategies.

Preparing for Demands of Daily Living

Reiff and Gerber (1994) stated, "For adults with learning disabilities, activities of day-to-day living offer concrete evidence of the persistence of learning disabilities through the lifespan" (p. 78). The challenges adults with LD faced in high school are evidenced in the challenges they encounter with everyday adult activities. For example, problems in reading and spelling affect daily activities, such as reading important documents and writing checks. Problems in math and organization make it hard to keep up with bills. Problems with depth perception can lead to difficulties in driving. Directionality problems result in getting lost frequently and problems in organization can affect many areas of daily life.

Unfortunately, many professionals still assume that individuals with LD do not need help in acquiring such life skills. Cronin et al. (2008), however, advocate reexamining curriculum and instruction of secondary programs for students with LD and tying content standards to adult domains (e.g., education/employment domain—writing a letter of application).

Process Considerations

In addition to content factors, there are also important considerations related to the processes that facilitate appropriate curriculum selection and implementation and linkages of appropriate people and programs. Such considerations include processes related to supporting students in the general education curriculum; ensuring person-centered, student-directed planning; collaborating with professionals and families; and establishing linkages with postsecondary service providers.

Supporting Students in General Education Classes

Many students with LD will need assistance meeting the demands in general education classes as well as the requirements for graduation (Benz et al., 2000). Personnel and structures to provide individualized tutoring, homework support, and encouragement to attend and succeed in school are important program considerations. School-wide tutoring and mentoring programs and graduation coaches can address these needs. In addition to providing individual supports to help students meet their immediate needs in general education, instruction (e.g., learning strategies) to equip them with skills to become more independent learners must also be provided.

Implementing Person-Centered, Student-Directed Transition Planning

Active student and family involvement in transition planning and skill development are recognized as important transition practices (Bassett & Li, 2008; Morningstar, Wehmeyer, & Dove, 2008); however, these are not easily achieved. These practices, nevertheless, will result in individualized services, ranging from employment preparation and independent living to postsecondary education preparation, consistent with the unique needs and goals of the student and his or her family.

School-based strategies for supporting student involvement in transition-related activities and planning include student-led conferences and student-centered planning sessions (e.g., Making Action Plans (MAPs), and student-directed Individualized Education Programs (IEPs) (Bassett & Li, 2008). Community-based approaches involve career explorations, service learning, involvement in work-study experiences, and connecting activities (e.g., community advisory groups, job fairs, workshops, and institutes). Additional strategies for increasing parent and family involvement include encouraging involvement of extended family members;

educating parents about their child's skills and abilities, work and community living options, and adult service agencies; providing increased professional support; and making available parent support programs (Morningstar et al., 2008; Trainor, 2005).

Collaborating

Successful transition planning, programs, and outcomes for youth with LD necessitate the effective communication and collaboration of many individuals: families and parents, special and general educators, guidance counselors, transition specialists, administrators, agency providers, postsecondary vocational and education personnel, and most importantly students themselves. Deshler & Schumaker (2006) noted that:

> The focus on transition planning for students with disabilities has substantively shifted in recent years. The shift has been from a specialized, professionally directed approach that is centered on the interaction of special education staff, vocational providers, and students to an inclusive student-centered approach that is supported through collaborative partnerships among students, special education and general education staff, families, employers, and community organizations.

(p. 264)

Collaborative partnerships involve the intentional efforts of middle and high school professionals to build partnerships, provide appropriate and challenging academic and career- and college-ready curriculum, implement effective models of instructional delivery, and deliver individualized transition supports that meet the needs of adolescents with LD. Collaborative teaming improves services to all students and is an ongoing process of shared planning, goals, decision making, and resources (Knackendoffel, 2007). Several models of collaboration in content delivery (e.g., team teaching, co-teaching) have been forwarded as effective practices. Academic and vocational content, leadership and service opportunities, and individualized learning and transition support available during the middle and high school years should be clearly articulated so comprehensive and collaborative planning can begin in middle school.

Linking Students and their Families with Adult Services

A final critical consideration in secondary transition planning for students with LD includes linkages with adult services and agencies. The manner in which services are obtained and provided at the postsecondary level is very different from the process used during secondary school. Often students with LD and their families do not know what services are available, the eligibility requirements for those services, or how to access them. This can result in a gap in or lack of services at a critical time in the lives of youth with LD.

For students with LD, vocational rehabilitation and postsecondary education and training linkages are highly relevant (Mellard & Lancaster, 2003). Vocational Rehabilitation (VR), funded by federal and state money, is a primary agency in helping individuals with disabilities find employment. Services provided by VR include vocational assessment, development of an Individualized Plan for Employment, support for educational services, acquisition of assistive technology, restoration services such as note takers and readers, and independent living services.

For students with LD, however, accessing VR services can be challenging because the VR definition of disability is different from the Individuals with Disabilities Education Improvement Act of 2004 (IDEA) one, and eligibility for services requires documentation that the LD results in a substantial impediment to employment (Mellard & Lancaster, 2003). Another important linkage is postsecondary education, including community and technical schools (Mellard & Lancaster, 2003). The types of services provided include development of academic, vocational, and technical skills through degree and non-degree programs; career assessment and counseling; and job placement.

Other linkages to consider for students with LD include adult education (e.g., General Educational Development Test (GED) and job-readiness programs) and centers for independent living (CILS) (advocacy training, independent skills development) (Mellard & Lancaster, 2003). Mellard and Lancaster recommended that in order to help students access these potentially important services, teachers, students, and parents should take the time to learn about the different systems and their requirements.

Current Issues Affecting the Transition Planning for Adolescents with LD

National, state, and local efforts have centered on the reform of traditional high school practices given unfavorable data on adolescent literacy, academic achievement, and drop-out rates (Clarke, 2008). Advocates and policy-makers are concerned that young adults are not adequately prepared to meet the demands needed for success in today's complex, global 21st century world. Resulting programmatic and policy initiatives have bearing on the secondary and transition needs of adolescents with LD (Deshler, Schumaker, Bui, & Vernon, 2006).

The high school drop-out rate has been described as an epidemic (Thomas & Date, 2006) with significant negative consequences including decreased employment and earnings potential, increased public assistance and dependency, heightened risk for incarceration, and increased health care costs (Alliance for Excellence in Education (AEE), 2008). The drop-out rate for adolescents with LD (28.3%) continues to signal a need for improved high school programs and supports (U.S. Department of Education, 2010). Recent educational reforms (e.g., increased performance standards, high stakes assessments for high school exit, increasing number and types of credits required for graduation), while important, have the potential to increase the drop-out rate for students with LD (National Council on Disability, 2004). Moreover, varying diploma options for high school graduation (e.g., standard diploma, IEP/special education diploma, and occupational diplomas) are available with potential positive and negative consequences for access to desirable post-school options (Burdette, 2007). Therefore, educators must ensure that programs and services are in place to assist students with LD in meeting standards leading to a valued diploma option that aligns with their post-school goals. The highest option appropriate for a student should be selected to maximize the postsecondary options available.

Simultaneously high school reform efforts centered on college and career readiness have sparked initiatives such as career academies, 21st century skills, and dual enrollment classes (Partnership for 21st Century Skills, 2003; Quint, 2006). Students with LD can greatly benefit from these programs. Special and general educators, including career and technology education professionals, must collaborate in the design and delivery of these initiatives and include relevant services in school-wide and transition-supported curricula.

Another school-wide system of support, response-to-intervention (RTI), has the potential to address students' academic and behavioral challenges impeding achievement at their earliest presence. RTI is an integrated, collaborative school-wide process of decision making providing preventive and increasingly intensive academic and behavioral interventions to improve school success and outcomes for struggling students (Duffy, 2007; Reschly & Wood-Garnett, 2009). IDEA 2004 specifies that RTI can be used as part of a comprehensive evaluation process to determine eligibility for special education services in the area of specific learning disabilities. The process of using RTI data for LD identification at the secondary level is not well known (Mastropieri & Scruggs, 2005) and the use of RTI data in developing secondary IEPs and transition plans is yet uncharted. While potentially promising, ongoing research is needed in order to inform practice impacting the academic and transition needs of youth with LD.

Two final issues center around post-school services and needs. The first is a documentation disconnect for postsecondary services. A major factor that influences successful transition from secondary to postsecondary education and services is having appropriate documentation of disability to access services (NJCLD, 2007). However, documentation compiled during secondary school often fails to meet the requirements of postsecondary institutions or rehabilitation service providers, who require specific documentation for eligibility determination, accommodations, and functional limitations and their impact on employment. Assessment changes brought on by education reform have a potential to widen the documentation disconnect, requiring thoughtful transition practices to ensure students and families have the information, resources, and documentation needed to access postsecondary services and supports.

Finally, in accessing postsecondary vocational rehabilitation services, students with LD are at risk of falling through the cracks to attain services because of an order of selection decision-making framework utilized by state vocational rehabilitation agencies (Bellini & Royce-Davis, 1999). Section 101 (a) (5) (A) of the Rehabilitation Act as amended indicates that if a vocational rehabilitation agency is unable to provide services to all eligible individuals who apply for services, an order of selection is required. Priority for services is afforded to those with the most significant disabilities. Determining the significance of LD is difficult and there exists a misconception that all learning disabilities are mild (U.S. State Education Department, 2002). With increasing fiscal challenges in state funding, the ability of students with LD to actualize transition needs for vocational rehabilitation may become increasingly challenging.

Summary and Recommendations

Secondary students with LD are at a critical juncture in their development and school experiences as they balance increased demands for autonomy and individualism, unique cognitive, learning and social needs, and increasing demands for challenging academic standards and 21st century skills. Given recent education reform and legislation, general and special education professionals are poised to provide a more comprehensive, collaborative school program that transfuses transition-sensitive considerations and skills across core, career and technical, and individualized curricula to both impact improved school and post-school outcomes for youth with LD and strengthen transition planning and programs. A list of selected recommendations for transition programming for secondary students with LD is provided in Table 24.1.

Table 24.1 Selected recommendations for transition considerations for students with LD

1 General and special educators must that ensure coordinated, ongoing curricular planning for students with LD begin as early as middle school (Repetto, Webb, Neubert, & Curran, 2006). Curricular plans should be updated annually given rapidly changing curricular options.

2 Valued postsecondary career options must be available for students with LD. STEM curriculum access and career exploration must be well planned throughout middle and high school. (Access STEM, 2010; AAAS, 2001.)

3 The impact of curricular choices on high school and postsecondary school options should be addressed in annual IEP conferences. Supplemental education programs, if needed to support attainment of challenging academic and/or career and college ready standards, should be considered annually.

4 Successful transition planning must include active involvement of content and career and technical education teachers. Special education professionals should broaden understanding of the transition needs of students with LD and collaborate with school personnel in developing more universal school-wide systems of transition supports, linking academic and transition planning instruction (Thoma et al., 2009).

5 When RTI is implemented in secondary schools, models should include transition considerations throughout all tiers of intervention. Increased knowledge and skills in drop-out prevention, career and college ready skills, and collaborative transition planning across general education and special education will be needed (Duffy, 2007).

6 Policy-makers, educators, families, and students should consider the implications of alternative diploma options for students with LD with regard to: (a) whether receiving something other than a standard high school diploma limits access to future postsecondary education, training, and/or employment; and (b) whether once a student receives a standard diploma, the student is no longer entitled to special education (Burdette, 2007).

7 IDEA 2004's Summary of Performance (SOP) provision should be utilized as a vehicle for summarizing students' academic achievement and functional performance as they relate to postsecondary service eligibility requirements (NJCLD, 2007).

8 Transition plans should address information required for the documentation of an LD for postsecondary services. Discrepancies in requirements should be outlined and potential solutions generated. Responsibilities and timelines should be identified beginning with the IEP/ITP and SOP of the anticipated final comprehensive evaluation during the secondary school years.

9 School professionals, families, and students must become knowledgeable about vocational VR services to knowledgably prepare for the transition process (Michaels, 2008). Professionals must ensure that students with LD are able to evaluate their abilities and limitations accurately so that they can articulate the impact of their LD on employment. Students must be able to describe and have some documentation of their functional limitations in communication, interpersonal skills, cognition, mobility, self-care, self-direction, work tolerance or work skills in such a way that shows they are an impediment to an employment outcome.

References

AccessSTEM (2010). The Alliance for Students with Disabilities in Science Technology Engineering, and Mathematics. The University of Washington, DO-IT. Retrieved from http://www.washington.edu/doit/Stem

Alliance for Excellence in Education (AEE) (2009). *Adolescent literacy*. Fact Sheet. Washington, DC. Retrieved from http://www.all4ed.org/files/AdolescentLiteracyFactSheet.pdf

Alliance for Excellent Education (AEA) (2008). Facts for education advocates: The economic impact of education. Fact Sheet. Washington, DC: Author. Retrieved from http://www.mdrc.org/publications/428/full.pdf

American Association for the Advancement of Science (2001). *In pursuit of a diverse science, technology, engineering, and mathematics workforce*. Washington, DC: Author.

Bassett, D., & Li, J. (2008). Student involvement in transition-related activities. In G. Blalock, J. Patton, P. Kohler, & D. Bassett (Eds.), *Transition and students with learning disabilities: Facilitating the movement from school to adult life* (2nd ed.) (pp. 51–78). Austin, TX: Hammill Institute on Disabilities.

Bellini, J. & Royce-Davis, J. (1999). Order of selection in vocational rehabilitation: Implications for the transition from school to adult outcomes for youths with learning disabilities. *Work: A Journal of Prevention, Assessment and Rehabilitation, 13* (1), 3–11.

Bender, W. N. (2008) *Learning disabilities: Characteristics, identification, and teaching strategies* (6th ed.). Upper Saddle River, NJ: Merrill.

Benz, M. R., Lindstrom, L. & Yovanoff, P. (2000). Improving graduation and employment outcomes of students with disabilities: Predictive factors and student perspectives. *Exceptional Children, 66,* 509–529.

Benz, M., Lindstrom, L., Unruh, D., & Waintrup, M. (2004). Sustaining secondary and transition programs in local schools. *Remedial and Special Education, 25*, 39–50.

Blackorby, J., Knokey, A., Wagner, M., Levine, P., Schiller, E., Sumi, C. (2007). What makes a difference? Influences on outcomes for students with disabilities. Retrieved from http://www.seels. net/info_reports/what_makes_difference.htm

Blackorby, J., & Wagner, M. (1996). Longitudinal post-school outcomes for youth with disabilities: Findings from the National Longitudinal Transition Study. *Exceptional Children, 62*, 399–413.

Briel, L, & Wehman, P. (2005). Career planning and placement. In E. Getzel & P. Wehman (Eds.). *Going to college: Expanding opportunities for people with disabilities* (pp. 291–305). Baltimore, MD: Paul H. Brookes Publishing Co.

Brinkerhoff, L. (2008). Making the transition to higher education: Opportunities for student empowerment. In G. Blalock, J. Patton, P. Kohler, and D. Bassett (Eds.). *Transition and students with learning disabilities: Facilitating the movement from school to adult life* (2nd ed.) (pp. 273–305). Austin, TX: Hammill Institute on Disabilities.

Bryan, T. (1997). Assessing personal and social status of students with learning disabilities. *Learning Disabilities Research and Practice, 12*, 63–76.

Burdette, P. (October 2007). *Diploma options for students with disabilities: Synthesis of the NCEO Document.* Alexandria, VA; Project Forum at the National Association of State Directors of Special Education. Retrievedfromhttp://www.projectforum.org/docs/DiplomaOptionsforSWD-SynthesisoftheNCDO Document.pdf

Caldarella, P., & Merrell, K. (1997). Common dimensions of social skills of children and adolescents: A taxonomy of positive social behaviors. *School Psychology Review, 26*, 265–279.

Carter, E., Trainor, A., Sun, Y., & Owens, L. (2009). Assessing the transition-related strengths and needs of adolescents with high-incidence disabilities. *Exceptional Children, 76*, 74–94.

Chambers, D., Rabren, K., & Dunn, C. (2009). A comparison of transition from high school to adult life of students with and without disabilities. *Career Development of Exceptional Individuals, 32* (1), 42–52.

Clarke, S. (2008). *Effective high school reform:* Alexandria, VA: Educational Research Service.

Cooper-Kahn, J., & Dietzel, L. (2008). *What is executive functioning?* Retrieved from http://www. ldonline.org/article/What_Is_Executive_Functioning%3F

Cronin, M., Lemoine, M., & Wheeler, S. (2008). Developing life skills. In G. Blalock, J. Patton, P. Kohler, and D. Bassett (Eds.). *Transition and students with learning disabilities: Facilitating the movement from school to adult life* (2nd ed.) (pp. 203–224). Austin, TX: Hammill Institute on Disabilities.

Day, S. & Edwards, B. (1996). Assistive technology for post-secondary students with learning disabilities. *Journal of Learning Disabilities, 29* (5), 486–492.

Deshler, D., Ellis, E., & Lenz, B. (1996). *Teaching adolescents with learning disabilities.* Denver, CO: Love.

Deshler, D. & Schumaker, J. (2006) *Teaching adolescents with disabilities; Accessing the general education curriculum.* Thousand Oaks, CA: Corwin Press.

Deshler, D., Schumaker, J., Harris, K.R., & Graham, S. (Eds.). (1999). *Advances in teaching and learning: Teaching every adolescent every day* (Vol. 3). Cambridge, MA: Brookline Books.

Deshler, D., Schumaker, J., Bui, Y., & Vernon, S. (2006). High schools and adolescents with disabilities: Challenges at every turn. In D.D. Deshler & J.B. Schumaker (Eds.), *Teaching adolescents with disabilities: Accessing the general education curriculum* (pp. 1–34). Thousand Oaks, CA: Corwin Press.

Dowdy, C. (1996). Vocational rehabilitation and special education: Partners in transition for individuals with learning disabilities. *Journal of Learning Disabilities, 29* (2), 137–147.

Duffy, H. (2007). *Meeting the needs of significantly struggling learners in high school: A look at approaches to tiered intervention.* Washington, DC: National High School Center. Retrieved from http://www.better-highschools.org/docs/NHSC_RTIBrief_08-02-07

Dunn, C. (2008). Transition planning for individuals with learning disabilities: A status report. In G. Blalock, J. Patton, P. Kohler, and D. Bassett (Eds.). *Transition and students with learning disabilities: Facilitating the movement from school to adult life* (2nd ed.) (pp. 17–49). Austin, TX: Hammill Institute on Disabilities.

Eaton, H. & Coull, L. (1997). *Transitions videos: Self-Advocacy and self-determination videos for students with learning disabilities, ADD/ADHD.* Vancouver, BC; Eaton Coull Learning Group, Ltd. Publishing.

Elksnin, N., & Elksnin, L. (1998). *Teaching occupational social skills.* Austin, TX: PRO-ED.

Field, S., (2008). Self-determination instructional strategies for youth with learning disabilities. In G. Blalock, J. Patton, P. Kohler, and D. Bassett (Eds.). *Transition and students with learning disabilities: Facilitating the movement from school to adult life* (2nd ed.) (pp. 167–201). Austin, TX: Hammill Institute on Disabilities.

Field, S., & Hoffman, A. (1994). Development of a model for self-determination. *Career Development for Exceptional Individuals, 17,* 159–169.

Gerber, P. J. (1998). Characteristics of adults with specific learning disabilities. In B. K. Lenz, N.A. Sturomski, & M. A. Corely (Eds,), *Serving adults with learning disabilities: Implications for effective practice.* Retrieved from http://www.ldonline.org/ld_indepth/adult/characteristics.html

Gersten, R., Chard, D., Jayanthi, M., Baker, S., Morphy, P., et al. (2008). *Math instruction for students with learning disabilities or difficulties learning math: A synthesis of the intervention research.* Portsmouth, NH: RMC Research Corporation, Center on Instruction.

Getzel, E., Gugerty, J., & McManus, S. (2006). Applications for youth with learning disabilities (pp. 475–504). In P. Wehman (Ed.) *Life Beyond the classroom: Transition strategies for young people with disabilities* (4th ed.). Baltimore, MD: Paul H. Brookes.

Hallahan, D., Lloyd, J., Kauffman, J., Weiss, M., & Martinez, E. (2005). *Learning disabilities: Foundations, characteristics, and effective teaching* (3rd ed.). Upper Saddle River, NJ: Merrill.

Harris, K.R., & Graham, S. (1996). *Making the writing process work: Strategies for composition and self-regulation.* Cambridge, MA: Brookline Books.

Harris, K.R., Graham, S., & Mason, L.H. (2003). Self-regulated strategy development in the classroom: Part of a balanced approach to writing instruction for students with disabilities. *Focus on Exceptional Children, 35,* 1–16.

Hock, M. (2009, June). Teaching methods: Instructional methods and arrangements effective for adults with learning disabilities. In J. M. Taymans (Ed.), *Learning to achieve: A review of the research literature on serving adults with learning disabilities* (pp. 193–208). National Institute for Literacy. Washington, DC.

Individuals with Disabilities Education Improvement Act of 2004 (IDEA), Pub. L. No. 108–446 104 Stat. 1142 (2004).

Kavale, K. & Forness, S. (1995). *The nature of learning disabilities: Critical elements of Diagnosis and classification.* Mahwah, NJ: Lawrence Erlbaum.

Knackendoffel, E. (2007). Collaborative teaming in the secondary school. *Focus on Exceptional Children, 40*(4), 1–20.

Kochar-Bryant, C, & Greene, G. (2009). *Pathways to successful transition for youth with learning disabilities.* Pearson: Columbus, OH.

Kortering, L. deBettencourt, L., & Braziel, P. (2005). Improving performance in high school algebra: What students with learning disabilities are saying. *Learning Disability Quarterly, 28*(3), 191–203.

Lehman, J., Cobb, B., & Tochterman, S. (2001). Exploring the relationship between transition and educational reform initiatives. *Career Development for Exceptional Individuals, 24*(2), 185–197.

Lerner, J. & Johns, B. (2009). *Learning disabilities and related mild disabilities: Characteristics, teaching strategies, and new directions* (11th ed.). Boston, MA: Houghton Mifflin.

Margalit, M., & Levin-Alyagon, M. (1994). Learning disability subtyping, loneliness, and classroom adjustment. *Learning Disability Quarterly, 17,* 297–310.

Mason, L., & Graham, S. (2008). Writing instruction for adolescents with LD: Programs of intervention research. *Learning Disabilities Research and Practice, 23*(2), 103–112.

Mastropieri, M., & Scruggs, T. (2001). Promoting inclusion in secondary classrooms. *Learning Disabilities Quarterly, 24,* 265–274.

Mastropieri, M., & Scruggs, T. (2005). Feasibility and consequences of response to intervention: Examination of the issues and scientific evidence as a model for the identification of individuals with learning disabilities. *Journal of Learning Disabilities, 38,* 525–531.

McGuire, J., Madaus, J., & Currie, J. (2000, October 20). *Secondary/post-secondary transition issues: Shall the twain ever meet?* Paper presented at the 22nd International CLD Conference on Learning Disabilities, Austin, TX.

Mellard, D., & Lancaster, P. (2003). Incorporating adult community services for students' transition planning. *Remedial and Special Education, 24*(6), 359–368.

Mercer, C., & Mercer, A. (2005). *Teaching students with learning problems* (7th ed.). Columbus, OH: Pearson/Merrill Prentice Hall.

Mercer, C., & Pullen, P. (2005). *Students with learning disabilities* (6th ed.). Columbus, OH: Pearson/Merrill Prentice Hall.

Michaels, C. (2008). Competency and transition to employment: Implications for students with learning disabilities. In G. Blalock, J. Patton, P. Kohler, and D. Bassett (Eds.). *Transition and students with learning disabilities: Facilitating the movement from school to adult life* (2nd ed.) (pp. 245–272). Austin, TX: Hammill Institute on Disabilities.

Michaels, C. & Barr, V. (2002). Best practices in career development programs for post-secondary students with learning disabilities: A ten-year follow-up. *Career Planning and Adult Development Journal, 18*(1), 61–79.

Miller, S., & Mercer, C. (1991). *Addition facts 0 to 9*. Lawrence, KS: Edge Enterprises.

Morningstar, M., Wehmeyer, M., & Dove, C. (2008). Role of families in enhancing transition outcomes for youth with learning disabilities. In G. Blalock, J. Patton, P. Kohler, and D. Bassett (Eds.). *Transition and students with learning disabilities: Facilitating the movement from school to adult life* (2nd ed.) (pp. 79–103). Austin, TX: Hammill Institute on Disabilities.

Murray, C., Goldstein, D. E., Nourse, S., & Edgar, E. (2000). The postsecondary school attendance and completion rates of high school graduates with learning disabilities. *Learning Disabilities Research & Practice, 15*(3), 119–127.

National Council on Disability (2004). *Improving educational outcomes for students with disabilities*. Washington, DC: Retrieved from http://www.ncd.gov/newsroom/publications/2004/pdf/educationoutcomes.pdf

National Joint Committee on Learning Disabilities (NJCLD). (1991). Learning disabilities: Issues on definition. *Asha, 33*, (Suppl. 5), 18–20.

National Joint Committee on Learning Disabilities (NJCLD). (2007). *The documentation disconnect for students with learning disabilities: Improving access to post-secondary disability services*. Retrieved from http://www.ldonline.org/about/partners/njcld

National Joint Committee on Learning Disabilities (NJCLD). (2008, June). *Adolescent literacy and older students with learning disabilities*. Retrieved from http://www.ldonline.org/njcld

National Mathematics Advisory Panel (NMAP). (2008). *Foundations for success: The final report of the National Mathematics Advisory Panel*. Retrieved from http://www2.ed.gov/about/bdscomm/list/mathpanel/report/final-report.pdf

Newman, L. (2006, July). *Facts from NLTS-2: General education participation and academic performance of students with learning disabilities*. Menlo Park, CA: SRI International. Retrieved from http://www.nlts2.org/fact_sheets/nlts2_fact_sheet_2006_07.pdf

O'Connor, M.P. (2009). Service works! Promoting transition success for students with disabilities through participation in service-learning. *Teaching Exceptional Children, 41*(6), 12–17.

Osgood, W., Foster, M., Flanagan, C., & Ruth, G. (2007). *On your own without a net: The transition to adulthood for vulnerable populations*. Chicago, IL: University of Chicago Press.

Partnership for 21st Century Skills (2003). *Learning for the 21st century: A report and mile guide for 21st century skills*. Washington, DC: Author.

Pierangelo, R. & Giuliani, G. (2004). Transition services in special education: A practical approach. Boston, MA: Allyn & Bacon.

Quint, J. (2006). *Meeting five critical challenges of high school reform: Lessons from research on three reform models*. New York: MDRC. Retrieved from http://www.mdrc.org/publications/428/full.pdf

Rabren, K., Dunn, C., & Chambers, D. (2002). Predictors of post-high employment among young adults with disabilities. *Career Development for Exceptional Individuals, 25*(1), 25–40.

Reiff, H. B., & Gerber, P. J. (1994). Social/emotional and daily living issues for adults with learning disabilities. In P. J. Gerber & H. B. Reiff (Eds.), *Learning disabilities in adulthood: Persisting problems and emerging issues* (pp. 72–81). Boston, MA: Andover Medical Publishers.

Reschly, D. J., & Wood-Garnett, S. (2009, September). *Teacher preparation for response to intervention in middle and high schools*. TQ Research and Policy Brief. Washington, DC: National Comprehensive Center for Teacher Quality.

Rosenthal, I. (1989). Model transition programs for learning disabled high school and college students. *Rehabilitation Counseling Bulletin, 33* (1), 54–66.

Sabornie, E., & deBettencourt, L. (2009). *Teaching students with mild and high-incidence disabilities at the secondary level* (3rd ed.). Columbus, OH: Pearson.

Scammacca, N., Roberts, G., Vaughn, S., Edmonds, M., Wexler, J., Reutebuch, C., et al. (2007). *Interventions for adolescent struggling readers: A meta-analysis with implications for practice*. Portsmouth, NH: RMC Research Corporation, Center on Instruction.

Scanlon, D., & Mellard, D. F. (2002). Academic and participation profiles of school-age dropouts with and without disabilities. *Exceptional Children, 68*, 239–258.

Schloss, P., Schloss, M., & Schloss, C. (2007). *Instructional methods for secondary students with learning and behavior problems* (4th ed.). Boston, MA: Allyn & Bacon.

Schumaker, J. (2009, January). *Teacher preparation and professional development in effective learning strategy instruction*. TQ Connection Issue Paper. Washington, DC: National Comprehensive Center for Teacher Quality.

Sitlington, P. (2008). Transition to life in the community. In G. Blalock, J. Patton, P. Kohler, and D. Bassett (Eds.). *Transition and students with learning disabilities: Facilitating the movement from school to adult life* (2nd ed.) (pp. 307–325). Austin, TX: Hammill Institute on Disabilities.

Smith, C. (2004). *Learning disabilities: The interaction of the students and their environments* (5th ed.). Boston, MA: Pearson.

Test, D., Mazzotti, V., Mustian, A., Fowler, C., Kortering, L., & Kohler, P. (2009). Evidence based secondary transition predictors for improving post-school outcomes for students with disabilities. *Career Development for Exceptional Individuals, 31*(3), 160–181.

Thoma, C., Bartholomew, C., & Scott, L. (2009). *Universal design for transition: A roadmap for planning and instruction.* Baltimore, MD: Paul H. Brookes Publishing.

Thomas, P., & Date, J. (November 20, 2006). Students dropping out of high school reaches epidemic levels. ABC News.

Trainor, A. (2005).Self-determination perceptions and behaviors of diverse students with learning disabilities during the transition planning process. *Journal of Learning Disabilities, 38* (3), 233–249.

U.S. Department of Education, Office of Special Education and Rehabilitative Services, Office of Special Education Programs (2010). *29th Annual Report to Congress on the Implementation of the Individuals with Disabilities Education Act, 2007.* Washington, DC: Author.

Wagner, M., Blackorby, J., Cameto, R., & Newman, L. (1993). *What makes a difference? Influences on post-school outcomes of youth with disabilities.* Menlo Park, CA: SRI International.

Wagner, M., Newman, L., & Cameto, R. (2004). *Changes over time in the secondary school experiences of students with disabilities. A report of findings from the National Longitudinal Transition Study (NLTS) and the National Longitudinal Transition Study-2 (NLTS2).* Menlo Park, CA: SRI International. Retrieved from http://www.nlts2.org/pdfs/changestime_compreport.pdf

Wagner, M., Newman, L., Cameto, R., Levine, P., & Marder, C. (2003). *Going to school: Instructional contexts, programs, and participation of secondary school students with disabilities.* Menlo Park, CA: SRI International. Retrieved from http://www.nlts2.org/reports/2003_12/index.html

Wehman, P. (2006). *Life beyond the classroom: Transition strategies for young people with disabilities* (4th ed.). Boston, MA: Paul H. Brookes Publishing Co.

Wehmeyer, M. (2007). *Promoting self-determination in students with developmental disabilities.* New York, NY: Guilford Press.

Wehmeyer, M., & Field, S. (2007). *Self-determination: Instructional and assessment strategies.* Thousand Oaks, CA: Corwin Press.

Zigmond, N. (1990). Rethinking secondary school programs for students with learning disabilities. *Focus on Exceptional Children, 1,* 77–83.

25

Transition Education for Adolescents with Intellectual Disability

Meg Grigal

UNIVERSITY OF MASSACHUSETTS–BOSTON

Ann Deschamps

TRANSCEN, INC.

As the field of special education has evolved over the past thirty-five years, the elements that comprise its practice have changed from those that were emphasized at its inception. Current practices in special education reflect a changing philosophy, one that approaches the education of students with disabilities from the point of view as to what students with disabilities need to transition successfully from the education system to adulthood (McLaughlin, 2010) and emphasize person-centered, inclusive, and outcome-oriented methodologies that promote self-determination (Polloway, Lubin, Smith, & Patton, 2010; Powers, Geenan, & Powers, 2009; Rusch & Millar, 1998; Wehmeyer, Agran, & Hughes, 1998). The title of this chapter, "Transition Education for Adolescents with Intellectual Disability", implies that the transition activities and outcomes for students with this disability label will be in some way different from students with other disability labels. Unfortunately, this is too often the case. While strides have been made to provide opportunities for people with intellectual disability to live and work in the community, too often these outcomes are not achieved (Butterworth, Smith, Cohen Hall, & Winsor, 2010; Lakin, Larson, Salmi, & Webster, 2010). However, promising models of practice have been developed and implemented at the local, state, and regional levels that support successful transition outcomes for students with intellectual disability (Allen, Ciancio, & Rutkowski, 2008; Certo, Luecking, Murphy, Brown, Courey, & Belanger, 2008; Hart, Grigal, Sax, Martinez, & Will, 2006). This chapter will provide an overview of the status of transition services for students with intellectual disability, including their current educational environments, expectations for anticipated outcomes, and adult outcomes. Challenges and barriers to successful transitions to adult life for students with intellectual disability will be identified and promising models of practice that address these challenges will be shared and discussed.

Definitions

What is Intellectual Disability?

According to Schalock et al. (2010), an intellectual disability is "characterized by significant limitations both in intellectual functioning and in adaptive behavior as expressed in conceptual, social, and practical adaptive skills. This disability originates before the age of 18" (Schalock et al., 2010, p. 1). Prior to the use of this term, people with intellectual disability were referred to with the disability label of "mental retardation." Some national and international professional and advocacy organizations have begun to eliminate the term mental retardation from their names, publications, and writings since it is so frequently used in the mainstream as pejorative. Some state agencies have also made attempts to reduce or eliminate the use of the words "mental retardation" from their names and mission statements; however, its removal varies greatly from state to state (Polloway et al., 2010). In 2010, Rosa's Law was passed in the United States that changed language in Federal law as well, replacing the term *mental retardation* with the term *intellectual disability* in federal legislation such as the Individuals with Disabilities Education Act, the Higher Education Opportunities Act (HEOA), the Elementary and Secondary Education Act, and the Rehabilitation Act of 1973.

What is Transition?

As has been discussed throughout this text, in general terms, transition is a formal planning process that assists students with disabilities to move from school into the adult world (Wehman, 2006). The Individuals with Disabilities Education Improvement Act of 2004 stated that the Individualized Education Program (IEP) team must create measurable postsecondary goals based upon age-appropriate transition assessments related to training, education, employment, and, where appropriate, independent living skills, and should reflect students' strengths, preferences, and interests. These goals should be reflected in an identified course of study composed of all of the courses and educational experiences that students will need to be prepared for their transition from school to the community. Finally, the IEP team must develop an educational plan that includes a coordinated set of activities with specific strategies to assist students to move from school into the community.

Current Education and Transition Services for Students with Intellectual Disability

The educational practices used to support secondary students with intellectual disability are far from uniform. One factor impacting the delivery of transition services involves the context in which students are educated. Depending upon states and districts, transition-age students with intellectual disability may be fully included in their high school general education classes, receive completely segregated instruction in a special education classroom or specialized school, or receive special education services somewhere in the middle of that continuum. According to Yu, Newman, & Wagner (2009), the majority of students with intellectual disability receive their secondary instruction in typical high school campuses and not special schools, with only 4% still attending segregated schools. Although special education services are increasingly provided in typical high school environments, this does not necessarily indicate that the majority of students with intellectual disability are receiving instruction in general education classroom settings.

Approximately one-third of course work done by students with intellectual disability would be considered part of the general education curriculum (Yu et al., 2009). A recent report from the National Longitudinal Transition Study 2 (NLTS-2, 2003) indicated that 92% of transition-age students with intellectual disability took at least one course in a separate special education setting in a semester. These "nonvocational special education classes" involved academic subjects (e.g., math, science, language, arts); study skills, in which students received help with homework and learned successful studying and test-taking strategies; and functional life skills that facilitated independent living. The educational setting for students with intellectual disability frequently dictates their access to transition-related activities such as career- and community-based instruction (Yu et al., 2009).

Compared to students without disabilities, students with intellectual disability are more likely to receive one-to-one instruction as opposed to whole-class instruction. This individualized instruction is often provided by an adult who is not their teacher, such as an instructional assistant or paraeducator (Broer, Doyle, & Giangreco, 2005; Giangreco, Edelman, Broer, & Doyle, 2001). Students with intellectual disability are also more likely to take part in community-based activities and go on field trips as part of their special education classes as opposed to accessing these activities in their general education classes (Yu et al., 2009).

The Impact of Expectations on Students with Intellectual Disability

Educational context is not the only factor that effects transition services for students with intellectual disability. The attitudes and expectations of parents and teachers have a significant impact on the path a student with an intellectual disability chooses after high school. The impact of low expectations was revealed in a study by Kraemer and Blacher (2001), who investigated the difference between parents' ideal and realistic goals for their children. Over 70% of parents of students with intellectual disability hoped their child would work independently or in a supported employment situation, but most presumed their child would realistically end up working in a segregated workshop. Higher expectations for academic and career success have been found to relate to better high school completion rates and higher postsecondary school attendance rates (Wagner, Newman, Cameto, Levine, & Marder, 2007). According to a report from the NLTS-2 (2003), youth with disabilities, in general, are much less likely to be expected by their families to continue their education after leaving high school. The type and severity of disability determined parents' levels of expectations, with the lowest level of expectations from parents of youth with intellectual or multiple disabilities, autism, and deaf–blindness, and the highest level of expectations from parents of youth with speech/language, visual or hearing impairments (Newman, 2005; NLTS-2, 2003).

However, the expectations for postsecondary education may be increasing for students with intellectual disability. Grigal and Neubert (2004) found that college was the most desired post-school outcome of 58% of parents of students with low-incidence disabilities, including students with intellectual disability. These high expectations were not reflected in parents' expectations for future employment, though, since full- or part-time work was not selected by a large percentage of this group of parents' most desired outcome for their child. In fact, of those parents who chose employment as an outcome, more chose segregated workshops as the desired post-school activity for their child than supported or competitive employment (Grigal & Neubert, 2004).

The occupational aspirations of youth with disabilities are more closely associated with their perceived efficacy than with their actual high school academic achievement (Wagner et al., 2007). Therefore it is reasonable to conclude that students with intellectual disability will do only as well as they are expected to do. If parents and teachers indicate to students with intellectual disability that they don't expect students to get a well-paying job, attend college or live independently, it's more than likely that the student will fulfill those expectations.

Employment Activities and Outcomes of Students with Intellectual Disability

The majority of students with intellectual disability receive some type of vocational training or work-based learning experiences while in high school to help them focus their personal career goals, and gain work-related skills (Guy, Sitlington, Larsen, & Frank, 2008; Hutchins & Renzaglia, 2002; Luecking & Fabian, 2000; Luecking & Gramlich, 2003). Indicators of quality work-based learning experiences are: (a) clear expectations of student activity at the workplace; (b) clearly defined roles of teachers and worksite supervisors; and (c) well-structured feedback on student performance (Luecking & Gramlich, 2003). The intention behind creating work-based or vocational training experiences is to get students with intellectual disability "ready" to work, ideally in a field of interest. Yet, this outcome is too often not achieved.

Accurate employment statistics for people with intellectual disability can be difficult to obtain due to inconsistent definitions of disability terms used by entities tracking employment. The American Community Survey uses the term "cognitive disability" while the U.S. Census uses the term "mental disability," both of which are defined differently but encompass individuals with intellectual disability. Regardless, the employment rate for people with intellectual disabilities is consistently lower than the employment rate for people without or with other disability types. In 2008, an estimated 23% of people with a cognitive disability were employed (Erickson, Lee, & von Schrader, 2010).

These bleak outcomes are mirrored by NLTS-2, which demonstrated that youth with intellectual disability were less likely to be employed than youth with other disability labels. While in school, 14% of students with intellectual disability worked only during the summer, 4% worked only during the school year, and 17% of students with intellectual disability worked during both the summer and the school year. Forty-three percent of working students with intellectual disability earned the minimum wage or more and the majority worked eight hours a week or less (Wagner et al., 2003). Among all disability groups, youth with intellectual disability had the lowest rate of paid employment (31%) outside of high school one year after exit. In spite of the increased focus on preparation for employment in secondary education, people with intellectual disability face significant challenges since they are less likely to be employed, work fewer hours, and earn less than other disability groups (Certo et al., 2008; Green & Brook, 2001; Luecking, 2010).

Post-Secondary Education for Students with Intellectual Disability

Students with and without disabilities and their adult counterparts have consistently demonstrated that further education correlates with successful employment or career outcomes (Wehman & Yasuda, 2005). Individuals with disabilities who have had any postsecondary education (PSE) are employed at double the rate of people with just a high school diploma (Gilmore, Bose, & Hart, 2001). Yet PSE is often omitted from transition planning for youth with intellectual disability. Youth with intellectual disability are one of the least likely groups of students (along with students with multiple disabilities) to enroll in postsecondary education four years after high school, with only 27% of students with intellectual disability enrolled in postsecondary education (Newman, Wagner, Cameto, & Knokey, 2009). Compare this to youth with hearing or visual impairments, who were three times more likely to enroll in PSE and students with autism or speech and language disabilities who were twice as likely to have continued their education after high school. Among students with intellectual disability who enrolled in college, 20% were in a two-year or vocational college or technical school, and a meager 4.6% were enrolled in a four-year college. Yet, just like their peers without disabilities, youth with intellectual disability can gain important benefits from postsecondary education. Data from the national vocational rehabilitation database (RSA 911) show that youth with intellectual disability who participated in postsecondary education were 26% more likely to leave vocational rehabilitation services with a paid job and earn a 73% higher weekly income (Migliore, Butterworth, & Hart, 2009).

The number of programs and services for students with intellectual disability in colleges across the country has increased (Gaumer, Morningstar, & Clark, 2004; Getzel & Wehman, 2005; Grigal & Hart, 2010a, Katovitch, 2009). A recent survey conducted by Think College documented over 250 programs in institutes of higher education that serve students with intellectual disability in 41 states (Hart & Grigal, 2010). Recent changes in the Higher Education Opportunities Act (HEOA) of 2008 have led to the creation and expansion of services and access to higher education for students with intellectual disability.

In 2010, the U.S. Department of Education's Office of Postsecondary Education awarded over $10.5 million to fund 27 model demonstration projects in two- and four-year institutions of higher education (IHEs) or consortia of institutions in 23 states (Duncan, 2010). These model demonstration projects, referred to as Transition and Postsecondary Programs for Students with Intellectual Disabilities or TPSIDs, would enable IHEs to create or expand high-quality inclusive model comprehensive transition and postsecondary programs for students with intellectual disability.

The HEOA (2008) also contained language expanding access to certain non-loan-based forms of financial aid (grants, work study) for students with intellectual disability. In 2010 new regulations were implemented allowing IHEs to apply to become approved as a Comprehensive Transition and Postsecondary Program (CTP), an eligible program for the Federal student aid programs. Once approved, these IHEs could provide students with intellectual disability access to Title IV Federal aid programs including Federal Pell Grants, Federal Work-Study (FWS), and Federal Supplemental Educational Opportunity Grants (FSEOG) programs. Students with ID would not have to meet the previous eligibility criteria of having a high school diploma, passing an ability to benefit test, or be seeking a degree in order to access these forms of financial aid; however, students and their families would have to meet the existing financial eligibility requirements for such federal student aid.

Barriers to Effective Transition Services and Successful Student Outcomes

While research has documented the steps, strategies, and crucial components for successful transition planning for students with intellectual disability (Test, Aspel, & Everson, 2006; Wehman, 2006; Kohler, 1996), too often these effective practices are not implemented in high schools (Grigal, Test, Beattie, & Wood, 1997; National Council on Disability, 2000). The National Council on Disability (2000) reported that "88% or 44 states failed to ensure compliance with transition requirements" (p. 89). Why is it that transition practices that we know to work are not used to support better outcomes for students with intellectual disability? The following provides a brief discussion of some the barriers that prevent students with intellectual disability from accessing documented best practices.

Little Involvement of Students with Intellectual Disability in Transition Planning

Chapter 6 provides a comprehensive overview of student involvement in transition planning, but it is worth just highlighting issues pertaining to this for students with intellectual disability. Over the past few decades, a number of instructional programs to promote student involvement have been developed and, to varying extents, evaluated (Agran, Blanchard, & Wehmeyer, 2000; Algozzine, Browder, Karvonen, Test, & Wood, 2001; Grigal, Neubert, Moon, & Graham, 2003; Shogren, Wehmeyer, Palmer, Soukup, Little, Garner, & Lawrence, 2007; Wehmeyer, Agran, & Hughes, 2000). Student involvement has been linked to more positive transition outcomes, including enhanced self-determination (see Chapter 13) (Wehmeyer et al., 2000). In a study measuring self-determination of individuals with intellectual and learning disabilities, Wehmeyer and Schwartz (1997) found that students with higher levels of self-determination had higher employment rates.

However, the translation of this knowledge into practice has been slow. Thomas, Rogan, & Baker (2001) found that teachers and parents put little effort into preparing students with disabilities, including students with intellectual disability, to become involved in their transition-planning process. The reported data suggest that many students with disabilities receive little or no instruction on involvement in the IEP process (Agran & Hughes, 2008). Most of the IEP goals for these youth appear to be based on adult recommendations, rather than on students' personal goals. Lack of student involvement translates to goals unrelated to their desires, which in turn affects motivation (Van Reusen & Bos, 1994) and, ultimately, outcomes (Wehmeyer & Palmer, 2003).

An increased emphasis on student involvement and self-determination for students with intellectual disability (Agran & Hughes, 2008) would ideally translate into an increase in the level of participation of youth with intellectual disability in their transition-planning meetings and goal identification. However, the current level of student involvement in the creation and monitoring of their transition-related IEP goals remains low (Agran & Hughes, 2008; Zhang & Stecker, 2000). Students with intellectual disability may be even less involved in their transition planning, less likely to provide input (less than half of those participating), and more likely to report no progress towards transition goals than are other students (Katsiyannis, Zhang, Woodruff, & Dixon, 2005). IDEA mandates student involvement in the transition-planning process and research reinforces the benefits of this involvement. However, the reality is that students with intellectual disability are, for the most part, not involved in the process.

Lack of Adequately Trained Staff

To effectively prepare students with disabilities, including students with intellectual disability, for the transition to adult life, it is important for transition professionals to understand essential competencies for transition service delivery (Anderson et al., 2003; Blalock et al., 2003; Defur & Taymans, 1995). Morningstar and Clark (2003) summarized these competencies into five categories:

- **Knowledge of principles and basic concepts of transition education and service**—knowledge and application of transition services requirements under IDEA as well as emerging and recommended practices focusing on transition planning and the Individualized Education Program (IEP).
- **Knowledge of models of transition education and services**—knowledge of specific program models that focus on individualized planning and align with general secondary education, including models of student-focused planning, student development, family involvement, and interagency collaboration, as described by leaders in the field.
- **Skills in using strategies for developing, organizing, and implementing transition education and services**—skills needed to implement effective models of transition, as well as transition assessment, service coordination, and curriculum planning within the context of general and special transition instructional programs.
- **Knowledge and use of collaboration competencies**—competence in service coordination with the complex array of agencies, programs, and services supporting young adults with disabilities.
- **Knowledge and skills to address systemic problems in transition services delivery**—capacity to understand and address barriers and strategies for planning, developing, implementing, and promoting transition services and programs at local, state, and federal levels.

Unfortunately, many education professionals charged with planning for and implementing transition services have little formal instruction in transition planning. A national survey of special education personnel preparation programs in the United States revealed that less than

50% of the personnel preparation instruction that teachers receive in higher education addresses transition standards (Anderson et al., 2003). This lack of training was acknowledged by teachers in a multi-state survey of special education teachers' perceptions of their transition competencies, which indicated that teachers felt that they lacked knowledge and skills related to some key transition areas such as employment (Benitez, Morningstar, et al., 2008).

If special education teachers feel unprepared, it is likely that the other primary instructional staff in most special education programs, including paraeducators, feel similarly unprepared. Paraeducators provide much of the direct service in transition-related activities (Blalock et al., 2003). Whitaker (2000) found that half the school districts in one state employed one or more paraprofessionals to assist students with intellectual disability in occupational education classes. However, these individuals receive very little training or preparation for this important role (Downing, Ryndak, & Clark, 2000).

As such, one factor contributing to the poor implementation of transition services for students with intellectual disability is the lack of adequate training and expertise of the staff charged with implementing them (Grigal & Hart 2010b; Li, Bassett, et al., 2009). Morningstar and Clark (2003) asserted that

> It is professionally unacceptable that we live in a society that demands some demonstration of competence through training and/or competency exams of certain workers (e.g., accountants, real estate brokers, hair stylists, plumbers, security guards, general contractors, to name a few), while at the same time permitting professionals who have little or no specific training or demonstrated competence to perform a wide range of tasks and roles in delivering transition education and services to students with disabilities.

> (p. 227)

The Increasing Burden of Compliance

Over the past fifteen years the Federal Government has provided an increasing amount of guidance as to how state and local jurisdictions should comply with the transition provisions. In 2004 the Individuals with Disabilities Improvement Act of 2004 (P.L. 108–446) contained new language related to transition services including a requirement to provide exiting students with a summary of performance (SOP) as well as including students' statement of their post-high school goals [(Section 614(c)(5)(B)(ii)]. The Office of Special Education Programs began requiring states to submit data on 20 indicators that were developed to ensure states were meeting the requirements of IDEA. Indicator 13 is the secondary transition indicator that requires the IEP to include appropriate measurable postsecondary goals based on age-appropriate transition assessment (Mazzotti, Rowe, Kelley, Test, Fowler, Kohler, & Kortering, 2009). Indicator 13 specifically states:

> Percent of youth with IEPs aged 16 and above with an IEP that includes appropriate measurable post-secondary goals that are annually updated and based upon an age appropriate transition assessment, transition services, including courses of study, that will reasonably enable the student to meet those post-secondary goals, and annual IEP goals related to the student's transition services needs. There also must be evidence that the student was invited to the IEP Team meeting where transition services are to be discussed and evidence that, if appropriate, a representative of any participating agency was invited to the IEP Team meeting with the prior consent of the parent or student who has reached the age of majority.

> (20 U.S.C. 1416(a)(3)(B))

The intention is to provide clear and specific guidance to the states and, ultimately, local school districts about how to implement the transition-planning provisions of the law. The addition of the Indicator 13 requirement and accompanying technical assistance efforts have focused school districts on the details of the transition-planning process including helping students articulate clear, measurable postsecondary education goals, effectively utilizing transition assessments that help students determine these goals, and documenting meaningful courses of study that assist in meeting the postsecondary goals. This requirement has also meant that schools systems are much more focused on exact wording of transition IEPs, interpretation of the government's words, and preparation for state and Federal auditors who enforce compliance. The goal for each local school district is compliance. While the increased specific guidance is well intended and comprehensively covers the transition process, attention to compliance sometimes takes valuable time away from teacher's direct interaction with students; that is, when the real transition planning takes place. A worthwhile objective is a balance between documentation of compliance for state and Federal governments and meaningful transition-planning activities among teachers and transitioning youth.

Limited or Lack of Agency Collaboration During Transition Planning

Transition planning is a collaborative effort involving students, family members, special education personnel, and community service providers (Noonan, Morningstar, & Gaumer-Erickson, 2008). Effective interagency collaboration means that school personnel, rehabilitation agencies, adult providers, workforce development organizations, family members, social service agencies, and other critical partners come to the table to braid their resources in order to ensure a seamless transition. Frequently no single agency has enough expertise or resources to effectively serve young adults transitioning from the school to life after school. This makes the combining of resources through interagency collaboration critical. In fact, not surprisingly, effective interagency collaboration has been associated with increased employment and postsecondary education outcomes for all disability populations (Noonan et al., 2008; Repetto, Webb, Garvan, & Washington, 2002).

Too often community providers and state agency personnel are not involved in transition planning until one or two years prior to the student's exit from high school (Agran, Cain, & Cavin, 2002). Unless school-system personnel and families establish relationships early on in the transition process, these essential members of the team will not be a part of the planning. This may lead to misinformation about the services available and a delay in accessing services upon leaving high school. Early collaboration activities can focus on information sharing or the provision of technical assistance to IEP team members regarding available services.

Promising Models of Practice

The barriers to effective transition planning are significant but not insurmountable. The following provides a description of four different promising models of practice that are being implemented throughout the country in very different settings. Each illustrates how preparing students with intellectual disability for life after high school can be done effectively and ultimately lead to positive outcomes.

Project Search

Project Search is a comprehensive three-part program providing employment and education opportunities for youth and adults with intellectual disability that includes a high school program, a vocational clinic, and an adult education program. One part of Project Search is the High School Transition Program (PS-HST), a one-year, community-based educational program for students with disabilities in their last year of high school. The program is for students with significant disabilities whose main goal after completing high school is competitive employment. It utilizes a process of workplace immersion that combines classroom instruction, career exploration, and on-the-job training and support for students.

Project Search started as a collaborative effort between the Ohio Rehabilitation Services Commission, the Cincinnati Children's Hospital, and three county school systems in Ohio. Students in the program spend their day working in a hospital in a variety of environments, trying different jobs. A typical school day includes:

- Employability skills class: students receive instruction in problem solving, teamwork, decision making, budgeting, check writing, resume writing, and other employability and daily living skills.
- Internship sites: students participate in non-paid internship sites throughout the host business/organization/university/hospital. They rotate through three or four different internships throughout the school year. They work at their assigned job for a four-and-a-half-hour period broken up by lunch.
- Lunch: Students are encouraged to eat with their co-workers and peers at their internship site. They choose whether to pack or purchase lunch.
- Reflection/planning/journal writing: Students have a chance to plan their week and address any concerns that might arise during the day. If available, students take public transportation home.

The goal of Project Search is to provide a real community-based work experience for each student. In addition to regular work, students participate in initial job orientation and training as well as shadowing other employees. They learn how to clock in and out, maintain appropriate work attire, and deal with supervisors providing constructive criticism. Each job rotation usually lasts eight to ten weeks, based on the needs of the employer. Individualized job development and placement in local businesses begin after the rotations are completed in different jobs in the hospital. Students are given support through job coaching and work-site accommodations with the ultimate goal of independent paid employment. At the end of the program, linkages are made to appropriate community services, such as the local rehabilitation services and/or the agency providing long-term funding for adults with developmental disabilities, in order to ensure a successful transition to work as well as retention and career advancement.

Project Search has an impressive track record with 82.5% of their students employed post-program in 2007/2008. Since the Ohio program started, the PS-HST program has become one of the most widely replicated transition programs in the country and has expanded to other businesses that reflect a broader range than the original program. More than 120 businesses in 39 US states, including California, Florida, Georgia, Indiana, Pennsylvania, and Washington, and several countries have already adopted the PS-HST approach. Sixty partnerships around the globe are working to implement this model for the youth with intellectual disability in their local communities (Allen et al., 2008).

Transition Service Integration Model

The Transition Service Integration Model (TSIM) creates a seamless transition process for transitioning-age youth with significant support needs—typically individuals labeled as having moderate or profound intellectual disability—by school systems subcontracting with private

Table 25.1 Benefits of the project search high school transition model (from http:// projectsearch.info)

Benefits to the students:

- Participation in a variety of internships in a high-status local business
- Acquire competitive, transferable and marketable job skills
- Gain increased independence, confidence and self-esteem
- Obtain on site and individualized instruction, support, and accommodations
- Linkage to vocational rehabilitation and other adult service agencies

Benefits to the host organization:

- Access to a new, diverse talent stream with skills that match the labor needs
- Gain interns/employees with disabilities who serve as role models for customers and give them a sense of hope, which is reflected in satisfaction surveys
- Access to a demographic of the economy with intense buying power: people with disabilities represent one of the fastest growing market segments in the US
- Experience increased local, regional, and national recognition through marketing of this unique program
- Performance and retention in some high-turnover, entry-level positions increase dramatically

agencies at the point of transition to facilitate individualized employment (Luecking & Certo, 2002). TSIM is designed to combine the resources of school and adult systems in sharing the costs of a student-driven approach to transition planning, resulting in integrated employment with wages paid directly by the employer.

In this model, during the student's last year in school, all services are entirely community-based with the cost paid by the local school district. The school system enters into a formal service contract with a local adult agency serving young adults with disabilities in the community. Staffing is provided by adult agencies that work in cooperation with school personnel to work directly in the community supporting students in different integrated work sites. After a complete orientation, the parents and the student choose to participate in TSIM. The employment experiences are dictated by the student's individual interests. Ultimately, school districts integrate their staff and resources with those of an adult agency, the state rehabilitation system, and the state developmental disabilities system before graduation to produce meaningful work outcomes and ensure support after graduation, resulting in a seamless transition (Certo et al., 2003).

The model uses the resources of transition partners for an uninterrupted, collaborative transition from public secondary education to employment in inclusive job settings and access to other integrated community environments. Components of the model include:

- A completely community-based class of 8–10 students with significant support needs in their last year of high school;
- A transition-planning process tailored to meet the needs of each individual student including effective interagency collaboration blending the resources of adult community agencies and state agencies;
- Paid employment experience and linkage to a community service provider before the point of transition, ensuring support in place after secondary school. In addition necessary linkages to education, employment, and other services as necessary are in place before the student exits secondary school.

The intent of TSIM is a seamless transition in the most literal sense. That is, youth are working in jobs they will keep upon exit from school and they are supported in these jobs by the same staff and same adult agency. Thus, the first day after school looks the same as the day before (Certo et al., 2003).

Fairfax County Public Schools Career and Transition Services

Fairfax County Public Schools (FCPS) in Fairfax, Virginia, provides comprehensive transition services to students with disabilities that have yielded quite impressive outcomes (Fairfax, 2006). FCPS is the largest school system in the state of Virginia and the 12th largest school system in the country. During 2008–2009 FCPS served 13,270 high school students with disabilities, of which 883 had a label of intellectual disability, 199 had the label of severe disability, and 1,913 had the label of autism (who also may have had intellectual disability). The mission of FCPS's Career and Transition Services is to empower a diverse population of students with the opportunities and resources necessary for transition to a variety of postsecondary options. Their philosophy is that successful transition is achieved through a continuum of instructional strategies, collaborative interdisciplinary team supports, utilization of technology, and awareness of and access to community resources. These services help students develop essential skills for self-determination, independent living, further education, and employment in order to maximize participation in their communities. Services include the following:

- Career Academy Support Services—each career and technical education center has a support team specifically to assist students with IEPs successfully complete course requirements;
- Career Assessment—evaluation and a wide range of assessments is offered, both formal and informal;
- Work Awareness and Transition (WAT) class—an elective course combining career exploration and introduction to work-based experiences. This is offered at the middle and high school levels;
- Job Coach Services—short-term support for high school students with IEPs transitioning to independent work;
- Employment and Transition Services (ETR)—a transition contact at each high school who provides assistance in postsecondary planning including linkages to postsecondary services;
- Office Technology and Procedures—elective high school course combining office skills instruction and work-based experience in a local business;
- Special Education Career Center—specialized career skills instruction in community settings.

In addition, the school system has a cooperative agreement in place with the local department of rehabilitation services and the community agency that provides long-term supports and funding for people with developmental disabilities. This ensures that these critical adult providers are working with the school system well before students exit high school with the goal of a seamless transition.

For over twenty years, FCPS has surveyed special education graduates to determine student outcomes and program effectiveness. In 2008, a total of 825 graduates were surveyed.

The survey found that 89% of those surveyed were employed and/or enrolled in postsecondary education. Forty percent were in paid employment (this included individuals working and attending postsecondary education). Of the 40%, 32% worked full-time and 68% worked part-time. Seventy-two percent were in postsecondary education; 11% were not in any meaningful activity (Cook, 2008).

The results of the 2007 and 2006 survey were similar. In 2007, 90% were employed and/or enrolled in postsecondary education (50% in paid employment, 71% in postsecondary education)(Cook, 2007a) and in 2006, 91% were employed and/or enrolled in postsecondary education (Cook, 2007b). The comprehensive services provided by FCPS reflect many of the suggested best practices in transition—early and effective planning, interagency collaboration, and use of dedicated and trained personnel in job development and training. This countywide program supports the premise that meaningful career and transition services can be provided in a public school setting with largely positive outcomes.

Dual Enrollment Transition Programs

Students with intellectual disability and other developmental disabilities (DD) can receive special education services under IDEA in most states up until the age of 21 (in Michigan until age 26). However, many students with intellectual disability are not motivated to stay in high school after age 18 while their peers move on to work or college. One emerging and promising model of practice addresses this issue by providing some transitioning youth with intellectual disability with an alternative to a high school environment for their final 2–3 years of special education (Dolyniuk, Kamens, Corman, DiNardo, Torato, & Rockoff, 2002; Hart et al., 2006). In the dual or concurrent enrollment transition programs, a local school system partners with a two- or four-year college to offer transition services to students with intellectual disability or other DD, age 18 to 21 years, on a college campus (Grigal, Neubert, & Moon, 2005; Hall, Kleinert, & Kearns, 2000). Students often spend their entire day at the college participating in a wide range of activities related to their transition goals including accessing college courses and engaging either in community-based work experiences such as job shadowing, time-limited internships, or working competitively in a paid job (Grigal et al., 2005; Grigal & Hart, 2010b; Neubert & Moon, 2006). Students may also learn and use self-determination skills, learn how to take public transportation or para-transit, and other skills needed for adult living (Hart, Grigal, & Weir, 2010; Neubert & Redd, 2008). Preliminary research on postsecondary education for individuals with intellectual disability is demonstrating improved employment and self-determination outcomes (Hart, Zimbrich, et al., 2005; Migliore et al., 2009; Zafft, Hart, & Zimbrich, 2004). Currently over 38 dual enrollment programs in 24 states have been identified in the country in two- and four-year colleges, as well as technical and trade schools (www.thinkcollege.net).

In 2005 the U.S. Department of Education, Office of Special Education Programs, funded a research and innovation project charged with demonstrating and researching exemplary practices supporting students with intellectual disability ages 18–21 in dual enrollment transition programs. Over the past five years this project, the Postsecondary Education Research Center Project has collected data from dual enrollment transition programs in two states, on 112 students with intellectual disability/DD from 36 high schools providing services in five college sites. Findings demonstrated that the students with intellectual disability in these dual enrollment programs attended 95 different typical college courses and 83% held paid jobs in integrated community settings while receiving transition services in the dual enrollment programs. Students with intellectual disability worked an average of 18 hours per week and earned an average of $7.90/hour. Upon exiting from the dual enrollment programs, 89% of students with intellectual disability intended to take more courses in a college or other adult learning environment, 84% exited with a paid job, and 91% exited connected with a community rehabilitation provider (Grigal & Hart, 2010b).

Dual enrollment programs serving youth with intellectual disability on college campuses can be the perfect nexus for the transition experience, providing opportunities for personal growth and development, interesting learning options, higher responsibility levels, access to adult learning and working environments, increased career opportunities, and new and expanded social networks (Grigal & Dwyre, 2009). However, there is a great deal of variability in the types of services provided and anticipated outcomes of existing dual enrollment experiences throughout the country (Hart & Grigal, 2010). Not all programs provide the same level of access to college courses or paid employment. Additionally, student access to such experiences is dependent upon dual enrollment program options being available in their community.

Lessons from Promising Models of Transition Practice

The models reviewed above represent only a handful of the existing models of promising practice that are occurring in the field of transition for students with intellectual disability. But these four examples reflect how very different systems can lead to successful transition outcomes. Project Search created a successful model that focused primarily on employment and was initially targeted at one type of work setting (a hospital), but it has now expanded to other business structures such as banks and universities. This model demonstrates the importance of partnering with businesses in the private sector and guiding students through meaningful internship experiences. The Transition Service Integration Model provides an example of how targeted state and local interagency partnerships, intentional well-orchestrated coordination, and early planning can lead to better student outcomes. It also shows the importance of family support for the ultimate outcomes of transition services since each family which agrees to have its child participate is committed to its child obtaining community employment. The Fairfax County Public School Transition Services demonstrates the importance of creating an infrastructure that supports transition services and builds capacity through course design, staffing structures, and field-based employment experiences. Additionally, the transition services provided by FCPS shows a commitment to high expectations for all students since its transition services are aimed at providing transition-age youth, regardless of their disability label, with successful employment and postsecondary outcomes. Finally, the dual enrollment model offers an alternative to the option of students with intellectual disability staying in a high school environment for seven years and creates a natural portal to an adult learning environment. Students with intellectual disability in the dual enrollment programs have the opportunity to alter their conception of what learning is from that of a passive participant in a special education program to that of an adult accessing desired knowledge in an institute of higher education. These programs have great potential to bridge the gap between secondary education and adult life and can lead not only to better employment outcomes but also to higher rates of postsecondary education access for students with intellectual disability.

All four examples integrate student-centered planning, youth empowerment and interagency collaboration as critical threads woven into the fabric of their program. Family education and involvement and linkages to necessary post-school services also are integrated into each model. The following highlights some of the critical markers of success in each of these promising models of transition service for students with intellectual disability:

Emphasis on Expanded Career Exploration Process

The purpose of work-based training experiences is to support the development of specific skills that students with intellectual disability need to acquire in order to obtain paid employment in a career of their choice (Grigal & Hart, 2010b). However, too often these experiences are in predetermined fields, settings of convenience and not related to systematic development of skills needed to obtain employment or the preferences and interests of the student. The promising models of practice demonstrate how the time students spend in unpaid job training activities as well as the quality of the work-based experiences can be deliberately structured to not only build the necessary career awareness to make an informed choice about a career path but also to build the skills that will transfer and ultimately lead to a paid job in a field of choice.

Commitment to Paid Work

Paid employment during high school is the hallmark of high-quality transition experiences since students with paid employment experience during high school are more likely to be employed as adults (Brewer, 2005; Luecking, 2010; Wagner, Newman, Cameto, & Levine, 2005). Without the support to gain paid employment experience in high school, many students with intellectual disability remain unemployed as adults. The students with intellectual disability in each of these promising models were expected to obtain paid employment as an outcome; therefore, each of the preparatory activities which students engaged in supported that potential outcome. In addition, many students participated in paid employment before graduation, building a resume reflective of their skills and experience before leaving high school. Arguably more important than the connection between secondary employment experiences and post-school success is the self-confidence that all students, including students with intellectual disability, experience when they have participated in a successful, meaningful paid work experience.

Highly Trained Staff in Job Development and Support

Each of the promising models of practice engaged staff who were well trained in job development and employment support. Any professional who supports students with intellectual disability needs to have a strong background in the areas of customized employment, building self-advocacy skills, and the ability to ensure that any negotiated employment relationship meets both the needs of the job seeker and those of the employer.

Increased Access to and Expectations for Post-Secondary Education

Students with intellectual disability receive the same benefits from postsecondary education as individuals without disabilities (Grigal & Hart, 2010). Providing access to adult learning experiences in college settings as part of the transition process better prepares students with intellectual disability to understand the potential impact of furthering their education once they leave high school. The dual enrollment transition programs provide an example of how student outcomes can be enhanced by expanding the learning environments to include college and other adult learning settings.

Emphasis on Youth Empowerment through Discovery and Self-Advocacy

Students with intellectual disability can help guide the direction of their transition plans towards desired adult outcomes. This only happens if the systems supporting these students provide opportunities for such advocacy to occur and honor students' input. While each of the models addressed youth empowerment and advocacy in different ways, each model provided students with intellectual disability the chance to provide input on the direction and ultimate outcomes of their transition experiences.

Conclusion

The transition experience for students with intellectual disability can vary considerably depending upon the expectations of their school system, their families, and in many cases, their own expectations. These expectations govern each aspect of a young adult's transition process from the type of planning activities that are conducted, the goals devised and outcomes anticipated, and the level of collaboration with community rehabilitation providers, state and local agencies, and local institutes of higher education. These expectations determine the settings in which students with intellectual disability will learn and the activities that will comprise their day, the kind of professionals who will educate these students, and the background and expertise of these professionals. As the field of special education continues to evolve in the language that guides its policy and the expectations that guide its practice, these changes will ideally bring forth new generations of educators. Successful transition outcomes for students with intellectual disability will require these educators to approach the potential of students with intellectual disability unburdened by assumptions of presumed deficiency but, instead, embracing certainty of their promise.

References

Agran, M., Blanchard, C., & Wehmeyer, M. L. (2000). Promoting transition goals and self-determination through student-directed learning: The Self-Determined Learning Model of Instruction. *Education and Training in Mental Retardation and Developmental Disabilities, 35*, 351–364.

Agran, M., Cain, H. M., & Cavin, M. D. (2002). Enhancing the involvement of rehabilitation counselors in the transition process. *Career Development for Exceptional Individuals, 25*, 141–155.

Agran, M., & Hughes, C. (2008). Asking student input: students' opinion regarding their individualized education program involvement. *Career Development for Exceptional Individuals, 31*, 69–76.

Algozzine, R., Browder, D., Karvonen, M., Test, D. W., & Wood, W. M. (2001). Effects of interventions to promote self-determination for individuals with disabilities. *Review of Educational Research, 71*, 219–277.

Allen, P., Ciancio, J., & Rutkowski, S. (2008). Transitioning students with disabilities into work. *Techniques: Connecting Education and Careers, 83*, 22–25.

American Association on Intellectual and Developmental Disabilities. (2009). Definition of Intellectual Disability. Retrieved July 12, 2009, from http://www.aamr.org/content_100.cfm?navID=21

Anderson, D., Kleinhammer-Tramill, P. J., Morningstar, M. E., Lehmann, J., Bassett, D., Kohler, P. D., et al. (2003). What's happening in personnel preparation in transition? A national survey. *Career Development for Exceptional Individuals, 26*, 145–160.

Benitez, D.T., Morningstar, M.E., & Frey, B.B. (2008). A multistate survey of special education teachers' perceptions of their transition competencies. *Career Development for Exceptional Individuals, 32*, 6–16.

Blalock, G., Kochhar-Bryant, C., Test, D., Kohler, P., White, W., Lehman, J., et al. (2003). The need for comprehensive personnel preparation in transition and career development: A position statement of the Division on Career Development and Transition. *Career Development for Exceptional Individuals, 26*, 91–110.

Brewer, D. (2005). *Working my way through high school: The impact of paid employment on transitioning students with disabilities* (Issue brief). Ithaca, NY: Cornell University, School of Industrial and Labor Relations Extension, Employment and Disability Institute. Retrieved February 15, 2010, from http://digitalcommons.ilr.cornell.edu/edicollect/109

Broer, S. M., Doyle, M. B., & Giangreco, M. F. (2005). Perspectives of students with intellectual disabilities about their experiences with paraprofessional support. *Exceptional Children, 71*, 415–430.

Butterworth, J., Smith, F. A., Cohen Hall, A., & Winsor, J. E. (2010). StateData: The National Report on Employment Services and Outcomes (2009). Boston, MA: Institute for Community Inclusion, University of Massachusetts.

Certo, N. J., Luecking, R. G., Murphy, S., Brown, L., Courey, S., & Belanger, D. (2008). Seamless transition and long-term support for individuals with severe intellectual disabilities. *Research and Practice for Persons with Severe Disabilities, 33*, 85–95.

Certo, N. J., Mautz, D., Pumpian, I., Sax, C., Smalley, K., Wade, H. et al. (2003). A review and discussion of a model for seamless transition to adulthood. *Education and Training in Developmental Disabilities, 38* (1), 3–17.

Cook, A. (2007). *Career and transition services 2007 survey of school leavers preliminary data.* Unpublished manuscript, Fairfax County Public Schools, Falls Church.

Cook, A. (2007a). *Career and transition services survey of special education school leavers 2006.* Unpublished manuscript, Fairfax County Public Schools, Falls Church.

Cook, A. (2008). *Career and transition services 2008 survey of school leavers preliminary data.* Unpublished manuscript, Fairfax County Public Schools, Falls Church.

DeFur, S. H., & Taymans, J. M. (1995). Competencies needed for transition specialists in vocational rehabilitation, vocational education, and special education. *Exceptional Children, 62,* 38–51.

Dolyniuk, C.A., Kamens, M.W., Corman, H., DiNardo, P. O. Totaro, R., & Rockoff, J. C. (2002). Students with developmental disabilities go to college: Description of a collaborative transition project on a regular college campus. *Focus on Autism and Other Developmental Disabilities, 17,* 236–241.

Downing, J., Ryndak, D., & Clark, D. (2000). Paraeducators in inclusive classrooms. *Remedial and Special Education, 21,* 171–181.

Duncan, A. (2010, October 5). U.S. Secretary of Education Duncan Announces $10.9 Million in Awards Under New Programs That Help Students with Intellectual Disabilities Transition to Postsecondary Education. Retrieved from http://www.ed.gov/news/press-releases/us-secretary-education-duncan-announces-109-million-awards-under-new-programs-he

Erickson, W., Lee, C., von Schrader, S. (2010, March 17). Disability Statistics from the 2008 American Community Survey (ACS). Ithaca, NY: Cornell University Rehabilitation Research and Training Center on Disability Demographics and Statistics (StatsRRTC). Retrieved from www.disability-statistics.org

Fairfax County Public Schools. (2006). *Transition tool kit for parents* (Publication). Retrieved April 1, 2010, from www.fcps.edu/dss/sei/careertransition/tool_kit_sections

Gaumer, A. S., Morningstar, M. E., & Clark, G. M. (2004). Status of community-based transition programs: A national database. *Career Development of Exceptional Individuals, 27,* 131–149.

Getzel, E. E., & Wehman, P. (2005). *Going to college: expanding opportunities for people with disabilities.* Baltimore, MD: Paul H. Brookes Publishing Co.

Giangreco, M. F., Edelman, S. W., Broer, S. M., & Doyle, M. B. (2001). Paraprofessional support of students with disabilities: Literature from the past decade. *Exceptional Children, 68,* 45–63.

Gilmore, D. S., Bose, J., & Hart, D. (2001). Postsecondary education as a critical step toward meaningful employment: Vocational rehabilitations role. *Research in practice, 7*(4), retrieved from http://www.communityinclusion.org/article.php?article_id=44. 27

Green, H., & Brooke, V. (2001). Recruiting and retaining the best from America's largest untapped talent pool. *Journal of Vocational Rehabilitation, 16,* 83–88.

Grigal, M., & Dwyre, A. (2010). Employment activities and outcomes of college-based transition programs for students with intellectual disabilities. *Think College Insight Brief, 3.* Boston, MA: Institute for Community Inclusion, University of Massachusetts.

Grigal, M., & Hart, D. (2010a). *Think college!: Postsecondary education options for students with intellectual disabilities.* Baltimore, MD: Paul H. Brookes Publishing Co.

Grigal, M., & Hart, D. (2010b). The missing link: The importance of employment. In M. Grigal & D. Hart (Eds.), *Think college!: postsecondary education options for students with intellectual disabilities* (pp. 259–272). Baltimore, MD: Paul H. Brookes Publishing Co.

Grigal, M., & Neubert, D. A. (2004). Parents' in-school values and post-school expectations for transition-aged youth with disabilities. *Career Development for Exceptional Individuals, 27*(1), 65–85.

Grigal, M., Neubert, D.A., & Moon, M.S. (2005). *Transition Services for students with significant disabilities in college and community settings: Strategies for planning, implementation, and evaluation.* Austin, TX: PRO-ED.

Grigal, M., Neubert, D.A., Moon, M.S., & Graham, S. (2003). Parents' and teachers' views of self-determination for secondary students with disabilities. *Exceptional Children, 70,* 97–112.

Grigal, M., Test, D., Beattie, J., & Wood, W. (1997). An evaluation of transition components of individualized education programs. *Exceptional Children, 63,* 357–372.

Guy, B., Sitlington, P.L., Larsen, M.D., and Frank, A.R. (2009). Preparation for employment: What are high schools offering? *Career Development for Exceptional Individuals. 32,* 30–41.

Hall, M., Kleinert, H.L., & Kearns, F.J. (2000). Going to college? Post-secondary programs for students with moderate and severe disabilities. *TEACHING Exceptional Children, 32,* 58–65.

Hart, D., Grigal, M., Sax, C., Martinez, D., & Will, M. (2006). Postsecondary education options for students with intellectual disabilities. *Research to Practice, 45*, 1–4.

Hart, D., & Grigal, M.(2010). The spectrum of options: Current practices. In M. Grigal & D. Hart (Eds.), *Think college!: postsecondary education options for students with intellectual disabilities* (pp. 49–86). Baltimore, MD: Paul H. Brookes Publishing Co.

Hart, D., Grigal, M., & Weir, C. (2010). Expanding the paradigm: Postsecondary education options for individuals with autism spectrum disorder and intellectual disabilities. *Focus on Autism and Other Developmental Disabilities, 25*, 134–150.

Hart, D., Zimbrich, K., & Parker, D. (2005). Dual enrollment as a postsecondary education option for students with intellectual disabilities. In E. E. Getzel, & P. Wehman (Eds.), *Going to college: Expanding opportunities for people with disabilities* (pp. 253–267). Baltimore, MD: Paul H. Brookes Publishing Co.

Higher Education Opportunity Act of 2008, Pub. L. No. 110–315 § 122 STAT. 3078 (2008).

Hutchins, M.P., & Renzaglia, A. (2002). Career development: Developing basic work skills and employment preferences. In K. Story, P. Bates, & D. Hunter (Eds.), *The road ahead: Transition to adult life for persons with disabilities.* St. Augustine, FL: TRN, Inc.

Individuals with Disabilities Education Improvement Act of 2004, PL 108–446, 20 U.S.C. §§ 1400 et seq.

Katovitch, D. M. (2009). *The power to spring up: postsecondary education opportunities for students with significant disabilities.* Bethesda, MD: Woodbine House.

Katsiyannis, A., Zhang, D., Woodruff, N., & Dixon, A. (2005). Transition supports to students with mental retardation: An examination of data from the National Longitudinal Transition Study 2. *Education and Training in Developmental Disabilities, 40*, 109–116.

Kohler, P.D. (1996). *Taxonomy for Transition Programming.* Champaign: University of Illinois.

Kraemer, B. R., & Blacher, J. (2001). Transition for young adults with severe mental retardation: School preparation, parent expectations, and family involvement. *Mental Retardation, 39*, 423–435.

Lakin, K.C., Larson, S.A., Salmi, P., & Webster, A. (2010). Residential services for persons with developmental disabilities: Statues and trends through 2009. Minneapolis: University of Minnesota, Research and Training Center on Community Living, Institute on Community Integration.

Li, J., Bassett, D. S., & Hutchinson, S. R. (2009). Secondary Special Educators' Transition Involvement. *Journal of Intellectual & Developmental Disability, 34*, 163–172.

Luecking, R. (2010). Preparing for what? Postsecondary education, employment, and community participation. In M. Grigal & D. Hart (Eds.), *Think college!: postsecondary education options for students with intellectual disabilities* (pp. 273–290). Baltimore, MD: Paul H. Brookes Publishing Co.

Luecking, R., & Certo, N. (2002). Integrating service systems at the point of transition for youth with significant disabilities: A model that works. *National Center on Secondary Education and Transition (NCSET), Information Brief, 1*(4).

Luecking, R., & Fabian, E. (2000). Paid internships and employment success for youth in transition. *Career Development for Exceptional Individuals, 23*, 205–221.

Luecking, R., & Gramlich, M. (2003). Quality work-based learning and postschool employment success. *National Center on Secondary Education and Transition (NCSET), Information Brief, 2*(2).

Mazzotti, V. L., Rowe, D. R., Kelley, K. R., Test, D. W, Fowler, C. H., Kohler, P. D. et al. (2009). Linking transition assessment and post-secondary goals: Key elements in the secondary transition planning process. *Teaching Exceptional Children, 42*, 44–51.

McLaughlin, M. J. (2010). Evolving interpretations of educational equity and students with disabilities. *Exceptional Children, 76*, 265–278.

Migliore, A., Butterworth, J., & Hart, D. (2009). *Postsecondary education and employment outcomes for youth with intellectual disabilities* (Fast Facts Series, No. 1). Retrieved October 12, 2009, from http://www.thinkcollege.net/publications

Morningstar, M. E., & Clark, G. M. (2003). The status of personnel preparation for transition education and services: What is the critical content? How can it be offered? *Career Development for Exceptional Individuals, 26*, 227–237.

National Council on Disability. (2000). *Transition and post-school outcomes for youth with disabilities: Closing the gaps to postsecondary education and employment.* Washington, DC: Author.

National Council on Disability. (2008). *The Rehabilitation Act: Outcomes for transition-age youth.* Washington, DC: Author. Retrieved October 28, 2008, from http://www.ncd.gov/newsroom/publications/index.htm

National Longitudinal Transition Study 2 (NLTS-2). (2003). *NLTS2 data brief: Youth employment, a report from the national longitudinal transition study-2.* Retrieved November 28, 2009 from http://www.ncset.org/publications/default.asp#nlts2

Neubert, D. A., & Moon, M.S. (2006). Postsecondary settings and services for students with intellectual disabilities: Models and Research Needs. *Focus on Exceptional Children, 39,* 4, 1–8.

Neubert, D. & Redd, V. A. (2008). Transition services for students with intellectual disabilities: A case study of a public school program on a community college campus. *Exceptionality,16,* 220–234.

Newman, L. (2005). Family expectations and involvement for youth with disabilities. *NLTS2 Data Brief, Reports from the National Longitudinal Transition Study, 4*(2).

Newman, L., Wagner, M., Cameto, R., & Knokey, A.M. (2009). *The post-high school outcomes of youth with disabilities up to 4 years after high school. A report of findings from the National Longitudinal Transition Study-2 (NLTS2)* (SRI Project P11182). Retrieved October 20, 2009, from www.nlts2.org/reports/2009_04/ nlts2_report_2009_04_complete.pdf

Noonan, P. M., Morningstar, M. E., & Gaumer-Erickson, A. (2008). Improving interagency collaboration: Effective strategies used by high-performing local districts and communities. *Career Development for Exceptional Individuals, 31,* 132–143.

Polloway, E. A., Lubin, J., Smith, J. D., & Patton, J. R. (2010). Mild intellectual disabilities: Legacies and trends in concepts and educational practices. *Education and Training in Mental Retardation and Developmental Disabilities, 45,* 54–68.

Powers, K., Geenen, S., & Powers, L. E. (2009). Similarities and differences in the transition expectations of youth and parents. *Career Development for Exceptional Individuals, 32,* 132–144.

Repetto, J. B., Webb, K. W., Garvan, C. W., & Washington, T. (2002). Connecting student outcomes with transition practices in Florida. *Career Development for Exceptional Individuals, 25,* 123–139.

Rusch, F. R., & Millar, D. M. (1998). Emerging transition best practices. In F. R. Rusch, & J. G. Chadsey (Eds.). *Beyond high school: Transition from school to work.* (pp. 36–59). Belmont, CA: Wadsworth.

Schalock, R. L., Borthwick-Duffy, S. A., Bradley, V. J., Buntinx, W. H. E., Coulter, D. L., Craig, E. M., et al. (2010). *Intellectual disability: Definition, classification, and systems of supports* (11th ed.). Washington, DC: American Association on Intellectual and Developmental Disabilities.

Shogren, K. A., Wehmeyer, M. L., Palmer, S. B., Soukup, J. H., Little, T. D., et al. (2007). Examining individual and ecological predictors of the self-determination of students with disabilities. *Exceptional Children, 73,* 488–509.

Test, D. W., Aspel, N., & Everson, J. (2006). *Transition methods for youth with disabilities.* Columbus, OH: Merrill/Prentice Hall.

Thomas, C., Rogan, P., & Baker, S. (2001). Student involvement in transition planning: Unheard voices. *Education and Training in Mental Retardation and Developmental Disabilities, 36,* 16–29.

Van Reusen, A. K., & Bos, C. S. (1994). Facilitating student participation in individualized education programs through motivation strategy instruction. *Exceptional Children, 60,* 466–475.

Wagner, M., Cadwallader, T. W., Newman, L., & Marder, C., Levine, P., Garza, N., et al. (2003). *Life outside the classroom for youth with disabilities. A report from the National Longitudinal Transition Study-2 (NLTS2)* (SRI Project P11182). Retrieved October 12, 2009, from www.nlts2.org/reports/2003_04-2/ nlts2_report_2003_04-2_complete.pdf

Wagner, M., Newman, L., Cameto, R., & Levine, P. (2005). *Changes over time in the early postschool outcomes of youth with disabilities. A report of findings from the National Longitudinal Transition Study (NLTS) and the National Longitudinal Transition Study-2 (NLTS2)* (SRI Project P11182). Retrieved October 12, 2009, from http://www.nlts2.org/reports/2005_06/nlts2_report_2005_06_ complete.pdf

Wagner, M., Newman, L., Cameto, R., Levine, P., & Marder, C. (2007). *Perceptions and expectations of youth with disabilities. A special topic report of findings from the National Longitudinal Transition Study-2 (NLTS2)* (SRI Project P11182). Retrieved October 12, 2009, from www.nlts2.org/reports/2007_08/ nlts2_report_2007_08_complete.pdf

Wehman, P. (2006). *Life beyond the classroom: Transition strategies for young people with disabilities.* Baltimore: Paul H. Brookes Publishing Co.

Wehman, P., & Yasuda, S. (2005). The need and the challenges associated with going to college. In E. E. Getzel & P. Wehman (Eds.), Going to college: Expanding opportunities for people with disabilities (pp. 3–23). Baltimore: Paul H. Brookes.

Wehmeyer, M. L. (1996). Self-determination as an educational outcome: Why is it important to children, youth and adults with disabilities? In D. J. Sands & M. L. Wehmeyer (Eds.), *Self-determination across the life span: Independence and choice for people with disabilities* (pp. 15–34). Baltimore: Paul H. Brookes.

Wehmeyer, M. L., Agran, M., & Hughes, C. (1998). *Teaching self-determination skills to students with disabilities: Basic skills for successful transition.* Baltimore, MD: Paul H. Brookes Publishing Co.

Wehmeyer, M. L., Agran, M., & Hughes, C. (2000). A national survey of teachers' promotion of self-determination and student directed learning. *Journal of Special Education, 34*, 58–68.

Wehmeyer, M. L., & Palmer, S. B. (2003). Adult outcomes for students with cognitive disabilities three-years after high school: The impact of self-determination. *Education and Training in Developmental Disabilities, 38*, 131–144.

Wehmeyer, M. L., & Schwartz, M. (1997). Self-determination and positive adult outcomes: A follow-up study of youth with mental retardation or learning disabilities. *Exceptional Children, 63*, 245–255.

Whitaker, S. D. (2000). Training needs of paraprofessionals in occupational education classes. *Career Development for Exceptional Individuals, 23*, 173–185.

Yu, J., Newman, L., & Wagner, M. (2009). *Facts from NLTS2: Secondary school experiences and academic performance of students with mental retardation* (SRI Project P11182). Retrieved October 12, 2009, from http://www.nlts2.org/fact_sheets/nlts2_fact_sheet_2009_07.pdf

Zafft, C., Hart, D. & Zimbrich, K. (2004). College Career Connection: A study of youth with intellectual disabilities and the impact of postsecondary education. *Education and Training in Developmental Disabilities, 39*, 45–53.

Zhang, D., & Stecker, P. (2000). *Infusing self-determination into transition planning: Current practice and recommendations.* Paper presented at the Annual Meeting of the American Association of Mental Retardation, Washington, D.C.

26

Transition Education for Adolescents Who Are Deaf or Hard of Hearing

John Luckner

UNIVERSITY OF NORTHERN COLORADO

A hearing loss of any type or degree can negatively impact the quantity as well as the quality of communication between individuals. The most debilitating effect occurs when a baby is born with a sensorineural hearing loss. Interactions between the baby and significant others are obstructed. The interference generally occurs because 95% of children with a hearing loss are born into hearing families who have little or no experience interacting with individuals who are deaf or hard of hearing (Mitchell & Karchmer, 2004). Specifically, most family members have grown up in our sound-oriented society and are used to communicating, mediating, and soothing babies, infants, and toddlers by talking, making noises, singing songs, or reading books to them. Other than making silly faces, family members have no experience or knowledge of how to communicate with the baby without using their voice.

Typical hearing babies are immersed in spoken language from the time of birth and even before (Mayberry, 2007). And almost every one of those babies becomes a fluent speaker of that language without ever being taught or consciously trying to achieve competence (Owens, 2010). In contrast, the presence of a hearing loss during the time period between birth and five years of age can negatively impact the acquisition of language because that developmental phase is considered an optimal and critical period for attaining language proficiency (Carney & Moeller, 1998). Consequently, the majority of children who are deaf or hard of hearing seldom arrive at school with the same extensive language skills or background knowledge as their hearing peers (Marschark, 2003). Unfortunately, schools require high levels of language ability in order to socialize, read, write, and access academic content. The possible effect of a hearing loss on communication and subsequent developmental areas is depicted in Figure 26.1. Additional factors that influence development include age of identification of the hearing loss, age of intervention, family involvement, degree of hearing loss, existence of an additional disability, and quality of educational programming.

This chapter is organized in the following manner. First, current trends that are positively affecting the education of individuals with a hearing loss are discussed. Second, educational and employment outcomes are reviewed. Third, a rationale for providing comprehensive transition planning and services is provided. Fourth, six specific obstacles that often interfere with learning and adaptation in adult functioning are introduced. Fifth, a model for facilitating the transition of students who are deaf or hard of hearing is presented. Finally, additional information about preparing students for postsecondary education as well as suggestions for working with students who require a life-skills focus are described.

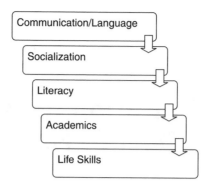

Figure 26.1 Potential impact of a hearing loss

Trends

In an effort to foster the development of age-appropriate communication and language skills and to offset the potential long-term impact of a hearing loss, three positive interventions have recently been implemented in the field of deaf education. Each is briefly described. First, as a result of universal newborn hearing screening (UNHS) 94% of newborn babies are being screened for hearing loss (Centers for Disease Control and Prevention, 2009). Prior to UNHS, most babies with a hearing loss were not identified until they were almost two years of age (Stein, Jabaley, Spitz, Stoakley, & McGee, 1990). Second, once a child has been identified as having a hearing loss through UNHS, the family can begin receiving early intervention services. Early intervention services are provided by knowledgeable and sensitive professionals who work with the family and caregivers to help them adapt their interactions so that the baby is provided access to the same quality-of-life experiences as hearing children (Sass-Lehrer & Bodner-Johnson, 2003). Research suggests that when children and families receive early intervention services, many of the children acquire near age-appropriate communication and language skills (e.g., Moeller, 2000; Yoshinaga-Itano & Gravel, 2001). Third, many children with either a severe or profound hearing loss are receiving cochlear implants. In the United States, approximately 15,500 children have received them (National Institute on Deafness and Other Communication Disorders, 2007). The U.S. Food and Drug Administration (FDA) allows children as young as 12 months of age to receive an implant. Early implantation and habilitation capitalizes on the plasticity of the brain and nervous system, stimulating and growing auditory neural connections throughout the brain as the foundation for spoken language, literacy, and academics (Cole & Flexer, 2007). Research indicates that early cochlear implantation and intensive habilitation are improving speech, language, and academic achievement (e.g., Marschark, Rhoten, & Fabich, 2007; Spencer, Gantz, & Knutson, 2004).

Education and Employment Outcomes

The educational and employment outcomes for individuals who are deaf or hard of hearing are mixed. In the past ten years, graduation rates with a regular high-school diploma have increased from 58% to 68% for students who are deaf or hard of hearing (U.S. Department of Education, 2009). As a result, individuals who are deaf or hard of hearing enroll in post-secondary education programs at a high rate (67%), which is similar to their hearing peers (Wagner, Newman, Cameto, & Levine, 2005). Yet, for a variety of reasons discussed later in this chapter, approximately 75% leave school without either a two-year or four-year degree (Lang, 2002; Marschark & Hauser, 2008; Stinson & Walter, 1997).

In the area of employment, some individuals who are deaf or hard of hearing have achieved great success. Professionals with a hearing loss are represented in almost every line of work (e.g., university president, actors, engineers, lawyers, physicians, professors, athletes) (Foster & MacLeod, 2003; Luckner & Stewart, 2003). However, many low-functioning individuals with a hearing loss can be found on the opposite end of the spectrum of career achievement. Most of these individuals have difficulty with communication, reading and writing, maintaining employment, social/emotional management, and living independently (Wheeler-Scruggs, 2002). The consequence of these deficits is illustrated by examining the data reported by the Social Security Administration (2007), which indicated that 54,263 individuals in the United States who are deaf or hard of hearing collect Supplemental Security Income (SSI). Additionally, as would be expected, a large number of individuals with a hearing loss function at some point along the continuum between being highly successful and in need of government support.

Rationale for Transition Planning

A general definition of transition is "passage from one form, state, style, or place to another" (*American Heritage Dictionary*, 1994, p. 854). Transitions, whether they occur for a toddler entering a preschool program or an elementary school student moving from a specialized school for students who are deaf to a program in her hometown where she will be one of only five students at the school with a hearing loss, can be stressful. Each transition involves unfamiliar people, settings, events, and requirements.

While every life transition is important and benefits from planning and collaboration, this chapter focuses primarily on helping youth who are deaf or hard of hearing transition from high school to a postsecondary education program and/or the work force as mandated in the Individuals with Disabilities Education Improvement Act of 2004 (PL 108–446). Effective transition planning and implementation are essential for four primary reasons. They (a) reduce the accompanying fear of change; (b) help assure that appropriate services are available and in place; (c) empower students and families to make choices in the best interests of the student and the family; and (d) help students create personally fulfilling lives.

The Individuals with Disabilities Education Improvement Act of 2004 (IDEA 2004) defines transition services as a coordinated set of activities for a child with a disability that:

(a) Is designed within a results-oriented process, which promotes movement from school to post-school activities, including postsecondary education, vocational training, integrated employment (including supported employment), continuing and adult education, adult services, independent living, or community participation;

(b) Is based upon the individual student's strengths, taking into account the student's preferences and interests; and

(c) Includes instruction, related services, community experiences, the development of employment and other post-school adult living objectives, and, when appropriate, acquisition of daily living skills and functional vocational evaluation (IDEA 2004, Sec. 602).

Three changes related to transition in IDEA 2004 are important to note:

(a) Initiation of transition services was moved from age 14 to age 16. However, IEP teams can determine if it is appropriate to begin earlier.

(b) Greater emphasis has been placed on transition outcomes determined through the development of goals based on transition assessments and the provision of transition services.

(c) A Summary of Performance (SOP), which is a summary of the student's academic and functional performance as well as recommendations for meeting the student's post-secondary goals, needs to be developed and completed during the final year of a student's high school education (Kochhar-Bryant, Shaw, & Izzo, 2009).

Potential Obstacles to Succeeding in Post-Secondary Education and in Finding Competitive Employment

A variety of factors individually or in combination may hinder the post-high school achievement of individuals who are deaf or hard of hearing. In this section several of the most frequently documented issues are noted and a short description of how each factor may interfere with optimal adult functioning is provided.

Language and Literacy Skill Deficits

In our current information-based society, being able to read is essential for (a) succeeding in school and work, (b) being an informed citizen, and (c) pursuing leisure interests (Luckner & Handley, 2008). As noted above, the initial impact of hearing loss occurs in the area of communication between children and their caregivers, which in turn has a significant effect on the development of language. Most hearing children acquire their language skills unintentionally through daily interactions (Burns, Griffin, & Snow, 1999; Landry & Smith, 2006). Specifically, research indicates that the quantity and quality of language input that young children have been exposed to at home during the first few years of life has a significant impact on their language development (Hart & Risley, 1995, 2003; Huttenlocher, Haight, Bryk, Seltzer, & Lyons, 1991; Rowe & Goldin-Meadow, 2009; Weizman & Snow, 2001; Wells, 1986), which in turn directly influences their long-term literacy success (Dickinson, McCabe, & Essex, 2006). The challenges that children who are deaf or hard of hearing experience in communicating with their caregivers and in acquiring language skills have led to the majority of students with a hearing loss graduating from high school with reading comprehension skills at approximately the fourth-grade level (e.g., Holt, Traxler, & Allen, 1997, Karchmer & Mitchell, 2003; Qi & Mitchell, 2007; Traxler, 2000). Futher, approximately 20% (some 2,000 annually) leave school with a reading level at or below second grade (Dew, 1999).

Experiential and Conceptual Knowledge Gaps

Learning has been defined as "a long-term change in mental representations or associations as a result of experience" (Ormrod, 2008, p. 4). Age-appropriate experiences help shape our intelligence, character, and interests. This happens because our brain is a highly dynamic organ that feeds on stimulation and experience and responds with the branching of nerve cells (Diamond & Hopson, 1998). Yet, too often, as a result of ineffective communication between parent and child, parent over-protectiveness, or a lack of understanding by parents about the importance of mediated experiences, many students who are deaf or hard of hearing grow up in homes where they are experientially impoverished (Marschark, Lang, & Albertini, 2002; Stewart & Kluwin, 2001; Stinson & Walter, 1997).

As individuals develop and encounter new experiences and information, they continually expand and revise their understanding of themselves and the world. That general knowledge is often summarized, stored, and retrieved in the form of concepts. Concepts are "a general category of objects, ideas, people, or events that share common characteristics" (Williams, 2009, p. 290). Some concepts (e.g., dog) are defined by observable characteristics and are easy to learn. Other concepts (e.g., intelligence) are defined by less obvious attributes. Concept knowledge also enhances the power of thought, facilitates generalization to new objects and events, and fosters efficient communication among individuals (Ormrod, 2008).

In addition to direct experiences, individuals also expand their conceptual knowledge by interacting with others to find out how they interpret the physical and social world. Because "most concepts are identified by a label—a word that symbolizes the concept and represents it in both thought and communication" (Ormrod, 2008, p. 249) —learners often acquire more sophisticated understanding when they exchange perspectives and build on one another's ideas. As a result of the difficulty of learning incidentally through overhearing others that individuals with any type of hearing loss have (Cole & Flexer, 2007), the lack of mediated experiences and the language delays noted above, as well as the limited number of individuals who can fluently interact with students who use sign language as their primary mode of communication, many students who are deaf or hard of hearing have gaps in their conceptual knowledge base. Unfortunately, experiential and conceptual knowledge gaps often make it more difficult for individuals to understand, learn, and remember information.

Lack of Independent and Responsible Behaviors

As individuals progress through their formal education it is anticipated that they will develop essential academic skills, social competence, and emotional regulation and become increasingly more independent and responsible. Some students who are deaf or hard of hearing grow up in home and school environments that are highly controlled, where they experience less freedom than their similar-age peers (Marschark et al., 2002; Willis & Vernon, 2002). In these settings, they become accustomed to adults making choices for them and rescuing them when a problem arises. Unintentionally, these well-meaning adults interfere with the natural process of making decisions and learning from successes and mistakes, essential preparation for adult functioning. The consequence of this is often a lack of motivation, which is a tendency to be attracted to, and to persist in situations that offer some challenge or opportunity to earn valued rewards through personal effort (Blocher, Heppner, & Johnston, 2001).

In order to be marketable in our information-based society, individuals need to be able to perform independently in five essential areas: gaining information, storing and retrieving information, expressing information, managing time, and self-advocating (Ellis & Lenz, 1996). Unfortunately, either because they have not been taught specific strategies or caring adults have not held them responsible for learning independently, many students who are deaf or hard of hearing have not become accomplished with these important life skills (Bonds, 2006; Calderon & Greenberg, 2003).

Dearth of Programming for Individuals with Additional Disabilities

Between 25% and 40% of students who have a hearing loss also have an additional disability (e.g., D'Zamko & Hampton, 1985; Gallaudet Research Institute, 2008; Knoors & Vervloed, 2003; Schildroth & Hotto, 1996). The occurrence of other disabilities in combination with a hearing loss creates learning problems that significantly add to the complexity of appropriately educating students who are deaf or hard of hearing. The presence of a disability in addition to a hearing loss often causes an interaction that exponentially compounds their special needs and often results in a variety of challenges across several domains (e.g., communication, cognition, affective social, behavior, physical abilities) (Jones, Jones, & Ewing, 2006).

Even though students with a hearing loss and an additional disability comprise a significant portion of the population receiving educational services, few teacher preparation programs focus on the unique needs of these students and a paucity of curriculum guides or professional materials is available for teachers who work with this population (Jones & Jones, 2003; Luckner & Carter, 2001). As a result, a large percentage of these individuals leave school with limited communication abilities, poor social and emotional skills, and experience difficulty living independently or maintaining employment (Bowe, 2003; Dew, 1999; LFD strategic work group, 2004; Wheeler-Scruggs, 2002).

Supplemental Security Income (SSI) Disincentive to Work

As previously noted, many individuals who are deaf or hard of hearing receive financial support in the form of SSI from the Social Security Administration. While a monthly check of $674 seems like a large sum of money to individuals still living at home with their parents, the quality of life it supports is very limited (Bowe, 2003). An annual salary of $8,088 makes it difficult to live independently and pay for rent, food, and transportation. Additionally, when individuals collect SSI and are not actively involved in postsecondary education or learning a career, they may experience difficulty developing the personal behaviors, knowledge, and skills needed in order to be hired at a later time when they no longer want to subsist on an income that is significantly below the poverty level. Also, the longer individuals remain out of the job market, the more difficult it is to become employed.

Employer and Co-Worker Attitudes

Many individuals with a hearing loss experience attitudinal and environmental barriers in gaining employment and career advancement (Foster & Macleod, 2003; Punch, Hyde, & Power, 2007). Some employers are reluctant to even interview an individual who is deaf or hard of hearing because they lack an understanding of the manifestations and consequences of a hearing loss and ways that hearing loss can be accommodated (Stika, 1997). Concomitantly, the expectations that employees will be able to use telephones, including the voice mail function, and the increased emphasis on teamwork that requires individuals to communicate in group situations, as well as the perceptions about possible costs for accommodations such as sign language interpreters, often cause employers to shy away from hiring or promoting individuals with a hearing loss (Laroche, Garcia, & Barette, 2000).

A Model for Facilitating the Transition of Students who are Deaf or Hard of Hearing

Figure 26.2, which is a revision of a model previously introduced by Luckner (2002), displays a six-stage approach to proactively address the barriers noted above as well as for fostering the attitudes, knowledge, and skills that students with hearing loss will require in order to successfully transition from school to adult roles. The essential aspects of each stage are discussed in the following sections.

Stage 1—Provide Exposure to Information about Careers and Facilitate the Development of Knowledge and Behaviors Related to Responsibility and Independence, Self-Determination; and Self-Advocacy

Career development is often characterized as a four-phase iterative process that continues throughout life as individuals discover new areas to explore or as they are required to adapt to

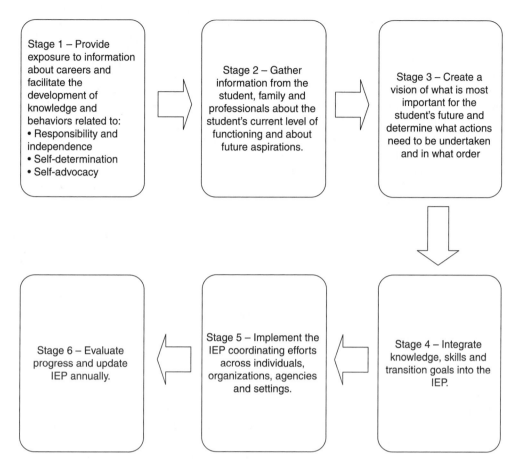

Figure 26.2 A model for facilitating the transition of students who are deaf or hard of hearing

changes in the world of work (Brolin & Loyd, 2004; Sitlington, Neubert, Begun, Lombard, & Leconte, 2007). The four stages include:

- Career awareness—students become knowledgeable about the existence of work, jobs, and careers as well as postsecondary education options, and participate in community and leisure activities.
- Career exploration—students begin to interact with various aspects of work such as accompanying adults to work, service learning, volunteering, and part-time jobs. Students begin to identify their interests, hobbies, abilities, and preferences.
- Career preparation—students seek to acquire knowledge and skills related to employability and living independently. They experience earning wages, managing finances, and refine career goals by establishing long-term goals and enrolling in courses that are aligned with their goals.
- Career assimilation—individuals strive to become lifelong learners who have the ability to work cooperatively with others, learn independently, and pursue additional training and education so they continue to become productive and marketable.

Career development resources appropriate for educators, students, and parents are provided at the websites of America's Career Resource Network (http://cte.ed.gov/acrn/default.aspx), the

Vocational Information Center (http://www.khake.com/index.html), and O★Net Online (http://online.onetcenter.org/). In addition, most states have a career information system available. Sitlington and colleagues (2007) have also developed a very useful "Career Development Checklist" and a list of "Relevant Assessment Questions for Career Development."

A variety of factors often interfere with the development of career awareness for students who are deaf or hard of hearing. First, hearing loss usually hinders an individual's ability to acquire knowledge via incidental learning. "Incidental learning is the process by which information is learned by virtue of passive exposure to events witnessed or overheard" (Calderon & Greenberg, 2003, p. 178). The information is not directly taught nor intended for instruction, yet important facts, behaviors, and beliefs are transmitted and absorbed either consciously or unconsciously. Much of the information related to the topics associated with the career awareness phase of development is overheard by hearing children listening to adults discuss daily events at dinner or while riding in the car.

Second, because 95% of children and youth who are deaf or hard of hearing are born into families with one or two hearing parents (Mitchell & Karchmer, 2004), the quantity and quality of conversations that occur between parents and children are often diminished (Evans, 1995; Wood & Wood, 1997). As a result, many children with hearing loss do not interact with their parents about many of the career awareness topics and don't have mediated experiences that help them develop the necessary attitudes and insight regarding the economic, psychological, and societal benefits of work.

Third, due to the previously discussed language and literacy challenges that often accompany hearing loss, many students do not have access to media such as books, television, radio, and newspapers. Many career awareness topics are introduced and illustrated through these popular outlets.

Responsibility means being able to distinguish right from wrong, to think and act rationally, and to be accountable for one's behavior (*Concise Oxford English Dictionary*, 2004). It is beneficial for professionals and family members to maintain an awareness that students who are deaf or hard of hearing should continue to advance along the "Responsibility Continuum" (Luckner, 1993) (see Figure 26.3) as they age, assuming more responsibility and independence over time. To do so, they will need to encourage the development of responsible behaviors while simultaneously refraining from rescuing students and not letting them experience the consequences of their decisions and actions. Simultaneously, adults will want to provide explicit instruction in skills for independent learning. Many students with a hearing loss demonstrate strategy deficits because they have not had the opportunity to overhear how adults or peers solve problems or approach learning tasks and because strategy instruction is not often included in students' Individualized Education Program (IEP) goals (Luckner, 1994). Examples of independent learning skills include time management, study skills, using an interpreter, expository text comprehension strategies, preparing for and taking tests, using the internet, and writing a

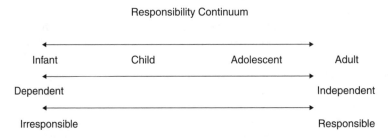

Figure 26.3 Responsibility continuum

research paper. These skills should be introduced via modeling, explanation, and the provision of feedback during elementary school, then practiced and refined throughout students' educational careers (Corno, 1992).

Wehmeyer (2006) recently defined self-determined behaviors as the "volitional actions that enable one to act as the primary causal agent in one's life and to maintain or improve one's quality of life" (p. 117). Examples of self-determined behaviors include self-awareness, self-regulation, goal setting and attainment, problem solving, decision-making, and choice making (Wehmeyer & Field, 2007). Professionals can promote the development of self-determination by teaching the skills that comprise self-determination, establishing environments that encourage students' self-determination, and promoting student involvement in IEP meetings.

Despite a paucity of research and resources specifically focused on self-determination and individuals who are deaf or hard of hearing, a variety of curriculum and resources are available that have been developed for students with mild, moderate, and severe disabilities which can be easily used with students who have hearing loss. Examples include Steps to Self-Determination (Hoffman & Field, 2006), ChoiceMaker Self-Determination Assessment (Martin & Marshall, 1995), and Take Charge for the Future (Powers, Ellison, Matuszewski, & Turner, 2004). Additionally, professionals can involve students in the development of IEP and transition goals as well as have students participate in IEP meetings (Velaski, 1999). The Self-Directed IEP (Martin, Marshall, Maxson, & Jerman (1996) is a useful resource in this context to achieve greater student involvement.

A four-level incremental approach for student involvement in IEP meetings adapted from Mason, McGahee-Kovac, & Johnson (2004) follows. Students would address each level as well as progress through the levels in accordance with their age, capability, and opportunities for practice.

Level 1—Students introduce everyone at the meeting to each other.

Level 2—Students present or read their goals for the future.

Level 3—Students explain their disability, share their individual strengths and challenges, and explain beneficial accommodations.

Level 4—Students lead and close the meeting.

Although self-advocacy is often viewed as a component of self-determination, self-advocacy skills become significantly more important in college and on the job. In particular, many of the services that students are entitled to during their PK-12 education may no longer be provided in postsecondary or work settings unless individuals understand the differences in their rights and responsibilities as they relate to issues such as applying, documenting a disability, requesting accommodations, applying for Vocational Rehabilitation Services, and securing transportation.

Self-advocacy has been defined as the "extent to which a student can identify supports needed to succeed and communicate that information effectively to others, including teachers and employers" (Friend, 2008, p. 524). Multiple strategies including role-playing, strategy instruction, and videos as well as published curricular packages can be used to teach self-advocacy skills (Test, Fowler, Brewer, & Wood, 2005).

Examples of self-advocacy skills that should be taught to students who are deaf or hard of hearing include:

- Using and maintaining hearing assistance technology;
- Employing strategies to address communication challenges (e.g., classroom discussions, noisy environments);

- Using an interpreter;
- Understanding legal rights and responsibilities in school, college or work as delineated in the Individuals with Disabilities Education Improvement Act (IDEA) of 2004; Section 504 of the Rehabilitation Act of 1973; and the Americans with Disabilities Act (ADA) of 1990;
- Recognizing when they need help;
- Knowing when and how to request help;
- Knowing appropriate accommodations and modifications;
- Asking for appropriate help from peers and adults;
- Completing application forms;
- Preparing for interviews;
- Expressing needs and wants effectively;
- Identifying and accessing local, state, regional, and national resources.

Stage 2—Gather Information from the Student, Family and Professionals about the Student's Current Level of Functioning and Future Aspirations

The process of assessment is conducted for a variety of purposes (e.g., to determine if a student is in need of special assistance or enrichment and to evaluate instructional programs). For transition planning, professionals are most interested in (a) identifying students' current level of functioning is specific areas, and (b) determining students' strengths, needs, preferences, and interests related to living, learning, and working after leaving high school (Sitlington, Neubert, & Clark, 2010).

Although most standardized tests provide limited information about employment and living independently, they do provide general information about students' present level of performance, subjects in which they perform well, plus potential data related to knowledge and skills needed in postsecondary education and training programs. The standardized assessments most often used with students who are deaf or hard of hearing are the Stanford Achievement Test Series, the Woodcock-Johnson III Test of Achievement, the Brigance Diagnostic Inventory of Essential Skills, and the Kaufman Test of Educational Achievement (Luckner & Bowen, 2006).

Many commercially developed transition-related assessment tests and procedures (e.g., adaptive behavior, aptitude, occupational interests), are available and can be used with students who are deaf or hard of hearing. Following is a brief description of a few assessments that target several domains of transition planning. For a more in-depth discussion on transition-related assessments see Clark (2007).

Transition Competence Battery for Deaf and Hard of Hearing Adolescents and Young Adults (TCB) (Reiman, Bullis, & Davis, 1993) is a standardized assessment tool that can be used to measure the work and social skills necessary to successfully work and live in the community for persons who are deaf or hard of hearing. The TCB can be used to generate curriculum objectives and transition activities for the IEP. It can also be used as a post-test to evaluate the results of transition planning.

The TCB was designed for individuals who are deaf or hard of hearing who primarily use sign communication or who possess limited English reading skills. It was not designed for individuals who are hard of hearing and high functioning or for individuals who have multiple disabilities in addition to a hearing loss. It can be administered to small groups (i.e., six to eight students) or individually to adolescents or young adults who are deaf or hard of hearing. Testing can include the total test battery administered over time or be broken up by subtests.

The TCB has two versions: a third-grade reading-level and illustrated written version and a video version. The video version employs a sign language interpreter who presents items using contact signing (sign communication using primarily English word order with American Sign Language (ASL) signs and ASL grammatical features). The TCB includes three subtests on employment (i.e., job-seeking skills, work adjustment skills, job-related social skills) and three subtests on independent living (i.e., money management skills, health and home skills, community awareness skills).

Transition Planning—Updated Version (TPI- UV) (Clark & Patton, 2006) was designed as a formal assessment and planning tool for use with students with disabilities in individualized educational planning. It focuses on the major areas of transition services planning that have emerged in the literature and from legislation. It has four forms: Student Form, Home Form, School Form, and Profile and Further Assessment Recommendations Form. The student, the student's parents or guardians, and one or more professionals at school participate in the assessment.

The TPI consists of 46 transition-planning statements, organized according to the following planning areas: Employment, Further Education/Training, Daily Living, Leisure Activities, Community Participation, Health, Self-Determination, Communication, and Interpersonal Relationships. Each planning area has three or more items related to knowledge, skills, or behaviors associated with successful adjustment in that area. The rater selects the level of agreement with statements that reflect the present level of performance or current level of functioning that the student consistently displays in each planning area. A scale of 0 (strongly disagree) to 5 (strongly agree) provides the rater a range of response on the extent of agreement to which the student has achieved and consistently performs the outcome represented in each item. In addition to the ratings of knowledge, skills, and behavior, each TPI form requests the rater to mark likely post-school settings (employment/further education or training, and living arrangement). Further, the Student Form includes a section with 15 questions eliciting responses regarding interests and preferences on current and future activities. A similar Parent Preferences and Interest Form is provided as an optional activity. The responses to these questions supplement ratings on present level of functioning to help focus planning on the student's preferences and interests as well as strengths and needs. On the Profile and Further Assessment Recommendations Form, the information obtained from all parties is summarized. A CD computer version is available. The Home Form is provided in four additional languages (Spanish, Mandarin, Japanese, and Korean). The Administration and Resource Guide includes an extensive list of over 600 sample goals that can be used for the development of IEP goals and objectives.

Person-Centered Planning is an informal transition assessment process. Person-centered planning refers to a family of approaches that brings together the student, family members, friends, and professionals to develop a plan of action that is based on the interests, aptitudes, knowledge, and skills of the student and is developed specifically so that the IEP goals, objectives, and action statements can easily be implemented (Clark, 2007; Kim & Turnbull, 2004). Sample questions that can be used for person-centered planning that draw from the work of Morningstar (1995) and Flexer, Simmons, Luft, & Baer (2001) include:

- At what age do you want to graduate from school?
- What kind of work or education do you hope to see yourself doing after you graduate from high school?
- Where do you want to live?
- What do you want to do with your free time?
- How will you get to work/school and around town?
- Who will be your friends?
- Are there postsecondary education or specific learning experiences that you want to have?

Stage 3—Create a Vision of What is Most Important for the Student's Future and Determine What Actions Need to be Undertaken and in What Order

Data gathered through formal and informal assessments provide the stimulus for developing a general framework that helps students successfully achieve their personal and professional goals. At a minimum, the areas of employment, continuing education, and community living should be addressed (Kochhar-Bryant et al., 2009). A more expansive view would address the six adult domains of (a) employment/education, (b) home and family, (c) leisure pursuits, (d) community involvement, (e) physical/emotional health, and (f) personal relationships and relationships (Cronin, Patton, & Wood, 2007).

The process of backward planning can help team members identify the actions that need to be undertaken each year prior to graduation for students to be ready to achieve their post-school goals. Consider a student who wants to get a job performing body repairs on automobiles and trucks when he completes school. It would be beneficial to develop a plan for him to gather more information about the job requirements, duties, education requirements, salary range, and career path for a collision repair technician. He would learn that a high school diploma or equivalent is expected and that certifications from the Inter-Industry Conference on Auto Collision Repair (ICAR) or Automotive Service Excellence (ASE) are preferred. In addition, a background in art, business, and automotive classes is useful. With the information about the knowledge and skills needed to become a collision repair technician, the student and the team can compare the knowledge and skills the student currently demonstrates and then work backwards to identify the knowledge, skills, and experiences the student needs to acquire over the next few years in order to successfully transition to employment in his chosen field. A similar backward planning process can be undertaken with the other adult domains noted above.

Stage 4—Integrate Knowledge, Skills and Transition Goals into the IEP

At the age of 14 or 16, depending on the state, students' IEPs must contain transition-related information about their:

- Present level of academic and functional performance;
- Measurable postsecondary goals that address education or training, employment, and, as needed, independent living;
- Goals and objectives related to the development of transition knowledge and skills;
- Planned course of study aligning the instruction, community-based experiences, life skills, and functional vocational evaluation if appropriate;
- Related and community-based services including supportive services needed to develop knowledge and skills as well as any agencies that will provide transition services (Kochhar-Bryant et al., 2009).

Each component is discussed in more detail below.

Present levels of performance is a summary of the assessments that have been conducted with students and should include the names of the assessments administered, who administered them, and when they were administered. As noted previously, the results of the assessments should be used to develop the postsecondary goals, annual goals, course of study, and related and community services. Two additional points need to be emphasized. First, it is important to include information about students' strengths, personal attributes, accomplishments, and aspirations for the future. Second, IDEA 2004 requires that students of 16 and older be invited to participate in meetings where their Individualized Education Programs (IEPs) are being developed. Consequently, data gathered through the assessment process should be made available to students and presented in a manner that they can understand. For example, vocabulary such as stanine scores, quartiles, and normal curve-equivalents should be avoided or explained to students prior to the IEP meeting.

Postsecondary goal statements are measurable outcomes that should be based on the results of the transition assessments and focus on what students will do after exiting the public school system. Following are a few examples of appropriate postsecondary goal statements:

- After graduation Liz will work in the fast food industry.
- After high school Nathan will attend college.
- Following graduation Harold will use public transportation to access the community.

Annual goals and objectives should relate to the development of transition knowledge and skills and should focus on what students will do or learn in the next year. In addition, they should specifically move students toward achievement of their postsecondary goals. An example of an annual goal is: Stanley will research the admission requirements for three colleges that offer a major in recreation and leisure, compare those requirements to his current course of study, and present his summary at his next IEP meeting.

Various transition-focused curricula are currently available for professionals to use with students and to identify transition-related goals and objectives. Examples include *Transition: It's All About Me* developed by the Postsecondary Education Programs Network (PEPNet), (n.d.) (www.pepnet.org/itransistion), *Whose Future Is It Anyway?* (Wehmeyer, Lawrence, Kelchner, Palmer, Garner, & Soukup, 2004) and *NEXT S.T.E.P: Student transition and Educational Planning* (Halpern, Herr, Doren, & Wolf, 2000). In addition, a K-12 scope and sequence of transition topics for students who are deaf or hard of hearing titled the *Transition Skills Guidelines* has been developed by the Laurent Clerc National Deaf Education Center (2006) (http://clerccenter2.gallaudet.edu/Transition/TSG.html). Finally, Internet resources such as the National Center on Secondary Education and Transition (http://www.ncset.org/) and the National Secondary Transition Technical Assistance Center (http://www.nsttac.org/) also have a wealth of resources for professionals to access.

The course of study should relate to students' postsecondary goals in each area (i.e., employment, postsecondary education, community living). Courses of study should provide a multi-year description of the specific coursework that will help students achieve their desired post-school goals. It should cover the time period from the first IEP that is in effect when students reach the age of 16 (or 14 if states have early transition procedures) until the year that students anticipate exiting school. It can be an individualized list of courses for each year (e.g., Year 1 age 15/16 ENG202: Literary Analysis and Composition II; MTH112: Pre-Algebra; HST202: Modern World Studies; SCI112: Earth Science; and BUS010: Business Communication and Career Exploration) and/or a narrative focusing on specific knowledge and skills to be learned (e.g., Kara will continue to participate in the college preparatory courses at the high school and receive support from the teacher of students who are deaf or hard of hearing in the areas of transition, self-advocacy, pre- and post-teaching of content vocabulary and concepts, and study skills for the next three years).

Related services include areas such as transportation, speech and language pathology, sign or oral interpretation, cued speech, note taking, tutoring, audiology, physical and occupational therapy, and psychological services. *Community-based services* include agencies that typically provide services such as vocational rehabilitation, public health, assistive technology, mental health, therapeutic recreation, employment, alcohol and substance abuse, transportation, and independent living. Students' IEPs should contain a statement of interagency responsibilities or any linkages required to ensure that students have the transition services they need from outside agencies. In addition, representatives from those agencies should be invited to IEP meetings.

Stage 5—Implement the IEP Coordinating Efforts across Individuals, Organizations, Agencies, and Settings

Communication and collaboration among students, families, and professionals are essential for implementation of the IEP including the specifically tailored transition goals and services. As noted earlier, families should be included in the assessment and planning process. In addition, they can help with career exploration activities, visits to vocational-technical schools and colleges, job-shadowing opportunities, paid work experiences, practicing independent living skills, using local public transportation and getting a driver's license as well as participating in community events. Family and professional partnerships improve outcomes for students and enhance satisfaction for both families and professionals (Epstein & Salinas, 2004).

Teamwork also needs to occur across service providers in order to appropriately deliver each student's course of study that includes postsecondary goals and related services (Morningstar, Kim, & Clark, 2008). For students who receive services in general education settings, teachers of students who are deaf or hard of hearing, general education teachers, and speech and language pathologists should implement a formal method of communication that allows them to coordinate their efforts and to reinforce and generalize the knowledge and skills being taught to students. Similarly, teachers of students who are deaf or hard of hearing will want to work in partnership with transition coordinators, general special education secondary educators, and life-skills teachers in order to provide services for the increasing number of students who suffer hearing loss as well as additional disabilities (Bruce, Dinatale, & Ford, 2008). Teachers also will want to partner with professionals who provide enrichment experiences for students who have gifts and talents, and with professionals with an expertise in English language learning to work with the growing population of students with hearing loss whose families do not use English as the primary language in the home (Rhoades, Price, & Perigoe, 2004). For students who receive services in a specialized program or school for students with hearing loss, similar professional communication and collaboration needs to occur. However, the particular individuals who need to be involved would likely be different. For example, dormitory staff as well as the content-subject teachers may play important roles in executing students' IEP goals and objectives related to transition.

IDEA 2004 also requires that school personnel develop linkages with community service agencies to better assist students in achieving their postsecondary goals. School and agency personnel formalize these linkages by developing an interagency agreement or a memorandum of understanding in an effort to provide comprehensive and seamless services for students as they transition from one phase of their lives to the next (Sitlington et al., 2010). The interagency agreements identify the roles and responsibilities of each agency involved with each student. Specifically, the cooperative agreement: (a) identifies the resources to be used; (b) identifies the goals, objectives, and activities; (c) identifies the expected results; and (d) establishes timelines for the activities (Kochhar-Bryant et al., 2009).

Stage 6—Evaluate Progress and Update IEP Annually

Students' progress can be examined and evaluated using a variety of methods including (a) monitoring and charting progress, (b) focused assessments, (c) portfolios, and (d) specific documents such as attendance reports and supervisor evaluations. Additionally, team members may want to reflect upon how well transition content is being acquired and the effectiveness of services and coordination efforts. Table 26.1 is an example of a questionnaire that can be used as stimulus for evaluating progress and planning.

Table 26.1 Transition implementation evaluation questionnaire for students who are deaf or hard of hearing

Directions: Team members – please evaluate the following actions with regard to the transition planning and services being provided for [student's name].

1. Promoting career development

Excellent ___   Satisfactory ___   Unsatisfactory ___   Needs immediate attention ___

2. Encouraging responsibility and independence

Excellent ___   Satisfactory ___   Unsatisfactory ___   Needs immediate attention ___

3. Fostering the development and use of self-determination skills

Excellent ___   Satisfactory ___   Unsatisfactory ___   Needs immediate attention ___

4. Developing self-advocacy skills

Excellent ___   Satisfactory ___   Unsatisfactory ___   Needs immediate attention ___

5. Collecting and examining transition-related information

Excellent ___   Satisfactory ___   Unsatisfactory ___   Needs immediate attention ___

6. Creating a shared vision of the student's future

Excellent ___   Satisfactory ___   Unsatisfactory ___   Needs immediate attention ___

7. Integrating knowledge, skills and transition goals into the IEP

Excellent ___   Satisfactory ___   Unsatisfactory ___   Needs immediate attention ___

8. Implementing and coordinating the IEP across individuals, organizations, agencies and settings

Excellent ___   Satisfactory ___   Unsatisfactory ___   Needs immediate attention ___

9. Evaluating progress and updating IEP annually

Excellent ___   Satisfactory ___   Unsatisfactory ___   Needs immediate attention ___

Additional Considerations

The model for facilitating the transition of students who are deaf or hard of hearing described above provides a general template for planning, implementing, and evaluating the transition services for students with hearing loss. In the following section additional information is provided specific to students who want to attend a postsecondary training program and to students who require a functional curriculum focusing on life skills.

Post-Secondary Education Focus

As noted earlier, more students with a hearing loss are graduating from high school with a regular diploma. As a result, increasing numbers of students with hearing loss are attending postsecondary education programs (Lang, 2002). Yet, due to the potential obstacles described above, approximately 25% of the individuals who start a postsecondary program graduate from a two-year or four-year program (Marschark, Lang, & Albertini, 2002; Stinson & Walter, 1997). This is an unfortunate occurrence because the U.S. Census Bureau reports that individuals' earnings generally increase in proportion to the educational level they attain. For example, individuals with an associate degree earn 33% more over their working life span than individuals with a high school diploma. Similarly, individuals with a bachelor's degree earn 31% more than individuals with an associate degree and 75% more than individuals with a high school diploma over their working life span (Day & Newburger, 2002). The lack of postsecondary training is also a concern because future employment demands will require a work force that is technologically advanced and able to acquire training beyond the high school level.

Recent research reported by Convertino, Marschark, Sapero, Sarchet, & Zupan (2009) examined the factors that predicted academic success of college students who are deaf or hard of hearing. The strongest predictor variables were the English, Natural Science, and Mathematics subscores of the American College Test (ACT), with the English subscore accounting for more than 80% of the variance. The authors concluded that high school academic preparation is a strong predictor of academic success for postsecondary students who are deaf or hard of hearing. Interestingly, neither audiological (i.e., degree of hearing loss) nor communicative (i.e., spoken language or American Sign Language skills) variables were predictive factors.

Given the importance of academic preparation for postsecondary programs, professionals will want to be proactive about helping students get ready to enter as well as succeed in their postsecondary education. Specific recommendations to consider that draw from the work of Dalke (1991), Tierney, Bailey, Constantine, Finkelstein, & Hurd (2009) and the Wisconsin Department of Public Instruction (2007) are:

- Offer courses and curricula that prepare students for college-level work and ensure that students understand what constitutes a college-ready curriculum by 9th grade.
- Engage students in career exploration activities.
- Facilitate students' understanding of their disability and how it affects learning and test taking.
- Utilize assessment measures to assist students in obtaining a clear picture of their strengths and needs as they relate to the demands of the postsecondary environment, and assist them in overcoming deficiencies as they are identified.
- Provide instruction and practice in self-advocacy.
- Encourage and support students' involvement in extracurricular activities.
- Provide instruction and practice in learning strategies, time management, study skills, stress management, and exam preparation.
- Facilitate students' involvement in volunteer and paid work experiences.
- Assist students in finding postsecondary programs that match their qualifications, interests, and goals.
- Surround students with adults and peers who build and support their college-going aspirations.
- Help students investigate eligibility requirements for Vocational Rehabilitation.
- Have students arrange to take the ACT or SAT tests and request accommodations if appropriate.
- Help students prepare their SOP documentation.
- Increase families' financial awareness, and help students apply for financial aid.
- Provide opportunities for students to explore and address issues related to the emotional factors involved in losing a familiar support system of family, friends, and teachers.
- Role-play interviews.
- Engage and support students in completing critical steps for completing the postsecondary application process and entry.
- Familiarize students with the physical environment of the campus and community.
- Identify and explain campus and community organization, agencies, and related support services that are available to students.

Two valuable websites that can be used to gather information about postsecondary training programs are the U.S. Department of Education's College Navigator website (http://nces.ed.gov/collegenavigator/) and the PEPNet College Guide (http://projects.pepnet.org/collegeguide/). A list of sources of financial aid for students to attend postsecondary training is available on the website of the Laurent Clerc National Deaf Education Center (http://clerc-center.gallaudet.edu/Clerc_Center/Information_and_Resources/Info_to_Go/Transition_to_Adulthood/Financial_Aid_.html).

Life-Skills Focus

As described previously, a large portion of the population of students who are deaf or hard of hearing have an additional disability. Risk factors can include any one or a combination of the following: being foreign born or having English as a second language, a lack of family support, inappropriate diagnosis, substance abuse, discrimination, inappropriate education, residence in a rural or low-income urban setting, and significantly below-average functioning, referred to as the Low Functioning Deaf (LFD)(LFD Strategic Work Group, 2004).

The LFD population, which has been estimated to be between 125,000 and 165,000 individuals, often have limited communication abilities, demonstrate poor social and emotional skills, experience difficulty maintaining employment, and cannot live independently without assistance or support. "Most LFD adults read below the second grade level with academic achievements below the fourth grade. These individuals are not likely to have high school diplomas and are typically unable to participate in college and other postsecondary vocational programs" (LFD Strategic Work Group, 2004, p. 1).

In an effort to prepare individuals who may require a more specialized plan of study than the general education or the postsecondary track set of courses, a special curriculum that focuses on adult outcomes may be necessary. Instruction in life skills, which have been defined as "specific competencies (i.e., knowledge, skills, and their application) of local and cultural relevance needed to perform everyday activities across a variety of settings" (Cronin et al., 2007, p. 2) is needed for many individuals because they are not being prepared for the multidimensional demands of adulthood. As a result, they become unemployed or underemployed, have restricted living options, and limited social interactions and activities (Bowe, 2003).

Similar to other forms of transition-related assessments, a variety of methods are available to determine a student's present level of performance as well as to monitor and evaluate an individual's progress. General types include formal testing, informal techniques such as observation, structured interviews, work-sample analysis, and performance assessments (Cronin et al., 2007). Frequently used commercially available instruments include the *Vineland-II Adaptive Behavior Scales—Second Edition* (Sparrow, Cicchetti, & Balla, 2005) and the *Adaptive Behavior Assessment System—Second Edition* (Harrison & Oakland, 2003).

Life-skills instruction can occur in a variety of ways depending on the needs of students. For example, content can be infused into existent courses, such as in a literacy class that requires students to provide details about how to use the public bus transportation schedule or to explain the directions and possible side effects of one of their medications. Another option is the development of a specific course such as "Daily Living Math," which could focus on topics like understanding paychecks, banking, and paying bills. A strand of courses is another possibility. Individual courses could focus on essential life skills such as interpersonal relations, physical and emotional health, personal finance, and leisure pursuits.

While many life skills can be taught in classroom settings, there may be advantages to learning and practicing specific skills in the natural environments in which they occur, such as the community in which the students live. Community-based instruction provides a level of applied experience that is often difficult to create in the classroom. Examples of community-based sites to consider include businesses (e.g., restaurants, laundromats, groceries), services (e.g., libraries, recreation centers), government agencies (e.g., Social Security office, motor vehicle), utilities (e.g., cable TV, electricity) and public transportation options.

Professionals also will want to consider arranging work-based learning opportunities for students. Typical options include:

- Cooperative Education—Students work half a day and attend academic and/or vocational classes the remainder of the day. An employee supervises students on the work site and a program coordinator from the school monitors students' progress.
- Internship Programs—Students work for an employer for a specific block of time to learn about the profession. Financial compensation, tasks to be completed, responsibilities, and length of internship vary.
- School-Based Enterprises—Groups of students participate in a school-sponsored endeavor to produce goods or services for sale or use.
- Supported Employment—A team of professionals as well as students and family members work collaboratively to support students to develop competitive work knowledge and skills in integrated settings. Support is provided in the form of placement, job coaches, transportation, assistive technology, specialized job training, and individually tailored supervision.

Summary

This is an exciting time for individuals who are deaf or hard of hearing. Trends such as newborn hearing screening in combination with early intervention, cochlear implants, and inclusive practices are providing opportunities for the development of communication competence and access to content knowledge and skills that infrequently occurred in the past. Increasing numbers of students are graduating from high school with regular diplomas and many continue their education by enrolling in a postsecondary training program.

These are also challenging times. The world of work continues to change. The number of high-paying, blue-collar jobs has decreased, while technical, professional, managerial, and administrative occupations are experiencing increased growth. Employers want to hire workers who have strong academic skills and good interpersonal skills, those who can work independently and who are reliable (Bronson, 2007). In addition, the majority of the predicted new jobs will require some postsecondary education (Goldberger, Lessell, & Biswas, 2005).

Professionals working with students who are deaf or hard of hearing need to work in collaboration with students and families as well as other professionals to make sure that transition planning is the focal point of the IEP. Planning for each phase of the educational process needs to be guided by individuals' current level of functioning, aspirations for the future, and the identification and provision of a personally meaningful education along with needed supports. Additionally, it is essential to not lose sight of the end target—that is, preparation for life after leaving or graduating from high school and the development of the appropriate attitudes, knowledge, and skills to successfully meet the demands of adult living.

References

American Heritage Dictionary (3rd ed.). (1994). New York: Dell Publishing.

Blocher, D. H., Heppner, M., & Johnston, J. (2001). *Career planning for the 21st century* (2nd ed.). Denver, CO: Love Publishing Company.

Bonds, B. G. (2006). School-to-work transitions. In D. F. Moores and D. S. Martin (Eds.). *Deaf learners: Developments in curriculum and instruction.* (pp. 145–160). Washington, DC: Gallaudet University Press.

Bowe, F. G. (2003). Transition for deaf and hard-of-hearing students: A blueprint for change. *Journal of Deaf Studies and Deaf Education, 8(4),* 486–493.

Brolin, D. E., & Loyd, R. J. (2004). *Career development and transition services: A functional life skills approach* (4th ed.). Upper Saddle River, NJ: Pearson Prentice Hall.

Bronson, E. (2007). Helping CTE students learn to their potential. *Techniques: Connecting Education and Careers, 82*(7), 2–4.

Bruce, S., Dinatale, P., & Ford, J. (2008). Meeting the needs of deaf and hard of hearing students with additional disabilities through professional teacher development. *American Annals of the Deaf, 153*(4), 368–375.

Burns, M. S., Griffin, P., & Snow, C. E. (1999). *Starting out right: A guide to promoting children's reading success*. Washington, DC: National Academy Press.

Calderon, R., & Greenberg, M. (2003). Social and emotional development of deaf children: Family, school and program effects. In M. Marschark & P. Spencer (Eds.). *Oxford Handbook of Deaf Studies, Language, and Education*. (pp. 177–189). New York, NY: Oxford University Press.

Carney, A. E., & Moeller, M. P. (1998). Treatment efficacy: Hearing loss in children. *Journal of Speech, Language, and Hearing Research, 41*(1), S61–S84.

Centers for Disease Control and Prevention. (2009). *Summary of 2007 National Early Hearing Detection & Intervention (EHDI) Program Data* (Version1). Retrieved July 17, 2009 from http://www.cdc.gov/ncbddd/ehdi/data.htm

Clark, G. M. (2007). *Assessment for transition planning* (2nd ed.). Austin, TX: PRO-ED.

Clark, G. M., & Patton, J. R. (2006). *Transition planning inventory: Updated version*. Austin, TX: PRO-ED.

Cole, E. B., & Flexer, C. (2007). *Children with hearing loss: Developing listening and talking birth to six*. San Diego, CA: Plural Publishing Inc.

Concise Oxford English Dictionary (11th ed.). (2004). New York, NY: Oxford University Press, Inc.

Convertino, C. M., Marschark, M., Sapere, P., Sarchet, T., & Zupan, M. (2009). Predicting academic success among deaf college students. *Journal of Deaf Studies and Deaf Education, 14*(3), 324–343.

Corno, L. (1992). Encouraging students to take responsibility for learning and performance. *The Elementary School Journal, 93*(1), 69–83.

Cronin, M. E., Patton, J. R., & Wood, S. J. (2007). *Life skills instruction: A practical guide for integrating real-life content into the curriculum at the elementary and secondary levels for students with special needs and who are placed at risk*. Austin, TX: Pro Ed.

Dalke, C. (1991). *Support programs in higher education for students with disabilities: Access for all*. Rockville, MD: Aspen.

Day, J. C., & Newburger, E. C., (July 2002). *The big payoff: Educational attainment and synthetic estimates of work-life earnings*. Retrieved January 14, 2010 from http://www.census.gov/population/www/socdemo/educ-attn.html

Dew, D. (Ed.). (1999). *Serving individuals who are low-functioning deaf: Report of the Twenty-Fifth Institute on Rehabilitation Issues*. Washington, DC: George Washington University.

Diamond, M., & Hopson, J. (1998). *Magic trees of the mind*. New York: Penguin Putnam Inc.

Dickinson, D. K., McCabe, A., & Essex, M. J. (2006). A window of opportunity we must open to all: The case for preschool with high-quality support for language and literacy. In D. K. Dickinson & S. B. Neuman (Eds.). *Handbook of early literacy research Volume 2* (pp. 11–28). New York, NY: The Guilford Press.

D'Zamko, M., & Hampton, I. (1985). *Personnel preparation for multihandicapped hearing-impaired students: A review of the literature. American Annals of the Deaf, 130*(1), 9–14.

Ellis, S., & Lenz, B. K. (1996). Perspectives on instruction in learning strategies. In D. Deshler, E. Ellis, & B. K. Lenz (Eds.), *Teaching adolescents with learning disabilities: Strategies and methods* (2nd ed.). (pp. 9–60). Denver, CO: Love Publishing.

Epstein, J. L., & Salinas, K. C. (2004). Partnering with families and communities. *Educational Leadership, 61*(8), 12–17.

Evans, J. F. (1995). Conversation at home: A case study of a young deaf child's communication experiences in a family in which all others can hear. *American Annals of the Deaf, 140* (4), 324–332.

Flexer, R.W., Simmons, T. J., Luft, P., & Baer, R. M. (2001). *Transition planning for secondary students with disabilities*. Upper Saddle River, NJ: Prentice-Hall Inc.

Foster, S., & Macleod, J. (2003). Deaf people at work: Assessment of communication among deaf and hearing persons in work settings. *International Journal of Audiology, 42*, S128–S139.

Friend, M. (2008). *Special Education: Contemporary perspectives for school professionals* (2nd ed.). Boston, MA: Pearson Education, Inc.

Gallaudet Research Institute (November 2008). *Regional and national summary report of data from the 2007-08 annual survey of deaf and hard of hearing children and youth*. Washington, DC: GRI, Gallaudet University.

Goldberger, S., Lessell, N., & Biswas, R. B. (September, 2005). *The right jobs: Identifying career advancement opportunities for low-skilled workers*. Retrieved December 2, 2009 from http:www.jff.org

Halpern, A. S., Herr, C. M., Doren, B., & Wolf, N. K., (2000). *NEXT S.T.E.P: Student transition and educational planning* (2nd ed.). Austin, TX: PRO-ED.

Harrison, P., & Oakland, T. (2003). *Adaptive behavior assessment system – Second edition*. San Antonio, TX: Psychological Corporation.

Hart, B., & Risley, T. R. (1995). *Meaningful differences in the everyday experiences of young American children*. Baltimore, MD: Paul H. Brookes.

Hart, B., & Risley, T. R. (2003). The early catastrophe: The 30 million word gap by age 3. *American Educator, 27*(1), 4–9.

Hoffman, A., & Field, S. (2006). *Steps to self-determination* (2nd ed.). Austin, TX: PRO-ED.

Holt, J., Traxler, C., & Allen, T. (1997). *Interpreting the scores: A user's guide to the 9th edition Stanford Achievement Test for educators of deaf and hard-of-hearing students* (Gallaudet Research Institute Technical Report No. 97-1). Washington, DC: Gallaudet University.

Huttenlocher, J., Haight, W., Bryk, A., Seltzer, M., & Lyons, T. (1991). Early vocabulary growth: Relation to language input and gender. *Developmental Psychology, 27*, 236–244.

Jones, T. W., Jones, J. K. (2003). Educating young deaf children with multiple disabilities. In B. Bodner-Johnson & M. Sass-Lehrer (Eds.). *The young deaf or hard of hearing child: A family-centered approach to early education.* (pp. 297–327). Baltimore, MD: Paul H. Brookes.

Jones, T. W., Jones, J. K., & Ewing, K. M. (2006). Students with multiple disabilities. In D. F. Moores and D. S. Martin (Eds.). *Deaf learners: Developments in curriculum and instruction.* (pp. 127–143). Washington, D.C.: Gallaudet University Press.

Karchmer, M.A., & Mitchell, R.E. (2003). Demographic and achievement characteristics of deaf and hard of hearing students. In M. Marschark & P. Spencer (Eds.). *Oxford handbook of deaf studies, language, and education.* (pp. 21–37). New York, NY: Oxford University Press.

Kim, K. H., & Turnbull, A. (2004). Transition to adulthood for students with severe intellectual disabilities: Shifting toward person-family interdependent planning. *Research & Practice for Persons with Severe Disabilities, 29*(1), 53–57.

Knoors, H., & Vervloed, M. P. J. (2003). Educational programming for deaf children with multiple disabilities: Accommodating special needs. In M. Marschark & P. Spencer (Eds.). *Oxford handbook of deaf studies, language, and education.* (pp. 82–94). New York, NY: Oxford University Press.

Kochhar-Bryant, C. A., Shaw, S., & Izzo, M. (2009). *What every teacher should know about transition and IDEA 2004.*Upper Saddle River, NJ: Pearson Education Inc.

Landry, S. H., & Smith, K. E. (2006). The influence of parenting on emerging literacy skills. In D. Dickinson & S. Neuman (Eds.), *Handbook of early literacy research: Volume 2* (pp. 135–148). New York, NY: The Guilford Press.

Lang, H. G. (2002). Higher education for deaf students: Research priorities in the new millennium. *Journal of Deaf Studies and Deaf Education, 7*(4), 267–280.

Laroche, C., Garcia, L. J., & Barette, J. (2000). Perceptions by persons with hearing impairment, audiologists, and employers of the obstacles to work integration. *Journal of the Academy of Rehabilitative Audiology, 33*, 63–90.

Laurent Clerc National Deaf Education Center. (2006). *Transition skills guidelines.* Retrieved July 16, 2009 from http://clerccenter2.gallaudet.edu/Transition/TSG.html

LFD strategic work group. (February, 2004). A model for a national collaborative service delivery system: Serving low functioning deaf youth and adults to assist them to be meaningfully employed and function independently at home and in the community. Retrieved June 4, 2009 from www.pepnet.org/training/train070824/LFD_Position_Paper_2-18-04.doc

Luckner, J. L. (1993, October). Unlocking the doors for developing self-esteem and personal responsibility. Paper presented at the Colorado State Symposium on Deafness, Colorado Springs, Colorado.

Luckner, J. L. (1994). Developing independent and responsible behaviors in students who are deaf or hard of hearing. *Teaching Exceptional Children, 26*(2), 13–17.

Luckner, J. L. (2002). *Facilitating the transition of students who are deaf or hard of hearing.* Austin, TX: PRO-ED.

Luckner, J. L., & Bowen, S. (2006). Assessment practices of professionals serving students who are deaf or hard of hearing: An initial investigation. *American Annals of the Deaf, 151*(4), 410–417.

Luckner, J. L., & Carter, K. (2001). Essential competencies for teaching students with hearing loss and additional disabilities. *American Annals of the Deaf, 146*(1), 7–15.

Luckner, J. L., & Handley, C. M. (2008). A summary of the reading comprehension research undertaken with students who are deaf or hard of hearing. *American Annals of the Deaf, 153*(1), 6–36.

Luckner, J. L., & Stewart, J. (2003). Self-assessments and other perceptions of successful adults who are deaf: An initial investigation. *American Annals of the Deaf, 148*(3), 243–250.

Marschark, M. (2003). Interactions of language and cognition in deaf learners: From research to practice. *International Journal of Audiology, 42*, 541–548.

Marschark, M., & Hauser, P. C. (2008). Cognitive underpinnings of learning by deaf and hard-of-hearing students: Differences, diversity, and directions. In M. Marschark & P. C. Hauser (Eds.). *Deaf cognition: Foundations and outcomes* (pp. 3–23). New York, NY: Oxford University Press, Inc.

Marschark, M., Lang, H. G., & Albertini, J. A. (2002). Educating deaf students: From research to practice. New York, NY: Oxford University Press.

Marschark, M., Rhoten, C., & Fabich, M. (2007). Effects of cochlear implants on children's reading and academic achievement. *Journal of Deaf Studies and Deaf Education, 12*(3), 269–282.

Martin, J. E., & Marshall, L. H. (1995). *ChoiceMaker self-determination instructional package.* Longmont, CO: Sopris West.

Martin, J. E., Marshall, L. H., Maxson, L., & Jerman, P. (1996). *The self-directed IEP.* Longmont, CO: Sopris West.

Mason, C. Y., McGahee-Kovac, M., & Johnson, L. (2004). How to help students lead their IEP meetings. *Teaching Exceptional Children, 36*(3), 18–24.

Mayberry, R. I. (2007). When timing is everything: Age of first-language acquisition effects on second-language learning. *Applied Psycholinguistics, 28*, 537–549.

Mitchell, R. E., & Karchmer, M. A. (2004). Chasing the mythical ten percent: Parental hearing status of deaf and hard of hearing students in the United States. *Sign Language Studies, 4*, 138–163.

Moeller, M. P. (2000). Early intervention and language development in children who are deaf and hard of hearing. *Pediatrics, 106*(3): E43.

Morningstar, M.E. (1995). *Planning for the future: A workbook to help young adults with disabilities, their families, and professionals to plan for living, working, and participating in the community.* Lawrence, KS: Department of Special Education, University of Kansas.

Morningstar, M. E., Kim, K. H., & Clark, G. M., (2008). Evaluating a transition personnel preparation program: Identifying transition competencies of practitioners. *Teacher Education and Special Education, 31*(1), 47–58.

National Institute on Deafness and other Communication Disorders. (2007, May). *Cochlear implants.* Retrieved May 2, 2009 from http://www.nidcd.nih.gov/health/hearing/coch.asp

Ormrod, J. E. (2008). *Human learning* (5th ed.). Upper Saddle River, NJ: Pearson Education, Inc.

Owens, R. E. Jr. (2010). *Language disorders: A functional approach to assessment and intervention* (5th ed.). Boston, MA: Pearson.

Postsecondary Education Programs Network (PEPNet), (n.d.). iTransition: It's all about me. Retrieved May 3, 2009 from www.pepnet.org/itransistion

Powers, L. E., Ellison, R., Matuszewski, J., & Turner, A. (2004). *Take Charge for the future.* Portland, OR: Portland University Regional Resource Center.

Punch, R., Hyde, M., & Power, D. (2007). Career and workplace experiences of Australian university graduates who are deaf or hard of hearing. *Journal of Deaf Studies and Deaf Education, 12*(4), 504–517.

Qi, S., & Mitchell, R. E. (April, 2007). Large-scale academic achievement testing of deaf and hard-of-hearing students: Past, present, and future. Paper presented at the Annual Meeting of the American Educational Research Association, April 10, 2007 in Chicago, Illinois.

Reiman, J., Bullis, M., & Davis, C. (1993). *Transition competence battery for deaf adolescents and young adults.* Santa Barbara, CA: James Stanfield.

Rhoades, E. A., Price, F., & Perigoe, C. B. (2004). The changing American family & ethnically diverse children with hearing loss and multiple needs. *The Volta Review, 104*(4), 285–305.

Rowe, M. L., & Goldin-Meadow, S. (2009). Differences in early gesture explain SES disparities in child vocabulary size in school entry. *Science, 323*, 951–953.

Sass-Lehrer, M., & Bodner-Johnson, B. (2003). Early intervention: Current approaches to family-centered programming. In M. Marschark and P. E. Spencer (Eds.). *Oxford handbook of deaf studies, language, and education* (pp. 65–81). New York, NY: Oxford University Press, Inc.

Schildroth, A. N., & Hotto, S. A. (1996). Changes in student and program characteristics, 1984–85 and 1994–95. *American Annals of the Deaf, 141*(2), 68–71.

Sitlington, P. L., Neubert, D. A., Begun, W. H., Lombard, R. C., & Leconte, P. J. (2007). *Assess for success: A practitioner's handbook for transition assessment* (2nd ed.). Thousand Oaks, CA: Corwin Press.

Sitlington, P. L., Neubert, D. A., & Clark, G. M. (2010). *Transition education and services for students with disabilities* (5th ed.). Upper Saddle River, NJ: Pearson Education Inc.

Social Security Administration. (2007). *Annual statistical report on the social security disability insurance program.* Washington, DC: Social Security Administration.

Sparrow, S. S., Cicchetti, D. V., & Balla, D. A., (2005). *Vineland-II adaptive behavior scales* (2nd ed.). Circle Pines, MN: American Guidance Service.

Spencer, L. J., Gantz, B. J., & Knutson, J. F. (2004). Outcomes and achievement of students who grew up with access to cochlear implants. *Laryngoscope, 114,* 1576–1581.

Stein, L., Jabaley, T., Spitz, R., Stoakley, D., & McGee, T. (1990). The hearing-impaired infant: Patterns of identification and habilitation revisited. *Ear and Hearing, 11,* 201–205.

Stewart, D. A., & Kluwin, T. N. (2001). *Teaching deaf and hard of hearing students: Content, strategies, and curriculum.* Boston, MA: Allyn and Bacon.

Stika, C. J. (1997). Living with hearing loss – Focus group results. Part II: Career development and work experiences. *Hearing Loss, 18*(6), 29–32.

Stinson, M., & Walter, G. (1997). Improving the retention for deaf and hard of hearing students: What the research tells us. *Journal of the American Deafness and Rehabilitation Association, 30*(4), 14–23.

Test, D. W., Fowler, C. H., Brewer, D. M., & Wood, W. M. (2005). A content and methodological review of self-advocacy intervention studies. *Exceptional Children 72*(1), 101–125.

Tierney, W. G., Bailey, T., Constantine, J., Finkelstein, N., & Hurd, N. F. (2009). *Helping students negotiate the path to college: What high schools can do: A practical guide* (NCEE #2009-4066). Washington, DC: National Center for Education Evaluation and Regional Assistance, Institute of Education Sciences, U.S. Department of Education. Retrieved from http://ies.ed.gov/ncee/wwc/publications/practice-guides

Traxler, C. B. (2000). The Stanford Achievement Test, 9th edition: National norming and performance standards for deaf and hard-of-hearing students. *Journal of Deaf Studies and Deaf Education, 5*(4), 337–348.

U.S. Department of Education, Office of Special Education and Rehabilitative Services, Office of Special Education Programs, (2009). *28th annual report to Congress on the implementation of the Individuals with Disabilities Education Act, 2006, vol.1,* Washington, D.C.: Author.

Velaski, A. (1999). It doesn't have to be like that: Getting the most from an IEP meeting. *Perspectives in Education and Deafness, 18*(1), 10–13.

Wagner, M., Newman, L., Cameto, R., & Levine, P. (2005). *After high school: A first look at the postschool experiences of youth with disabilities.* Menlo Park, CA: SRI International.

Wehmeyer, M. L. (2006). Self-determination and individuals with severe disabilities: Reexamining meanings and misinterpretations. *Research and Practice in Severe Disabilities, 30,* 113–120.

Wehmeyer, M. L., & Field, S. L. (2007). *Self-determination: Instructional and assessment strategies.* Thousand Oaks, CA: Corwin Press.

Wehmeyer, M. L., Lawrence, M., Kelchner, K., Palmer, S., Garner, N., & Soukup, J. (2004). *Whose future is it anyway? A student-directed transition planning process* (2nd ed.). Lawrence, KS: Beach Center on Disability, University of Kansas.

Weizman, Z. O., & Snow, C. E. (2001). Lexical input as related to children's vocabulary acquisition: Effects of sophisticated exposure and support for meaning. *Developmental Psychology, 37*(2), 265–279.

Wells, G. (1986). *The meaning makers: Children learning language and using language to learn.* Portsmouth, NH: Heinemann.

Wheeler-Scruggs, K. (2002). Assessing the employment and independence of people who are deaf and low functioning. *American Annals of the Deaf, 147*(4), 11–17.

Williams, C. B. (2009). *No limits: A practical guide for teaching deaf and hard of hearing students.* Hillsboro, OR: Butte Publications, Inc.

Willis, R. G., & Vernon, M. (2002). Residential psychiatric treatment of emotionally disturbed deaf youth. *American Annals of the Deaf, 147,* 31–37.

Wisconsin Department of Public Instruction (2007, September). *Opening doors to postsecondary education and training.* Retrieved November 11, 2009, from http://dpi.state.wi.us/sped/pdf/tranopndrs.pdf

Wood, D., & Wood, H. (1997). Communicating with children who are deaf: Pitfalls and possibilities. *Language, Speech, and Hearing Services in Schools, 28,* 348–354.

Yoshinaga-Itano, C., & Gravel, J.S. (2001). The evidence for universal newborn hearing screening. *American Journal of Audiology, 10,* 62–64.

27

Transition Education for Adolescents Who Are Blind or Have Low Vision

Karen E. Wolffe

CAREER COUNSELING & CONSULTATION, LLC

Jane Erin

UNIVERSITY OF ARIZONA

The provision of services to young adults in transition from school to work and adult life is not a new concept. Projects have focused on this population for many years within the education and rehabilitation communities. Beginning in the mid–1970s, the federal government passed numerous pieces of legislation that demonstrated a commitment to the career development of people with disabilities and mandated their inclusion in meaningful education and rehabilitation experiences (for example, PL 93–112, Rehabilitation Act of 1973; PL 94–142, the Education for All Handicapped Children Act of 1975; PL 94–482, Vocational Education Act of 1976; and PL 95–207, Career Education Incentive Act of 1977). Both the Rehabilitation Act and the Education for All Handicapped Children Act, which became the Individuals with Disabilities Education Act and more recently, the Individuals with Disabilities Education Improvement Act, have been consistently improved over time through the reauthorization process, and the federal government's intent to promote full inclusion of people with disabilities in society has thus been reinforced legislatively.

In 1990 the Americans with Disabilities Act (PL 101–336) was signed into law extending protections under the provisions of the Rehabilitation Act to all people with disabilities and guaranteeing access to public buildings, programs, transportation, telecommunications, and employment. However, in spite of these legislative efforts, positive employment outcomes for young adults who are blind or have low vision have been elusive. The most recent Department of Education-funded longitudinal study of special education students, graduates, parents, and educators, which compares results from the Department's first supported study, the National Longitudinal Transition Study (NLTS), with the second, NLTS2, indicated that fewer youth who were blind or had low vision were working at the point they were interviewed in 2003 than those interviewed in 1987 (Wagner, Newman, Cameto, & Levine, 2005). In the 2009 NLTS2 outcomes report, which analyzed results from 2005 interviews that occurred at the height of U.S. economic prosperity, youth with visual impairments were employed at a rate of 43% compared to 66% of nondisabled youth. Other than youth with mental retardation, emotional disturbance, orthopedic impairments, or deaf/blindness, youth with visual impairments were the least likely to be employed. In addition, they worked the fewest hours per week (22.8) of any of the youth with disabilities who were employed (Newman, Wagner, Cameto, &

Knokey, 2009). These low employment rates are particularly disappointing when one considers that these same young adults with visual impairments were almost as likely to graduate from high school and attend postsecondary training as their nondisabled peers (Newman et al., 2009; Wagner, D'Amico, Marder, Newman, & Blackorby, 1992; Wagner et al., 2005). Added to this documented concern in the NLTS and NLTS2 is the fact, long in evidence, that the number of students reported by school districts to the federal government and categorized as visually impaired does not include students with other disabilities, who are likely not doing as well as the 25% or so represented in these studies (Kirchner & Smith, 2005).

Students with Visual Impairments

Students with visual disabilities are occasionally totally blind, but more often have low vision. Many of the students have additional disabilities as well. There are no data available that give unequivocal population numbers, as noted above, because the data collected on special education students capture those students with visual impairments only, and those with visual impairments and additional disabilities are typically coded as students with multiple disabilities. Consequently, data from a variety of sources are necessary to understand the incidence of blindness or low vision in children and adolescents.

An American Foundation for the Blind study completed in 1998 estimated 93,600 children, 0–21 years, were receiving special education services that were vision-related (Kirchner & Diament, 1999). Of these children, approximately 55,200 were considered legally blind, and 5,600 were braille readers (Kirchner & Diament, 1999).

More recent data collected by the American Printing House for the Blind (APH) indicated that as of January 1, 2007, 58,388 students who were legally blind were attending a documented program in education or rehabilitation for at least 20 hours per week at less than the college level (C. Amback, personal communication, September 24, 2008). Students who are legally blind and have concomitant cognitive, physical, or sensory disabilities are included in this estimate. Students with low vision less severe than legal blindness or students who were not voluntarily reported to the APH by education or rehabilitation programs were not included in this estimate.

A fairly recent Center for Disease Control (CDC) study of eight-year-olds in the Atlanta area compares rates of visual impairment (20/70 acuity or worse) for 1996 and 2000, finding the rate in that short period stayed almost constant (1.4 and 1.2/1000), the level long estimated to apply nationally to children (Bhasin, Brocksen, Avchen, & Braun, 2006). However, a shift in diagnoses is noted. According to findings of *The Model Registry of Early Childhood Visual Impairment*, Cortical Visual Impairment (CVI) is by far the leading diagnosis, with over 30% of the children currently receiving services reportedly having CVI. Retinopathy of Prematurity (ROP), CVI, Optic Nerve Hypoplasia (ONH), and Albinism combined account for 63% of the children and nearly 60% of the children are multiply impaired, with cerebral palsy as the leading systemic diagnosis, in this sample (www.blindbabies.org/registry.htm). This implies that while estimates of the population can be extrapolated from Census data for transition-age youths with visual impairments, it is likely to be an underestimate of the young adults with visual impairments and additional disabilities—a number that would likely be half again as large.

The breakdown of functionally blind students versus those with impaired but functional vision is that 80–90% of the students classified as visually impaired have some functional vision (Corn & Koenig, 1996). The percentage of visually impaired students with multiple disabilities who are served in the educational system is estimated at 66% by the National Center on Birth Defects and Developmental Disabilities (CDC, 2004). While many of these students will be eligible for rehabilitation services leading to work following their public-school experience, some are too severely disabled to move into competitive employment and will more likely receive services from alternative agencies providing supported or sheltered employment. If students cannot benefit from employment, they may still be eligible for adult services that focus on supported or sheltered living and community-based activities other than work.

In this chapter, young adults with visual impairments and additional disabilities are discussed as well as individuals who are only blind or have low vision. However, the primary focus of the chapter is on youth considered eligible for rehabilitation services. The estimated size of this population can be derived from the annual Rehabilitation Administration Services (RSA) data, which are based on rehabilitation-case service reports. According to RSA data, approximately 10,000 consumers between 14 and 24 years of age with visual impairments exited the vocational rehabilitation program between 2000 and 2004; therefore, it is anticipated that at least 2,000 to 2,500 young adults are currently eligible for federally mandated rehabilitation services annually. While the reauthorization of IDEA in 2004 changed the minimum age from 14 to 16 years when transition planning is required for students in the public schools, the Act left in place the provision that students with more severe disabilities could receive transition services earlier if determined appropriate by the Individual Education Program (IEP) team.

The Unique or Disability-Specific Needs of Students with Visual Impairments

Youth who are blind or have low vision need instruction in both the standard academic or general curriculum and in disability-specific skills such as braille and travel skills since their visual impairments change the way they obtain information about the world around them. These disability-related skill sets are known in the field of education for visually impaired children as the *Expanded Core Curriculum* (ECC). Nine content areas constitute the ECC: access skills (also known as compensatory academic skills), including communication modes; orientation and mobility; social interaction skills; independent living skills; recreation and leisure skills; career education; use of assistive technology; visual efficiency skills; and self-determination (Hatlen, 1996; Huebner, Merk-Adam, Stryker, & Wolffe, 2004). Each of these areas is described briefly below, as detailed in Hatlen (1996) and Huebner et al. (2004).

Access Skills (also known as Compensatory Skills)

These are the critical skills that students with visual impairments need to be successful in accessing the general education curriculum and include concept development, organizational skills, and communication skills (speaking and listening, reading and writing with braille or print, or using alternative communication systems such as sign language, pictorial systems, or calendar box systems). Also included is skill development in using tactile graphics, raised-line drawings, maps or graphs as well as recorded materials (digital books, reading machines, recording devices).

Orientation and Mobility

These skills enable children and adolescents who are visually impaired to orient to their surroundings (i.e., to determine where they are in relationship to the things and people in their environment). Travel skills enable them to move independently and safely in the environment, use sighted guide techniques, and travel with a long cane or dog guides. Students are also taught techniques for travel using any remaining vision they may have, which may include the use of optical devices such as hand-held telescopes known as *monoculars*.

Social Interaction

These are skills needed to respond appropriately to others and participate actively in social situations. Children with visual impairments are unable to casually observe how people interact and socialize with one another so typically need to be taught these skills. Social interaction skills that may require instruction include learning when and how to use nonverbal communication (body language and facial expressions) such as smiling, frowning, nodding, winking, shrugging, and so forth. This also includes instruction in specific social skills such as shaking hands; turning toward others when speaking or being spoken to; using language to make a request, decline assistance, or express a need; expressing emotion and affection appropriately; participating appropriately in conversations in various situations, etc.

Independent Living

These skills enable individuals to manage their home environments and personal lives. The chores they are expected to perform, depending on their ages and abilities, include personal hygiene and grooming (including clothing care), eating properly (with appropriate utensils and table manners), planning and preparing meals, taking care of the household (organizing and cleaning living spaces, taking out the trash or washing dishes, etc.), money and time management, and other related skills.

Recreation and Leisure

These skills help adolescents with visual impairments to identify and choose from the array of choices available to them in recreation and leisure. They need to be taught games and activities at an age-appropriate level and encouraged to actively participate in physical and social recreational activities. They need to be made aware of and exposed to physical activities that are specially designed for individuals with visual impairments (goal ball, for example), activities that require little or no adaptation (playing Dominoes, wrestling or swimming, for example), and activities that require adaptation for full enjoyment (e.g., playing cards or board games).

Sensory Efficiency

These skills help students maximize the use of their senses, including any functional vision, hearing, touch, smell, and taste. Examples of sensory efficiency skills include learning to use touch, vision, hearing, or smelling to identify people, places (kitchen, living room, gymnasium, or swimming pool) or personal items; learning to use optical devices effectively; learning to use auditory aids appropriately; learning how to discriminate between tastes or smells to tell the difference between similar things such as salt and sugar or shampoo and conditioner; or learning how to differentiate between textures and colors to sort laundry.

Assistive Technology

In this area, students learn to use assistive technology (devices designed with speech or braille output and/or screen magnification) effectively to access mainstream technology such as computers or other electronic equipment with standard visual displays. Assistive technology includes reading and writing devices, calculators and other math and science tools, as well as navigation devices. Such devices make it easier for students with visual impairments to function effectively in school, at home, and in the workplace.

Career Education

These skills enable students who are visually impaired to recognize that they can contribute to their families and the larger society in a meaningful way and become workers as adults. These skills include assuming responsibilities at home and school, understanding the concept of working for a reward, exploring and expressing preferences about career/life roles, learning about job tasks and career paths, developing interests and abilities that are vocationally related, and finding and securing employment.

Self-Determination

These skills enable students to become effective advocates for their own needs and goals. Skills include learning to make choices, expressing preferences to others, describing one's disability, and explaining the adaptations or accommodations needed to function efficiently and independently.

Many of the aforementioned skills may seem critical for all students with disabilities rather than just students with visual impairments. While skill development in such areas as self-determination, career education, socialization, independent living, and assistive technology is, in fact, necessary for many students with special needs; what is truly different for students with visual impairments is how the content is presented. Most general and special education instruction is presented visually: teachers demonstrate skills they want students to emulate; they point to pictures and text describing skill sets under discussion; they show videos and films of concepts; they place students at computer stations where they can interact with material presented visually; they present information in writing, pictorially, or graphically so students can see what is expected of them. For students without sight or with severely impaired sight, this visual teaching technique does not work well. Students with impaired vision must receive their instruction via alternative modalities; specifically, with tactual, auditory, and kinesthetic techniques. Or, the visual medium must be made accessible to the students using their remaining functional vision: typically, through enlargement or enhancement of images. Instructional staff working with students with visual impairments must understand the content in the expanded core curriculum and be able to modify the learning environment or adapt the teaching materials.

Professionals who Provide Educational Services to Students with Visual Impairments

Students who are blind or have low vision are usually educated in public schools in classrooms with their sighted peers (American Printing House for the Blind, 2009). Only a few require more intensive services from specialized schools for students who are blind, have low vision, or come from separate classrooms in the public schools. Special education services that are needed because of a visual impairment are provided by two types of professionals: teachers of students with visual impairments (TVIs) and certified orientation and mobility specialists (COMS). These professionals are usually itinerant (traveling to students' neighborhood schools), and they provide educational support for a designated amount of time each week, as specified on the students' IEPs. They may work directly with a student in or out of the classroom, or they may support the classroom teacher by consulting and providing materials for a student. When students with visual impairments enter high school, they assume more responsibility for obtaining their own specialized equipment and materials. At that point, the teacher of students with visual impairments and the orientation and mobility instructor might not need to conduct instruction at a specific time but instead be available, as needed, to support the student in planning and implementing appropriate educational adaptations.

Teachers of students with visual impairments are responsible for meeting the students' general educational needs related to a visual impairment. They have received university instruction, usually at the graduate level, to qualify for their state's teaching certificate in visual impairment. They provide instruction and adapted materials to support the students' academic needs; examples are tactile graphics for mathematics, instruction in the use of magnification devices to read the whiteboard, or instruction in braille. They also provide instructional support in nonacademic areas that are affected by a visual impairment, including social skills, career development, and use of technology (Koenig & Holbrook, 2000).

When a student nears the end of high school, the teacher of students with visual impairment is responsible for assuring that career planning is taking place and that the student is developing skills to lead to a future occupation. TVIs are familiar with ways in which a visual impairment can affect a student's ability to apply for a job and be employed. Specific instruction in social skills, such as entry and exit from a conversation, eye contact, body orientation, and describing one's own visual impairment, can be helpful in preparing a student to interact in the workplace (Erin & Wolffe, 1999; Sacks & Wolffe, 1992). When the student has additional disabilities that make competitive employment unlikely, the TVI participates with other educational personnel to identify possible postsecondary options, including supported employment or participation in community and residential activities (Wolffe, 1998).

Certified orientation and mobility instructors receive a degree or post-degree certification to teach orientation and travel skills to people who are blind or have low vision. They are nationally certified by the Academy for Certification of Vision Rehabilitation and Education Professionals (http://www.acvrep.org/). Their roles include instruction in basic concepts and skills such as body awareness and orientation in familiar environments as well as travel skills in all of the environments in which a student participates (Griffin-Shirley, Trusty, & Rickard, 2000). While younger children usually require more emphasis on concept development and travel within the immediate school and home environments, older students will need to travel independently in the community and be able to familiarize themselves with new environments.

Some students will learn to use a long cane, the slender white extended cane used for travel by many people who are blind, under the guidance of an orientation and mobility instructor. Not only is cane travel essential for students who have little or no vision, but it is often useful to students who have usable vision, who may prefer the use of a cane in crowded or poorly lighted areas or when they want others to be aware that they have a visual impairment. In addition, students with low vision may benefit from the use of low-vision devices such as monoculars to view distant information such as a bus number or a sign.

Often an orientation and mobility instructor will assess older high school students in future environments such as a community college campus. Tactile, visual, or auditory maps may be introduced to provide an understanding of the layout of a new environment so that students can travel without assistance once they are familiar with the location of desired destinations. Orientation and mobility instructors will also provide instruction in how to manage transportation since most people with visual impairments do not drive. They teach travel by bus as well as other options for transportation such as shared rides or paratransit systems. For students with some vision, techniques for travel will be assessed and taught; these can include scanning at intersections, following markings on the street, and making decisions about traffic conditions (Fazzi & Naimy, 2010). For a young person who is visually impaired and preparing to enter the workforce, independent travel is an important skill for obtaining and continuing employment (Erin & Wolffe, 1999; Wolffe, 2004).

Sometimes students with visual impairments receive services from paraprofessionals (also known as aides or classroom assistants). The role of the paraprofessional varies widely. Some are trained and hired as braille transcribers and spend most of their time developing braille and tactile materials. These individuals usually work with students who are blind. They have been trained in the use of the braille code, often through completion of the transcriber's course through the Library of Congress. These paraprofessionals are highly skilled employees, and in some schools they are paid more than paraprofessionals without specific training in visual impairments (see information about pay scales at http://www.nrcpara.org/forum/wages).

Other paraprofessionals are employed to support the skills taught by a TVI. They may work with an adolescent on reading activities, or on practicing skills such as moving through the cafeteria line, putting on a coat, or improving keyboarding speed. Paraprofessionals may also provide physical assistance to students with multiple disabilities. It is important that their work be guided by a TVI who has assessed the student and can monitor the educational activities (Koenig & Holbrook, 2000); they should not be the primary skill instructor listed on the student's IEP.

A survey of teachers of students who are blind or have low vision and the paraprofessionals who work with them indicated that the most common activity for paraprofessionals was preparing materials, both in braille and large print (McKenzie & Lewis, 2008). Other common responsibilities reported in this study included supervising meals (more often reported by teachers), behavioral management, feeding, supervising students on buses, and performing assessments and clerical tasks.

It is rarely beneficial to assign a full-time aide to a student with a visual impairment. Students with visual impairments need the opportunity to learn by doing, and both the student and fellow classmates can learn from assisting one another. When an adult is close to a student throughout the classroom day, other students are discouraged from interacting with the student. When a paraprofessional is needed, that aide may need to be assigned to a classroom rather than an individual student (Miller & Levack, 1997; Russotti & Shaw, 2004). The TVI works closely with the paraprofessional to help the aide understand when the student needs assistance and when the aide should distance herself from the child. This is especially true when a student has reached secondary school and is assuming responsibility for managing his or her own materials; however, this responsibility begins well before the secondary level when the classroom teacher expects the student to manage personal materials and request assistance from others in the classroom when necessary.

Educational Support from Families and Service Providers

Although professionals in visual impairment work to ensure that students receive appropriate services related to their blindness or low vision, the transition process will not be successful without a unified team approach. The student as well as family members, general and special educators, related service providers such as occupational and physical therapists, and rehabilitation professionals must collaborate to achieve the goals that have been established for successful transition. Academic and vocational assessments can provide the groundwork for the team to consider postsecondary goals and to identify the necessary actions for a student to move toward those goals. If a student has specific career objectives, the team must assure that there are realistic experiences related to the student's stated interests and goals. These experiences might include job shadowing or volunteer experiences arranged in collaboration with the vocational counselors in the school setting. For example, a student may have been encouraged toward a stereotypical goal such as becoming a musician because the general public has heard of blind musicians, rather than being encouraged to consider all the ramifications such a choice will entail: the need for extensive practice in addition to talent and interest; self-marketing; planning for where, how, and when to audition; financial investment in musical instruments and lessons; related mobility requirements (moving in and out of clubs or performing on stage, for instance); and independent living requirements since such jobs often require extensive travel or moving to another city or state rather than staying in one's home community. Team members need to provide realistic and specific feedback throughout the school years so students know their strengths and weaknesses compared to the abilities of others with similar goals.

Although the student's educational team will include qualified professionals in visual impairment, the student's main teachers are general educators. Part of the role of the TVI and O & M specialist is to work with classroom teachers to emphasize the simple adaptations that will make their lessons accessible to a student with a visual impairment. Simple strategies like reading material from the whiteboard while writing or describing items in a laboratory demonstration can make a lesson understandable for a student with a visual impairment; however, the general education teacher will need to understand that advanced planning is required for the TVI to prepare appropriate materials in braille, large print, electronic file, or tactile graphic. Older students should be encouraged to communicate directly with the classroom teacher about how they learn best. Not only does this ensure that the student's needs are met when the TVI is not around, but it also provides personal advocacy experience that the student will need in the workplace or college.

Sometimes educators with no experience with students who have visual impairments do not know how much work or academic performance to expect (Spungin, 2002). A person with a visual impairment can perform similarly to sighted peers. Although adaptations may be needed, students should be expected to reach the same standards as their sighted peers unless another disability requires modification of content and curriculum. An analysis of data from 41 young people with visual impairments by McDonnall and Crudden (2009) revealed that academic performance was strongly related to later employment. This finding supports the importance of establishing clear academic goals to prepare the student for work, especially in reading and mathematics.

In addition, general educators have a responsibility to involve students in classroom activities and to encourage them to respond actively as members of the class. Students with visual impairments often appear passive or unengaged to their classroom teachers, as indicated in a study by Bardin and Lewis (2008). This lack of involvement sends a message to others, even if unintentionally, that the student is uninterested.

Consistent expectations among family members and teachers also convey the message to students who are blind or have low vision that they must complete classroom activities and assignments as required even though this sometimes requires more time or alternative approaches (Mangold, 1982; Wolffe, 1999). Families send a powerful message that they expect their child to work as an adult by requiring the child to perform routine tasks at home and complete homework assignments. Some families may not have accurate perceptions of what a person with a visual impairment can do (McConnell, 1999), and they may need information about their student's capabilities that can translate into higher expectations for postsecondary experiences. Conversely, others may have heard positive comments and praise from their student's teachers and may not understand how their son's or daughter's abilities compare to the general population.

Families can be instrumental in building connections with work environments. Individuals with visual impairments use formal job-seeking networks less frequently than sighted peers and more often rely on friends and family to assist with work opportunities (Nagle, 2001). As members of the educational team, families can convey their own understanding of their student's strengths and weaknesses but should consider the information they receive from the team about the necessary skills that will provide the best chances for future work opportunities.

Service personnel such as occupational and physiotherapists can provide information on physical abilities and adaptations that should be implemented when the team considers postsecondary opportunities. Rehabilitation counselors are also essential members of the team; they can describe the types of services that will be available when the student leaves high school and work with educational personnel to plan for transition (Rubin & Roessler, 2008). States vary in the support they offer to students entering college or the workplace. Rehabilitation counselors can respond to specific questions, such as what types of assistive technology will be provided, whether orientation and mobility services will be available for orientation to college campuses, and whether a student is eligible for a postsecondary rehabilitation program. While it is considered a best-practice approach to involve a rehabilitation professional in an adolescent's educational planning in secondary school, it is not mandatory in education or rehabilitation law. What is required is a Memorandum of Understanding (MOU) between education and rehabilitation entities in a community, spelling out what each agency will provide. In many states, a rehabilitation counselor or transition coordinator will attend students' IEP meetings following their 16th birthday. This collaboration between education and rehabilitation personnel appears to help ensure a smooth transition from secondary school into postsecondary training and work.

When an adolescent has multiple disabilities along with a visual impairment, the team will include other special education personnel who can provide input on the student's cognitive, physical, emotional, and communicative abilities. The team will consider community-based experiences and adult residential needs, and professionals in visual impairment will offer input on adaptations related to the student's visual impairment when changes to new environments take place. Representatives of other agencies, including providers in developmental disabilities, will be regularly included on the team as the student nears transition to adulthood.

Transition-age Youth Characteristics

Two lifestyles studies, one quantitative and one qualitative, were undertaken by Wolffe and Sacks to analyze similarities and differences among youth (15–21 years old) who were blind, had low vision, and the sighted. For their quantitative study, the researchers interviewed young adults and their parents three times in eighteen months and addressed four domains: academics, activities of daily living, social, and vocational (Sacks, Wolffe, & Tierney, 1998; Wolffe & Sacks, 1997). As a follow-up, the researchers used ethnographic techniques and observed three of the participants during a typical day and validated the findings in an earlier qualitative study (Sacks & Wolffe, 1998).

The results of these studies indicated that students who were blind or sighted received comparable grades (As and Bs), while the low-vision students received Bs and Cs. There were marked differences between the groups in terms of homework, however. The students with visual impairments reported receiving less homework than the sighted students and the visually impaired students tended to study at school with the help of instructional personnel while the sighted students tended to study out of school and with friends. In terms of activities of daily living, all of the students took care of themselves, their money, and their schedules (time management). The most obvious differences between the groups were in home management responsibilities: performing household chores, grocery shopping, cleaning, cooking, and general housekeeping responsibilities. Having better vision tended to equate to youth's greater levels of responsibility at home (Wolffe & Sacks, 1997).

In the social-skills area, these young adults differed in the intensity level (passive, mid or high) of their activities. Young people with low vision tended to be involved in the fewest activities and were the least likely to be in social situations with lots of other people (high-level activities). The sighted students were the most active socially. One of the most promising findings in the vocational area was that almost all of the students (88% of the students who were blind and 94% of the students with sight or low vision) had worked for pay. However, while 81% of the sighted students reported finding their own jobs, only 31% of the low-vision students and 19% of the blind students did so (Wolffe & Sacks, 1997).

In a replication of the lifestyles study completed with Canadian youth (Shaw, Gold, & Simson, 2005; Shaw, Gold, & Wolffe, 2007), the researchers noted that although Canadian youth with visual impairments had worked for pay, there were significant differences between partially sighted participants—78% of whom had worked for pay—and blind participants—61% of whom had worked for pay. There were also significant differences between blind and partially sighted participants in terms of who was currently working for pay: 35% of partially sighted and 20% of blind participants (29% of the combined groupings) were currently employed. These findings are not unlike what the researchers engaged in NLTS and NLTS2 found in their analyses of follow-up data with U.S. youth (Newman et al., 2009; Wagner, D'Amico et al., 1992; Wagner et al., 2005).

Findings from NLTS and NLTS2, which span the period from 1981 to the present (NLTS2 is scheduled to conclude in 2010), provide the most comprehensive view to date of the characteristics of students with visual impairments in the transition process. However, as noted earlier, students in the NLTS and NLTS2 do not typically have additional disabilities. Young adults with visual impairments who were out of school tended to be living with a parent or guardian in the first and second NLTS cohorts (1987 and 2003); the respective percentages were 76% and 81%. While there was no statistically significant change over time, the percentages for individuals who were blind or had low vision are slightly higher compared to other young adults with disabilities. In the most recent NLTS2 report (Newman et al., 2009), there is steady progress with 19% of youth with visual impairments living independently and 18% living semi-independently (with a spouse, a partner, or a roommate). By comparison, 28% of youth in the general population and 25% of youth with other disabilities were living independently. More young adults with visual impairments were living semi-independently, presumably in dormitories, than any of their peers with other disabilities (the range is 0.2% for youth with mental retardation to 13% for youth with hearing impairments).

In terms of social involvement, there is an increase noted from 37% of young adults with visual impairments participating in community groups in 1987 to 45% in 2003. However, of even greater positive note was the increase in volunteer work activities or community service for these young adults: only 12% of the 1987 cohort reported this type of activity while in the 2003 cohort, 54% were engaged in volunteer work or community service—a statistically significant increase of 42%. In the most recent NLTS2 report, 46% were participating in community groups and 67% were engaged in volunteer work or community service. Young adults with visual impairments had a significantly higher rate of participation in volunteer or community service activities than did those in seven other disability categories: $p < 0.001$ compared with youth with learning disabilities, mental retardation, emotional disturbances, other health impairments, or autism, $p < 0.01$ for hearing impairment or orthopedic impairment (Newman et al., 2009).

Concerns evidenced in NLTS and NLTS2 about the mediocre level of general social involvement (less than 50% of young adults with visual impairments are participating in community groups) are mirrored in the lifestyle studies performed in the United States (Wolffe & Sacks, 1997) and Canada (Gold, Shaw, & Wolffe, 2010; Shaw et al., 2005; Shaw, Gold, et al., 2007). In the Wolffe and Sacks study (1997), students with low vision appeared to be involved in the fewest activities and were the least likely to be in social situations that involved group interactions (high-level activities). Student and parent data indicated the sighted students in this sample were the most active socially. An Analysis of Variance for high-level social activities indicated significant effects between groups for students and for parents. Mean differences between the groups indicated that the groups were relatively equal for mid-level activities; however, students who were blind had the greatest involvement in passive activities. The Canadian lifestyles study showed comparable results: Histograms suggested a pattern of greater engagement in passive and mid-level social activities than in high-level social activities for the participants (all of whom were blind or had low vision) (Shaw et al., 2005). Career and rehabilitation counselors have long understood the importance of social skills and social networks both for finding and maintaining employment. Therefore, it is essential that young adults with visual impairments develop strong social skills and that they participate in social activities in their communities (Bolles & Brown, 2001; Crudden, McBroom, Skinner, & Moore, 1998; Fesko & Temelini, 1997; Roy, Dimigen, & Taylor; Sacks & Wolffe, 1992; Wolffe, 1997).

Also of interest is the finding that 37% of the Canadian participants who were blind and partially sighted (N=330) reported that they were actively looking for work. Although, when they were asked how much time they spent on a daily basis looking for work, the respondents stated they spent "one hour or less" per day on their job searches, 26% reported that they had not submitted any applications in the past year, and 41% said that they had not had any interviews in the previous year (Shaw et al., 2005; Shaw et al., 2007).

Results reported in the NLTS and NLTS2 related to employment were introduced earlier in this chapter. While the most recent data (from the 2005 interviews with youth and parents) indicated that 43% of the youth with visual impairments were working at the point when they were interviewed, they were working the fewest number of hours per week (22.8) of any of the working youth. When queried, they were the most likely group (81%) of young workers with disabilities to want to work full-time. They earned an average salary of $7.90 an hour and 38% of those employed were receiving benefits. Overall, they liked their jobs (42%) or had a fair perception of the work (40%) and almost universally (98%) felt well treated on the job. This group of young adults with disabilities were the most likely to make their employers aware of their disability; however, only 16% received job accommodations.

Transition-age youth with visual impairments are likely to graduate and attend college or university programs. In the 2005 NLTS2 interviews, 78% of visually impaired students indicated that they had or were enrolled in postsecondary training (56% in two-year programs, 12% in vocational training programs, and 44% in four-year programs). Of those who were enrolled at the time of the interviews, the vast majority (97%) stated that they were working toward degrees; however, only 12% had completed their program of study within four years of high school graduation. By comparison, 45% of youth with emotional disturbance, 41% with speech/language impairments, and 30% with other health impairments had completed their studies. While 43% of the youth with visual impairments were working, they were working fewer hours than any other group of young adults with disabilities (Newman et al., 2009). Throughout the published studies, youngsters with visual impairments seem to be experiencing difficulty with social engagement and tend to be living with their families or semi-independently in dormitories rather than independently.

In order to improve these outcomes, it is imperative that transition programs be designed to meet these students' disability-specific needs. Characteristics of programs that have proven successful in effecting change within this population are discussed next.

Transition Program Characteristics

Elements that have been identified as leading to success in transition programs for students with visual impairments include: assessment and programming that is outcome oriented;

disability-specific skill development, including reading and writing with braille or optical devices, O&M skills, use of assistive technology, and the like; structured pre-employment skills training that includes self-initiated job searches, skill building connected to future work (transferable skills), student diversity, goal setting, limited use of supports, and self-advocacy instruction; paid or volunteer work experiences for students; collaboration between education (secondary and postsecondary) and rehabilitation personnel; and program evaluation (McDonnall & Crudden, 2009; Nagle, 2001; Wolffe, 1997). Each of these elements is described in the following sections.

Outcome-Oriented Assessment and Programming

These necessitate that students identify what they are interested in doing following high school: where they plan to live, what they plan to do for work, what training they need to accomplish, and what help they anticipate needing from others. They then need to develop plans while still in school to prepare for these eventualities. An informal assessment tool, the *Transition Competencies Checklist*, is specific to the population of students with visual impairments, including those with additional disabilities, and is available upon request from the first author of this chapter. This tool has students self-evaluate in ten areas: understanding work; leisure and social skills; problem-solving skills; self-advocacy skills; compensatory skills (also known as alternative techniques); knowledge of careers and sources of career information; understanding ability level; mastery of career counseling content areas (self-awareness, career exploration, job-seeking skills, job maintenance, employment skills); evidence of work experience; and understanding employers' concerns) (Wolffe, 2001).

Alternative Skills or Disability-Specific Skills

These are described in an earlier section of this chapter related to the *Expanded Core Curriculum*. These are the skills that enable youth with visual impairments to integrate into training or work environments with their nondisabled peers while using techniques that do not rely on vision, such as reading and writing with braille or optical devices, using assistive technology, traveling without sight or with impaired sight using appropriate tools and techniques, living independently, taking care of oneself and one's home, and so forth.

Pre-Employment Skills Training

Pre-employment skills training for youth with visual impairments needs to include self-awareness (based on both the young adults' perceptions of their strengths and weaknesses and input from others), career exploration (which includes gaining information about the diversity of jobs available and what those jobs entail), job-seeking skills (especially how to handle paperwork and interactions, such as interviews without visual cues), and job maintenance skills (work habits and behaviors expected of all workers). Young adults with visual impairments need to be encouraged to self-initiate in their job searches since one of the concerns evidenced in research (Wolffe & Sacks, 1997) has been that others (teachers, counselors, significant adults) in the lives of youth have been more likely to secure jobs for these students than the students themselves. Another area of importance is skill building that encourages transferable skills. The mainstream career literature reports that young adults without disabilities can anticipate changing careers a minimum of seven times in their lifetime (Bolles, 2009); therefore, it is imperative that youth with disabilities develop skills that are viable in present and future work.

This would include a broad understanding of technology and how it is changing to meet the needs of a diverse workforce as well as developing soft skills: the work habits and behaviors that all employers expect of their workers (attendance, punctuality, trustworthiness, self-initiative, working cooperatively, following directions, and so forth). Students with visual impairments need to be encouraged to set achievable goals and make limited use of supports, which will be expected of them in a work environment. Finally, students with visual impairments can benefit from programs where they are encouraged to learn and apply self-advocacy skills, such as practicing disclosure of disability, with an emphasis on how the students can perform competitively with or without accommodations.

Ongoing Evaluation of the Program Components

Strong programs include *ongoing evaluation of the program components* using both internal and external evaluators to ensure a nonbiased report of the program's strengths and weaknesses. Change in students' perceptions of employment readiness and growth in areas they have identified as important to their career progress need to be documented as well as more discrete outcomes such as employment. Details about employment outcomes, such as the number of hours being worked, rate of pay, benefits received, and type of work being performed, tell only part of the story. Researchers also need to know how these young adults secured their jobs, what types of accommodations have enabled them to be successful on the job, and what amount of time and effort they had to exert to become and remain employed.

Paid or Volunteer Work Experiences

Paid or volunteer work experiences for students are a key element in successful transition programs. It may well be that increases in rates of employment over time are related to corresponding increases in the involvement of students with disabilities in volunteer and community work as well as paid work while still in school. This is an area that requires further research, but the initial results of projects like the NLTS2 are promising.

Collaboration between Education and Rehabilitation Personnel

One of the most critical elements for successful transition programs is a *strong collaboration between education (secondary and postsecondary) and rehabilitation personnel*. With collaboration between service providers, young adults who are blind or have low vision can make seamless transitions from childhood to adult roles and responsibilities. Educators can share with the team their perceptions of how the students learn best, whether they demonstrate strong work habits, and how they apply their knowledge, abilities, and talents in academic settings. Personnel from postsecondary training institutions can help students understand what content, skills, and study habits will be required in their next learning environment, and they can prepare accordingly. This is particularly important because most of the students with visual impairments will have received special education services in primary and secondary educational settings and may not be well prepared for postsecondary independent study. Finally, it is important to include rehabilitation personnel in transition planning and when implementing adult activities because they are well-versed in labor market considerations These include what jobs are available in the desired geographic areas, what options and support are available to prepare for the type of careers sought, what employers expect of their employees, what accommodations are reasonable and how to acquire them for work, and so forth.

A Model Transition Program

Researchers have followed a promising approach to providing transition services that was initiated in Florida in 2002. The results of that effort provide insight into the effectiveness of the programmatic elements outlined above (Jorgensen-Smith & Lewis, 2004; Lewis, Bardin, & Jorgensen-Smith, 2009). The approach, which is being used by the Florida Division for Blind Services (DBS) to provide transition services, involves collaboration between DBS, community-based rehabilitation service providers, and educators working in districts referring students to summer transition projects. DBS workers were introduced to the principles of the *Transition Tote System* (Wolffe & Johnson, 1997) and exposed to the career education needs of children and adolescents with visual impairments including the elements of successful programs. They, in turn, worked with community-based providers and established three summer transition programs.

All of the program participants in the summer transition programs completed a self-assessment tool for young adults, the *Transition Competencies Checklist* (Wolffe, 2001), and set goals for their training based on the pre-test results. The *Transition Competencies Checklist*, introduced above, is a self-report tool, which addresses ten transition areas of concern. The students used the *Checklist* to identify their strengths and weaknesses and set goals for their training based on the information they gleaned from the tool. The staff used the *Transition Tote System* to provide instruction in career education concepts and also provided disability-specific skills training in all of their transition projects to meet the students' reported needs.

In addition to using the *Transition Tote* materials, the service providers decided to adhere to the guidelines proposed as critical to successful transition programs. Therefore, their transition programs included: collaboration among agencies; job-readiness training (including self-initiated job searches, the acquisition of transferable skills, the inclusion of diverse groups of young people, the limited use of supports, the development of realistic goals, and instruction in self-advocacy); paid work; internal and external evaluation; and enthusiastic service providers. DBS contracted with three private rehabilitation agencies to pilot the project.

Results of the pilot project focused on program evaluation. Formative and summative data for each of the pilot sites and feedback from the participants—exit interviews and focus groups—were collected. Once the pilot projects were completed, the data collected were analyzed and the work group considered how to infuse what they had learned into a statewide implementation plan (Jorgensen-Smith & Lewis, 2004). In a one-year post-training follow-up study, Lewis and her colleagues (Lewis, Bardin, et al., 2009) used the *Transition Competencies Checklist* to measure changes in the students' perceived transition abilities. They reported that the students who participated in the transition program scored higher ratings in the areas where they had participated in structured learning: understanding of work based on real-life experiences, self-advocacy, knowledge of career options, ratings of their future level of dependency, mastery of career counseling areas, and ratings of their overall transition competencies one year after having completed the summer transition program. The students showed evidence of having retained content that was presented to them via the structured learning approach (using the *Transition Tote* materials), but not in other areas of instruction (alternative skills such as O&M, social skills, and self-advocacy, etc.) a year following training.

When the researchers looked at students based on their modes of reading (braille versus print), prior work experience, and gender, they found no differences in the students' overall transition competencies. These results were unexpected since previous studies have found differences between the employment rates of students with low vision and those who are blind (Houtenville, 2003; Shaw et al., 2007). These researchers found that individuals with low vision were more likely to be employed than those who were blind. While unexpected, the finding that students' prior work experience was not significantly correlated to positive outcomes may have been an artifact of the decision by Lewis and her colleagues not to include the two sections of the *Transition Competencies Checklist* that related to work experience in the overall transition competencies score (Lewis et al., 2009). Another surprising finding was the lack of gender differences found in this sample of students since there is contradictory evidence in the literature (D'Amico, 1991; Newman, 1991; Newman et al., 2009; Wagner, 1992; Wagner, Cadwallader, & Marder, 2003).

Overall, this model transition project and its evaluation lend credence to several notions related to ongoing service provision for students with visual impairments:

- A structured learning approach may be most productive for retaining content for students with visual impairments.
- Collaborative programming that involves rehabilitation and education personnel may facilitate the transition process for students.
- Instruction in self-advocacy skills is an important component of pre-employability skills training in preparation for the transition from school to work.
- Without structured learning, important skills such as problem-solving skills, social and leisure skills, and compensatory skills may not be adequately reinforced to be applied long-term.

While more research is needed, this preliminary evaluation of a model transition program for students with visual impairments seems to validate much of the work and previous research in the area of transition for these students. Table 27.1 provides resources to support instruction in these key areas, including specific curricula in career education and transition skill development.

Table 27.1 Resources

Resources: internet sites

www.careerconnect.org AFB's fully accessible online employment resource, which offers students with visual impairments and their families as well as those who work with them access to more than 1,000 successfully employed blind and visually impaired adults who are willing to discuss their jobs, the tools they use to perform on the job, how they secured and maintain employment, or any other relevant queries. CareerConnect also offers a variety of audio/video media: On Your Mark, Get Set. . .Go to Work, a series of videos that explore early work experiences of young adults with visual impairments; Aaron's Adventures in Employment, a combination of videos and old-time radio dramas chronicling the adventures of a visually impaired teenager going to work for the first time; interactive features that enable youths to develop a personal data sheet (to help in completing applications) and build a resume.

www.tsbvi.edu/REC2 web Texas School for the Blind and Visually Impaired provides an informational website that includes education resources on a wide variety of topics, including careers and transition.

Resources: publications

Attmore, M. (1990). *Career perspectives: Interviews with blind and visually impaired professionals.* New York, NY: AFB Press.

This is the first in a series of short books produced by AFB that focus on successfully employed blind and visually impaired workers. All of the jobs performed by workers in this book require college training.

Erin, J. N. & Wolffe, K. E. (1999). *Transition planning for students with visual disabilities.* Austin, TX: PRO-ED.

This book is one in a series produced by PRO-ED that focuses on transition issues. In Transition Planning for Students with Visual Disabilities, the authors cover six major issues in the transition process: functional academic skills, housing, transportation, employment, and leisure and recreational issues.

(Continued)

Table 27.1 Continued.

Joffe, E. (1999). *A practical guide to the ADA and visual impairment*. New York, NY: AFB Press.

In this book, the author describes the unique needs of people who are blind or visually impaired and how they can be addressed through the implementation of the ADA. Checklists for employers, architects, and service providers are included that identify key elements of the law with appropriate accommodations or modifications for people with visual impairments.

Kendrick, D. (1993). *Jobs to be proud of*. New York, NY: AFB Press.

This is the second in a series of short books produced by AFB that focus on successfully employed workers who are visually impaired. The jobs being performed by workers in this book do not require college training.

Kendrick, D. (1998). *Teachers who are blind or visually impaired*. New York, NY: AFB Press.

This is another in the series of short books produced by AFB that focus on successfully employed workers who are visually impaired. The jobs being performed by workers in this book involve work in educational settings.

Kendrick, D. (2000). *Business owners who are blind or visually impaired*. New York, NY: AFB Press.

This short book in the series produced by AFB focuses on successfully employed entrepreneurs who are visually impaired and who work as day care and flower shop owners, foreign language tutor and translator, tax preparer and bookkeeper, and environmental engineer.

Kendrick, D. (2001). *Health care professionals who are blind or visually impaired*. New York, NY: AFB Press.

This short book in the series produced by AFB focuses on successfully employed workers in health care settings who are blind or have low vision.

McBroom, L. W. (1996). *Transition activity calendar for students with visual impairments*. Starkville: Rehabilitation Research and Training Center on Blindness and Low Vision, Mississippi State University.

This booklet is written in a checklist format and spells out the activities in which college-bound students with visual impairments need to be engaged, from junior high through high school.

Sacks, S. Z., & Silberman, R. K. (Eds.). (1998). *Educating students who have visual impairments with other disabilities*. Baltimore, MD: Paul Brookes.

Chapter 11 in this book deals specifically with transition planning for students with visual impairments who have additional disabilities.

Sacks, S. Z., & Wolffe, K. E. (Eds.). (2006). *Teaching social skills to students with visual impairments: From theory to practice*. New York, NY: AFB Press.

This edited book describes the development of social skills in children and adolescents with visual impairments and provides activities to teach these skills. Assessment techniques and tools as well as instructional resources are also included.

Trief, E., & Feeney, R. (2005). *College bound: A guide for students with visual impairments*. New York, NY: AFB Press.

This book details the activities that young people need to accomplish in preparation for college.

Wolffe, K. E. (Ed.). (1999). *Skills for success: A career education handbook for children and adolescents with visual impairments*. New York, NY: AFB Press.

This book guides families and professionals in developing activities that will lead to careers for children with visual impairments, including those with multiple disabilities. The introduction provides an overview of key issues to prepare students for careers, and subsequent chapters present activities that are appropriate for preschoolers, elementary students, secondary students, and middle school students. Each section includes suggestions for students who have multiple disabilities.

Wolffe, K. E., & Terlau, M. T. (2011). *Navigating the rapids of life: The transition tote system* (2nd edition). Louisville, KY: American Printing House for the Blind.

This set of materials for youth with visual impairments comprises a pre-employment structure-learning curriculum in the following content areas: self-awareness, career exploration, job seeking, and job maintenance. Materials include *The Student Manual*, which comes in the tote – a backpack that features organizational tools designed with students who are blind or have low vision in mind; *The Teacher Guide*, which explains to teachers and other caregivers how to modify the lessons of the curriculum for students with greater challenges; and a video, *Navigating the Rapids of Life*, which covers four domains (home, school, community, work) and shows children and young adults (10 to 26 years old) actively engaged in each domain.

Wolffe, K. E. (1997). *Career counseling for people with disabilities: A practical guide to finding employment.* Austin, TX: PRO-ED.

This book is designed for counselors working with adults who are disabled and interested in employment. Although not specific to people with visual impairments, many of the activities and resources are pertinent.

Note: In addition to the aforementioned booklets and books, many articles related to the transition process for youth with visual impairments are available, the bulk of them in the *Journal of Visual Impairment & Blindness*, published by American Foundation for the Blind in both print and electronic formats.

Resources: organizations

American Foundation for the Blind (http://www.afb.org/) is a multiservice nonprofit organization that provides information for individuals with visual impairments of all ages, their families, and the professionals who work with them. AFB's CareerConnect website can put visually impaired individuals in contact with working adults with visual impairments; the online magazine AccessWorld provides current information on mainstream and assistive technology; and the Public Policy and Policy Research link provides information on policy and advocacy efforts related to visual impairment.

American Printing House for the Blind (http://www.aph.org/) is a nonprofit organization that develops products for students who are blind or have low vision. APH receives federal funds to produce textbooks in print and large type as well as other educational materials. They produce many products that facilitate transition, including assistive technology, braille equipment and materials, and products related to career development and independent living.

Specialized Schools for the Blind. Many states have specialized schools that provide resources for students who are blind or have low vision. Many schools maintain websites that are available to families and professionals and provide short-term services or summer programs that can assist students with transition to adulthood. Many of these specialized schools also work with local public schools to meet the needs of students educated in their districts. Member schools in the Council of Schools for the Blind can be found at http://www.cosb1.org/. Texas School for the Blind and Visually Impaired maintains a public information website that includes information on career education and transition at http://www.tsbvi.edu/recc/ce.htm. Perkins School for the Blind in Boston offers a career education website at http://www.perkins.org/resources/scout/transition/career-exploration.html.

Hadley School for the Blind (http://www.hadley.edu/). This correspondence school for people with visual impairments provides credit courses for high school students and adults. A course in Finding Employment is offered for adults, and many courses will support career development for secondary and post-secondary students.

National Federation of the Blind (http://www.nfb.org/nfb/) and American Council of the Blind (http://www.acb.org/) are national organizations of and for people who are blind and visually impaired. Members advocate for issues related to blindness/visual impairment, publish relevant materials, and hold national and local conferences.

References

American Printing House for the Blind. Distribution of eligible students based on the Federal Quota Census of January 7, 2008. Retrieved from http://www.aph.org/fedquotpgm/dist09.html

Bardin, J.A., & Lewis, S. (2008). A survey of the academic engagement of students with visual impairments in general education classes. *Journal of Visual Impairment & Blindness, 102*, 472–483.

Bhasin, T. K., Brocksen, S., Avchen, R. N., Braun, K. V. N. (2006). Prevalence of four developmental disabilities among children aged 8 years – Metropolitan Atlanta Developmental Disabilities Surveillance Program, 1996 and 2000 (*Morbidity and Mortality Weekly Reports*, Jan. 27, 2006). Washington, DC: U.S. Government Printing Office.

Bolles, R. N. (2009). *What color is your parachute?* Berkeley, CA: Ten Speed Press.

Bolles, R. N., & Brown, D. S. (2001). *Job-hunting for the so-called handicapped or people who have disabilities*. Berkeley, CA: Ten Speed Press.

CDC – Centers for Disease Control and Prevention (2004). Vision impairment: What is vision impairment? Retrieved February 12, 2011, from http://www.cdc.gov/ncbddd/dd/vision2.htm

Corn, A. L., & Koenig, A. J. (Eds.). (1996). *Foundations of low vision: Clinical and functional perspectives*. New York: AFB Press.

Crudden, A., McBroom, L. W., Skinner, A. L., & Moore, J. E. (1998). *Comprehensive examination of barriers to employment among persons who are blind and visually impaired*. Mississippi State, MS: Mississippi State University, Rehabilitation Research and Training Center on Blindness & Low Vision.

D'Amico, R. (1991). The working world awaits: Employment experiences during and shortly after secondary school. In M. Wagner, L. Newman, R. D'Amico, E. D. Jay, P. Butler-Nalin, C. Marder, et al. (Eds.). *Youth with disabilities: How are they doing? The first comprehensive report from the National Longitudinal Transition Study* (pp. 8.1–8.53). Menlo Park, CA: SRI International.

Erin, J. N. & Wolffe, K. E. (1999). *Transition planning for students with visual disabilities*. Austin, TX: PRO-ED.

Fazzi, D., & Naimy, B. (2010). Orientation and mobility for children and youths with low vision. In A.L. Corn & J. N. Erin (Eds.). *Foundations of low vision: Clinical and functional perspectives, 2nd edition*. New York: AFB Press.

Fesko, S. L., & Temelini, D. J. (1997). What consumers and staff tell us about effective job search practices. In F. Menz, J. Eggers, V. Brooke (Eds.), *Vocational rehabilitation research: Lessons for improving employment of people with disabilities*. (pp. 135–160). Menomonie, WI: Rehabilitation Research and Training Center, Stout Vocational Rehabilitation Institute, University of Wisconsin-Stout.

Gold, D., Shaw, A., & Wolffe, K. E. (2010). The social lives of Canadian youths with visual impairments. *Journal of Visual Impairment & Blindness, 104*, 431–443.

Griffin-Shirley, N., Trusty, S., & Rickard, R. (2000). Orientation and mobility. In Alan Koenig and M. Cay Holbrook (Eds.), Foundations of Education, Second Edition, Volume II: Instructional Strategies for Teaching Children and Youth with Visual Impairments, (pp. 529–568). New York: AFB Press.

Hatlen, P. (1996). The core curriculum for blind and visually impaired students, including those with additional disabilities. *RE:view, 28*, 25–32.

Houtenville, A. J. (2003). A Comparison of the Economic Status of Working-Age Persons with Visual Impairments and Those of Other Groups. *Journal of Visual Impairment and Blindness, 97*(3), 133–148.

Huebner, K. M., Merk-Adam, B., Stryker, D., & Wolffe, K. (2004). *The national agenda for the education of children and youths with visual impairments, including those with multiple disabilities (revised)*. New York: AFB Press.

Jorgensen-Smith, T., & Lewis, S. (2004). Meeting the challenge: Innovation in one state rehabilitation system's approach to transition. *Journal of Visual Impairment & Blindness, 98*, 212–227.

Kirchner, C., & Diamant, S. (1999). Estimate of number of visually impaired students, their teachers, and orientation and mobility specialists: Part 1. *Journal of Visual Impairment & Blindness. 93*, 600–606.

Kirchner, C., & Smith, B. (2005). Transition to what? Education and employment outcomes for visually impaired youth after high school. *Journal of Visual Impairment and Blindness, 99*, 499–504.

Koenig, A., & Holbrook, M.C. (2000). Professional practice. In M. Cay Holbrook and Alan Koenig (Eds.), Foundations of Education, Second Edition, Volume I: History and Theory of Teaching Children and Youth with Visual Impairments (pp. 260–276). New York: AFB Press.

Lewis, S., Bardin, J. A., & Jorgensen-Smith, T. (2009). After one year: Self-reported transition skills of teens with visual impairments. *AER Journal: Research and Practice in Visual Impairment and Blindness, 2*, 84–96.

Mangold, S. S. (Ed.). (1982). A teachers' guide to the special educational needs of blind and visually handicapped children. New York: American Foundation for the Blind.

McConnell, J. (1999). Parents, adolescents, and career plans of visually impaired students. *Journal of Visual Impairment & Blindness, 93*, 498–515.

McDonnall, M.C., & Crudden, A. (2009). Factors affecting the successful employment of transition-aged youths with visual impairments. *Journal of Visual Impairment & Blindness, 103*, 329–341.

McKenzie, A., & Lewis, S. (2008). The role and training of paraprofessionals who work with students who are visually impaired. *Journal of Visual Impairment & Blindness, 102*, 459–471.

Miller, C., & Levack, N. (1997). *A paraprofessional's handbook for working with students who are visually impaired.* Austin, TX: Texas School for the Blind and Visually Impaired.

Nagle, K. (2001). Transition to employment and community life for youths with visual impairments: Current status and future directions. *Journal of Visual Impairment & Blindness, 95*, 725–738.

Newman, L. (1991). Social activities. In M. Wagner, L. Newman, R. D'Amico, E. D. Jay, P. Butler-Nalin, C. Marder, & R. Cox (Eds.). *Youth with disabilities: How are they doing? The first comprehensive report from the National Longitudinal Transition Study* (pp. 8.1–8.53). Menlo Park, CA: SRI International.

Newman, L., Wagner, M., Cameto, R., and Knokey, A.-M. (2009). *The post-high school outcomes of youth with disabilities up to 4 years after high school. A report from the National Longitudinal Transition Study–2 (NLTS2) (NCSER 2009–3017).* Menlo Park, CA: SRI International.

Roy, A. W. N., Dimigen, G., & Taylor, M. (1998). The relationship between social networks and the employment of visually impaired college graduates. *Journal of Visual Impairment & Blindness, 92*, 423–432.

Rubin, S. E., & Roessler, R. T. (2008). *Foundations of the vocational rehabilitation process* (6th ed.). Austin, TX: PRO-ED.

Russotti, J., & Shaw, R. (2004). When you have a visually impaired student in your classroom: A guide for paraeducators. New York: AFB Press.

Sacks, S. Z., & Wolffe, K. (1992). The importance of social skills in the transition process for students who are visually impaired, *Journal of Vocational Rehabilitation, 2* (1), 46–55.

Sacks, S. Z., & Wolffe, K.E. (1998). Lifestyles of adolescents with visual impairments: An ethnographic analysis. *Journal of Visual Impairment & Blindness, 92* (1), 7–17.

Sacks, S. Z., Wolffe, K. E., & Tierney, D. (1998). Lifestyles of students with visual impairments: Preliminary studies of social networks. *Exceptional Children, 64* (4), 463–478.

Shaw, A., Gold, D., & Simson, H. (2005). *The status of Canadian youth who are blind or visually impaired: A study of lifestyles, quality of life and employment.* Toronto, ON: Canadian National Institute for the Blind.

Shaw, A., Gold, D., & Wolffe, K. (2007). Employment-related experiences of youths who are blind or visually impaired: How are these youths faring? *Journal of Visual Impairment & Blindness, 101*, 7–21.

Spungin, S. J. (Ed.). (2002). *When you have a visually impaired student in your classroom: A guide for teachers.* New York: AFB Press.

Wagner, M. (1992). *Being female: A secondary disability?* Paper presented at the annual meeting of the American Educational Research Association: San Francisco, CA.

Wagner, M., Cadwallader, T., & Marder, C. (2003). *Life outside of the classroom for youth with disabilities.* Menlo Park, CA: SRI International.

Wagner, M., D'Amico, R., Marder, C., Newman, L., & Blackorby, J. (1992). *What happens next? Trends in postschool outcomes of youth with disabilities.* Menlo Park, CA: SRI International.

Wagner, M., Newman, L., Cameto, R., & Levine, P. (2005). *Changes over time in the early postschool outcomes of youth with disabilities.* Menlo Park, CA: SRI International.

Wolffe, K. (1997). The key to successful school-to-work programs for blind or visually impaired students. *Journal of Visual Impairment & Blindness (Suppl.), 91*, 5–7.

Wolffe, K. E. (1998). Transition planning and employment outcomes for students who have visual impairments with other disabilities. In S. Z. Sacks and R. Silberman (Eds.). *Educating students who have visual impairments with other disabilities.* Baltimore, MD: Paul Brookes.

Wolffe, K. E. (Ed.). (1999). *Skills for success: A career education handbook for children and adolescents with visual impairments.* New York: American Foundation for the Blind.

Wolffe, K. E. (2001). *Transition competencies checklist.* Austin, TX: author.

Wolffe, K. (2004). Transitioning young adults from school to public transportation. *EnVision: A publication for parents and educators of children with impaired vision, 8*, 7–9.

Wolffe, K. E., & Johnson, D. (1997). *Navigating the rapids of life: The transition tote system.* Louisville, KY: American Printing House for the Blind.

Wolffe, K., & Sacks, S. Z. (1997). The social network pilot project: A quantitative comparison of the lifestyles of blind, low vision, and sighted young adults. *Journal of Visual Impairment & Blindness, 91* (3), 245–257.

Wolffe, K. E. & Terlau, M. T. (2011). *Navigating the rapids of life: The transition tote system* (2nd ed.). Louisville, KY: American Printing House for the Blind.

28

Transition Education for Adolescents with Emotional and Behavioral Disorders

Erik W. Carter

VANDERBILT UNIVERSITY

Deanne K. Unruh

UNIVERSITY OF OREGON

Introduction

Adolescence represents a critical juncture in the lives of young people. The experiences youth have during the secondary years can play a prominent role in shaping the skills and attitudes they acquire, the goals they pursue, and the success they attain in and after high school. Through a broad array of high school, community-based, and home activities, youth develop essential competencies, discover and deepen their interests, focus their aspirations, establish critical relationships, and acquire new supports that will prepare them for adulthood. These experiences can help youth envision and transition toward an array of exciting outcomes, including attending college, beginning an interesting career, getting a place of one's own, and participating in the life of one's community.

Youth with emotional and behavioral disorders (EBD) hold these same aspirations for their lives—both during and after high school. Yet, more than virtually any other group of adolescents, the life outcomes these youth anticipate often never materialize. A consistent finding of longitudinal and follow-up research studies is that disappointing outcomes in the areas of employment, postsecondary education, independent living, and community participation are both widespread and persistent (Karpur, Clark, Caproni, & Sterner, 2005; Osgood, Foster, Flanagan, & Ruth, 2007; Zigmond, 2006). Many schools, families, and communities struggle to ensure that these youth leave high school with the experiences and relationships they need to chart a course characterized by success and personal satisfaction. As a result, these youth remain especially vulnerable to negative outcomes that extend into and throughout adulthood.

The National Longitudinal Transition Study-2 (NLTS-2) provides one of the most comprehensive sources of information on the in- and post-school experiences of youth with EBD (Newman, Wagner, Cameto, & Knokey, 2009). And the portrait this study paints is quite bleak (see Figure 28.1). The early work experiences of many young adults with EBD are defined by unemployment, job instability, limited benefits, and overall dissatisfaction. For example, only 63% of young adults who had received special education services under the category of emotional

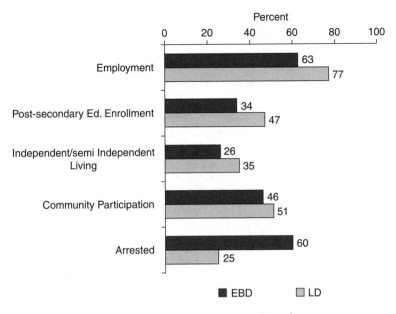

Figure 28.1 Post-school outcomes for youth with EBD at least four years out
Source: Based on Newman, Wagner, Cameto, & Knokey, 2009

disturbance (ED) had been employed at any time since leaving high school up to four years earlier and only 42% were employed at the time they were interviewed. Despite the strong association between postsecondary enrollment, expanded career options, and increased earnings, only 34% of youth with ED had enrolled in any type of postsecondary school (e.g., community college, technical school, university) up to four years after leaving high school. Only one quarter (26%) of young adults with EBD had lived independently or semi-independently since leaving high school. Although community participation can enhance quality of life, nearly 55% of these young adults had not taken lessons outside of school, volunteered, or participated in a community group (e.g., hobby clubs, religious groups, sports teams) during the previous year. Furthermore, more than one third experienced some form of criminal justice system involvement (e.g., arrested, jailed) during the previous two years and more than one third had been involved in violence-related activities in the past (e.g., physical fights, carrying a weapon, gang involvement).

These disappointing outcomes reinforce the necessity of designing and delivering high-quality transition services and supports to youth with EBD throughout secondary school and extending into early adulthood. Numerous empirical studies and model demonstration programs have shown that the in- and post-school outcomes these youth attain can be substantially improved through the delivery of well-designed transition services and supports (see Cheney & Bullis, 2004; Clark & Unruh, 2009). Indeed, the knowledge base describing important elements of effective transition services and supports for youth with EBD has deepened substantially over the last two decades.

In this chapter, we review important elements of effective transition services and supports for youth with EBD. Although the transition practices and policies discussed throughout this *Handbook on Transition* are certainly relevant for youth with EBD, in this chapter we emphasize and expand upon some of those elements of transition education that may be particularly salient for this segment of the adolescent population. In detailing these components, we draw upon key components identified in the empirical literature and model demonstration programs for youth with EBD.

Given the myriad needs of and complex challenges encountered by youth with EBD, effective transition education should address at least two broad emphases. First, transition education must focus on equipping youth with the skills, knowledge, and attitudes that will increase their competence and build their confidence. Explicit instruction should be directed toward equipping youth to leave high school with an array of skills—including social, self-determination, employment-related, and academic skills—that will expand their future opportunities, promote successful engagement in employment and postsecondary education, and enhance their overall quality of life. Second, transition efforts must focus on establishing a meaningful and coordinated system of informal and formal supports for youth with EBD. Even when provided high-quality instructional experiences, most youth with EBD will additionally require individualized supports that enable them to connect to, participate actively within, and maintain involvement in a multitude of high school, workplace, postsecondary education, and community environments. A narrow focus on skill-instruction to the exclusion of arranging individualized supports will typically be insufficient to meet the multifaceted transition needs of many youth with EBD. These two areas of emphasis are both essential and can coalesce to create a comprehensive framework of transition education. Indeed, current secondary transition models emphasize the importance of coupling instructional efforts with the establishment of quality supports (Kohler & Field, 2003; National Alliance for Secondary Education and Transition [NASET], 2005; Test, Fowler, et al., 2009). The remainder of this chapter highlights aspects of transition education that may be particularly instrumental in enhancing skills and establishing sufficient supports for youth with EBD.

Throughout this chapter, we refer to individuals with EBD as those young people whose behavioral and/or emotional challenges impede their in- and post-school outcomes and who require specialized services and supports to participate successfully in school, work, and/or community activities. Although students who are receiving special education services under the disability category of *emotional disturbance* have been a dominant focus of transition efforts, the number of youth who would benefit from transition programming is much greater than these students, including those youth receiving clinical diagnoses (e.g., schizophrenia, depression), those without disabilities who evidence risk for EBD, and those who are adjudicated within the juvenile justice system. Indeed, many have argued that youth with EBD are tremendously under-identified and/or underserved (Walker, Nishioka, Zeller, Severson, & Feil, 2000), and this appears to be particularly true among transition-age youth. The considerable heterogeneity evidenced among youth with the EBD label highlights the importance of individualized, developmentally appropriate, and culturally responsive transition services and supports.

Enhancing Relevant Skills

High school represents an opportune time for youth to develop critical skills and attitudes that will prepare them to successfully assume future adult roles. The experiences youth with EBD have within and beyond the classroom can provide rich opportunities for them to acquire, practice, and refine important transition-related skills, including social, self-determination, vocational, and academic skills. Unfortunately, youth with EBD often have fairly limited access to these important learning opportunities during high school and many leave school unprepared to meet the expectations of postsecondary, work, and community settings (Clark & Unruh, 2009; Wagner & Davis, 2006).

Individualized, student-focused planning has long been advocated as an essential starting point for designing instruction that is relevant to the needs, interests, and long-term goals of youth with disabilities. This is especially true for youth with EBD, who may evidence a wide range of behavioral needs and strengths. For example, their disabilities may manifest themselves in myriad ways, as internalizing behaviors (e.g., depression, anxiety) or externalizing behaviors (e.g., noncompliance, aggression). At the same time, youth with EBD are served within a broad range of settings, including diverse school classrooms (e.g., general education, resource, or self-contained classrooms), alternative schools, community-based programs, day-treatment programs, and juvenile correction centers. This heterogeneity in needs and learning contexts necessitates careful consideration of which competencies and supports will be most essential for particular students. Individualized planning is essential for determining which skills are most critical to teach and the contexts (e.g., classrooms, community activities, workplaces) within which those competencies can be taught most effectively and efficiently. Formal and informal transition assessments of students' strengths, needs, interests, and goals for the future represent the starting point for identifying those skills, attitudes, and behaviors most essential for students to attain, as well as the experiences most appropriate for developing those competencies. Although the hallmark of special education services is individualized education, we discuss four skill domains that may be important for transition planning teams to consider.

Social and Interpersonal Skills

The extent to which youth and young adults demonstrate critical social and interpersonal skills may influence their attainment of important transition outcomes during and after high school (Benz, Yovanoff, et al., 1997; Test, Mazzotti, et al., 2009). For example, greater social competence can contribute to academic success, enhanced relationships with peers and adults, development of social capital, and greater overall well-being. Social skills also are critical to success in the workplace, as demonstration of adequate interpersonal skills on the job is a primary consideration of employers related to hiring, promotion, and retention (Carter & Wehby, 2003). Finally, the adequacy of youths' social-related skills may influence their capacity to recruit needed supports and services and advocate effectively for their needs during and after leaving high school.

Yet, social skills deficits represent a prominent characteristic of youth with EBD. These youth typically experience considerable difficulty establishing and maintaining satisfying and positive relationships with peers and adults (Cullinan, 2004). Research indicates that high school students with EBD have low levels of social competence and school adjustment, as well as higher levels of problem behaviors and disciplinary contacts than youth with learning and other high-incidence disabilities (Cullinan & Sabornie, 2004; Lane, Carter, Pierson, & Glaeser, 2006).

For youth who experience inabilities or difficulties performing critical social skills, transition education should incorporate social skills training (SST) components. Such interventions typically "emphasize the acquisition, performance, generalization, and/or maintenance of prosocial behaviors and the reduction or elimination of competing problem behaviors" (Cook et al., 2008, p. 133). Although it is often presumed that the social and behavioral challenges of youth with EBD are resistant to intervention by the time they reach adolescence, recent meta-analyses suggest that social skills training can be effective for many secondary students and that social-related deficits may not be quite as firmly entrenched as sometimes presumed (Cook et al., 2008).

The following issues should be considered when designing social skills instruction for transition-age youth with EBD. First, social skills instruction should start early, particularly for students evidencing an early onset trajectory of behavioral challenges. But even for "late starters"—those whose behavioral challenges do not emerge during adolescence—social skills training should be offered early in and throughout secondary school. Second, interventions should be based on sound assessments to ensure they are addressing the specific nature of social skills deficits (e.g., acquisition, fluency, maintenance, motivation). Third, appropriate social skills are contextually determined. The array of contexts within which youth must demonstrate these skills extends beyond the classroom and into an array of work and community-based settings. For example, Johnson, Bullis, Benz, & Hollenbeck (2004) highlight four work-related social skills that are essential to long-term employment success: locus of control, problem solving, teamwork, and communication. Instructional efforts should emphasize those social-related skills needed to meet the behavioral demands and expectations of the particular setting in which the student participates, both in the present and in the future.

Self-determination Skills

Over the last two decades, self-determination has emerged as an important element to be infused throughout transition education for youth with disabilities. Equipping youth with skills, attitudes, and opportunities to play an active and prominent role in determining their future and the course of action that will take them there is widely considered an essential component of comprehensive transition education. Self-determination refers broadly to having the capacities and opportunities to steer one's own life in ways and directions that contribute to a personally satisfying life (Field, Martin, Miller, Ward, & Wehmeyer, 1998). As adolescents approach adulthood, they are expected to assume greater responsibility for managing their own behavior and learning as well as to have a more prominent voice in their own educational and transition planning.

For youth with EBD, efforts to promote self-determination hold particular importance. The reluctance of many youth with EBD to identify as having a disability at the workplace, college classroom, or other out-of-school contexts (Newman et al., 2009) increases the importance of possessing the capacity to recruit or deliver support for oneself. Moreover, many young people with EBD are ineligible for, unaware of, or have difficulty accessing formal adult services and supports, requiring them to advocate for their needs with limited external assistance.

Yet, research indicates that many youth with EBD evidence limited self-determination. Relative to their peers with other high-incidence disabilities, youth with EBD may have less knowledge about self-determination and the behaviors it requires, diminished ability to engage in self-determined behavior, and limited confidence regarding the efficacy of their efforts to be self-determining (Cameto, Levine, & Wagner, 2004; Carter, Lane, Pierson, & Glaeser, 2006; Carter, Trainor, Sun, & Owens, 2009). For youth served within alternative programs or juvenile justice facilities, self-determination may be even more diminished (Houchins, 2002; Van Gelder, Sitlington, & Pugh, 2008). Because self-determination is typically evidenced within interpersonal interactions (e.g., with peers, teachers, parents, employers), the social skills deficits exhibited by many youth—along with their challenging behaviors—may further limit effective self-determination.

At the same time, the opportunities youth with EBD are provided to acquire those skills, attitudes, and knowledge that enhance the acquisition of self-determination skills may be particularly limited—both within and beyond the classroom. Although the availability of self-determination-related curricula and resources has expanded considerably, secondary teachers often report having limited training and professional development opportunities related to promoting self-determination (Thoma, Nathanson, Baker, & Tamura, 2002). Moreover, students' individualized education programs (IEPs) infrequently contain instructional goals addressing self-determination, and instructional efforts may remain limited for these youth (Carter, Lane, Pierson, & Stang, 2008; Powers et al., 2005).

Although self-determination instruction is considered an essential element of the secondary transition curriculum, empirical guidance for promoting self-determination among youth with

EBD is still evolving. Carter (2011) reviewed several promising approaches for enhancing the self-determination of youth with EBD. First, students' self-determination capacities and opportunities should be assessed throughout the transition-planning process. Second, component skills identified during the assessment process that can enhance self-determination should be emphasized as instructional priorities. For example, goal setting, problem solving, self-management, self-advocacy, decision making, and self-evaluation can all be systematically taught and typically are combined within comprehensive instructional packages (e.g., Cobb, Lehman, Newman, Gonchar, & Alwell, 2009; Mooney, Ryan, Uhing, Reid, & Epstein, 2005). Third, self-determination should be taught and supported throughout all aspects of the transition-planning process, but particularly within IEP meetings. Fourth, youth should be taught to apply self-determination skills within the environments where they will ultimately need them. In addition to addressing self-determination instruction within the general education curriculum, secondary teachers should provide instruction within other community-based learning contexts (e.g., worksites, service-learning projects, community-based sites). Fifth, it is essential to acknowledge the role families play in fostering self-determination. Collaborating with parents and caregivers to prioritize self-determination skills and reinforce their use across school and home settings is an important aspect of culturally responsive transition instruction. Finally, a foundation for self-determination should be established early in, and continue throughout, students' educational careers.

Employment-related Skills

Although academic success is typically prioritized within current accountability movements, a secondary curriculum that concurrently emphasizes career development and work-based learning experiences is regularly cited as an important component of high-quality transition programs (Cheney & Bullis, 2004; NASET, 2005). Early work and career development experiences— whether school-sponsored or occurring beyond the school day—can provide youth with an engaging and effective context for acquiring and refining an array of important social, self-determination, and other functional skills, as well as enhancing general and occupationally specific work-related skills. At the same time, career preparatory experiences offer youth opportunities to explore and discover their career interests, learn essential work and collaborative values, establish relationships in their community, strengthen their resumes, and heighten future expectations related to college and careers. Moreover, early work experiences during high school constitute one of the most prominent predictors of improved post-school employment outcomes (Test, Mazzotti et al., 2009). Youth with EBD who take part in school-sponsored or after-school work experiences, have internships, enroll in vocational classes, or hold after-school and summer jobs may be better positioned to obtain work after high school.

Yet, high-quality adolescent career development experiences remain elusive for many youth with EBD. During high school, youth with EBD have limited involvement in vocational coursework, school-based enterprises, job shadowing, internships, work-study programs, and out-of-school jobs (Carter, Trainor, Ditchman, Sweeden, & Owens, 2011; Wagner & Davis, 2006). Moreover, concerns about the quality of existing experiences and their alignment with students' needs and goals for the future have frequently been raised. Although these students' social and behavioral challenges can make both finding and maintaining employment more difficult, youth with EBD also have relatively few opportunities to acquire important job search and occupational skills that promote meaningful work experiences.

Youth with EBD should have access to secondary school experiences that integrate rigorous academic instruction with relevant career development experiences. Classroom-based instruction should focus on promoting awareness of potential career paths and requirements, enhancing occupation-specific knowledge, and teaching academic and collateral skills that will be required within the workplace. At the same time, connecting youth with EBD to community-based work experiences offers an important avenue for teaching essential work-related skills, attitudes, and behaviors. Indeed, supported work opportunities in the community may also provide more authentic contexts for enhancing students' career-related competencies, facilitating generalized learning, and creating community connections. Community-based work experiences, however, should be individually designed to reflect students' interests and goals for the future, as well as to enhance their motivation. Instructional efforts should target those work-related social and interpersonal skills that are especially critical to long-term success and satisfaction on the job. Finally, because youth with EBD may be reluctant to receive individualized support at the workplace from a job coach or school staff, it may be necessary to explore alternative or supplemental avenues for providing work-related instruction and ongoing feedback (e.g., job clubs, mentor relationships, off-site meetings).

Academic Competence

A number of opportunities in adulthood may be directly or indirectly influenced by students' academic achievement during high school. Although postsecondary enrollment is among the most obvious of these opportunities, the academic-related skills students possess can also influence their future career pathways and potential for advancement. Moreover, high school diploma options and graduation requirements are directly linked to academic performance during high school. Thus, strengthening the academic competence and confidence should receive additional emphasis within transition education for youth with EBD.

Many youth with EBD leave high school without the necessary coursework and adequate instruction to meet the demands associated with entry into or success in college (Wagner & Davis, 2006). Descriptive research indicates that adolescents with EBD show pronounced academic deficits relative to their same-age peers without disabilities, often performing far below grade level in core content areas such as reading, math, and science (Lane et al., 2006). Moreover, these youth are perceived to be less academically competent than students with other high-incidence disabilities, which may lead to diminished expectations regarding access to the general curriculum and future postsecondary opportunities.

Youth with EBD should have access to rigorous learning opportunities that communicate high expectations and challenge students to reach their potential. Although this emphasis on increasing academic rigor is a central element of reform efforts to strengthen secondary education for all students, it is particularly important for youth with EBD. Relatively limited attention has focused on academic interventions for students with EBD at the high-school level (Lane & Carter, 2006). Instead, social and behavioral interventions typically dominate the educational programs of adolescents with EBD to the general neglect of an academic curricular focus. Interestingly, these academic deficits may contribute to or further exacerbate the behavioral challenges these youth experience (Hinshaw, 1992). Because students' academic trajectories often are established quite early, preparation for postsecondary education must also begin early and be coupled with encouragement and high expectations for such future educational attainments. This means ensuring youth are accessing the coursework needed to gain entry into college or preferred careers, as well as providing youth with effective academic instruction. Although the academic evidence-base for adolescents with EBD is still in relative infancy, it is important to presume that youth with EBD can benefit from strong instruction. Secondary educators should carefully consider the supports, accommodations, and modifications youth with EBD will need within the classroom to benefit maximally from these instructional efforts. Providing instruction on self-regulation and self-management strategies may be particularly advantageous for this group of youth (Mooney et al., 2005). Finally, because many youth with EBD have difficulty seeing the relevance of high school to their lives and future, designing authentic learning opportunities that integrate academic content with real-life application may be particularly important to establishing a motivating learning context. Indeed, both early dropout and high absenteeism may be linked to students' perceptions of the relevance of school.

Establishing Meaningful Supports

Enhancing the transition-related skills, knowledge, and attitudes of youth with EBD is essential to improving the quality and impact of students' in- and post-school experiences. Yet, many adolescents with disabilities will also require a constellation of formal and informal supports to help them realize their goals for life after high school. Although well-crafted supports are instrumental for all youth with disabilities, the importance of establishing an individualized and coordinated system of supports is only magnified for youth experiencing emotional and behavioral difficulties. In the following section, we highlight some of those supports that may be particularly beneficial to consider for youth with EBD, including (a) establishing a coordinated service system, (b) supporting student involvement in the transition process, (c) enhancing family involvement, (d) providing behavioral and other mental health services, (e) connecting youth to vocational supports, and (f) developing pro-social networks.

Coordinating Services Across Systems

Wagner and Davis (2006) reported data from the National Longitudinal Transition Study-2 indicating that many youth with EBD do not receive the supportive services that individuals with emotional and behavioral difficulties are likely to require and benefit from. In addition to those services and supports provided in and through the school system, an array of community-based services may be requisite to address the needs of the whole child, particularly those needs related to behavioral outcomes (Wagner & Davis, 2006). Addressing these needs may require the active involvement by the youth and family along with additional service partners, including child welfare, child and adult mental health services, substance abuse treatment, and juvenile justice. Unfortunately, navigating these multiple service systems can be quite difficult for youth and young adults with EBD and their families, resulting in considerable gaps within and across these service systems (Davis, Green, & Hoffman, 2009). For example, although youth may continue to receive special education services through age 21, eligibility for some community support services ends at age 18 and those new adult-serving programs that begin often have different eligibility requirements. Moreover, these adult and community-based services often have philosophies and service approaches that differ substantially from those offered by schools, requiring transition staff to learn about and negotiate these services while supporting a youth's transition process. Services for transition-age youth with EBD often cross the cusp between child- and adult-focused services. Some child services end with no adult services (e.g., special education, child welfare). Other services (e.g., child mental health, juvenile justice system) have counterparts in the adult system, which often are quite different in service eligibility and philosophy than their child-serving counterparts. To compound this problem, age and definition eligibility often differ within and across agencies.

Community-based agencies identified to work with transition-age youth need to be developmentally and culturally appropriate and provide a continuous stream of services across the transition-age years (Davis et al., 2009). Transition staff working with youth with EBD should be knowledgeable about and develop relationships with a diverse array of community-based supports in their community to help youth access and navigate needed services. To support this process, a thorough understanding of the eligibility requirements for each of the local agencies is requisite to ensure appropriate matches are made between the youth and service agency. Developing procedures that facilitate sharing of information across multiple agencies is critical for coordinating efforts and addressing clear gaps in services. The procedures for information sharing may need to be revisited periodically to ensure the process is not cumbersome, that confidentiality is maintained, and that current policies are adhered to. In addition, knowledge of the various evaluations or assessments used by these agencies to define eligibility is also helpful. Schools and local service agencies can review the eligibility evaluations used to define service eligibility for transition-age youth. With this review, transition staff can then develop an assessment battery used for transition planning that will, in addition, be helpful for community agencies to define eligibility. Having up-to-date and available evaluations may assist in timely access of community services for youth with EBD.

Supporting Student Involvement

As noted in the previous section, teaching youth with disabilities self-determination and advocacy skills is a recommended component of high-quality transition services. At the same time, most youth with EBD will require ongoing support and meaningful opportunities to take an active and leading role in designing and working toward their transition plan. Youth-driven educational planning is important to ensuring that transition programs reflect the individualized interests, preferences, strengths, and needs of a student with EBD. Through their active involvement in the transition-planning process, students may be more likely to buy in to the process, be motivated to work toward the goals, and perceive that transition services and supports are meeting their needs (Seiler, Orso, & Unruh, 2009). Supporting youth-driven planning also helps students make decisions about their lives and experience natural consequences of their choices.

Although supporting meaningful student involvement in the transition assessment and planning process is firmly situated as recommended transition practice, many youth with EBD are not actively engaged in this important aspect of transition education. Drawing upon findings from the National Longitudinal Transition Study-2, Cameto et al. (2004) reported that approximately 6% of adolescents with EBD did not attend their own educational planning meeting; 30% were present but provided little input; 53% were considered by their teachers to be moderately active participants; and only 11% were reported to have taken a leadership role. Active student involvement in both the transition assessment and planning process may provide an engaging and motivating context for enabling students to learn about and communicate their strengths and needs. Supporting such involvement, however, likely will require a shift in approach for many secondary educators. Youth with EBD likely have had few opportunities to assume leadership roles and will benefit from advance preparation and practice.

In addition, students and families can be invited to contribute to the evaluation process in schools to improve transition programming (Dresser et al., 2009). Students' perceptions of received services and assessments of additional transition services needed can provide authentic evaluation data that are youth-focused and may point to program strengths or deficits leading to program continuation and/or improvement.

Family Support and Involvement

A successful transition to adulthood for youth with EBD can be enhanced when family involvement is encouraged and actively supported (Clark & Hart, 2009; Lane & Carter, 2006; Unruh, Povenmire-Kirk, & Yamamoto, 2009). In fact, Powers et al. (2007) reported that youth with disabilities identified help and encouragement from their families as among the most important factors contributing to a successful transition. Families represent a natural source of support for youth beyond high school, long after school services have ended. However, 13% of youth with EBD live with individuals other than their biological parents (e.g., relatives, foster-care providers, residential treatment programs), the highest rate of any other disability group (Wagner et al., 2003). Therefore, for some youth with EBD, the term "family" encompasses a broader definition that may include foster care parents, residential care providers, extended relatives, or other key individuals who provide a positive influence in the life of the youth. When biological family members are not involved in the lives of youth, transition staff should query youth to identify key players who will serve in the familial role if needed (Clark & Hart, 2009). Transition personnel may need to help the youth define individuals in their life who have a positive influence and who have long-lasting connections with the youth.

Developing collaborative relationships with family members or other key individuals in the lives of youth with EBD is essential (Osher & Osher, 2002). By the age of transition, some family members may be worn down and negative about prior involvement with school personnel or feel blamed for their youth's behavior. Secondary transition staff should recognize that parents may bring prior expectations—both positive and negative—to their interactions with school staff. To foster family involvement in service coordination and participation in the transition planning, several strategies can be utilized to encourage participation. Removing barriers that may prevent family participation in the transition planning and service coordination is integral for increasing family participation. For example, schools might support the transportation needs of families, time meetings around work constrictions, or help arrange for child care needs (Anderson & Matthews, 2001). Families can also provide guidance to ensure that culturally appropriate transition plans and services are implemented for youth. Moreover, schools can draw upon the family's experiences and perspectives to help utilize a strength-based assessment to identify a youth's interests, strengths, and future goals; help families locate and utilize developmentally and culturally appropriate community support systems (e.g., child and/or adult mental health services, vocational rehabilitation); and provide graduated support for the youth as they progress toward greater independence (Clark & Hart, 2009).

At times, families of youth with EBD may themselves benefit from access to set of additional stabilization resources (Unruh, Waintrup, Canter, & Smith, 2009). Almost one third of families of youth with EBD live in poverty, more than families of youth served under other disability categories (Wagner et al., 2003). Resources such as housing and access to food banks may be required to support some families' stability. In addition, based on the unique needs of the family, referrals to community agencies (e.g., mental health, substance abuse treatment) for family members may support a youth's maintained stability in the community by adding to the strength of the overall family. Knowledge of a broad range of community resources for referral sources based on the unique needs of each family can strengthen the transition services provided to youth with EBD.

Behavioral Health Services

As discussed earlier, a coordinated care system across schools, families, mental health, vocational services, and postsecondary education is critical for successful transition programming. Although behavioral health services were addressed in the discussion of a coordinated care system, it is important to emphasize the specific need for collaboration between schools and mental health services separately. Access to and receipt of behavioral health services has historically been low for students with EBD (Wagner, Friend, et al., 2006) even though many youth with EBD would benefit substantially from these services during their secondary years. Access

467

to services, however, is hampered by the lack of coordinated services across child and adult mental health services (Davis et al., 2009). For example, a school transition team may face challenges in serving youth with EBD when mental health services change dramatically from child-serving to adult-serving at the age of 18. There are multiple obstacles that special education staff need to be aware of when assisting youth with EBD to access needed mental health services. For example, depending on the state, eligibility for child mental health services may not transfer to adult services based on varying eligibility definitions that allow access to mental health services. In addition, services in the child and adult service agencies may not always be developmentally appropriate. For example, child mental health services may not include practices that can support a youth to work toward adult independence. On the other hand, adult services may provide services that target older adults (e.g., 30 and 60 years of age). If a youth attends group sessions with adults in this age range, their needs are dramatically different based on their developmental age, and services are neither appealing nor appropriate to the youth. Differing philosophies between child and adult mental health providers may impact the school's transition team. For example, a child-serving agency may readily include the family and school in the service coordination process. When adult services are provided, the mental health provider may not as readily include the school and family in the treatment process since their services are specifically targeting the individual. In summary, school-based transition services for youth with EBD should support access to behavioral health services, whether these services are accessed in the school setting or the community. These services need to be (a) continuous across a varying definition of child or adult services, (b) age and developmentally appropriate, and (c) appealing to youth (Davis et al., 2009).

Vocational Supports

Connecting youth with EBD to competitive employment experiences has long been identified as an essential feature of transition services (Bullis & Cheney, 1999, Cheney & Bullis, 2004). Competitive or paid employment provides natural consequences—both positive and negative— for learning the appropriate social and employment skills needed to both find and maintain a job. Employment-related transition strategies that support competitive employment may consist of (a) ensuring an appropriate job-match is determined for the youth, (b) supporting the youth in the workplace, and (c) utilizing community-based employment agencies.

Appropriate employment settings based on the needs of the youth with EBD should be defined purposefully and with care (Waintrup & Unruh, 2008). Bullis and Fredericks (2002) provide guidelines for selecting employment sites based on various needs manifested by youth with EBD. For example, students with anger management difficulties may need support identifying work environments that do not acerbate their anger "hot buttons." Students also need assistance implementing strategies that minimize or make accommodations for specific stressors related to their behaviors. Job-matching for specified behaviors is particularly important for students who may have a history of theft, aggression and/or assault, inappropriate sexual behaviors, running away, fire setting, suicide, drug and alcohol issues, prior abuse, attendance problems, or hygiene problems (Bullis & Fredericks, 2002).

To support work-related social skill instruction, transition staff may need to provide targeted employer/employee interventions with the youth and/or with the combined student and employer (e.g., methods to mediate a situation between employer and employee, how to ask for time off). These contextual situations help youth transfer to and practice in real-life situations the social skills taught in the school setting. If a youth is experiencing difficulties on the job, transition staff may want to intercede to support the youth's decision-making process. Additionally, to increase a student's self-advocacy and ensure the transition plan is youth-driven, transition personnel need to work with the youth to define whether and how a transition staff will interact with a student's employer. Some youth may not want the stigma of receiving additional or external supports on the job, preferring instead to discuss and problem solve work-based situations with the transition staff outside of the workplace. Other students may appreciate having transition staff interacting with the employer to support a youth's access to and success within an employment setting. The choice of level of interaction needs to be that of the students.

In addition, connections to community-based support services such as vocational rehabilitation and workforce investment act agencies should be made to support the employment-related goals of students with EBD. These agencies can provide additional monetary support to provide career assessments, training costs, interview clothing, job coaches (if needed), tax credits to employers to employ individuals eligible for either vocational rehabilitation or workforce investment funds, and additional individual supports based on the needs of the job. Secondary transition staff should develop strong, collaborative relationships with these community partners to help youth with EBD gain access to these valuable services. Some strategies for developing strong relationships were described previously, but most importantly include understanding the eligibility requirements of the agency, what services the agency can provide and then aligning the needs of the youth with the appropriate employment-related agency. In addition, educating employment-related agencies about the needs of youth with EBD is important. Employment-related caseworkers (e.g., vocational rehabilitation counselors) need to be aware of and educated in aligning the employment goals around the specific needs of the youth with EBD. Also, youth with EBD may typically be on a caseworker's caseload for longer periods of time than their other clients due to the intensity and length of services needed to work toward a positive service outcome.

Supportive Social Networks

Youth with EBD may need additional support to develop pro-social networks that support successful transitions. Research has shown that individuals who exhibit high-risk behaviors may increase these behaviors with continued access and/or exposure to other individuals exhibiting similar behaviors (Thornberry & Krohn, 1997). Concern has been raised that providing educational or treatment programming in groups of individuals with challenging behaviors may actually increase an individual's propensities for negative behaviors as opposed to reducing the targeted behaviors, a goal of the group-based intervention (Dishion, McCord, & Poulin, 1999). Helping individual youth develop pro-social networks in their community is important to support healthy social development. Pro-social networks may naturally occur through the implementation of other transition goals (e.g., employment or postsecondary education). For example, youth who become involved in work experiences outside of the school setting may develop friendships through the workplace which may transfer to additional positive activities outside of work in the community (e.g., going to the gym together, attending local concerts). If these pro-social networks do not naturally emerge, transition personnel may work with the youth and family to encourage participation in positive activities that may increase the likelihood of developing pro-social friends. Again, the student's interests and preferences should be ascertained so that community activities align with those of greatest interest to youth.

Peer mentoring is an additional strategy that may support youth with EBD throughout the transition process. Peer mentors who have similar experiences and who have successfully transitioned to young adulthood may provide positive encouragement and modeling to youth with EBD. Incorporating peer mentoring as part of a transition program, however, needs to be completed purposefully and with care. Peer mentors should be trained and monitored to ensure that they are maintaining their own recovery and do not cross personal boundaries with their mentees. In addition, purposeful activities with common goals need to be structured to develop meaningful mentoring interactions. Peer mentors can help youth with EBD assess and articulate specific preferences, and strengths needed to develop a youth-driven transition plan.

Future Research Directions

Recognizing that the evidence base of transition practices for youth with EBD remains somewhat limited, it is imperative that future researchers focus increased attention on the unique needs of this segment of the youth population. For example, even though service coordination across multiple agencies is typically required to meaningfully implement the transition plans of youth with EBD, Test, Fowler, and colleagues (2009) noted that studies examining the efficacy of interagency collaboration remain absent from the literature. To help guide future research endeavors, Clark, Koroloff, Geller, & Sondheimer (2008) recommended a set of research emphases focusing on the transition-related needs of youth and young adults with EBD. Their research framework includes four avenues of research needed to ultimately improve the transition outcomes of youth with EBD.

Research Examining the Population Characteristics, Service Utilization, and Developmental Trajectories of Youth and Young Adults with EBD

Relatively little is known about the developmental trajectory of these youth through early adolescence and into young adulthood. Comparisons of these trajectories to peers with other disabilities or without disabilities could provide further information from which to develop targeted interventions for youth with EBD.

Research on the Development and Adaptation of Interventions Specifically for Youth with EBD

As noted by Test and colleagues (2009), rigorous research is needed to evaluate new and existing interventions to clearly define a set of evidence-based practices for youth with disabilities in general, as well as to specifically test theoretically relevant interventions for youth with EBD.

Research Evaluating the Impact of Educational and Adult-system Services and Supports on the In- and Post-school Achievements of Youth with EBD

Service coordination across schools and multiple agencies appear to be critical for the transition process for youth with EBD. To fully understand how service coordination components (e.g., vocational rehabilitation, receipt of mental health services) operate and impact youth with EBD outcomes, these various components should be evaluated individually and within intervention packages to better understand the effectiveness of broad school/community programs on the long-term outcomes for employment, education, and quality of life of youth with EBD.

Research on the Implementation of Effective Program or Transition Service Systems

Research on the dissemination, implementation, and sustainability of evidence-based practices is in its infancy, specifically for youth with EBD. Based on the multiple service gaps noted in this chapter, as the field develops further evidence-based practices, it is essential to test how the various policies, level of coordinated services, and strength of implementation for interventions reliant on service coordination impact transition programming. Understanding how various policies and coordinated service systems, or lack thereof, impact the fidelity of implementation of transition practices and impact on outcomes of youth with EBD can guide needed policy change.

Through such studies, the transition field can gain a further understanding of the unique developmental process for youth with EBD and, as importantly, develop and test interventions across services systems to ensure program effectiveness with this population.

Summary

The experiences and relationships youth with EBD have during secondary school and early adulthood can make a substantial difference in the quality of life they experience into adulthood. Equipping youth with transition-related skills that increase their competence and confidence, as well as establishing a comprehensive network of individually designed supports and services, represents important elements of effective transition programming. To improve the in-school experiences and post-school outcomes of youth with disabilities, the efforts of multiple stakeholder groups—including policy makers, program administrators, parents, and youth themselves—are needed. Figure 28.2 includes example action steps these individuals might take to improve the quality and impact of transition services (Unruh & Clark, 2009). Although the field still has much to learn about how best to support successful transitions for this population of youth, it is clear that quality transition programming is critical to the long-term success and well-being of youth.

Policy-related decision makers at local, state, and federal levels

- Initiate Memorandum of Understandings (MOUs) across agencies targeting transition-age youth
- Redefine the age of transition—from ages 14 or 16 through ages 25 or 30—to ensure continuity of services
- Mandate implementation of evidence-based services and supports
- Designate a portion of contracted or grant-driven program funds to evaluation and program improvement.

School and program administrators

- Communicate high expectations for young people with EBD
- Value, support, and conduct data-based decision-making evaluation activities for program improvement
- Implement hiring practices that recruit staff committed to transition-age youth with EBD
- Ensure staff have sufficient resources to deliver high-quality transition services and supports (e.g., access to ongoing training with TA, adequate compensation).

Transition teachers and program staff

- Participate in data-based evaluation activities for program improvement
- Embrace and implement evidence-based practices for youth with EBD
- Develop relationships and working partnerships with families and local service partners
- Value the cultural diversity of students and consider cultural appropriateness of services during decision-making processes
- Value the voice of students and families to support their active involvement in all aspects of transition planning and education.

(Continued)

Parents and advocates

- Advocate to state and local-level policy makers for transition-age services for youth with EBD
- Be an active participant in youth and young adults' IEP process and transition plan
- Assist youth to advocate to clarify their strengths, interests, and preferences during the transition-planning process
- Assist youth in selecting and accessing appropriate support services
- Honor the need for their growth towards independence.

Youth and young adults with EBD

- Participate in quality assurance/evaluation activities of transition programs
- Become a peer mentor
- Articulate to your strengths, preferences, and goals to transition staff
- Inform program staff, administrators, and policy makers about the appropriate service needs of youth with EBD.

Figure 28.2 "Calls for action" to improve outcomes of youth with EBD
Source: Adapted from Unruh & Clark (2009)

References

Anderson, J.A., & Matthews, B. (2001). We care . . . for students with emotional and behavioral disorders and their families. *TEACHING Exceptional Children, 33*(5), 34–39.

Benz, M., Yovanoff, P., & Doren, B. (1997). School-to-work components that predict postschool success for students with and without disabilities. *Exceptional Children, 63,* 151–165.

Bullis, M., & Cheney, D. (1999). Vocational and transition interventions for adolescents and young adults with emotional or behavioral disorders. *Focus on Exceptional Children, 31,* 1–29.

Bullis, M., & Fredericks, H.D. (Eds.) (2002). *Providing effective vocational/transition services to adolescents with emotional and behavioral disorders.* Champaign-Urbana, IL: Research Press.

Cameto, R., Levine, P., & Wagner, M. (2004). *Transition planning for students with disabilities.* Menlo Park, CA: SRI International.

Carter, E. W. (2011). Promoting self-determination among transition-age youth with emotional/behavioral disorders: Promising practices. In D. Cheney (Ed.), *Transition of students with emotional and behavioral disabilities* (2nd ed. pp.51–78). Champaign, IL: Research Press.

Carter, E. W., Lane, K. L., Pierson, M., & Glaeser, B. (2006). Self-determination skills of transition-age youth with emotional disturbances and learning disabilities. *Exceptional Children, 72,* 333–346.

Carter, E. W., Lane, K. L., Pierson, M. R., & Stang, K. K. (2008). Promoting self-determination for transition-age youth: Views of high school general and special educators. *Exceptional Children, 75,* 55–70.

Carter, E. W., Trainor, A. A., Ditchman, N., Sweeden, B., & Owens, L. (2011). Community-based work experiences of adolescents with high-incidence disabilities. *The Journal of Special Education, 45,* 89–103.

Carter, E. W., Trainor, A. A., Sun, Y., & Owens, L. (2009). Assessing the transition-related strengths and needs of adolescents with high-incidence disabilities. *Exceptional Children, 76,* 74–94.

Carter, E. W., & Wehby, J. H. (2003). Job performance of transition-age youth with emotional and behavioral disorders. *Exceptional Children, 69,* 449–465.

Cheney, D., & Bullis, M. (2004). The school-to-community transition of adolescents with emotional and behavioral disorders. In R. B. Rutherford, M. M. Quinn, & S. R. Mathur (Eds.), *Handbook of research in emotional and behavioral disorders* (pp. 369–384). New York: Guilford Press.

Clark, H. B., & Hart, K. (2009). Navigating the obstacle course: An evidence-supported community transition system. In H. B. Clark & D. K. Unruh (Eds.), *Transition to adulthood for young people with emotional and/or behavioral difficulties: An evidenced-based handbook* (pp. 47–116). Baltimore, MD: Paul H. Brookes.

Clark, H. B., Koroloff, N., Geller, J., & Sondheimer, D.L. (2008). Research on transition to adulthood: Building the evidence base to inform services and supports for youth and young adults with serious mental health disorders. *Journal of Behavioral Health Services and Research, 35*(4), 365–372.

Clark, H. B., & Unruh, D. K. (Eds.). (2009). *Transition of youth and young adults with emotional or behavioral difficulties.* Baltimore, MD: Paul H. Brookes.

Cobb, B., Lehman, J., Newman-Gonchar, R., & Alwell, M. (2008). Self-determination for students with disabilities: A narrative meta-synthesis. *Career Development for Exceptional Individuals, 32,* 108–114.

Cook, C. R., Gresham, F. M., Kern, L., Barreras, R. B., Thornton, S., & Crews, S. D. (2008). Social skills training for secondary students with emotional and/or behavioral disorders: A review and analysis of the meta-analytic literature. *Journal of Emotional and Behavioral Disorders, 16,* 131–144.

Cullinan, D. (2004). Classification and definition of emotional and behavioral disorders. In R. B. Rutherford, M. M. Quinn, & S. R. Mathur (Eds.), *Handbook of research in emotional and behavioral disorders* (pp. 32–53). New York: Guilford Press.

Cullinan, D., & Sabornie, E. J. (2004). Characteristics of emotional disturbance in middle and high school students. *Journal of Emotional and Behavioral Disorders, 12,* 157–167.

Davis, M., Green, M., & Hoffman, C. (2009). The service system obstacle course for transition-age youth and young adults. In H. B. Clark & D. K. Unruh (Eds.), *Transition to adulthood for young people with emotional and/or behavioral difficulties: An evidenced-based handbook* (pp. 25–46). Baltimore, MD: Paul H. Brookes.

Dishion, T. J., McCord, J., & Poulin, F. (1999). When interventions harm: Peer groups and problem behavior. *American Psychologist, 54,* 755–764.

Dresser, K. L., Zucker, P. J., Orlando, R. A., Krynski, A. A., White, G., et al. (2009). Collaborative approach to quality improvement in process, progress, and outcomes: Sustaining a responsive and effective transition system. In H. B. Clark & D. K. Unruh (Eds.), *Transition to adulthood for young people with emotional and/or behavioral difficulties: An evidenced-based handbook* (pp. 263–290). Baltimore, MD: Paul H. Brookes.

Field, S. S., Martin, J. E., Miller, R. J., Ward, M., & Wehmeyer, M. L. (1998). Self-determination for persons with disabilities: A position statement of the Division on Career Development and Transition. *Career Development for Exceptional Individuals, 21,* 113–128.

Hinshaw, S. P. (1992). Externalizing behavior problems and academic underachievement in childhood and adolescence: Causal relationships and underlying mechanisms. *Psychological Bulletin, 111,* 127–155.

Houchins, D. E. (2002). Self-determination knowledge instruction and incarcerated students. *Emotional and Behavioral Difficulties, 7,* 132–151.

Johnson, M., Bullis, M., Benz, M., & Hollenbeck, K. (2004) *Working at gaining employment skills: A job-related social skills curriculum for adolescents.* Longmont, CO: Sopris West.

Karpur, A., Clark, H. B., Caproni, P., & Sterner, H. (2005). Transition to adult roles for students with emotional/behavioral disturbances: A follow-up study of student exiters from steps-to-success. *Career Development for Exceptional Individuals, 28,* 36–46.

Kohler, P. D., & Field, S. (2003). Transition-focused education: Foundation for the future. *The Journal of Special Education, 37,* 174–183.

Lane, K. L., & Carter, E.W. (2006). Supporting transition-age youth with and at risk for emotional and behavioral disorders at the secondary level: A need for further inquiry. *Journal of Emotional and Behavioral Disorders, 14,* 66–70.

Lane, K. L., Carter, E. W., Pierson, M., & Glaeser, B. (2006). Academic, social, and behavioral profiles of high school students with emotional disturbance and learning disabilities. *Journal of Emotional and Behavioral Disabilities, 14,* 108–117.

Mooney, P., Ryan, J. B., Uhing, B. M., Reid, R., & Epstein, M. H. (2005). A review of self-management interventions targeting academic outcomes for students with emotional and behavioral disorders. *Journal of Behavioral Education, 14,* 203–331.

National Alliance for Secondary Education and Transition (NASET). (2005). *National standards and quality indicators: Transition toolkit for systems improvement.* Minneapolis: University of Minnesota, National Center on Secondary Education and Transition.

Newman, L., Wagner, M., Cameto, R., & Knokey, A. (2009). *The post-high school outcomes of youth with disabilities up to 4 years after high school: A report from the National Longitudinal Transition Study-2 (NLTS2)* Menlo Park, CA: SRI International.

Osgood, D. W., Foster, E. M., Flanagan, C., & Ruth, G. R. (Eds.). (2007). *On your own without a net: The transition to adulthood for vulnerable populations.* Chicago: University of Chicago Press.

Osher, T. W., & Osher, D. M. (2002). The paradigm shift to true collaboration with families. *Journal of Child and Family Studies, 11,* 47–60.

Powers, K. M., Gil-Kashiwabara, E., Geenan, S. J., Powers, L., Balandran, J., & Palmer, C. (2005). Mandates and effective transition planning practices reflected in IEPs. *Career Development for Exceptional Individuals, 28,* 47–59.

Powers, L. E., Garner, T., Valnes, B., Squire, P., Turner, A., et al. (2007). Building a successful adult life: Findings from youth-directed research. *Exceptionality, 15*, 45–56.

Seiler, D., Orso, S., & Unruh, D. K. (2009). Partnerships for youth transition. In H. B. Clark & D. Unruh (Eds.), *Transition to adulthood for young people with emotional and/or behavioral difficulties: An evidenced-based handbook* (pp. 117–140). Baltimore, MD: Paul H. Brookes.

Test, D. W., Fowler, C. H., Richter, S. M., White, J., Mazzotti, V., et al. (2009). Evidence-based practices in secondary transition. *Career Development for Exceptional Individuals, 32*, 115–128.

Test, D. W., Mazzotti, V. L., Mustian, A. L., Fowler, C. H., Kortering, L., & Kohler, P. (2009). Evidence-based secondary transition predictors for improving postschool outcomes for students with disabilities. *Career Development for Exceptional Individuals, 32*, 160–181.

Thoma, C. A., Nathanson, R., Baker, S. R., & Tamura, R. (2002). Self-determination: What do special educators know and where do they learn it? *Remedial and Special Education, 23*, 242–247.

Thornberry, T. P., & Krohn, M. D. (1997). Peers, drug use, and delinquency. In D. M. Stoff, J. Breiling, & J. D. Maser (Eds.), *Handbook of antisocial behavior* (pp. 218–233). New York: Wiley.

Unruh, D. K., & Clark, H.B. (2009). Futures focus: Practice, program system, policy and research. In H. B. Clark & D. K. Unruh (Eds.), *Transition to adulthood for young people with emotional and/or behavioral difficulties: An evidenced-based handbook* (pp. 325–344). Baltimore, MD: Paul H. Brookes.

Unruh, D., Povenmire-Kirk, T. & Yamamoto, S. (2009). Perceived barriers and protective factors of juvenile offenders on their developmental pathway to adulthood. *Journal of Correctional Education, 60*, 201–224.

Unruh, D. K., Waintrup, M., Canter, T., & Smith, S., (2009). Special service systems for serving youth in the juvenile justice system. In H. B. Clark & D. K. Unruh (Eds.), *Transition to adulthood for young people with emotional and/or behavioral difficulties: An evidenced-based handbook* (pp. 189–208). Baltimore,: Paul H. Brookes.

Van Gelder, N., Sitlington, P. L., & Pugh, K. M. (2008). Perceived self-determination of youth with emotional and behavior disorders: A pilot study of the effect of different educational environments. *Journal of Disability Policy Studies, 19*, 182–190.

Wagner, M., & Davis, M. (2006). How are we preparing students with emotional disturbances for the transition to young adulthood? Findings from the National Longitudinal Transition Study-2. *Journal of Emotional and Behavioral Disorders, 14*, 86–98.

Wagner, M., Friend, M., Bursuck, W.D., Kutash, K., Duchnowski, A.J., Sumi, W. C., et al. (2006). Educating students with emotional disturbances: A national perspective on school programs and services. *Journal of Emotional and Behavioral Disorders, 14*, 12–30.

Wagner, M., Marder, C., Levine, P., Cameto, R., Cadwallader, T., et al. (2003). *The individual and household characteristics of youth with disabilities.* Menlo Park, CA: SRI International.

Waintrup, M., & Unruh, D. (2008). Career development programming strategies for transitioning incarcerated adolescents to the world of work. *Journal of Correctional Education, 59*, 127–144.

Walker, H.M., Nishioka, V., Zeller, R., Severson, H., & Feil, E. (2000). Causal factors and potential solutions for the persistent under-identification of students having emotional or behavioral disorders in the context of schooling. *Assessment for Effective Intervention, 26*, 29–40.

Zigmond, N. (2006). Twenty-four months after high school: Paths taken by youth diagnosed with severe emotional and behavioral disorders. *Journal of Emotional and Behavioral Disorders, 14*, 99–107.

29

Transition Education for Adolescents with Serious Mental Health Conditions

Janet S. Walker

L. Kris Gowen

PORTLAND STATE UNIVERSITY

Introduction

The period of transition to adulthood is a time of life that typically brings many challenges as young people are expected to move into roles and relationships that reflect increasing independence and responsibility. These challenges are particularly pronounced for young people who experience serious mental health conditions (SMHC) during transition. Compared to their peers, young people with SMHC tend to fare worse educationally and economically, and they are more likely to have legal troubles or become parents at a young age (U.S. Government Accountability Office, 2008). What is more, many of the young people who experience SMHC are vulnerable and/or at risk in other ways. For example, rates of SMHC are elevated among young people who are homeless or who have had experience in the child welfare or juvenile justice systems (Courtney & Dworsky, 2005; Garland, Hough, McCabe, Yeh, Wood, & Aarons, 2001; James & Glaze, 2006; Shufelt & Cocozza, 2006; Unger & Kipkke, 1997; Vander Stoep, Beresford, Weiss, McKnight, Gauee, & Cohen, 2000).

In recent years, attention has been drawn to the fact that existing mental health and related services are not effectively meeting the needs of young people with SMHC (Kessler et al., 2005; Pottick, Bilder, Vander Stoep, Warner, & Alvarez, 2008; U.S. Government Accountability Office, 2008). This is due in part to the lack of services that are attractive to, and developmentally appropriate for, older adolescents and young adults. Additionally, policy and funding barriers often make it difficult for young people who want to receive services to access and/or continue in care.

Our goal in this chapter is to describe empirically supported and promising community-based programs or approaches that are designed to promote positive development and to achieve better outcomes for young people with SMHC. We provide detail regarding the nature of the challenges that these young people face as well as some of the challenges that systems and providers have to deal with in trying to serve the population. We then describe recent theory and research on positive development, particularly as it applies to older adolescents and young or "emerging" adults. The next section of the chapter describes a series of empirically supported and promising programs, including programs specifically designed to serve highly vulnerable populations of transition-age young people, such as those who are homeless and those who are transitioning out of the juvenile justice system. Throughout these sections, we describe how these various approaches are connected to central themes in the research and theory on positive development during late adolescence and early adulthood. Finally, we review some questions and implications raised by considering programs and interventions from a positive development perspective.

Many Challenges

Among young people ages 14 to 30 in the United States, it is likely that at least 1 in 15 has an SMHC, and the rate may be much higher. The Government Accountability Office (GAO) recently estimated that at least 2.4 million young adults age 18–26—or 6.5% of the total population in that age range—had a serious mental illness (2008). The report notes, however, that this is likely an underestimate since certain subpopulations with high rates of mental illness—such as homeless or incarcerated young people—were not included in the figure. For youth ages 14 to 18 years, estimates of the percentage with serious emotional or behavioral disorders typically range from 5 to 10, although some estimates put the rate even higher (Burns, 2002; Friedman, Katz-Leavy, Manderscheid, & Sondheimer, 1998; Mark & Buck, 2006; National Institute of Mental Health, 2006).

Though exact figures are hard to come by, there is no doubt that many of these young people face multiple challenges. For example, according to the 2008 GAO report, among young adults with serious mental illness, 89% had two or more diagnoses, 56% had four or more, and 32% had a co-occurring diagnosis of substance abuse or dependence. For the younger cohort, studies have estimated that upwards of 40% have had a substance use disorder at some point, and that about 20% have a current co-occurring disorder (Aarons, Brown, Hough, Garland, & Wood, 2001; Manteuffel, Stephens, Sondheimer, & Fisher, 2008; Turner, Muck, Muck, Stephens, & Sukumar, 2004). Rates of SMHC are particularly high among youth from low-income households and those who receive public services in any sector, and many of these young people receive services from multiple systems (Garland et al., 2001; Manteuffel et al., 2008; Mark & Buck, 2006).

Youth and young adults in vulnerable populations are particularly likely to have a significant mental health condition, including 45–65% of homeless youth and young adults (Unger & Kipkke, 1997; Vander Stoep, Beresford, Weiss, McKnight, Gauee, & Cohen, 2000); at least 50% of foster youth and young adult former foster youth (Courtney & Dworsky, 2005; Garland et al., 2001); and at least 50% of youth and upwards of 60% of young adults involved in juvenile justice or corrections, respectively (James & Glaze, 2006; Shufelt & Cocozza, 2006). Significant proportions of these youth have multiple challenges. For example, one study of young adults who had been foster youth found that 20% had symptoms of three or more mental disorders (Courtney & Dworsky, 2005), while other studies have found that, among youth in juvenile justice who have mental health disorders, half or more also have co-occurring substance use disorders (Garland et al., 2001; Skowyra & Cocozza, 2006; Teplin, Abram, McClelland, Dulcan, & Mericle, 2002).

Finally, the transition years are the time of greatest vulnerability for young people with SMHC, when they are likely to have their highest levels of risk and challenge, including risk of arrest and criminal involvement and peaking substance use (Davis, Banks, Fisher, & Grudzinskas, 2004; Davis & Vander Stoep, 1997; Garland et al., 2001; Vander Stoep et al., 2000). Furthermore, the typical age of onset for psychotic disorders comes during these transition years, and, overall, adult mental health disorders have their highest rates of incidence in early adulthood (Pottick et al., 2008).

Ample and growing evidence points to the many ways that young people with SMHC fare worse than their peers in terms of educational attainment, career success, and community integration (Davis et al., 2004; Davis & Vander Stoep, 1997; Vander Stoep et al., 2000). These young people have high school completion rates even lower than students with other disabilities (56% vs. 72%), and only 36% are employed two years after high school. Approximately one-third (34%) attend postsecondary programs, compared to 60% of youth overall; this is in spite of the fact that 70–80% aspire to participate in education after high school (Wagner, Newman, Cameto, Levine, & Marder, 2007). Youth with mental health conditions are also more likely than their peers to become young parents. More than half have been arrested at least once, and 43% have been on probation or parole (NLTS-2, 2006–2008).

Growing evidence indicates that existing services and systems do not serve these young people adequately. There is a steady decrease in service utilization across the transition-age groups (Pottick et al., 2008), and among adults, those in the youngest cohort are least likely to get treatment (Kessler et al., 2005). Discontinuities between child- and adult-serving systems are significant contributors to this drop-off in utilization, which is most pronounced precisely at the age when young people lose eligibility for child systems at age 18–22, depending on state of residence (Davis & Koroloff, 2006; Pottick et al., 2008). As they cross the divide between child and adult services, young people face different and usually more restrictive requirements for adult programs. Even where young people are eligible, transition to adult services often means the end of established relationships with providers from children's systems (Davis & Koroloff, 2006; U.S. Government Accountability Office, 2008; Vander Stoep et al., 2000). Separate child and adult finance streams—and competition between child and adult systems for the same funds—discourage shared planning and restrict options for creating specialized programs and strategies to serve young people across the transition-age (Clark, Koroloff, Geller, & Sondheimer, 2008; Davis & Sondheimer, 2005; Pottick et al., 2008).

The unattractiveness of typical adult services to the younger population likely also contributes to the decrease in service utilization. For example, the GAO report quoted a state official who said that more than half of the eligible young adults who had received mental health services as children chose not to receive them as adults, and SAMHSA has reported that young adults have the lowest help-seeking behavior of any age group (U.S. Department of Human Services Substance Abuse and Mental Health Services Administration, 2007). Young people do not necessarily feel comfortable in settings dominated by older adults, and this discomfort may be exacerbated by changes in treatment approach between child and adult services. Additionally, young people often experience typical adult services as not well adapted to their needs or culture, and providers report having difficulty finding adequate age-appropriate mental health services for their clients (Davis, 2007; Jivanjee, Kruzich, & Gordon; Sieler, Orso, & Unruh, 2010; U.S. Government Accountability Office, 2008). Other factors may inhibit young people from even approaching adult services. The stigmatization and self-stigmatization associated with seeking treatment is particularly pronounced among young people of transition-age, and acts as a significant deterrent to help-seeking (Biddle, Donovan, Sharp, & Gunnell, 2007; Vogel, Wade, & Haake, 2006). Young people who have "graduated" from child services often have had unpleasant experiences that lead them to avoid services once they are able to make their own decisions. Adolescents often find mental health and related services stigmatizing, blaming, and coercive: planning is often undertaken without input from the young person, and youth often do not agree with the goals of treatment (Amodeo & Collins, 2007; Center for Mental Health Services, 2006; Federation of Families for Children's Mental Health & Keys for Networking Inc., 2001; Garland, Lewczyk-Boxmeyer, Gabayan, & Hawley, 2004). Finally, there are few programs and intervention approaches that specifically respond to the developmental needs and challenges of the transition-age population as outlined above. Adult providers are not usually trained in adolescent and emerging adult development, and so they are unprepared to work with young adults with SMHC, who tend to be less developmentally mature than their age alone would suggest (Pottick et al., 2008; U.S. Government

Accountability Office, 2008). More generally, interventions designed or adapted for this age range are relatively unstudied, and the evidence base is underdeveloped (Clark et al., 2008; Kurtines, Ferrer-Wreder, Berman, Lorente, Silverman, & Montgomery, 2008). It thus remains the unfortunate truth that the combination of high risk and inadequate response jeopardizes the life chances of this highly vulnerable segment of the population.

Given the evidence outlined above, it is clear that more research is needed in order to identify, develop, and evaluate interventions that are developmentally appropriate, attractive to young people, and effective in achieving positive outcomes. In the next few pages, we use a review of research, theory, and related literature to develop a description of key features of interventions that are consistent with all of these criteria.

Development During Transition

Though the legal age of adulthood in Western societies is typically 18, the transition to full biological, cognitive, and social maturity is not typically achieved until at least the mid-20s. During the transition period, there is significant brain development that is qualitatively different from the development in childhood and early adolescence. The most notable change is the maturation of the frontal lobe, the seat of "higher" functions such as self-control, emotional regulation, organization and planning (Giedd, Blumenthal, & Jeffries, 1999; Sowell, 2001). Alongside brain development comes cognitive development, particularly in capacities to think abstractly, make reasoned judgments, process information efficiently, and self-reflect (Zarrett & Eccles, 2006). These are precisely the capacities that young people need to successfully navigate the challenges of transition.

This transition period brings a unique set of challenges as young people move away from subordinate and dependent relationships with parents and other adults, toward relationships that reflect increasing maturity and responsibility in the family and community. The earlier part of this period, ages 14 to 18 or so, is often described as "youth," while the later part, ages from the late teens to the mid- or even late 20s, is increasingly known as "emerging adulthood" (Arnett, 2004; Obradovic, Burt, & Masten, 2006). While emerging adults in Western cultures clearly differ from youth—particularly in terms of their level of independence, freedom and mobility— the fundamental developmental tasks are similar. These developmental tasks of transition have been enumerated and listed in a variety of ways over the years (Masten & Coatsworth, 1998), as have the lists of assets or competencies that support accomplishing developmental tasks (Eccles & Gootman, 2002; Hawkins, Letcher, Sanson, Smart, & Toumbourou, 2009; Lerner & Benson, 2003; Schwartz, Cote, & Arnett, 2009). Across these various lists, however, there is a fairly high degree of recent consensus about several interrelated types of assets or capacities that are crucial for successful development during this time period (Catalano, Berglund, Ryan, Lonczak, & Hawkins, 2004; Guerra & Bradshaw, 2008; Larson, 2000; Riediger, Freund, & Baltes, 2005; Schwartz et al., 2009; Zarrett & Eccles, 2006). This level of agreement across the lists is explained by the fact that the authors rely on scientifically-derived evidence as a basis for enumerating assets and capacities. These four key types of developmental assets are:

- Developing a positive identity and a sense of purpose, including self-determination, efficacy and empowerment;
- Acquiring the capacity, motivation, and self-control to make decisions and carry out plans consistent with personally meaningful goals;
- Acquiring skills that provide a sense of mastery, aid in leveraging resources, and contribute to the ability to take on adult roles; and
- Developing supportive relationships and pro-social connectedness.

Positive Development, Resilience, and Recovery

While a focus on developmental tasks of different life stages is long-standing, a relatively recent trend in the field has been the coalescing of a "positive development" (PD) approach that focuses on actively promoting thriving and well-being across the life span (Bronstein, Davidson, Keyes, & Moore, 2003; Seligman & Csikszentmihalyi, 2000). A major thrust of PD theory and research has been to identify characteristics of thriving and well-being that are invariant across widely diverse world cultures. The PD approach has been characterized as nothing less than a paradigm shift because of its explicit turn away from a focus on correcting deficits and preventing negative outcomes and toward a focus on strengths and enhancing healthy development (Barton, Watkins, & Jarjoura, 1997; Bronstein et al., 2003; Kurtines et al., 2008). Positive development has been most clearly described as it applies to youth. This approach, called positive youth development (PYD), has a growing theory and research base; however, recent years have seen the beginnings of an approach to the study of positive development in "emerging adulthood" as well (Arnett, 2004; Obradovic et al., 2006; Schwartz et al., 2009). These PD approaches for youth in transition focus on how to prepare young people for adulthood by actively promoting the four types of assets and capacities described above.

A key element of the PD approach is the idea that development is heavily influenced by environment and that positive development is promoted through the interplay between individual capacities and supportive relationships, settings, and institutions. There is emerging consensus and research support regarding the key features of settings that support development of the capacities needed during the transition period (Catalano et al., 2004; Guerra & Bradshaw, 2008; Larson, 2000). Such environments are psychologically and physically safe; they provide connection to pro-social adults and peers; they allow for opportunities to build skills; and they provide a balance between structure and flexibility, so that while there are clear expectations, there are also opportunities for young people to set goals and make decisions and plans about how to reach those goals. In short, what facilitates successful development during transition is when young people and their environments interact in ways that build the capacities, motivation, and skills that young people need in order to become constructive agents of their own development.

Young people with SMHC may well lag behind their peers in terms of their developmental "age." A key feature of emotional or behavioral disorders is difficulty in developing self-control and self-regulation. Furthermore, many of these young people have personal histories characterized by inadequate exposure to settings that support positive development. As noted above, child and adolescent services and systems—including mental health, special education, child welfare, and juvenile justice—are frequently experienced as deficit-based, paternalistic, compliance-driven and/or coercive, and offer little opportunity for young people to set goals or make decisions. Furthermore, many of these young people have been traumatized, abused, and/or exploited. This implies not only that they have been significantly connected to *anti*social adults and/or peers, but also that their emotional and cognitive development has been put at risk. Traumatic experience, and the resulting stress, has a cumulative, detrimental impact on the developing brain (Shonkoff & Phillips, 2000), particularly in the areas of executive function and emotional and self-regulation that are so essential for successful development during the transition years.

Interventions rooted in positive development thus appear to be an ideal way to approach the challenges experienced by young people with SMHC. Indeed, PD is becoming increasingly popular—and research supported—in youth development programs and prevention efforts aimed at young people from various cultural backgrounds and with different risk profiles.

Among professionals who focus on youth and young adults, there is a growing awareness of the literature on assets and PYD and of the large body of resilience research. These studies show that, across cultural subpopulations, young people with higher levels of assets are far more likely to thrive—both as adolescents and as adults—despite multiple challenges and significant adversity (e.g., Condly, 2006; Iwaniec, Larkin, et al., 2006).

In recent years, more focused efforts have emerged to use PD approaches in targeted interventions with young people who experience serious disabilities or who have "problem behavior" (e.g., Amodeo & Collins, 2007; Bradshaw, Brown et al., 2006; Kurtines et al., 2008). Yet incorporation of PD elements into interventions with struggling youth of transition-age—including those with SMHC—is still relatively rare and under-researched. On the other hand, for this age group generally the intervention literature is very underdeveloped (Clark & Unruh, 2010; Kurtines et al., 2008). The only evidence-supported practice specifically targeted at transition-age young people with SMHC is the Transition to Independence (TIP) model, which is entirely consistent with a PYD approach and has an explicit focus on enhancing protective factors (assets), youth-driven planning, and positive, supportive relationships (Haber, Karpur, Deschenes, & Clark, 2008). More generally, the appropriateness of a PD approach for this population—particularly the emphasis on strengths and assets combined with individualized, youth-driven planning—is increasingly recognized in consensus statements (e.g., Altschuler, Stangler, Berkley, & Burton, 2009; Gagnon & Richards, 2008; e.g., Institute of Medicine, 2006), definitions of promising practices (Clark & Unruh, 2010; Davis, 2007) and federal initiatives aimed at this population (Frakera & Rangarajan, 2009).

Crucially, a focus on positive development resonates with what youth and young adults with SMHC want for themselves: to take charge of their own lives; to develop positive connections to others; to have a sense of optimism, empowerment, and efficacy; and to have the opportunity to pursue personally meaningful goals (Anthony, 1993; Jivanjee, Kruzich, et al., 2008; Sieler, Orso, & Unruh, 2010). Indeed, PD elements are at the very core of definitions of recovery in mental health, with their emphasis on strengths, hope, empowerment, well-being, community integration, and support from positive peers and family (Gagne, White, & Anthony, 2007; Ralph & Corrigan, 2005). It is not hard to see recovery as essentially a PD approach for people with SMHC, and thus it is perhaps not surprising that the types of programs, environments, and settings that are seen as helpful in supporting recovery are quite similar to those that support PD more generally (O'Connell, Tondora, Croog, Evans, & Davidson, 2005; Ridgeway & Press, 2004).

In sum, research, theory, and expert consensus suggest that there is a need to develop and test programs and interventions that are rooted in a PD approach. In addition, these programs should be attractive to young people and designed to promote positive outcomes in areas that include education, career, social support, mental health, and quality of life. Such programs and interventions would act to build assets in each of the four key areas.

Positive Identity, Sense of Purpose, Efficacy, Empowerment, Self-Determination

The PD approach outlined above suggests that effective programs to support transition-aged youth with SMHC would include an individualized approach that focuses on supporting young people to identify and move toward personally meaningful goals. This begins with envisioning a positive future identity (Who do I want to become?). Pursuing goals promotes a sense of purpose, and making progress toward those goals contributes to building feelings of efficacy, empowerment, and self-determination. These three are related concepts that reference the individual's ability to act as the primary causal agent in pursuing personally meaningful goals (Powers, Sowers, Turner, Nesbitt, Knowles, & Ellison, 1996; Wehmeyer, 1996), though empowerment also includes the additional dimension of acting as an agent for change in the broader community (Walker, Thorne, Powers, & Gaonkar, 2010). Self-determination has been identified as one of the key predictors of postsecondary success for youth with disabilities. Randomized controlled studies, as well as other research (see the review in Test, Fowler, & Brewer, 2005) have demonstrated the benefit of self-determination enhancing interventions for these youth and young adults.

Capacity, Motivation, Self-Control, and Confidence to Make Decisions and Carry Out Plans

In order to experience success in reaching personally meaningful goals, young people need to develop persistence and self-control, as well as specific skills related to decision-making and follow-through. Having these capacities and skills increases the likelihood that they will gain confidence in their decision-making and planning capabilities, and that they will persevere, even in the face of inevitable setbacks.

Skills for Adult Roles and Leveraging Resources

In order to reach their goals and to assume adult roles, young people with SMHC need opportunities to learn a wide range of specific skills. For example, many young people need to develop skills related to finding and maintaining housing and employment. Other needed skills can range from seeking and evaluating information, to enlisting help from others, to presenting ideas to a group, to requesting accommodations and supports.

Supportive Relationships and Pro-social Connectedness

A PD perspective further suggests that young people with SMHC will benefit from learning specific strategies for increasing and maintaining interpersonal support from positive peers, family, providers, and people in the community. Young people can learn specific steps and skills that can help them increase the quality and the extent of their interpersonal networks, as well as the amount of emotional, instrumental, and informational support available to them.

Using a PD perspective suggests that the development of these four types of assets are important recovery-oriented outcomes in and of themselves, as well as mediators of longer-term outcomes related to education, employment, mental health, and general quality of life. Indeed, a review of the available research on community-based programs and interventions for transition-age young people with SMHC reveals a common focus on asset building as described above. Also consistent with the PD perspective is that many of the programs and interventions include a focus on changing the settings around the youth so that the settings are more likely to encourage young people to develop or express strengths and assets. Below, we describe a series of empirically supported and promising approaches, and highlight the ways in which these approaches reflect a PD perspective.

Promising Programs

To date, very few programs specifically support the lives of transition-aged youth with SMHC, and even fewer programs have been evaluated for effectiveness. However, some programs are backed by enough empirical evidence that they can be considered as either "supported" or "promising" practices for improving the outcomes in this population. These programs (listed alphabetically), along with their outcomes, are briefly described in this section.[1]

Achieve my Plan!

Achieve my Plan! (AMP) is an intervention designed for use in any context in which a young person with a mental health condition is involved in a team-planning process. Human service and educational agencies and systems often convene teams to work collaboratively on plans for serving young people—typically those with high levels of need and/or involved in multiple systems—as they approach the transition into adulthood. These kinds of planning teams include IEP teams, wraparound teams, youth/family decision teams, and so on. AMP aims to increase the extent to which youth are involved and engaged in planning, the extent to which the plans that are produced reflect participating youths' own goals and perspectives, and the extent to which the young people are actively involved in carrying out action steps for their plans. In turn, this greater engagement with the planning process is expected to impact therapeutic alliance, treatment engagement, and mental health outcomes. One of the unique features of AMP is that the intervention was developed in collaboration with an advisory board that included youth, caregivers, and service providers.

An AMP coach works one-on-one with a young person to prepare him or her to participate actively and constructively in the team meetings. The coaching is more intensive prior to the first meeting and becomes less intensive over time. Other team members, particularly the person who is in charge of facilitating the team meeting, also receive AMP training and ongoing coaching so that they can become skilled in creating a team atmosphere that is conducive to and supportive of meaningful youth participation.

AMP was piloted with youth in two wraparound programs and youth in a high school/day treatment program (Walker, Geenen, Thorne, & Powers, 2009). Despite the relatively small sample size, the data show positive results. For example, analyses of pre- and post-data from video recordings of team meetings show improvements in the quality of youth participation, the supportiveness of adults toward youth, and overall team task focus. Pre- and post-data from assessments with youth showed significant improvement in perceptions of participation in planning. As assessed by the Youth Empowerment Scale (Walker et al., 2010), youth also indicated they were more confident both in managing their own mental health and in working with service providers to optimize their services and supports. Overall empowerment also increased. A randomized controlled trial of AMP is currently underway to test AMP's effect on more distal outcomes, including therapeutic alliance, quality of life, recovery and mental health.

The Community Reinforcement Approach at Homeless Youth Drop-in Centers

Slesnick and colleagues (2007) provided counseling to homeless youth in a drop-in center rather than a counseling or mental health clinic. Drop-in centers traditionally offer homeless youth access to food, clothing, recreation, health care, and other services. The Community Reinforcement Approach (CRA), a comprehensive behavioral program that utilizes social, recreational, familial, and vocational resources to support the young adult (Meyers & Squires, 1995), was used to treat the young adults over the course of six months. CRA programs also stress the importance of the client taking a leadership role in his or her treatment.

Findings indicate that youth participating in CRA (N=172) had lower rates of substance use and internalizing problems, compared to youth receiving treatment as usual. They also had increased social stability and housing at the 12-month follow-up when compared to baseline. This study provided initial evidence that mental health services and substance use treatment can be integrated successfully and effectively into drop-in services for homeless youth.

Early Assessment and Support Alliance (EASA)

EASA is a program designed to help youth and young adults maintain normal life trajectories when psychotic symptoms first occur. EASA focuses its interventions on mobilizing family and community resources in order to assist young people in achieving their goals. To accomplish this, services are strengths-focused and oriented toward goals the young people find relevant and personally meaningful, such as getting through school, resolving conflicts, paying off debts, or regaining proficiency in areas where they once excelled but in which they are now struggling. In addition, a supported employment specialist meets with each EASA participant, and occupational therapists are also on staff to offer support as needed.

An evaluation of EASA has shown dramatic decreases in hospitalization rates for its participants; for the one-year period following EASA's inception at the beginning of 2008, EASA served 340 young people and their families. Of those young people served, 42% needed hospitalization in the three months prior to intake; after participating in EASA, only 7% required hospitalization in the following three months and 3% were hospitalized after two years (Sale, 2008). Evaluation of EASA also indicates that the longer youth have been involved in EASA, the more likely they are to be either working or in school (Sale & Melton, 2010).

My Life

The My Life intervention uses a self-determination enhancement approach to improve the outcomes of transition-age youth in both special education and foster care. The primary focus of this model is to facilitate youths' self-determination through recognizing their accomplishments, encouraging them to learn from mentors, and promoting their acquisition of self-regulation strategies (Geenen, Powers, Hogansen, & Pittman, 2007). My Life provides youth with about 50 hours of coaching in self-determination skills for achieving their personal transition goals. They also participate in three or four mentoring workshops with young adults who have foster care experience and who are working or in college. Additionally, each youth develops an individualized transition plan that he or she presents in an interagency transition planning meeting. The goals of My Life are to increase quality of life, engagement in transition planning, educational attainment, employment, and stability of living situations among its participants.

In a pilot study of My Life, 60 youth (age 17) who were both receiving special education services and under the guardianship of child welfare were recruited. Of those participants, 29 completed the program, and 31 were randomized into a control group, where they received usual care. After a 12-month follow-up, young people participating in the intervention had better educational and employment outcomes than those in the control group. My Life participants also reported significantly greater levels of competence, empowerment, and social belonging in a quality-of-life measure.

Rehabilitation, Empowerment, Natural Supports, Education, and Work (RENEW)

RENEW is designed to support youth with emotional or behavioral disorders to achieve the following outcomes: high-school completion, employment, postsecondary education and training, and community inclusion. Five principles guide its practice: (a) promote self-determination; (b) increase community inclusion; (c) provide unconditional care; (d) provide strengths-based services; (e) provide flexible resources. RENEW employs a "toolbox" approach to working with young people, providing access to an array of services, such as personal futures planning, alternative education options, and mentoring. Young people receive specific services that fit with their particular goals and needs.

In its demonstration project, RENEW served 72 young people, ages 16 through 21, each of whom had an EBD diagnosed by a mental-health professional. In comparing pre- and post-intervention data, young people showed improvement in education and employment outcomes. At the beginning of RENEW, 7% of participants had completed high school; after three years, 63% had completed high school or its equivalent (compared to a national rate of 56%), and another 17% were on track to finish. Of the 42 youth who completed high school, 18 (43%) enrolled in postsecondary education; overall, postsecondary education enrollment in youth with EBD is 34% (Wagner et al, 2007). Regarding employment, 71 of the 72 RENEW participants obtained jobs in competitive settings with "typical" wages (Malloy, Drake, Abate, & Cormier, 2010).

Strategies Teaching Adolescent Young Offenders to Use Transition Skills (Project STAY OUT)

STAY OUT is an Oregon-based program designed to support incarcerated youth with EBD by offering system-wide service delivery in order to decrease recidivism and increase rates of employment and education outcomes for these youth. STAY OUT begins while the youth still resides in the correctional facility and continues after his or her release. Services are managed by a transition specialist who coordinates with different agency staff such as vocational rehabilitation counselors, parole officers, mental health professionals, and education staff. Four characteristics form the foundation for service delivery:

(a) Facilitated, self-directed planning and decision-making for youth;
(b) System collaboration to provide access to community resources;
(c) Dedication to increasing positive family and peer support;
(d) Continued development of youths' employment, educational, and independent living skills.

Developing a positive relationship between the transition specialist and the youth is critical to program success (Unruh, Waintrup, & Canter, 2010).

An evaluation of STAY OUT was conducted based on the outcomes of the 508 youth served between 1999 and 2007. Six-month post-release, 63% of STAY OUT participants were engaged (defined as being either employed and/or in school and not recidivated), as compared to only 35% in the general juvenile justice population.

The Transition to Independence Process (TIP) Model

The TIP model involves youth and young adults (ages 14–29), their families, and other friends or allies in a process that facilitates the young people's movement toward greater self-sufficiency and successful achievement of their goals. Young people are encouraged to explore their interests and futures as related to a series of transition domains: employment and career, education, living situation, personal effectiveness/well-being, and community-life functioning. The seven guidelines for the TIP model are: (a) engage young people through relationship development, person-centered planning, and a focus on their future; (b) tailor services and supports to meet the needs of young participants by building on their strengths; (c) prioritize personal choice and social responsibility in young people; (d) ensure a safety net of support by involving a young person's loved ones and wider community; (e) enhance a young person's competencies so that they can achieve greater self sufficiency; (f) maintain an outcome focus; and (g) involve young people and their social supports in the TIP system at the practice, program, and community levels (Clark, 2004).

The TIP model was evaluated in a year-long school-based program (Karpur, Clark, Caproni, & Sterner, 2005). Those who graduated from the program were less likely to be incarcerated or on probation, and more likely to be enrolled in postsecondary education than a matched sample of youth with EBD who did not participate in the program (3% vs. 12%, and 9% vs. 28%, respectively). In a multi-state project in which the TIP model was implemented across sites, participants showed significant increases in employment and educational advancement and significant decreases in mental health interference and criminal justice involvement (Haber, Karpur, Deschenes, & Clark, 2008).

Connecticut's Young Adult Services Program (YAS)

In 1997, Connecticut's Department of Mental Health and Addiction Services established the YAS Program, designed to help those over 18 with moderate to severe symptoms of mental illness transition smoothly from children's mental health care and into adult services. YAS includes clinical, residential, case management, vocational, and social rehabilitation supports that are guided by three major principles: (a) services must be comprehensive and integrated because focusing on one issue without supporting other aspects of a young adult's life is ineffective; (b) facilitating young adults' transitions from highly supervised and structured programs into community settings in which they experience higher degrees of autonomy is essential, and; (c) participants should not be removed from YAS since it is important to provide young adults with opportunities to form secure attachments given the traumas many of them have previously experienced. In addition, services to young adults incorporate both strengths-focused treatment planning (SFTP—defined as assessing a client's social and cognitive strengths, and incorporating them into the treatment plan) and community-focused treatment planning (CFTP—defined as setting a goal of increasing client residential and community supports).

In an evaluation of YAS, 60 clients (average age of 20 years) who had aged out of institutional settings such as foster care or residential treatment were assessed. Most (95%) had known histories of severe and sustained abuse, 95% had been in foster and/or residential care, half had diagnosed learning disabilities, and many had been incarcerated. Three treatment variables were related to improved outcomes. Longer tenure in YAS was significantly associated with a higher quality of life, greater satisfaction with services, client reports of higher functioning, and lower reported loneliness. After controlling for both demographic variables and time in YAS, two additional treatment characteristics predicted positive outcomes. Based on chart reviews, higher rates of SFTP were significantly associated with higher quality of life, and higher rates of CFTP were significantly associated with fewer arrests and fewer symptoms (Styron et al., 2006).

Promising Programs and a PD Perspective

A positive development perspective is clearly evident in a number of the principles and components that are central elements of the programs and interventions described above. As can be seen in Figure 29.1,[2] all of the promising programs explicitly focus on enhancing at least two of the four types of assets. In terms of the range of asset types promoted, TIP and AMP appear to be the most comprehensive of the eight outlined in that they both address all four positive development assets for transition-age youth and young adults. Regarding which assets are most likely to be addressed by programs, all eight of the promising programs focus on the development of supportive relationships and pro-social connectedness. This indicates a shared recognition that young adults need to know how to leverage natural supports and work with others in order to achieve successful outcomes. The next most common asset area addressed across

Asset	Program							
	AMP	CRA	EASA	My Life	RENEW	STAY OUT	TIP	YAS
Positive identity, sense of purpose, efficacy, empowerment, self-determination.	X			X	X		X	
Capacity, motivation, self-control, and confidence to make decisions and carry out plans.	X	X		X	X	X	X	X
Skills for adult roles and leveraging resources.	X		X			X	X	
Supportive relationships and pro-social connectedness.	X	X	X	X	X	X	X	X

Figure 29.1 Developmental assets represented in promising programs for Transition-age youth with serious mental health conditions

programs was teaching young people to develop the capacity to make decisions and move toward goals. This combination of emphasis on two asset areas—building supportive relationships and learning to make decisions—highlights the balancing act that is at the center of the transition age: the need to increase independence and take on aspects of a new identity while also maintaining social connectedness and community ties.

In contrast, the asset least likely to be addressed across promising programs was "skills for adult roles." While all programs addressed at least one adult-related skill, few were explicit in addressing skills across a variety of domains. Instead, many programs (e.g., RENEW, YAS), appeared to focus on narrow goals and outcomes rather than a breadth of skills.

Other Community-based Approaches

Besides the promising programs described above, which offer some evidence of their effectiveness, other approaches have the potential to be effective for youth and young adults either because of their success with adults with mental health conditions and/or because of their perceived developmental appropriateness for youth and young adults.

Supported Employment

In Supported Employment, individuals with severe disabilities (including mental health conditions) work to gain competitive employment that they find personally meaningful. Key components of Supported Employment include job coaches, assistance with transportation, assistive technology, specialized job training, and individually tailored supervision. Although no Supported Employment program targeting transition-aged youth with SMHC has yet been evaluated, Supported Employment has been shown to be effective for adults with serious mental illness across several studies; more specifically, in experimental studies. For example, 58% of those who received supported employment achieved competitive employment, compared to 21% of those in a control group (usually traditional vocational rehabilitation; see Bond, Drake, Mueser, & Becker, 1997, for a review). Given the importance young adults place on being employed, Supported Employment is a good candidate for evaluating—and, if necessary, adapting—for that population.

Clubhouse Model

A Clubhouse is a planned community where staff and mental health consumers work together doing daily activities and chores to provide services and basic needs (e.g., meals, companionship) to its members. In this manner, Clubhouses often provide transitional employment opportunities for people with serious mental health conditions. As with Supported Employment programs, the Clubhouse model has not been evaluated specifically for its effectiveness with transition-age young people with SMHC. However, Clubhouses seem to be developmentally appropriate for young adults since they provide opportunities for participants to learn skills such as working in a community, doing daily chores, and following through with responsibilities—all tasks relevant to becoming an adult. Additionally, Clubhouses have been shown to be effective; in a randomized-controlled study, adults (average age = 38 years) who participated in a Clubhouse had significantly higher wages and remained competitively employed for significantly more weeks per job than adults who received Assertive Community Treatment, a more clinically oriented intervention that includes some vocational focus (Shonebaum, Boyd, & Dudek, 2006).

Peer Support Services

Peer support is social, emotional, and/or instrumental support that is offered professionally by a person with a mental health condition to others sharing a similar mental health condition (Solomon, 2004). Endorsement for these services is evident in such documents as a 2008 position statement issued by Mental Health America, which calls on states to incorporate peer support services—including adolescent peer services—into community-based mental health and substance abuse treatments (MHA, 2008). Although there is no consistent evidence that peer support services are *more* effective than support delivered by mental health professionals, neither is there any evidence that they are *less* effective (Rogers, Farkas, Anthony, Kash, & Maru, 2010), or that they cause detrimental effects (Simpson & House, 2002); additionally, there is some evidence that peer-delivered services increase engagement and retention of clients (Rogers et al., 2010). Given that these services are potentially effective, that they may increase client engagement, that they offer employment opportunities for people recovering from mental health conditions, and that consumer advocacy groups see them as an essential element of a comprehensive service system, it seems that peer support services warrant further implementation and evaluation. Peer support approaches may be particularly appropriate for youth and young adults because of their higher reliance on peers over family during this developmental phase. Having peer support may also ameliorate the stigmatization and social isolation often felt by young adults with mental health conditions.

Specific peer support services designed for youth and young adults are lacking, however, and warrant further efforts.

Conclusion

This chapter uses Positive Development as a theoretical framework for understanding shared characteristics of promising community-based programs for youth and young adults with serious mental health conditions. Four essential assets for successful transition to adulthood that capture the essence of PD were identified from the literature: (a) developing a positive identity and sense of purpose; (b) acquiring the capacity to make decisions consistent with personally meaningful goals; (c) acquiring skills that contribute to the ability to take on adult roles; and (d) developing supportive relationships and pro-social connectedness. Our review of the small number of promising programs and interventions that are specifically designed for transition-age youth with serious mental health conditions indicates that these approaches typically include an explicit focus on one or more of these asset areas. The most common ways in which these programs focus on building assets are through promoting supportive social relationships and helping young people develop the confidence to make decisions.

Viewing these programs in terms of the assets they promote raises some interesting questions. For example, several of the programs focus on one or two specific domains of success in young adults (usually employment and/or education), rather than helping to build the more general skills needed to function in adult roles, or supporting well-being or community among program participants. It has been suggested that programs designed for young adults should prioritize meeting the developmental needs of emerging adults such as identity formation, exploration, and increased responsibility—the process of becoming an adult—over more concrete outcomes such as getting a job (Tanner, 2010).

A PD perspective also draws attention to the idea that asset development for young people is promoted through the interplay between individual capacities and supportive relationships, settings, and institutions. A number of the programs described here recognize the need for working with the young person's social, interpersonal, and organizational/institutional environments in order to increase environmental support for asset building. These programs demonstrate a shared awareness that, for young people who are struggling, it may not be enough to teach skills or provide an entrée into a new role. A young person may not be able to exercise the skills or take advantage of an open door if the surrounding environments are not supportive. Researchers working in the area of positive development have identified features of supportive environments, and this information may be helpful to ongoing efforts to develop effective programs and interventions for young people with SMHCs. Beyond this, the PD approach's focus on environments provides insight regarding the types of settings that, even though they are not specifically designed as programs or interventions for young people with SMHCs, they nonetheless provide conditions that are likely to support their positive development.

From this review, it is apparent that there are few community-based programs specifically designed to support youth and young adults with serious mental health conditions and even fewer that have any evidence of effectiveness. More rigorous studies need to be conducted in order to consider both what approaches are best for working with this population and what outcomes should be stressed in order to optimize long-term success. In recognition of this need for further study, recent initiatives focused on transition-age youth with mental health needs have been funded by major federal entities. For example, in late 2009, two Research and Training Centers on transition-age youth with serious mental health conditions were funded by the National Institute on Disability and Rehabilitation Research and the Substance Abuse and Mental Health Services Administration (SAMHSA); SAMHSA has also funded two series of demonstration projects: first the Partnership for Youth Transition (2002–2006), and currently the Healthy Transitions Initiative (2009–2013). In 2008, the U.S. Government Accountability Office published a report, *Young Adults with Serious Mental Illness: Some States and Federal Agencies Are Taking Steps to Address Their Transition Challenges* (2008), which called attention to the challenges these young people face when trying to access services and engage in meaningful life activities. Such efforts point to the fact that the mental health field acknowledges youth and young adults as a separate population, with specific needs and strengths to consider in order to develop appropriate, meaningful, and effective interventions.

Notes

1 Please note that community- rather than school-based programs are highlighted where possible because school-based programs are the focus of Chapter 28, 'Transition Education for Adolescents with Emotional Behavioral Disorders'.
2 The process of identifying the types of assets promoted by each of these programs or interventions relied primarily on publicly available written descriptions of programs. In some cases, the developers of the programs responded to requests for further information. Therefore, this figure reflects a conservative estimate of the extent to which these promising approaches focus on building the various asset types.

References

Aarons, G. A., Brown, S. A., Hough, R. L., Garland, A. F., & Wood, P. A. (2001). Prevalence of adolescent substance use disorders across five sectors of care. *Journal of the American Academy of Child & Adolescent Psychiatry, 40*(4), 419.

Altschuler, D., Stangler, G., Berkley, K., & Burton, L. (2009). *Supporting youth in transition to adulthood: Lessons learned from child welfare and juvenile justice.* Washington, DC: Georgetown University Center for Juvenile Justice Reform.

Amodeo, M., & Collins, M. E. (2007). Using a positive youth development approach in addressing problem-oriented youth behavior. *Families in Society: The Journal of Contemporary Social Services, 88*(1), 75–85.

Anthony, W. (1993). Recovery from mental illness: The guiding vision of the mental health service system in the 1990s. *Psychological Rehabilitation Journal, 16*, 11–24.

Arnett, J. J. (2004). *Emerging adulthood:The winding road from the late teens through the twenties.* New York: Oxford University Press.

Barton, W. H., Watkins, M., & Jarjoura, R. (1997). Youth and communities: Toward comprehensive strategies for youth development. *Social Work, 42*, 483–494.

Biddle, L., Donovan, J., Sharp, D., & Gunnell, D. (2007). Explaining non-help-seeking amongst young adults with mental distress: A dynamic interpretive model of illness behaviour. *Sociology of Health & Illness, 29*(7), 983–1002.

Bond, G. R., Drake, R. E., Mueser, K. T., & Becker, D. R. (1997). An update on supported employment for people with serious mental illness. *Psychiatric Services, 48*, 335–346.

Bradshaw, C. P., Brown, J. S., & Hamilton, S. F. (2006). Applying Positive Youth Development and Life-Course Research to the Treatment of Adolescents Involved With the Judicial System. *Journal of Addictions & Offender Counseling, 27*(1), 2–16.

Bronstein, M. H., Davidson, L., Keyes, C. L. M., & Moore, K. A. (Eds.). (2003). *Well-being: Positive development across the life course.* Mahwah, NJ: Lawrence Erlbaum Associates.

Burns, B. J. (2002). Reasons for hope for children and families: A perspective and overview. In B. J. Burns & K. Hoagwood (Eds.), *Community treatment for youth: Evidence-based intervention for severe emotional and behavioral disorders* (pp. 3–15). New York: Oxford University Press.

Catalano, R. F., Berglund, M. L., Ryan, J. A. M., Lonczak, H. S., & Hawkins, J. D. (2004). Positive youth development in the United States: Research findings on evaluations of positive youth development programs. *The Annals of the American Academy of Political and Social Science, 592*, 98–124.

Center for Mental Health Services. (2006). Who's in control over treatment decisions: Caregiver and youth perceptions. *EvalBrief: Systems of Care, 8*(5), 1–4.

Clark, H. B. (2004). *Transition to Independence Process System Development and Operations Manual.* Tampa, FL: University of South Florida.

Clark, H. B., Koroloff, N., Geller, G., & Sondheimer, D. L. (2008). Research on transition to adulthood: Building the evidence base to inform services and supports for youth and young adults with serious mental health disorders. *Journal of Behavioral Health Services & Research, 35*(4), 365–372.

Clark, H. B., & Unruh, D. K. (Eds.). (2010). *Transition of youth and young adults with emotional or behavioral difficulties: An evidence-based handbook.* Baltimore, MD: Brookes Publishing.

Condly, S. J. (2006). Resilience in children: A review of literature with implications for education. *Urban Education, 41*(3), 211–236.

Courtney, M. E., & Dworsky, A. (2005). *Midwest evaluation of the adult functioning of former foster youth.* Chicago, IL: The University of Chicago, Chapin Hall Center for Children.

Davis, M. (2007). *Pioneering transition programs: The establishment of programs that span the ages served by child and adult mental health.* Rockville, MD: Substance Abuse and Mental Health Services Administration, Center for Mental Health Services.

Davis, M., Banks, S., Fisher, W., & Grudzinskas, A. (2004). Longitudinal patterns of offending during the transition to adulthood in youth from the mental health system. *Journal of Behavioral Health Services & Research, 31*(4), 351–366.

Davis, M., & Koroloff, N. (2006). The great divide: How public mental health policy fails young adults. In W. H. Fisher (Ed.), *Community based mental health services for children and adolescents* (Vol. 14, pp. 53–74). Oxford, UK: Elsevier Sciences.

Davis, M., & Sondheimer, D. L. (2005). State child mental health efforts to support youth in transition to adulthood. *Journal of Behavioral Health Services & Research, 32,* 27–42.

Davis, M., & Vander Stoep, A. (1997). The transition to adulthood for youth who have serious emotional disturbance: Development transition and young adult outcomes. *The Journal of Mental Health Administration, 24,* 400–427.

Eccles, J., & Gootman, J. A. (2002). Personal and social assets that promote well-being. In J. Eccles & J. A. Gootman (Eds.), *Community programs to promote youth development.* Washington, DC: National Academy Press.

Federation of Families for Children's Mental Health & Keys for Networking Inc. (2001). *Blamed and ashamed: The treatment experiences of youth with co-occurring substance abuse and mental health disorders and their families.* Washington, DC: Author.

Frakera, T., & Rangarajan, A. (2009). The Social Security Administration's youth transition demonstration projects. *Journal of Vocational Rehabilitation, 30,* 223–240.

Friedman, R. M., Katz-Leavy, J. W., Manderscheid, R. W., & Sondheimer, D. (1998). Prevalence of serious emotional disturbance: An update. In R. W. Manderscheid & M. J. Henderson (Eds.), *Mental health: United States* (pp. 110–112). Rockville, MD: Substance Abuse and Mental Health Services Administration.

Gagne, C., White, W., & Anthony, W. A. (2007). Recovery: A common vision for the fields of mental health and addictions. *Psychiatric Rehabilitation Journal, 31*(1), 32–37.

Gagnon, J. C., & Richards, C. (2008). *Making the right turn: A guide about improving transition outcomes of youth involved in the juvenile corrections system.* Washington, DC: Institute for Educational Leadership, National Collaborative on Workforce and Disability for Youth.

Garland, A. F., Hough, R. L., McCabe, K. M., Yeh, M., Wood, P. A., & Aarons, G. A. (2001). Prevalence of psychiatric disorders in youths across five sectors of care. *Journal of the American Academy of Child & Adolescent Psychiatry, 40*(4), 409.

Garland, A. F., Lewczyk-Boxmeyer, C. M., Gabayan, E. N., & Hawley, K. M. (2004). Multiple stakeholder agreement on desired outcomes for adolescents' mental health services. *Psychiatric Services, 55,* 671–676.

Geenen, S., Powers, L.E., Hogansen, J. & Pittman, J. (2007). Youth with disabilities in foster care: Developing self-determination within a context of struggle and disempowerment. *Exceptionality, 15*(1), pp. 17–30.

Giedd, J. N., Blumenthal, J., & Jeffries, N. O. (1999). Brain development during childhood and adolescence: a longitudinal MRI study. *Nature Neuroscience, 2,* 861–863.

Guerra, N. G., & Bradshaw, C. P. (2008). Linking the prevention of problem behaviors and positive youth development: Core competencies for positive youth development and risk prevention. *New Directions for Child & Adolescent Development, 2008*(122), 1–17.

Haber, M. G., Karpur, A., Deschenes, N., & Clark, H. B. (2008). Predicting improvement of transitioning young people in the Partnerships for Youth Transition Initiative: Findings from a multi-site demonstration. *Journal of Behavioral Health Services and Research, 35,* 488–513.

Hawkins, M. T., Letcher, P., Sanson, A., Smart, D., & Toumbourou, J. W. (2009). Positive development in emerging adulthood. *Australian Journal of Psychology*, *61*(2), 89–99.

Institute of Medicine. (2006). *Improving the quality of health care for mental and substance-use conditions*. Washington, DC: The National Academies Press.

Iwaniec, D., Larkin, E., & Higgins, S. (2006). Research review: Risk and resilience in cases of emotional abuse. *Child & Family Social Work*, *11*(1), 73–82.

James, D. J., & Glaze, L. E. (2006). *Mental health problems of prison and jail inmates*. Washington, DC: Bureau of Justice Statistics.

Jivanjee, P., Kruzich, J., & Gordon, L. (2008). Community integration of transition-age individuals: Views of young adults with mental health disorders. *Journal of Behavioral Health Services & Research*, *35*(4), 402–418.

Karpur, A., Clark, H. B., Caproni, P., & Sterner, H. (2005). Transition to adult roles for students with emotional/behavioral disturbances: A follow-up study of student exiters from steps to success. *Career Development for Exceptional Individuals*, *28*, 36–46.

Kessler, R. C., Demler, O., Frank, R. G., Olfson, M., Pincus, H. A., Walters, E. E. . . .Zaslavsky, A. M. (2005). Prevalence and treatment of mental disorders, 1990 to 2003. *New England Journal of Medicine*, *352*(24), 2515–2523.

Kurtines, W. M., Ferrer-Wreder, L., Berman, S. L., Lorente, C. C., Silverman, W. K., & Montgomery, M. J. (2008). Promoting positive youth development: New directions in developmental theory, methods, and research. *Journal of Adolescent Research*, *23*, 233–244.

Larson, R. W. (2000). Toward a psychology of positive youth development. *American Psychologist*, *55*, 170–183.

Lerner, R. M., & Benson, P. L. (Eds.). (2003). *Developmental assets and asset-building communities: Implications for research, policy, and practice*. New York, NY: Kluwer.

Malloy, J. M., Drake, J., Abate, K., & Cormier, G. M. (2010). The RENEW model of futures planning, resource development, and school-to-career experiences for youth with emotional or behavioral disorders. In D. Cheney (ed.) *Transition of Secondary Students with Emotional or Behavioral Disorders* (2nd ed.), 267–304.

Manteuffel, B., Stephens, R. L., Sondheimer, D. L., & Fisher, S. K. (2008). Characteristics, service experiences, and outcomes of transition-aged youth in systems of care: Programmatic and policy implications. *The Journal of Behavioral Health Services & Research*, *35*, 469–487.

Mark, T. L., & Buck, J. A. (2006). Characteristics of U.S. youths with serious emotional disturbance: Data from the National Health Interview Survey. *Psychiatric Services*, *57*, 1573–1578.

Masten, A. S., & Coatsworth, J. D. (1998). The development of competence in favorable and unfavorable environments. *American Psychologist*, *53*, 205–220.

Meyers, R. J., & Squires, D. D. (1995). The Community Reinforcement Approach: A guideline developed for the Behavioral Health Recovery Management project. Accessed online September 2, 2010 at http://www.bhrm.org/guidelines/CRAmanual.pdf

MHA (2008). Position statement 37: The role of peer support services in the creation of recovery-oriented mental health systems. Accessed online September 2, 2010 at http://www.nmha.org/go/position-statements/37

National Institute of Mental Health. (2006). *The numbers count: Mental disorders in America*. Washington, DC: Author.

NLTS-2. (2006–2008). Findings from the National Longitudinal Transition Study.

Obradovic, J., Burt, K. B., & Masten, A. S. (2006). Pathways of adaptation from adolescence to young adulthood. *Annals of the New York Academy of Sciences*, *1094*(1), 340–344.

O'Connell, M., Tondora, J., Croog, G., Evans, A., & Davidson, L. (2005). From rhetoric to routine: Assessing perceptions of recovery-oriented practices in a state mental health and addiction system. *Psychiatric Rehabilitation Journal*, *28*(4), 378–386.

Pottick, K. J., Bilder, S., Vander Stoep, A., Warner, L. A., & Alvarez, M. F. (2008). U.S. patterns of mental health service utilization for transition-age youth and young adults. *Journal of Behavioral Health Services & Research*, *35*(4), 373–389.

Powers, L. E., Sowers, J., Turner, A., Nesbitt, M., Knowles, E., & Ellison, R. (1996). Take charge: A model for promoting self-determination among adolescents with challenges. In L. E. Powers, G. H. S. Singer & J. Sowers (Eds.), *On the road to autonomy: Promoting self-competence for children and youth with disabilities* (pp. 291–322). Baltimore, MD: Brookes Publishing.

Ralph, R. O., & Corrigan, P. W. (2005). *Recovery in mental illness: Broadening our understanding of wellness*. Washington, DC: American Psychological Association.

Ridgeway, P., & Press, A. (2004). *Assessing the recovery-orientation of your mental health program: A user's guide for the Recovery-Enhancing Environment Scale (REE)*. Lawrence, KS: University of Kansas, School of Social Welfare.

Riediger, M., Freund, A. M., & Baltes, P. B. (2005). Managing life through personal goals: Intergoal facilitation and intensity of goal pursuit in younger and older adulthood. *Journals of Gerontology Series B: Psychological Sciences & Social Sciences, 60B*(2), P84–P91.

Rogers, E. S., Farkas, M., Anthony, W., Kash, M., & Maru, M. (2010). *Systematic review of peer-delivered services literature 1989–2009*. Boston, MA: The Center for Psychiatric Rehabilitation. Accessed online September 7, 2010 at http://drrk.bu.edu/research-syntheses/psychiatric-disabilities/supported-education

Sale, T. (2008). EAST helps people with psychosis out west. *Behavioral Healthcare, June*, 28–31.

Sale, T., & Melton, R. (2010). Early psychosis intervention in Oregon: Building a positive future for this generation. *Focal Point: Youth, Young Adults, and Mental Health, 24*, 25–28.

Schwartz, S. J., Cote, J. E., & Arnett, J. J. (2009). Identity and agency in emerging adulthood: Two developmental routes in the individualization process. *Youth & Society, 37*, 201–229.

Seligman, M. E. P., & Csikszentmihalyi, M. (2000). Positive psychology. *American Psychologist, 55*(1), 5.

Shonebaum, A. D., Boyd, J. K., & Dudek, K. J. (2006). A comparison of competitive employment outcomes for the Clubhouse and PACT models. *Psychiatric Services, 57*, 1416–1420.

Shonkoff, J., & Phillips, D. A. (Eds.). (2000). *From neurons to neighborhoods: The science of early childhood development*. Washington, DC: National Academy Press.

Shufelt, J. L., & Cocozza, J. J. (2006). *Youth with mental health disorders in the juvenile justice system: Results from a multi-state prevalence study*. Delmar, NY: National Center for Mental Health and Juvenile Justice.

Sieler, D., Orso, S., & Unruh, D. K. (2010). Creating options for youth and their families. In H. B. Clark & D. K. Unruh (Eds.), *Transition of youth and young adults with emotional or behavioral difficulties: An evidence-based handbook*. Baltimore, MD: Brookes Publishing.

Simpson, E. L., & House, A. O. (2002). Involving users in the delivery and evaluation of mental health services: Systematic review. *British Medical Journal, 325*, 1265–1269.

Skowyra, K., & Cocozza, J. (2006). *Blueprint for change: A comprehensive model for the identification and treatment of youth with mental health needs in contact with the juvenile justice system*. Mahwah, NJ: The National Center for Mental Health and Juvenile Justice Policy Research Associates.

Slesnick, N., Prestopnik, J.L., Meyers, R.J., & Glassman, M. (2007). Treatment outcomes for street-living, homeless youth. *Addictive Behavior, 2*(6), 1237–1251.

Solomon, P. (2004). Peer support/peer provided services underlying processes, benefits, and critical ingredients. *Psychiatric Rehabilitation Journal, 27*, 392–401.

Sowell, E. R. (2001). Improved memory functioning and frontal lobe maturation between childhood and adolescence: a structural MRI study. *Journal of the International Neuropsychological Society, 7*, 312.

Styron, T. H., O'Connell, M., Smalley, W., Rau, D., Shahar, G., Sells, D. et al., (2006). Troubled youth in transition: An evaluation of Connecticut's special services for individuals again out of adolescent mental health programs. *Children and Youth Services Review, 28*, 1088–1101.

Tanner, J. (2010). Is there a developmentalist in the house? Using developmental theory to understand the service needs of emerging adults. *Focal Point: Youth, Young Adults, and Mental Health, 24*, 8–12.

Teplin, L., Abram, K., McClelland, G., Dulcan, M., & Mericle, A. (2002). Psychiatric disorders in youth in juvenile detention. *Archives of General Psychiatry, 59*, 1133–1143.

Test, D. W., Fowler, C. H., & Brewer, D. M. (2005). A content and methodological review of self-advocacy intervention studies. *Exceptional Children, 72*(1), 101–125.

Turner, W. C., Muck, R. D., Muck, R. J., Stephens, R. L., & Sukumar, B. (2004). Co-occurring disorders in the adolescent mental health and substance abuse treatment systems. *Journal of Psychoactive Drugs, 36*(4), 455–462.

Unger, J. B., & Kipkke, M. D. (1997). Homeless youths and young adults in Los Angeles: Prevalence of mental health problems and the relationship between mental health and substance abuse disorders. *American Journal of Community Psychology, 25*(3), 371–394.

Unruh, D., Waintrup, M., & Canter, T. (2010). Project STAY OUT: A facility-to-community transition intervention targeting incarcerated adolescent offenders. In D. Cheney (ed.) *Transition of Secondary Students with Emotional or Behavioral Disorders*, 2nd edition, 347–374

U.S. Department of Human Services Substance Abuse and Mental Health Services Administration. (2007). *What a difference a friend makes: Social acceptance is key to mental health recovery* (SMA 07-4257). Accessed online April 1, 2009, from http://mentalhealth.samhsa.gov/publications/allpubs/SMA07-4257/default.asp

U.S. Government Accountability Office. (2008). *Young adults with serious mental illness: Some states and federal agencies are taking steps to address their transition challenges* (GAO Publication No. 08-678). Washington, DC: Author.

Vander Stoep, A., Beresford, S., Weiss, N., McKnight, B., Cauce, M., & Cohen, P. (2000). Community-based study of the transition to adulthood for adolescents with psychiatric disorders. *American Journal of Epidemiology, 152*, 352–362.

Vogel, D. L., Wade, N. G., & Haake, S. (2006). Measuring the self-stigma associated with seeking psychological help. *Journal of Counseling Psychology, 53*(3), 325–337.

Wagner, M., Newman, L., Cameto, R., Levine, P., & Marder, C. (2007). *Perceptions and expectations of youth with disabilities. A special topic report of findings from the National Longitudinal Transition Study-2 (NLTS2)* (NCSER 2009-3017). Menlo Park, CA: SRI International. Accessed online January 3, 2011 at http://ies.ed.gov/ncser/pdf/20073006.pdf

Walker, J. S., Geenen, S., Thorne, E., & Powers, L. E. (2009). Improving outcomes through interventions that increase youth empowerment and self-determination. *Focal Point: Research, Policy, and Practice in Children's Mental Health, 23*(2), 13–16.

Walker, J. S., Thorne, L., Powers, L. E., & Gaonkar, R. (2010). Development of a scale to measure the empowerment of youth. *Journal of Emotional and Behavioral Disorders, 18*, 51–59.

Wehmeyer, M. L. (1996). Self-determination as an educational outcome: Why is it important to children, youth, and adults with disabilities? In D. J. Sands & M. L. Wehmeyer (Eds.), *Self-determination across the life span: Independence and choice for people with disabilities* (pp. 17–36). Baltimore, MD: Brookes Publishing.

Zarrett, N., & Eccles, J. (2006). The passage to adulthood: Challenges of late adolescence. *New Directions for Youth Development, 111*, 13–28.

List of Contributors

Editors

Michael L. Wehmeyer, Ph.D. is Professor of Special Education; Director, Kansas University Center on Developmental Disabilities; and Senior Scientist, Beach Center on Disability, all at the University of Kansas. His research focuses on self-determination; access to the general education curriculum for students with severe disabilities; conceptualizing intellectual disability, supports, and support need measurement; and technology use by people with cognitive disabilities.

Kristine Wiest Webb, Ph.D. is Professor in the Department of Exceptional Student and Deaf Education at the University of North Florida. Her research interests involve transition to postsecondary education, family involvement in the transition process, and teacher preparation in the area of transition.

Contributing Authors

W. Drew Andrews, Ed.D. is a Special Education Teacher in Duval County, Florida. His research interests include implementation of effective practices in transition programs and program development.

Diane S. Bassett, Ph.D. is Professor of Special Education at the University of Northern Colorado. Her research interests include educational reform and transition, self-determination, blending standards and transition-focused strategies, and transition to postsecondary education.

Michael R. Benz, Ph.D. is Professor of Special Education and Director of the Center on Disability and Development at Texas A&M University. His research interests include transition services and outcomes.

LaVerne Albright Buchanan, Ed.D. is Senior Associate at TransCen, Inc., Rockville, Maryland. Her areas of consultation and technical assistance include best practices for school-to-work, transition and career development, service learning, drop-out prevention and program evaluation.

Erik W. Carter, Ph.D. is Associate Professor of Special Education at Vanderbilt University. His research addresses secondary transition services, self-determination, peer relationships, and access to the general curriculum.

Terrence Cavanaugh, Ph.D. is Associate Professor at the University of North Florida. His areas of work include educational technology, reading technology, assistive technology, and teacher education.

Sarah A. Celestin, Ed.D. is Project Director at the University of Delaware's Center for Disabilities Studies. Her research interests include access to the general education curriculum, alternative assessments, and transition planning for students with significant intellectual disability.

Christina M. Curran, Ph.D. is Assistant Professor of Special Education at the University of Northern Iowa. Her research interests involve transition practices for middle and high school students with learning and high incidence disabilities, universal design and curricular access for secondary students, and inclusive teacher preparation.

Sharon deFur, Ed.D. is Professor of Special Education in the School of Education at the College of William and Mary, Williamsburg, VA. Her research interests focus on secondary and transition education issues for youth and young adults with disabilities, their families, and their teachers.

Ann Deschamps, Ed.D. is Senior Associate at TransCen, Inc. The focus of her work is building the capacity of school systems to improve transition services for all students with IEPs.

Bonnie Doren, Ph.D. is Senior Research Associate in the College of Education at the University of Oregon. Her research interests include establishing predictors of school and post-school outcomes, addressing the career development and transition needs of young women with disabilities, and development of self-advocacy and self-determination skills in the context of transition planning for students with disabilities.

Cari Dunn, Ph.D. is Professor of Special Education in the Department of Special Education, Rehabilitation, and Counseling at Auburn University. Her research interests relate to secondary curriculum and transition for students with high incidence disabilities and preparation of secondary special education teachers.

Laura T. Eisenman, Ph.D. is Associate Professor of Special Education and Disability studies at the University of Delaware. Her research interests include inclusive high school practices that facilitate self-determination and transitions of youth with disabilities and postsecondary education opportunities for youth with intellectual disabilities.

Jane Erin, Ph.D. is Professor of Special Education with specialization in education of students with visual impairments at the University of Arizona. Her primary research interests are literacy of blind and visually impaired students and educational services for students who have visual impairments.

Sharon Field, Ed.D. is Professor (Clinical) of Educational Leadership and Policy Studies and Co-Director of the Center for Self-Determination and Transition for the College of Education, Wayne State University, Detroit, MI. Her research interests include strategies to support self-determination and the application of findings from positive psychology to educational settings.

K. Brigid Flannery, Ph.D. is Senior Research Associate/Associate Professor at the University of Oregon. Her research interests involve transition planning, access to postsecondary education and training, and positive behavior support at the high school level.

Elizabeth Evans Getzel, MA is Director of Postsecondary Education Initiatives at the Virginia Commonwealth University RRTC. Her research interests involve transition, career development, postsecondary education, and employment for individuals with disabilities.

L. Kris Gowen, Ph.D., Ed.M. is Senior Research Associate at the Regional Research Institute of Human Services, Portland State University. Her research interests involve the sexual and mental health of youth and young adults, and providing unbiased services for youth of all sexual and gender orientations.

Meg Grigal, Ph.D. is the Co-Director of Think College and a Senior Research Fellow at the Institute for Community Inclusion at University of Massachusetts, Boston. Her research interests involve transition, employment, and postsecondary education for individuals with intellectual and developmental disabilities.

Cheryl Hanley-Maxwell, Ph.D. is Professor of Rehabilitation Psychology and Special Education and an Associate Dean in the School of Education at the University of Wisconsin-Madison. Her research interests include secondary special education reform, transition, vocational preparation for students with disabilities and supported employment.

Margaretha Vreeburg Izzo, Ph.D. is Professor of Psychiatry, Associate Director of the Ohio State University Nisonger Center, and Program Director of the Special Education and Transition Division. Her research focuses on school-to-work transition and postsecondary education for students with intellectual disability.

David R. Johnson, Ph.D. is Director of the Institute on Community Integration and Birkmaier Professor of Educational Leadership, College of Education and Human Development at the University of Minnesota. His research has focused on special education and transition policy and services, studies on the post-school outcomes of students with disabilities, cost–benefit analysis of employment programs, and secondary and postsecondary student engagement and drop-out prevention strategies.

Carol A. Kochhar-Bryant, Ph.D. is Professor of Special Education and Chair of the Department of Special Education and Disability Studies at the George Washington University, Washington, DC. Her research interests involve transition to postsecondary education and employment for students with disabilities, adolescent social-emotional development, and integrating the developmental sciences into leadership preparation.

Larry Kortering, Ph.D. is Co-Principal Investigator for National Secondary Transition Technical Assistance Center (NSTTAC) and a Professor in Special Education at Appalachian State University. His ongoing research and related work focuses on school completion, improving secondary programs and best practices in transition services for youth with disabilities, with an emphasis on developing interventions and services that prove responsive to the student consumer.

Lauren Lindstrom, Ph.D. is Associate Professor of Human Services in the College of Education at the University of Oregon. Her research interests include post-school employment outcomes, career development, and gender equity.

John Luckner, Ed.D. is Professor in the School of Special Education at the University of Northern Colorado. His research interests include transition, literacy, and the provision of appropriate services for students who are deaf or hard of hearing and their families.

Richard G. Luecking, Ed.D. is President of TransCen, Inc., a non-profit organization dedicated to education and employment success of people with disabilities. He is the author of numerous trade and academic publications on topics related to school-to-work transition and employment of people with disabilities.

James E. Martin, Ph.D. is the Zarrow Family Professor of Learning Enrichment and is the Director of the Zarrow Center at the University of Oklahoma. His research interest focuses upon infusing self-determination practices into transition education as a means to improve post-school outcomes of students with disabilities.

Dr. Mary E. Morningstar, Ph.D. is Associate Professor in the Department of Special Education at the University of Kansas and Director of the Transition Coalition. Dr. Morningstar coordinates the online transition master's program as well as the teacher licensure program for students with significant disabilities.

Debra A. Neubert, Ph.D., is Professor of Special Education at the University of Maryland. Her research interests involve transition assessment and transition to college.

Patricia M. Noonan, Ph.D. is Assistant Research Professor at the University of Kansas Center for Research on Learning. Her research interests involve large-scale multi-site evaluation of tiered school reform initiatives, professional development in secondary special education/transition, and intra- and interagency collaboration.

Wendy Parent-Johnson, Ph.D., CRP is a Research Professor at the Kansas University Center on Developmental Disabilities, University of Kansas. Her research interests involve supported/customized employment and transition from school to work for individuals with severe disabilities, with an emphasis on creative funding and support strategies, individual and family involvement, job coach training and leadership, interagency collaboration and service delivery issues, and systems change.

Karen B. Patterson, Ph.D. is Associate Professor and Chair of Exceptional Student and Deaf Education Department at the University of North Florida. Her research interests include teacher preparation, positive academic and behavioral interventions, and developmental disabilities.

Amy M. Pleet, Ed.D. is Coordinator of Inclusion Consulting at the Center for Secondary Teacher Education, University of Delaware. Her research interests include family engagement, secondary inclusion effectiveness, and student ownership/self-determination.

Jeanne B. Repetto, Ph.D., is Associate Professor in the School of Special Education, School Psychology and Early Childhood at the University of Florida. Her research interests involve transition, middle school education, healthcare transition and at-risk learners in online learning.

Sharon Richter, Ph.D. is Assistant Professor of Special Education at Appalachian State University. Her research interests include secondary transition and self-determination for students with intellectual disabilities.

Janice Seabrooks-Blackmore, Ph.D. is Associate Professor of Special Education at the University of North Florida. Her research interests relate to quality pre-service teacher preparation, transition, person-centered planning strategies, and learning strategies for adolescents with mild disabilities in secondary settings.

Brenda Smith Myles, Ph.D. is a consultant with the Autism Research Center and the Ohio Center for Autism and how Incidence. Her research focuses on Asperger syndrome, educating students with ASD, and transition for youth with ASD.

Daniel E. Steere is a professor in the Department of Special Education and Rehabilitation at East Stroudsburg University of Pennsylvania. His interests include teacher preparation and the development of effective transition services.

Pamela Sherron Targett, M.Ed. is Director of Special Projects at the RRTC at Virginia Commonwealth University. Her special interests are transition to employment for students with the most severe disabilities, innovative ways to create employer partnerships and develop jobs, and implementing supported employment services for individuals with traumatic brain injury.

David W. Test, Ph.D. is principal investigator for National Secondary Transition Technical Assistance Center (NSTTAC) and Professor of Special Education at the University of North Carolina at Charlotte. His research interests involve transition to adulthood, self-determination, and applied behavior analysis.

Colleen A. Thoma, Ph.D. is Professor of Special Education at Virginia Commonwealth University. Her research interests involve universal design for learning and transition; personnel preparation to support student self-determined transition planning; and the transition from school to postsecondary education.

Audrey A. Trainor, PhD, is Associate Professor of Special Education at the University of Wisconsin, Madison. Her current research interests include high incidence disabilities, transition, diversity and equity, and cultural and social capital.

Deanne K. Unruh, Ph.D., is Sr. Research Associate in the College of Education at the University of Oregon. Her interests include developing interventions to support adolescents, specifically youth with emotional/behavioral difficulties and/or involved in the juvenile justice system, in their transition to adulthood.

Allison R. Walker, Ph.D. is Assistant Professor of Special Education at the University of North Carolina, Wilmington. Her interests involve the transition of students from culturally and linguistically diverse backgrounds to postsecondary settings and self-determination, specifically self-advocacy.

Janet S. Walker, Ph.D. is Research Associate Professor in the School of Social Work at Portland State University, and Director of the Research and Training Center on Pathways to Positive Futures. Her work focuses on the development and replication of programs that promote positive development for youth and young adults with high levels of risk and/or need.

Donna L. Wandry, Ph.D., is Professor and Chair, Department of Special Education, West Chester University of Pennsylvania. Her research interests involve special education legislation, movement from school to adult life for students with disabilities, and systems change in transition.

Paul Wehman, Ph.D. is Professor of Physical Medicine and Chair of the Research Division. He also has a joint appointment in the Departments of Special Education and Disability Policy and Rehabilitation Counseling at Virginia Commonwealth University. He is part of a group of professionals, researchers, and advocates dedicated to the hiring, advancement, and retention of individuals with significant disabilities in competitive employment, with a concentration on services to persons with physical disabilities such as spinal cord injury and traumatic brain injury and who are typically underrepresented populations in employment and rehabilitation.

Gwendolyn Williams, Ph.D. is Associate Professor of Special Education and Program Chair at West Texas A&M University. Her research interests include transition services, behavior management, assistive technology, and effective instruction for students with moderate to severe disabilities.

Karen E. Wolffe, Ph.D., CRC, manages a private practice as a career counselor and consultant in Austin, TX. Her research and writing interests include the importance of career education, social skills development, transition issues, employment for people with disabilities, and access in the workplace for people with visual impairments.

Dan Dalun Zhang, Ph.D., is Associate Professor of special education at Texas A&M University. His current interests include promotion of positive transition outcomes, self-determination, and individuals with disabilities in the juvenile justice system.

Index

Page numbers in bold indicate figures and tables